1·31·83

INVESTIGATIONS
INTO THE MILITARY
AND ANTHROPOLOGICAL STATISTICS
OF AMERICAN SOLDIERS

This is a volume in the
Arno Press Collection

THE AMERICAN MILITARY EXPERIENCE

See last pages of this volume
for a complete list of titles.

INVESTIGATIONS

IN THE

MILITARY AND ANTHROPOLOGICAL STATISTICS

OF

AMERICAN SOLDIERS.

BENJAMIN APTHORP GOULD

ARNO PRESS
A New York Times Company
New York • 1979

Editorial Supervision: RITA LAWN

Reprint Edition 1979 by Arno Press, Inc.

Reprinted from a copy in the University of Virginia Library

AMERICAN MILITARY EXPERIENCE
ISBN for complete set: 0-405-11850-3
See last pages of this volume for titles.

Manufactured in the United States of America

Library of Congress Cataloging in Publication Data

Gould, Benjamin Apthorp, 1824-1896.
Investigations in the military and anthropological statistics of American soldiers.

(American military experience)
Reprint of v. 2 of the 1869 ed. of the U.S. Sanitary Commission's Sanitary memoirs of the War of the Rebellion, published for the commission by Hurd and Houghton, New York.
1. United States--History--Civil War, 1861-1865--Medical and sanitary affairs--Statistics. 2. United States. Army--Statistics. 3. Soldiers--United States--Statistics. 4. Anthropometry--United States.
I. Title. II. Series. III. Series: United States Sanitary Commission. Sanitary memoirs of the War of the Rebellion ; v. 2.
E631.G68 1979 973.7'75 78-22380
ISBN 0-405-11857-0

SANITARY MEMOIRS

OF THE

WAR OF THE REBELLION.

COLLECTED AND PUBLISHED

BY THE

UNITED STATES SANITARY COMMISSION.

INVESTIGATIONS

IN THE

MILITARY AND ANTHROPOLOGICAL STATISTICS

OF

AMERICAN SOLDIERS.

BY

BENJAMIN APTHORP GOULD,

PH. DR.; MEMBER OF THE NATIONAL ACADEMY OF SCIENCES; PRESIDENT OF THE AMERICAN ASSOCIATION FOR THE ADVANCEMENT OF SCIENCE; MEMBER OR CORRESPONDENT OF THE ACADEMIES OR SCIENTIFIC SOCIETIES OF BOSTON, CHERBOURG, GÖTTINGEN, MARBURG, NASHVILLE, NEW ORLEANS, PHILADELPHIA, ETC.; ASSOCIATE OF THE ROYAL ASTRONOMICAL SOCIETY OF LONDON, ETC.;

ACTUARY TO THE U. S. SANITARY COMMISSION.

NEW YORK:

PUBLISHED FOR THE U. S. SANITARY COMMISSION,

BY HURD AND HOUGHTON.

Cambridge: Riverside Press.

1869.

RIVERSIDE, CAMBRIDGE:
STEREOTYPED AND PRINTED BY
H. O. HOUGHTON AND COMPANY.

UNITED STATES SANITARY COMMISSION.

		DATE OF APPOINTMENT.
Rev. H. W. Bellows, D. D. . .	New York	June 9, 1861.
Alexander Dallas Bache, LL. D.	Washington, D. C. .	"
William H. Van Buren, M. D. .	New York	"
Wolcott Gibbs, M. D.	Cambridge, Mass. . .	"
* Robert C. Wood, M. D., U. S. A.	. . . .	"
† George W. Cullum, U. S. A. .	. . . .	"
‡ Alexander E. Shiras, U. S. A.	. . . .	"
Samuel G. Howe, M. D. . . .	Boston, Mass. . . .	"
Elisha Harris, M. D.	New York	June 12, 1861.
Cornelius R. Agnew, M. D. . .	New York	"
George T. Strong, Esq. . . .	New York	June 13, 1861.
John S. Newberry, M. D. . . .	Cleveland, O. . . .	June 14, 1861.
Frederick Law Olmsted, Esq.	New York . . .	June 20, 1861.
Rt. Rev. Thomas M. Clark . .	Providence, R. I. . .	July 30, 1861.
Horace Binney, Jr., Esq. . . .	Philadelphia, Pa. . .	July 30, 1861.
§ Hon. R. W. Burnett	Cincinnati, O. . . .	Dec. 5, 1861.
Hon. Mark Skinner	Chicago, Ill. . . .	Dec. 7, 1861.
§ Hon. Joseph Holt	Washington, D. C. .	Jan. 23, 1863.
Rev. James H. Heywood . . .	Louisville, Ky. . . .	Jan. 23, 1863.
‖ Fairman Rogers, Esq. . . .	Philadelphia, Pa. . .	Feb. 6, 1863.
J. Huntington Wolcott, Esq. .	Boston, Mass. . . .	June 13, 1863.
Charles J. Stillé, Esq. . . .	Philadelphia, Pa. . .	Jan. 15, 1864.
Ezra B. McCagg, Esq.	Chicago, Ill. . . .	Mar. 9, 1864.

* Resigned, December, 1864.

† Resigned, February, 1864.

‡ Resigned, December 17th, 1864.

§ These gentlemen never took their seats.

‖ Resigned, 1864.

PREFACE.

THE discussions and inferences submitted in the present volume are offered with the diffidence and distrust which must necessarily accompany the results of investigations in a field entirely new to the inquirer, and regarding subjects with which the tenor of his previous pursuits had left him comparatively unacquainted; and the author is not without apprehensions lest the magnificent range of the statistics here embodied may serve to render the short-comings in their discussion more prominent.

A very unexpected invitation, from the Sanitary Commission in June 1864, to take charge of their statistics, was placed upon such grounds and urged in such a way that it became difficult to persist in declining; and the temptation to connect one's name, however remotely, with an institution so deeply rooted in a nation's affections, and of which the name is so thoroughly interwoven with memories and associations of philanthropy, wisdom, and self-sacrifice, was irresistible.

The statistical investigations, already made or undertaken by the Sanitary Commission, under the superintendence of Mr. Elliott, indicated directions in which such inquiries might be effectively prosecuted; and the field for useful research appeared almost boundless. An examination into the class of investigations already begun confirmed this impression, and the uniformly ready and most gratifying acquiescence, by the Commission and its officers, in all the recommendations made for the development and furtherance of these researches has afforded unfailing support and encouragement. Other lines of investigation would have been pursued, and those here presented would have been elaborated more thoroughly, had continued access to the archives of the War Department and other opportunities for the collection of information, been permitted by Mr. Stanton, then Secretary of War. The discussion of the Hospital Statistics, both in their military and their medical relations, the collection of regimental returns from the rolls of the Adjutant General, the statistics of colored troops, and the physical characteristics of the prisoners of war, are among the inquiries which it thus became necessary to abandon. The data here discussed form, consequently, only a portion of those which the Sanitary Commission had hoped to present as an incidental contribution to military and anthropological knowledge. They may fairly claim whatever merit belongs to an exhaustive collection of facts, wherever this has been possible, or to laborious and continued effort for their acquisition in other cases. These statistics greatly surpass in amount all that has been previously gathered on the same subjects, and it may be long before opportunity again offers for an equal collection of similar material. On the other hand, the proper reduction, elaboration, and discussion of this grand store of numerical data demands special training and peculiar gifts. No pains have been spared in their elaboration, and the enormous amount of work bestowed on the materials will be apparent only to those who are in some degree familiar with arithmetical computations. But the variety of the topics is great; and medical and physiological knowledge of a high order is needed for eliciting such information as they may contain, as well as for deducing the best results. The author trusts that in a critical judgement of his portion of the work, the suddenness of the call upon him, and his want of previous medical training or experience may be allowed for, and that his earnest endeavors to improve opportunities at his control for opening new lines of research, and for collecting information which might otherwise be lost, may be offset against any defects in the series of questions or the treatment of the materials collected. All these materials, both in their original form, and in the several stages of their subsequent tabulation or computation have been carefully preserved, accessible to other investigators.

The limited time and means available for the reductions have compelled the omission of very many interesting inquiries for which ample opportunities are afforded by the materials in our possession. These are in many cases indicated in those portions of the present volume which treat of kindred subjects; among them the influence of occupation and social position upon stature, the ancestry of the native Americans included in our measurements, and its possible relation to their physical development, the change of the relative dimensions of the different parts of the body in consequence of normal growth, and the relation of pulse and respiration to weight, ought especially to be mentioned. That our materials may tempt to some future researches on these and other topics is earnestly to be hoped.

In general, in this discussion of our materials a disquisition upon the subjects examined has not been aimed at. Neither a history of the question, nor any statement of the present condition of the problem has been undertaken in any case; and it will be seen that where historical references or scientific explanations have been offered, it has been in consequence of some apparent necessity for the sake of proper presentation of our own results. The few pages in the eighth chapter concerning the nature, significance, and proper interpretation of mean or average results, and the existence and determination of types, seemed called for in a treatise where almost all the physical determinations are given in the form of mean values.

The anthropological results here given are of course restricted in their very nature, pertaining as they do, not merely to one sex only, but to those ages, for that sex, in which the physical changes are least marked. Comparatively few of our inferences extend to ages not within the limits of military service, where the physical organization has nearly or quite attained its full development, and the decline has not yet fairly commenced.

It has been more than once stated how much we regret that the measurements here recorded were not uniformly made in units of the metric system, which is already in universal use among scientists, and is destined soon to be the uniform standard of the civilized world. The discussion and presentation of results, so far as is possible, in the same units in which the observations are made is dictated by every consideration of fitness; but to promote convenience, in translating inches and pounds into their metric equivalents, tables for such conversion are appended to our volume.

Since the nature of the contents precludes a full and convenient Index to the work, the place of such an index is here supplied by an extremely full Synopsis or abstract of the contents, which may serve to record the whole range of discussion of each subject in detail, and furnish all needful means of reference. The difficulty of obtaining a connected view of the course of an investigation or argument, which is interspersed with numerous and extensive tables, seemed to point to this as the most desirable course. This synopsis or syllabus indicates not merely the topics discussed in the text, but the general tenor of their treatment.

The history of each of the several researches of which the results are here offered is briefly given in the preliminary remarks; but the general history of the work would be very incomplete, without reference to the important part borne by the two gentlemen who have successively acted as chief clerks of the Statistical Bureau of the Commission, to the great acceptance of all with whom they were thus associated.

Mr. T. J. O'Connell, a gentleman of Irish birth, and a graduate of the University of Dublin, who, with the assistance of a single clerk, had carried on the statistical work subsequent to Mr. Elliott's departure for Europe in the summer of 1863, became the chief clerk upon the reorganization of the Bureau a year later, and managed the details of the work with discretion and unsurpassed fidelity. His health, already seriously impaired by service in the army, in which he had enlisted as a private soldier upon the outbreak of the rebellion, gave way during the early part of the succeeding winter. His resignation was for some months declined, while he was temporarily relieved from duty, but at his own earnest desire his office was filled in April 1865. Before the close of that year he died, leaving an honorable name, associated in the minds of those who knew him with the memory of a high-toned character, and unassuming ability.

In May 1865, Mr. Lucius Brown, who had provisionally filled Mr. O'Connell's place for the two previous months, assumed its duties definitely, and has continued in charge of the office since that time. All of the extended computations and tabulations have been carried on under his immediate supervision, the numerous executive details have been superintended by him alone, and there is not a page of this volume, which has not been submitted to his accurate critical inspection. Upon his assiduous care the value of these results has in a great measure depended, and the labor and solicitude of the Actuary have been much lightened by the consciousness that the precision and consistency of all details of statement would find their severest critic in his own office, before the manuscript had passed into the printer's hands.

A list of clerks who have been engaged upon this work is given upon another page. All of these have rendered effective service; some in visiting the State capitals, and there collecting the statistics which are here elaborated; some in tabulating, classifying, or assorting the materials; others in the very laborious computations which they have entailed.

In conclusion, the author begs leave to acknowledge the cordial support of all the members of the U. S. Sanitary Commission through this somewhat arduous undertaking, prosecuted in their behalf, for which they have provided all needful supplies, and all possible encouragement. To the General Secretaries of the Commission, Dr. J. Foster Jenkins, and John S. Blatchford, Esq., he would especially express his gratitude for numberless acts of kindness, and unfailing courtesy and assistance.

CAMBRIDGE, *July* 1868.

To the following persons who labored faithfully and effectively in gathering, tabulating, assorting or computing the statistical materials given in this volume, our best acknowledgements are due:—

Messrs. T. J. O'Connell,
Lucius Brown,
John N. Stockwell,
C. W. Pritchett,
Edwin A. Wilson,
John P. Brown,
Edward D. Chaloner,
Edward A. Phalen,
Arthur Searle,
G. M. Finotti,
J. D. Dinneen,
Jas. H. Sutherland,
N. Trudeau,
Edward S. Holden,
W. J. Handy,
L. F. Papanti,
Hermann E. Clow,
Loring E. Beckwith,
George H. Miller,
George F. Buckley,
Thomas J. Sullivan,
F. L. Hayes,
W. W. Parker,
F. B. Brown,
Erving Winslow,
Wm. Irving Gilliss,
Albert A. Brooke,
Charles Brockway,
Beverly R. Codwise,
J. D. Barclay, Jr.,
Octavius Cate,

Messrs. O. B. Dodge,
Wm. B. Oliver,
W. W. Magee,
George T. Chase,
George Brown,
Frank Sutton,
Sherwood Hough,
James H. Stewart,
Horatio D. Jarves,
Samuel J. Bradlee,
Cyrus Pitts,
George F. Sutherland,
S. G. Rowland,
Charles W. Abrams,
R. A. Lampher,
J. H. Tierney,
John B. Hyde,

Misses C. Alice Baker,
S. E. Rhoades,
Mary C. Wells,
Caroline L. Sawyer,
L. C. Bragg,
Ellen W. Sawyer,
Susan M. Lane,
Sarah S. Lane,
Elizabeth M. Lane,
Emma L. Clarke,
Gertrude H. Mason,
Emma L. Hutchins,
Mary T. Peabody,
Ellen Green.

Especial mention seems due to the services of Messrs. Stockwell and J. P. Brown, to whom the more difficult computations were intrusted, and by the former of which almost all the calculations in the third and fourth chapters were made, — of Rev. C. W. Pritchett, who had charge of the results of the Camp Inspections, — of Messrs. Wilson, Phalen, Sutherland, and Brockway, whose discretion and good judgement secured for our undertaking the good will of the many officers with whom they were brought in contact while visiting the several capitals of Loyal States, — and of Mr. E. D. Chaloner, who labored effectively in the work for three years, but who has not lived to see its completion.

CONTENTS.

CHAPTER I.

Military Population and Enlistments in the Loyal States, as deduced from Official Reports.

CHAPTER II.

Nativity of United States Volunteers.

CHAPTER III.

Ages of the Original Volunteers.

CHAPTER IV.

Ages of Recruits.

CHAPTER V.

Statures.

CHAPTER VI.

Complexions. Color of Hair and Eyes.

CHAPTER VII.

CHAPTER VIII.

Mean Dimensions of Body.

CHAPTER IX.

Mean Proportions of Body.

CHAPTER X.

Dimensions and Proportions of Head.

CHAPTER XI.

Weight and Strength.

CHAPTER XII.

Pulmonary Capacity.

CHAPTER XIII.

Respiration and Pulse.

CHAPTER XIV.

Vision.

CHAPTER XV.

Miscellaneous Characteristics.

CHAPTER XVI.

MILITARY SERVICE.

STATISTICS OF AMERICAN SOLDIERS.

CHAPTER I.

MILITARY POPULATION AND ENLISTMENTS IN THE LOYAL STATES, AS DEDUCED FROM OFFICIAL REPORTS.

At almost every stage of our inquiries, it becomes desirable to obtain some tolerably close information concerning the General Statistics of the volunteer army, — comprising also those of the white male inhabitants of military age, within those States by which our volunteer army was chiefly furnished. For obvious reasons no accurate knowledge can be obtained; yet the materials exist in published documents for deducing approximate estimates, which seem sufficiently near the truth to serve for most practical purposes.

The present chapter aims at affording such an estimate, together with references to the various sources of information from which the adopted numbers are derived.

1. *Military Population.*

"The Census of the Population of the United States in 1860," gives[1] a table of the white males of military age, or what we will call for brevity the "military population," in each State. A table deduced from the actual enumeration, by the formulas given in our third chapter, would differ but slightly from this, and the numbers for the individual Territories may be readily deduced in the same way.

The State of West Virginia, established and organized during the war from fifty counties previously belonging to Virginia, but which were thoroughly loyal, ought manifestly to be included in the same class with the other loyal States. Deducing the number of its military population from the census returns for the several counties by ages, we obtain somewhat less than 64 600; while the ratio of its total male population to that of Virginia before the separation,

[1] Page xvii.

would give about 67 500. We adopt 66 000 as its military population in 1860.

Separating from the other loyal States and Territories those on the Pacific coast and its vicinity, which, although they aided the national government with moral and pecuniary support, were yet too remote from the scenes of military operations to contribute any considerable number of men for active service in our principal campaigns,[1] we find the military population of the United States in 1860, to have been essentially as follows: —

Loyal States, excepting California and Oregon		4 285 105
West Virginia		66 000
Colorado, Dakotah, and Nebraska Territories		30 065
District of Columbia		12 797
Total military population furnishing the volunteers		4 393 967
California and Oregon	185 756	
Nevada, New Mexico, Utah, Washington Terr.'s	46 149	
Loyal military population on Pacific and vicinity		231 905
Military population of insurgent States		998 193
Total military population of United States		5 624 065

This estimate, of course, includes the very large number[2] exempted from enrollment. The total white male population between 20 and 45 years, neither exempt from military duty nor serving 1865 May 1, was by the enrollment[3] about 2 254 000,[4] which would seem to indicate that rather more than one half of that number was exempt, although of military age.

2. *Growth of Military Population*

The rate of increase in 1860 for the white population of the free States was about 41 per cent.[5] in the decade, which corresponds to 3.51 per centum annually. The immigration to the same States was about 0.37 per centum, which gives 3.14 per cent. as the increase, while the mortality[6] was 1.21 per cent.; so that the natural increase of the population, before deducting the deaths, is represented by about 4.35 per centum.

[1] California raised in all about 15 700 men; Oregon, one battalion cavalry, about 1 800 men; Nevada, one each of cavalry and infantry, about 1 200 men.

[2] *Provost Marshal General's Report*, 1866, p. 144.

[3] Thirteen counties of West Virginia and three Territories, with a military population at nome of perhaps 28,000, are not included in this enrollment.

[4] *Provost Marshal General's Report*, pp. 2, 144, 159.

[5] *Census*, p. vii.

[6] *Ibid.* p. xlv.

In forming our estimates of the increase of military population during the war, we may, with sufficient accuracy for our purpose, consider the number of white males in the loyal States, who arrived at the ages of 18 and 45 respectively, as increasing by one twenty-fifth part in each successive year.

The total number of alien passengers to the United States in 1860,[1] corresponding very well with the average during the preceding lustrum,[2] was 153 640. The number of arrivals from foreign countries [3] after that year was —

In 1861	112 705
In 1862	114 475
In 1863	199 811
In 1864	221 535

six sevenths of which may be considered as of alien passengers.[4] The statistics of many preceding years indicate 58 in 100 as the proportion of males among immigrants to this country. The records of emigrants to Canada through the United States, and of settlers in this country making subsequent voyages across the Atlantic, indicate [5] that the number of alien passengers should be diminished by about 14½ per cent. to determine the actual number of immigrants. Of the total number of male immigrants, about 66 per cent. are between the ages of 18 and 45 years.

We are thus warranted in assuming $0.58 \times 0.855 \times 0.66$, or 0.327, as that proportion of the total number of alien passengers to the United States, which represents the male immigrants of military age. Eight ninths of these [6] was about the proportion settling in the free States previous to the war, and we are therefore warranted in assuming that 30 in each hundred alien passengers before 1861, and 33 in each hundred during the war, were males of military age immigrating to the loyal States of the Atlantic slope.

We thus obtain for the immigrant military population: 46 092 in 1860; 31 879 in 1861; 32 380 in 1862; 56 518 in 1863; 62 663 in 1864; making a total number of 229 532 to the close of the year 1864.

Our estimate of the annual increase of the military population of the loyal States will then assume the following form, after deducting from the supposed numbers attaining the ages of 18 and 45 respectively, the numbers, belonging to these classes, who from our

1 *Census*, p. xxv. 2 *Ibid.* p. xxi.

3 For these figures I am indebted to the courtesy of Hon. J. C. Cox, Chief Clerk of the Department of the Interior.

4 *Census*, p. xxi. 5 *Ibid.* p. xxi. 6 *Ibid.* p. xxx.

other data may be inferred to have been already in the army. The deaths in that portion of the military population which was not in the army may be represented by the proportion (deduced for time of peace) of 0.86 per centum.

	1860–1	1861–2	1862–3	1863–4	1864–5
Number attaining the age of 18 years	215 020	212 630	217 600	226 740	237 710
Number attaining the age of 45 years	98 928	95 600	95 560	94 930	95 170
Deaths in military population not in the army . . .	37 676	35 518	33 712	32 955	33 230
Natural increase during the year	78 416	81 512	88 328	98 855	109 310
Increase during the year by immigration	46 092	31 879	32 380	56 518	62 663
Total increase of military population . . .	124 508	113 391	120 708	155 373	171 973

In this estimate it will be remarked that no account whatever is taken of arrivals other than by regular immigration at our own seaports. There is, however, reason to believe that, apart from all other influences, the spirit of sympathy with a republic struggling for the maintenance of free institutions, brought many volunteers to our army from continental Europe, thus modifying the figures just deduced; and that large numbers, animated by a kindred impulse, came to our support from the neighboring British provinces. Indeed, the number from Canada, Nova Scotia, and New Brunswick, appears to have been some tens of thousands.

3. *Total Enlistments and Discharges.*

From the able and carefully prepared "Report of the Provost Marshal General,"[1] the figures here given are deduced by diminishing the total number on pages 161–63.

1st, by the number of Negroes supposed to be included in the total, namely: —

Volunteers after July 1, 1863[2]	37 394
Supposed drafted after July 1, 1863[3]	4 000
Five regiments from loyal States, 1862–63[4] . . .	5 200
	46 594

[1] Ex. Doc. War Department, 39th Congress, 1st Session.
[2] Pages 43, 45. [3] Pages 43, 46. [4] Estimated from p. 68.

Credits for naval enlistments before February, 1864[1] . 67 334
Naval enlistments after that date[2] 37 340

104 674

3d, by the number of enlistments at unknown dates for unknown periods[3] 63 322
4th, by credits allowed states in adjustment of quotas, 1864–65[4] 35 290

Combining the various data of enlistments for different terms of service and under different calls, we find, approximately, taking July 1 as the commencement of the statistical year: —

	Enlistments exclusive of "veterans"	Enlistments of "veterans," furloughed upon re-enlistment	Enlistments expired
Before July 1, 1861[5]	170 326	–	–
1861 to 1862 . . .	652 238	–	93 326
1862 to 1863 . . .	527 423	–	102 595
1863 to 1864 . . .	500 194	136 507	90 077
After July 1, 1864 .	418 562	11 869	584 376
	2 268 743	148 376	870 374

So that but for casualties, about 1 400 000 would have been in service at the close of the war.

The total number of the Enlistment Table upon page 163 of the "Provost Marshal General's Report" is thus assumed to be made up as follows: —

Enlistments of white soldiers exclusive of "Veteran Volunteers	2 268 743
Enlistments of "Veteran Volunteers"[6]	148 376
Enlistments in Navy and Marine Corps	104 674
Enlistments of colored troops supposed to be included . .	46 594
Enlistments of unknown or uncertain character . .	63 322
Credits allowed by adjustment	35 290
Number of drafted men who paid commutation[7] . .	86 724
Grand Total of Enlistment Table	2 753 723

1 *Provost Marshal General's Report*, p. 72.
2 *Ibid.* pp. 43, 45.
3 *Ibid.* p. 161.
4 *Ibid.* p. 43.
5 The estimated number of 3-years' men enlisted before July 1861, in all 72 regiments and 10 batteries (pp. 7, 8), is 77 000, which is here added to the 3-months' men.
6 *Ibid.* p. 163.
7 *Ibid.* p. 43.

4. *Strength of the Army at Different Dates.*

The Provost Marshal General gives[1] the numerical force of the army as follows: —

1862, March 31	637 126
1863, January 1	918 191
1864, January 1	860 737
1865, January 1	959 460

which data constitute the only published information of a trustworthy character as to the national forces under arms during the contest.

For the end of the war, or May 1, 1865, the Secretary's Report for 1866 gives[2] the number of troops then serving in the volunteer army as	1 034 000
There being in the regular army[3] about	22 000
Making the total number about	1 056 000
And since the number of colored troops[4] was not far from	120 000
We may assume the number of white troops then serving as	936 000

Farther knowledge being on many accounts desirable and the Secretary of War being still unwilling to afford the Sanitary Commission either additional information or access to the sources whence it might be derived, the following estimate has been prepared with some labor. Though of course not strictly correct, it is believed to be a close approximation to the truth, and worthy of reliance for practical purposes, — the numbers being expressed in thousands.

[1] *Provost Marshal General's Report*, p. 102.
[2] Page 1.
[3] *Provost Marshal General's Report*, p. 102.
[4] *Ibid.* p. 69.

TABLE I.

Strength of the United States Army.

Date	White Vol's from Loyal States, excluding Pacific Coast			Colored Troops	Veteran Reserve Corps	Regular Army	White Vol's from States not before included	In Transit and Rendezvous	Totals
	From Returns	Estimated	Totals						
1861, June	3	166	169	–	–	16	2	–	187
July	9	202	211		–	17	3	–	231
August	23	203	226		–	18	4	–	248
September	60	263	323	–	–	19	10	1	353
October	77	332	409	–	–	20	10	2	441
November	86	384	470	–	–	21	10	2	503
December	90	452	542	–	–	22	10	2	576
1862, January	80	462	542	–	–	22	10	3	577
February	118	460	578	–	–	23	10	3	614
March	238	360	598	–	–	23	12	4	637
April	254	347	601	–	–	23	11	4	639
May	222	370	592	–	–	24	11	4	631
June	223	333	556	–	–	24	10	4	594
July	217	359	576	–	–	24	14	4	618
August	400	245	645	–	–	24	15	4	688
September	522	263	785	1	–	25	15	4	830
October	618	229	847	1	–	25	14	4	891
November	705	172	877	2	–	25	14	4	922
December	729	144	873	3	–	25	14	3	918
1863, January	758	99	857	3	–	25	14	3	902
February	743	97	840	3	–	25	15	3	886
March	727	87	814	3	–	25	17	3	862
April	691	104	795	4	–	25	17	3	844
May	654	98	752	6	1	25	17	3	804
June	606	120	726	14	2	25	19	3	789
July	602	92	694	22	6	25	22	8	777
August	593	77	670	30	10	25	25	15	775
September	599	70	669	37	14	25	28	25	798
October	614	71	685	39	18	25	31	30	828
November	618	67	685	40	19	25	36	36	841
December	622	73	695	41	20	25	36	44	861
1864, January	626	88	714	43	21	24	36	42	880
February	644	97	741	44	22	24	33	38	902
March	682	105	787	46	23	24	30	34	944
April	673	132	805	55	24	24	29	30	967
May	660	172	832	64	25	24	28	25	998
June	680	146	826	74	26	23	22	20	991

TABLE I. — (*Continued.*)

Strength of the United States Army.

Date	White Vol's from Loyal States excluding Pacific Coast.			Colored Troops	Veteran Reserve Corps.	Regular Army	White Vol's from States not before included.	In Transit and Rendezvous.	Totals
	From Returns	Estimated.	Totals						
1864, July	672	129	801	83	27	23	20	17	971
August . . .	627	131	758	93	28	23	25	15	942
September . .	611	130	741	102	30	23	28	10	934
October . . .	621	120	741	106	30	22	30	6	935
November. . .	627	128	755	109	30	22	26	3	945
December. . .	590	177	767	112	30	22	27	1	959
1865, January . . .	–	763	763	115	29	22	27	2	958
February . . .	–	765	765	116	29	22	29	6	967
March	–	774	774	118	28	22	29	9	980
April	–	832	832	120	27	22	31	24	1 056

Taking as a basis those troops (col. 1) for which the regimental monthly returns of loss and gain had been transcribed[1] before the Secretary's order in September 1865, forbidding our farther access to the rolls, estimates for the remainder were formed after a careful study of all published sources of information, expressed or implied, and are given in column two. The reports of the Adjutant Generals of the several States afforded a means of inferring the number of regiments in service at the close of each month. The strength of those regiments not included in our official returns was estimated as unchanged until April 1862, when recruiting ceased, and up to which date the losses of the early regiments are assumed to have been compensated by additional enlistments. From April until August, 1862, the figures are derived from special estimates. Subsequent to August 1862, the strength of regiments reported in other months is used, after correction for the average loss or gain during the interval; but when no report whatever has been found for a regiment, the average strength of other regiments from the same State during the same month is generally adopted.

[1] These comprise all white volunteers from loyal States not on the Pacific coast, up to the beginning of 1865, for which the monthly returns were on file at the War Department in September of that year, together with those additional ones which were on file at the State capitals, — access to these latter having been courteously granted, and all needful facilities cordially afforded in every case.

This mode of estimation will not, it is believed, be much in error, when, as in the present case, the aggregate is taken from a considerable number of regiments or battalions separately considered.

The sum of these two columns is given in column three, headed "Total," and represents the best attainable estimate of the strength at the close of each successive month, of the white volunteer troops, exclusive of those recruited in insurgent States or furnished by the Pacific coast. To these, besides the white volunteers thus excluded, are to be added the regular army, the colored troops, and, after April 1863, the "Veteran Reserve Corps;" as well as the number (very considerable at one period) of soldiers at the various military rendezvous, and on the way to their regiments.

The number of colored troops to June 1863, is inferred from the number of regiments in service, as reported by the Provost Marshal General.[1] For later dates it is estimated from the Annual Reports of the Secretary of War, partly from the total strength reported, partly from general statements as to the recruiting service, and partly from the number recruited between given dates, allowance being made of course for reported casualties.

5. *Casualties.*

The whole number of casualties during the forty-eight months of the war, among 2 480 000 white soldiers, was 858 000,[2] or, on an average, nearly 18 000 a month. Of these nearly 400 000 must have occurred prior to July 1863, or about 15 000 monthly.

The total number of deaths in the same service was about 250 000, making the ratio of deaths to the whole number of casualties as 100 to 343.

In the appended estimates the monthly rate of mortality has been deduced from the summaries of the regimental returns to the Adjutant General; and the total number of deaths from an application of this rate to the whole number of white troops under consideration.

1 *Provost Marshal General's Report*, pp. 67, 68.

2 *Ibid.* pp. 78, 79.

TABLE II.

Estimated Death-Rate and Total Deaths for Troops here considered.

Month	Death-Rate per 1 000	Total Number of Deaths	
1861.			
Before July,		1 000 [1]	
1861, July .	2.24	511	
August	1.75	427	
Sept. .	2.25	772	
Oct. .	2.88	1 241	
Nov. .	3.59	1 770	
Dec. .	5.87	3 322	
1862, Jan. .	6.59	3 737	
Feb. .	5.36	3 237	
March .	5.30	3 312	
April .	8.24	5 175	
May .	7.99	4 954	
June .	9.56	5 583	34 041
July .	7.15	4 319	
August	10.12	6 811	
Sept. .	8.73	7 106	
Oct. .	7.86	6 885	
Nov. .	5.53	5 010	
Dec. .	9.72	8 758	
1863, Jan. .	8.47	7 496	
Feb. .	7.21	6 258	
March .	6.57	5 532	
April .	5.61	4 617	
1863, May .	8.93	6 965	
June .	6.07	4 577	74 334

Month	Death-Rate per 1 000	Total Number of Deaths	
July .	10.87	7 902	
August	7.54	5 353	
Sept. .	8.05	5 788	
Oct. .	5.52	4 085	
Nov. .	6.12	4 566	
Dec. .	4.80	3 667	
1864, Jan. .	3.72	2 902	
Feb. .	3.35	2 690	
March .	3.64	3 076	
April .	4.57	3 926	
May .	13.00	11 453	
June .	13.92	12 096	67 504
July .	1085	9 125	
August	10.23	8 142	
Sept. .	8.79	6 803	
Oct. .	8.06	6 198	
Nov. .	5.26	4 103	
Dec. .	6.04	4 772	
1865, Jan. .	5.58	4 391	
Feb. .	5.62	4 457	
March .		6 500[1]	
April .		7 500[1]	61 991
			238 870

The total number of deaths in the service, exclusive of those which occurred after muster-out, but resulted from military service, is given by the Provost Marshal General,[2] as follows: —

	White Vols	Regulars	Colored Troops	Total
Officers .	7 047	240	260	7 547
Men . .	238 458	4 639	29 038	272 135
Total .	245 505	4 879	29 298	279 682

The total resulting from our estimates, 239 000 officers and men among the white troops here specially considered, is found to be in

[1] Assumed.

[2] *Provost Marshal General's Report*, pp. 73–83.

close accordance with the figures deducible from the aggregate for the war officially given.

6. *Annual Enlistments and Discharges.*

The first column of the annexed table presents the number of enlistments here deduced, and the second the number from States here specially considered. Those classed in our summary as uncertain, 63 322 in number, were mostly enlisted after July 1862, and furnished by Southern or Pacific States, and the Territories. Colorado appears to have provided 2 000 of them, early in 1864, and these are therefore added in the table to the 637 000 previously obtained. The regular army contained at the outbreak of the war about 16 000 men.

The third column gives the estimated number of discharges, whether by disbandment or muster-out of the organization, or in consequence of personal disabilities.

TABLE III.

Enlistments and Discharges during each Year of the War.

	Enlistments		Discharges	
	Total	From States here considered	Returned Home	Died in Service
Before July, 1862	822 500	810 000	207 000	35 000
1862–3	527 500	517 000	271 000	74 000
1863–4	637 000	639 000	432 000	68 000
After July 1, 1864	430 000	430 000	358 000	62 000
	2 417 000	2 396 000	1 268 000	239 000

7. *Number of Reenlistments.*

Of the 93 326 original volunteers for three months, at the outbreak of the insurrection, we assume from various indications, that 60 000 men reenlisted during the year 1861–2.

During the first eighteen months of the war, the number of discharges for disability was large, and about the close of the year 1862 many men, who had already served and been discharged, reenlisted in other regiments, and not unfrequently from other States.

We assume a little less than one tenth of those enlisting during the year 1862–3, or 50 000 out of 517 000, to be men who have already served in the army.

During the year 1863–4, the Provost Marshal General[1] gives 136 000 as the number of "veteran" enlistments. There seem to have been about 503 000 other enlistments, of which we consider 64 000, or about one eighth, to represent men who had already served, making the total number of reenlistments about 200 000. Recruiting officers at the East represent that about one fourth of the men enlisting during the last two years of the war had already served in the army. But at the West the men enlisting during the same period were largely new recruits.

Finally, in the year 1864–5 the veteran reenlistments were 12 000; and if we suppose 48 000 of the remaining 418 000 enlistments to belong to men who had already seen service, the total number of reenlistments will have been 60 000.

8. *General Schedule.*

We have now attained the means of forming a tolerably correct estimate of the general statistics of the war, including the character of the population at home, as well as the strength of the army at the commencement of each official year. These numbers, it will be remembered, pertain only to *white soldiers from those loyal States and Territories already specified*, excepting perhaps a few regulars: and for convenience they are expressed in thousands of men.

[1] *Provost Marshal General's Report*, p. 43.

TABLE IV.

Statistics of Military Population and Army, annually from 1860 *till* 1865.

Date	Military Population not in Army		Enlistments during Year		Returned from Army	Died in Service	Force in Army
	Had not served	Had served	New Men	Reenlistments			
July 1, 1860	4 378	–	–	–	–	–	16
" 1861	4 333	–	170	–	–	1	185
" 1862	3 868	145	580	60	207	34	584
" 1863	3 525	363	467	50	271	74	756
" 1864	3 246	590	439	200	432	68	895
May 1, 1865	3 024	883	370	60	358	62	905
	–	–	2 026	370	1 268	239	–

Incorporating with the numbers above given those of other troops in service, we obtain the total strength of the army: and the following table presents the statistics in a form more comprehensive, though less adapted for the deduction of general laws. The "complete military population" includes those serving in the field and the navy, but otherwise only pertains to the territory already specified. For the numbers in the naval service I am indebted to the courtesy of Dr. P. J. Horwitz, U. S. N., Chief of the Bureau of Medicine and Surgery.

TABLE V.

General Statistics of Military Population, White and Colored Troops, and Navy.

Date	Complete Military Population	Growth	Military Population not in Army	Enlistments during Year	White Troops not included above	Colored Troops	Total Army	Navy
July 1, 1860	4 394	–	4 378	–	–	–	16	–
" 1861	4 518	125	4 333	170	2	–	187	20
" 1862	4 597	113	4 013	640	10	–	594	26
" 1863	4 644	121	3 888	517	19	14	789	40
" 1864	4 731	155	3 836	639	22	74	991	44
May 1, 1865	4 812	143	3 907	430	31	120	1 056	33
	–	657	–	2 396	–	–	–	–

The total number of enlistment credits was, as will be shown in the next chapter, about 2 760 000; of which 86 700 were for men who paid commutation. The actual enlistments of white soldiers were not far from 2 480 000; those of colored troops, including 7 122 white officers, were [1] 186 017 and those of sailors [2] 118 044.

[1] *Provost Marshal General's Report*, p. 69.

[2] *Report of Bureau of Equipment and Recruiting*, 1865–66, p. 200.

CHAPTER II.

NATIVITY OF UNITED STATES VOLUNTEERS.

1. *Nature of the Investigation. Available Materials.*

THE materials available for forming a trustworthy estimate of the nativities, and even the nationality of our soldiers have been very meager, and estimates which have been made by different persons at different times, have varied to an almost incredible extent. It has even been alleged, and that repeatedly, in unfriendly foreign publications and addresses, that the greater part of our armies was composed of Europeans, attracted by the bounties paid, or by other influences; while Americans, who knew the sources from which our army was chiefly recruited, and who had themselves either enlisted, or given fathers, sons, or brothers to the defense of the nation, may not improbably have been led to overrate the proportion of purely American birth.

When it is remembered how very considerable is the number of American citizens born in Europe, especially among the inhabitants of our Atlantic cities and several of the Western States, and it is farther borne in mind how promptly these classes responded to the call of their adopted country, — accepting the unwonted duties as readily as the well known privileges of citizenship, — it is manifest that the records of nativity, even were they complete, would only indirectly guide to the knowledge of the nationality of our volunteers. The only proper course for the inquiry seems to be, a determination of the nativity of the army from the best available sources of information, and a comparison of the numbers thus obtained with corresponding statistics of population afforded by the latest census.

It was not until the war had been waged for some time that the State or country of birth was systematically required upon the enlistment-rolls. At first it was recorded in but very few of the States,— often no information of the sort was demanded; and even where the enlistment-rolls were prepared with care, the place of residence was frequently given in the stead of the place of birth.

Various considerations, connected with bounties, with State aid, and with the quotas of the respective towns, actually led, in many instances, to a change in the form of the enlistment-blanks, by substituting a column for legal residence or place of enlistment, in the place of that originally provided for the nativity.

These facts have much impeded all endeavors to acquire an accurate knowledge of the nativities and original nationalities of our soldiers. Only two sources of information have seemed trustworthy: first, the actual records, in those instances where the needful facts were noted, and secondly, such information as could be derived from commanding officers or adjutants of regiments. And here the inquiry is embarrassed by other obstacles. Our soldiers enlisted for periods varying from three months to three years; very many of them enlisted anew at the expiration of their first period of service; and cases are not uncommon in which the same volunteer enlisted several times. Instances have indeed occurred, of five successive different enlistments by the same man. To discriminate these cases and avoid the repetition of the same records, has proved difficult, except for certain special organizations, such as Gen. Hancock's "First Army Corps" and the "Veteran Reserve Corps."

The first million of men, comprising chiefly those soldiers whose ages are discussed in our chapter upon the "*Ages of Volunteers*," were mostly drawn from the population under the immediate stimulus of the first patriotic emotions. At that time the moral influences affecting enlistment were essentially different from those which came into play at a later period. The pressure of repeated calls for troops had not that stringency which was felt when our supply of able-bodied men became seriously impaired, when the number left at home became inadequate for the needs of the community, and when the alternative presented itself between the offer of large bounties or the acceptance of a conscription. Most of the patriotic men who could go to the war had already gone, and the chief available source for new troops, beside the annual supply of young men attaining military age, consisted in that class of men who could be tempted by the large bounties, or were influenced directly or indirectly by the pressing danger of conscription. It is to troops raised under these latter circumstances, after the activity of the Provost Marshal General's Bureau had commenced, that most of the official records of nativity belong. How very much larger was the purely American element among the earlier troops needs not to be recalled to any one then in the country; and a mere mention of the circumstances will readily make manifest to any inquirer that, to a large extent, the only statistics attainable will understate the proportion of soldiers of native birth.

This obstacle to the attainment of an accurate result might be obviated to some extent by a resort to the other method of investigation, namely, application to the original officers of regiments. This course has been attempted, but with less success than was anticipated. The large number of officers who lost their lives in the service, the length of time that has elapsed since the outbreak of the war, the grave duties which promotion to higher offices has since entailed on most of the survivors, the difficulty of obtaining their present address, are among the impediments which will be recognized at once. Still the endeavor has been made, and letters of inquiry have been addressed to about one thousand commanding officers of regiments whose nativities are not to be found upon the records. The replies, though comparatively few and often meager, have been most kindly afforded us where our letters seem to have reached the officers intended, and have, in general, proved very serviceable; and when, as in a few instances, records have been subsequently found, or when estimates for the same regiment have been received from different persons, the accordance has been found so satisfactory as to justify a reliance upon the results thus obtained.

2. *Statistics of Enlistments and Reenlistments.*

The total number of actual enlistments and commissions for army and navy during the war, excluding colored troops, cannot have differed very much from 2 585 000. In the national credits to the several States, the military and naval enlistments were combined, thus offering an additional embarrassment to our inquiry; but, from the best information attainable after a careful scrutiny of official records, it would seem probable that about 2 480 000 of these enlistments were for the army. If from this number we could deduct the number of reenlistments (also unknown), we should have the total number of different white volunteer soldiers, the State or county of whose birth we seek. The nativities of about 1 205 000 of these have been collected by us, from the records at the national and State capitals; and those of the remainder, or about 905 000, are to be determined from other sources. For about 293 000 of these, the answers received from regimental officers afford a tolerably good estimate, and for the remainder we must resort to reasonable inference.

Our results are given in Table I.

TABLE I.

Enlistments from the Several States.

		Grand Total	Commuted	Men actually Furnished	Naval Enlistments	Soldiers Furnished	Colored Troops	White Soldiers	Reenlistments
Maine	U. S.	71 745	2 007	69 738	3 097	64 708	104	64 604	–
	State	72 945	2 000	70 945	6 754	64 191	115	64 076	3 400[a]
New Hampshire	U. S.	34 605	692	33 913	371	33 025	125	32 900	–
	State	34 560	–	–	–	32 986[b]	–	–	2 005
Vermont	U. S.	35 246	1 974	33 272	103	32 653	120	32 533	–
	State	34 238	1 971	32 267	215[c]	32 052	239	31 813	1 961
Massachusetts	U. S.	151 785	5 318	146 467	16 834	126 236	3 966	122 270	–
	State	159 165	5 318	153 847	26 317	127 530	5 486	122 044	10 356
Rhode Island and Connecticut . .	U. S.	80 981	1 978	79 003	1 804	74 895	3 601	71 294	–
	State	78 891	1 922	76 969	2 788	74 181	–	–	6 125
New York	U. S.	464 156	18 197	445 959	28 427	404 748	4 125	400 623	–
	State	473 443[d]	18 183	455 260	41 090	414 170	5 829	408 341	20 897
New Jersey	U. S.	79 511	4 196	75 315	1 858	67 186	1 185	66 001	–
	State	88 305[e]	–	–	4 853	–	3 092	–	2 954
Pennsylvania	U. S.	366 326	28 171	338 155	9 529	323 846	8 612	315 234	–
	State	361 903	–	–	–	–	–	–	17 495[f]

Delaware	U. S.	13 651	1 386	12 265	79	12 171	954	11 217	–
	State	–	–	–	–	–	–	–	–
Maryland	U. S.	49 731	3 678	46 053	2 217	42 128	8 718	33 410	–
	State	–	–	–	–	–	–	–	–
District of Columbia	U. S.	16 872	338	16 534	558	15 181	3 269	11 912	–
	State	–	–	–	–	–	–	–	–
West Virginia	U. S.	32 003	0	32 003	–	32 003	196	31 807	–
	State	31 884	0	31 884	–	31 884	213	31 671	3 100
Kentucky	U. S.	78 540	3 265	75 275	5	74 961	23 703	51 258	–
	State	89 413[g]	–	–	–	–	25 438	–	8 000
Ohio	U. S.	317 133	6 479	310 654	1 076	307 380	5 092	302 288	–
	State	366 626[h]	6 290	360 336	–	–	–	–	30 000
Indiana	U. S.	195 147	784	194 363	71	193 285	1 537	191 748	–
	State	251 437[i]	785	250 652	–	–	1 500	–	13 181
Illinois	U. S.	258 217	55	258 162	1 171	255 938	1 811	254 127	–
	State	271 297[k]	55	271 242	1 500	269 742	2 500	267 242	25 000
Michigan	U. S.	90 119	2 008	88 111	–	87 613	1 387	86 226	–
	State	92 729	1 982	90 747	483	90 264	1 453	88 811	5 545
Wisconsin	U. S.	96 118	5 097	91 021	–	90 888	165	90 723	–
	State	–	–	–	–	–	437	90 942	10 784
Minnesota	U. S.	25 034	1 032	24 002	–	23 999	104	23 895	–
	State	25 031	1 109	23 922	0	–	39	23 883	1 445

TABLE I.—(*Continued.*)

Enlistments from the Several States.

		Grand Total	Commuted	Men actually Furnished	Naval Enlistments	Soldiers Furnished	Colored Troops	White Soldiers	Reenlistments
Iowa	U. S.	75 860	67	75 793	–	75 788	440	75 348	–
	State	80 000	–	–	–	–	600	79 400	6 850
Missouri	U. S.	108 773	–	108 773	134	108 756	8 344	100 412	–
	State	110 000[l]	–	–	–	–	–	–	4 000
Kansas	U. S.	20 097	2	20 095	–	20 095	2 080	18 015	–
	State	–	–	–	–	–	–	–	–
Other States and Territories	U. S.	183 130[m]	–	183 130	–	–	–	–	–
	State	–	–	–	–	–	–	–	–

a 3533 Veteran Volunteers. *Report of the Secretary of War*, 1865, page 21.
b Not including one battalion.
c Of 1215 "regulars, marines, and seamen," 1000 are counted as for the army.
d Including 15 987 "emergency men."
e Including 8957 not credited by United States.
f 18 607 Veteran Volunteers. *Report of the Secretary of War*, 1865, page 21.
g Not including State troops.
h Probably 40 000 or 50 000 of this number represent militia called out on emergency and not regularly enlisted into the U. S. service.
i 50 000 were State troops paid by the United States.
k About 15 000 "emergency men" not credited.
l Not including State troops.
m This is obtained by increasing the 92 073 from page 163, by 91 057 Negroes assumed to have been furnished by these States, but not included in the table there given. This latter number is obtained thus: —

Total number of colored troops from all the States (not including 7122 white officers) (page 69)	178 895
Total number of colored troops from States already considered (as shown in general summary)	87 838
Remainder	91 057

The summaries are intended to present in as condensed a form as may well be, the data available for the formation of trustworthy estimates. For each State two sets of numbers are given, the first derived from the excellent and comprehensive "Report of the U. S. Provost Marshal General," and the second deduced from the data published by the Adjutant Generals of the several States, or courteously furnished to us from their files. In most cases, as might be anticipated, the numbers recorded in the archives of the State are larger than those at the War Department at Washington, inasmuch as the former give all the enlistments recorded, while the latter mostly refer to those only for which credit was allowed toward the State quotas. The number of men who paid commutation is, of course, more accurately given by the federal officers; while on the other hand, the figures representing the naval enlistments given by the Provost Marshal General are those found on pages 71, 72 of his "Report," and only include the equivalent, in three-years' men, of those, prior to February, 1864, for which sufficient legal evidence was brought to warrant their inclusion with the credits of the State.

The number of "soldiers furnished" in the column of figures from the "Provost Marshal General's Report" is taken from pages 78, 79; that of "men actually furnished" being taken from page 163. Although, from the fact that a special line is given for colored troops on page 79, it would seem that they were not comprised in the numbers of the last column on that page, yet a careful study of the figures leads to the conviction that they are in fact there included. The differences between the numbers given on these two pages, when compared with the number of naval enlistments according to the State authorities, and with the number of colored troops furnished by the States, according to independent sources of information, leave no room for doubt on this point;[1] the case being made very clear by those States which, like Missouri, Kentucky, and Kansas, furnished the relatively largest supply of colored troops.

Therefore, although on comparing the table of colored troops, page 69, with that on page 163, it might be inferred that the table on page 79 contains no colored troops among the State forces, it appears, nevertheless, beyond reasonable doubt, that they are so included.

The estimate of the total number of reenlistments is the most

[1] If the colored troops are included in the table, page 163, they must also be included in the last column on page 78. But a comparison with the figures given on pages 43, 44, with those on page 163, shows conclusively that they are so included in the latter.

difficult step of all, and the attainment of accurate knowledge on this point is probably impossible. No official information seems to exist, except in some isolated cases, for other organizations than those which, like the "Veteran Volunteers," the "Veteran Reserves," and the "First Army Corps," consisted exclusively of reenlisted men, or those regiments which reenlisted in a body. To attain the best possible estimates, it is requisite, first, to form some approximate judgment as to the total number of reenlistments, and then to apportion these among the several States, according to the most satisfactory information which could be collected.

The basis of the total estimate of reenlistments was as follows: —

Veterans enlisted under calls of February 1 and March 14, 1864 [1]	136 507
Additional veterans, under call of July 18, 1864 [2] . . .	11 869
Enlisted in "Veteran Reserve Corps" [3]	60 508
Enlisted in "First Corps" (Hancock's), about . . .	9 116
Estimated number of original three-months' men who reenlisted upon expiration of their first term, in 1861	60 000
Estimated number enlisting anew during the war after discharge for disability, etc., about	92 000
	370 000

The difficulties in the way of any closer approach to accuracy are great, and it may be questioned whether data exist for any very trustworthy estimation of the last two items. Still these cannot apparently be far from the truth. That no means exist of determining the number of reenlistments from materials in the War Department, may be inferred from a remark of the Provost Marshal General, page 58.

"In filling the different calls," he says, "each accepted enlistment was credited, instead of limiting the credit to the actual number of persons who entered the service anew; and hence, to determine the number of men actually entering the service for the first time under the different calls, the number credited should be reduced in the same ratio that the enlistments of the same persons have been repeated. The extent of this reduction cannot be calculated at this time, or even estimated with sufficient accuracy to be useful."

To assign these 370 000 reenlistments to their respective States,

1 *Provost Marshal General's Report*, p. 43. 2 *Ibid.* 3 *Ibid.*, p. 79.

4 Compare *ibid.* p. 79 with *Report of Secretary of War*, 1866, p. 86. Of 3 183 casualties to August 1865, about 1 700 are assumed to have occurred before May 1.

the numbers obtained from the Adjutant Generals of all the States, excepting Maryland, Delaware, and Kansas, and from the "Report of the Secretary of War"[1] for these States and the District of Columbia, were similarly increased in such a ratio as to bring their resultant total up to the required number. Exceptions to this rule were, however, made for Massachusetts, Kentucky, Ohio, Illinois, Wisconsin, and Missouri, for which six States special means of information were found. For Kentucky and Wisconsin, the original estimate seems to conform to that afforded by other sources of information.

We have thus the following table, in which the first column of figures is that obtained from the State records, and the second that to which careful investigation leads as the most probable numbers for all reenlistments, recorded or not; and there is reason to believe that they are near approximations to the truth.

Reenlistments.

State	Recorded No.	Probable No.	State	Recorded No.	Probable No.
Maine . . .	3 400	9 291	Kentucky .	8 000	8 000
New Hamp. .	2 005	5 479	Ohio . . .	30 000	45 000
Vermont . .	1 961	5 359	Indiana . .	13 181	36 018
Massachusetts	10 356	15 000	Illinois . .	25 000	36 000
R. I. and Conn.	6 125	16 737	Michigan .	5 545	15 152
New York . .	20 897	57 102	Wisconsin .	10 784	10 784
New Jersey .	2 954	8 072	Minnesota .	1 445	3 949
Pennsylvania	17 495	47 806	Iowa . . .	6 850	18 719
Delaware . .	404	1 104	Missouri .	4 000	15 000[2]
Maryland . .	2 003	5 473	Kansas . .	425	1 161
Dist. Columbia	118	323			
West Virginia	3 100	8 471	Total . .	176 048	370 000

3. *Collection of Nativities.*

In the General Summary of Enlistments, which follows, the results are presented as inferred from the data already given, together with a statement of the number of troops for which it has been found possible to collect the nativities.

All nativities recorded on the descriptive muster-rolls at the State

[1] 1865, p. 21.

[2] Adjutant General Simpson believes that there were probably as many as 10 000 reenlistments among the German population of Missouri; but in this "German population" he counts all members of German families who retain their ancestral usages, — whether American-born or not.

capitals have been transcribed there by the agents of the Commission, who have been furnished with all needful facilities in every instance. In some cases special rolls have been found to exist, giving information as to the birthplace of the troops.

For regiments not thus described, attempts were made, as already mentioned, to obtain the desired information by application to officers who commanded them at an early period of their history. The addresses of these officers, generally their first Colonel, Lieutenant-Colonel, or Adjutant, having been obtained from the Adjutant

TABLE II.

General Summary of Enlistments.

State	Grand Total	Commuted	Served	Navy	No. Soldiers	Colored
Maine	72 945	2 007	70 938	6 754	64 184	115
New Hampshire . .	34 500	692	33 808	380	33 428	125
Vermont . . .	34 500	1 974	32 526	215	32 311	239
Massachusetts .	157 600	5 318	152 282	26 317	125 965	5 486
R. I. and Conn. .	80 000	1 978	78 022	2 788	75 234	3 601
New York . . .	460 000	18 197	441 803	41 100	400 703	5 829
New Jersey . .	79 500	4 196	75 304	4 853	70 451	3 092
Pennsylvania . .	370 000	28 171	341 829	13 929	327 900	8 612
Delaware . . .	13 600	1 386	12 214	129	12 085	954
Maryland . . .	49 000	3 678	45 322	3 217	42 105	8 718
Dist. of Columbia	16 800	338	16 462	842	15 620	3 269
West Virginia .	32 000	–	32 000	–	32 000	213
Kentucky . . .	80 000	3 265	76 735	155	76 580	25 438
Ohio	318 000	6 479	311 521	1 576	309 945	5 092
Indiana . . .	195 000	784	194 216	271	193 945	1 537
Illinois	257 000	55	256 945	1 500	255 445	2 500
Michigan . . .	91 000	2 008	88 992	483	88 509	1 453
Wisconsin . . .	96 000	5 097	90 903	200	90 703	437
Minnesota . . .	25 000	1 032	23 968	–	23 968	104
Iowa	76 000	67	75 933	–	75 933	600
Missouri . . .	109 000	–	109 000	234	108 766	8 344
Kansas	20 100	2	20 098	–	20 098	2 080
California . . .	15 700	–	15 700	–	15 700	–
Other States and Territories . .	167 357	–	167 357	–	167 357	91 057
Total	2 850 602	86 724	2 763 878	104 943	2 658 935	178 895

General of the State, circular letters were forwarded them, asking for the best estimate which they could make. About 1000 such letters were sent in all, to which about 350 answers have been received. In some cases full records were thus obtained, and in most cases where answers were received, the estimates kindly communicated seem entitled to great reliance. The number of troops whose nativities are derived from these sources are separately indicated in the table; and in the last column is given the number of volunteers from each State whose nativities could not be obtained at all.

TABLE II. — (*Continued.*)

General Summary of Enlistments.

State	White Soldiers	Reenlistments	Different White Soldiers	Nativities already obtained			Nativities not obtained
				Recorded	Estimated	Total	
Maine . . .	64 069	9 300	54 800	52 325	–	52 325	2 475
N. Hampshire.	33 303	5 500	27 800	26 832	–	26 832	968
Vermont . .	32 072	5 300	26 800	24 072	2 728	26 800	–
Massachusetts.	120 479	15 000	105 500	49 776	21 093	70 869	34 631
R. I. and Conn.	71 633	16 700	54 900	41 318	12 864	54 182	718
New York . .	394 874	57 100	337 800	230 267	3 142	233 409	104 391
New Jersey . .	67 359	8 100	59 300	18 875	–	18 875	40 425
Pennsylvania .	319 288	47 800	271 500	77 425	54 943	132 368	139 132
Delaware . .	11 131	1 100	10 000	–	–	–	10 000
Maryland . .	33 387	5 500	27 900	7 337	–	7 337	20 563
Dist. of Colum.	12 351	400	12 000	–	–	–	12 000
West Virginia	31 787	8 500	23 300	17 562	3 541	21 103	2 197
Kentucky . .	51 142	8 000	43 100	19 955	23 145	43 100	–
Ohio	304 853	45 000	259 900	108 288	87 570	195 858	64 042
Indiana . . .	192 408	36 000	156 400	118 254	19 362	137 616	18 784
Illinois . . .	252 945	36 000	216 900	188 832	–	188 832	28 068
Michigan . .	87 056	15 100	72 000	23 322	37 859	61 181	10 819
Wisconsin . .	90 266	10 800	79 500	55 136		55 136	24 364
Minnesota . .	23 864	3 900	20 000	18 056	–	18 056	1 944
Iowa	75 333	18 700	56 600	54 611	–	54 611	1 989
Missouri . .	100 422	15 000	85 400	58 259	27 141	85 400	–
Kansas . . .	18 018	1 200	16 800	11 411	–	11 411	5 389
California . .	15 700	–	15 700	–	–	–	15 700
Other States and Terr's	76 300	–	76 300	3 159	–	3 159	73 141
Total . . .	2 480 040	370 000	2 110 200	1 205 072	293 388	1 498 460	611 740

4. *Results and Inferences regarding Nativities of the Volunteer Army.*

The numbers in the last column of Table II. have been distributed among the different nativities in the proportions of those troops from the same State whose nativities were obtained, excepting for Massachusetts, where the proportion deduced from officers' estimates was used, inasmuch as the small number of recorded nativities belonged to regiments of a different character, and for New Jersey. For Delaware and the District of Columbia, in neither of which any nativities were recorded, the distribution was made according to the combined ratios resulting from the recorded nativities in Pennsylvania, Maryland, and West Virginia. And finally, for California and the troops classed as from "other States and Territories," the distribution was adopted which results from the remainder of the statistics, so that the proportions for the total armies are not affected thereby.

It will be readily perceived that the principles adopted are such as to lead to an underestimate of the American element, by applying the relative nativities of troops recruited during the latter part of the war to the unregistered soldiers who volunteered at the outbreak of the struggle. Still, as it is clearly out of the question to form any trustworthy numerical estimate of the influence of this mode of estimation, it seems the better course to give the resultant figures, after calling attention to this source of inaccuracy in the inferences.

We thus arrive at the following table of nativities for the volunteers from the several States, the colored troops being, of course, omitted, as also the navy, and the 92 000 volunteers from States and Territories not here considered. The word "volunteers" is here used in the official signification, as denoting the citizen soldiery in distinction from regular soldiers, and not, as in a subsequent chapter, in distinction from recruits.

TABLE III.

Nativities of United States Volunteers.

Place of Enlistment	Native Americans	British Americans	English	Irish	Germans	Other Foreigners	"Foreigners" not otherwise designated	Total No. different White Soldiers
Maine . . .	48 135	3 217	779	1 971	244	454	–	54 800
New Hampshire	19 759	2 362	1 147	2 699	952	881	–	27 800
Vermont . .	22 037	2 713	325	1 289	86	208	142	26 800
Massachusetts .	79 560	2 917	2 306	10 007	1 876	1 591	7 243	105 500
R. I. and Conn.	37 190	1 697	2 234	7 657	2 919	2 129	1 074	54 900
New York . .	203 622	19 985	14 024	51 206	36 680	11 555	728	337 800
New Jersey . .	35 496	2 692	2 491	8 880	7 337	2 051	353	59 300
Pennsylvania .	222 641	1 339	3 503	17 418	17 208	3 532	5 859	271 500
Delaware . .	8 306	45	127	582	621	130	189	10 000
Maryland . .	22 435	155	403	1 400	3 107	400	–	27 900
Dist. of Colum.	9 967	54	152	698	746	156	227	12 000
West Virginia	21 111	35	248	550	869	284	203	23 300
Kentucky . .	38 988	67	117	1 303	1 943	181	501	43 100
Ohio . . .	219 949	1 589	2 619	8 129	20 102	3 149	4 363	259 900
Indiana . . .	141 454	760	1 248	3 472	7 190	1 374	902	156 400
Illinois . . .	168 983	4 404	5 953	12 041	18 140	7 379	–	216 900
Michigan . .	54 830	3 136	1 310	3 278	3 534	1 251	4 661	72 000
Wisconsin . .	47 972	3 371	3 703	3 621	15 709	5 124	–	79 500
Minnesota . .	11 977	1 371	614	1 140	2 715	2 183	–	20 000
Iowa	48 686	995	1 015	1 436	2 850	1 618	–	56 600
Missouri . .	46 676	359	761	4 362	30 899	2 343	–	85 400
Kansas . . .	13 493	269	429	1 082	1 090	437	–	16 800
Grand Total .	1 523 267	53 532	45 508	144 221	176 817	48 410	26 445	2 018 200

To compare these proportions with those existing in the population, Table IV. has been prepared, showing the numbers which would have been found for each nativity, had no enlistments taken place except from those who were inhabitants of the United States in 1860, and had those of every nativity enlisted in the same ratio.

This is the only comparison of the kind which existing statistics permit, but it fails of perfect applicability, for the reason that the numbers of the military population of foreign birth had increased through immigration during the subsequent five years by about 230 000.

TABLE IV.

Distribution of United States Volunteers according to the Nativities of the Population, in 1860.

Place of Enlistment	Native Americans	British Americans	English	Irish	Germans	Other Foreigners	"Foreigners" not otherwise designated	Total No. different White Soldiers
Maine . . .	51 526	1 533	234	1 337	34	132	4	54 800
New Hampshire	26 012	382	195	1 088	35	88	–	27 800
Vermont . .	24 009	1 345	139	1 149	19	136	3	26 800
Massachusetts .	83 033	2 338	2 060	16 017	860	1 160	32	105 500
R. I. and Conn.	44 480	527	1 344	7 124	824	596	5	54 900
New York . .	249 759	4 873	9 346	43 911	22 591	7 301	19	337 800
New Jersey .	48 041	104	1 454	5 686	3 097	917	1	59 300
Pennsylvania .	230 478	332	4 435	19 242	13 173	3 832	8	271 500
Delaware . .	8 988	4	175	644	139	50	–	10 000
Maryland . .	23 707	18	229	1 345	2 373	227	1	27 900
Dist. of Colum.	9 535	12	203	1 433	643	172	2	12 000
West Virginia	22 652	7	76	305	194	66	–	23 300
Kentucky . .	40 297	29	211	1 043	1 276	242	2	43 100
Ohio	222 852	799	3 691	8 671	18 984	4 879	24	259 900
Indiana . . .	142 593	370	1 087	2 862	7 793	1 662	33	156 400
Illinois . . .	175 583	2 562	5 313	11 145	16 647	5 552	98	216 900
Michigan . .	57 418	3 568	2 518	2 939	3 793	1 761	3	72 000
Wisconsin . .	51 045	1 865	3 138	5 134	12 729	5 585	4	79 500
Minnesota . .	13 066	947	409	1 515	2 172	1 890	1	20 000
Iowa	47 689	698	968	2 358	3 239	1 646	2	56 600
Missouri . .	72 509	226	804	3 490	7 105	1 251	15	85 400
Kansas . . .	14 796	156	221	614	682	310	21	16 800
Grand Total .	1 660 068	22 695	38 250	139 052	118 402	39 455	278	2 018 200

Another fruitful source of apparent excess of the foreign element in the army is to be found in the large number of foreigners, who, attracted by the large local bounties frequently offered, enlisted for the purpose of obtaining the bounty-money, and then deserted without serving. It is beyond question that cases were of not rare occurrence where the same person enlisted very many times, securing bounty in each case, and being, of course, recorded every time as a new volunteer.[1]

[1] "As soon as large *local* bounties were offered and paid in advance, a set of desperate characters presented themselves, who would enlist and 'jump' bounties as often as opportunities presented. A man now in the Albany penitentiary, undergoing an imprisonment

The recorded number of deserters was 268 530, although the Provost Marshal General considers that about one fourth of these were subsequently accounted for.[1] More than 76 000 were arrested, but probably as many as 125 000 different enlistments failed to yield soldiers to the army, although they led to their entry upon the official records.

In this connection it may not be amiss to quote the words of General Fry:[2] —

"It appears beyond dispute that the crime of desertion is especially characteristic of troops from large cities, and of the districts which they supply with recruits. The ratio per thousand of desertions to credits throughout the loyal States is 62.51. . . .

"It is probable that a more minute examination of the statistics of the army than has yet been made, would reveal the fact that desertion is a crime of foreign, rather than native birth, and that but a small proportion of the men who forsook their colors were Americans. It is a notorious circumstance that the great mass of the professional bounty-jumpers were Europeans. In general, the manufacturing States, as, for instance, Massachusetts, Connecticut, Rhode Island, New York, and New Jersey, rank high in the column of desertion; and this result is to be attributed not only to the fact that such States are dotted with towns and cities, but to the secondary fact that these towns and cities are crowded with foreigners. The respectable and industrious part of this population did, indeed, produce a mass of faithful troops; but with these were mixed a vast number of adventurers unworthy of any country, who had no affection for the republic, and only enlisted for money."

To sum up the results of this investigation, we find that of the 2 018 000 different white volunteers recorded from the loyal States exclusive of the Pacific Coast, about 1 523 000 were probably native Americans, while an equable representation of the population of these States in 1860 would have given 1 660 000 native Americans. But this takes no account either of the normal immigration subsequent to that date, nor of the number of unarrested deserters which would alone have made these numbers equal, and which chiefly consisted of foreigners. Any attempt to allow for these influences alone could not fail to show as large a proportion of natives in the ranks of the army, as in the military population remaining at home. The proportion of native Americans among the officers was of course much larger than this.

of four years, confessed to having 'jumped the bounty' *thirty-two times*."—*Provost Marshal General's Report*, p. 153

[1] *Ibid.* p. 89.

[2] *Ibid.* p. 75.

CHAPTER III.

AGES OF VOLUNTEERS.

1. *Introductory.*

On taking charge of the Statistical Department of the United States Sanitary Commission, in August, 1864, it was found that considerable progress had been made in collecting the ages of the soldiers of our volunteer regiments, — an investigation which had been suggested and commenced by Mr. Elliott, the accomplished and skilful statistician, who, not very long before, had relinquished the direction of this Bureau of the Commission.

Although the best use to be made of the materials appeared somewhat uncertain, it did not seem proper to discontinue inquiries already so far advanced; and the large experience of Mr. Elliott in matters connected with vital statistics gave assurance that valuable as well as interesting results were likely to be deduced from a thorough study of these data.

The collection of these materials was therefore continued and completed, by means of the muster-rolls on file at the War Department in Washington, to which access was courteously afforded by General E. D. Townsend, Acting Adjutant-General, and Colonel Samuel Breck, who was in charge of the rolls. Tables have thus been formed for twenty-seven States, Territories, or geographical groups, exhibiting the number of men at each year of age in the volunteer organizations, at the time of their muster into the service of the United States. The officers are tabulated as a distinct class; and the three arms of the military service — infantry, cavalry, and artillery — have been treated separately.

The original collection of the materials was principally made by M. T. J. O'Connell, until lately the efficient and accurate chief clerk of the Statistical Department, and was completed by Mr. E. A. Wilson, prior to the order of Mr. Secretary Stanton debarring the Sanitary Commission from access to the archives. The greater part of the computations has been performed by Mr. Stockwell alone, with great care, perseverance, and ability.

The recruits who joined these original regiments after their first organization and acceptance into the national service are not included; and the limits of the investigation have excluded all drafted men, substitutes, etc. Moreover, many regiments belonging within these limits are omitted, because organized since the collection of the data for the States to which they belong; but the number of these is comparatively small, and inadequate to exert any sensible effect upon the results. The degree of completeness may be seen by the following table, which shows the number and date of the latest regiment included in the collection.

Arkansas	2d	Infantry,	latest.
California	4th	"	1862, Feb.
Connecticut	28th	"	1862, Nov.
Delaware	2d	"	1861, Dec.
Illinois	131st	"	1864, June.
Indiana	115th	"	1863, Aug.
Iowa	48th	"	1865.
Kansas	15th	"	1863.
Kentucky	52d	"	1864.
Louisiana	N. O. Vols.		1864, May.
Maine	28th	Infantry	1864.
Maryland	10th	"	1864, June.
Mass.	59th	"	1864, July.
Michigan	27th	"	1864, Aug.
Minnesota	10th	"	1864, Aug.
Mississippi	Marine Brig.		only organ'n.
Missouri	34th	Infantry	1862, Dec.
Nevada	1st	"	1864, June.
N. Hampshire	18th	"	1864, Sept.
New Jersey	25th	"	1862, Sept.
N. Mexico	4th	"	1863.
New York	177th	"	1863, June.
Ohio	128th	"	1863, Aug.
Pennsylvania	155th	"	1863, Jan.
Rhode Island	12th	"	1862, Oct.
Tennessee	8th	"	1864.
Vermont	16th	"	1862, Oct.
W. Virginia	15th	"	1862, Sept.
Wash. Terr.	1st	"	only reg't
Wisconsin	53d	"	1864.

The total number of volunteers whose ages have thus been investigated is 1 049 457, of whom 1 012 273 were enlisted men, and 37 184 were commissioned officers. All except $1\frac{1}{2}$ per centum (.01495) of the men, and $3\frac{1}{3}$ per centum (.0331) of the officers, were between the ages of 18 and 46 years at the date of their enlistment or commission. Those beyond these limits have not been included in the determination of the general formulas, so that these depend upon the statistics of ages for 1 032 600 men, of whom 35 953 were commissioned officers.*

The results have proved amenable to law in a higher degree than I had ventured to anticipate. Residual discordances exist, of course, between the numbers for each year of age, as derived from the tabulated records, and those indicated by the general formulas deduced from the whole series; yet where these discordances attain any essential magnitude, they may almost invariably be made to yield instructive and useful information.

The results attained, for that portion of the population who thus rushed to the field at their country's call, naturally suggest analogous inquiries regarding the white male population of the United States, and especially relative to the population of that portion of the country which furnished the volunteers under consideration. And it was not until after many unavailing efforts to obtain information as to the distribution of our population by ages, that the great deficiency of our knowledge of the facts and laws relative to this very important subject became manifest.

The only published attempt, of which I am aware, to classify the population of the United States according to years of age is very crude, and the method pursued yields results quite at variance from the truth. The only trustworthy facts are contained in the summaries of the census-returns; and the groups into which the population is there divided are altogether too large to permit the desired laws to be deduced with ease. It is earnestly to be hoped that in future census-publications the groups may be so made as to include intervals of age not greater than five years.

It thus became important, if only for the sake of comparison between the ages of the volunteer troops and that of the population whence they sprung, to subject the census of 1860 to a similar discussion. And I cannot but think that the results elicited might be advantageously employed, so far as they apply and extend, for the life-tables of our insurance and annuity offices. The life-curve for our American population is clearly diverse from the curve on which the present English tables are based;

* The prescribed limits of military age at the commencement of the rebellion were 18 and 45 years; but the large proportional number at the age of 45 seems to indicate that the law was so interpreted as to permit the acceptance of volunteers whose age at their last birthday did not exceed 45 years.

and it is a source of regret that the proper limits of the present investigation forbid its extension into the tempting fields of inquiry which their comparison suggests.

The fact which first attracts attention among the results of this research is the marked diversity between the distribution of the ages of officers and that of the enlisted men. Each follows a clearly manifest law; in each case the law is deducible with close approximation to the truth; so also is the law governing the ages of our population; yet each of the three is utterly different from the other two. The sources of the diversity may well be made the object of careful research, and not without a reasonable probability of useful results. Certain discordances between the recorded and the computed numbers for a few particular ages will be considered hereafter.

2. *Ages of the Enlisted Men.*

The grand total of the rank and file of the volunteers whose ages are included in this discussion is shown in the following tabular view, which exhibits the recorded age at last birthday for the entire number; although, as already stated, those under 18 or over 45 (last birthday), 15 626 in all, have been excluded from the general discussion. These excluded cases represent two classes, viz. the boys, chiefly drummers, musicians, &c., and the men who, although past the legal age, were so sturdy or earnest that the enrolling officers did not, at that time of great national peril, feel justified in insisting on an absolute compliance with the legal qualifications.

In the column entitled "Miscellaneous" are included all those organizations which do not belong strictly within the three principal arms of the military service, such as Engineers, Sharpshooters, Mounted Infantry, Coast Guards, Marine Brigades, &c., together with a few regiments or battalions for which the statistics were received after the special computations for Infantry, Cavalry, and Artillery had been completed, so that their incorporation with these would have required a repetition of the calculations without producing any essential change in the result.

TABLE I.

Classified Summary of Enlisted Volunteers.

Age at last birthday.	ACTUAL NUMBER OF MEN.				Total at each year of age.
	Infantry.	Cavalry.	Artillery.	Miscellaneous.	
13	113	5	0	9	127
14	288	15	2	25	330
15	636	49	21	67	773
16	2053	232	61	412	2758
17	4653	638	226	908	6425
18	103420	15013	5400	9642	133475
19	71226	9767	3439	5783	90215
20	56238	7864	2627	4329	71058
21	75978	12081	4416	4661	97136
22	57485	9096	3107	3703	73391
23	48954	7806	2759	3198	62717
24	40852	6361	2163	2719	52095
25	36383	5724	2012	2507	46626
26	31292	4831	1768	2352	40243
27	26369	4192	1505	2220	34286
28	27196	4318	1525	2273	35312
29	18833	2845	1087	1748	24513
30	21937	3251	1213	1959	28360
31	12814	2053	796	2301	17954
32	17038	2450	931	1548	21967
33	13678	1950	753	1598	17979
34	12004	1679	724	1333	15740
35	14558	2130	836	1456	18980
36	10437	1541	702	1377	14057
37	8782	1268	477	1293	11820
38	10025	1416	579	1326	13346
39	7200	979	416	1001	9596
40	10886	1441	649	1019	13995
41	5634	822	320	659	7435
42	8369	1199	535	826	10929
43	7900	1079	533	828	10340
44	12274	1851	796	1149	16070
45	5509	954	289	260	7012
46	737	105	45	80	967
47	541	74	34	63	712
48	532	73	31	63	699
49	354	60	17	38	469
50 & over.	1942	203	68	153	2366

The relative excess of the numbers at certain particular ages, and the corresponding defect at others, strikes the attention at the first glance. To the former class belong the ages, 21 years, most years divisible by 5 (excepting 20 and 45), and those divisible by 2; to the latter class belong most of those years of age whose last digit is 1 or 9. By determining the general law of distribution, we may obtain the measure of this excess, and thus throw light upon the origin of these discordances.

The following facts are also manifest, or readily deducible: —

Of the whole number, 1 012 273, about 1 per centum (.0102), were below, and a little more than one half as many (.0052) were above, the limits of military age, interpreted as between the ages 18 and 46.

Of the number 996 647, within these limits, —

The average age at last birthday is . . . . . $25^{y}.3250$
The average age at time of enlistment is . . . 25.8083
The age above and below which the numbers are equal is 23.477
There were of the age 18 years . . . . . 13.27 per cent.
under 21 years . . . . . 29.52 "
under 25 years . . . . . 58.34 "
under 30 years . . . . . 76.57 "

The very close accordance of the proportional numbers for the total force of about a million of men from all the loyal States, with those deduced* by Mr. Elliott for less than 51 000 men from the single State of Massachusetts, is very striking. Tables for the individual States and groups of States, herewith presented, unite in corroborating the inference that this distribution is due to no special local influences, but to a general and overruling law, which varies but slightly through widely distant regions of our country, and seems scarcely affected by any influences dependent upon immigration from abroad.

This law, which was found by Mr. Elliott to hold good also for the Massachusetts troops, shows the number of volunteers (en listed men, not including officers) at each successive year of age to form a series of which the first differences are in geometrical progression.

When the ratio of this geometrical progression is unity, the

* "*On the Military Statistics of the United States of America,*" Proceedings of the International Statistical Congress, V Session, 1863, p. 32.

progression becomes arithmetical; when, as in the present case, it is less than unity, we have a decreasing rate of change.

Let this ratio be denoted by h, and the number of men at any given year of age be

$$x_n = b + c\,(1 - h)\,h^n \qquad (1)$$

so that the total number at and over that age will be

$$s_n = a - b\,n + c\,h^n \qquad (2)$$

in which n denotes the excess of the age above 18 years, at which epoch

$$s_0 = a + c.$$

The constants a, b, c, h are to be determined, and we have

$$\Delta x_0 = c\,(1 - h)^2, \qquad \Delta x_n = c\,h^n\,(1 - h)^2, \qquad \Delta_m x_{m\,n} = c\,h^{m\,n}\,(1 - h^m)^2$$

whence

$$h^n = \frac{\Delta_m x_{mn}}{\Delta_m x_{(m+1)\,n}} \qquad (3)$$

which enables us to determine h from the most convenient equidistant portions of the series.

The variation of the fundamental equation (2) gives for any change in the values of the constants

$$\partial s_n = \partial a - n\,\partial b + h^n\,\partial c + n\,c\,h^{n-1}\,\partial h, \qquad (4)$$

by means of which, after an approximate value of h has been deduced from (3), and corresponding values of a, b, c derived from the numerical data for any four years, the corrected values of all four constants may be derived by the method of least squares.

The total number up to any given age, or the definite sum from x_0 to x_n, is evidently

$$s_0 - s_n = b\,n + c\,(1 - h^n) = \Sigma_0^n x \qquad (5)$$

so that

$$-\,n + \frac{c}{b}\,h^n = \frac{1}{b}\,(c - \Sigma_0^n x)$$

or by (2)

$$= \frac{1}{b}\,(s_n - a). \qquad (6)$$

Since the numerical values deduced from the tables belong not to the age n years, but to that age which corresponds to the average for all the individuals between n and $n+1$ years, the constants deduced hold good also for the series of these mean ages; the successive annual arguments being really at intervals differing slightly from one year.

The age t corresponding to this average may be deduced for any year with sufficient accuracy for all practical purposes, by putting $n=t$ in the first member of equation (6), and using in the last member the value of $s_{n+\frac{1}{2}}$ instead of s_n, which gives

$$-t+\frac{c}{b}h^t=\frac{1}{b}(s_{n+\frac{1}{2}}-a). \qquad (7)$$

Similarly we may find the age corresponding to the average for any period of years. For this purpose we replace $s_{n+\frac{1}{2}}$ in the last member of the equation (7) by

$$\tfrac{1}{2}(s_n+s_{n'})=a-\tfrac{1}{2}b(n+n')+\tfrac{1}{2}c(h^n+h^{n'})$$

and the corresponding value of t is the age equivalent to the average of the period included between n and n'.

Proceeding as above described, and, after the first approximate determination of h, a, b, c, from four conveniently situated and equidistant observed values of s_n, obtaining improved values for all four constants by the method of least squares, the formulas derived from the grand total of all the enlisted men of military age as presented in Table I. are these, which express the relative numbers for every ten thousand: —

$$x_n= \qquad +77.04 \quad +1156.0\cdot 0.85362^n$$
$$s_n=2102.8-77.04\,n+7897.2\cdot 0.85362^n.$$

With these values the fourth and seventh columns of Table II. are computed, the third and sixth columns showing the "observed," or recorded numbers, reduced to the same scale; and the fifth and eighth columns exhibiting the discordances between the calculated and observed values.

These discordances, although in one sense regular, inasmuch as the larger ones are apparently not the result of so-called accident, or, in other words, of the use of numbers insufficient to eliminate discordances of no palpable significance, are in another sense markedly devoid of regularity, inasmuch as the positive and negative signs alternate freely, and no decided indication seems to exist of a systematic deviation of the general formula.

TABLE II.

Grand Total of Enlisted Men.

Age at last birthday.	Number.	Proportion at and over given age. Observed.	Proportion at and over given age. Calculated.	Difference. (C. — O.)	Proportion at given age. Observed.	Proportion at given age. Calculated.	Difference. (C. — O.)
13	127						
14	330						
15	773						
16	2758						
17	6425						
18	133475	10000	10000	0	1339	1233	−106
19	90215	8661	8767	+106	905	1064	+159
20	71058	7756	7703	− 53	713	919	+206
21	97136	7043	6784	−259	975	796	−179
22	73391	6068	5988	− 80	736	691	− 45
23	62717	5332	5297	− 35	629	601	− 28
24	52095	4703	4696	− 7	523	524	+ 1
25	46626	4180	4172	− 8	468	460	− 8
26	40243	3712	3712	0	404	403	− 1
27	34286	3308	3309	+ 1	344	355	+ 11
28	35312	2964	2954	− 10	354	315	− 39
29	24513	2610	2641	+ 31	246	280	+ 34
30	28360	2364	2361	− 3	285	250	− 35
31	17954	2079	2111	+ 32	181	225	+ 44
32	21967	1898	1886	− 12	221	203	− 18
33	17979	1677	1683	+ 6	181	185	+ 4
34	15740	1496	1498	+ 2	158	169	+ 11
35	18980	1338	1329	− 9	191	156	− 35
36	14057	1147	1173	+ 26	141	144	+ 3
37	11820	1006	1029	+ 23	118	134	+ 16
38	13346	888	895	+ 7	133	126	− 7
39	9596	755	769	+ 14	96	118	+ 22
40	13995	659	651	− 8	141	112	− 29
41	7435	518	539	+ 21	74	107	+ 33
42	10929	444	432	− 12	109	103	− 6
43	10340	335	329	− 6	104	99	− 5
44	16070	231	230	− 1	161	96	− 65
45	7012	70	134	+ 64	70	93	+ 23
46	967						
47	712						
48	699						
49	469						
50 & over.	2366						

The trustworthiness of the equations from which the "calculated" numbers in this table are derived will be readily estimated upon inspection of the two columns which exhibit the difference between the calculated and observed numbers at the different years of age; and the substitution of the numerical values of the constants in equations (6) and (7) enables us to determine without difficulty the actual average age which corresponds to any given "age last birthday."

Making these numerical substitutions, the equations assume the form

$$-n + 102.507\,(0.85362)^n = -27.2949 + 0.01298027\,s_n \qquad (8)$$

$$t - 102.507\,(0.85362)^t = -27.2949 + 0.01298027\,s_{n+\frac{1}{2}} \qquad (9)$$

and yield at once the true ages corresponding to the average of the ages "at last birthday," which will be found as follows: —

Age last birthday.	Corresponding average age.
18	18.4814
23	23.4828
28	28.4850
33	33.4885
38	38.4924
43	43.4956
45	45.4968

Intermediate values may be found by interpolation with all needful accuracy.

Tables similar to Table II. prepared for each arm of the service independently, and for nine States or groups of States, and numbered as Tables III. to XIV. inclusive, are appended.

Such tables were originally constructed for a much larger number of groups; but these twelve will abundantly suffice to make manifest all the marked phenomena which the more detailed series has brought to light.

TABLE III.

United States Volunteer Infantry.

Age at last birthday.	Number at each year of age.	Proportion at and over specified age.		Difference. (C. — O.)	Proportion at each year of age.		Difference. (C. — O.)
		Observed.	Calculated.		Observed.	Calculated.	
13	113						
14	288						
15	636						
16	2053						
17	4653						
18	103420	10000	10000	0	1337	1252	− 85
19	71226	8663	8748	+ 85	921	1078	+157
20	56238	7742	7670	− 72	727	921	+194
21	75978	7015	6749	−266	983	802	−181
22	57485	6032	5947	− 85	743	694	− 49
23	48954	5289	5253	− 36	633	602	− 31
24	40852	4656	4651	− 5	528	524	− 4
25	36383	4128	4127	− 1	470	458	− 12
26	31292	3658	3669	+ 11	405	401	− 4
27	26369	3253	3268	+ 15	341	353	+ 12
28	27196	2912	2915	+ 3	352	312	− 40
29	18833	2560	2603	+ 43	244	276	+ 32
30	21937	2316	2327	+ 11	284	247	− 37
31	12814	2032	2080	+ 48	166	221	+ 55
32	17038	1866	1859	− 7	220	200	− 20
33	13678	1646	1659	+ 13	177	181	+ 4
34	12004	1469	1478	+ 9	155	166	+ 11
35	14558	1314	1312	− 2	188	152	− 36
36	10437	1126	1160	+ 34	135	141	+ 6
37	8782	991	1019	+ 28	114	131	+ 17
38	10025	877	888	+ 11	130	123	− 7
39	7200	747	765	+ 18	93	116	+ 23
40	10886	654	649	− 5	141	110	− 31
41	5634	513	539	+ 26	73	105	+ 32
42	8369	440	434	− 6	108	101	− 7
43	7900	332	333	+ 1	102	97	− 5
44	12274	230	236	+ 6	159	94	− 65
45	5509	71	142	+ 71	71	91	+ 20
46	737						
47	541						
48	532						
49	354						
50	1942						

TABLE IV.

United States Volunteer Cavalry.

Age at last birthday.	Number at each year of age.	Proportion at and over specified age.		Difference. (C. — O.)	Proportion at each year of age.		Difference. (C. — O.)
		Observed.	Calculated.		Observed.	Calculated.	
13	5						
14	15						
15	49						
16	232						
17	638						
18	15013	10000	10000	0	1295	1240	− 55
19	9767	8705	8760	+ 55	842	1074	+232
20	7864	7863	7686	−177	682	931	+249
21	12081	7181	6755	−426	1042	808	−234
22	9096	6139	5947	−192	784	703	− 81
23	7806	5355	5244	−111	673	612	− 61
24	6361	4682	4632	− 50	549	534	− 15
25	5724	4133	4098	− 35	494	467	− 27
26	4831	3639	3631	− 8	417	410	− 7
27	4192	3222	3221	− 1	360	360	0
28	4318	2862	2861	− 1	372	318	− 54
29	2845	2490	2543	+ 53	245	281	+ 36
30	3251	2245	2262	+ 17	280	250	− 30
31	2043	1965	2012	+ 47	176	223	+ 47
32	2450	1789	1789	0	211	200	− 11
33	1950	1578	1589	+ 11	168	180	+ 12
34	1679	1410	1410	0	145	163	+ 18
35	2130	1265	1247	− 18	184	148	− 36
36	1541	1081	1098	+ 17	133	135	+ 2
37	1268	948	963	+ 15	109	124	+ 15
38	1416	839	839	0	122	115	− 7
39	979	717	724	+ 7	84	107	+ 23
40	1441	633	618	− 15	124	100	− 24
41	822	509	518	+ 8	71	94	+ 23
42	1199	438	426	− 12	103	89	− 14
43	1079	335	337	+ 2	93	85	− 8
44	1851	242	252	+ 10	160	81	− 79
45	954	82	170	+ 88	82	78	− 4
46	105						
47	74						
48	73						
49	60						
50	203						

TABLE V.

United States Volunteer Artillery.

Age at last birthday.	Number at each year of age.	Proportion at and over specified age.		Difference. (C. — O.)	Proportion at each year of age.		Difference. (C. — O.)
		Observed.	Calculated.		Observed.	Calculated.	
14	2						
15	21						
16	61						
17	226						
18	5400	10000	10000	0	1275	1179	− 96
19	3439	8725	8821	+ 96	812	1024	+212
20	2627	7913	7797	−116	620	891	+271
21	4416	7293	6906	−387	1042	776	−266
22	3107	6251	6130	−121	734	678	− 56
23	2759	5517	5452	− 65	651	593	− 58
24	2163	4866	4859	− 7	511	521	+ 10
25	2012	4355	4338	− 17	475	459	− 16
26	1768	3880	3879	− 1	417	405	− 12
27	1505	3463	3474	+ 11	355	359	+ 4
28	1525	3108	3115	+ 7	360	320	− 40
29	1087	2748	2795	+ 47	257	286	+ 29
30	1213	2491	2509	+ 18	286	257	− 29
31	796	2205	2252	+ 47	188	232	+ 44
32	931	2017	2020	+ 3	220	211	− 9
33	753	1797	1809	+ 12	178	193	+ 15
34	724	1619	1616	− 3	171	177	+ 6
35	836	1448	1439	− 9	197	163	− 34
36	702	1251	1276	+ 25	166	151	− 15
37	477	1085	1125	+ 40	113	142	+ 29
38	579	972	983	+ 11	137	133	− 4
39	416	835	850	+ 15	98	126	+ 28
40	649	737	724	− 13	153	119	− 34
41	320	584	605	+ 21	76	114	+ 38
42	535	508	491	− 17	126	109	− 17
43	533	382	382	0	126	105	− 21
44	796	256	277	+ 21	188	102	− 86
45	289	68	175	+107	68	100	+ 32
46	45						
47	34						
48	31						
49	17						
50	68						

TABLE VI.

Ages of Maine, New Hampshire, Vermont, and Connecticut Vol's.

Age at last birthday.	Number at each year of age.	Proportion at and over specified age.		Difference. (C. — O.)	Proportion at each year of age.		Difference. (C. — O.)
		Observed.	Calculated.		Observed.	Calculated.	
13	3						
14	10						
15	27						
16	95						
17	223						
18	11694	10000	10001	+ 1	1522	1245	−277
19	6541	8478	8756	+278	852	1071	+219
20	5311	7626	7685	+ 59	691	923	+232
21	7477	6935	6762	−173	976	800	−176
22	5356	5959	5962	+ 3	699	685	− 14
23	4614	5260	5277	+ 17	604	598	− 6
24	3824	4656	4679	+ 23	500	519	+ 19
25	3357	4156	4160	+ 4	440	453	+ 13
26	2988	3716	3707	− 9	390	397	+ 7
27	2590	3326	3310	− 16	338	350	+ 12
28	2762	2988	2960	− 28	361	307	− 54
29	1881	2627	2653	+ 26	245	273	+ 28
30	1983	2382	2380	− 2	259	243	− 16
31	1362	2123	2137	+ 14	177	218	+ 41
32	1609	1946	1919	− 27	210	196	− 14
33	1427	1736	1723	− 13	185	178	− 7
34	1141	1551	1545	− 6	149	163	+ 14
35	1355	1402	1382	− 20	176	149	− 27
36	1046	1226	1233	+ 7	136	138	+ 2
37	989	1090	1095	+ 5	127	128	+ 1
38	1005	963	967	+ 4	131	118	− 13
39	817	832	849	+ 17	107	115	+ 8
40	969	725	734	+ 9	127	108	− 19
41	604	598	626	+ 28	77	102	+ 25
42	882	521	524	+ 3	115	97	− 18
43	870	406	427	+ 21	113	95	− 18
44	1789	293	332	+ 39	233	90	−143
45	459	60	242	+182	60	88	+ 28
46	50						
47	38						
48	34						
49	23						
50 & over.	60						

TABLE VII.

Ages of Massachusetts Volunteers.

Age at last birthday.	Number at each year of age.	Proportion at and over specified age.		Difference. (C. — O.)	Proportion at each year of age.		Difference. (C. — O.)
		Observed.	Calculated.		Observed.	Calculated.	
12	4						
13	4						
14	26						
15	44						
16	101						
17	289						
18	6894	10000	10000	0	1269	1145	−124
19	4582	8731	8855	+124	846	1002	+156
20	3604	7885	7853	− 32	666	877	+211
21	5429	7219	6976	−243	1003	771	−232
22	3860	6216	6205	− 11	713	678	− 35
23	3203	5513	5527	+ 14	592	597	+ 5
24	2871	4921	4930	+ 9	530	528	− 2
25	2474	4391	4402	+ 11	457	467	+ 10
26	2232	3934	3935	+ 1	412	415	+ 3
27	1962	3522	3520	− 2	362	370	+ 8
28	2041	3160	3150	− 10	377	330	− 47
29	1411	2783	2820	+ 37	260	296	+ 36
30	1564	2523	2524	+ 1	288	267	− 21
31	988	2235	2257	+ 22	183	242	+ 59
32	1233	2042	2015	− 27	228	219	− 9
33	1041	1814	1796	− 18	193	200	+ 7
34	980	1621	1596	− 25	181	184	+ 3
35	1213	1440	1412	− 28	224	169	− 55
36	761	1216	1243	+ 27	141	157	+ 16
37	699	1075	1086	+ 11	129	146	+ 17
38	828	946	940	− 6	153	137	− 16
39	600	793	803	+ 10	111	129	+ 18
40	838	682	674	− 8	155	122	− 33
41	440	527	552	+ 25	81	116	+ 35
42	658	446	436	− 10	122	110	− 12
43	596	324	326	+ 2	110	106	− 4
44	859	214	220	+ 6	159	102	− 57
45	296	55	118	+ 63	55	98	+ 43
46	28						
47	14						
48	16						
49	9						
50 & over.	33						

TABLE VIII.

Ages of New York Volunteers.

Age at last birthday	Number. at each year of age.	Proportion at and over specified age. Observed.	Calculated.	Difference. (C. — O.)	Proportion at each year of age. Observed.	Calculated.	Difference. (C. — O.)
13	17						
14	63						
15	153						
16	448						
17	699						
18	19737	10000	10000	0	1087	1173	+ 86
19	16233	8913	8827	− 86	894	1019	+125
20	11286	8019	7808	−211	621	887	+266
21	20227	7398	6922	−476	1114	773	−341
22	13689	6284	6149	−135	754	675	− 79
23	11516	5530	5774	+244	634	592	− 42
24	9488	4896	4882	− 14	523	520	− 3
25	8648	4373	4363	− 10	476	459	− 17
26	7285	3897	3904	+ 7	401	406	+ 5
27	6223	3496	3498	+ 2	343	360	+ 17
28	6652	3153	3138	− 15	366	322	− 44
29	4552	2787	2816	+ 29	251	289	+ 38
30	5474	2536	2527	− 9	301	260	− 41
31	3287	2235	2267	+ 32	181	236	+ 55
32	4533	2054	2031	− 23	249	215	− 34
33	3330	1805	1816	+ 11	184	197	+ 13
34	3135	1621	1619	− 2	173	182	+ 9
35	3885	1448	1437	− 11	114	168	+ 54
36	2872	1234	1269	+ 35	158	157	− 1
37	2201	1076	1112	+ 36	121	146	+ 25
38	2709	955	966	+ 11	149	139	− 10
39	1858	806	827	+ 21	103	132	+ 29
40	3157	703	695	− 8	173	126	− 47
41	1268	530	569	+ 39	70	121	+ 51
42	2302	460	448	− 12	127	116	− 11
43	2068	333	332	− 1	114	112	− 2
44	3148	219	220	+ 1	173	109	− 64
45	831	46	111	+ 65	46	106	+ 60
46	87						
47	41						
48	53						
49	23						
50 & over.	103						

TABLE IX.

Ages of Pennsylvania Volunteers (including Reserves).

Age at last birthday.	Number at each year of age.	Proportion at and over specified age.		Difference. (C. — O.)	Proportion at each year of age.		Difference. (C. — O.)
		Observed.	Calculated.		Observed.	Calculated.	
13	23						
14	51						
15	85						
16	241						
17	486						
18	13052	10000	10000	0	1137	1339	+202
19	11410	8863	8661	−202	994	1131	+137
20	8234	7869	7530	−339	717	959	+242
21	13336	7152	6571	−581	1161	814	−347
22	9376	5991	5757	−234	816	694	−122
23	7696	5175	5063	−112	670	595	− 75
24	6061	4505	4468	− 37	528	510	− 18
25	5375	3977	3958	− 19	468	441	− 27
26	4420	3509	3517	+ 8	385	382	− 3
27	3576	3124	3135	+ 11	311	334	+ 23
28	3817	2813	2801	− 12	332	293	− 39
29	2644	2481	2508	+ 27	230	260	+ 30
30	2926	2251	2248	− 3	255	232	− 23
31	2029	1996	2016	+ 20	177	208	+ 31
32	2375	1819	1808	− 11	207	188	− 19
33	1903	1612	1620	+ 8	166	173	+ 7
34	1657	1446	1447	+ 1	144	158	+ 14
35	2089	1302	1289	− 13	182	147	− 35
36	1490	1120	1142	+ 22	130	138	+ 8
37	1290	990	1004	+ 14	112	130	+ 18
38	1434	878	874	− 4	125	124	− 1
39	1141	753	750	− 3	99	118	+ 19
40	1692	654	632	− 22	147	113	− 34
41	918	507	519	+ 12	80	109	+ 29
42	1431	427	410	+ 17	124	106	− 18
43	1318	303	307	+ 4	115	103	− 12
44	1674	188	206	+ 18	146	101	− 45
45	480	42	105	+ 63	42	99	+ 57
46	73						
47	46						
48	49						
49	36						
50 & over.	109						

TABLE X.

Ages of Ohio Volunteers.

Age at last birthday.	Number at each year of age.	Proportion at and over specified age.		Difference. (C. — O.)	Proportion at each year of age.		Difference. (C. — O.)
		Observed.	Calculated.		Observed.	Calculated.	
13	21						
14	44						
15	103						
16	470						
17	1476						
18	23495	10000	10000	0	1567	1359	−208
19	14986	8433	8641	+208	999	1143	+144
20	12358	7434	7498	+ 64	825	963	+138
21	12819	6609	6535	− 74	855	815	− 40
22	10499	5754	5720	− 34	700	692	− 8
23	9297	5054	5028	− 26	620	590	− 30
24	7327	4434	4438	− 6	489	505	+ 16
25	6502	3945	3933	− 12	430	435	+ 5
26	5678	3515	3498	− 17	382	377	− 5
27	4739	3133	3121	− 12	316	329	+ 13
28	4997	2817	2792	− 25	333	289	− 44
29	3570	2484	2503	+ 19	238	256	+ 18
30	3960	2246	2247	+ 1	264	228	− 36
31	2596	1982	2019	+ 37	174	206	+ 32
32	3029	1808	1813	+ 5	201	187	− 14
33	2669	1607	1626	+ 19	178	171	− 7
34	2302	1429	1455	+ 26	154	159	+ 5
35	2659	1275	1296	+ 21	178	148	− 30
36	2216	1097	1148	+ 51	147	139	− 8
37	1830	950	1009	+ 59	123	132	+ 9
38	1959	827	877	+ 50	130	125	− 5
39	1424	697	752	+ 55	95	120	+ 25
40	1880	602	632	+ 30	126	116	− 10
41	1097	476	516	+ 40	73	113	+ 40
42	1513	403	403	0	101	110	+ 9
43	1337	302	293	− 9	89	108	+ 19
44	2070	213	185	− 28	138	106	− 32
45	1128	75	79	+ 4	75	104	+ 29
46	202						
47	161						
48	145						
49	104						
50 & over.	471						

TABLE XI.

Ages of Indiana Volunteers.

Age at last birthday.	Number at each year of age.	Proportion at and over specified age.		Difference. (C. — O.)	Proportion at each year of age.		Difference. (C. — O.)
		Observed.	Calculated.		Observed.	Calculated.	
13	13						
14	16						
15	39						
16	162						
17	578						
18	11178	10000	10000	0	1608	1446	−162
19	7175	8392	8554	+162	1032	1223	+191
20	6478	7360	7331	− 29	932	1035	+103
21	6398	6428	6296	−132	920	877	− 43
22	5580	5508	5419	− 89	802	744	− 58
23	4562	4706	4675	− 31	656	632	− 24
24	3782	4050	4043	− 7	544	538	− 6
25	3216	3506	3505	− 1	462	460	− 2
26	2707	3044	3045	+ 1	390	394	+ 4
27	2269	2654	2651	− 3	326	337	+ 11
28	2272	2328	2314	− 14	327	290	− 37
29	1513	2001	2024	+ 23	217	251	+ 34
30	1799	1784	1773	− 11	259	218	− 41
31	1013	1525	1555	+ 30	145	190	+ 45
32	1230	1380	1365	− 15	177	166	− 11
33	1046	1203	1200	− 3	151	146	− 5
34	871	1052	1053	+ 1	125	130	+ 5
35	962	927	923	− 4	138	116	− 22
36	666	789	806	+ 17	96	104	+ 8
37	589	693	702	+ 9	85	94	+ 9
38	656	608	608	0	94	86	− 8
39	428	514	522	+ 8	62	79	+ 17
40	683	452	443	− 9	98	73	− 25
41	371	354	370	+ 16	53	68	+ 15
42	482	301	302	+ 1	69	64	− 5
43	471	232	238	+ 6	68	60	− 8
44	682	164	178	+ 14	98	57	− 41
45	457	66	121	+ 55	66	55	− 11
46	70						
47	37						
48	50						
49	24						
50 & over.	146						

TABLE XII.

Ages of Michigan Volunteers.

Age at last birthday.	Number. at each year of age.	Proportion at and over specified age.		Difference. (C. — O.)	Proportion at each year of age.		Difference. (C. — O.)
		Observed.	Calculated.		Observed.	Calculated.	
13	3						
14	9						
15	27						
16	112						
17	299						
18	5862	10000	10000	0	1523	1279	−244
19	3437	8477	8721	+244	893	1098	+205
20	2767	7584	7623	+ 39	719	943	+224
21	3727	6865	6680	−185	968	812	−156
22	2802	5897	5868	− 29	728	700	− 28
23	2337	5169	5168	− 1	607	605	− 2
24	1963	4562	4563	+ 1	510	524	+ 14
25	1724	4052	4039	− 13	448	455	+ 7
26	1568	3604	3584	− 20	407	396	− 11
27	1297	3197	3188	− 9	337	346	+ 9
28	1335	2860	2842	− 18	347	304	− 43
29	923	2513	2538	+ 25	240	268	+ 28
30	989	2273	2270	− 3	257	237	− 20
31	695	2016	2033	+ 17	180	211	+ 31
32	843	1836	1822	− 14	219	188	− 31
33	614	1617	1634	+ 17	160	169	+ 9
34	527	1457	1465	+ 8	137	153	+ 16
35	668	1320	1312	− 8	173	140	− 33
36	481	1147	1172	+ 25	125	128	+ 3
37	411	1022	1044	+ 22	107	118	+ 11
38	458	915	926	+ 11	119	109	− 10
39	313	796	817	+ 21	81	102	+ 21
40	466	715	715	+ 0	121	96	− 25
41	256	594	619	+ 25	67	91	+ 24
42	403	527	528	+ 1	105	86	− 19
43	400	422	442	+ 20	104	83	− 21
44	825	318	359	+ 41	214	79	−135
45	398	104	280	+176	104	77	− 27
46	44						
47	23						
48	26						
49	14						
50 & over.	61						

TABLE XIII.

Ages of Illinois Volunteers.

Age at last birthday.	Number at each year of age.	Proportion at and over specified age.		Difference. (C. — O.)	Proportion at each year of age.		Difference. (C. — O.)
		Observed.	Calculated.		Observed.	Calculated.	
13	5						
14	23						
15	65						
16	250						
17	539						
18	10167	10000	10080	+ 80	1070	942	−128
19	8348	8930	9138	+208	879	1043	+164
20	7076	8051	8095	+ 44	745	958	+213
21	8709	7306	7137	−169	916	858	− 58
22	7441	6390	6279	−111	783	766	− 17
23	6872	5607	5513	− 94	723	677	− 46
24	6019	4884	4836	− 48	634	600	− 34
25	5315	4250	4236	− 14	559	529	− 30
26	4441	3691	3707	+ 16	468	465	− 3
27	3810	3223	3242	+ 19	401	410	+ 9
28	3677	2822	2832	+ 10	387	358	− 29
29	2622	2435	2474	+ 39	276	315	+ 39
30	2869	2159	2159	0	302	276	− 26
31	1847	1857	1883	+ 26	194	242	+ 48
32	2076	1663	1641	− 22	219	211	− 8
33	1666	1444	1430	− 14	175	185	+ 10
34	1508	1269	1245	− 24	159	162	+ 3
35	1568	1110	1083	− 27	165	142	− 23
36	1243	945	941	− 4	131	124	− 7
37	944	814	817	+ 3	99	110	+ 11
38	1056	715	707	− 8	111	96	− 15
39	725	604	611	+ 7	77	87	+ 10
40	1040	527	524	− 3	109	77	− 32
41	607	418	447	+ 29	64	69	+ 5
42	816	354	378	+ 24	86	64	− 18
43	734	268	314	+ 46	77	59	− 18
44	1075	191	255	+ 69	113	54	− 59
45	737	78	201	+123	78	50	− 28
46	88						
47	86						
48	78						
49	45						
50 & over.	237						

TABLE XIV.

Ages of Wisconsin and Iowa Volunteers.

Age at last birthday.	Number at each year of age.	Proportion at and over specified age.		Difference. (C. — O.)	Proportion at each year of age.		Difference. (C. — O.)
		Observed.	Calculated.		Observed.	Calculated.	
13	11						
14	22						
15	79						
16	369						
17	829						
18	11083	10000	10000	0	1485	1221	−264
19	6440	8515	8779	+264	863	1048	+185
20	4874	7652	7731	+ 79	653	902	+249
21	7082	6999	6829	−170	949	778	−171
22	5271	6050	6050	0	707	673	− 34
23	4240	5343	5377	+ 34	569	585	+ 16
24	3718	4774	4792	+ 18	499	510	+ 11
25	3260	4275	4282	+ 7	437	447	+ 10
26	2953	3838	3835	− 3	396	393	− 3
27	2675	3442	3442	0	359	345	− 14
28	2495	3083	3097	+ 14	334	310	− 24
29	1844	2749	2787	+ 38	247	277	+ 30
30	1973	2502	2510	+ 8	264	250	− 14
31	1472	2238	2260	+ 22	196	227	+ 31
32	1674	2042	2033	− 9	224	207	− 17
33	1432	1818	1826	+ 8	192	191	− 1
34	1237	1626	1635	+ 9	166	177	+ 11
35	1359	1460	1458	− 2	182	165	− 17
36	1154	1278	1293	+ 15	155	155	0
37	1022	1123	1138	+ 15	137	146	+ 9
38	1104	986	992	+ 6	148	139	− 9
39	873	838	853	+ 15	117	133	+ 16
40	967	721	720	− 1	130	128	− 2
41	670	591	592	+ 1	90	124	+ 34
42	886	501	468	− 33	119	120	+ 1
43	950	382	348	− 34	127	117	− 10
44	1374	255	231	− 24	184	114	− 70
45	531	71	117	+ 46	71	112	+ 41
46	113						
47	108						
48	115						
49	76						
50 & over.	632						

The agreement of these several special results with those deduced from their aggregate is remarkable. Only in one case, that of the Illinois troops, has the simple formula

$$s_n = a - bn + ch^n$$

failed to give all desired accordance between theory and observation; and throughout the whole series the same peculiarities in the residuals are recognizable. In this connection I may add, what is in itself very significant, that attempts to deduce a law of distribution of age for troops recruited in Missouri, Kentucky, Tennessee, and Virginia have proved fruitless, and only small success was attainable for the Maryland volunteers. The inference is obvious, that the volunteering of troops from these States was not subject to the undisturbed influence of any statistical law. In the case of Illinois troops, a curious anomaly manifested itself in the residuals, namely, a cyclical or periodic term. This was found to be represented with sufficient accuracy by adding to the formula a term $d \sin \sqrt{n} \cdot 68°$, in which $d = 314$. I know of no satisfactory interpretation of this expression, but it has been used in the preparation of the table for that State.

In Table XV. is presented a summary of the results deduced from the special groups presented in Tables II. to XIV. All the constants are reduced to the same scale, and hold good for 10 000 troops of the ages 18 to 45 at last birthday, inclusive. The mean ages, as here given, refer, not to the last birthday, but to the actual date of enlistment.

The values of the constants for these special tables have been determined from a smaller number of equations of condition than were used for the grand total. In that each year was specially used; in these the results were deduced from eight normal places.

TABLE XV.

Constants deduced for Special Classes of Volunteers.

Class.	Number of Soldiers		Mean age at enlistment		a	b	c	h
	Of all ages.	Of military age.	For all.	For 18 to 45.				
Total Enlisted Men	1012273	996647	25.8362	25.8083	2102.8	77.04	7897.2	0.8536
Total Infantry	785120	773271	25.7827	25.7484	2080.0	75.84	7920.0	0.8514
Total Cavalry	117405	115951	25.8110	25.7795	1595.0	57.90	8405.0	0.8593
Total Artillery	42862	42357	26.1576	26.1202	2239.0	81.20	7761.0	0.8585
Me., N.H., Vt., Conn.	76445	75881	25.8792	25.8423	2112.0	73.06	7889.0	0.8514
Massachusetts	54705	54137	26.0561	26.0943	2016.0	76.40	7984.0	0.8662
New York	183281	181594	26.1308	26.1642	2390.5	88.86	7609.5	0.8575
Pennsylvania	116043	114844	25.8227	25.8331	2477.4	90.20	7523.0	0.8340
Ohio	153133	149936	25.4936	25.3859	2625.0	96.08	7375.0	0.8287
Indiana	70673	69536	24.7100	24.6858	1175.0	42.18	8825.0	0.8409
Michigan	39107	38489	25.5290	25.5276	1827.0	61.30	8173.0	0.8510
Illinois	96409	95003	25.9369	25.8935	2023.0	70.66	8057.0	0.8558
Wisconsin and Iowa	76987	74613	26.1571	25.9991	2737.0	100.20	7263.0	0.8456

In considering the residuals, the most striking feature is the excess of the recorded numbers at 18 and 21, which latter excess is counterbalanced by a deficiency at 20 and to some extent at 19 also. The explanation of this is readily found in the facts that enlistments of youths under 18 are not valid without the formal consent of parents, and that 21 is the period at which minority ceases. There can be no reasonable doubt that these residuals furnish the measure of the number under 18 and under 21, who misstated their age to the mustering officer. At the age of 18 the discordance is less marked than at 21, since the inducements to misstate operated near this age in different directions, many of those at 18 probably representing themselves as 21 years old, while their number was made good by others who untruly declared themselves as having completed their 18th year.

The excess of the recorded number at 21 averages $1\frac{4}{5}$ per cent., that deficiency at 20 is about 2 per cent., and at 19 about $1\frac{3}{5}$ per cent. The number recorded for 18 years is in excess by 1 per cent., although it varies very considerably in the different groups.

A large excess, representing the number of those who from similar motives understated their ages, is also to be seen at the age of 44 in most States, corresponding to an analogous deficiency at 45. This varies, however, in different States, owing in all probability to the different interpretation by the mustering officers of that provision of the law which precluded the acceptance of men over 45 years old. The average, in the more elaborately calculated table for the grand total, places the number at 44 in excess of the computed number by two thirds of its whole amount, and leaves that at 45 in defect by one fourth part.

For all other ages than those enumerated, the regular excess or defect of the residuals furnishes apparently the measure of the accuracy with which the ages were stated or recorded. It will be seen that at those ages which correspond to what are called round numbers, such as those divisible by 10, also, though to a less extent, at those divisible by 5, and in a still less but yet recognizable degree, at those divisible by 2, the recorded numbers are in excess; while the adjacent numbers, especially those ending in 1, 9, and 7, are in defect. The natural tendency which every one will recognize, and which inclines us to make use of certain more habitually employed numbers, rather than to use a minuteness repugnant to some persons, furnishes an adequate and, as I believe, the true explanation.

It will be readily noted that where any two of the above-named principles conflict, the residual is diminished; and that where they act in combination it is increased.

Lines showing the computed and the enrolled numbers of enlisted men are given on Chart *A*, and readily manifest these facts to the eye. The other data upon this chart are given for comparison, and will be referred to hereafter. It will be borne in mind that the numbers given do not, by a large amount, represent the actual numbers of enlisted volunteers or of volunteer officers, nor probably so much as two fifths of the total number of our soldiers in the struggle for national existence. They are relative quantities, deduced from only those data cited at the commencement of this paper, and illustrate, not the actual numbers for our troops, but the relative distribution of their ages.

The same results are presented in another form upon Chart *B*, which exhibits, for the enlisted men, the officers, and the white male population, the *proportion at and over the specified ages* and under 45 years, for each 10 000 men of military age.

Charts C and D show the law by which the ratios of officers and enlisted men to the white male population vary with the age. All the numbers are reduced to the scale of ten thousand of population at 18 years, Chart C being constructed in reference to the whole United States, and Chart D to the Loyal States only.

3. *Ages of Officers.*

The total number of officers of all ages is 37 184, that of those between 18 and 46 being 35 953.

On comparing the numbers at the several ages with the formula

$$s_n = a - bn + ch^n$$

we find at once that for certain ages the value of h would be an impossible one; and that for other years, which would yield possible values, these values are so discordant and the residuals to which they lead become so large that it is manifest that the curve can be represented neither by this nor by any similar law.

Many trials have led to the empirical formula

$$s_n = a - bn^{k'} + c \sin n^k \theta \qquad \text{(A)}$$

as that which best represents the character of the curve. The extremely complicated manner, however, in which the six constants of this equation enter into the formula renders the attainment of a solution from six equations, by any direct process, a matter of great difficulty and inconvenience. Of course the constant a represents the value of s_n for $n = 0$, so that the problem really consists in the determination of the five quantities b, c, k', k, and θ. Graphic representations of the curve, by showing the points at which the third term becomes $= 0$, facilitated the approximate determination of these constants, and thus equations of condition were formed which have led to quite satisfactory values, giving an agreement between the formula and the observed numbers nearly if not quite as good as that obtained for the enlisted men by the formula already described.

Subsequently, investigations made for the purpose of extending this formula to the ages from 46 to 50 showed a deviation for these later years. This deviation seems only to be reconciled by the employment of an additional term containing two more constants, and the term thus found proves applicable to all ages above 30, essentially diminishing the residuals for all subsequent years.

The formula then stands for each 10 000 officers

$$s_n = 10\,000 - 736\,n^{0.75} + 1259 \sin n^{0.536} \times 45°.64 + 100 \sin (n - 12)\, 18°$$

in which the last term is only to be employed for positive values of $n - 12$, that is, for ages above 30 years.

The near agreement of this formula with the observations will be recognized on Table XVI., which exhibits for each year of age from 18 to 50, as well as for those above 50, the actual and the proportionate observed number of officers, both at, and at and over, the given age, together with the corresponding numbers as deduced from the formula, and the discordances between Computation and Observation.

The dissimilarity of the curves thus found for officers and for enlisted men is most striking, as will be perceived by reference to Charts *A* and *B*. The chief discordance for the officers' curve is for the age of 18 years, at which, or at 19, the formula seems to fail. This is probably due in part to the fact that comparatively few officers were commissioned under the age of legal maturity, so that the law governing the distribution by age ought not to be regarded as applicable below 21 years.

TABLE XVI.

Ages of Officers of United States Volunteers.

Age at last birthday.	Number at given age.	Proportion at given age			Number at and over given age.	Proportion at and over given age		
		Observed.	Calculated.	Difference. (C. — O.)		Observed.	Calculated.	Difference. (C. — O.)
13								
14								
15	1				37183			
16	5				37182			
17	5				37177			
18	178	48	−164	−212	37172	10000	10000	0
19	409	110	+233	+123	37094	9952	10164	+212
20	687	185	351	+166	36685	9842	9931	+ 89
21	1630	439	443	+ 4	35998	9657	9580	− 77
22	1839	495	500	+ 5	34368	9218	9137	− 81
23	2101	565	537	− 28	32529	8723	8637	− 86
24	2234	601	557	− 44	30428	8158	8100	− 58
25	2161	581	567	− 14	28194	7557	7543	− 14
26	2114	569	563	− 6	26033	6976	6976	0
27	1968	529	555	+ 26	23919	6407	6413	+ 6
28	2071	557	536	− 21	21951	5878	5858	− 20
29	1756	472	516	+ 44	19880	5321	5322	+ 1
30	1836	494	457	− 37	18124	4849	4806	− 43
31	1429	384	430	+ 46	16288	4355	4349	− 6
32	1613	434	405	− 29	14859	3971	3919	− 52
33	1422	383	381	− 2	13246	3537	3514	− 23
34	1324	356	359	+ 3	11824	3154	3133	− 21
35	1434	386	335	− 51	10500	2798	2774	− 24
36	1221	328	313	− 15	9066	2412	2439	+ 27
37	1031	277	291	+ 14	7845	2084	2126	+ 42
38	1033	278	269	− 9	6814	1807	1835	+ 28
39	813	219	245	+ 26	5781	1529	1566	+ 37
40	874	235	222	− 13	4968	1310	1321	+ 11
41	557	149	197	+ 48	4094	1075	1099	+ 24
42	656	176	171	− 5	3537	926	902	− 24
43	485	130	148	+ 18	2881	750	731	− 19
44	598	161	124	− 37	2396	620	583	− 37
45	478	130	100	− 30	1798	459	459	0
46	217	58	86	+ 28	1320	329	359	+ 30
47	184	50	70	+ 20	1103	271	273	+ 2
48	175	47	58	+ 11	919	221	203	− 18
49	121	33	55	+ 22	744	174	145	− 29
50 & over.	523	141	90	− 51	523	141	90	− 51

The mean age at last birthday for all the officers is . 30.4406 y
" " " for those between 18 & 45 29.8338
and the mean age of the mean at last birthday is . 29.45
or about 29.94 at the time of their muster into the service. Above and below this age the number of officers was equal.

The annexed Table XVII. exhibits the relative proportions of officers to the enlisted men, and of these to the white male population of the whole United States and of the Loyal States respectively, as given by the census of 1860, taken less than one year before the call to arms.

The caution must here be repeated, that the "proportion of enlisted men to the population," as here given, does not at all apply to the armies of the nation during the rebellion. It relates solely to the number of volunteer troops here considered; and this Table XVII. is presented simply to make manifest the laws according to which the ratios of enlisted men to the population, and the ratios of officers to men, varied with the age.

TABLE XVII.

Relative Proportions of Officers, Enlisted Men, and White Male Population at same age, for the first million of Volunteers.

AGE.	Proportion of Officers to Enlisted Men.	Proportion of Enlisted Men to Population of U. States.	Proportion of Enlisted Men to Population of Loyal States.	AGE.	Proportion of Officers to Enlisted Men.	Proportion of Enlisted Men to Population of U. States.	Proportion of Enlisted Men to Population of Loyal States.
18	0.001	0.448	0.570	32	0.072	0.100	0.128
19	0.007	0.393	0.502	33	0.074	0.093	0.119
20	0.013	0.345	0.442	34	0.076	0.088	0.112
21	0.019	0.305	0.391	35	0.077	0.084	0.105
22	0.025	0.269	0.363	36	0.078	0.080	0.100
23	0.031	0.239	0.308	37	0.077	0.077	0.096
24	0.037	0.212	0.275	38	0.075	0.075	0.093
25	0.043	0.190	0.246	39	0.073	0.074	0.090
26	0.048	0.170	0.221	40	0.068	0.073	0.088
27	0.054	0.154	0.199	41	0.062	0.073	0.088
28	0.059	0.139	0.180	42	0.057	0.073	0.087
29	0.063	0.127	0.164	43	0.049	0.074	0.087
30	0.065	0.116	0.150	44	0.041	0.075	0.088
31	0.068	0.107	0.138	45	0.033	0.076	0.089

4. *Population of the United States and of the Loyal States.*

The great and unexpected dissimilarity between the law of distribution of age for officers and for men led, as I have already mentioned, to an investigation of the ages of the white male population, both of the whole United States, and of the Loyal States considered by themselves. And, in the absence of any distinct criterion, those States which were free from slavery in 1860, together with Delaware, Maryland, Kentucky, and Missouri, have been classed as Loyal States. The territory of West Virginia, eastern Tennessee, &c., is thus excluded, although inhabited by a thoroughly loyal population, which contributed about twenty of the regiments here computed; and about ten other regiments, included in our data, were raised in States not accounted loyal. But all these are offset by the very considerable portion of the inhabitants of the four Slave States above named, from which the insurgent army was reinforced.

The only materials available for the inquiry are contained in the tables, derived from the official census of the United States in 1860. Of course it is the male population alone which has any relation to the present research.

The difficulty of deducing from these meagre details the number of males at each year of military age is apparent at the first glance. Had the classification between the ages of 20 and 50 been in six groups of five years each, instead of three groups of ten years, the facility and accuracy of the investigation would have been incomparably greater. As it is, the only available data are contained in the second column of the following tables, XVIII. and XIX. These tables give, in column 3, the results of the formulas obtained for representing the observed numbers given in column 2. The degree of correctness of these formulas may be estimated by means of column 4, which shows the excess of the calculated number over the number given by the census, in decimals of the latter. The accordance for ages above 20 years is remarkably good. Beyond 50 years the agreement is not so close as between 20 and 50, but is nevertheless quite tolerable; but the comparison is omitted here as not pertinent to the subject, since none of the census-numbers for groups of ages above 50 have been employed in the computation.

The other columns require no explanation. It will be remembered that the numbers of enlisted men and officers here given are merely those belonging to the original volunteer regiments at the time of their enlistment, excluding all recruits, substitutes, drafted men, etc. Also, that the numbers apply only to those regiments which had been mustered into the United States service prior to the collection of our data, as shown on page 2.

TABLE XVIII.

White Male Population of the United States in 1860.

Comparison between Computed and Observed Ages.

Age at last birthday.	White Male Population of the United States.		Difference. (C. — O.)	Enlisted Men of first volunteers.	Officers of first volunteers.	Ratio to White Male Population.	
	Census.	Computed.				Men.	Officers.
10 – 15	1 578 274	1 547 730	–0.0193				
15 – 20	1 391 950	1 422 340	+0.0245				
18 – 20		553 360		219 200	587	0.395	0.0011
20 – 30	2 465 276	2 436 770	–0.0116	529 809	18 561	0.217	0.0076
30 – 40	1 847 259	1 847 810	0.0000	165 292	13 156	0.090	0.0071
40 – 45		807 860		63 667		0.079	
40 – 50	1 215 031	1 216 690	+0.0014		4 868		0.0040
18 – 45		5 645 800		977 968			

TABLE XIX.

White Male Population of the Loyal States in 1860.

Comparison between Computed and Observed Ages.

Age at last birthday.	White Male Population of the Loyal States.		Difference. (C. — O.)	Enlisted Men of first volunteers.	Officers of first volunteers.	Ratio to White Male Population.	
	Census.	Computed.				Men.	Officers.
10 – 15	1 211 521	1 179 260	–0.0266				
15 – 20	1 095 934	1 110 770	+0.0135				
18 – 20		435 100		219 200	587	0.502	0.0014
20 – 30	1 971 486	1 956 890	–0.0075	529 809	18 561	0.271	0.0095
30 – 40	1 517 736	1 517 720	0.0000	165 292	13 156	0.109	0.0087
40 – 45		664 510		63 667		0.096	
40 – 50	996 481	996 350	0.0000		4 868		0.0049
18 – 45		4 574 220		977 968			

The formulas which thus represent the number of white males from the age of 10 years upwards are, —

for the United States

$$x = 445\,440 \sin (134° \, 34' + (y - 10) \cdot 52')$$

for the Loyal States

$$x = 257\,870 \sin (111° \, 6'.1 + (y - 10) \cdot 80'.2)$$

in which x is the number at the year of age y.

Assuming these values to be correct, we find the distribution of the white male population in 1860 to have been as represented in Tables XX. and XXI.

These tables show, for the United States and the Loyal States respectively, the actual numbers: — first, at each year of age from 15 to 50, inclusive; secondly, at and over each year of age from 15 to 50, inclusive; thirdly, at and over each year within the limits of military age from 18 upwards, and also the corresponding relative or proportional numbers, using those for 18 years as the units.

Subsequent investigation has led to the detection of a formula totally different in structure from those above given, but which, although its agreement with the census-numbers within the years of military age is by no means so close as these afford, yet represents the various censuses of the United States and those of foreign countries throughout the period of human life with a degree of precision never before attained, so far as I am aware. It represents the number of infants under one year as well as, and indeed better than, the number at middle life or advanced years; and I cannot avoid the conviction that this formula affords an important step toward the true mathematical expression of what we may call the life-curve. Modifications will doubtless be made in it; indeed, it manifestly gives the numbers too small for the ages under 5 years, over 70 years, and between 20 and 45 years, while those of later childhood and youth on the one side, and of advanced maturity on the other, are in excess. But the discordances are small, and I hardly think that any expression of equal simplicity will be found which will represent the life-curve more closely.

Of this formula, which is simply

$$s_n = a \sin n\, k^n\, \theta$$

where s_n represents the sum of all under the age n, a is the total number, and k, θ are two constants characteristic of the especial population under examination, details and applications are given in the Appendix ; where also are tables exhibiting the distribution of the total white population of the United States, as given by this law. The values differ slightly from those in Tables XX. and XXI., which, for the census of 1860 at least, seem to be more accurate within the limits to which they are extended, although the corresponding numbers beyond these limits would be less accordant with observation.

TABLE XX.

White Male Population of the United States in 1860.

Age at last birthday.	Actual Number			Relative Number		
	At the given age.	At and over given age.	At and over given age and under 46.	At the given age.	At and over given age.	At and over given age & under 46.
15	294 770	8 252 612				
16	289 680	7 957 842				
17	284 530	7 668 162				
18	279 320	7 383 632	5 645 800	10 000	10 000	10 000
19	274 040	7 104 312	5 366 480	9 811	9 622	9 505
20	268 700	6 830 272	5 092 440	9 620	9 251	9 020
21	263 290	6 561 572	4 823 740	9 426	8 887	8 544
22	257 820	6 298 282	4 560 450	9 230	8 530	8 078
23	252 300	6 040 462	4 302 630	9 033	8 181	7 621
24	246 720	5 788 162	4 050 330	8 833	7 839	7 174
25	241 090	5 541 442	3 803 610	8 631	7 505	6 737
26	235 380	5 300 352	3 562 520	8 427	7 179	6 310
27	229 640	5 064 972	3 327 140	8 222	6 860	5 893
28	223 840	4 835 332	3 097 500	8 014	6 549	5 486
29	217 990	4 611 492	2 873 660	7 804	6 246	5 090
30	212 090	4 393 502	2 655 670	7 593	5 951	4 704
31	206 140	4 181 412	2 443 580	7 380	5 664	4 328
32	200 140	3 975 272	2 237 440	7 165	5 385	3 963
33	194 100	3 775 132	2 037 300	6 949	5 114	3 609
34	188 020	3 581 032	1 843 200	6 731	4 851	3 265
35	181 890	3 393 012	1 655 180	6 512	4 596	2 932
36	175 710	3 211 122	1 473 290	6 291	4 350	2 610
37	169 500	3 035 412	1 297 580	6 068	4 112	2 299
38	163 250	2 865 912	1 128 080	5 845	3 882	1 999
39	156 970	2 702 662	964 830	5 620	3 661	1 710
40	150 640	2 545 692	807 860	5 393	3 448	1 432
41	144 290	2 395 052	657 220	5 166	3 244	1 165
42	137 900	2 250 762	512 930	4 937	3 049	909
43	131 470	2 112 862	375 030	4 707	2 862	665
44	125 020	1 981 392	243 560	4 476	2 684	432
45	118 540	1 856 372	118 540	4 244	2 515	210
46	112 030	1 737 832		4 011	2 354	
47	105 500	1 625 802		3 777	2 202	
48	98 940	1 520 302		3 542	2 059	
49	92 360	1 421 362		3 307	1 925	
50	85 760	1 329 002		3 072	1 800	

TABLE XXI.

White Male Population of the Loyal States in 1860.

Age at last birth-day.	Actual Number			Relative Number			Prop. to W. Male Pop. of United States.
	At the given age.	At and over given age.	At and over given age and under 46.	At the given age.	At and over given age.	At and over given age & under 46.	
15	228 120	6 675 533					7 739
16	225 270	6 447 413					7 776
17	222 280	6 222 143					7 812
18	219 160	5 999 863	4 574 220	10 000	10 000	10 000	7 846
19	215 940	5 780 703	4 355 060	9 853	9 634	9 521	7 880
20	212 600	5 564 763	4 139 120	9 700	9 275	9 049	7 912
21	209 130	5 352 163	3 926 520	9 542	8 920	8 584	7 943
22	205 550	5 143 033	3 717 390	9 379	8 572	8 127	7 973
23	201 870	4 937 483	3 511 840	9 211	8 229	7 678	8 001
24	198 070	4 735 613	3 309 970	9 038	7 893	7 237	8 028
25	194 160	4 537 543	3 111 900	8 859	7 563	6 804	8 054
26	190 150	4 343 383	2 917 740	8 676	7 239	6 379	8 078
27	186 040	4 153 233	2 727 590	8 488	6 922	5 963	8 101
28	181 820	3 967 193	2 541 550	8 296	6 612	5 555	8 123
29	177 500	3 785 373	2 359 730	8 099	6 309	5 157	8 141
30	173 100	3 607 873	2 182 230	7 898	6 013	4 769	8 162
31	168 590	3 434 773	2 009 130	7 692	5 725	4 391	8 179
32	163 990	3 266 183	1 840 540	7 483	5 444	4 022	8 194
33	159 300	3 102 193	1 676 550	7 269	5 170	3 663	8 207
34	154 530	2 942 893	1 517 250	7 051	4 905	3 315	8 219
35	149 680	2 788 363	1 362 720	6 829	4 647	2 977	8 229
36	144 730	2 638 683	1 213 040	6 604	4 398	2 650	8 237
37	139 720	2 493 953	1 068 310	6 375	4 157	2 334	8 243
38	134 620	2 354 233	928 590	6 143	3 924	2 029	8 246
39	129 460	2 219 613	793 970	5 907	3 699	1 735	8 247
40	124 230	2 090 153	664 510	5 668	3 484	1 452	8 247
41	118 920	1 965 923	540 280	5 426	3 277	1 180	8 242
42	113 550	1 847 003	421 360	5 181	3 078	920	8 234
43	108 110	1 733 453	307 810	4 933	2 889	672	8 223
44	102 620	1 625 343	199 700	4 683	2 709	436	8 209
45	97 080	1 522 723	97 080	4 430	2 538	212	8 190
46	91 480	1 425 643		4 174	2 376		8 165
47	85 830	1 334 163		3 916	2 224		8 136
48	80 130	1 248 333		3 656	2 081		8 099
49	74 400	1 168 203		3 394	1 947		8 055
50	68 640	1 093 803		3 130	1 823		8 001

The results present some curious contrasts between the life-curves for the total population in the loyal States and in the insurgent States, which may be best recognized by reference to the appended chart, marked *E*. This chart exhibits the number of white males at each year of age from 18 to 50, corresponding to each 10 000 at the age of 18. It will be seen at once that the curvature of the line representing the population of the insurgent States is in the direction opposite to that of the lines belonging to the loyal States and to the whole country. The dotted line is straight, and shows what the distribution would be, did it follow a regular arithmetical progression. To what extent this difference may be due to immigration from Europe, which has been chiefly to the Free States, I will not undertake to estimate. We have seen, however, that the law of distribution of our volunteer troops according to ages was essentially the same for those States to which immigration is greatest as for those to which it is least.

The construction of all the curves laid down on the accompanying charts will be manifest without explanation. For those ordinates which belong to the respective ages they give the corresponding numbers.

APPENDIX TO CHAPTER III.

ON THE AGES OF A POPULATION.

In the course of the preceding investigation, the interesting question as to the general distribution of a population by ages became prominent; and the inquiry continually suggested itself, how far any simple formula might be capable of representing the observed numbers for all ages of life. This has incidentally led to the detection of what seems to be the true law, which, although not strictly pertaining to the subject in hand, seems yet to possess sufficient practical value and importance in its indirect bearing to justify its introduction here,—the more especially, since endeavors to obtain information on this point elsewhere have proved fruitless.

It appears that, in a population at all homogeneous in its character, the number of persons under the age n years may be represented by the simple expression

$$N = a \sin n k^n \theta$$

in which a denotes the total number of the population, while k and θ are constants peculiar to the country and epoch. The quantity θ is an angle somewhat larger than 1°, and k is a number, generally a little less than unity.

For the special case $k = 1$, the formula becomes

$$N = a \sin n \theta$$

containing only one unknown quantity, the angle θ, to be determined by investigation.

A very peculiar characteristic of this law is recognizable in the circumstance that the number at any given age appears to be strictly proportional to the whole population; so that the expectation of life, for the average individual, is as well represented as is the general distribution by ages of the total number of individuals, of whom the population is composed.

Investigating the values of the constants k and θ for the people of the United States at each of the last four enumerations, we find

Date	k	θ
1830	0.9918	2°.0524
1840	0.9921	1°.9747
1850	0.9932	1°.8361
1860	0.9941	1°.7307.

The census of 1820 is not sufficiently distinct, in the assortment by ages, to permit a determination of the constants, but the indications are clear that a proper enumeration would have afforded results in conformity with the preceding series; the value of k being smaller, and that of θ larger than for the population in 1830.

The curious fact thus becomes evident, that our population has, during the last forty years or more, been gradually assimilating itself to the normal type represented by $k = 1$; growing, or developing itself, so to speak, toward a compliance with the simple law

$$N = a \sin n\,\theta$$

in which the value of θ indicates the longevity of the people, since, according to the formula, the entire population becomes extinct at the age when $n\theta = 90°$.

How far immigration has affected the values of the constants for the United States we will not now inquire. Were the tendency to immigrate independent of age, no appreciable influence could be traced to this source; and the character of the immigration into this country seems to have been such as to exhibit no overwhelming excess or deficiency for any one period of life, except that there is certainly a deficiency in the relative number at the most advanced ages. But the accessions to our population from Ireland and Germany appear to have been in most cases by families, and not composed chiefly of persons in the prime of life or fullness of strength, as is the case in very new countries.

The English people appearing to afford a fair specimen of a permanent and normal population, the last two censuses of England and Wales were examined, and with the following result:—

Date	k	θ
1851	0.9957	1°.4702
1861	0.9962	1°.4316.

Thus a similar phenomenon is manifested by the English enumerations to that exhibited by the American census-returns; the values of k approaching unity, and those of θ diminishing. The smaller value of the angle θ

indicates a longer duration of life in that country; but k, the modulus of the change by geometric progression, was not larger for England in 1851 than it bids fair to be for the United States in ten years from the present time.

Passing next to the French population, we find the value $k = 1$ as the result alike of the last three enumerations, the values of θ being

in 1851	1°.0553
" 1856	1°.0556
" 1861	1°.0473.

The remarkable peculiarity of the life-curve for France, as regards the small infantile mortality, is well exhibited by the chart *F*, which shows the number living, at each year of age, for every million in the population. The several curves of this chart represent the distribution of ages for the United States in 1830 and 1860, (those for the intermediate decades being omitted to avoid confusion,) for England in 1861, and for France. The English curve for 1851 would differ too slightly from that for 1861 to be conveniently distinguished on the chart; and the French curves for 1851, 1856, and 1861 would be undistinguishable from one another.

The chart *G* shows the corresponding values of *N*, (the number under each year of age,) for each nation, and clearly manifests the differences in the law, corresponding to the diversity in the constants.

The tables of population deduced from the census-returns already cited, together with the values given by the formula, are here appended, reduced however, in each case, to the scale of 100,000 of population. The differences are given in decimals of the census-numbers, and the accordance between the formula and the recorded numbers will be manifest at the first inspection. The chief discrepancies will be found in the French tables, for the ages

exceeding 50, in the census of 1851
" 55, " " " " 1856
" 60, " " " " 1861.

This curious circumstance and the nature of the discordances suggest some historical explanation; which the disturbed condition of the French nation at the period corresponding to the birth of this portion of the population seems to render plausible.

TABLE XXII.

Ages of the Population of the United States, as deduced from the Census Returns of 1830 *and* 1340.

AGE.	Census of 1830.			Census of 1840.		
	Proportional numbers.		Difference. (C. — O.)	Proportional numbers.		Difference. (C. — O.)
	Observed.	Calculated.		Observed.	Calculated.	
0 – 5	17977	17082	−0.050	17437	16334	−0.063
5 – 10	14576	15254	+0.046	14173	14651	+0.034
10 – 15	12452	13280	+0.014	12094	12931	+0.069
15 – 20	11147	11318	+0.024	10911	11205	+0.027
20 – 30	17752	17244	−0.029	18155	17456	−0.038
30 – 40	10908	11287	+0.035	11597	11790	+0.017
40 – 50	6886	6932	+0.007	7320	7466	+0.020
50 – 60	4308	3973	−0.078	4365	4389	+0.005
60 – 70	2525	2100	−0.168	2449	2343	−0.043
70 – 80	1104	992	−0.100	1132	1067	−0.058
80 & over	365	540		367	368	

TABLE XXIII.

Ages of the Population of the United States, as deduced from the Census Returns of 1850 *and* 1860.

AGE.	Census of 1850.			Census of 1860.		
	Proportional numbers.		Difference. (C. — O.)	Proportional numbers.		Difference. (C. — O.)
	Observed.	Calculated.		Observed.	Calculated.	
0 – 1	2751	3170	+0.152	2998	3003	+0.002
1 – 5	12070	12215	+0.012	12300	11608	−0.056
5 – 10	13836	14102	+0.019	13117	13484	+0.028
10 – 15	12292	12564	+0.022	11588	12206	+0.053
15 – 20	10892	10990	+0.009	10625	10853	+0.021
20 – 30	18562	17505	−0.057	18242	17692	−0.030
30 – 40	12368	12225	−0.012	13012	12760	−0.019
40 – 50	8130	8019	−0.013	8496	8618	+0.014
50 – 60	4903	4883	−0.041	5214	5366	+0.029
60 – 70	2667	2695	+0.010	2910	2953	+0.015
70 – 80	1147	1250	+0.090	1158	1261	+0.089
80 & over	382	382		340	196	

TABLE XXIV.

Ages of the Population of England and Wales, as deduced from the Census Returns of 1851 *and* 1861.

AGE.	Census of 1851.			Census of 1861.		
	Proportional numbers.		Difference. (C. — O.)	Proportional numbers.		Difference. (C. — O.)
	Observed	Calculated.		Observed.	Calculated.	
0 – 5	13006	12533	−0.035	13352	12245	−0.083
5 – 10	11590	11800	+0.018	11588	11575	−0.001
10 – 15	10616	10987	+0.034	10415	10819	+0.040
15 – 20	9832	10079	+0.013	9688	10007	+0.032
20 – 25	9441	9114	−0.036	9317	9108	−0.023
25 – 30	8307	8170	−0.017	7932	8178	+0.030
30 – 35	7168	7179	+0.001	6950	7282	+0.046
35 – 40	6083	6273	+0.030	6111	6352	+0.038
40 – 45	5393	5378	−0.003	5638	5506	−0.024
45 – 50	4440	4546	+0.023	4617	4705	+0.019
50 – 55	3934	3782	−0.040	3995	3820	−0.046
55 – 60	2919	3061	+0.046	3039	3245	+0.063
60 – 65	2668	2426	−0.100	2751	2512	−0.095
65 – 70	1815	1841	+0.014	1862	1910	+0.025
70 – 75	1386	1332	−0.041	1391	1355	−0.026
75 – 80	809	876	+0.076	794	869	+0.086
80 – 85	410	481	+0.173	394	435	+0.104
85 & over.	183	142		146	77	
Total,	100000	100000		100000	100000	

FORMULAS

For 1851, $N = 100\,000 \sin n\, (0.99575)^n \,.\, 1^\circ.4702.$

1861, $N = 100\,000 \sin n\, (0.99616)^n \,.\, 1^\circ.4316.$

TABLE XXV.

Ages of the Population of France,

as deduced from the Census Returns of 1851, 1856, *and* 1861.

AGE.	Census of 1851.			Census of 1856.			Census of 1861.		
	Proportional numbers.		Difference. (C. — O.)	Proportional numbers.		Difference. (C. — O.)	Proportional numbers.		Difference. (C. — O.)
	Observed.	Calculated.		Observed.	Calculated.		Observed.	Calculated.	
0 – 5	9291	9208	−0.009	9568	9200	−0.038	9677	9124	−0.088
5 – 10	9216	9130	−0.009	9120	9119	0.000	8767	9052	+0.032
10 – 15	8800	8946	+0.016	8821	8965	+0.016	8668	8898	+0.027
15 – 20	8805	8716	−0.010	8530	8736	+0.024	8701	8722	+0.002
20 – 25	8326	8437	+0.013	8077	8427	+0.043	8237	8374	+0.017
25 – 30	8020	8036	+0.002	8075	8051	−0.003	7857	8005	+0.019
30 – 35	7565	7616	+0.007	7575	7614	+0.005	7421	7564	+0.019
35 – 40	7188	7105	−0.012	7255	7092	−0.022	7098	7071	−0.004
40 – 45	6596	6534	−0.009	6656	6526	−0.020	6625	6514	−0.017
45 – 50	5869	5890	+0.004	6041	5902	−0.023	6155	5900	−0.041
50 – 55	5782	5233	−0.095	5317	5228	−0.017	5382	5254	−0.024
55 – 60	4390	4512	+0.028	4838	4503	−0.069	4559	4518	−0.009
60 – 65	3670	3753	+0.023	3734	3753	+0.005	4160	3790	−0.090
65 – 70	2785	2954	+0.059	2757	2958	+0.076	2941	3016	+0.025
70 – 75	1952	2148	+0.100	1902	2145	+0.128	1940	2218	+0.143
75 – 80	1062	1313	+0.239	1088	1312	+0.205	1123	1398	+0.245
80 – 85	480	468	−0.025	453	468	−0.033	490	568	+0.159
85 & over.	203	1		193	1		199	14	
Total,	100000	100000		100000	100000		100000	100000	

FORMULAS

For 1851, $N = 100\,000 \sin n\ (1^\circ.0553)$.

1856, $N = 100\,000 \sin n\ (1^\circ.0556)$.

1861, $N = 100\,000 \sin n\ (1^\circ.0473)$.

The agreement of the observed numbers with those given by our formula is indicated by the quantities in the columns headed *C.* — *O.* (i. e. Computed *minus* Observed), and appears to be entirely within the limits of probable error in the enumeration, — if we except those discordances for the French census already alluded to. It affords a strong argument for belief that the true form of the normal life-curve is closely represented by the sine-formula.

The only other statistics of ages for European populations, which have been conveniently accessible, are contained in the abstract of the Prussian census of 1852, given by Brachelli, in the second volume of his *Deutsche Staatenkunde.* A discussion of the numbers there recorded gives

$$k = 0.9960, \qquad \theta = 1^\circ.4702,$$

these values being closely similar to those for England and Wales in 1851.

It is manifest that if the number under any given age n be represented by the expression

$$N = a \sin n\, k^n\, \theta$$

the number between the ages n and $n+1$ will be expressed by

$$2\,a \sin \tfrac{1}{2} k^n\,(k\,n + k - n)\,\theta.\ \cos \tfrac{1}{2} k^n\,(k\,n + k + n)\,\theta,$$

and the mortality at the same period, by the finite difference of this quantity.

But when k becomes unity, these values are greatly simplified, and we have

Population under the age n years	$= a \sin n\,\theta$
Population at " " " "	$= 2\,a \sin \frac{1}{2}\theta \cos (n + \frac{1}{2})\,\theta$
Mortality " " " " "	$= 4\,a \sin^2 \frac{1}{2}\,\theta \sin (n + 1)\,\theta.$

According to the formula here presented, the life-curve for advanced ages bears no similarity to an asymptote, but ceases abruptly when the quantity $n\,k^n\,\theta = 90^\circ$; or for the case of $k = 1$, when $n = \frac{90^\circ}{\theta}$. This indicates that all ages above this limit are exceptional, and to be regarded in the same light as deviations from the theoretical number at other periods of life.

The many paths of research afforded by the residual discordances from the formula must be passed by on this occasion, with the single remark that they offer indications of abundant reward for any explorer.

CHAPTER IV.

AGES OF RECRUITS.

1. *Nature of the Problem.*

To determine the law of distribution for recruits according to ages, in the same manner as we have already done for the volunteers, is impossible. The large inroads made upon the younger portion of the military population, by the enlistment of volunteers, materially changed the character of that population; and each successive subsequent call for troops not only tended to increase the irregularity of distribution of ages among the men left at home, but drew from the community as new recruits a class whose ages were themselves irregularly distributed, in consequence of the great disturbance of symmetry already existing in the military population. This process several times repeated gave a distribution of ages, in the aggregate of the recruits, which is subject to no simple law, and threatened to baffle all attempts at intelligent investigation.

Since the official musters have not always been so recorded as to permit the separate investigation of recruits enlisted in the different years, we must content ourselves with the consideration of only two general classes, "Volunteers" and "Recruits;" adopting for the former the definition given in the last chapter, and referring all other white troops furnished by the States, including reenlisted volunteers, to the latter class.

Our problem then becomes the following: — first, to determine as nearly as possible, from the information deduced by the discussion of Ages of Volunteers, what were the ages of the men enlisted during each successive year of the war; then, by comparing the aggregate of these with the numbers collected from the official muster-rolls, to learn how far our adopted law of enlistment by ages, as derived from volunteer troops, is corroborated by these records of ages of recruits, and what modification of the formula is requisite for producing the closest possible accordance between the computed and the observed numbers.

The ages of the military population in each successive year are an essential element in this investigation, inasmuch as the number enlisting at any given age must be dependent upon the total number at that age in the community; so that in the theoretical distribution of a certain number of recruits according to ages, it is not the absolute number at each age, but the tendency to enlist at that age, which must be inferred from the formula. In other words, whenever the normal distribution of ages in the population has been disturbed, the formula tells us not the actual, but the proportionate number enlisting at each year of age; and in the absence of other information, the total number of enlistments in each year must be so distributed among the several military ages, as to assign to each a number whose ratio to the military population of that age, then at home, follows the law indicated by the formula.

It thus becomes necessary for the success of the investigation, that the statistics of population upon which the calculations are based should be specially adapted to the object in view; and a close approach to the truth in the fundamental formula adopted becomes doubly important.

2. *Fundamental Statistics.*

In the general schedule of statistics of the war given in Chapter I., which must, from its very nature, be only approximate, the total number of troops enlisting in each year was deducted from the number of males of military age previously at home. This course, although in accordance with the object there in view, was not strictly accurate, inasmuch as it was based upon the erroneous assumption that the enlisted men were all within the limits of military age prescribed by law. In the present research this assumption is inadmissible, and it becomes necessary to prepare more detailed estimates, by increasing the military population at home, at any epoch, by the probable number of men who had already enlisted, but were not between the ages of eighteen and forty-five at the time of enlistment; also by distinguishing subsequent enlistments of men not within these limits of age, and separately considering the deaths at home of those who had, and of those who had not, served in the army.

The following table has consequently been used in the computations of this chapter. It is accordant with the schedules of Chapter I. except in this special reference to irregular enlistments. In the fourth column is given, under the heading "Natural Growth," the excess of the number of white males, attaining the age of eighteen, over the number of those arriving at forty-five years; the sum of the two classes of deaths deducted from the sum of the increases, by natural growth and by immigration, showing the actual, or net, increase of the military population. The deaths among men who had served in the army are here assumed to be essentially in the same proportion as among those who had not served. This is doubtless an underestimate, since the effect of wounds, exposure, and exhaustion must have manifested themselves in an increased rate of mortality; but in the absence of numerical data, little account is here taken of this influence, which would probably produce small perceptible effect upon the results of the present inquiry. The numbers are given in thousands, as before, and those of the last line are recorded as though the army were not disbanded until July 1865.

TABLE I.

Military Population and Enlistments.

Date	Military Population at Home						New Enlistments		Reenlistments
	Had not served	Had served	Increase by		Deaths		Military Age	Not of Military Age	
			Natural Growth	Immigration	Not served.	Served			
1860, July 1	4 378	–	–	–	–	–	–	–	–
1861, April 1	4 472	–	87	35	28	–	–	–	–
1861, July 1	4 338	–	29	11	9	–	165	5	–
1862, July 1	3 890	145	117	32	34	2	563	17	60
1863, July 1	3 563	363	122	32	31	3	450	17	50
1864, July 1	3 302	590	132	56	28	5	421	18	200
1865, July 1	3 126	882	143	62	27	6	354	16	60

3. *Method of Investigation.*

The formula deduced from the grand total of the ages of volunteers gave the number of men in each 10 000, at and over any given year of age at the time of enlistment, as

$$s_n = 2103 - 77.0\,n + 7897\,(0.85362)^n$$

n being the excess above eighteen years. But this formula also indicated a decided excess of the recorded numbers for the ages eighteen, twenty-one, and forty-four, as also a deficiency at the ages nineteen and twenty; owing, without doubt, to misrepresentations.

In the hope of attaining numerical values of still greater precision, the computation was repeated, after modifying the original data by about one half the amount of the supposed misstatements. The results were quite satisfactory, showing not merely a smaller series of discordances between the calculated and the observed numbers, but a somewhat nearer approach to equality between the excess at twenty-one years, and the deficiency at nineteen and twenty. This gave encouragement for a repetition of the process, using as a correction to the recorded numbers, three fourths of the amount of misstatement as deduced from the second approximation; and gave a result which seems to express the distribution of ages of volunteers, taken as an aggregate, as closely as any formula attainable. This was assumed as the basis of the present investigation, and is as follows: —

(First assumed) $$s_n = 2068 - 77.5\,n + 7932\,(0.85588)^n$$

It must now be noted, that the volunteers, of whom we have the recorded ages of somewhat more than one million, were chiefly enlisted before the middle of the year 1863. The total number, up to 1863 July 1, was 1 327 000, and we may roughly suppose 800 000 enlistments to have taken place from a normal population prior to July 1862, and 520 000 to have been made a year later from the military population left at home after the withdrawal of these 800 000.

Following this hypothesis, and deducting from the military population in April 1861, such a number of men at each year of age as our assumed formula indicates for a total force of 800 000 men (making allowance, however, for enlistments above and below the established limits of age, in the proportions indicated by the official records in Table II., Chapter III.), we obtain the distribution of ages which may be presumed to have existed in the military population at home, after the departure of these men to the army. Then all the ages of this "disturbed population" being increased by one year, the second installment of volunteers is to be distributed according to ages. This is accomplished by using the assumed formula and the original population to determine the ratio of enlistment to military population for each year of age, in the mode employed for Table XVII., Chapter III., and applying these ratios to the disturbed population, after multiplying them by such fraction as shall make the total resultant number just 520 000. Adding now the numbers for each age thus obtained for the two installments, we obtain a calculated series quite different from that which the assumed formula would give if employed directly to assign the distribution of the whole 1 320 000 men at once. But from this series we may deduce a new formula, possessing the property that if so applied to the whole 1 320 000 directly, it will indicate the same distribution which the assumed formula gives if it is applied first to 800 000, and the ratios thus deduced for an undisturbed population are then used to obtain the ages of 520 000 more, from the population as disturbed by the withdrawal of the 800 000, one year previous. This new expression is as follows: —

(Hypothetical formula) $$s_n = 2011 - 76.2n + 7989\ (0.87052)^n$$

What we desire, however, is neither of the formulas yet obtained, but such a one that if employed as we have just now used that first assumed, — namely, for the two installments separately, each from its proper population, — it will give essentially the same distribution that our assumed formula gives when applied to the aggregate of all the volunteers at once. In short, we need a law of ages which shall occupy precisely the same relation to an assumed law, in which this latter stands to the "hypothetical" law just deduced.

This we may very nearly obtain by applying with reversed signs, to the numerical values in the formula first assumed, the differences between the values in this and in the hypothetical formula. We thus obtain an expression which represents the actual tendency to enlistment on the part of our volunteers as closely as it seems practicable to deduce it by numerical processes from existing data; and which we shall adopt, for discovering the number of men, at each year of age withdrawn from the home population during each year of the War of the Rebellion. It is the following: —

(Adopted formula) $$s_n = 2125 - 78.8n + 7875\ (0.84124)^n$$

or $$x_n = 78.8 + 1250\ (0.84124)^n$$

4. *Changes of Home Population during the War.*

The results deducible from the principles here laid down may readily be presented in tabular form, and the course of the investigation will easily be followed after a few preliminary comments.

For greater simplicity and convenience of computation, only so many of the men within the limits of military age as have never served in the army, and only original enlistments, are first considered, in investigating the condition of the military population during the successive years of the war; all necessity of considering the men returning home from the army being thus obviated. The reenlisted men are then classified by themselves, and assorted according to age by following that law of distribution which prevailed at the time of their first enlistment. This procedure assumes the proportion of reenlistments to original enlistments to have been the same at each age, — an assumption perhaps not strictly warrantable, and only to be defended by showing the inapplicability of any other principle; but the results of the investigation seem to indicate that this assumption cannot be far from correct.

A slight obstacle exists to the ready determination of the white male population, at each age, remaining at home in July 1862, inasmuch as the interval between this epoch and the preceding one is not twelve, but fifteen, months. This difficulty is mostly obviated by adding three fourths of the military population at each age n in April 1861, corrected by subtracting the enlistments and deaths during the next fifteen months, to one fourth of the military population at the age $n - 1$, similarly corrected; — the sum of these two quantities, increased by the immigration at the age n during the next fifteen months, being used for the military population at the age $n + 1$ in July 1862.

For the age sixteen years, in July 1862, the number of white males sixteen years old, a year and a quarter previously, is increased by one twentieth part to correspond with the normal annual growth of four per cent.

The mortality of the population at home is assumed to follow the same laws as in 1860, for which year the statistics of mortality have been so thoroughly discussed by Dr. Jarvis, in the Results of the United States Census,[1] and the adopted number of deaths is such as corresponds to the military population in the previous year, diminished by one half of the enlistments during the year. The adopted table of mortality has been prepared by determining the ratio of the deaths of males within given periods of age, in the loyal States, to the total number of males at the same ages in the

[1] *Statistics of the U. S. in* 1860 (*including Mortality, Property, etc.*), *being the Final Exhibit of the Eighth Census.* Washington, 1866. Table IV. pp. 44–46.

same region, as computed in Chapter III., Table XXI.; and then obtaining the ratio for each year of age by interpolation. It is here appended.

TABLE II.

Mortality of Military Population at Home.

Age	Mortality	Age	Mortality	Age	Mortality	Age	Mortality	Age	Mortality
15	0.0050	21	0.0077	27	0.0082	33	0.0085	39	0.0094
16	.0055	22	.0079	28	.0082	34	.0086	40	.0097
17	.0060	23	.0080	29	.0082	35	.0087	41	.0100
18	.0065	24	.0080	30	.0083	36	.0088	42	.0103
19	.0070	25	.0081	31	.0083	37	.0090	43	.0105
20	0.0074	26	0.0081	32	0.0084	38	0.0092	44	0.0108

Immigrants are distributed according to ages, in our table, by the same law which prevailed for the military population in the United States before the war. This unquestionably does not represent the true distribution of their ages; still it will serve as a sufficiently near approximation to the true numbers, for all the purposes of our present investigation.

TABLE III.

Unenlisted Military Population and Enlistments in each Year, using Formula for Ages of Volunteers.

FIRST PART.

Age	White Military Population, April 1861	Enlistments to July 1862	Deaths	Immigrants	White Military Population, July 1862	Enlistments to July 1863	Deaths	Immigrants
16	225 000	2 100	1 500	2 200	238 450	1 670	1 300	1 630
17	222 000	10 700	1 600	2 100	227 210	8 280	1 340	1 610
18	218 900	97 470	1 400	2 100	214 730	72 540	1 180	1 590
19	215 700	82 910	1 500	2 100	144 540	42 160	880	1 560
20	212 400	70 670	1 600	2 000	130 480	32 940	860	1 540
21	208 900	60 370	1 700	2 000	139 920	30 680	970	1 510
22	205 300	51 700	1 800	2 000	147 150	28 120	1 060	1 490
23	201 600	44 410	1 800	2 000	152 560	25 500	1 120	1 460
24	197 800	38 280	1 800	1 900	156 390	22 960	1 160	1 430
25	193 900	33 110	1 800	1 900	159 040	20 600	1 200	1 400
26	189 900	28 770	1 800	1 800	160 470	18 440	1 220	1 370
27	185 800	25 130	1 800	1 800	161 050	16 520	1 250	1 350
28	181 600	22 060	1 700	1 800	160 780	14 810	1 260	1 320
29	177 300	19 470	1 700	1 700	159 800	13 320	1 250	1 280
30	172 900	17 300	1 700	1 700	158 260	12 020	1 250	1 250
31	168 400	15 470	1 700	1 600	156 050	10 880	1 240	1 220
32	163 800	13 930	1 600	1 600	153 500	9 910	1 240	1 190
33	159 100	12 640	1 600	1 500	150 510	9 070	1 240	1 150
34	154 400	11 550	1 600	1 500	147 210	8 360	1 230	1 120
35	149 500	10 630	1 600	1 400	143 560	7 750	1 210	1 080
36	144 600	9 860	1 500	1 400	139 560	7 230	1 190	1 050
37	139 600	9 220	1 500	1 300	135 550	6 790	1 180	1 010
38	134 500	8 670	1 500	1 300	131 270	6 420	1 170	970
39	129 300	8 210	1 500	1 200	126 670	6 100	1 160	940
40	124 100	7 830	1 500	1 200	121 970	5 840	1 150	900
41	118 800	7 500	1 400	1 100	117 080	5 610	1 140	860
42	113 400	7 230	1 400	1 100	112 210	5 430	1 120	820
43	108 000	7 000	1 400	1 000	107 060	5 260	1 100	780
44	102 500	6 810	1 300	1 000	101 890	5 130	1 070	740
45 to 50	428 400	9 000	4 600	4 100	418 900	6 660	4 570	3 100
18 to 45	4 472 000	728 200	43 200	43 000	3 889 260	450 390	31 100	32 380
16 to 50		750 000	50 900			467 000	38 310	

TABLE III.

Unenlisted Military Population and Enlistments in each Year, using Formula for Ages of Volunteers.

SECOND PART.

Age	Military Population July 1863	Enlistments to July 1864	Deaths	Immigrants	Military Population July 1864	Enlistments to May 1865	Deaths to July 1865	Immigrants to July 1865
16	248 000	1 810	1 360	2 840	257 920	1 710	1 410	3 160
17	237 110	9 020	1 400	2 810	247 670	8 550	1 460	3 110
18	219 200	77 240	1 180	2 770	229 500	73 430	1 260	3 070
19	142 600	43 380	860	2 730	143 550	39 660	880	3 020
20	103 060	27 140	670	2 680	101 090	24 170	670	2 980
21	98 220	22 460	680	2 640	77 930	16 180	550	2 930
22	109 780	21 880	790	2 590	77 720	14 060	570	2 880
23	119 460	20 820	880	2 550	89 700	14 200	670	2 830
24	127 400	19 520	940	2 500	100 310	13 950	760	2 770
25	133 700	18 070	1 010	2 450	109 440	13 430	830	2 720
26	138 640	16 620	1 050	2 400	117 070	12 740	900	2 660
27	142 180	15 210	1 100	2 350	123 370	11 990	960	2 600
28	144 630	13 900	1 120	2 300	128 220	11 190	1 000	2 550
29	146 020	12 690	1 140	2 240	131 910	10 410	1 030	2 480
30	146 510	11 600	1 160	2 190	134 430	9 670	1 060	2 420
31	146 240	10 630	1 160	2 130	135 940	8 970	1 080	2 360
32	145 150	9 770	1 170	2 070	136 580	8 350	1 100	2 300
33	143 540	9 020	1 170	2 010	136 280	7 780	1 120	2 230
34	141 350	8 370	1 170	1 950	135 360	7 280	1 130	2 160
35	138 740	7 820	1 170	1 890	133 760	6 840	1 130	2 100
36	135 680	7 330	1 160	1 830	131 640	6 460	1 130	2 020
37	132 190	6 910	1 160	1 770	129 020	6 120	1 130	1 950
38	128 590	6 560	1 150	1 700	125 890	5 830	1 120	1 880
39	124 650	6 260	1 140	1 630	122 580	5 590	1 120	1 810
40	120 340	6 020	1 130	1 560	118 880	5 390	1 120	1 740
41	115 880	5 790	1 120	1 500	114 750	5 200	1 120	1 660
42	111 190	5 620	1 110	1 430	110 470	5 060	1 110	1 590
43	106 480	5 460	1 090	1 360	105 890	4 930	1 090	1 510
44	101 480	5 330	1 070	1 300	101 290	4 830	1 070	1 440
45 to 50	410 770	6 750	4 480	5 410	404 950	6 030	4 420	6 000
18 to 45	3562 900	421 420	28 550	56 520	3 302 570	353 710	26 710	62 660
16 to 50		439 000	35 790			370 000	34 000	

We have now the means — by summing the enlistments at each age, deduced by the preceding calculations, and combining them with the reenlistments of successive years, distributed as already explained — of obtaining the ages of recruits, as calculated by the formula adopted for the volunteers. The degree of accordance between the distribution of ages, thus obtained, and that actually derived from official records, will afford a criterion for estimating the extent to which the law connecting the ages of our volunteers, or first million of soldiers, with their tendency to enlist, is also applicable to the recruits, or last million and a quarter of troops. Of course we can only consider in the calculation those within the limits of military age.

TABLE IV.

Ages of Recruits,
as derived from Formula for Ages of Volunteers.

Age	Original Enlistments 1863–5	Reenlistments				Aggregate Recruits	Proportionate Numbers		
		1862	1863	1864–5	Total		Calculated	Recorded	C.–R.
Under 18	21 090	1 030	140	–	1 170	22 260	–	–	
18	150 670	7 800	710	720	9 230	159 900	1 410	1 563	–153
19	83 040	6 630	6 500	3 700	16 830	99 870	880	848	+ 32
20	51 310	5 650	5 530	33 790	44 970	96 280	849	707	+142
21	38 640	4 830	4 710	28 740	38 280	76 920	678	905	–227
22	35 940	4 140	4 020	24 500	32 660	68 600	605	686	– 81
23	35 020	3 550	3 450	20 930	27 930	62 950	555	587	– 32
24	33 470	3 060	2 960	17 920	23 940	57 410	506	504	+ 2
25	31 500	2 650	2 550	15 400	20 600	52 100	459	443	+ 16
26	29 360	2 300	2 220	13 270	17 790	47 150	416	390	+ 26
27	27 200	2 020	1 920	11 480	15 420	42 620	376	347	+ 29
28	25 090	1 760	1 670	9 970	13 400	38 490	339	352	– 13
29	23 100	1 560	1 470	8 710	11 740	34 840	307	254	+ 53
30	21 270	1 380	1 300	7 640	10 320	31 590	278	281	– 3
31 to 35	70 170	4 280	3 950	22 940	31 170	101 340	894	772	+122
35 to 45	119 350	6 640	5 850	32 360	44 850	164 200	1 448	1 361	+ 87
Over 45	12 780	720	1 050	7 930	9 700	22 480	–	–	–
18 to 45	775 130	58 250	48 810	252 070	359 130	1 134 260	10 000	10 000	–
16 to 50	809 000	60 000	50 000	260 000	370 000	1 179 000	–	–	–

5. *Final Inferences.*

The discrepancies between the calculated and recorded numbers, after reduction to the scale of 10 000, are of the same order of magnitude as those found in Chapter III., between the calculated and recorded numbers of volunteers at the several ages ; and are indeed somewhat larger than those there found for the grand total of enlisted men. But it is manifest that if the tendency to enlistment for the recruits were governed by a law depending on their age, to the same extent as was found to hold good for the volunteers, the present more detailed method of investigation ought to show a decidedly closer accordance between theory and observation than was there manifested.

The algebraic form of the law being apparently as good as could be expected, attention was directed to discovering what modification of the numerical values would bring about a closer accordance with the recorded numbers. This investigation, being necessarily indirect, tedious, and in great measure tentative, need not be described; but it resulted in modifying the formula by some slight change in the numbers.

We thus obtain for the law of enlistment of recruits by ages —

(Formula for Recruits)
$$s_n = 1631 - 62.8n + 8369\ (0.8353)^n$$
$$x_n = 62.8 + 1378.4\ (0.8353)^n$$

The second part of Table III. thus requires modification throughout ; and the following tables (V. and VI.) which result from the employment of the "formula for recruits" in distributing all enlistments since July 1863 by ages, seem to present the facts in the most trustworthy form ; — the first part of Table III., as given on page 80 remaining unchanged.

TABLE V.

Unenlisted Military Population and Enlistments in each Year, using Formula for Ages of Recruits.

Age	Mil'y Population July 1863	Enlistments to July 1864	Deaths	Immigrants	Mil'y Population July 1864	Enlistments	Deaths to July 1865	Immigrants to July 1865
16	248 000	2 010	1 360	2 840	257 920	1 920	1 410	3 160
17	237 110	9 910	1 400	2 810	247 470	9 480	1 460	3 110
18	219 200	83 920	1 180	2 770	228 610	80 230	1 260	3 070
19	142 600	46 680	860	2 730	136 870	41 070	880	3 020
20	103 060	28 920	670	2 680	97 790	25 150	670	2 980
21	98 220	23 680	680	2 640	76 150	16 830	550	2 930
22	109 780	22 820	790	2 590	76 500	14 570	570	2 880
23	119 460	21 480	880	2 550	88 760	14 630	670	2 830
24	127 400	19 890	940	2 500	99 650	14 260	760	2 770
25	133 700	18 200	1 010	2 450	109 070	13 610	830	2 720
26	138 640	16 530	1 050	2 400	116 940	12 780	900	2 660
27	142 180	14 940	1 100	2 350	123 460	11 890	960	2 600
28	144 630	13 460	1 120	2 300	128 490	10 960	1 000	2 550
29	146 020	12 130	1 140	2 240	132 350	10 070	1 030	2 480
30	146 510	10 930	1 160	2 190	134 990	9 230	1 060	2 420
31	146 240	9 880	1 160	2 130	136 610	8 460	1 080	2 360
32	145 150	8 960	1 170	2 070	137 330	7 770	1 100	2 300
33	143 540	8 160	1 170	2 010	137 090	7 140	1 120	2 230
34	141 350	7 470	1 170	1 950	136 220	6 600	1 130	2 160
35	138 740	6 880	1 170	1 890	134 660	6 120	1 130	2 100
36	135 680	6 380	1 160	1 830	132 580	5 710	1 130	2 020
37	132 190	5 950	1 160	1 770	129 970	5 360	1 130	1 950
38	128 590	5 590	1 150	1 700	126 850	5 050	1 120	1 880
39	124 650	5 290	1 140	1 630	123 550	4 800	1 120	1 810
40	120 340	5 030	1 130	1 560	119 850	4 590	1 120	1 740
41	115 880	4 800	1 120	1 500	115 740	4 400	1 120	1 660
42	111 190	4 630	1 110	1 430	111 460	4 250	1 110	1 590
43	106 480	4 480	1 090	1 360	106 880	4 120	1 090	1 510
44	101 480	4 350	1 070	1 300	102 270	4 020	1 070	1 440
45 to 50	410 770	5 650	4 480	5 410	406 050	4 930	4 420	6 000
18 to 45	3 562 900	421 430	28 550	56 520	3 300 690	353 670	26 710	62 660
All		439 000	35 790			370 000	34 000	

Hence we deduce the following Table VI. for the true ages of recruits, in the stead of Table IV. It will be observed that the excess of recorded ages at twenty-one years is very nearly compensated by a corresponding deficit at nineteen and twenty; so that we may be warranted in regarding these discrepancies, and also the excess at eighteen years, as representing very closely the actual amount of misrepresentation at these ages.

TABLE VI.

Ages of Recruits,
as deduced from most probable Formula.

Age	Original Enlistments			Reenlistments 1862–5	Aggregate Recruits	Proportionate Numbers		
	1863–4	1864–5	Total			Calc'd	Recorded	C.—R.
Under 18	11 920	11 400	23 320	1 170	24 490			
18	83 920	80 230	164 150	9 230	173 380	1 529	1 563	− 34
19	46 680	41 070	87 750	16 830	104 580	922	848	+ 74
20	28 920	25 150	54 070	44 970	99 040	873	707	+166
21	23 680	16 830	40 510	38 280	78 790	695	905	−210
22	22 820	14 570	37 390	32 660	70 050	618	686	− 68
23	21 480	14 630	36 110	27 930	64 040	565	587	− 22
24	19 890	14 260	34 150	23 940	58 090	512	504	+ 8
25	18 200	13 610	31 810	20 600	52 410	462	443	+ 19
26	16 530	12 780	29 310	17 790	47 100	415	390	+ 25
27	14 940	11 890	26 830	15 420	42 250	372	347	+ 25
28	13 460	10 960	24 420	13 400	37 820	333	352	− 19
29	12 130	10 070	22 200	11 740	33 940	299	254	+ 45
30	10 930	9 230	20 160	10 320	30 480	269	281	− 12
31 to 35	34 470	29 970	64 440	31 170	95 610	844	772	+ 72
35 to 45	53 380	48 420	101 800	44 850	146 650	1 292	1 361	− 69
Over 45	5 650	4 930	10 580	9 700	20 280			
18 to 45	421 430	353 670	775 100	359 130	1 134 230	10 000	10 000	
16 to 50	439 000	370 000	809 000	370 000	1 179 000			

By the process described in Chapter III., page 39 we may now compute for the recruits also the true age, *t*, corresponding to the averages of any given "Age last birthday," and shall find that the modification of the formula produces in no case a greater change than three units in the third decimal place. But the untrue returns for the ages eighteen to twenty-one inclusive affect the result materially, and we may obtain data for deducing values entitled to much confidence, by comparing the recorded numbers with those indicated by our formula.

A combination of the true ages of those recorded as of any

given age at the last birthday, will give the following values, which acquire importance from their effect upon the investigation of the law of growth in stature.

Recorded Age last birthday	Corresponding Average Age
18	18.460
19	19.482
20	20.482
21	21.179
25	25.486
30	30.487
35	35.490
40	40.494
45	45.497
31 to 35	32.870
35 to 45	39.558

6. *Ages of the Army in each Year.*

In closing the present chapter, it may not be amiss to present an estimate of the ages of the troops here considered, who were serving in the national army in each successive year of the rebellion ; — the present investigations affording all needed data. And by combining our results for volunteers, recruits, and reenlisted men, we arrive at the following schedule, which cannot differ much from the truth.

TABLE VII.

Ages of White Volunteer Army from Loyal States (excluding Pacific Coast).

Age last Birthday	July 1862	July 1863	July 1864	May 1865
16	800	600	750	685
17	4 855	4 130	4 890	4 595
18	40 960	32 370	38 025	35 420
19	68 300	70 300	72 775	70 265
20	58 155	75 685	80 590	75 380
21	49 620	64 320	76 050	72 305
22	42 435	56 490	65 305	65 270
23	36 390	49 505	58 645	56 825
24	31 310	43 340	52 340	52 025
25	27 035	37 955	46 520	47 180
26	23 435	33 285	41 245	42 510
27	20 410	29 250	36 545	38 140
28	17 870	25 785	32 400	34 145
29	15 725	22 830	28 775	30 550
30	13 920	20 305	25 620	27 350
31	12 410	18 140	22 895	24 525
32	11 135	16 305	20 550	22 065
33	10 060	14 750	18 540	19 935
34	9 160	13 425	16 825	18 095
35	8 400	12 305	15 355	16 510
36	7 760	11 355	14 110	15 135
37	7 230	10 560	13 055	13 980
38	6 780	9 895	12 170	12 990
39	6 390	9 320	11 430	12 160
40	6 070	8 840	10 795	11 480
41	5 805	8 435	10 260	10 880
42	5 575	8 095	9 805	10 380
43	5 385	7 810	9 430	9 960
44	5 230	7 565	9 115	9 615
45 and over	9 390	17 050	24 190	28 645
	568 000	740 000	879 000	889 000

We are thus enabled to determine for the total white volunteer army, at each of the four dates comprised in the foregoing table, a tabular view of the mean age, the probable age for any individual, and the proportionate number of men below certain specified limits of age. This is analogous to the similar exhibit for the ages of the "Volunteers," in our restricted sense of the term, presented in the preceding chapter.[1] The gradual increase of the average age, from year to year, which is manifested by the annual changes in the distribution of the numbers at each age in Table VII. is shown, in a form perhaps more striking to the general reader, by the subjoined figures.

	July 1862	July 1863	July 1864	May 1865
	y	y	y	y
Average age last birthday	25.104	25.766	26.067	26.321
Average age at date	25.590	26.252	26.553	26.807
Age above and below which the numbers were equal	23.96	24.76	25.11	25.49
Percentage under 20 years last birthday	19.76	14.30	13.06	12.36
Percentage under 25 years last birthday	59.16	54.58	52.32	50.00
Percentage under 30 years last birthday	78.06	75.34	74.18	72.51

[1] Page 35.

CHAPTER V.

STATURES.

1. *Statistics Collected, and Mode of Discussion.*

THE descriptive muster-rolls of the army promised to afford such valuable materials for studying the law of growth, as well as the mean stature belonging to different States and nativities, that steps were taken in November 1864 to obtain these important data from the military archives of the several States. Blanks were accordingly prepared, upon which the nativity, age, and height of each soldier could be easily transcribed, as well as the regiment or other organization into which he enlisted; and clerks were sent to the capitals of the loyal States to collect these records.

The desired facilities were accorded by the Adjutant-Generals with a ready courtesy and cordiality for which the grateful thanks of the Commission are due; and in almost every instance personal kindness and assistance were offered and given to an extent which we should not have presumed to solicit. The Ages of Recruits, investigated in the preceding chapter, were mostly obtained in this way, as well as the Nativities discussed in Chapter II.; and this collection of materials was continued until all the records available had been transcribed. The number might probably have been still farther increased by additional records in the federal archives at Washington, had not all opportunity for such inquiries been refused the Commission by the Secretary of War; but it is not probable that the results would have been appreciably modified by this relatively small increase of material. It is much to be regretted that the records of stature are so meagre for the first years of the war.

The facts indicated by the records of the State of New York rendering it desirable that similar information should be obtained concerning the men enlisting in the naval service, application for access to the naval records was made to the late Commander Albert N. Smith, Chief of the Bureau of Equipment and Recruiting, who in the most courteous manner afforded all requisite opportunities and assistance in our work.

The height, age, and nativity were thus collected for each one of nearly a million and a quarter of men, namely, for

1 104 841	white soldiers;
39 615	colored soldiers;
83 800	white sailors;
4 000	colored sailors:
1 232 256	in all.

These records were then tabulated and assorted by distributing the records from each office according to nativities, and grouping, for each nativity, those of each age according to height; all under seventeen years and all over thirty-five being aggregated, as well as those of the four years of age between thirty-one and thirty-five. Similarly the heights under sixty-one inches were grouped in one column, as were also those over seventy-five inches; but these were singly considered in taking the corresponding mean heights. A little less than one fifth of all under the height of sixty-one inches were under the age of eighteen years. No limit of stature appears to have been established for volunteer troops, and the rule of the Board of Enrollment was that "the matter of stature should be considered only in the general examination as to the physical fitness of the man for military service." For the regular army the minimum height was established in August 1861 at sixty-three inches, but this has no appreciable bearing on the results here found.

The number under sixty-one inches was 5445, out of 1 104 841, or a little less than one half of one per centum; the corresponding numbers for soldiers of twenty-one years and upward being 2524 out of 753 666; or one third of one per cent. The full table of ages for the under-statures will be given hereafter. Since the heights were never recorded more minutely than to the nearest quarter of an inch, they were assorted by quarter-inches.

It soon became evident that a very large proportion of the measurements were given to the nearest inch only, and that the number recorded at the half inch greatly exceeded the sum of those given for the uneven quarters. The influence of this crude method of measuring manifests itself to some extent in our results, especially in those pertaining to the law of growth. Indeed there is no department of our statistical work in which the tendency to the employment of round numbers is not prominently exhibited, in some manner analogous to that already described in the consideration of the Ages of Volunteers. It is doubtless attendant upon all statistical inquiries, if indeed not inherent in all quantitative determinations requiring human judgement to any extent, though decreasing with the training of the observer; and the scientific inquirer can only hope so to arrange his methods of investigation as to reduce the effect of this source of error to a minimum, without eliminating it entirely.

To obviate the danger of vitiating too large an amount of work by any accidental error in grouping, the materials from the more populous States were tabulated in successive installments; forty thousand being as large a number as it was found advisable to assort at once, although in some cases this number was exceeded. These successive installments, or "counts," followed the order in which the records were transcribed, but not necessarily that in which the men enlisted; so that the results obtained from consecutive counts afforded only a rough approximation to those which a strictly historical classification would have yielded. A classification by years of enlistment would have afforded a means of obtaining results of high interest and value; but for some States this was impossible, and for the others it would have entailed an additional amount of labor, altogether precluded by financial considerations.

It has been seen how very large a proportion of our soldiers were under the age of legal majority, and how rapidly their relative number decreased for increasing ages. The slightest consideration shows moreover that the mean stature of the enlisted men would fall far short of indicating the stature belonging to years of full development, or even to their mean age, since the growths before and after this mean age are at different rates. And, since the earliest inferences from the present research led to the conviction that the age of full stature was a much later one than is generally supposed, and that this age probably varied for different States and countries, it became still more clearly important that the typical stature for each should be deduced only from the statistics for ages subsequent to the attainment of maximum stature. It seems remarkable that this precaution should have been so little regarded by investigators. The mean stature of the white soldiers here considered would be increased by nearly three eighths of an inch by excluding from the computation those under the age of twenty-four years; and the average heights of those above and those below that age differ by more than two thirds of an inch.

There is reason to believe that the average stature of the volunteer soldiers (using this term in the sense in which it was employed in Chapter III., to designate the original members of volunteer organizations) was decidedly greater than that of the recruits who subsequently enlisted, and it is therefore a source of much regret that so large a proportion of our material is afforded by the latter only. The successive "counts" for different States indicate a decided tendency to diminution of the average stature as the war went on; and it is doubtless owing to this fact that the mean statures afforded by the present investigation, which comprises all those volunteers whose statures were recorded, range much higher than those given in the excellent report[1] of Dr. Baxter, Chief Medical Officer of the Provost Marshal General's Bureau, inasmuch as these latter are deduced from the statistics of less than 350 000 soldiers, all of whom were recruits, substitutes, or drafted men.

The regulations prescribe that the heights be taken with a measuring rod, while the men are without clothing. There is doubtless some difference in the average results obtained by different examining surgeons, but these must vanish from the mean of measurements by so many different officers. The most appropriate distribution of the soldiers according to nativities was a question of some difficulty, since it was necessary to decide upon the mode of distribution, before the relative numbers were known. The following eighteen classes were adopted, and although this division might with advantage be somewhat modified in the light of our present knowledge, it has, to preserve uniformity, been retained for all the statistics of the Commission.

A. The six New England States.
B. New York, New Jersey, and Pennsylvania.
C. Ohio and Indiana.
D. Michigan, Wisconsin, and Illinois.
E. Slave States, not including F and G_2.
F. Kentucky and Tennessee.
G_1. Free States west of the Mississippi.
G_2. Slave States west of the Mississippi.
H. British America, exclusive of Canada.
I. Canada.
J. England.
K. Scotland.
L. Ireland.
M. France, Belgium, and Switzerland.
N. Germany.
O. Scandinavia.
P. Spain, Portugal, and Spanish America.
Q. Miscellaneous.

[1] Pages 698, 699.

All statures exceeding 76¾ inches (195 centimeters) have been regarded as excessive, and especial inquiries have been instituted to verify the truth of the records in such cases. In about one sixth part of the number the records have proved erroneous, generally by one foot; for about one fourth of the entire number the record has been corroborated; and attempts to obtain farther information have failed in the remaining instances.

2. *Heights at each Age, by States of Enlistment.*

The general table here appended exhibits the Mean Heights, in inches for each age, of somewhat more than 1 100 000 soldiers, distinguishing them by the States in which they enlisted; and it furthermore shows, in every instance, the number of men from which this mean height was deduced. The number of men is given in a lighter type, just above the corresponding stature. Thus it will be seen that the mean stature of the 17 563 men from West Virginia was 68.425 inches, while that of the 18 875 men from New Jersey was 66.575 inches, or nearly two inches less.

The great discordances between the mean statures of men from different States seemed to follow no simple geographical rule, nor yet to depend upon the character of the respective populations historically considered, with reference either to the original stock or to later immigration. It seems needless to present here the special tables, showing the number of men at each age and each height, for the several States, although such tables exist in our archives.

TABLE I.

Mean Heights at each Age, by States of Enlistment.

Age last birthday	Maine	New Hampshire	Vermont	Massachusetts	Rhode Island and Connecticut	New York	New Jersey	Pennsylvania	Maryland	West Virginia
Under 17	79 63.701	86 62.414	59 63.721	60 62.933	84 63.084	725 63.280	22 62.898	413 65.044	50 62.495	94 65.356
17	134 66.917	91 66.312	156 66.372	126 65.865	145 65.346	1365 65.287	49 65.220	1377 65.590	88 64.636	244 66.945
18	9524 66.966	3190 66.703	4084 66.720	5313 66.181	4513 66.169	25 203 66.103	984 65.602	10 953 65.974	1026 65.996	3441 67.335
19	4390 67.856	1972 67.062	1907 67.553	3764 66.706	3021 66.696	14 980 66.575	1275 66.007	7007 66.614	676 66.764	1609 68.380
20	3465 68.226	1830 67.287	1643 67.627	2828 67.007	2575 66.912	10 961 66.980	1458 66.309	6152 67.166	565 67.388	1308 68.607
21	5411 68.279	3184 67.235	2764 67.741	5131 67.101	4204 66.927	19 306 67.241	1934 66.602	6424 67.305	694 67.582	1479 68.592
22	3539 68.339	2280 67.331	1657 67.797	3090 67.217	3316 67.094	13 263 67.306	1760 66.646	4766 67.352	528 67.471	1217 68.668
23	2947 68.547	1828 67.525	1411 67.878	2379 67.259	2769 67.358	10 810 67.372	1404 66.785	4139 67.414	504 67.960	952 69.040
24	2420 68.432	1334 67.447	1179 67.848	1999 67.281	2198 67.307	9067 67.384	1253 66.747	3544 67.451	360 67.992	807 68.966
25	2167 68.489	1292 67.441	975 67.805	1695 67.319	1999 67.319	8229 67.325	1020 66.713	2907 67.536	286 67.830	712 68.742
26	1904 68.447	1019 67.604	863 67.964	1545 67.210	1712 67.410	7169 67.457	894 66.558	2723 67.594	267 67.757	576 68.915
27	1696 68.618	962 67.682	769 68.071	1350 67.296	1489 67.432	6526 67.424	763 66.727	2484 67.529	242 68.084	477 68.613
28	1668 68.559	998 67.590	740 68.106	1409 67.216	1638 67.466	6518 67.423	781 66.684	2506 67.530	218 67.776	482 68.988
29	1143 68.561	695 67.751	506 67.993	1061 67.405	1148 67.385	4491 67.455	521 66.688	1898 67.575	183 67.728	337 69.111
30	1264 68.461	730 67.788	537 67.968	1113 67.169	1233 67.239	5177 67.341	608 66.657	1873 67.639	163 67.637	393 68.897
31-34	3482 68.555	1864 67.894	1598 68.091	2848 67.444	3256 67.389	14 482 67.478	1577 66.889	5924 67.665	482 67.712	1078 68.937
35 & over	7081 68.587	3466 67.956	3215 67.772	5144 67.394	6005 67.446	29 736 67.394	2572 66.810	12 671 67.573	1001 67.747	2357 68.778
Total	52 314 68.122	26 821 67.402	24 063 67.613	40 855 67.050	41 305 67.088	188 008 67.085	18 875 66.575	77 761 67.136	7333 67.312	17 563 68.425

TABLE I. — (*Continued.*)

Mean Heights at each Age, by States of Enlistment.

Age last birthday	Kentucky	Ohio	Indiana	Illinois	Michigan	Wisconsin	Minnesota	Iowa	Missouri	Louisiana
Under 17	144 65.625	494 64.304	270 64.596	1168 64.326	298 65.727	243 65.247	74 65.314	152 64.484	431 62.854	24 59.250
17	260 66.119	1136 65.828	634 66.610	2527 66.004	660 66.142	514 66.035	161 65.585	384 65.951	736 66.122	12 64.208
18	4563 66.662	19 601 66.665	21 935 66.870	28 635 66.638	3145 66.530	6892 66.789	812 66.316	6886 66.862	7280 66.957	122 65.373
19	2099 67.685	9331 67.528	10 519 67.723	16 547 67.620	1612 67.317	3438 67.502	324 67.309	2566 67.926	4102 67.861	108 66.306
20	2069 68.274	8199 67.836	9435 68.111	13 130 68.121	1732 67.568	2958 67.830	254 67.980	1615 68.309	3783 68.217	97 66.789
21	1794 68.426	7636 68.098	9705 68.351	14 919 68.247	1670 67.823	3715 68.012	558 67.821	2198 68.612	4486 68.227	121 66.926
22	1619 68.608	6190 68.175	7835 68.483	13 024 68.396	1288 68.000	2799 68.093	310 68.276	1519 68.667	3614 68.387	137 66.668
23	1383 68.707	5669 68.217	6789 68.487	11 332 68.396	1269 68.082	2475 68.044	273 68.264	1329 68.616	3313 68.429	116 67.293
24	1212 68.907	4922 68.203	6012 68.408	10 118 68.441	1159 68.054	2334 67.922	257 68.158	1166 68.702	2747 68.475	108 67.431
25	1026 68.530	4243 68.252	4890 68.536	9097 68.387	909 67.915	1996 68.068	232 68.046	1063 68.691	2790 68.275	135 66.909
26	861 68.899	3857 68.266	4283 68.495	7753 68.426	873 68.055	1788 67.857	220 67.604	956 68.735	2526 68.269	113 67.077
27	716 68.802	3563 68.295	3738 68.476	6647 68.421	729 68.085	1783 67.932	232 68.252	967 68.512	2042 68.411	118 66.981
28	742 68.894	3601 68.269	3929 68.527	6646 68.398	797 67.881	1807 67.787	267 67.808	870 68.861	2143 68.363	140 67.093
29	490 68.763	2706 68.261	2769 68.498	4833 68.452	649 67.865	1423 67.986	225 68.019	696 69.037	1453 68.261	102 67.201
30	642 68.927	2938 68.300	3000 68.546	5257 68.344	661 67.953	1587 67.789	229 68.199	790 68.780	1925 68.176	127 67.238
31–34	1342 68.784	8541 68.369	8361 68.632	13 453 68.454	1884 67.985	4868 67.832	794 67.916	2148 68.876	4776 68.328	311 67.006
35 & over	3031 68.817	15 661 68.367	14 147 68.422	23 421 68.306	3987 67.931	10 582 67.621	1475 67.771	4299 68.656	9350 68.247	691 66.986
Total	23 993 68.160	108 288 67.838	118 251 68.062	188 507 67.970	23 322 67.615	51 202 67.652	6697 67.625	29 604 68.131	57 497 68.033	2582 66.831

3. *Heights at each Age by Nativities.*

The soldiers of each State being assorted by nativities, according to the schedule already described, and the results for each nativity then aggregated, we obtain a table similar in form to that given in the last section, but showing the mean height at each age, not by the State of enlistment, but by the State or country of birth. It may, however, not be without interest for the statistician, if a

TABLE II.

Natives of New England States, by Heights and Ages.

Height	Under 17	17	18	19	20	21	22	23	24
in.									
Under 61	89	18	97	35	27	29	24	16	23
61	27	11	71	22	11	10	6	5	5
61½	15	4	71	23	15	19	3	5	7
62	24	24	225	66	17	26	25	13	22
62½	12	13	174	55	48	30	25	13	20
63	30	56	951	236	123	183	107	80	75
63½	10	29	710	204	114	163	120	74	56
64	30	51	1 665	513	276	417	222	214	172
64½	12	44	1 182	429	292	365	230	191	184
65	46	73	2 319	867	534	784	522	401	295
65½	20	30	1 289	554	378	622	359	323	263
66	28	80	2 752	1 241	924	1 242	783	626	516
66½	8	30	1 393	754	502	738	483	389	331
67	18	71	2 473	1 253	967	1 351	850	711	617
67½	7	43	1 313	755	614	946	582	528	424
68	14	56	2 317	1 399	1 111	1 537	1 112	893	705
68½	7	28	1 037	731	598	859	561	496	415
69	10	43	1 575	997	913	1 377	886	813	636
69½	10	21	731	550	410	667	460	439	360
70	7	27	1 125	775	746	1 036	715	682	573
70½	3	16	407	358	304	466	330	287	244
71	2	16	547	455	435	673	450	449	333
71½	1	8	181	160	169	252	175	187	138
72	3	7	323	308	287	448	342	297	275
72½	–	7	70	64	82	111	100	61	65
73	–	1	115	93	106	189	148	99	99
73½	–	–	34	34	42	82	57	51	33
74	–	2	39	39	52	70	56	50	51
74½	–	–	14	11	11	25	22	19	12
75 & over	–	–	19	20	32	35	35	29	30
Total	433	809	25 219	13 001	10 140	14 752	9 790	8 441	6 979

few of the special tables be here given, showing the number of soldiers at each year of age for particular nativities, and to avoid too great diffuseness, we will give these tables for four nativities only, and will aggregate the measures recorded to quarter-inches with those given for the half-inches. The General Table VI. follows these and exhibits the mean heights at each age for the several nativities.

TABLE II. — (*Continued.*)

Natives of New England States, by Heights and Ages.

Height	25	26	27	28	29	30	31-34	35 and over	Total
in.									
Under 61	15	12	11	9	2	9	25	36	477
61	2	7	4	8	5	9	11	19	233
61½	7	5	5	4	5	5	13	26	232
62	29	10	13	10	6	15	25	54	604
62½	13	13	8	15	13	9	27	57	545
63	40	54	50	33	40	43	103	221	2 425
63½	56	59	49	38	31	39	71	155	1 978
64	160	136	102	111	80	85	235	477	4 946
64½	147	114	115	118	73	69	224	435	4 224
65	276	240	184	179	144	164	410	962	8 400
65½	217	191	152	180	128	139	412	731	5 988
66	407	425	362	326	252	272	697	1 630	12 563
66½	302	263	222	209	174	149	505	1 034	7 486
67	552	530	460	423	316	351	914	1 944	13 801
67½	408	337	304	274	203	223	672	1 346	8 979
68	703	550	566	530	355	412	1 221	2 449	15 930
68½	365	335	320	293	243	209	642	1 326	8 465
69	553	475	463	446	366	342	977	2 171	13 043
69½	289	270	226	243	190	190	553	1 035	6 644
70	462	455	413	441	301	281	1 007	2 089	11 135
70½	259	194	196	212	128	163	422	908	4 897
71	301	261	288	264	211	192	676	1 247	6 800
71½	122	114	115	116	71	94	250	523	2 676
72	213	227	178	197	156	147	426	931	4 765
72½	61	50	39	49	40	24	95	204	1 122
73	78	90	76	94	47	49	163	347	1 794
73½	30	35	37	20	28	28	62	127	700
74	36	41	38	32	33	27	87	160	813
74½	18	18	9	11	4	6	22	54	256
75 & over	27	19	25	17	14	9	54	84	449
Total	6 148	5 530	5 030	4 902	3 659	3 754	11 001	22 782	152 370

TABLE III.

Natives of New York, New Jersey, and Pennsylvania, by Heights and Ages.

Height	Under 17	17	18	19	20	21	22	23	24
in.									
Under 61	217	69	316	110	69	100	66	61	38
61	57	31	214	75	41	44	36	27	17
61½	23	25	239	85	50	58	27	24	20
62	67	120	609	168	97	121	92	62	53
62½	18	56	552	205	87	108	90	50	46
63	160	260	2 059	699	350	384	243	207	193
63½	56	126	1 266	482	267	282	196	178	142
64	146	389	3 673	1 318	775	926	539	460	434
64½	46	152	1 789	835	464	580	392	289	237
65	140	381	4 462	1 976	1 341	1 585	1 065	893	725
65½	56	142	1 903	982	721	851	662	503	440
66	136	438	5 065	2 691	1 887	2 412	1 621	1 441	1 147
66½	55	133	1 814	1 087	872	1 103	764	653	546
67	84	297	4 113	2 427	1 878	2 621	1 872	1 625	1 292
67½	27	105	1 621	960	946	1 277	874	750	711
68	66	255	3 717	2 396	2 157	3 157	2 102	1 816	1 566
68½	29	63	1 248	899	769	1 116	855	776	645
69	47	165	2 339	1 762	1 540	2 333	1 636	1 409	1 258
69½	16	36	739	593	551	823	592	529	506
70	25	97	1 585	1 349	1 337	1 880	1 419	1 270	1 115
70½	5	23	418	366	413	515	390	362	343
71	14	43	724	666	683	1 046	793	738	634
71½	3	14	230	170	174	306	257	219	173
72	3	26	411	399	479	672	531	507	429
72½	1	5	71	74	73	104	87	100	65
73	2	7	106	116	139	224	160	163	152
73½	–	–	35	26	52	67	53	60	29
74	2	2	35	56	68	105	82	89	74
74½	–	–	12	8	17	18	15	12	11
75 & over	–	–	13	23	21	71	48	48	41
Total	1 501	3 460	41 378	23 003	18 318	24 889	17 559	15 321	13 082

TABLE III. — (*Continued.*)

Natives of New York, New Jersey, and Pennsylvania, by Heights and Ages.

Height	25	26	27	28	29	30	31–34	35 and over	Total
in.									
Under 61	37	45	21	31	24	20	77	179	1 480
61	25	15	13	14	14	13	41	68	745
61½	14	21	12	8	11	13	26	70	726
62	35	23	33	27	25	22	75	106	1 735
62½	37	34	27	29	20	23	68	129	1 579
63	127	97	117	109	60	88	215	439	5 807
63½	102	101	82	85	42	58	198	331	3 994
64	304	265	243	214	202	163	542	1 034	11 627
64½	202	208	162	183	128	139	392	720	6 918
65	608	497	486	481	367	349	962	2 136	18 454
65½	379	313	312	262	183	202	617	1 143	9 671
66	913	893	800	738	547	591	1 665	3 408	26 393
66½	460	422	394	369	276	260	786	1 539	11 533
67	1 104	1 090	927	873	617	629	1 866	3 820	27 135
67½	559	485	506	473	364	341	1 005	1 905	12 909
68	1 327	1 234	1 123	1 108	839	844	2 549	4 915	31 171
68½	577	496	426	461	337	340	1 014	1 922	11 973
69	1 157	1 017	911	893	703	684	2 070	4 364	24 288
69½	451	441	332	337	295	296	855	1 621	9 013
70	947	887	836	790	611	653	1 943	3 906	20 650
70½	284	282	252	265	188	205	656	1 160	6 127
71	533	489	466	452	359	357	1 097	2 193	11 287
71½	158	149	153	149	113	117	340	655	3 380
72	403	365	289	288	253	283	806	1 592	7 736
72½	58	49	58	46	38	46	166	221	1 262
73	139	146	99	122	81	105	303	523	2 587
73½	38	35	30	36	31	25	78	135	730
74	57	63	52	47	55	46	174	236	1 243
74½	5	10	11	13	6	8	26	54	226
75 & over	34	34	27	24	24	24	71	144	647
Total	11 074	10 206	9 200	8 927	6 813	6 944	20 683	40 668	273 026

TABLE IV.

Natives of Ohio and Indiana,
by Heights and Ages.

Height	Under 17	17	18	19	20	21	22	23	24
in.									
Under 61	131	44	264	63	55	33	23	29	21
61	34	19	175	48	24	21	11	11	10
61½	1	14	94	14	17	10	17	13	9
62	53	56	445	107	79	59	26	32	22
62½	11	21	253	68	29	35	27	12	20
63	83	132	1 651	379	221	161	110	94	87
63½	11	57	728	182	99	87	83	63	45
64	106	219	3 178	885	553	456	304	261	245
64½	16	67	1 174	326	263	199	133	94	130
65	96	250	4 490	1 371	1 015	848	666	536	432
65½	25	79	1 417	526	400	390	293	209	236
66	104	280	5 880	2 268	1 671	1 610	1 098	905	795
66½	30	66	1 595	671	587	584	431	362	281
67	66	264	5 089	2 335	1 839	1 782	1 300	1 168	950
67½	23	96	1 635	851	690	744	546	509	439
68	64	219	4 991	2 702	2 452	2 461	1 941	1 719	1 421
68½	12	54	1 332	804	692	785	585	545	457
69	37	141	3 273	2 093	1 814	1 978	1 572	1 400	1 147
69½	8	34	901	647	589	626	563	517	423
70	31	112	2 656	1 907	1 934	2 041	1 709	1 576	1 325
70½	3	11	503	459	421	476	428	391	330
71	13	41	1 260	986	1 026	1 246	1 022	846	728
71½	1	10	302	243	298	342	290	235	203
72	4	32	843	690	810	946	815	781	717
72½	1	4	118	97	120	129	126	120	100
73	1	8	251	252	279	401	298	264	226
73½	1	3	62	75	72	94	75	63	80
74	–	5	99	128	151	183	152	139	108
74½	–	1	18	21	19	47	33	35	37
75 & over	–	3	54	60	80	99	80	84	42
Total	966	2 342	44 731	21 258	18 299	18 873	14 757	13 013	11 066

TABLE IV.—(*Continued.*)

Natives of Ohio and Indiana, by Heights and Ages.

Height	25	26	27	28	29	30	31–34	35 and over	Total
in.									
Under 61	24	13	18	13	7	15	25	52	830
61	9	8	5	4	5	1	15	24	424
$61\frac{1}{2}$	9	7	4	9	3	1	7	22	251
62	17	10	14	14	13	11	26	32	1 016
$62\frac{1}{2}$	20	18	10	10	7	3	27	28	599
63	46	72	34	47	35	31	84	100	3 367
$63\frac{1}{2}$	41	35	38	27	24	27	49	69	1 665
64	156	147	143	112	76	69	186	321	7 417
$64\frac{1}{2}$	87	72	71	70	36	44	126	174	3 082
65	367	322	255	265	184	166	447	613	12 323
$65\frac{1}{2}$	172	178	123	108	91	73	211	317	4 848
66	651	545	516	473	305	292	903	1 181	19 477
$66\frac{1}{2}$	225	185	187	164	119	137	346	462	6 432
67	752	613	593	609	395	400	1 116	1 496	20 767
$67\frac{1}{2}$	352	288	258	251	179	210	540	756	8 367
68	1 196	976	866	921	551	618	1 643	2 305	27 046
$68\frac{1}{2}$	446	347	309	296	231	201	583	841	8 520
69	933	827	779	794	573	578	1 504	2 195	21 638
$69\frac{1}{2}$	353	345	280	272	220	207	587	799	7 371
70	1 119	941	816	840	592	678	1 804	2 664	22 745
$70\frac{1}{2}$	298	281	211	216	203	180	475	752	5 638
71	604	560	510	487	363	355	1 087	1 498	12 632
$71\frac{1}{2}$	188	170	162	152	104	106	321	493	3 620
72	559	524	415	422	285	379	997	1 452	10 671
$72\frac{1}{2}$	88	60	74	63	55	43	166	193	1 557
73	201	187	182	185	121	134	398	572	3 960
$73\frac{1}{2}$	70	76	64	44	32	38	103	153	1 105
74	96	102	80	73	65	60	182	284	1 907
$74\frac{1}{2}$	22	26	28	16	12	19	50	64	448
75 & over	61	43	54	62	39	26	134	152	1073
Total	9 162	7 978	7 099	7 019	4 925	5 102	14 142	20 064	220 796

TABLE V.

Natives of Ireland, by Heights and Ages.

Height	Under 17	17	18	19	20	21	22	23	24
in.									
Under 61	24	11	49	20	17	28	27	16	8
61	7	4	31	21	15	26	15	15	12
61½	4	2	48	32	35	26	39	18	11
62	3	8	76	57	38	51	43	36	16
62½	1	7	85	88	48	82	68	38	34
63	5	12	247	164	101	141	112	108	87
63½	1	8	195	145	116	196	127	106	92
64	5	21	442	348	231	362	260	220	186
64½	5	5	236	228	213	321	258	203	158
65	5	22	493	486	344	623	491	401	329
65½	4	5	241	249	273	425	364	270	228
66	4	20	541	523	435	885	690	525	462
66½	4	7	212	251	256	474	398	312	280
67	3	12	365	475	433	843	705	599	447
67½	2	6	183	231	260	435	409	296	246
68	2	15	330	351	420	766	648	556	480
68½	3	1	113	166	155	332	339	258	234
69	–	3	154	238	219	502	479	431	301
69½	–	5	57	104	99	197	208	180	136
70	2	6	95	152	175	355	306	262	245
70½	–	–	48	43	45	129	107	110	87
71	–	4	51	70	89	151	161	112	127
71½	–	1	12	24	14	51	51	44	36
72	–	1	26	31	37	81	65	63	68
72½	–	–	3	3	6	18	19	11	11
73	–	–	7	10	12	28	31	21	19
73½	–	–	–	3	4	9	7	10	4
74	–	–	2	4	2	10	12	10	8
74½	–	1	–	1	1	1	–	1	1
75 & over	–	–	3	1	2	2	6	3	7
Total	84	187	4 345	4 519	4 095	7 550	6 445	5 235	4 360

TABLE V.—(*Continued.*)

Natives of Ireland,
by Heights and Ages.

Height	25	26	27	28	29	30	31–34	35 and over	Total
in.									
Under 61	17	9	13	14	4	17	36	61	371
61	6	5	11	4	6	6	10	34	228
61½	12	7	15	14	–	9	22	38	332
62	33	22	19	17	10	24	44	99	596
62½	43	22	35	30	22	29	48	105	785
63	96	87	70	71	32	88	151	349	1 921
63½	98	79	59	68	29	74	106	256	1 755
64	186	168	131	147	86	148	282	722	3 945
64½	146	112	116	135	88	114	237	551	3 126
65	376	246	239	284	179	285	543	1 353	6 699
65½	271	171	186	178	128	165	337	805	4 300
66	459	443	380	458	284	458	836	2 057	9 460
66½	286	248	195	225	152	191	457	868	4 816
67	490	402	437	477	258	424	843	1 810	9 023
67½	288	224	228	244	163	225	457	919	4 816
68	515	433	407	452	259	458	890	1 947	8 929
68½	234	183	159	210	126	156	384	663	3·716
69	352	284	271	295	176	246	573	1 276	5 800
69½	140	139	110	120	91	102	259	442	2 389
70	270	219	206	198	110	221	440	931	4 193
70½	86	58	73	90	40	51	167	239	1 373
71	118	80	108	112	70	103	221	431	2 008
71½	47	31	38	41	22	37	75	170	694
72	54	48	51	58	30	59	111	212	995
72½	14	12	12	10	4	8	22	39	192
73	20	12	12	26	11	12	32	66	319
73½	6	6	4	5	6	7	14	30	115
74	7	3	6	7	11	7	13	32	134
74½	1	2	2	3	1	3	2	8	28
75 & over	8	5	3	1	2	3	9	15	70
Total	4 679	3 760	3 596	3 994	2 400	3 730	7 621	16 528	83 128

TABLE VI.

Mean Heights at each Age, by Nativities.

Age last birthday	A New England	B New York, N. J., and Penn.	C Ohio and Indiana	D Michigan, Wisconsin, and Ill.	E Slave States not incl. F and G_2	F Kentucky and Tennessee	G_1 Free States west of the Miss.	G_2 Slave States west of the Miss.	H British Amer. not incl. Canada	I Canada
Under 17	433 63.520	1501 64.206	966 64.505	886 64.819	187 64.169	219 65.250	62 64.762	230 63.346	7 63.357	78 64.125
17	809 66.210	3460 65.677	2342 66.251	1764 66.096	441 66.101	444 66.235	127 65.963	358 66.186	19 65.737	202 65.364
18	25 219 66.726	41 378 66.287	44 731 66.880	18 219 66.698	6223 66.867	7560 66.924	1746 66.709	4277 66.848	542 66.137	4036 65.892
19	13 001 67.465	23 003 66.967	21 258 67.785	8914 67.736	3394 67.711	3742 68.034	513 67.829	2091 67.802	420 66.792	2958 66.596
20	10 140 67.840	18 318 67.444	18 299 68.157	6834 68.205	2802 68.127	3441 68.552	365 68.561	1764 68.344	380 67.281	2287 66.953
21	14 752 67.922	24 889 67.639	18 873 68.427	7120 68.395	3414 68.207	3558 68.640	363 68.481	1851 68.410	871 67.425	3708 67.034
22	9790 68.021	17 559 67.742	14 757 68.565	5426 68.504	2814 68.294	3090 68.897	197 68.657	1309 68.592	588 67.389	2748 67.356
23	8441 68.174	15 321 67.847	13 013 68.638	4120 68.610	2474 68.466	2815 68.950	136 68.360	990 68.766	492 67.581	2117 67.385
24	6979 68.135	13 082 67.878	11 066 68.617	3584 68.628	2050 68.624	2495 69.028	88 68.557	712 68.776	403 67.742	1671 67.516
25	6148 68.146	11 074 67.969	9162 68.700	2633 68.669	1881 68.577	2192 68.946	55 68.150	655 68.777	325 67.901	1433 67.544
26	5530 68.184	10 206 68.000	7978 68.751	2073 68.699	1640 68.707	1946 69.163	34 67.890	467 68.597	272 67.698	1264 67.459
27	5030 68.269	9200 67.974	7099 68.753	1633 68.737	1407 68.620	1635 69.050	27 67.907	342 69.132	244 67.834	1058 67.630
28	4902 68.316	8927 68.012	7019 68.774	1434 68.792	1498 68.791	1701 69.202	21 67.298	322 68.967	251 67.784	1124 67.500
29	3659 68.286	6813 68.082	4925 68.837	993 68.804	1085 68.870	1218 69.039	15 67.867	231 69.276	171 67.822	750 67.465
30	3754 68.169	6944 68.099	5102 68.906	993 68.917	1191 68.837	1416 69.098	7 68.143	218 68.563	158 68.429	774 67.417
31–34	11 001 68.359	20 683 68.134	14 142 68.959	2277 68.949	3609 68.802	4041 69.356	22 67.545	544 68.926	446 68.135	1875 67.696
35 and over	22 782 68.300	40 668 68.096	20 064 68.980	2293 68.781	8579 68.854	8821 69.274	33 68.098	677 68.866	731 68.063	3615 67.300
Total	152 370 67.834	273 026 67.529	220 796 68.169	71 196 67.877	44 689 68.255	50 334 68.605	3811 67.419	17 038 67.964	6320 67.501	31 698 67.066

It is thus manifest that the variation of stature for different classes of troops is clearly shown, whether we arrange them by the

TABLE VI.—(*Continued.*)

Mean Heights at each Age, by Nativities.

Age last birth-day	J England	K Scotland	L Ireland	M France, Belgium, and Switzerland	N Germany	O Scandinavia	P Spain, Portugal, and Sp. America	Q Miscellaneous	Totals
Under 17	79 63.503	10 63.300	84 62.586	15 62.000	182 62.033	13 63.423	3 64.917	15 61.500	4970 64.186
17	144 64.526	35 64.736	187 65.344	18 65.556	358 64.638	43 65.849	5 64.000	43 64.802	10 799 65.902
18	2238 65.822	481 65.909	4345 65.818	335 65.524	5498 65.654	557 66.299	50 65.845	667 65.653	168 102 66.570
19	1703 66.192	330 66.614	4519 66.309	254 65.881	4266 66.249	337 67.194	39 65.103	505 66.320	91 247 67.298
20	1655 66.503	328 66.918	4095 66.612	279 65.923	4197 66.572	346 67.391	61 66.361	466 66.327	76 057 67.693
21	2638 66.579	470 67.036	7550 66.809	428 66.507	5563 66.723	494 67.281	99 65.929	692 66.507	97 333 67.774
22	2161 66.683	446 67.166	6445 67.030	327 66.602	4900 66.887	457 67.382	112 66.277	625 66.754	73 751 67.906
23	1827 66.945	391 67.306	5235 67.071	329 66.810	4446 66.898	346 67.638	74 66.087	524 66.714	63 091 67.996
24	1625 66.848	358 67.518	4360 67.144	382 66.768	4384 66.849	399 67.728	61 66.459	497 66.563	54 196 67.995
25	1462 66.903	343 67.317	4679 67.106	369 66.430	4344 66.823	324 67.912	60 66.062	524 66.485	47 663 67.981
26	1192 66.954	338 67.306	3760 67.131	314 66.525	4094 66.811	297 67.618	44 66.625	453 66.795	41 902 68.014
27	1166 67.048	305 67.206	3596 67.192	270 66.818	3553 66.841	295 67.558	46 66.120	387 66.775	37 293 68.022
28	1259 66.945	333 67.696	3994 67.206	352 66.668	3990 66.760	308 67.298	44 65.727	421 66.790	37 900 68.010
29	899 67.090	265 67.366	2400 67.202	285 66.817	3106 66.751	209 67.522	26 66.202	279 67.215	27 329 68.041
30	1090 67.019	315 67.582	3730 67.103	287 66.700	3581 66.778	275 67.534	35 66.386	377 66.698	30 247 67.973
31–34	2905 66.999	821 67.453	7621 67.242	830 66.592	10 488 66.785	659 67.502	58 66.328	1047 66.719	83 069 68.072
35 and over	5994 66.990	1744 67.647	16 528 67.090	1735 66.714	22 071 66.718	1423 67.299	80 66.153	2054 66.826	159 892 67.957
Total	30 037 66.741	7313 67.258	83 128 66.951	6809 66.534	89 021 66.660	6782 67.337	897 66.111	9576 66.596	1 104 841 67.639

States of enlistment, or by the nativities of the men. But the fact, that the variations are more marked when the assortment is made by nativities, is conspicuous. To permit this comparison to be made with greater ease, the annexed table has been prepared. Its materials are identical with those of Table I., but the States of enlistment have been combined in the same groups as those of the classification by nativities.

TABLE VII.

Mean Heights at each Age, by Regions in which Enlisted.

Age last birthday	New England	New York, N. J., and Penn.	Ohio and Indiana.	Michigan, Wisconsin and Ill.	Slave States not incl. F and G_2	Kentucky and Tennessee	Free States west of the Miss	Slave States west of the Miss.	Totals
Under 17	368 63.141	1160 63.900	764 64.407	1709 64.702	144 64.361	144 65.625	226 64.757	455 62.664	4970 64.186
17	652 66.152	2791 65.435	1770 66.108	3701 66.033	332 66.334	260 66.119	545 65.842	748 66.091	10 799 65.902
18	26 624 66.606	37 140 66.051	41 536 66.773	38 672 66.656	4467 67.027	4563 66.662	7698 66.805	7402 66.931	168 102 66.570
19	15 054 67.194	23 262 66.555	19 850 67.631	21 597 67.579	2285 67.902	2099 67.685	2890 67.857	4210 67.821	91 247 67.298
20	12 341 67.454	18 571 66.989	17 634 67.983	17 820 68.019	1873 68.239	2069 68.274	1869 68.264	3880 68.189	76 057 67.693
21	20 694 67.480	27 664 67.212	17 341 68.240	20 304 68.169	2173 68.270	1794 68.426	2756 68.452	4607 68.193	97 333 67.774
22	13 882 67.562	19 789 67.259	14 025 68.347	17 111 68.317	1745 68.306	1619 68.608	1829 68.601	3751 68.324	73 751 67.906
23	11 334 67.739	16 353 67.332	12 458 68.365	15 076 68.312	1456 68.666	1383 68.707	1602 68.556	3429 68.391	63 091 67.996
24	9130 67.689	13 864 67.344	10 934 68.316	13 611 68.319	1167 68.666	1212 68.907	1423 68.604	2855 68.436	54 196 67.995
25	8128 67.708	12 156 67.325	9133 68.404	12 002 68.298	998 68.480	1026 68.530	1295 68.576	2925 68.212	47 663 67.981
26	7043 67.742	10 786 67.417	8140 68.387	10 414 68.297	842 68.548	861 68.899	1176 68.524	2639 68.218	41 902 68.014
27	6266 67.841	9773 67.396	7301 68.388	9159 68.299	719 68.434	716 68.802	1199 68.461	2160 68.333	37 293 68.022
28	6453 67.786	9805 67.391	7530 68.404	9250 68.234	700 68.610	742 68.894	1137 68.614	2283 68.285	37 900 68.010
29	4553 67.809	6910 67.430	5475 68.381	6905 68.301	520 68.623	490 68.763	921 68.788	1555 68.192	27 329 68.041
30	4877 67.703	7658 67.360	5938 68.424	7505 68.192	556 68.529	642 68.927	1019 68.650	2052 68.118	30 247 67.973
31–34	13 048 67.870	21 983 67.485	16 902 68.499	20 205 68.261	1560 68.558	1342 68.784	2942 68.617	5087 68.247	83 069 68.072
35 and over	24 911 67.873	44 979 67.410	29 808 68.393	37 990 68.076	3358 68.471	3031 68.817	5774 68.430	10 041 68.160	159 892 67.957
Total	185 358 67.485	284 644 67.065	226 539 67.955	263 031 67.876	24 896 68.097	23 993 68.160	36 301 68.037	60 079 67.981	1 104 841 67.639

It will be seen at a glance how essentially the two tables differ from one another; the statures of the nativity-tables for American States being reduced in the enlistment-tables in consequence of the admixture of foreigners, and the amount of their difference for different regions being also essentially modified by reason of the inequality in their respective proportions of foreigners and Americans.

Careful examination will disclose the fact that, for Americans, both the State of enlistment (which in a majority of cases is the State where the physical growth has in great measure taken place) and the State of birth (which indicates the ancestry) seem to exert a marked influence upon the stature. In other words, the genealogical stock and the region where the men have been reared combine to prescribe the stature, and the rate and duration of growth.

This is made especially manifest by the tables XII. and XIII. given hereafter, for comparing the stature of natives of certain sections of the country, who enlisted in the place of their birth, with that of natives of the same sections enlisting elsewhere; also by Table XIV., which shows the extent to which the mean stature of natives of some foreign countries varies with the region in which they enlisted. The subject is more fully considered, in our section concerning the Full Stature.

4. *Law of Growth.*

The statistics here presented are perhaps the first which have been collected on a scale sufficiently large, and with sufficient detail of classification, to permit definite conclusions regarding the age at which the maximum stature is normally attained, and the rate of growth for the years immediately preceding this age. Thirty years ago, Quetelet, in his classic work "*Sur l'Homme*,"[1] expressed the belief that the growth of man was not entirely at an end even at the age of twenty-five years; but his opinion was based upon statistics derived from the one city of Brussels; namely, nine hundred instances, for ages between nineteen and twenty-six, from municipal registers of an enrollment in 1816, and the remainder from recent measurements of students of the university. The results of the present research corroborated this opinion from the beginning, and indeed tended to fix the epoch of maximum stature much later than even Quetelet seems to have suspected. More copious data and more thorough investigation now leave small

[1] Pages 14, 24, 42. See also Liharžik, *Proceedings of the Vienna Academy of Sciences*, XLIV. p. 632.

doubt upon this point, although the increase of stature after the age of twenty-three years is relatively quite small.

Examination of the materials collected leads to the following inferences for white soldiers.

1. That the rate of growth undergoes a sudden diminution at about the age of twenty years, the increase of stature continuing nevertheless uninterruptedly until about the age of twenty-four.

2. That for a year or two after this latter epoch the height remains nearly stationary, if indeed it does not diminish, after which a slight increase again manifests itself, and continues until the full stature is attained.

3. That the normal epoch of maximum stature must generally be placed, at least for American States,[1] as late as thirty years, but that it varies for different classes of men.

4. That the annual variations after twenty-three years, or thereabouts, are of an order of magnitude not much larger than the possible errors of the determinations themselves; and that the epochs of the changes vary considerably for different States and nativities; so that these are less conspicuous in the total of a large number of different classes, than when the soldiers from a particular State, or those of a particular nativity, are considered by themselves.

Since the fluctuations of the total height during the several ages from twenty-three to thirty-four, at last birthday, are generally comprised within a range not much exceeding the tenth of an inch, or less than three millimeters, it becomes necessary to inquire whether these fluctuations do actually represent some natural law, or whether they can be regarded as fortuitous, and explained on the assumption either of inadequate data, or of want of accuracy in the original measurements. But since the minimum number at any year of age exceeds 27 000, the first of these assumptions may safely be rejected; not so, however, with the second, for a little reflection will show that the regularity of the curve of growth might thus be seriously impaired.

The most natural means of testing this question would seem to be by an examination of the several groups in which our materials have been classified, in order to determine how far they severally corroborate the inference indicated by their total. Of such groups we have three series, namely: in thirty-eight "counts," the largest of which contains less than 54 000 men; then according to

[1] The only apparent exceptions are natives of the Slave States, excluding Kentucky and Tennessee; but here the maximum appears at twenty-nine and the number of men is small.

twenty States of enlistment; and finally according to eighteen nativities. The number of times at which the highest mean stature occurred for any year of age (no matter how small its excess above the mean height for any other year), was as follows: —

Age	22	23	24	25	26	27	28	29	30	31–34	35 and over	Total
By Counts .	3	2	3	0	4	5	3	4	4	7	3	
By States .	2	0	2	0	0	3	2	2	1	7	1	20
By Nativities	1	1	0	1	1	1	1	4	1	6	1	18
In all .	6	3	5	1	5	9	6	10	6	20	5	76

The argument from independent probabilities thus corroborates the inference derived from the totals, regarding the epoch of maximum stature. It becomes yet stronger when we consider that in three out of the six instances of maxima at twenty-two, these are derived from a number of men too small to be entitled to any considerable weight, the same being the case with two out of the five maxima at twenty-four. And it may perhaps be most strongly appreciated, if the number of men be also taken into account, as when the ages of maximum stature deduced from the classification by nativities are presented in the following form: —

Age		Nativities			
35 and upwards	for	1	comprising	220 796	men.
31–34	"	6	"	661 752	"
30	"	1	"	6 320	"
29	"	4	"	101 340	"
28	"	1	"	7 313	"
27	"	1	"	6 809	"
26	"	1	"	897	"
25	"	1	"	6 782	"
23	"	1	"	89 021	"
22	"	1	"	3 811	"
		18		1 104 841	

The last of these values is manifestly entitled to no weight; but all other natives of the United States excepting the classes E and G_2, together with the Irish and Canadians, are comprised in the first two groups, numbering nearly nine elevenths of the whole. The Southerners (not including Kentucky or Tennessee) and the English composed most of those for whom the maximum is at twenty-nine, and the Germans form the large class whose maximum appears at twenty-three.

If the classification by States be similarly analyzed, we find that 767 366, or somewhat less than eight elevenths of the whole number, are to be found in the two groups for which the greatest mean stature belongs to an age above thirty years (last birthday).

The fact, that this highest mean stature exceeds the mean stature for any other year by only a very slight amount, impairs in no degree the correctness of our inference that such a maximum actually exists. Indeed, if we confine ourselves to the first six nativities of our schedule, which include all the native Americans (United States), excepting less than 21 000 who were born west of the Mississippi River, and comprise more than eight elevenths of all the white soldiers whose descriptive musters we possess, and if for these we compare the height at twenty-six years, last birthday (which represents the mean stature at 26.486 years of age), with the full stature subsequently attained, we find the excess of the latter to be —

Nativity	Number of Men	Excess of Full Stature
		inches
A. New England	152 370	0.175
B. New York, New Jersey, and Pennsylvania	273 026	0.134
C. Ohio and Indiana	220 796	0.229
D. Michigan, Wisconsin, and Illinois . .	71 196	0.250
E. Slave States not including F and G_2	44 689	0.163
F. Kentucky and Tennessee	50 334	0.193
	812 411	0.148

As regards the more delicate question concerning the slight depression of the curve of stature at about the age of twenty-four years, a similar mode of research affords a similar corroboration. An inspection of the mean results themselves, as indicated together with the empirical curves on Charts H and I, will show the character and amount of this disturbance of regularity in the curve. Of the eighteen groups according to nativity, two only, B and D, fail to make this temporary diminution of height distinctly manifest. The variations may be seen from the appended table, which gives the mean change of stature for each of four consecutive years of age; the ages cited being for "last birthday," and therefore requiring in the mean an increase by nearly half a year. The total number of men comprised in the several nativities has been given above.

Nativity	22-23	23-24	24-25	25-26	26-28	28 to maximum
	inches	inches	inches	inches	inches	inches
A	+0.153	−0.039	+0.011	+0.038	+0.132	+0.043
B	+0.105	+0.031	+0.091	+0.031	+0.012	+0.122
C	+0.073	−0.021	+0.083	+0.051	+0.023	+0.206
D	+0.106	+0.018	+0.041	+0.030	+0.093	+0.157
E	+0.172	+0.158	−0.047	+0.130	+0.084	+0.079
F	+0.053	+0.078	−0.082	+0.217	+0.039	+0.154

It will be perceived at once that those two nativities which exhibit no negative sign in the annual variations between twenty-three and a half and twenty-five and a half show nevertheless smaller positive values than the regular curve would imply.

Arranging in a similar manner the annual variations of mean stature for the men enlisted in the several States, we obtain analogous results. The values from those nine States, for whose soldiers the maximum stature occurred after the age of thirty, are here presented: —

State	22-23	23-24	24-25	25-26	26-28	28 to maximum
	inches	inches	inches	inches	inches	inches
New Hampshire	+0.194	−0.078	−0.006	+0.163	−0.014	+0.366
Massachusetts.	+0.042	+0.022	+0.038	−0.109	+0.006	+0.228
New York . .	+0.066	+0.012	−0.059	+0.132	−0.034	+0.055
New Jersey. .	+0.139	−0.038	−0.034	−0.155	+0.126	+0.205
Pennsylvania .	+0.062	+0.037	+0.085	+0.058	−0.064	+0.135
Kentucky . .	+0.099	+0.200	−0.377	+0.369	−0.005	+0.033
Ohio	+0.042	−0.014	+0.049	+0.014	+0.003	+0.100
Indiana . . .	+0.004	−0.079	+0.128	−0.041	+0.032	+0.105
Illinois . . .	+0.000	+0.045	−0.054	+0.039	−0.028	+0.056

These results seem to warrant the inference, that, during a period commencing near the age of twenty-three or twenty-four, a temporary diminution of the rate of growth occurs. Whether the apparent diminution of stature be real, or whether, taken in connection with the mean values for preceding and following years, it is to be interpreted as an accidental fluctuation about a nearly stationary mean value, we will not venture to decide. Did a complete arrest of growth take place, this would doubtless manifest itself as a diminution of stature, in consequence of consolidation of the cartilages and intervertebral substance, such as sets in after the attainment of the full stature, and is indeed manifested in the diurnal fluctuations of the height of individuals.

The variation of the epoch of this point of flexure in the curve of stature for different classes, will be manifest in the various tables already given, as well as its tendency to obliterate the phenomenon in the curve for their total. The dots near the curves upon Charts H and I present the mean values for each age as obtained directly from the recorded observations.

After various unsuccessful attempts to obtain a formula which should represent in some simple form the law of growth between the ages of seventeen and thirty-eight years, this endeavor has been abandoned. Such a formula would have small value unless it represented equally well the law for earlier ages; and the investigation of this interesting topic, from our military statistics, is of course impossible. Should the statistical labors of the Sanitary Commission stimulate to the acquisition of anthropological statistics of youth, for which our schools and colleges afford so great facilities, the material thus collected, combined with that discussed in the present volume, may render possible a thorough discussion of the laws of human growth, not only in stature, but in the various other dimensions here recorded. And by distributing its measuring apparatus to educational and scientific institutions in different parts of the country, the Commission trusts that it may have done something toward aiding these much needed inquiries.

It remains to construct by empirical means the best approximation to the curve of growth deducible from our collected data for the various nativities. For this, graphic methods have proved the most available, and the tables following indicate the resultant stature for each actual age, for the soldiers of the several nativities enlisted in the national army. The same values are represented on the charts H and I, upon each of which the total for all the soldiers is also shown. The dots near the curves upon these charts indicate the observed mean values, and in those cases where danger of confusion exists between the values for different nativities, the letters indicating the nativities are also appended.

TABLE VIII.

Mean Statures at each Age, for fourteen Nativities.

Actual Age	New England	New York, New Jersey, Pennsylvania	Ohio and Indiana	Michigan, Wisconsin, Illinois	Slave States excluding Kentucky & Tenn.	Kentucky and Tennessee	British Provinces	England
	in.	in.	in.	in.	in.	in.	in.	in.
16	64.24	64.00	64.46	64.63	63.95	64.87	63.81	63.38
17	65.41	65.11	65.48	65.45	65.33	65.58	64.84	64.37
18	66.33	65.95	66.54	66.38	66.44	66.55	65.68	65.39
19	67.16	66.70	67.39	67.38	67.37	67.58	66.37	66.04
20	67.64	67.25	67.97	68.02	68.01	68.31	66.81	66.35
21	67.89	67.58	68.33	68.32	68.28	68.67	67.09	66.55
22	68.03	67.73	68.51	68.47	68.40	68.84	67.28	66.70
23	68.10	67.80	68.62	68.56	68.49	68.95	67.42	66.81
24	68.14	67.85	68.66	68.63	68.57	69.00	67.52	66.90
25	68.14	67.90	68.67	68.66	68.64	69.03	67.57	66.94
26	68.16	67.94	68.69	68.70	68.68	69.05	67.58	66.97
27	68.20	67.98	68.73	68.73	68.74	69.09	67.58	67.00
28	68.25	68.01	68.78	68.77	68.77	69.12	67.58	67.02
29	68.29	68.05	68.82	68.80	68.80	69.15	67.57	67.03
30	68.32	68.09	68.86	68.84	68.82	69.20	67.59	67.03
31	68.34	68.11	68.90	68.87	68.82	69.23	67.61	67.03
32	68.35	68.12	68.92	68.90	68.83	69.25	67.62	67.03
33	68.35	68.13	68.94	68.91	68.84	69.27	67.62	67.03
34	68.35	68.14	68.95	68.91	68.84	69.28	67.61	67.02
35	68.36	68.14	68.96	68.90	68.84	69.29	67.61	67.02
36	68.36	68.14	68.97	68.89	68.84	69.29	67.60	67.01
37	68.35	68.13	68.97	68.87	68.84	69.28	67.58	67.01
38	68.34	68.12	68.98	68.84	68.84	69.28	67.57	67.00
39	68.32	68.10	68.98	68.81	68.83	69.27	67.55	67.00
40	68.30	68.08	68.98	68.79	68.83	69.26	67.53	66.99

8

TABLE VIII. — (*Continued.*)

Mean Statures at each Age, for fourteen Nativities.

Actual Age	Sootland	Ireland	France, Belgium, Switzerland	Germany	Scandinavia	All Others	Mean of all
	in.	in.	in.	in.	in.	in.	in.
16	–	64.10	63.83	–	64.16	–	64.16
17	64.26	64.94	64.60	63.98	65.14	64.09	65.26
18	65.47	65.58	65.25	65.27	66.12	65.31	66.23
19	66.34	66.09	65.75	66.04	66.83	65.98	67.01
20	66.83	66.47	66.12	66.44	67.21	66.30	67.52
21	67.03	66.76	66.41	66.68	67.43	66.51	67.77
22	67.16	66.97	66.60	66.82	67.54	66.61	67.89
23	67.26	67.07	66.73	66.91	67.61	66.63	67.97
24	67.33	67.10	66.77	66.90	67.67	66.62	68.00
25	67.38	67.09	66.76	66.86	67.69	66.64	67.99
26	67.41	67.11	66.73	66.82	67.68	66.67	67.99
27	67.43	67.14	66.72	66.80	67.65	66.70	68.01
28	67.44	67.19	66.73	66.78	67.60	66.74	68.02
29	67.45	67.21	66.74	66.78	67.56	66.76	68.02
30	67.46	67.22	66.74	66.79	67.54	66.78	68.02
31	67.46	67.23	66.74	66.80	67.53	66.79	68.02
32	67.47	67.22	66.74	66.80	67.52	66.80	68.02
33	67.47	67.22	66.74	66.79	67.52	66.80	68.01
34	67.48	67.21	66.73	66.79	67.51	66.80	68.01
35	67.48	67.20	66.73	66.78	67.50	66.80	68.00
36	67.49	67.19	66.72	66.77	67.49	66.80	68.00
37	67.50	67.17	66.71	66.76	67.48	66.80	68.00
38	67.51	67.15	66.70	66.75	67.46	66.79	67.99
39	67.52	67.13	66.70	66.74	67.44	66.79	67.99
40	67.52	67.09	66.69	66.73	67.41	66.78	67.98

These tables may be employed with advantage in referring the mean stature of a class of men, whose mean age is known or may be estimated, to their corresponding mean stature for any other age. But, like other averages, though correct for the type or the mean of all, they are by no means necessarily correct for individual cases, nor indeed for groups of considerable size, if belonging only to some one subdivision of the general class.

The variation manifest in the age of full stature for soldiers of different nativities appears to be, to a considerable extent at least, a normal phenomenon. The growth in height clearly continues longest for natives of the United States (excepting the farthest southern portion) and the Irish population, for all of whom the maximum appears to be decidedly later than thirty-one years. For natives of the southern part of the Southern States, and for natives of the British provinces on this continent other than Canada,[1] it is found at twenty-nine or thirty; then come the English, Scotch, French, Spanish, Scandinavians, and Germans, in successive gradations, the latter attaining their full stature at twenty-three. Furthermore, if, instead of the assortment by nativities, we consult that made by States of enlistment, we find the age of greatest stature to be at twenty-four years, or earlier, for the troops of Missouri, Wisconsin, and Minnesota, all of which contain a large Teutonic element in their population. Similar inferences may be deduced from the results of different counts for the troops of some of the larger States, especially Illinois and New York; but the discussion of these is omitted as being too minute for a general statistical investigation, — especially since such slight differences in the measurement are to be considered.

It will have been remarked that the whole of this investigation is based upon the assumption, that, where the number of men discussed is sufficiently large, we may obtain by computing the mean stature for different men, at the several ages involved, the same results as though we had obtained the mean stature of the same body of men in successive years. This assumption seems a reasonable one, and is entirely justifiable; yet the objection may logically be urged that it takes for granted an equal vitality among men of different statures, since if the mortality rate were slightly less for tall men than for shorter ones, this circumstance would produce an apparent increase of height in successive years, by reason of the increase in the proportional number of tall men.

To meet this objection, so far as it applies to the inference which

[1] The province which bore this name prior to 1866.

these researches appear to warrant, that the growth in stature continues in general until the thirtieth year, or even later, it might be urged, that so far as any deductions may be drawn from existing statistics, these seem to indicate that the maximum vitality belongs to the average stature, so that the influence of such a source of inaccuracy would be in the direction opposite to that which our results imply.[1] Indeed this same argument has been used[2] to explain the observed gradual diminution of mean stature after the age of forty years. But a much more satisfactory disposition of this doubt is afforded by the series of manuscript tables (nearly 700 in all), in which for each class of men considered, the number is given who were found of each given height and age. From these tables (of which the summaries for four nativities have already been given in Tables II., III., IV., and V., and the remainder of which afford the same result), it may readily be perceived that the relative number at the higher statures slowly increases with the age, in the same proportion in which that at the lower statures diminishes; whereas, were our results appreciably influenced by a difference in the vitality, or mortality, for different statures, the increase of the relative number having the higher statures would not be commensurate with the decrease of the relative number of men of less height. And, furthermore, the relative number of very tall or very short men, at ages when the full stature is approximately attained, say at twenty-four and upwards, would systematically change on this account, as the ages increase, which is not found to be the case.

The facts here presented are those upon which our knowledge of the Law of Growth for the average man within the limits of military age must chiefly depend. But our discussion would be incomplete, did it omit to recognize and illustrate the truth, that inferences drawn from the mean of all the men at each year of age, may not always represent the facts for the average man with perfect correctness. This is well illustrated by Lehmann, in an able and ingenious memoir,[3] in which he treats of the possibility of applying to individual cases the laws which have been deduced for the average man. That these laws may fail to indicate phenomena

[1] Since the average excess, above the mean height, for "tall men," is much greater than the average defect in height for "short men," an equal mortality for men above and below the medium stature would diminish the aggregate excess above the mean, more than the aggregate deficiency below it; and thus occasion a decrease in the mean stature, year by year, unless this were compensated by annual growth. The diminution in mean stature, after attainment of the age of maximum, may be in part owing to some influence of this nature.

[2] Quetelet, *Physique Sociale*, II. 31.

[3] *Schumacher's Jahrbuch*, 1841, p. 137; 1843, p. 146.

even of a strikingly marked character, occurring in every individual, and yet so masked in the averages as actually to escape notice, will be manifest when we consider the so-called "shoot" or sudden increase of growth, which occurs at, or just preceding, the chief epoch of physical development. The rate of increase in stature seems to diminish, regularly or nearly so, from birth, until the time at which the shoot takes place; it is then suddenly augmented by a very considerable amount, after which it diminishes again. If then the growth of any individual be represented by a curve for which the abscissas are the years of age, and the ordinates are the corresponding statures, this curve will consist of two distinct branches, each of them concave toward the axis of abscissas; the two branches meeting in a cusp where the shoot commences. Yet inasmuch as the epoch of the shoot is extremely variable, fluctuating between the eleventh and the nineteenth year of age, the tokens of its occurrence disappear from the corresponding curve of mean growth. This latter manifests a nearly even progression during the ages in question, and rises at the average age for the shoot scarcely more rapidly than at adjacent ages, since the sudden accession of growth does not in the majority of cases occur at the average age. All indications of a sudden change in the rate of growth are wanting in the curve of mean stature; so that the investigator, who studies the Law of Growth solely by the mean results from many individuals, might easily allow one of the most salient and unfailing phenomena connected with this law to escape unnoticed.

The very impressive suggestion has been made by Burdach, that the phenomena at this epoch of chief physical development may be regarded as equivalent to a new birth. Indeed it is an epoch more marked, in its physical relations, than is that of birth; and the form of the curve of stature corroborates this philosophic idea. And we are thus naturally led to the query, whether there may not perhaps be other epochs at which a sudden accession takes place in the rate of development in stature. Statistics are as yet inadequate for determining whether any such accession probably accompanies the second dentition; but the curious depression in the curve of stature at about the twenty-fourth year, of which we have spoken, suggests a suspicion that some secondary "shoot," on a much diminished scale, may occur at this age.

Indeed, it would seem by no means an unreasonable conjecture that several such shoots may normally occur in the regular course of life; and, moreover, that the idea thrown out by Lehmann and others, may not be unfounded, which suggests that the growth in stature may never be brought to full termination. The diminution in height with advancing years — first pointed out by Quetelet as occurring after the age of about forty years, and, according to our own statistics, beginning at a yet earlier date — may be considered as brought about by the predominance of influences in this direction by no means inconsistent with the existence of a slight continuance of growth. Such influences are the permanent consolidation of the cartilages, and of the intervertebral substance, analogous to the temporary compression, which is well known to follow long-continued standing or subjection to heavy weights; the less vigorous and erect carriage of the body; perhaps also a chronic curvature of certain parts, all of which may coexist with an actual continuance of growth in stature. It may be true that the increase in length of the larger bones is at the epiphyses, and that the complete ossification of these epiphyses is usually completed by the twenty-first year; yet we have evidence that the increase in stature usually continues for many years after this age, so that there must be some other mode of increase in height, perhaps by growth in the spinal column, perhaps by growth of the bones, as bones, after the disappearance of their cartilage.

Should these views be correct, it would not be difficult to explain an actual diminution of stature at about the twenty-fourth year, as apparently indicated by our mean values, but not otherwise readily explicable. For while the occurrence of a shoot at this age would impart to the curves of growth for individuals the appearance of a reentering angle at the corresponding point, and might produce in the curve for the average an apparent depression, in consequence of the change of curvature, yet it could not effect an actual diminution of stature. But if other influences are simultaneously at work, which would diminish the actual height were it not for a continuance of growth, these might easily attain a temporary preponderance, and a real diminution thus take place.

5. *Full Stature.*

The height of the full-grown man has been the subject of as wide a diversity of statement, and seems as completely undetermined even for any one nationality, as the law of the growth by which it is attained. Among the values given by the principal investigators within the author's knowledge, the following may be cited, all the numbers being here reduced to centimeters and to English (American) inches.

	centimeters.	inches
Buffon[1] (mean value)	169.2	66.60
Tenon,[2] from 60 men between the ages of 25 and 45, measured at Massy	166.5	65.55
Quetelet,[3] from 900 men enrolled for draft at Brussels	168.41	66.30
Quetelet,[4] from 9500 Belgian militia (province of Brabant)	163.80	64.49
Quetelet,[5] from 69 convicts at the penitentiary of Vilvorde	166.40	65.51
Hargenvilliers,[6] from French conscripts (20 years old)	161.50	63.58
Quetelet,[7] from 80 students at Cambridge, England (measured in shoes)[8]	174.21	68.60
Forbes,[9] from Scotch students at Edinburgh (ditto)	173.45	68.30
Silbermann,[10] from 559 conscripts in one Paris *arrondissement*	164.34	64.70
Carus,[11]	171.20	67.40
Schadow,[12] from his own measures	172.60	67.96
Zeising,[13] from his own measures and Quetelet's . .	173.00	68.11
Liharžik,[14] from 300 selected men in Vienna . .	175.00	68.90
Danson,[15] from 733 Liverpool prisoners, aged 25 and upwards	168.80	66.46

1 *Histoire Naturelle*, ed. Sonnini, XVIII. 432.

2 *Annales d'Hygiène*, X. 27.

3 *Sur l'Homme*, II. pp. 13, 23.

4 *Ibid.* p. 11.

5 *Ibid.* p. 17.

6 *Recherches et considerations sur la formation et le recrutement de l'armée en France*, Paris, 1817, p. 65 (Villermé, *Ann. d'Hygiène*, I. 352).

7 *Sur l'Homme*, II. p. 21.

8 Dr. A. S. Thomson states (*Contributions to Nat. Hist. of the New Zealand Race of Men*, Journal Statistical Soc., London, XVII. 27) that these students, like those at Edinburgh, whose height is recorded by Prof. Forbes, were measured in their shoes, and that an inch should be deducted on that account. This has been done for the value here given, and the same estimate is adopted for the Edinburgh shoes.

9 *Proceedings Royal Society of Edinburgh*, I. 160; *Lond. and Edinb. Phil. Mag.*, X. 200.

10 *Sur les proportions du corps humain*, Comptes Rendus de l'Acad. des Sciences, XLII. 496.

11 *Proportionslehre*, Leipsic, 1854.

12 *Polyklet*, Berlin, 1834–35, p. 61. (See Zeising, p. 881.)

13 *Ueber die Metamorphosen in den Verhältnissen der menschlichen Gestalt*, Nova Acta Acad. Imp. Nat. Cur., XXVI. 805.

14 *Der Bau und das Wachsthum des Menschen*, Sitzungsberichte der Wiener Akad. XLIV. 2, p. 636.

15 *Statistical Observations relative to Growth of the Human Body*, Journal Statistical Soc. London, XXV. 24.

Coolidge,[1] mean of 100 U. S. soldiers,[2] natives of

	centimeters	inches
Indiana	175.58	69.125
Kentucky	175.96	69.275
Ohio	175.37	69.044
Tennessee	176.11	69.335
Maine	174.69	68.777
Vermont and New Hampshire	173.58	68.341
Massachusetts and Connecticut	173.19	68.185
North Carolina	176.22	69.377
Georgia	177.61	69.926
South Carolina	175.96	69.275
Alabama	175.71	69.176
Virginia	175 22	68.986
New York	172.23	67.806
Pennsylvania	172.99	68.107
New Jersey and Delaware .	172.24	67.811
Maryland	174.13	68.556
Illinois	175.85	69.235
Missouri	174.23	68.594

The exceedingly wide range of these data, can scarcely be accounted for by any one influence. Nor, indeed, are the means afforded in most cases for determining to what extent the variations are fortuitous, and in what measure they are due to differences in the classes of men under consideration, or how far they may be dependent upon the employment of different limits of age, in those cases where limits were regarded.

Even for our vastly more copious statistics, the ages for which the corresponding mean heights may be properly used in determining the full stature of the average man, remain somewhat uncertain. It seems to be shown by the present investigation, that these ages differ greatly for different nationalities, and even for different classes of the same people. The suggestion of Villermé[3] that the stature is greater, and the growth sooner completed, all other things being equal, in proportion as the country is richer, and the comfort of its inhabitants more general, seemed from his data quite plausible; but it is not supported as a general law by the information here collected. It was based upon the hypothesis "that misery, that is to say the circumstances which accompany it, dimin-

1 *Statistical Report on Sickness and Mortality of U. S. Army, in the years* 1840–56, p. 633.

2 These soldiers were taken in the order in which they were entered on the Adjutant-General's books. Recruits under 65 inches high were not accepted at the time; but, for the small amount by which this rule could have affected the determination of the mean stature, see Hammond's *Military Hygiene*, p. 29.

3 *Sur la taille de l'homme en France.* Annales d'Hygiène, I. 386.

ishes the stature and retards the epoch of complete development of the body." Misery, in its here intended sense of excessive poverty, affecting the supply of nutriment, physical protection from weather, and needful rest, hardly exists in the United States; yet the epoch of full development appears to be later in this than in any other country. The fact, however, that privations or exposure will "stunt" or prevent the attainment of the normal height is beyond question, and appears to explain the results obtained for sailors, as will be mentioned hereafter.

Whether in deducing the measure of the completed stature, or full height, we shall use the same limits of age for all the classes of men considered, and what these limits shall be in any case, thus become questions of some difficulty. To afford a clearer oversight of the values resulting from the adoption of different limits, two tables are here presented; the first showing the mean heights of soldiers of the several States, and the second, the mean heights of soldiers of different nativities.

TABLE IX.

Mean Statures for different Periods of Age.
By States.

State	21–23	24–26	27–30	31–34	35 & over	31 & over	24 & over
Maine . . .	11 897 68.363	6491 68.455	5771 68.556	3482 68.555	7081 68.587	10 563 68.576	22 825 68.537
N. Hampshire .	7292 67.338	3645 67.489	3385 67.692	1864 67.894	3466 67.956	5330 67.934	12 360 67.736
Vermont . .	5832 67.790	3017 67.867	2552 68.044	1598 68.091	3215 67.772	4813 67.878	10 382 67.916
Massachusetts .	10 600 67.170	5239 67.272	4933 67.268	2848 67.444	5144 67.394	7992 67.412	18 164 67.333
R. I. and Conn.	10 289 67.097	5909 67.341	5508 67.389	3256 67.389	6005 67.446	9261 67.426	20 678 67.392
New York . .	43 379 67.294	24 465 67.386	22 712 67.411	14 482 67.478	29 736 67.394	44 218 67.421	91 395 67.409
New Jersey . .	5098 66.668	3167 66.683	2673 66.691	1577 66.889	2572 66.810	4149 66.840	9989 66.750
Pennsylvania .	15 329 67.349	9174 67.521	8761 67.563	5924 67.665	12 671 67.573	18 595 67.601	36 530 67.572
Maryland . .	1726 67.659	913 67.872	806 67.829	482 67.712	1001 67.747	1483 67.736	3202 67.798
West Virginia	3648 68.735	2095 68.876	1689 68.885	1078 68.937	2357 68.778	3435 68.828	7219 68.855
Kentucky . .	4796 68.569	3099 68.780	2590 68.852	1342 68.784	3031 68.817	4373 68.807	10 062 68.810
Ohio	19 495 68.157	13 022 68.237	12 808 68.281	8541 68.369	15 661 68.367	24 202 68.367	50 032 68.312
Indiana . . .	24 329 68.432	15 185 67.474	13 436 68.511	8361 68.632	14 147 68.422	22 508 68.500	51 129 68.495
Illinois . . .	39 275 68.339	26 968 68.419	23 383 68.404	13 453 68.454	23 421 68.306	36 874 68.360	87 225 68.389
Michigan . .	4227 67.954	2941 68.011	2836 67.946	1884 67.985	3987 67.931	5871 67.948	11 648 67.964
Wisconsin . .	8989 68.046	6118 67.950	6600 67.870	4868 67.832	10 582 67.621	15 450 67.687	28 168 67.787
Minnesota . .	1141 68.051	709 67.951	953 68.060	794 67.916	1475 67.771	2269 67.821	3931 67.903
Iowa	5046 68.630	3185 68.709	3323 68.777	2148 68.876	4299 68.656	6447 68.729	12 955 68.736
Missouri . .	11 413 68.336	8063 68.341	7563 68.309	4776 68.328	9350 68.247	14 126 68.274	29 752 68.301
Louisiana . .	374 66.946	356 67.124	487 67.127	311 67.006	691 66.986	1002 66.992	1845 67.053
Totals . .	234 175 67.876	143 761 67.996	132 769 68.011	83 069 68.072	159 892 67.957	242 961 67.996	519 491 68.000

TABLE X.

Mean Statures for different Periods of Age. By Nativities.

Nativity	21–23	24–26	27–30	31–34	35 & over	31 & over	24 & over
New England .	32 983 68.016	18 657 68.153	17 345 68.264	11 001 68.359	22 782 68.300	33 783 68.319	69 785 68.261
N. Y., N. J., and Penn. .	57 769 67.725	34 362 67.943	31 884 68.035	20 683 68.134	40 668 68.096	61 351 68.109	127 597 68.046
Ohio and Indiana . . .	46 643 68.529	28 206 68.682	24 145 68.809	14 142 68.959	20 064 68.980	34 206 68.971	86 557 68.832
Michigan, Wisconsin, & Ill.	16 666 68.520	8290 68.658	5053 68.801	2277 68.949	2293 68.781	4570 68.865	17 913 68.751
Slave States not incl. F & G_2	8702 68.308	5571 68.632	5181 68.771	3609 68.802	8579 68.854	12 188 68.838	22 940 68.773
Kentucky and Tennessee .	9463 68.816	6633 69.041	5970 69.102	4041 69.356	8821 69.274	12 862 69.300	25 465 69.186
Free States west of Miss. R.	696 68.507	177 68.302	70 67.739	22 67.545	33 68.098	55 67.877	302 68.094
Slave States west of Miss. R.	4150 68.552	1834 68.731	1113 69.003	544 68.926	677 68.866	1221 68.892	4168 68.851
Brit. Amer. not incl. Canada	1951 67.453	1000 67.781	824 67.931	446 68.135	731 68.063	1177 68.090	3001 67.943
Canada . . .	8573 67.224	4368 67.508	3706 67.512	1875 67.696	3615 67.300	5490 67.435	13 564 67.480
England . .	6626 66.714	4279 66.896	4414 67.020	2905 66.999	5994 66.990	8899 66.993	17 592 66.976
Scotland . .	1307 67.161	1039 67.383	1218 67.472	821 67.453	1744 67.647	2565 67.585	4822 67.513
Ireland . . .	19 230 66.954	12 799 67.126	13 720 67.174	7621 67.242	16 528 67.090	24 149 67.138	50 668 67.145
France, Belgium, & Switzerland	1084 66.628	1065 66.579	1194 66.745	830 66.592	1735 66.714	2565 66.675	4824 66.671
Germany . .	14 909 66.829	12 822 66.828	14 230 66.790	10 488 66.785	22 071 66.718	32 559 66.739	59 611 66.771
Scandinavia .	1297 67.412	1020 67.754	1087 67.471	659 67.502	1423 67.299	2082 67.363	4189 67.486
Spain, Portugal, & Span. Amer.	285 66.107	165 66.359	151 66.081	58 66.328	80 66.153	138 66.227	454 66.227
Miscellaneous .	1841 66.650	1474 66.607	1464 66.820	1047 66.719	2054 66.826	3101 66.790	6039 66.752
Totals . .	234 175 67.876	143 761 67.996	132 769 68.011	83 069 68.072	159 892 67.957	242 961 67.996	519 491 68.000

It would hence seem that the well-known phenomenon of a decrease in height after the age of forty-five or fifty years, exerts but a small influence here. Indeed the total number of the men here considered who were over forty-five years old at enlistment amounts only to about 13 300, out of 159 892 who were upwards of thirty-five, and of 242 961 who were upwards of thirty-one years of age; so that an average diminution of stature by a centimeter, or 0.39 inches, among those older than forty-five, would diminish the mean height by only 0.033 inches for those of thirty-five and over, and by 0.022 inches for those who had passed the age of thirty-one.

Notwithstanding the uncertainty of the upper limit, the ages 'thirty-five and over' are probably best adapted to our purpose, where the number of cases available is sufficiently large; but for a considerable number of the nativities this is not the case. Consequently the most appropriate method of obtaining the average full stature for any nativity seems, under the circumstances, to be by taking the mean height of all over thirty-one years, when the number in this category is sufficiently large to afford a trustworthy estimate; but where the number falls short of about 3500, by fixing the limit of age at the latest year which will afford that number of men, provided, however, that it be not placed earlier than the age of apparent maximum for the State or country under consideration. There seems no occasion for hesitancy as to adopting this rule, since it so happens that those nativities for which the age of full growth is the latest, are also those for which we possess the most copious statistics; so that by determining our results in this way, we are most likely to obtain the same values which would be afforded by an increased number of men at thirty-one and over.

We thus arrive at the measures of full stature for the average man of the several classes, and will, as before, assort them both by their States and by nativities, giving the numerical values in inches and centimeters.

TABLE XI.

Full Statures.
By States and by Nativities.

State of Enlistment.	Number	Height Inches	Height Centim.	Nativity	Number	Height Inches	Height Centim.
Maine . . .	10 563	68.576	174.18	New England . .	33 783	68.319	173.53
New Hamp. .	5 330	67.934	172.55	N. Y., N. J., & Penn.	61 351	68.109	173.00
Vermont . .	4 813	67.878	172.41	Ohio and Indiana	34 206	68.971	175.19
Massachusetts	7 992	67.412	171.22	Mich., Wis., & Ill.	4 570	68.865	174.91
R. I. and Conn.	9 261	67.426	171.26	Slave States excl.			
New York . .	44 218	67.421	171.25	of Ken. & Tenn.	13 409	68.843	174.86
New Jersey .	4 149	66.840	169.76	Kentucky & Tenn.	12 862	69.300	176.02
Pennsylvania	18 595	67.601	171.70	British Provinces .	6 667	67.551	171.58
West Virginia	3 828	68.835	174.84	England	8 899	66.993	170.16
Kentucky . .	4 373	68.807	174.77	Scotland	3 478	67.579	171.65
Ohio	24 202	68.367	173.65	Ireland	24 149	67.138	170.53
Indiana . . .	22 508	68.500	173.99	France, Belgium,			
Illinois . .	36 874	68.360	173.63	& Switzerland .	3 759	66.697	169.41
Michigan . .	5 871	67.948	172.59	Germany . . .	32 559	66.739	169.51
Wisconsin .	15 450	67.687	171.92	Scandinavia . .	3 790	67.461	171.35
Minnesota . .	3 674	67.885	172.43	Spain and Miscell.	4 421	66.766	169.58
Iowa . . .	6 447	68.729	174.57				
Missouri . .	14 126	68.274	173.41				

A comparison of these values can hardly fail to suggest the suspicion, that the full stature for a given nativity may be different in the different States, and this is strongly corroborated by the comparison of the special nativity-tables made for the men of each several State. Indeed the evidence thus obtained falls but little short of demonstration. These special tables, of which there are eighteen for each one of the thirty-eight counts for those States whose troops are here discussed, are of course too voluminous for publication in this place. The character of their indications in this respect may be seen from two tables which permit a comparison between the mean heights for natives of the New England States and for natives of New York, enlisting in their native States, and those of the same nativities who enlisted at the West.

TABLE XII.

Stature of Natives of New England.
By Ages and Regions where Enlisted.

Age	Enlisted in New England		Enlisted at West		Excess of Height at West
	Number	Height	Number	Height	
		in.		in.	in.
Under 18	888	65.232	281	65.612	0.380
18	22 539	66.765	1 913	66.636	–
19	11 403	67.506	1 034	67.550	0.044
20	8 901	67.835	873	68.135	0.300
21	13 076	67.943	991	68.115	0.172
22	8 362	68.047	941	68.268	0.221
23	7 135	68.170	882	68.262	0.092
24	5 735	68.115	883	68.413	0.298
25	5 022	68.163	821	68.249	0.086
26	4 492	68.174	746	68.488	0.314
27	4 031	68.277	702	68.489	0.212
28	3 951	68.279	684	68.628	0.349
29	2 928	68.243	554	68.621	0.378
30	2 968	68.168	569	68.508	0.340
31–34	8 545	68.358	1 748	68.527	0.169
35 & over	16 910	68.302	3 857	68.448	0.146

From these tables and other similar ones which might be formed from our statistics, the deduction is palpable, that agencies connected with the State furnishing the men to the national army, produced a decided effect upon the stature, superposed upon whatever other influences may have proceeded from the particular stock from which the men sprang.

It is not difficult to form conjectures regarding the nature of these agencies. A large proportion of those enlisting in other than their native States had doubtless migrated in childhood, while their constitution, and especially their osseous development, was readily affected by external influences. Whether these were climatic, social, or alimentary, it is perhaps premature to discuss at present. That residence in the Western States, during the years of growth, tends to produce increase of stature, seems established; and the indications are strong that the same is the case with many of the Southern States. It would moreover appear that those States which show for their natives the highest statures, are those which

TABLE XIII.

Stature of Natives of New York.[1]
By Ages and Regions where Enlisted.

Age	Enlisted in New York		Enlisted in the West		Excess of Height at West
	Number	Height	Number	Height	
		in.		in.	in.
Under 18	1 711	64.823	1 504	65.473	0.650
18	18 680	66.307	11 040	66.604	0.297
19	9 288	66.900	6 175	67.506	0.606
20	6 303	67.369	5 445	67.889	0.520
21	10 884	67.614	6 512	68.101	0.487
22	6 750	67.700	5 437	68.179	0.479
23	5 660	67.736	5 098	68.270	0.534
24	4 700	67.795	4 619	68.246	0.451
25	3 949	67.819	4 163	68.343	0.524
26	3 549	67.906	3 945	68.321	0.415
27	3 183	67.856	3 559	68.347	0.491
28	2 895	67.930	3 607	68.359	0.429
29	2 099	67.926	2 879	68.447	0.521
30	2 181	67.947	3 027	68.391	0.444
31–34	6 632	67.981	8 504	68.459	0.478
35 & over	12 874	67.902	17 318	68.401	0.499

tend most strongly to increase the stature of those who remove thither during the period of development. The westward course of population precludes any trustworthy inferences regarding the converse of this statement. And furthermore, it is evident that the relative stature for different States follows no manifest geographical law.

The suggestion that calcareous districts, by furnishing a more abundant and continuous supply of lime for the bones while growing, promote their development, and thus tend to increase the stature, seems to afford a partial explanation for this phenomenon; but it gives by no means a complete solution of the problem, for the variations of stature are not by any means proportionate to the amount of calcareous formations near the surface of the soil. Thus the marked differences, in the average statures of the natives, be-

[1] This table includes a few natives of New Jersey and Pennsylvania, but not in numbers sufficient to affect the result in any way.

tween Maine and New Hampshire, and between Vermont and New York, cannot be accounted for on this theory.

An instructive and interesting table may be formed, by presenting the full stature of natives of those European countries which have contributed most largely to our population, namely, Ireland and Germany, — as obtained from enlistments in different States, — side by side with the corresponding statures for natives of the same States enlisting at home. Such a table is here presented for men of twenty-eight years and upwards, this limit being adopted in order to obtain an adequate number of men.

TABLE XIV.

Full Statures of Irish and Germans, enlisting in various States, compared with those of Natives enlisting at home.

State of Enlistment	Natives of Ireland		Natives of Germany		Natives of the Region	
	No.	Stature	No.	Stature	No.	Stature
		in.		in.		in.
Maine	829	67.262	83	67.922	12 263	68.781
New Hampshire . .	746	66.610	299	66.373	5 239	68.418
Vermont	413	67.078	34	66.596	4 832	68.172
Massachusetts . .	2 304	66.834	570	66.329	6 535	67.705
New York	12 138	67.068	8 196	66.527	26 681	67.930
Pennsylvania . . .	1 863	67.060	3 259	66.639	17 283	67.883
Indiana	1 340	67.268	2 475	66.842	6 887	68.979
Missouri	1 625	67.584	5 700	66.965	1 293	69.085

The adjoining States of Ohio and Indiana have in general been considered together in these investigations, as "Nativity C." Circumstances led, however, to the separation of the natives of these two States, during the assortment of about two thirds of the Indiana soldiers. This has made it possible to give the figures for these soldiers in the last table; and here also a comparison of the results, obtained from these groups separately, illustrates the same principle which is manifested by our other statistics. The relative smallness of the difference between the statures of natives of these two States might reasonably be supposed to elude detection under the circumstances, yet for the mean heights we find —

TABLE XV.

Statures of Natives of Ohio and Indiana, enlisting in Indiana.

Age		Under 21	21-23	24-26	27-30	31-34	35 and over
Natives of Indiana	Number	18 248	9200	4900	3784	2017	2239
	Height	67.424	68.628	68.774	68.891	69.095	68.929
Natives of Ohio	Number	4962	3341	2204	1930	1287	1882
	Height	67.263	68.456	68.614	68.668	68.865	68.787
Excess for Indiana		0.161	0.172	0.160	0.223	0.230	0.142

It is needless to occupy more space with illustrations of this principle, which the foregoing tables will have made manifest, and which might be deduced by a comparison of the mean heights for any nativity in different States. And the fact must be conceded, that the full stature for any class of men is dependent both upon their lineage and their residence during the period of development.

The separate consideration of the men drawn from rural and from urban districts would be full of instruction; and some attempts have been made to follow out this question; but the character of our data renders it a matter of so much difficulty, to say the least, that these endeavors were reluctantly abandoned.

The social classes to which the men belonged would afford another basis for useful classification, and the relations of stature and other physical characteristics to the special parentage, occupation, and education, as also the mutual relations of stature, complexion, and temperament, are among the problems of which our statistics would permit the discussion, and which were among those which we desired to include in the present chapter. But the limited outlay, which the Sanitary Commission has felt warranted in devoting to the present researches, is inadequate to the proper investigation of these points.

It has been already stated that the measures [1] of eighty students between eighteen and twenty-five years old at Cambridge (England) gave a mean stature of 69.60 inches, and that similar measures of more than ten times that number at the Edinburgh Univer-

[1] Made according to a prevailing usage by a tradesman in the town, and recorded to quarters of an inch.

sity by Prof. Forbes, gave the mean stature as 68.70; but that from each of these values an inch ought to be deducted because the young men were measured in their shoes or boots.

The rapid movements of our army on one occasion temporarily prevented the prosecution of measurements in the field, and the opportunity was improved to make various bodily measurements of the older students of the universities at Cambridge (Massachusetts) and New Haven, for comparison with the corresponding ones of men of the same age in the army.

The results of these measures will be given in the proper place; here the statures only need be adduced. They comprise all members of the Senior and Junior class who could be conveniently collected, and a few members of the professional schools, taken as opportunity offered, no selection whatever being made. The ages are for the last birthday, and the heights were measured to tenths of inches.

TABLE XVI.

Heights and Ages
of Harvard and Yale Students.

Age	63–64	64–65	65–66	66–67	67–68	68–69	69–70	70–71	71–72	72–73	73–74	over 74
17	–	–	–	1	1	1	–	–	–	–	–	–
18	–	2	2	–	–	1	1	–	1	–	–	–
19	1	5	7	6	4	5	7	1	2	1	–	–
20	3	3	6	6	8	15	14	7	7	2	2	–
21	–	4	7	11	13	9	11	13	1	1	–	–
22	3	1	7	6	6	5	6	6	2	–	1	1
23	2	1	–	1	1	1	4	–	2	–	–	1
24	–	2	–	1	3	5	1	–	3	1	–	1
25	–	1	–	3	1	2	2	–	–	2	–	–
26	–	1	–	2	–	–	–	–	1	–	–	1
27	–	–	1	–	–	1	–	2	1	–	–	–
Over 27	–	–	2	–	–	–	–	–	2	–	–	–
Total	9	20	32	37	37	45	46	29	22	7	3	4

The resultant mean statures are —

Age	Height in.	Height c.	Number
17	67.467	171.37	3
18	67.143	170.54	7
19	67.354	171.08	39
20	68.411	173.76	73
21	68.037	172.81	70
22	67.900	172.46	44
23	68.208	173.25	13
24	68.918	175.05	17
25	68.300	173.48	11
26	68.660	174.40	5
27	69.180	175.72	5
Above 27	68.600	174.24	4
Total	68.099	172.97	291

And may be classified thus: —

Age	Height in.	Height c.	Number
17–20	67.976	172.66	122
21–23	68.007	172.74	127
24–26	68.673	174.43	33
27 & over	68.922	175.06	9
Total	68.099	172.97	291

The two extremes were 63.1 inches for one young man of twenty years, and 77.4 inches for one of twenty-two years.

We may sum up many of our general inferences regarding the full stature, in a few closing sentences.

That the stature of a population is not in ordinary cases affected by the temperature of the region which it inhabits, as was supposed by Buffon,[1] may be regarded as established by the small influence which the latitude appears to exert. The statistics here collected show how slight any such influence must be within the territory of the United States; for the differences of stature here seem altogether independent of climatic agencies, as will be perceived from a very cursory inspection of Table XI. For South America the same fact is established by the researches of D'Orbigny,[2] who especially discards this theory with emphatic repetition. For Europe the non-dependence of stature upon latitude is too well known to require illustration, and although there is a wide diversity between the statures of the Latin and the Teutonic races, it is in the direction opposite to that which this theory implies.[3]

1 *Histoire Naturelle*, ed. Sonnini, XVIII. 302.
2 *L'Homme Americain*, I. 94, 95, 99.
3 Quetelet, *Systême Social*, pp. 25, 26.

That stature is not a distinctive characteristic of nationality is demonstrated with equal certainty by these statistics. Our tables XII. to XV. show incontestably the agency of some local influence, by exhibiting the difference in stature between men, of the same stock and nativity, reared in different States. The same conclusion was forced upon D'Orbigny by his South American investigations,[1] and the statistics of conscription in France and Prussia also make this truth manifest by showing the wide diversity in the mean stature of men of the same race, and born in districts by no means remote from each other.

That the stature depends in any controlling degree upon the domestic circumstances of a population, as affected by abundance or need of the comforts of life, according to the opinion of Villermé,[2] can scarcely be maintained after consideration of the facts here presented, although the effects of privation or exposure upon the physical growth are doubtless recognizable.

That the stature is chiefly affected by the elevation of the districts inhabited, as suggested by D'Orbigny, who attributes [3] the supposed inferior stature in mountainous regions to the prolonged influence of a rarefied atmosphere, seems equally untenable. Among the tallest men of Kentucky, Tennessee, and West Virginia, are the dwellers upon the slopes of the Alleghanies; the Green Mountains of Vermont furnish a race of men among the tallest in all the New England States; yet on the other hand the prairies and level fields of Indiana and Illinois afford a population of preeminent stature. The tallest men of France inhabit the slopes of the Jura.

That all the influences here considered, — climate, nationality, comfort, elevation, — may contribute in some measure to affect the stature is more than probable; that both ancestral and local influences are recognizable is certain. And although we cannot succeed in determining what is the chief agent, it may not be without value that we furnish evidence of what it is not.

6. *Stature of Sailors.*

The assortment of one of the installments, or "counts," of the New York soldiers indicated for all the ages, without exception, a mean height less by more than an inch, than that given by the other counts for the same State. Examination revealed the fact

[1] *L'Homme Americain*, I. 395.

[2] *Annales d'Hygiène*, I. 386.

[3] *L'Homme Americain*, I. 98, 103.

that these records contained the statistics of about 25 000 sailors, enlisted for the naval service in New York city, and credited to the State, so that they had been recorded with the soldiers. The special discussion of the heights of these men showed a stature for the sailors less than that for the soldiers enlisted at the same time, by amounts varying systematically with the age, but averaging an inch and a quarter.

Comparing the results for each year of age directly with one another, we find the mean statures of soldiers enlisted in the State of New York to surpass those of sailors enlisted in the same State by the following amounts.

Age	Excess in	Age	Excess in.
Under 17	1.496	25	1.282
17	2.367	26	1.369
18	1.993	27	1.273
19	1.506	28	1.235
20	1.425	29	1.214
21	1.384	30	1.249
22	1.345	31–34	1.213
23	1.277	35 & over	1.247
24	1.302		
	Total . . .	1.292	

The large excess at the age of seventeen, taken in connection with the gradual diminution of this excess for subsequent ages, seems to point both to a postponement of the development in stature, and to a permanent arrest of this development to a considerable extent.

Steps were immediately taken to procure the ages and heights of sailors enlisted elsewhere, and through the ready aid of Dr. P. J. Horwitz, Chief of the Naval Bureau of Medicine and Surgery, and of Commander A. N. Smith, Chief of the Bureau of Equipment and Recruiting, statistics were obtained without difficulty for about 62 000 additional sailors, 4000 of them being negroes. The naval musters classify most of the men in the three divisions, "ordinary seamen," "seamen," and "landsmen." In our tabulations the two former have been combined under the title "seamen;" and the accompanying tables, XVII., XVIII., XIX., and XX., present the results for seamen, landsmen, and for the New York naval musters, as originally assorted, and for the several classes combined. With the "landsmen" are combined the miscellaneous classes, such as "firemen," "coal-heavers," "boys," etc., etc. The number of men from which each result was deduced is indicated in a lighter type, as in the Tables I. and VI.

It will be perceived at a glance that the stature of "landsmen" exceeds that of "seamen," which latter also exceeds that of the sailors, credited to New York.

The remarks already made while considering the Law of Growth, and the Full Stature, throw sufficient light upon this phenomenon, which appears at first so remarkable. The privations and exposures of a nautical life evidently exert a stunting effect upon the development, and the class of sailors enlisted at a great sea-port like New York, might reasonably be supposed to contain a larger proportion of "old salts," that is to say of men bred to seamanship from early youth. The effect of the sailor's life in delaying the growth, is indicated by the great difference between the statures of soldiers and sailors at the ages of seventeen and eighteen years, as already shown.

The attainment of full stature seems to be earliest for seamen, for whom our statistics indicate twenty-eight years as the corresponding age; and latest for landsmen, for whom it does not occur until "thirty-five and upwards." For the combination of the two in the New York naval musters, it is at the intermediate age, 31–34.[1]

[1] It may not be without interest if the mean ages at which sailors of different nativities attained their full stature be here appended, although the small number from which the inferences for some of the classes must be deduced precludes any great reliance upon the results. It will be perceived that, in general, the age of full stature is latest for "Landsmen," earliest for "Seamen," and intermediate for the combination of the two classes, in the enlistments at New York city, for the several nativities as well as for their aggregate; also that this fact is generally more marked, the greater the number of men from which the result is obtained. The ages here are for "last birthday," as recorded.

Nativity	Seamen		New York Sailors		Landsmen		Total	
	Age	No.	Age	No.	Age	No.	Age	No.
A	28	372	23	263	30	108	30	446
B	28	274	31–34	486	35 & over	300	31–34	1318
C, D, G_1	24	132	31–34	6	35 & over	39	35 & over	135
E, F, G_2	24	95	29	34	30	56	30	156
H, I	29	84	30	20	29	26	29	127
J	28	121	30	52	27	58	31–34	445
K	29	35	28	39	35 & over	52	28	110
L	29	141	27	275	29	160	29	493
M, P	30	23	26	16	27	8	27	40
N	26	89	26	53	23	53	26	175
O	25	66	27	35	29	6	27	91
Q	19	18	27	31	29	3	27	95
Total	28	1095	31–34	1632	35 & over	1692	29	2436

TABLE XVII.

Heights of Sailors,
by Ages and Nativities.

Age	New England				New York, New Jersey, and Pennsylvania			
	Seamen	Lands-men	N. Y. Sailors	Total	Seamen	Lands-men	N. Y. Sailors	Total
Under 17	14 64.696	363 61.504	74 62.358	451 61.743	6 63.458	291 60.379	414 61.801	711 61.233
17	43 64.669	280 63.513	47 64.032	370 63.713	14 64.357	158 63.203	340 62.928	512 63.052
18	234 65.637	868 65.298	55 64.964	1157 65.350	106 65.597	453 65.280	363 64.247	922 64.910
19	223 66.054	526 65.811	51 65.515	800 65.860	140 66.370	368 66.381	297 65.084	805 65.900
20	245 66.093	435 66.320	55 65.941	735 66.216	177 66.548	364 66.447	316 65.553	857 66.138
21	942 66.586	1411 66.641	486 66.157	2839 66.540	437 66.510	1068 66.573	2152 65.909	3657 66.175
22	762 66.432	754 66.810	339 66.197	1855 66.543	435 66.600	699 66.654	1218 65.994	2352 66.302
23	646 66.512	481 66.760	263 66.659	1390 66.626	376 66.607	493 66.744	834 66.110	1703 66.403
24	522 66.589	334 66.939	215 66.194	1071 66.619	387 66.651	393 66.755	716 66.224	1496 66.474
25	503 66.600	269 66.958	172 66.263	944 66.641	337 66.522	338 66.759	539 66.103	1214 66.402
26	409 66.549	203 66.860	137 65.954	749 66.524	293 66.687	257 66.751	430 66.156	980 66.471
27	363 66.721	181 67.054	111 65.766	655 66.651	256 66.543	195 66.774	295 66.057	746 66.411
28	372 67.136	185 67.039	124 65.978	681 66.899	274 66.970	197 67.018	327 66.344	798 66.725
29	279 66.944	107 66.860	82 66.064	468 66.770	200 66.723	139 66.926	216 66.363	555 66.634
30	266 67.020	108 67.148	72 66.569	446 66.978	169 66.768	132 66.841	200 65.990	501 66.477
31-34	685 66.687	245 67.137	193 66.470	1123 66.748	521 66.965	311 66.818	486 66.436	1318 66.735
35 & over	1244 66.834	269 66.989	334 66.499	1847 66.796	855 66.697	300 67.140	599 66.177	1754 66.595
Total	7752 66 599	7019 66.124	2810 66.080	17 581 66.327	4983 66.640	6156 66.206	9742 65.678	20 881 66.063

TABLE XVII. — (*Continued.*)

Heights of Sailors, by Ages and Nativities.

Age	Northwestern States				Slave States			
	Seamen	Lands-men	N. Y. Sailors	Total	Seamen	Lands-men	N. Y. Sailors	Total
Under 17	21 64.345	165 61.000	8 61.125	194 61.367	4 65.875	154 60.054	21 61.762	179 60.384
17	46 64.674	85 63.229	5 64.950	136 63.781	11 65.909	103 65.041	13 63.308	127 64.939
18	233 66.038	355 63.549	8 63.562	596 65.594	49 65.663	286 66.055	28 63.393	363 65.797
19	173 67.366	164 66.299	5 64.600	342 66.814	53 66.953	213 66.979	27 65.426	293 66.831
20	177 67.133	108 66.917	9 66.083	294 67.021	68 67.099	220 67.048	35 65.643	323 66.906
21	247 67.817	132 67.430	57 66.487	436 67.526	154 66.617	437 67.056	208 65.826	799 66.651
22	167 67.445	100 67.177	37 66.872	304 67.287	132 66.841	289 67.283	140 65.682	561 66.779
23	130 67.863	73 67.314	23 66.022	226 67.499	92 67.111	234 67.947	83 65.928	409 67.349
24	132 68.097	52 67.274	31 66.161	215 67.619	95 67.524	207 67.699	70 65.404	372 67.222
25	103 67.791	42 66.423	12 66.625	157 67.336	72 66.674	126 67.262	78 66.474	276 66.886
26	75 67.577	43 67.610	14 65.250	132 67.341	81 67.046	146 67.808	64 66.348	291 67.275
27	68 67.654	26 67.269	12 66.312	106 67.408	79 66.921	83 66.958	55 66.059	217 66.717
28	48 67.714	41 67.591	11 65.864	100 67.460	68 66.908	97 67.531	76 66.158	241 66.922
29	43 67.570	20 68.100	7 67.036	70 67.668	56 67.286	63 67.583	34 66.574	153 67.250
30	42 67.315	25 67.530	7 64.679	74 67.139	50 67.050	56 68.594	50 66.305	156 67.365
31-34	94 67.646	66 67.909	6 67.125	166 67.732	132 67.062	191 67.817	111 66.077	434 67.142
35 & over	88 67.810	39 68.135	8 66.156	135 67.806	327 66.870	192 68.359	161 66.304	680 67.157
Total	1887 67.321	1536 65.870	260 66.003	3683 66.623	1523 66.904	3097 66.896	1254 65.851	5874 66.675

TABLE XVII. — (*Continued.*)

Heights of Sailors, by Ages and Nativities.

Age	British Provinces				England			
	Seamen	Lands-men	N. Y. Sailors	Total	Seamen	Lands-men	N. Y. Sailors	Total
Under 17	2 62.750	21 62.738	10 63.350	33 62.924	-	29 60.224	21 60.976	50 60.540
17	8 64.656	31 64.669	11 61.523	50 63.975	11 64.455	22 62.591	24 61.698	57 62.575
18	57 65.342	162 64.679	12 63.021	231 64.756	49 64.015	79 64.291	35 63.214	163 63.977
19	84 65.958	145 65.816	15 65.817	244 65.865	69 64.924	52 64.731	40 63.369	161 64.475
20	114 66.485	108 66.743	23 65.630	245 66.518	87 65.256	65 65.285	54 64.694	206 65.118
21	340 66.605	264 66.820	106 66.429	710 66.659	250 65.313	183 65.587	320 65.054	753 65.270
22	277 66.893	192 67.443	81 66.571	550 67.037	262 65.421	137 65.443	174 65.394	573 65.418
23	223 66.805	112 66.944	52 66.582	387 66.815	193 65.710	91 65.566	167 65.488	451 65.599
24	154 66.818	79 67.161	34 66.110	267 66.830	160 65.752	93 65.573	131 65.441	384 65.602
25	154 66.854	73 66.969	31 65.669	258 66.744	175 66.127	80 65.787	112 65.708	367 65.925
26	114 67.004	48 67.432	24 66.708	186 67.077	123 65.878	65 65.558	81 65.855	269 65.794
27	111 66.626	43 67.110	18 66.486	172 66.733	123 66.122	58 66.466	83 65.349	264 65.955
28	130 66.896	55 66.668	20 67.325	205 66.877	121 66.277	53 65.925	94 65.628	268 65.979
29	84 67.253	26 67.875	17 67.647	127 67.433	86 66.166	43 66.064	49 65.347	178 65.916
30	72 67.212	31 67.331	20 67.650	123 67.313	84 65.703	49 65.633	52 66.029	185 65.776
31-34	182 67.209	56 67.232	35 67.150	273 67.206	208 66.071	114 66.362	123 65.764	445 66.061
35 & over	220 66.984	62 66.875	24 66.917	306 66.957	352 65.700	116 66.390	161 65.929	629 65.886
Total	2326 66.781	1508 66.569	533 66.316	4367 66.651	2353 65.695	1329 65.494	1721 65.272	5403 65.511

TABLE XVII. — (*Continued.*)

Heights of Sailors,
by Ages and Nativities.

Age	Scotland				Ireland			
	Seamen	Lands-men	N. Y. Sailors	Total	Seamen	Lands-men	N. Y. Sailors	Total
Under 17	-	6 62.417	7 62.429	13 62.423	2 66.125	71 60.437	39 61.212	112 60.808
17	1 65.000	7 61.536	4 65.687	12 63.208	9 63.861	53 63.632	42 61.095	104 62.627
18	8 64.687	28 63.732	1 65.500	37 63.986	68 64.952	235 64.428	76 63.914	379 64.357
19	14 65.304	18 65.056	8 64.250	40 64.981	93 66.341	254 65.658	88 65.560	435 65.784
20	23 64.696	12 65.771	12 65.104	47 65.074	160 65.916	277 66.144	184 65.649	621 65.939
21	66 65.989	50 65.455	84 65.158	200 65.506	365 65.990	1010 66.387	997 66.010	2372 66.167
22	60 65.904	38 66.441	56 65.527	154 65.899	445 66.129	778 66.711	738 66.156	1961 66.370
23	62 65.512	25 65.690	38 66.336	125 65.798	357 66.089	547 66.573	535 66.078	1439 66.269
24	55 66.405	31 66.476	48 65.958	134 66.261	285 66.377	419 66.625	423 66.370	1127 66.467
25	60 66.137	20 65.975	45 65.378	125 65.838	282 66.368	386 66.492	455 66.087	1123 66.297
26	49 65.766	19 65.882	30 65.042	98 65.566	253 66.508	361 66.648	332 66.217	946 66.459
27	39 66.391	23 65.750	25 66.390	87 66.221	203 66.282	254 66.485	275 66.484	732 66.428
28	45 66.094	26 67.000	39 67.128	110 66.675	243 66.353	321 66.540	293 66.252	857 66.389
29	35 66.900	9 66.000	21 66.155	65 66.535	141 66.814	160 66.863	192 66.391	493 66.665
30	36 66.042	15 67.283	31 66.411	82 66.409	179 66.485	228 66.658	205 66.116	612 66.426
31–34	82 66.299	37 66.939	64 65.898	183 66.288	363 66.492	427 66.728	385 66.278	1175 66.508
35 & over	171 66.515	52 67.365	97 66.361	320 66.606	531 66.264	487 66.560	446 66.075	1464 66.305
Total	806 66.119	416 66.007	610 65.842	1832 66.001	3979 66.255	6268 66.343	5705 66.040	15 952 66.213

TABLE XVII.—(*Continued.*)

Heights of Sailors,
by Ages and Nativities.

Age	Latin Races				Germany			
	Seamen	Lands-men	N. Y. Sailors	Total	Seamen	Lands-men	N. Y. Sailors	Total
Under 17	–	5 58.250	–	5 58.250	1 67.000	17 60.162	7 60.357	25 60.490
17	–	4 61.438	2 61.500	6 61.458	5 64.900	19 63.487	10 62.150	34 63.301
18	4 63.625	11 64.886	5 62.450	20 64.025	39 65.256	79 64.104	18 64.333	136 64.465
19	12 64.333	19 64.605	4 64.812	35 64.536	53 64.835	50 65.115	21 64.940	124 64.966
20	17 64.824	6 64.833	6 64.667	29 64.793	66 65.723	49 66.296	44 65.943	159 65.961
21	43 65.017	32 65.281	27 64.426	102 64.944	150 65.897	84 66.339	190 65.508	424 65.810
22	31 65.202	18 64.736	22 64.364	71 64.824	207 66.377	61 66.324	149 65.745	417 66.302
23	37 65.743	13 64.981	24 65.177	74 65.426	154 66.266	53 66.995	131 65.798	338 66.199
24	46 65.837	13 65.096	16 65.547	75 65.647	140 66.389	44 66.716	79 65.911	263 66.300
25	41 65.207	16 65.250	23 65.033	80 65.166	136 66.006	29 66.000	72 66.156	237 66.051
26	20 65.175	9 66.222	16 65.891	45 65.639	89 66.857	33 66.311	53 66.759	175 66.724
27	28 66.125	8 67.000	4 64.125	40 66.100	79 66.206	32 66.781	54 66.347	165 66.364
28	27 65.778	11 66.182	12 65.146	50 65.715	113 66.270	31 66.065	47 66.261	191 66.234
29	17 65.176	4 66.875	7 64.786	28 65.321	87 66.241	30 66.633	36 66.472	153 66.373
30	23 66.696	6 65.583	13 65.000	42 66.012	54 65.903	29 66.078	36 65.250	119 65.748
31–34	44 65.670	12 66.312	21 64.750	77 65.519	139 66.365	65 66.015	96 66.310	300 66.272
35 & over	69 65.250	23 66.098	32 64.297	124 65.161	210 66.435	99 66.697	88 66.014	397 66.468
Total	459 65.457	210 65.207	234 64.765	903 65.220	1722 66.189	804 65.919	1131 65.828	3657 66.018

TABLE XVII.—(*Continued.*)

Heights of Sailors, by Ages and Nativities.

Age	Scandinavia				Miscellaneous			
	Seamen	Lands-men	N. Y. Sailors	Total	Seamen	Lands-men	N. Y. Sailors	Total
Under 17	–	3 61.000	–	3 61.000	1 66.000	19 59.039	8 63.781	28 60.643
17	2 62.125	–	–	2 62.125	2 64.375	5 62.100	4 60.375	11 61.886
18	9 66.556	10 63.925	2 65.375	21 65.190	17 64.956	21 64.750	8 63.344	46 64.582
19	15 66.417	2 66.875	4 63.937	21 65.988	18 66.250	20 64.275	15 64.933	53 65.132
20	36 65.958	6 66.542	15 65.933	57 66.013	32 64.937	13 64.827	17 64.794	62 64.875
21	63 66.421	18 66.069	73 65.949	154 66.156	91 65.354	38 65.079	78 64.782	207 65.088
22	120 66.065	10 67.400	107 65.834	237 66.017	75 65.667	25 66.200	85 64.818	185 65.349
23	72 65.997	9 65.694	64 66.379	145 66.147	47 64.989	21 64.964	67 65.627	135 65.302
24	66 66.223	6 65.542	58 65.884	130 66.040	59 65.877	25 65.040	59 64.725	143 65.255
25	66 66.958	11 66.341	67 65.974	144 66.453	72 65.562	26 66.269	83 65.684	181 65.720
26	56 66.406	7 66.679	40 65.681	103 66.143	49 65.745	22 66.159	49 65.281	120 65.631
27	49 66.602	7 65.964	35 67.014	91 66.712	55 65.450	9 65.972	31 66.274	95 65.768
28	52 66.538	11 67.068	51 66.010	114 66.353	27 65.565	10 65.125	45 65.594	82 65.527
29	37 66.561	6 67.917	29 66.069	72 66.476	30 65.583	3 69.500	41 65.537	74 65.716
30	54 66.847	7 66.714	19 66.224	80 66.688	30 65.633	10 65.125	28 65.554	68 65.526
31-34	98 66.398	13 66.885	56 66.446	167 66.452	88 65.213	16 65.531	56 65.540	160 65.359
35 & over	146 66.214	15 65.467	109 66.275	270 66.197	98 65.727	38 66.329	70 65.075	206 65.617
Total	941 66.352	141 66.135	729 66.094	1811 66.231	791 65.501	321 65.080	744 65.211	1856 65.312

TABLE XVIII.

Heights of Landsmen,
by Periods of Age and Nativities.

Nativity	Under 21	21–23	24–26	27–30	31–34	35 and over	31 and over	24 and over
New England . .	2472 64.827	2646 66.711	806 66.925	581 67.031	245 67.137	269 66.989	514 67.059	1901 66.994
N. Y., N. J., and Penn.	1634 64.714	2260 66.635	988 66.755	663 66.892	311 66.818	300 67.140	611 66.976	2262 66.855
Northwestern States	877 64.696	305 67.320	137 67.119	112 67.594	66 67.909	39 68.135	105 67.993	354 67.528
Slave States . . .	976 65.426	960 67.341	479 67.617	299 67.582	191 67.817	192 68.359	383 68.089	1161 67.764
British Provinces .	467 65.421	568 67.055	200 67.156	155 67.126	56 67.232	62 66.875	118 67.044	473 67.118
England	247 64.016	411 65.535	238 65.641	203 66.037	114 66.362	116 66.390	230 66.376	671 66.013
Scotland	71 64.085	113 65.838	70 66.171	73 66.541	37 66.939	52 67.365	89 67.188	232 66.678
Ireland	890 64.921	2335 66.539	1166 66.588	963 66.607	427 66.728	487 66.560	914 66.639	3043 66.609
Latin Races, etc. .	45 63.717	63 65.063	38 65.428	29 66.379	12 66.313	23 66.098	35 66.171	102 65.953
Germany	214 64.474	198 66.510	106 66.394	122 66.395	65 66.015	99 66.697	164 66.427	392 66.408
Scandinavia . . .	21 64.536	37 66.338	24 66.240	31 66.903	13 66.885	15 65.467	28 66.125	83 66.449
Miscellaneous . .	78 63.080	84 65.384	73 65.815	32 65.773	16 65.531	38 66.329	54 66.093	159 65.901
Total	7992 64.843	9980 66.667	4325 66.757	3263 66.836	1553 66.947	1692 66.984	3245 66.966	10 833 66.853

TABLE XIX.

Heights of Seamen,
by Periods of Age and Nativities.

Nativity	Under 21	21–23	24–26	27–30	31–34	35 and over	31 and over	24 and over
New England . .	759 65.834	2350 66.516	1434 66.581	1280 66.952	685 66.687	1244 66.834	1929 66.782	4643 66.767
N. Y., N. J., and Penn.	443 66.153	1248 66.571	1017 66.618	899 66.755	521 66.965	855 66.697	1376 66.799	3292 66.731
Northwestern States	650 66.538	544 67.714	310 67.869	201 67.580	94 67.646	88 67.810	182 67.725	693 67.747
Slave States . . .	185 66.580	378 66.815	248 67.121	253 67.024	132 67.062	327 66.870	459 66.925	960 67.002
British Provinces .	265 65.989	840 66.753	422 66.882	397 66.953	182 67.209	220 66.984	402 67.086	1221 66.972
England	216 64.828	705 65.462	458 65.929	414 66.091	208 66.071	352 65.700	560 65.838	1432 65.940
Scotland	46 64.886	188 65.805	164 66.116	155 66.339	82 66.299	171 66.515	253 66.445	572 66.322
Ireland	332 65.783	1167 66.073	820 66.414	766 66.450	363 66.492	531 66.264	894 66.357	2480 66.405
Latin Races, etc. .	33 64.500	111 65.311	107 65.472	95 65.995	44 65.670	69 65.250	113 65.414	315 65.609
Germany	164 65.308	511 66.203	365 66.360	333 66.188	139 66.365	210 66.435	349 66.407	1047 66.321
Scandinavia . .	62 66.032	255 66.133	188 66.536	192 66.646	98 66.398	146 66.214	244 66.288	624 66.473
Miscellaneous . .	70 65.279	213 65.384	180 65.715	142 65.539	88 65.213	98 65.727	186 65.484	508 65.581
Total	3225 65.940	8510 66.399	5713 66.550	5127 66.665	2636 66.650	4311 66.571	6947 66.601	17 787 66.603

TABLE XX.

Heights of Sailors,
by Periods of Age and Nativities.

Nativity	Under 21	21-23	24-26	27-30	31-34	35 and over	31 and over	24 and over
New England . .	3513 65.012	6084 66.560	2764 66.601	2250 66.816	1123 66.748	1847 66.796	2970 66.778	7984 66.727
N. Y., N. J., and Penn.	3807 64.459	7712 66.264	3690 66.449	2600 66.568	1318 66.735	1754 66.595	3072 66.655	9362 66.550
Northwestern States	1562 65.447	966 67.444	504 67.458	350 67.418	166 67.732	135 67.806	301 67.765	1155 67.526
Slave States . . .	1285 65.473	1769 66.853	939 67.140	767 67.020	434 67.142	680 67.157	1114 67.151	2820 67.112
British Provinces .	803 65.507	1647 66.822	711 66.863	627 67.036	273 67.206	306 66.957	579 67.074	1917 66.983
England	637 64.077	1777 65.401	1020 65.769	895 65.917	445 66.061	629 65.886	1074 65.958	2989 65.881
Scotland	149 64.398	479 65.709	357 65.922	344 66.470	183 66.288	320 66.606	503 66.491	1204 66.316
Ireland	1651 64.978	5772 66.261	3196 66.405	2694 66.458	1175 66.508	1464 66.305	2639 66.395	8529 66.419
Latin Races, etc. .	95 63.982	247 65.054	200 65.452	160 65.820	77 65.519	124 65.161	201 65.299	561 65.502
Germany . . .	478 64.802	1179 66.039	675 66.323	628 66.210	300 66.272	397 66.468	697 66.349	2000 66.296
Scandinavia . . .	104 65.623	536 66.092	377 66.226	357 66.545	167 66.452	270 66.197	437 66.295	1171 66.349
Miscellaneous . .	200 64.119	527 65.234	444 65.546	319 65.643	160 65.359	206 65.617	366 65 504	1129 65.560
Total	14 284 64.908	28 695 66.330	14 877 66.454	11 991 66.562	5821 66.621	8132 66.546	13 953 66.577	40 821 66.528

The argument that the exigencies of naval service would promote enlistments among the shorter class of men, by preference, since these are in general the most agile and active, so that thus an apparent inferiority of stature may be exhibited in the mean, — may be entitled to some weight in diminishing the amount of effect to be attributed to other influences. But it can hardly do more than this, since the differences are the largest at those ages where, by reason of incomplete stature, no such tendency to natural selection exists. This argument is, however, especially precluded by a comparison of the mean statures of soldiers and sailors, after omitting from the data all those whose stature exceeds some limit not inconsistent with perfect nautical convenience. Such a comparison, for men whose stature does not exceed 66 inches, gives, for all ages, results in conformity with those already obtained from the whole number of cases.

7. *Stature of other Races of Men.*

For discussing the stature of other races than our own, comparatively few materials are known to the writer.

Tenon, in his manuscript notes, written about the year 1783, and posthumously edited by Villermé, says,[1] that the mean height of the Laplanders is 138 centimeters (54.3 inches), and that of the Patagonians, from 175.9 to 202.9 (69¼ to 79⅞ inches), — the range of variation for a people diminishing with the stature.

Pauw states[2] that the average height of the Esquimaux is but 130 centimeters.

Rollin, the surgeon of La Perouse's expedition, gives[3] the stature of some of the inhabitants of the shores of the Pacific Ocean in 1786 and 1787, as follows, for full grown males: —

	Inches	Centimeters
Natives of Concepcion, in Chile	65.1	165
" " Monterey, in California,	66.6	169
" " Baie des Français,[4]	67.1	171
Tartars of Saghalien Island,	63.9	162
" " Mouth of Amoor River,	61.8	157

Humboldt, in his "Personal Narrative,"[5] states that the ordinary stature of the Chayma race of Indians is about 62 inches, or 157 centimeters.

The statures of the Caribes of the Orinoco, Humboldt found[6] to range in general from 5 feet 6 in. to 5 feet 10 in., old French measure, being equivalent to a mean of 72.47 inches, or 184 centimeters. But he himself[7] regards this stature as an exceptional one for the race to which they belong, favorable circumstances having doubtless increased their normal stature.[8]

A summary of authorities concerning the great stature of the Patagonians, or at least of one tribe of the Patagonian Indians, which, according to Falkner, was the Puelche tribe, may be found in Lawrence's "Lectures on Man,"[9] — according to which there

[1] *Annales d'Hygiène*, X. 27.

[2] *Recherches philosophiques sur les Americains*, I. 259.

[3] *Voyage of La Perouse*, English Translation, 2d ed., III. 222, 247.

[4] "Cross Sound," near Sitka, in Alaska.

[5] *Personal Narrative*, Williams's Translation, III. 222; *Voyage*, 8vo ed. III. 277.

[6] *Voyage*, 8vo. ed., IX. 11. [7] *Ibid.* III. 355. [8] *L'Homme Americain*, II. 294.

[9] *Lectures on Physiology, Zoology, and the Natural History of Man*, by W. Lawrence, London, 1822, pages 378, 389.

would seem to be small doubt that men much exceeding six feet in stature were common on the Patagonian coast in the last century; and the evidence seems to be strong that many individuals exceeded 78 inches, and that some surpassed 80 inches in height. But a more thorough and exhaustive monograph, on the history and bibliography of the statements regarding the stature of these men, may be found in the treatise [1] of Alcide d'Orbigny, who lived for eight months [2] among this tribe, on the banks of the Rio Negro, where, besides studying the habits and characteristics of the natives, he measured a very large number of them. In his remarkable work on the South American man, the fruit of eight years of sojourn among the Indian races,[3] and four years more of study, we find the mean stature of thirty-nine tribes of the aborigines of South America, classified by tribes, branches, and races. D'Orbigny says that he did not meet with a single man who surpassed the stature of 192 centimeters (75.6 inches), and that the mean stature of the full-grown Patagonians was found [4] to be 173 centimeters (68.1 inches). That of the Puelche tribe was [5] 170 centimeters, few being found below the height of 162 centimeters (63.8 inches), and some attaining 180 centimeters (70.9 inches). A probable explanation of the exaggerated accounts of the stature of this really tall race of men is given by D'Orbigny, who says that the breadth of their shoulders, their bare heads, and the manner in which they drape themselves from head to foot in the skins of wild animals, produce such an illusion, that his own party had attributed to them an excessive stature, before any actual comparison or measurement became possible.

The mean statures and maximum limits for seven groups of Indians were found by D'Orbigny [6] to be as follows: —

		Mean m.	Upper Limit. m.
Ando-Peruvian	Peruvian	1.597	1.700
	Antisian	1.645	1.760
	Araucanian	1.641	1.730
Pampean	Pampean[7]	1.688	1.920
	Chiquitean	1.663	1.760
	Moxean	1.670	1.785
Brasilio-Guaranian		1.620	1.730

1 *L'Homme Americain, de l'Amerique Méridionale*, Paris, 1839, II. 26–75.
2 *Ibid.* I. xiv.; II. 67.
3 *Ibid.* I. xxvii.
4 *Ibid.* II. 67.
5 *Ibid.* II. 78.
6 *Ibid.* I. 90, 102.
7 Of the Pampean tribes the Patagonians were tallest, a large number of them giving as the average stature 173 centimeters; the upper limit being as above, 192 centimeters. The average heights of the Puelches was 170 centimeters; while that of the Mataguayos, who formed the smallest tribes of the Pampean branch, was 167 centimeters.

Dr. A. S. Thomson has also given[1] some interesting statistics regarding the New Zealanders, and found the mean height of 147 men of this race, of different ages, to be $66\frac{3}{4}$ inches, or 169.5 centimeters.

Freycinet says[2] that the stature of the Bushmen is but four French feet, or 51.16 inches (129.9 centimeters), which seems, however, to be rather below their actual stature.

Du Chaillu reports[3] the existence of a race in the interior of equatorial Africa, called Obongoes, whose mean stature does not exceed 56 inches (142 centimeters). He measured the height of several women, but was able to measure but one man. His stature was 54 inches.

Copious materials for determining the stature of the Negro race, as it is in the United States, must exist in the War Department, derived from the descriptive musters of the 180 000 men, enlisted[4] in the national armies during the later years of the rebellion. The same antagonism of the Hon. Secretary of War towards the Sanitary Commission which has so materially impeded its work in other respects, and has deprived its Statistical Department of large opportunities, has here also restricted our materials to the 40 000 colored soldiers enlisted by the several States, and the 4000 colored sailors; but the number of these who are of mixed race is so large, and the relative amount of the mixture is so diverse, that this number is inadequate for a thorough investigation of the subject. Several widely different varieties of the negro race are to be found among the recently enslaved population of the Southern States, and these are mixed with each other, with the white, and sometimes with the different Indian races, to an extent which precludes the attainment of statistical results based upon intelligent classification, unless from a much larger number of cases than is at our disposal. In the height-tables given in the report of the Provost Marshal General, the colored soldiers do not appear to have been separately considered; but there is ground for expectation that the extended discussion of the Medical and Vital Statistics of the Provost Marshal's Bureau, for which an appropriation has been made by Congress, and which has been intrusted to the very competent hands of Dr. J. H. Baxter, late Chief Medical

1 *Contributions to the Natural History of the New Zealand Race of Men*, Journal Statistical Society, XVIII. 27.

2 Péron, *Voyage aux Terres Australes*, II. 308.

3 *Journey to Ashango Land*, p. 319.

4 *Provost Marshal General's Report*, p. 69.

Officer of the Bureau, and author of the valuable tables already published, will largely contribute to our knowledge of this and kindred subjects.

After some fruitless endeavor to obtain satisfactory results by treating the pure negroes and the mulattoes separately, it was decided to assort them in two classes only, namely, those born in the Free States, and those born in the Slave States. The mean results from these two classes differ so little from each other, that it has also appeared advisable to combine the two tabulations. The tables accordingly present the two classes separately, and their aggregates.

TABLE XXI.

Mean Heights of Colored Soldiers, by Ages.

Age	Natives of Free States		Natives of Slave States		Total	
	Number	Height	Number	Height	Number	Height
		in.		in.		in.
Under 17	8	63.400	340	63.368	348	63.369
17	44	63.847	422	64.602	466	64.531
18	961	65.439	4 016	65.581	4 977	65.554
19	777	65.807	2 889	66.096	3 666	66.035
20	561	66.219	2 533	66.575	3 094	66.510
21	745	66.454	2 433	66.784	3 178	66.707
22	517	66.691	2 119	67.057	2 636	66.985
23	471	66.752	1 682	66.886	2 153	66.857
24	411	66.965	1 450	67.072	1 861	67.048
25	399	67.006	1 606	67.082	2 005	67.066
26	290	66.559	1 111	67.333	1 401	67.173
27	294	67.147	925	67.302	1 219	67.265
28	262	66.943	945	67.144	1 207	67.100
29	200	67.062	555	67.290	755	67.229
30	219	66.918	997	67.032	1 216	67.011
31 34	522	66.872	1 747	67.257	2 269	67.168
35 & over	1 397	67.125	5 767	67.108	7 164	67.111
Totals	8 078	66.538	31 537	66.685	39 615	66.655

Grouping the same data by periods of age, we find —

TABLE XXII.

Mean Heights of Colored Soldiers,
by Periods of Age.

Age	Natives of Free States		Natives of Slave States		Total	
	Number	Height	Number	Height	Number	Height
Under 21	2 351	65.710	10 200	65.859	12 551	65.831
21-23	1 733	66.606	6 234	66.904	7 967	66.840
24-26	1 100	66.872	4 167	67.145	5 267	67.088
27-30	975	67.023	3 422	67.178	4 397	67.144
31 & over	1 919	67.056	7 514	67.143	9 433	67.125
24 & over	3 994	66.998	15 103	67.151	19 097	67.119
Total	8 078	66.538	31 537	66.685	39 615	66.655

These figures indicate a somewhat inferior stature, but a rather longer continuance of growth for men of color, born in the Northern States. It will be borne in mind, in this connection, that the negro population in the North was chiefly confined to the States of the Atlantic seaboard, there being an extremely small number of this race in the Free States west of New York and Pennsylvania. Consequently those regions of the Free States, which produce the tallest men, were almost unrepresented among the black soldiers, and the small excess in stature, of negroes born in the Southern States, corresponds with that found for white natives of the same regions. The indications are also that the diminution of stature after attainment of the maximum, begins sooner and is more marked at its commencement, than is the case for the white race. How far this phenomenon is real, and if real, to what extent it may be explained by the condition of the Southern negroes, are difficult questions to decide.

In considering the law of growth deducible from these statistics of negro-stature, it must be remembered that the recorded ages are not as correct as for the whites. A large number of the blacks at the South are unable to state their age, and to a very considerable extent this must have been a subject of estimate by the mustering officer. This fact is well illustrated by the series of numbers of men at the several years of age in Table XXI. For natives of the Free States it will be seen that the successive numbers follow a law closely similar to that deduced for white soldiers; even the relative excess at twenty-one years and the corresponding deficiency at twenty being clearly manifest; while on the other hand the numbers for successive ages among the natives of Slave States are much farther from the regular gradations of an equable law. The corresponding mean statures must of course be somewhat affected.

For the colored sailors our data assume the following form: —

TABLE XXIII.

Mean Heights of Colored Sailors, by Ages.

Age	Natives of Free States		Natives of Slave States		Total	
	Number	Height	Number	Height	Number	Height
Under 17	56	61.768	105	62.069	161	61.964
17	40	64.013	75	64.077	115	64.054
18	104	64.954	161	64.887	265	64.913
19	79	65.111	158	65.359	237	65.276
20	71	66.035	229	65.762	300	65.827
21	203	65.789	299	65.738	502	65.759
22	136	66.075	241	66.009	377	66.033
23	110	65.918	189	66.209	299	66.102
24	72	65.951	148	66.373	220	66.235
25	83	66.307	160	66.437	243	66.393
26	48	66.380	103	66.570	151	66.510
27	41	66.585	89	66.090	130	66.246
28	56	66.473	79	65.981	135	66.183
29	46	65.462	47	66.463	93	65.968
30	40	67.269	97	66.224	137	66.529
31-34	89	66.337	133	66.641	222	66.519
35 & over	131	66.309	282	66.936	413	66.737
Total	1 405	65.753	2 595	65.867	4 000	65.827

TABLE XXIV.

Mean Heights of Colored Sailors, by Periods of Age.

Age	Natives of Free States		Natives of Slave States		Total	
	Number	Height	Number	Height	Number	Height
		in.		in.		in.
Under 21	350	64.591	728	64.775	1 078	64.715
21-23	449	65.908	729	65.950	1 178	65.934
24 26	203	66.198	411	66.448	614	66.315
27-30	183	66.418	312	66.159	495	66.255
31 & over	220	66.320	415	66.842	635	66.661
Total	1 405	65.753	2 595	65.867	4 000	65.827

The inferences already deduced, from comparison of the statures of sailors with those of soldiers, receive an entire corroboration from the statistics of negroes. Here too we find a great disparity between the statures of these two classes at all ages — the difference amounting to more than an inch for persons under twenty-one years, and gradually decreasing year by year. And the deduction is unavoidable, that the stature is permanently stunted and its rate of growth also affected by the influences of a nautical life.

Many minor indications of these tables will suggest themselves to the careful student; but the number of colored sailors upon which our inferences must be based is only 4000 in all, and does not warrant a more minute discussion.

After the close of the war full measurements were taken of about five hundred Indians of military age, belonging mostly to the Iroquois[1] people, and dwelling on their reservation near Buffalo. None were measured but those claiming and appearing to have no admixture of white blood; how far this assumption is correct must remain a matter of conjecture. All available men of this class above twenty-one years old were measured, as were also some below this limit of age, but no attempt was made at other discrimination or selection, so that the mean results fairly represent the

1 The Iroquois, or Six Nations, all originally belonged within the limits of the State of New York, and are composed of the Mohawk, Seneca, Oneida, Cayuga, Onondaga, and Tuscarora tribes.

Iroquois men. The dimensions in general will be given in their place, but the statures are presented here. The ages are probably correct.

TABLE XXV.

Heights and Ages of Iroquois Indians.

Age	Under 64	64–65	65–66	66–67	67–68	68–69	69–70	70–71	71–72	72–73	73–74	Over 74
16	–	–	–	–	–	1	–	–	–	–	–	–
18	–	–	–	2	–	–	–	–	–	–	–	–
19	–	–	–	1	1	–	–	2	1	1	–	–
20	–	–	3	1	3	1	–	–	–	1	1	–
21	–	1	1	3	3	5	–	–	–	1	–	–
22	–	–	6	8	10	5	1	–	–	–	–	–
23	–	–	4	1	14	7	3	1	1	1	–	–
24	–	–	2	2	22	7	5	1	–	2	–	–
25	–	–	1	2	4	4	–	3	–	–	–	–
26	–	–	4	8	14	12	5	1	1	–	–	–
27	–	–	1	–	8	12	2	3	2	–	–	–
28	1	1	2	2	16	12	3	1	–	–	–	–
29	–	–	–	3	14	11	5	4	1	1	–	–
30	–	–	–	–	5	7	6	3	1	–	–	–
31-34	–	–	–	2	24	21	11	4	3	3	–	–
35 & over	1	4	2	5	26	47	24	11	3	1	1	2
Total	2	6	26	40	164	152	65	34	13	11	2	2

The resultant mean statures are —

Age	Height	Number	Age	Height	Number
	in.			in.	
16	68.400	1	25	68.093	14
18	66.300	2	26	67.842	45
19	69.517	6	27	68.668	28
20	67.980	10	28	67.624	38
21	67.579	14	29	68.423	39
22	67.110	30	30	68.877	22
23	67.984	32	31-34	68.665	68
24	68.093	41	35 & over	68.583	127

and may be classified thus: —

Age	Height	Number
	in.	
16–20	68.311	19
21–23	67.564	76
24–26	67.980	100
27–30	68.317	127
31 & over	68.612	195

The two extremes were 61.4 for one man twenty-eight years old, and 75.7 for one over thirty-five. It will be perceived that the statures of these New York Indians are greater than those of natives of New York enlisted in the State, and that the growth of red men continues, like that of white and black men, until after the thirtieth year of age.

8. *Extremes of Stature.*

It has already been stated that all statures exceeding 76¾ inches (195 centimeters) have been regarded as excessive, and inquiries specially instituted to test their correctness, as also that the records have thus been found erroneous in about one sixth part of the cases. These excessive statures have been regarded as worthy of particular investigation, and no pains have been spared in investigating them. So too all statures below 61 inches (155 centimeters) have seemed worthy of separate tabulation, although here the defect of stature has been in a very large number of instances due to immaturity of age. Thus out of the 5445 instances among 1 104 841 enlistments (being less than the half of one per centum), where the height was below this limit of 61 inches, there were 1027 who were below the age of eighteen, and 1216 who gave their age as eighteen last birthday. Of these it has already been proved that a very considerable proportion had not probably attained this age. Of those who registered their age as nineteen and upwards, only 3202, or about two sevenths of one per cent. of the entire number were below this stature.

We will first consider the extremely large statures, under which title all are comprehended whose height amounts to 75 inches (190.5 centimeters). There are of this class 3613 instances, or about one third of one per cent.

From the distribution of statures of French conscripts, published by Hargenvilliers in 1817 in the pamphlet already cited, Quetelet has computed[1] that out of each million of men there were —

[1] *Theorie des Probabilités*, p. 148.

1186 at and over the stature of 191.5, and below that of 131.5 centim.
26 at and over the stature of 201.5, and below that of 121.5 centim.
1 at and over the stature of 211.5, and below that of 111.5 centim.

Liharžik, in his elaborate and learned work on "Proportionality in Nature as based upon the Square numbers," gives[1] the minimum height observed for a dwarf, as 86 centimeters (33.86 inches), and as the maximum height that of the "giant" Murphy, which was 210 centimeters, or 82.7 inches.

Several well authenticated cases are on record, of men largely exceeding eight feet in height, reaching the stature of 255 to 259 centimeters, also of well-proportioned dwarves from 75 to 92 centimeters.

On the other hand, our own data show for each million of men —

3270	at and	over the	stature of	75	inches, or	190.5	centimeters
1180	"	"	"	76	"	193.0	"
360	"	"	"	77	"	195.6	"
169	"	"	"	78	"	198.1	"
47	"	"	"	79	"	200.7	"
22	"	"	"	80	"	203.2	"
11	"	"	"	81	"	205.7	"
7	"	"	"	82	"	208.3	"
6	"	"	"	83	"	210.8	"
2	"	"	"	84	"	213.4	"

These numbers are, however, derived from enlisted men of all ages, and if we restrict ourselves to the men between twenty and twenty-one years of age, we find, for each million of men, the proportionate numbers as follows: —

2761	at and over	75	inches, or	190.5	centimeters.
1012	"	76	"	193.0	"
342	"	77	"	195.6	"
171	"	78	"	198.1	"
92	"	79	"	200.7	"
53	"	80	"	203.2	"
26	"	81	"	205.7	"
13	"	82	"	208.3	"
13	"	83	"	210.8	"

thus indicating a larger proportion of extreme cases than were found among the French conscripts. The tables here appended show the entire number of extremely high statures found, after correcting the errors discovered by special inquiry. The first,

[1] *Das Quadrat die Grundlage aller Proportionalität in der Natur*, etc., Vienna, 1865, p. 211.

(XXVI.,) shows the actual number at each year of age, by gradations of single inches, and is followed by a corresponding one which presents the same data in the form of proportional numbers for each 100 000 men of the same age. The line entitled "Total" in this table (XXVII.), indicates the proportional number at each height, without reference to the age. The next pair of tables is similar to these, except that the division into groups is by States of Enlistment instead of Age; while the two following these give in like manner the classification by Heights and Nativities, and the next two that by Ages and Nativities. Doubtless many other enlisted men passed the limit of 75 inches by growth subsequent to enlistment, and an estimate on this point may be attained by means of Table XXXIV., which is based upon the same materials as Table XXXIII., but presents the proportional numbers at and over 75 inches for each 10 000 men of the same age, as well as of the same nativity, thus indicating the increase of the relative numbers with increasing years. The headings are to be understood as including the first-named and excluding the last-named stature.

TABLE XXVI.

Number of Soldiers upwards of 75 Inches tall, by Heights and Ages.

Age.	75-76	76-77	77-78	78-79	79-80	80-81	81-82	82-83	83-84	84-85	Total
17	5	–	–	–	–	–	–	–	–	–	5
18	103	31	8	6	2	2			1	–	153
19	108	56	10	5	4	–			–	–	183
20	133	51	13	6	3	2	1	–	1	–	210
21	226	71	16	8	3	–	1	–	1	–	326
22	176	61	17	11	1	2	–	–	–	1	269
23	156	63	16	12	2	–	1	–	–	–	250
24	142	52	14	9	–	–	–	1	–	–	218
25	120	62	10	11	2	–	–	–	2	–	207
26	108	51	14	3	1	1	–	–	–	–	178
27	100	38	13	8	–	–	–	–	–	0	159
28	99	46	10	7	–	–	–	–	–	1	163
29	72	35	7	2	1	–	–	–	–	–	117
30	65	29	9	6	1	–	–	–	–	–	110
31–34	277	104	22	17	3	1	–	–	–	–	424
35 & over	419	156	32	24	5	4	1	–	–	–	641
Total	2309	906	211	135	28	12	4	1	5	2	3613

TABLE XXVII.

Proportional number of Tall Men, in each 100 000 *of same Age, by Heights and Ages.*

Age	75-76	76-77	77-78	78-79	79-80	80-81	81-82	82-88	83-84	84-85	Total
17	46	–	–	–	–	–	–	–	–	–	46
18	61	18	5	4	1	1	–	–	1	–	91
19	119	61	11	6	4	–	–	–	–	–	201
20	175	67	17	8	4	3	1	–	1	–	276
21	232	73	17	8	3	–	1	–	1	–	335
22	239	83	23	15	1	3	–	–	–	1	365
23	247	100	25	19	3	–	2	–	–	–	396
24	262	96	26	16	–	–	–	2	–	–	402
25	252	130	21	23	4	–	–	–	4	–	434
26	258	122	34	7	2	2	–	–	–	–	425
27	268	102	35	21	–	–	–	–	–	–	426
28	262	121	26	18	–	–	–	–	–	3	430
29	263	128	26	7	4	–	–	–	–	–	428
30	215	96	30	20	3	–	–	–	–	–	364
31-34	333	125	26	21	4	1	–	–	–	–	510
35 & over	262	97	20	15	3	3	1	–	–	–	401
Total	209	82	19	12	3	1	0.5	0	0.5	0	327

TABLE XXVIII.

Number of Soldiers upwards of 75 *Inches tall, by Heights and States of Enlistment.*

Height	Me.	N. H.	Vt.	Mass.	R. I. & Conn.	N. Y.	N. J.	Penn.	Md.	W. Va.
75-76	147	34	40	29	39	169	7	82	9	72
76-77	47	12	12	2	18	61	2	27	1	18
77-78	9	2	4	3	1	5	–	6	1	3
78-79	8	1	–	–	1	3	–	2	1	1
79-80		1	1	2	1	–	1	1	1	–
80-81	1	–	1	–	–	–	–	–	–	–
81-82	–	–	–	–	–	–	–	–	–	–
82-83	–	–	–	–	–	–	–	–	–	–
83-84	–	–	–	–	–	–	–	–	–	–
84-85	–	–	–	–	–	–	–	–	–	–
Total	212	50	58	36	60	238	10	118	13	94

TABLE XXIX.

Proportional Number of Tall Men in each 100 000 *from same State, by Heights and States of Enlistment.*

Height	Me.	N. H.	Vt.	Mass.	R. I. & Conn.	N. Y.	N. J.	Penn.	Md.	W. Va.
75-76	281	127	166	71	95	90	37	105	123	410
76-77	90	45	50	5	44	32	11	35	14	102
77-78	17	7	17	7	2	3	–	8	13	17
78-79	15	4	–	–	2	2	–	3	14	6
79-80	–	4	4	5	2	–	5	1	13	–
80-81	2	–	4	–	–	–	–	–	–	–
81-82	–	–	–	–	–	–	–	–	–	–
82-83	–	–	–	–	–	–	–	–	–	–
83-84	–	–	–	–	–	–	–	–	–	–
84-85	–	–	–	–	–	–	–	–	–	–
Total	405	187	241	88	145	127	53	152	177	535

TABLE XXVIII. — (*Continued.*)

Number of Soldiers upwards of 75 *Inches tall, by Heights and States of Enlistment.*

Height	Ky.	Ohio	Ind.	Ill.	Mich.	Wis.	Minn.	Iowa	Mo.	La.	Total
75-76	100	241	367	541	32	96	8	102	188	6	2 309
76-77	29	111	159	14	34	248	31	5	72	3	906
77-78	7	24	35	12	6	53	15	1	23	1	211
78-79	6	13	26	6	2	41	9	–	15	–	135
79-80	1	2	6	1	1	5	1	2	1	–	28
80-81	–	1	2	1	3	3	–	–	–	–	12
81-82	–	–	1	1	–	2	–	–	–	–	4
82-83	–	–	1	–	–	–	–	–	–	–	1
83-84	–	–	1	–	–	3	1	–	–	–	5
84-85	–	1	–	–	–	–	–	–	1	–	2
Total	143	393	598	576	78	451	65	110	300	10	3 613

TABLE XXIX. — (*Continued.*)

Proportional Number of Tall Men in each 100 000 *from same State, by Heights and States of Enlistment.*

Height	Ky.	Ohio	Ind.	Ill.	Mich.	Wis.	Minn.	Iowa	Mo.	La.	Total
75-76	417	223	310	287	137	187	120	345	327	232	209
76-77	121	102	134	7	146	484	463	17	125	116	82
77-78	29	22	30	6	26	104	224	3	40	39	19
78-79	25	12	22	3	8	80	134	–	26	–	12
79-80	4	2	5	1	4	10	15	7	2	–	3
80-81	–	1	2	1	13	6	–	–	–	–	1
81-82	–	–	1	1	–	4	–	–	–	–	0.5
82-83	–	–	1	–	–	–	–	–	–	–	–
83-84	–	–	1	–	–	6	15	–	–	–	0.5
84-85	–	1	–	–	–	–	–	–	2	–	–
Total	596	363	506	306	334	881	971	372	522	387	327

TABLE XXX.

Number of Soldiers upwards of 75 *Inches tall, by Heights and Nativities.*

Height	New Eng.	N. Y., N. J., and Penn.	Ohio and Indiana	Mich., Wis., and Ill.	Slave States not including F and G_2	Ken. and Tenn.	Free States W of Miss. River	Slave States W of Miss. River	British Prov. excl. of Canada	Canada
75-76	302	414	663	202	189	274	4	60	11	40
76-77	106	173	295	76	52	103	2	22	4	11
77-78	22	32	68	25	14	26	–	8	–	2
78-79	12	14	35	21	11	18	1	7	–	3
79-80	5	8	7	2	2	2	–	–	–	–
80-81	2	3	1	3	–	1	–	–	–	–
81-82	–	1	1	1	–	1	–	–	–	–
82-83	–	–	1	–	–	–	–	–	–	–
83-84	–	–	2	2	–	1	–	–	–	–
84-85	–	2	–	–	–	–	–	–	–	–
Total	449	647	1 073	332	268	426	7	97	15	56

TABLE XXXI.

Proportional Number of Tall Men, in each 100 000 *of same Nativity, by Heights and Nativities.*

Height	New Eng.	N. Y., N. J., and Penn.	Ohio and Indiana	Mich., Wis, and Ill.	Slave States not including F and G_2	Ken. and Tenn.	Free States W. of Miss. River	Slave States W. of Miss. River	British Prov. excl. of Canada	Canada
75-76	198	152	301	284	423	545	105	352	174	126
76-77	70	63	134	107	117	205	53	129	63	35
77-78	15	12	31	35	31	52	–	47	–	6
78-79	8	5	16	29	25	36	26	41	–	10
79-80	3	3	3	3	4	4	–	–	–	–
80-81	1	1	–	4	–	2	–	–	–	–
81-82	–	–	–	1	–	2	–	–	–	–
82-83	–	–	–	–	–	–	–	–	–	–
83-84	–	–	1	3	–	2	–	–	–	–
84-85	–	1	–	–	–	–	–	–	–	–
Total	295	237	486	466	600	848	184	569	237	177

TABLE XXX. — (*Continued.*)

Number of Soldiers upwards of 75 *Inches tall, by Heights and Nativities.*

Height	Eng.	Scot.	Ire-land.	Fr., Belg., & Switz.	Ger.	Scand.	Spain, etc.	Miscel.	Total
75-76	18	7	46	5	58	9	2	5	2 309
76-77	9	4	16	4	25	4	–	–	906
77-78	3	2	2	1	6	–	–	–	211
78-79	1	–	4	2	5	1	–	–	135
79-80	–	–	1	1	–	–	–	–	28
80-81	–	–	1	–	–	1	–	–	12
81-82	–	–	–	–	–	–	–	–	4
82-83	–	–	–	–	–	–	–	–	1
83-84	–	–	–	–	–	–	–	–	5
84-85	–	–	–	–	–	–	–	–	2
Total	31	13	70	13	94	15	2	5	3 613

TABLE XXXI. — (*Continued.*)

Proportional Number of Tall Men, in each 100 000 *of same Nativity, by Heights and Nativities.*

Height	Eng.	Scot.	Ire-land	Fr., Belg., & Switz.	Ger.	Scand.	Spain, etc.	Miscel.	Total
75-76	60	96	55	73	65	132	223	52	209
76-77	30	55	19	59	28	59	–	–	82
77-78	10	27	3	15	7	–	–	–	19
78-79	3	–	5	29	6	15	–	–	12
79-80	–	–	1	15	–	–	–	–	3
80-81	–	–	1	–	–	15	–	–	1
81-82	–	–	–	–	–	–	–	–	0.5
82-83	–	–	–	–	–	–	–	–	–
83-84	–	–	–	–	–	–	–	–	0.5
84-85	–	–	–	–	–	–	–	–	–
Total	103	178	84	191	106	221	223	52	327

TABLE XXXII.

Number of Soldiers upwards of 75 Inches tall, by Ages and Nativities.

Age	New Eng.	N. Y., N. J., and Penn.	Ohio and Indiana	Mich., Wis., and Ill.	Slave States not including F and G_2	Ken. and Tenn.	Free States W. of Miss. River	Slave States W. of Miss. River	British Prov. excl. of Canada
17	–	–	3	1	–	–	–	1	–
18	19	13	54	22	12	14	–	6	–
19	20	23	60	27	10	21	2	7	1
20	32	21	80	25	12	23	2	7	–
21	35	71	99	46	14	25	1	11	2
22	35	48	80	31	16	28	–	11	1
23	29	48	84	26	19	20	–	12	1
24	30	41	42	28	19	25	1	8	3
25	27	34	61	21	11	22	–	9	3
26	19	34	43	20	19	20	–	3	1
27	25	27	54	14	9	13	–	3	–
28	17	24	62	15	11	23	–	3	–
29	14	24	39	5	11	12	–	2	–
30	9	24	26	15	12	13	–	1	–
31–34	54	71	134	22	28	73	1	5	1
35 & over	84	144	152	14	65	94	–	8	2
Total	449	647	1 073	332	268	426	7	97	15

TABLE XXXII. — (*Continued.*)

Number of Soldiers upwards of 75 Inches tall, by Ages and Nativities.

Age	Canada	Eng.	Scot.	Ireland	Fr., Belg., & Switz.	Ger.	Scand.	Spain, etc.	Miscel.	Total
17	–	–	–	–	–	–	–	–	–	5
18	2	4	–	3	1	3	–	–	–	153
19	4	–	–	1	1	5	1	–	–	183
20	2	–	2	2	–	2	–	–	–	210
21	5	2	1	2	3	9	–	–	–	326
22	5	2	–	6	2	3	1	–	–	269
23	1	1	–	3	–	5	1	–	–	250
24	6	–	2	7	1	5	–	–	–	218
25	5	2	2	8	1	1	–	–	–	207
26	5	3	1	5	–	4	–	–	1	178
27	5	2	1	3	–	3	–	–	–	159
28	1	–	1	1	–	5	–	–	–	163
29	3	–	–	2	–	3	1	–	1	117
30	–	1	1	3	–	3	2	–	–	110
31–34	5	5	–	9	1	12	3	–	–	424
35 & over	7	9	2	15	3	31	6	2	3	641
Total	56	31	13	70	13	94	15	2	5	3 613

TABLE XXXIII.

Proportional Number of Tall Men in each 100 000 *of same Nativity, by Ages and Nativities.*

Age	New Eng.	N. Y., N. J., and Penn.	Ohio and Indiana	Mich., Wis., and Ill.	Slave States not including F and G[2]	Ken. and Tenn.	Free States W. of Miss. River	Slave States W. of Miss. River	British Prov. excl. of Canada
17	–	–	1	1	–	–	–	6	–
18	12	5	24	31	27	28	–	35	–
19	13	8	27	38	22	42	53	41	16
20	21	8	36	35	27	46	53	41	–
21	23	26	45	65	31	50	26	64	31
22	23	18	36	44	35	55	–	64	16
23	19	18	38	36	43	40	–	70	16
24	20	15	19	39	43	50	26	47	47
25	18	12	28	29	25	44	–	53	47
26	12	12	20	28	43	40	–	18	16
27	17	10	24	20	20	26	–	18	–
28	11	9	28	21	25	46	–	18	–
29	9	9	18	7	25	24	–	12	–
30	6	9	12	21	27	26	–	6	–
31-34	36	26	61	31	62	145	26	29	16
35 & over	55	52	69	20	145	186	–	47	32
Total	295	237	486	466	600	848	184	569	237

TABLE XXXIII. — (*Continued.*)

Proportional Number of Tall Men in each 100 000 *of same Nativity, by Ages and Nativities.*

Age	Canada	Eng.	Scot.	Ireland	Fr., Belg., & Switz.	Ger.	Scand.	Spain, etc.	Miscel.	Total
17	–	–	–	–	–	–	–	–	–	–
18	6	13	–	4	14	3	–	–	–	14
19	13	–	–	1	15	6	15	–	–	17
20	6	–	27	2	–	2	–	–	–	19
21	16	7	14	2	44	10	–	–	–	29
22	16	7	–	7	29	3	15	–	–	24
23	3	3	–	4	–	6	15	–	–	23
24	19	–	27	8	15	6	–	–	–	20
25	16	7	27	10	15	1	–	–	–	19
26	16	10	14	6	–	5	–	–	10	16
27	16	7	14	4	–	3	–	–	–	14
28	3	–	14	1	–	6	–	–	–	15
29	9	–	–	2	–	3	15	–	10	11
30	–	3	14	4	–	3	29	–	–	10
31-34	16	16	–	11	15	14	44	–	–	38
35 & over	22	30	27	18	44	35	88	223	32	58
Total	177	103	178	84	191	106	221	223	52	327

TABLE XXXIV.

Proportional number of Tall Men in each 10 000 *of same Age and Nativity.*

Age	New Eng.	N. Y., N. J., and Penn.	Ohio and Indiana	Mich., Wis., and Ill.	Slave States not including F and G_2	Ken. and Tenn.	Free States W. of Miss. River	Slave States W. of Miss. River	British Prov. excl. of Canada
17	–	–	13	6	–	–	–	28	–
18	7	3	12	12	19	18	–	14	–
19	15	10	28	30	29	56	39	33	24
20	32	11	44	37	43	67	55	40	–
21	24	28	52	65	41	70	28	59	23
22	36	27	54	57	57	91	–	84	17
23	34	31	65	63	77	71	–	121	20
24	43	31	38	78	93	100	114	112	74
25	44	31	67	80	58	100	–	137	92
26	34	33	54	96	116	103	–	64	37
27	50	29	76	86	64	80	–	88	–
28	35	27	88	105	73	135	–	93	–
29	38	35	79	50	101	98	–	87	–
30	24	35	51	151	101	92	–	46	–
31–34	49	34	95	97	78	181	454	92	22
35 & over	37	35	76	61	76	107	–	118	27
Total	29	24	49	47	60	85	18	57	24

TABLE XXXIV. — (*Continued.*)

Proportional Number of Tall Men in each 10 000 *of same Age and Nativity.*

Age	Canada	Engl.	Scotl.	Ireland	France, etc.	Germ.	Scand.	Spain, etc.	Miscel.	Total
17	–	–	–	–	–	–	–	–	–	5
18	5	18	–	7	30	5	–	–	–	9
19	13	–	–	2	39	12	30	–	–	20
20	9	–	61	5	–	5	–	–	–	28
21	13	8	21	3	70	16	–	–	–	33
22	18	9	–	9	61	6	22	–	–	36
23	5	5	–	6	–	11	29	–	–	40
24	36	–	56	16	26	11	–	–	–	40
25	35	14	58	17	27	2	–	–	–	43
26	40	25	30	13	–	10	–	–	22	42
27	47	17	33	8	–	8	–	–	–	43
28	9	–	30	2	–	12	–	–	–	43
29	40	–	–	8	–	10	48	–	36	43
30	–	9	32	8	–	8	73	–	–	36
31-34	27	17	–	12	12	11	45	–	–	51
35 & over	19	15	11	9	17	14	42	250	15	40
Total	18	10	18	8	19	11	22	22	5	33

During the investigation of the correctness of the records for cases of extreme height, a very considerable number of similar cases among the earlier volunteers were brought to our knowledge; and it seems probable that the proportion of very tall men, among the troops whose descriptive musters are not on file, was at least not inferior to that among the later enlistments from which our statistics are necesssarily derived.

Among our own data 51 cases of statures not less than 80 inches were recorded; but many of these were found erroneous on special investigation. Great exertions were made to obtain information regarding others, who are recorded as follows on the official musters: —

Regiment	Height	Age	Place of Birth
Unassigned Maine Infantry .	80 inches	26	Maine,
7th Vermont Infantry . . .	80 "	40	Vermont,
128th New York Infantry . .	81 "	21	Ireland,
100th Ohio Infantry	84 "	22	New York,

Regiment	Height	Age	Place of Birth
169th Ohio Infantry	80 inches	37	Ireland,
29th Indiana Infantry . . .	80½ "	20	Ohio,[1]
59th Indiana Infantry . . .	83¾ "	30	Indiana,
59th Indiana Infantry . . .	83½ "	38	Indiana,
81st Indiana Infantry . . .	80½ "	23	Indiana,
89th Indiana Infantry . . .	82 "	24	Ohio,
153d Indiana Infantry . . .	83 "	25	Ohio,
1st Indiana Artillery	80 "	31	Kentucky,
31st Illinois Infantry	81½ "	21	Tennessee,
106th Illinois Infantry . . .	83¾ "	25	Illinois,
109th Illinois Infantry . . .	80 "	22	Illinois,
149th Illinois Infantry . . .	83½ "	18	Ohio,
Unassigned Illinois Infantry .	80 "	18	Illinois,
Unassigned Illinois Infantry .	83 "	20	Illinois,
Unassigned Illinois Infantry .	80 "	20	Illinois,
11th Michigan Cavalry . .	80 "	22	New York,
1st Michigan Artillery . .	81½ "	20	Michigan,
8th Wisconsin Infantry . .	80 "	20	New York,[2]
46th Wisconsin Infantry . .	80 "	39	Norway,
46th Wisconsin Infantry . .	80 "	39	New York,
26th Missouri Infantry . . .	84¾ "	28	Pennsylvania.

The tallest man for whose stature the testimony is complete and unimpeachable, is Lieutenant Van Buskirk, of the 27th Indiana Infantry. General Silas Colgrove, formerly colonel of that regiment, writes that he has frequently seen him measured, and that his stature was fully 82½ inches, without shoes, or 209.5 centimeters. General Colgrove adds that he was a brave man, and bore the fatigues of marching as well as most men of ordinary stature.

Corporal Ira Stout, of the 50th Indiana Infantry, Company E, was 24 years of age, and 81 inches high (205.7 centimeters) at the date of his enlistment, September 1861. He was born in Ohio County, Indiana, was a farmer by occupation, had blue eyes, light hair, and fair complexion. This information is corroborated by Captain Percy Rous, his commanding officer, who states that the man was soon discharged on account of disability, and had done but little marching at the time.

Colonel Gregory, of the 29th Indiana Infantry, has obtained for us precise information from Captain Charles Ream, of Company K, concerning one of his men, for whom he confirms the record. The somewhat inappropriate name of this man was John Bunch; he was born in Ohio, and at his enlistment, September 1861, was

[1] Confirmed. [2] Confirmed.

20 years old, 80½ inches tall (204.5 centimeters), by occupation a farmer, with hazel eyes, light hair, and light complexion. He was a notorious skulker, was never with the regiment in a single battle, and deserted in August 1862. He was known in the regiment as the "United States Ramrod."

Colonel M. W. Tappan, of the 1st New Hampshire Infantry (3 months' regiment), believes our information to be correct in the case of Joseph H. Harris, of that regiment, also 80½ inches (204.5 centimeters) in height, aged 26 years, born in Vermont, by occupation a mechanic, eyes blue, hair brown, complexion dark.

Captain J. B. Redfield, formerly commanding Company A of the 8th Wisconsin Volunteers, vouches for the record concerning a man in that company, Andrew J. Sanders, who was born in New York, and was at his enlistment 20 years old, and 80 inches (203.2 centimeters) in height.

These are the five tallest men whose cases are well identified, but only two of them, Bunch and Sanders, are included in our tables. The circumstance that three of them are from Indiana, may be perhaps explained by the especially careful inquiries which were made in that State, on account of the high average stature of its inhabitants. The testimony is overwhelming that very tall men do not bear the fatigues of a campaign so well as persons of ordinary stature; that they are less capable of performing long marches, and are more frequently on the sick list at other times.[1]

The statistics for persons of under-stature are neither so interesting nor valuable as those for very tall men, even if we consider only those whose small size is not fairly attributable to the non-attainment of full stature. The number of men under 61 inches who have reached the age of 23½ years (23 last birthday), is 1951, or about thirteen twenty-fourths of the number of men 75 inches tall. Of the whole number of "short men," about 54 per centum were under 21 years of age, and the number of those whose subsequent growth would carry them past the limit of 61 inches cannot well be determined. But if we assume the number who would remain below this limit after attaining their full stature to be proportional to the number of men who have reached the age of 25 without reaching the height of 61 inches, we should have 3692 as the number of men included in our statistics, whose full stature

1 The general conviction of medical men seems to be decided, that the mortality among tall men is greater than among short men. Thus, Sir George Ballingall, in his *Outlines of Military Surgery*, 5th ed., p. 34, says, "Tall men are more subject to disease generally, and especially to diseases of the chronic class, than men of medium size, and they are frequently the first to fail under fatigue."

would not attain this height. In the tables presenting the statistics of enlisted men under 61 inches, the line of Totals shows the effect of growth after enlistment in a striking manner, since the relative numbers continue to diminish until the age of 29. Here too the effect of misstatement of age appears in a very distinct form in the numbers for 20 and 21 years. On the other hand, the number of men who were less than 75 inches high at the time of their enlistment, but who must have passed that limit of stature in their subsequent growth, is doubtless quite considerable. This is abundantly shown by the last column of Table XXVI., which exhibits a progressive increase of the actual number of tall men until the age of 21, although the total number of enlistments rapidly decreases with the age after 18; and by Table XXVII., in which a progressive increase of the relative number is manifest until the age of 25 at last birthday. Applying, as before, to our whole number of men, the ratio deduced from the records of men above 25, we should find 4747 as the probable number of men whose stature was not less than 75 inches, and our numbers would thus be changed from 3613 tall and 5445 short, to 4747 tall and 3692 short men.

The disproportion between these two classes of men in the population is probably yet greater than these figures would indicate, inasmuch as the tendency to enlist cannot have been so great for very tall as for very short men. Obvious considerations of comfort and incommensurate exposure point to this inference, so that in all likelihood the very tall men were much less fully represented in the army than in the population.

No especial scrutiny has been instituted to test the accuracy of the records for short men excepting in some extreme cases; but the indications are, that could we deal with an equally large number of men who had attained their full stature, taken at random from the population, the number of those whose stature attains the limit of 75 inches would be found nearly, if not quite, twice as large, and that of those who reach the limit of 76 inches one half as large, as the number of those whose full stature falls short of 61 inches.

Among the descriptive musters of very short men there are four cases of men at ages near, or subsequent to, that of full stature, whose height did not exceed 53¾ inches (or 136.5 centimeters).

The shortest man for whom the record is satisfactorily verified was a member of the 192d Ohio Infantry; at the time of enlistment he was 24 years old, and 40 inches in height. Colonel F. W.

Butterfield, his commanding officer, vouches for the correctness of this record. He also assures us that he knew the man well, and that there was no soldier in his command who could endure a greater amount of fatigue or exposure.

In the musters of the 128th Indiana Infantry is described a man 44 years old and 49 inches in height. General R. P. De Hart, formerly colonel of this regiment, confirms the statement, and states that the man was a good soldier, and able to bear the hardships of a campaign as well as men of medium stature.

One man is recorded as 39½ inches in height, but concerning him we have not succeeded in obtaining special information.

Four tables will suffice for these statistics. Both for the States where enlisted, and for the Nativities, one table gives the actual number of men below 61 inches, recorded at each age, and another, analogous to Table XXXIV., shows the corresponding proportional number for each 10 000 men of the same class.

TABLE XXXV.

Number of Soldiers below 61 *Inches in Height, by Ages and States.*

Age	Me.	N. H.	Vt.	Mass.	R. I. & Conn.	N. Y.	N. J.	Penn.	Md.	W. Va.
Under 17	17	21	8	15	24	165	5	19	17	11
17	3	1	4	5	6	55	–	17	6	1
18	35	13	9	24	29	288	8	58	17	14
19	14	11	1	10	8	123	5	29	3	1
20	8	11	3	7	7	86	6	11	2	1
21	14	10	8	11	9	121	6	21	3	5
22	5	5	3	10	14	87	11	22	–	1
23	4	6	4	1	7	79	2	18	1	1
24	10	6	4	11	9	55	6	8	2	2
25	3	4	5	4	8	60	4	6	–	–
26	3	2	3	8	6	57	3	5	–	–
27	3	4	1	4	5	33	2	3	–	–
28	1	5	–	6	6	45	4	4	–	–
29	–	–	–	–	4	21	3	6	–	–
30	1	2	1	4	5	41	1	1	1	–
31–34	6	5	–	9	13	117	1	20	2	–
35 & over	11	10	7	16	9	212	21	28	–	2
Total	138	116	61	145	169	1 645	88	276	54	39

TABLE XXXV.—(*Continued.*)

Number of Soldiers below 61 *Inches in Height, by Ages and States.*

Age	Ky.	Ohio	Ind.	Ill.	Mich.	Wis.	Minn.	Iowa	Mo.	La.	Totals
Under 17	13	80	45	153	1	7	6	20	123	14	764
17	12	27	12	50	2	8	10	8	35	1	263
18	99	81	187	179	18	33	13	36	73	2	1 216
19	25	24	45	39	5	21	1	11	20	–	396
20	14	26	30	33	5	14	1	9	8	–	282
21	8	14	13	27	12	17	–	7	18	1	325
22	12	7	15	25	6	7	1	2	13	2	248
23	8	19	13	31	3	6	–	2	10	–	215
24	4	14	22	15	–	6	2	2	3	–	181
25	13	12	15	11	4	4	–	1	12	–	166
26	4	6	12	9	5	9	2	–	8	–	142
27	4	7	13	11	3	9	–	4	4	–	110
28	2	7	9	9	3	6	1	1	4	–	113
29	1	9	4	8	7	5	–	–	2	1	71
30	4	11	5	7	4	3	–	1	8	–	100
31-34	4	25	19	24	8	18	3	2	14	–	290
35 & over	13	39	42	57	16	32	4	10	32	2	563
Total	240	408	501	688	102	205	44	116	387	23	5 445

TABLE XXXVI.

Proportional Number of Short Men in each 10 000 *of same Age and State.*

Age	Me.	N. H.	Vt.	Mass.	R. I. & Conn.	N. Y.	N. J.	Penn.	Md.	W. Va.
Under 17	2152	2442	1356	2500	2857	2276	2273	460	3400	1170
17	224	110	256	397	414	403	–	123	682	41
18	37	41	22	45	64	114	81	53	166	41
19	32	56	5	27	26	82	39	41	44	6
20	23	60	18	25	27	78	41	18	35	8
21	26	31	29	21	21	63	31	33	43	34
22	14	22	18	32	42	66	62	46	–	8
23	14	33	28	4	25	73	14	43	20	10
24	41	45	34	55	41	61	48	23	56	25
25	14	31	51	24	40	73	39	21	–	–
26	16	20	35	52	35	79	34	18	–	–
27	18	42	13	30	34	51	26	12	–	–
28	6	50	–	43	37	69	51	16	–	–
29	–	–	–	–	35	47	58	32	–	–
30	8	27	19	36	40	79	16	5	61	–
31–34	17	27	–	32	40	81	6	34	41	–
35 & over	15	29	22	31	15	71	82	22	–	8
Total	26	43	25	35	41	87	47	35	74	22

TABLE XXXVI. — (*Continued.*)

Proportional Number of Short Men in each 10 000 *of same Age and State.*

Age	Ky.	Ohio	Ind.	Ill.	Mich.	Wis.	Minn.	Iowa	Mo.	La.	Totals
Under 17	903	1619	1667	1310	34	288	811	1316	2854	5833	1537
17	461	238	189	198	30	156	621	208	475	833	243
18	217	41	85	62	57	48	160	52	100	164	72
19	119	26	43	24	31	61	31	43	49	–	43
20	68	32	32	25	29	47	39	56	21	–	37
21	45	18	13	18	72	46	–	32	40	83	33
22	74	11	19	19	47	25	32	13	36	146	34
23	58	33	19	27	24	24	–	15	30	–	34
24	33	28	37	15	–	26	78	17	11	–	33
25	127	28	31	12	44	20	–	9	43	–	35
26	46	15	28	12	57	50	91	–	32	–	34
27	56	20	35	17	41	50	–	41	20	–	29
28	27	19	23	14	38	33	37	11	19	–	30
29	20	33	14	17	108	35	–	–	14	98	26
30	62	37	17	13	60	19	–	13	42	–	33
31–34	30	29	23	18	42	37	38	9	29	–	35
35 & over	43	25	30	24	40	30	27	23	34	29	35
Total	100	38	42	36	44	40	66	39	67	89	49

TABLE XXXVII.

Number of Soldiers below 61 *Inches in Height, by Ages and Nativities.*

Age	New Eng.	N. Y., N. J., and Penn.	Ohio and Indiana	Mich., Wisc., and Ill.	Slave States not including F and G2	Ken. and Tenn.	Free States W. of Miss. River	Slave States W. of Miss. River	British Prov. excl. of Canada
Under 17	89	217	131	77	33	23	15	51	2
17	18	69	44	24	9	25	7	16	–
18	97	316	264	115	56	94	22	42	7
19	35	110	63	27	9	29	5	7	3
20	27	69	55	19	7	11	1	4	2
21	29	100	33	16	13	10	2	11	6
22	24	66	23	15	3	13	1	6	1
23	16	61	29	14	7	13	–	2	2
24	23	38	21	8	6	8	–	2	3
25	15	37	24	5	6	10	–	2	–
26	12	45	13	4	2	6	1	–	1
27	11	21	18	5	2	3	–	–	–
28	9	31	13	1	3	1	–	–	2
29	2	24	7	2	1	1	–	1	–
30	9	20	15	1	4	1	–	–	–
31-34	25	77	25	4	10	9	1	2	1
35 & over	36	179	52	4	12	11	–	1	2
Total	477	1 480	830	341	183	268	55	147	32

TABLE XXXVII. — (*Continued.*)

Number of Soldiers below 61 *Inches in Height, by Age and Nativity.*

Age	Canada	Engl.	Scotl.	Ireland	France, etc.	Germ.	Scand.	Spain, etc.	Miscel.	Total
Under 17	6	20	2	24	6	59	3	–	6	764
17	3	11	–	11	1	21	1	1	2	263
18	28	30	3	49	3	80	–	1	9	1 216
19	15	13	5	20	3	43	–	1	8	396
20	9	10	5	17	3	40	–	1	2	282
21	18	18	1	28	2	33	1	2	2	325
22	10	11	4	27	2	37	1	2	2	248
23	9	12	2	16	3	26	1	–	2	215
24	3	14	2	8	5	32	1	2	5	181
25	8	8	–	17	2	26	–	–	6	166
26	9	6	1	9	2	25	4	–	2	142
27	2	4	1	13	1	25	–	–	4	110
28	3	3	–	14	3	29	1	–	–	113
29	3	3	2	4	4	16	–	–	1	71
30	4	4	3	17	3	18	1	–	–	100
31 34	4	15	4	36	9	57	2	–	9	290
35 & over	21	26	10	61	13	120	6	1	8	563
Total	155	208	45	371	65	687	22	11	68	5 445

TABLE XXXVIII.

Proportional Number of Short Men in each 10 000, *of same Age and Nativity.*

Age	New Eng.	N. Y., N. J., and Penn.	Ohio and Indiana	Mich., Wisc., and Ill.	Slave States not including F and G_2	Ken. and Tenn.	Free States W. of Miss. River	Slave States W. of Miss. River	British Prov. excl. of Canada
Under 17	2 055	1 446	1 356	869	1 765	1 050	2 419	2 217	2 857
17	222	199	188	136	204	563	551	447	–
18	38	76	59	63	90	124	126	98	129
19	27	48	30	30	26	77	97	33	71
20	27	38	30	28	25	32	27	23	53
21	20	40	17	22	38	28	55	59	69
22	24	38	16	28	11	42	51	46	17
23	19	40	22	34	28	46	–	20	41
24	33	29	19	22	29	32	–	28	74
25	24	33	26	19	32	46	–	30	–
26	22	44	16	19	12	31	294	–	37
27	22	23	25	31	14	18	–	–	–
28	18	35	18	7	20	6	–	–	80
29	5	35	14	20	9	8	–	43	–
30	24	29	29	10	34	7	–	–	
31-34	23	37	18	18	28	22	454	37	22
35 & over	16	44	26	17	14	12	–	15	27
Total	31	54	38	48	41	53	144	86	51

TABLE XXXVIII. — (*Continued.*)

Proportional Number of Short Men in each 10 000 *of same Age and Nativity.*

Age	Canada	Engl.	Scotl.	Ireland	France, etc.	Germ.	Scand.	Spain, etc.	Miscel.	Total
Under 17	769	2 532	2 000	2 857	4 000	3 242	2 308	–	4000	1 537
17	149	664	–	588	556	587	233	2000	465	243
18	69	134	62	113	90	145	–	200	135	72
19	51	76	151	44	118	101	–	256	158	43
20	39	60	152	41	107	95	–	164	43	37
21	48	68	21	37	47	59	20	202	29	33
22	36	51	90	42	61	75	22	179	32	34
23	42	66	51	31	91	58	29	–	38	34
24	18	86	56	18	131	73	25	328	101	33
25	56	55	–	36	54	60	–	–	114	35
26	71	50	30	24	64	61	135	–	44	34
27	19	34	33	36	37	70	–	–	103	29
28	27	24	–	35	85	73	32	–	–	30
29	40	33	75	17	140	51	–	–	36	26
30	52	37	95	46	104	50	36	–	–	33
31-34	21	52	49	47	108	54	30	–	86	35
35 & over	58	43	57	37	75	54	42	125	39	35
Total	49	69	61	45	95	77	32	123	71	49

The extent to which mean statures, computed directly from data, military or otherwise, from which all cases below a given limit have been excluded, are affected by such restriction of the fundamental data, may be estimated from the statistics here presented. By far the greater portion of the materials available for determining or comparing the statures of different people or races are derived from military records, and a neglect of proper regard to the conditions under which the statistics are collected, may easily result in error as gross and as absurd as that occasioned by the failure to record that an inch or more of the registered height of English and Scottish students was the handiwork of the shoemaker, who had thus succeeded in adding at least a part of a cubit to their stature.

Similar to these precautions is the other one, regarding the needfulness of which these researches will leave no room for doubt, that only persons of the same age, or of full stature, be compared with each other, in determining differences due to race, or nation, or class. The mean age corresponding to a given stature is also a very false guide unless the limits of age be quite narrow, or unless those ages only be taken into account, which may afford guaranty of an approximate attainment of the full stature.

SUPPLEMENTARY NOTES.

As these pages are passing through the press, the author has succeeded in obtaining, through the kindness of his friends Dr. S. Weir Mitchell and Dr. John H. Packard, of Philadelphia, a copy of the *Récueil de Mémoires de Médecine, de Chirurgie et de Pharmacie Militaires*, for March and July 1863, forming parts of Vols. IX. and X., and containing Boudin's learned and valuable memoir, "*Études ethnologiques sur la taille et le poids de l'homme chez divers peuples*": a memoir, without some reference to which the present chapter would be incomplete, yet which sundry efforts had previously failed to procure. Since it is too late to incorporate any of the results of M. Boudin's researches in the body of the chapter, it may not be regarded as inappropriate, to devote a few paragraphs, in the form of supplementary notes, to such of the new materials which he has given, as have an especial bearing upon the results of our own inquiries.

§ 3. *Heights by Nativities.* — The mean stature of French conscripts, from 1818 to 1828 inclusive, is stated to have been 165.7 centimeters (65.24 inches), their mean age being 20½ years, and the limit of stature 157 centimeters (61.81 inches). And from the other data here given Mr. Elliott finds [1] the mean stature of the conscripts from 1831 to 1862 to be 165.5 centims. (65.16 inches), the mean age remaining the same, but the minimum of stature having been reduced to 156 centimeters.

Our statistics (Tables VI., VIII.) have shown that for the natives of France, Belgium, etc., aged 20 at last birthday, who enlisted in our army, the mean height was 66.24 inches, or 168.24 centimeters, being greater by 1.08 inches, or 2.74 centimeters, than that found in France.

It is true that the Belgians and Swiss have been aggregated with the French in constructing our table, but the French form much the largest proportion, while their combination with Belgians would tend to decrease the resultant mean, inasmuch as the Belgian stature is less than the French.[2]

From these facts the inference appears legitimate that the mean stature of the natives of France who enlisted in the American army during their twenty-first year was nearly three centimeters greater than

1 *Milit. Stat. of U. S. A.*, Berlin, 1863, p. 16. 2 *Recueil de Mémoires*, etc., X. 27–31.

that of the conscripts of the same age in their native country, notwithstanding that all below the stature of 156 centimeters were rejected in France, while no such rejections were made in this country. Thus we are again led to the conclusion, which so many other considerations have forced upon us, that the natives of European countries who enlisted in America were on the average taller than those who enlisted at home; just as the mean height of men born in Massachusetts and enlisting in Indiana was found greater than that of Massachusetts men who enlisted in their native State.[1]

The statistics of relative stature of Irish, English, and French, quoted from Marshall,[2] and derived from the official documents of the recruiting offices, have afforded results so widely at variance with those deduced from our own materials, that some little investigation has seemed well bestowed in eliciting the sources of discrepancy.

From our Table VI. it will be seen that among our soldiers the stature of natives of Ireland somewhat exceeded that of natives of England, at nearly every age.[3] Yet the statistics of recruits to the British army in 1860, as given in the official documents cited[4] indicate the reverse, provided we assume that those who enlisted in England were all English, and those who enlisted in Ireland all Irish.

We have in our Table V. an assortment by Age and Stature of the Irish-born soldiers in the American army; and an easy means is thus afforded for collating our results directly with the British official statistics. These are given in columns 2, 3, and 4 of the subjoined table, and show the relative number of men at each stature enlisting in Ireland, England, and Scotland. The fifth column gives the actual number of Irish enlisting in the American army, whose heights and ages we possess; while the sixth gives the relative number of those exceeding 64 inches in stature, and is directly comparable with the column of Irish recruits to the British army.

1 See Tables XII. to XV.

2 *Military Miscellany, — a History of the Recruiting of the Army*, etc. London, 1846.

3 Similar results were afforded by Prof. Forbes's measures of students given in the *Lond. and Ed. Phil. Mag.* X. 200.

4 *Récueil de Mémoires*, etc., IX. 191, 2.

TABLE XXXIX.

Comparative Distribution of Irish Soldiers, by Stature.

Height	British Recruits, 1860			Irish in U. S. Army	
	English	Scotch	Irish	Actual	Relative
inches					
Below 64	–	–	–	7 960	–
64-65	2 458	2 475	3 235	8 448	1 124
65-66	2 276	2 026	2 238	12 380	1 647
66-67	1 995	1 785	1 622	14 058	1 870
67-68	1 368	1 397	1198	13 792	1 835
68-69	845	1 083	852	11 080	1 474
69-70	519	571	478	7 386	983
70-71	320	372	260	4 473	595
71-72	159	176	89	2 196	292
72 & over	60	115	28	1 355	180
Total	10 000	10 000	10 000	83 128	10 000

An instant's comparison of the relative number of Irish of any given stature, in the British and American armies, will suffice to show the uncertainty of any deductions which do not account for the totally different distribution of the numbers, or at least eliminate its influence upon the mean stature. An adequate explanation of this diversity is afforded by Table XL., which shows the enormous difference of the distribution by age, in the two armies. The 2d and 3d columns exhibit the actual number of Irish, at each age, recorded in our own army, both before and after excluding those whose stature was below 64 inches; while the 4th, which is formed like the 5th, and is comparable with it, is obtained from the preceding one, by reducing the numbers to decimals of their total.

TABLE XL.

Comparative Distribution of Irish Soldiers, by Age.

Age last birthday	In the United States Army			British Recruits
	Total	Excluding all below 64 in.		Relative
		Actual	Relative	
Below 17	84	36	5	101
17	187	124	17	433
18	4 345	3 393	451	2 501
19	4 519	3 818	508	1 283
20	4 095	3 609	480	1 272
21	7 550	6 819	907	848
22	6 445	5 884	783	756
23	5 235	4 788	637	534
24	4 360	4 007	533	580
25 & upward	46 308	42 690	5 679	1 692
Total	83 128	75 168	10 000	10 000

It will thus be seen that, while nearly 56 per cent. of the Irish in the American army were above the age of 25 years, about an equal proportion of the British recruits with whom they are compared had not attained their 21st year. In the absence of other information, we naturally assume that the distribution of the Irish by age was the same as that of the English and Scotch recruits, and we need no farther information to account for the wide diversity in the distribution by stature of the Irish in the two armies.

If now we may suppose, what the numbers in Table XXXIX. certainly suggest, that the Irish recruits to the British army were in general younger than the English recruits, the preceding argument is rendered yet stronger, while an explanation is afforded of the discordant inferences regarding the relative stature of English and Irish, as drawn from the American and the British statistics.

Considering next the difference in stature between the English and French armies, the numbers given by Marshall, page 89, and cited[1] by Boudin, would indicate the enormous difference of about five inches, or 12 centimeters. This is quoted as an illustration of "how far the stature is independent of welfare or misery, and how strictly on the other

1 *Récueil de Mémoires*, etc., IX. p. 181.

hand it is subordinated to the race; in other words, how great a part is played by hereditary transmission."

In the table alluded to, only four men in each 1000 of the British army are given as below the height of 66 inches, indicating that the troops were recruited with this stature as the minimum limit; while in the French army, 735 in each thousand were below this limit, and the distribution of only 265 remains for comparison with that of 996 British soldiers. Add to this that the French conscripts are taken at the age of 20 years, while nearly one half of the British recruits appear to have been older, and $22\frac{3}{4}$ per cent. of them were more than 24 years old. Moreover this exhibit is totally contradicted by the tables of stature subsequently given for the French army,[1] and the British recruits in 1860.[2] Whether the former gives the actual stature at the time or the stature at enlistment of the men then in the army is not clear. On the former supposition, it would be improper to compare the actual statures of the army with those of the British recruits at the time of enlistment; but, on the other hand, the minimum stature admitted was 156 centimeters in the one case, and 64 inches, or more than $162\frac{1}{2}$ centimeters, on the other. Yet notwithstanding these serious obstacles to a fair comparison, we find that in the assortment by inches of stature, the largest group is between 64 and 65 inches for the soldiers of each nation.

The attempt to deduce any results of value from a comparison of data obtained under such exceedingly different circumstances is simply preposterous, and no better illustrations than those here considered can be found of the erroneous inferences to which the statistical investigator may conduct the incautious student. It was from the consideration of inferences drawn from the collocation of such incongruous data that Bischoff, in a publication[3] which, like that of Boudin, has just been received, was led to say, "I have arrived at the conviction that the materials, which the statistics of recruiting apparently afford on the grandest scale, for estimating the condition of a people as regards development and health, and for comparing it with others, are practically as good as useless, and have consequently already led to many false deductions."

§ 5. *Full Statures.* — Mr. Boudin arrives at the same result to which we have been led in the present investigation, namely, that the influences of comfort or deprivation upon the stature of a community are by no means so controlling as Villermé, and others following him, have supposed, and that the race, or stock, is a much more potent element in determining the stature. But his estimate of the effect of local influences acting upon the individual during the period of his growth, is very far below that which the present investigations seem to render indisputable.[4]

1 *Recueil de Mémoires*, etc. IX. p. 184. 2 *Ibid*, p. 191.

3 Bischoff, *Ueber die Brauchbarkeit der veröffentlichten Resultate des Recrutirungs Geschäftes*, etc., Munich, 1867, p. 10. 4 See pages 126, 127.

§ 7. *Stature of other Races of Men.* — Mr. Boudin quotes[1] from Pauw[2] the mean stature of the Esquimaux as 130 centimeters, and from the "Foreign Quarterly Review"[3] (as cited by Marshall), the mean stature and weight of two Sepoy regiments. For the stature of these the mean value is[4] 173.3 for the Bengal, and 168.2 for the Madras, native infantry; but as 66 inches (167.6 centimeters) was the established minimum stature, the result has an anthropological value only so far as it manifests the difference of stature between the native populations of Bengal and Madras.

§ 8. *Extremes of Stature.* — In a very elaborate discussion[5] of the geographical distribution in France of exceptionally tall men, with a historical and ethnical investigation as to the races from which the present population of the several districts is derived, Mr. Boudin finds new ground for the conviction that the differences of stature observable in different localities are to be attributed to ethnological in a higher degree than to physiological influences.

Thus the recruits of minimum stature are[6] from three to four times more numerous in Brittany than Normandy; in three departments of Franche-Comté the proportion of stature above 1732 millimeters is found to be more than three times greater than in three other contiguous departments, nearly adjacent to the former. There were, according to the statistics of 1836–40 inclusive, only 18 departments in which were found men surpassing 189.5 centimeters in stature (74.61 inches), the number of these amounting on the average to $3\frac{4}{9}$ in each 10 000 recruits, although the proportion was 16 in 10 000 for the department of Vosges; while statures surpassing 192.2 (75.67 inches) occurred[7] in only 5 departments; the average proportion in these being $3\frac{2}{5}$ in 10 000, but in Vosges alone twice this number.

The departments which afford the largest number of exceptionally tall men are not necessarily the same as those in which the number exceeding the average stature was a maximum. In the latter class Doubs takes the lead, in the former Vosges. These districts are on the slopes of the Jura.

In Belgium and Prussia similar inferences are deducible. Thus the Belgian military statistics of the ten years 1840–50 show the exemptions for insufficient stature in eastern Flanders and in Namur to be in the proportion of 187 to 56. And the Prussian statistics of the decade preceding show the ratio of similar exemption in Silesia to be $4\frac{1}{2}$ times greater than in Westphalia.

These facts are thoroughly analogous to those elicited in our own investigations; but the effect of geographical, or rather of local, influences upon the stature may be regarded as demonstrated by our statistics, quite as thoroughly as is that of race or stock.

[1] IX. p. 203. [2] *Recherches Philosophiques sur les Américains*, I. 259.
[3] XXXIII. 397. [4] Page 193. [5] X. 12–31. [6] X. 15. [7] X. 16

CHAPTER VI.

COMPLEXIONS: COLOR OF HAIR AND EYES.

1. *Available Records.*

In the early part of the war there was, as has been already stated, a very large number of soldiers for whom no descriptive muster-rolls were made out in such a form as to indicate any of their physical characteristics. And when subsequently the statures were recorded, these were not always accompanied by records of complexion, color of eyes, or color of hair, until an advanced stage of the war.

The records of these physical characteristics are, however, too copious not to prove instructive to the anthropologist, and perhaps may prove serviceable for the investigation of problems yet unsolved, besides possessing much value as a basis for a physical knowledge of our nation. The clerks who were stationed at the several State capitals were therefore instructed to tabulate these descriptions, so far as could well be done without incurring too great expense, or neglecting the collection of other statistics which were regarded as more important.

In gathering these data no attempt was made at an exhaustive collection, such as was desired for the nativities and the statures; but it was simply proposed to tabulate a number sufficiently large to afford the means for a near estimate of the proportions of the different classes, and of the manner and degree with which they vary for different races and in different regions. In this way the statistics have been collected for about 668 000 men, of whom the complexions, color of hair, and color of eyes are classified in the tables here given.

The volunteers proper are kept distinct from the recruits, the former term being used, as in the discussion of their ages, to designate the original members of the several State organizations, while the latter includes all who subsequently joined these organizations. The numbers of the two classes were not far from equal; but it is to be remarked that for the reasons already stated, the earlier volunteers are not included in our statistics ; while of the recruits, the omissions are generally of the later ones, inasmuch as the clerks in transcribing usually followed the order in which the descriptions were recorded, and ceased collecting when the number transcribed seemed adequate for the purposes in view.

The results of these researches are presented in two modes: first, according to the States by which the troops were furnished, and secondly, according to the nativity of the men, without reference to the State of enlistment. The assortment by nativities is identical with that employed for the investigation of statures, there being eighteen classes for white soldiers.

2. *Color of Hair.*

TABLE I.

Color of Hair. Original Volunteers, by States.

State of Enlistment	Black	Dark	Brown	Light	Sandy	Red	Gray	Totals
Maine . . .	6 178	13 352	11 681	6 189	1 186	203	502	39 291
New Hampshire	2 178	3 371	7 297	4 224	754	163	124	18 111
Vermont . .	1 995	2 234	5 351	2 420	489	105	112	12 706
Massachusetts .	2 114	4 556	6 621	4 644	516	133	103	18 687
Connecticut .	2 306	3 727	5 716	3 592	713	133	278	16 465
Pennsylvania .	3 263	8 968	5 964	5 431	1 316	762	272	25 976
West Virginia	2 412	4 234	1 981	4 447	567	494	147	14 282
Kentucky . .	2 202	4 384	1 076	5 185	458	504	100	13 909
Ohio	8 835	15 392	12 780	15 190	2 170	2 579	323	57 269
Indiana . . .	8 197	18 166	8 429	17 347	2 077	3 425	518	58 159
Illinois . . .	10 170	15 722	15 864	19 548	2 120	3 706	688	67 818
Michigan . .	1 073	1 829	3 347	2 085	274	291	54	8 953
Wisconsin . .	3 918	4 812	12 461	7 622	1 103	240	267	30 423
Iowa	2 491	3 212	4 051	2 954	591	185	452	13 936
Missouri . .	4 341	6 390	6 992	8 529	2 256	383	442	29 333
Total . . .	61 673	110 349	109 611	109 407	16 590	13 306	4 382	425 318

TABLE II.

Color of Hair.
Recruits, by States.

State of Enlistment	Black	Dark	Brown	Light	Sandy	Red	Gray	Totals
Maine . . .	2 591	4 742	8 130	3 085	492	162	131	19 333
New Hampshire	1 430	570	5 487	866	267	66	75	8 761
Vermont . .	1 304	1 566	3 945	1 535	340	63	41	8 794
Massachusetts .	2 797	5 730	10 374	5 047	741	382	284	25 355
Connecticut .	1 943	2 937	7 672	2 096	543	206	191	15 588
New York . .	5 985	11 655	22 264	9 269	1 718	650	612	52 153
Pennsylvania .	5 376	14 406	13 900	9 352	1 866	1 241	376	46 517
West Virginia	484	1 053	219	870	71	67	21	2 785
Kentucky . .	701	1 937	365	2 294	188	205	23	5 713
Ohio	875	1 872	1 975	1 900	232	266	39	7 159
Indiana . . .	671	2 052	1 173	1 498	271	309	51	6 025
Illinois . . .	244	444	748	441	43	67	21	2 008
Michigan . .	1 832	3 745	8 396	3 757	556	491	84	18 861
Wisconsin . .	2 560	2 610	8 766	4 169	647	114	156	19 022
Iowa	644	1 127	1 327	993	244	51	40	4 426
Missouri . .	68	131	149	154	34	3	3	542
Total . . .	29 505	56 577	94 890	47 326	8 253	4 343	2 148	243 042

TABLE III.

Color of Hair.
U. S. Soldiers, by States.

State of Enlistment	Black	Dark	Brown	Light	Sandy	Red	Gray	Totals.
Maine . . .	8 769	18 094	19 811	9 274	1 678	365	633	58 624
New Hampshire	3 608	3 941	12 784	5 090	1 021	229	199	26 872
Vermont . .	3 299	3 800	9 296	3 955	829	168	153	21 500
Massachusetts .	4 911	10 286	16 995	9 691	1 257	515	387	44 042
Connecticut .	4 249	6 664	13 388	5 688	1 256	339	469	32 053
New York . .	5 985	11 655	22 264	9 269	1 718	650	612	52 153
Pennsylvania .	8 639	23 374	19 864	14 783	3 182	2 003	648	72 493
West Virginia	2 896	5 287	2 200	5 317	638	561	168	17 067
Kentucky . .	2 903	6 321	1 441	7 479	646	709	123	19 622
Ohio	9 710	17 264	14 755	17 090	2 402	2 845	362	64 428
Indiana . . .	8 868	20 218	9 602	18 845	2 348	3 734	569	64 184
Illinois . . .	10 414	16 166	16 612	19 989	2 163	3 773	709	69 826
Michigan . .	2 905	5 574	11 743	5 842	830	782	138	27 814
Wisconsin . .	6 478	7 422	21 227	11 791	1 750	354	423	49 445
Iowa	3 135	4 339	5 378	3 947	835	236	492	18 362
Missouri . .	4 409	6 521	7 141	8 683	2 290	386	445	29 875
Total . . .	91 178	166 926	204 501	156 733	24 843	17 649	6 530	668 360

TABLE IV.

Color of Hair.
Original Volunteers, by Nativities.

Nativity	Black	Dark	Brown	Light	Sandy	Red	Gray	Totals
A	13 364	24 852	33 042	19 551	3 195	819	1 060	95 883
B	9 821	18 266	19 607	15 766	2 824	2 172	984	69 440
C	16 616	30 631	21 117	31 315	4 212	5 383	496	109 770
D	3 935	6 157	6 417	8 216	797	1 304	52	26 878
E	3 315	5 516	2 841	5 274	689	708	289	18 632
F	3 925	7 147	2 387	7 704	918	986	283	23 350
G_1	170	269	347	329	34	27	2	1 178
G_2	947	1 558	1 244	1 967	357	135	19	6 227
H	258	513	698	410	73	19	20	1 991
I	1 162	1 419	2 109	1 075	186	114	44	6 109
J	1 043	1 954	3 015	2 230	429	249	165	9 085
K	260	450	599	501	106	59	55	2 030
L	2 637	4 875	5 795	3 743	966	513	455	18 984
M	298	375	420	312	50	38	33	1 526
N	3 325	5 387	8 490	9 144	1 449	673	359	28 827
O	131	314	740	1 178	152	59	13	2 587
P	17	15	4	3	–	–	–	39
Q	449	651	739	689	153	48	53	2 782
Total	61 673	110 349	109 611	109 407	16 590	13 306	4 382	425 318

TABLE V.

Color of Hair.
Recruits, by Nativities.

Nativity	Black	Dark	Brown	Light	Sandy	Red	Gray	Totals
A	5 273	9 016	19 060	8 020	1 277	472	378	43 496
B	10 449	21 767	32 510	16 898	3 009	1 669	698	87 000
C	1 961	4 367	4 666	4 067	668	543	65	16 337
D	1 129	1 600	3 653	2 012	219	174	13	8 800
E	885	1 877	1 281	1 310	178	143	54	5 728
F	765	1 865	599	2 055	195	189	29	5 697
G_1	67	149	211	174	20	5	7	633
G_2	97	177	188	150	23	7	–	642
H	494	879	1 645	472	92	52	22	3 656
I	1 736	2 248	4 806	1 278	277	106	59	10 510
J	1 022	1 937	4 335	1 568	333	152	105	9 452
K	259	523	1 192	400	134	66	39	2 613
L	2 888	5 696	11 105	3 481	1 039	522	449	25 180
M	362	443	631	163	34	12	18	1 663
N	1 469	3 251	7 417	4 242	573	192	176	17 320
O	61	178	703	712	129	20	8	1 811
P	113	101	59	11	2	1	4	291
Q	475	503	829	313	51	18	24	2 213
Total	29 505	56 577	94 890	47 326	8 253	4 343	2 148	243 042

TABLE VI.

Color of Hair.
U. S. Soldiers, by Nativities.

Nativity	Black	Dark	Brown	Light	Sandy	Red	Gray	Totals
A	18 637	33 868	52 102	27 571	4 472	1 291	1 438	139 379
B	20 270	40 033	52 117	32 664	5 833	3 841	1 682	156 440
C	18 577	34 998	25 783	35 382	4 880	5 926	561	126 107
D	5 064	7 757	10 070	10 228	1 016	1 478	65	35 678
E	4 200	7 393	4 122	6 584	867	851	343	24 360
F	4 690	9 012	2 986	9 759	1 113	1 175	312	29 047
G_1	237	418	558	503	54	32	9	1 811
G_2	1 044	1 735	1 432	2 117	380	142	19	6 869
H	752	1 392	2 343	882	165	71	42	5 647
I	2 898	3 667	6 915	2 353	463	220	103	16 619
J	2 065	3 891	7 350	3 798	762	401	270	18 537
K	519	973	1 791	901	240	125	94	4 643
L	5 525	10 571	16 900	7 224	2 005	1 035	904	44 164
M	660	818	1 051	475	84	50	51	3 189
N	4 794	8 638	15 907	13 386	2 022	865	535	46 147
O	192	492	1 443	1 890	281	79	21	4 398
P	130	116	63	14	2	1	4	330
Q	924	1 154	1 568	1 002	204	66	77	4 995
Total	91 178	166 926	204 501	156 733	24 843	17 649	6 530	668 360

The corresponding relative proportions for each State and each nativity may be more readily seen from the following tables, in which the several numbers are reduced to the scale of 1000. The degree of reliance to be placed upon these results may be readily estimated by reference to the tables of absolute numbers, from which they are deduced.

TABLE VII.

Color of Hair.

Proportionate Numbers for different States.

State of Enlistment	Black	Dark	Brown	Light	Sandy	Red	Gray	Totals
Maine . . .	149	309	338	158	29	6	11	1 000
N. Hampshire.	134	147	476	189	38	9	7	1 000
Vermont . .	153	177	432	184	39	8	7	1 000
Massachusetts.	111	234	386	220	28	12	9	1 000
Connecticut .	132	208	418	177	39	11	15	1 000
New York . .	115	223	427	178	33	12	12	1 000
Pennsylvania .	119	322	274	204	44	28	9	1 000
West Virginia	170	310	129	311	37	33	10	1 000
Kentucky . .	148	322	74	381	33	36	6	1 000
Ohio	151	268	229	265	37	44	6	1 000
Indiana . . .	138	315	150	294	36	58	9	1 000
Illinois . . .	149	232	238	286	31	54	10	1 000
Michigan . .	105	200	422	210	30	28	5	1 000
Wisconsin . .	131	150	429	239	35	7	9	1 000
Iowa	171	236	293	215	45	13	27	1 000
Missouri . .	147	218	239	291	77	13	15	1 000
Total . . .	136	250	306	235	37	26	10	1 000

TABLE VIII.

Color of Hair.
Proportionate Numbers for different Nativities.

Nativity	Black	Dark	Brown	Light	Sandy	Red	Gray	Totals
A	134	243	374	198	32	9	10	1 000
B	130	256	333	209	37	24	11	1 000
C	147	278	204	281	39	47	4	1 000
D	142	217	282	287	29	41	2	1 000
E	172	304	169	270	36	35	14	1 000
F	162	310	103	336	38	40	11	1 000
G_1	131	231	308	278	30	17	5	1 000
G_2	152	253	208	308	55	21	3	1 000
H	133	247	415	156	29	13	7	1 000
I	174	221	416	142	28	13	6	1 000
J	111	210	396	205	41	22	15	1 000
K	112	209	386	194	52	27	20	1 000
L	125	239	383	164	45	23	21	1 000
M	207	256	330	149	26	16	16	1 000
N	104	187	345	290	44	19	11	1 000
O	43	112	328	430	64	18	5	1 000
P	394	352	191	42	6	3	12	1 000
Q	185	231	314	201	41	13	15	1 000
Total	136	250	306	235	37	26	10	1 000

3. *Color of Eyes.*

TABLE IX.

Color of Eyes.
Volunteers by States.

State of Enlistment	Blue	Gray	Hazel	Dark	Black	Totals
Maine . . .	17 847	6 820	6 783	2 828	5 013	39 291
New Hampshire	9 692	2 957	2 327	1 599	1 536	18 111
Vermont . .	7 222	1 833	860	1 288	1 503	12 706
Massachusetts	9 477	3 279	3 101	1 515	1 316	18 688
Connecticut .	8 274	3 418	1 227	2 083	1 462	16 464
Pennsylvania	8 330	9 176	3 261	4 098	1 111	25 976
West Virginia	6 176	3 644	1 118	1 819	1 526	14 283
Kentucky . .	6 388	3 085	1 291	1 321	1 823	13 908
Ohio	22 698	16 601	6 680	6 523	4 766	57 268
Indiana . . .	24 714	14 928	7 690	5 557	5 258	58 147
Illinois . .	30 275	16 608	8 137	7 213	5 571	67 804
Michigan . .	4 534	1 980	915	611	905	8 945
Wisconsin .	16 256	6 343	2 995	2 834	1 995	30 423
Iowa	6 620	3 192	1 669	1 210	1 241	13 932
Missouri . .	13 505	7 175	3 372	3 132	2 129	29 313
Total . . .	192 008	101 039	51 426	43 631	37 155	425 259

TABLE X.

Color of Eyes.
Recruits by States.

State of Enlistment	Blue	Gray	Hazel	Dark	Black	Totals
Maine . . .	8 971	3 220	4 525	1 275	1 342	19 333
New Hampshire	3 575	2 225	2 183	420	358	8 761
Vermont . .	4 723	1 355	894	820	1 004	8 796
Massachusetts	12 783	4 839	4 532	1 834	1 367	25 355
Connecticut .	6 984	3 874	2 746	1 219	763	15 586
New York . .	24 342	13 314	3 910	7 326	3 261	52 153
Pennsylvania .	14 829	16 626	7 047	6 743	1 273	46 518
West Virginia	1 158	754	325	325	223	2 785
Kentucky . .	2 754	1 230	494	591	644	5 713
Ohio	2 632	2 261	1 055	691	519	7 158
Indiana . .	2 374	1 653	1 237	474	286	6 024
Illinois . . .	897	518	334	169	89	2 007
Michigan . .	9 977	4 261	1 673	1 749	1 200	18 860
Wisconsin . .	10 101	3 658	2 240	1 758	1 265	19 022
Iowa . . .	1 857	1 196	706	362	305	4 426
Missouri . .	236	133	66	63	45	543
Total . .	108 193	61 117	33 967	25 819	13 944	243 040

TABLE XI.

Color of Eyes.
U. S. Soldiers by States.

State of Enlistment	Blue	Gray	Hazel	Dark	Black	Totals
Maine . . .	26 818	10 040	11 308	4 103	6 355	58 624
New Hampshire	13 267	5 182	4 510	2 019	1 894	26 872
Vermont . .	11 945	3 188	1 754	2 108	2 507	21 502
Massachusetts	22 260	8 118	7 633	3 349	2 683	44 043
Connecticut .	15 258	7 292	3 973	3 302	2 225	32 050
New York . .	24 342	13 314	3 910	7 326	3 261	52 153
Pennsylvania .	23 159	25 802	10 308	10 841	2 384	72 494
West Virginia	7 334	4 398	1 443	2 144	1 749	17 068
Kentucky . .	9 142	4 315	1 785	1 912	2 467	19 621
Ohio	25 330	18 862	7 735	7 214	5 285	64 426
Indiana . . .	27 088	16 581	8 927	6 031	5 544	64 171
Illinois . . .	31 172	17 126	8 471	7 382	5 660	69 811
Michigan . .	14 511	6 241	2 588	2 360	2 105	27 805
Wisconsin . .	26 357	10 001	5 235	4 592	3 260	49 445
Iowa . . .	8 477	4 388	2 375	1 572	1 546	18 358
Missouri . .	13 741	7 308	3 438	3 195	2 174	29 856
Total . . .	300 201	162 156	85 393	69 450	51 099	668 299

TABLE XII.

Color of Eyes.
Volunteers by Nativities.

Nativity	Blue	Gray	Hazel	Dark	Black	Totals
A	47 633	16 632	13 295	8 321	10 001	95 882
B	29 193	18 837	8 280	8 126	4 994	69 430
C	45 834	29 033	13 565	11 339	9 989	109 760
D	11 901	6 415	3 428	2 512	2 606	26 862
E	8 206	4 545	1 904	2 028	1 944	18 627
F	10 777	5 209	2 506	2 113	2 740	23 345
G_1	479	324	176	98	97	1 174
G_2	2 746	1 504	785	585	605	6 225
H	1 015	379	309	158	129	1 990
I	2 760	1 290	698	677	684	6 109
J	4 514	2 078	1 091	862	538	9 083
K	1 012	535	225	159	98	2 029
L	9 820	5 004	1 873	1 452	836	18 985
M	522	364	228	257	155	1 526
N	12 819	7 674	2 610	4 267	1 458	28 828
O	1 764	444	137	182	60	2 587
P	6	5	8	10	10	39
Q	1 007	767	308	485	211	2 778
Total	192 008	101 039	51 426	43 631	37 155	425 259

TABLE XIII.

Color of Eyes.
Recruits by Nativities.

Nativity	Blue	Gray	Hazel	Dark	Black	Totals
A	21 890	7 777	7 558	3 318	2 956	43 499
B	35 737	24 954	10 248	11 632	4 432	87 003
C	6 747	4 464	2 470	1 547	1 110	16 338
D	4 112	2 021	877	923	867	8 800
E	2 321	1 518	816	653	421	5 729
F	2 689	1 223	530	617	638	5 697
G_1	236	189	112	53	43	633
G_2	243	168	93	72	65	641
H	1 602	769	786	285	214	3 656
I	4 415	2 331	1 856	1 109	799	10 510
J	4 232	2 325	1 548	877	463	9 445
K	1 206	645	376	224	161	2 612
L	12 486	7 073	3 367	1 614	639	25 179
M	525	353	385	225	175	1 663
N	7 700	4 463	2 321	2 229	609	17 322
O	1 246	310	141	80	34	1 811
P	73	56	46	55	61	291
Q	733	478	437	306	257	2 211
Total	108 193	61 117	33 967	25 819	13 944	243 040

TABLE XIV.

Color of Eyes.
U. S. Soldiers by Nativities.

Nativity	Blue	Gray	Hazel	Dark	Black	Totals
A	69 523	24 409	20 853	11 639	12 957	139 381
B	64 930	43 791	18 528	19 758	9 426	156 433
C	52 581	33 497	16 035	12 886	11 099	126 098
D	16 013	8 436	4 305	3 435	3 473	35 662
E	10 527	6 063	2 720	2 681	2 365	24 356
F	13 466	6 432	3 036	2 730	3 378	29 042
G_1	715	513	288	151	140	1 807
G_2	2 989	1 672	878	657	670	6 866
H	2 617	1 148	1 095	443	343	5 646
I	7 175	3 621	2 554	1 786	1 483	16 619
J	8 746	4 403	2 639	1 739	1 001	18 528
K	2 218	1 180	601	383	259	4 641
L	22 306	12 077	5 240	3 066	1 475	44 164
M	1 047	717	613	482	330	3 189
N	20 519	12 137	4 931	6 496	2 067	46 150
O	3 010	754	278	262	94	4 398
P	79	61	54	65	71	330
Q	1 740	1 245	745	791	468	4 989
Total	300 201	162 156	85 393	69 450	51 099	668 299

TABLE XV.

Color of Eyes.
Proportionate Numbers for different States.

State of Enlistment	Blue	Gray	Hazel	Dark	Black	Totals
Maine . . .	458	171	193	70	108	1 000
New Hampshire	494	193	168	75	70	1 000
Vermont . .	555	148	82	98	117	1 000
Massachusetts .	506	184	173	76	61	1 000
Connecticut .	476	228	124	103	69	1 000
New York . .	467	255	75	140	63	1 000
Pennsylvania .	319	356	142	150	33	1 000
West Virginia	430	258	84	126	102	1 000
Kentucky . .	466	220	91	97	126	1 000
Ohio	393	293	120	112	82	1 000
Indiana . . .	422	258	139	94	87	1 000
Illinois . . .	447	245	121	106	81	1 000
Michigan . .	522	224	93	85	76	1 000
Wisconsin . .	533	202	106	93	66	1 000
Iowa	462	239	129	86	84	1 000
Missouri . .	460	245	115	107	73	1 000
Total . . .	449	243	128	104	76	1 000

TABLE XVI.

Color of Eyes.

Proportionate Numbers for different Nativities.

Nativity	Blue	Gray	Hazel	Dark	Black	Totals
A	499	175	150	83	93	1 000
B	415	280	119	126	60	1 000
C	417	266	127	102	88	1 000
D	449	237	121	96	97	1 000
E	432	249	112	110	97	1 000
F	464	221	105	94	116	1 000
G_1	396	284	159	84	77	1 000
G_2	435	243	128	96	98	1 000
H	464	203	194	78	61	1 000
I	432	218	154	107	89	1 000
J	472	238	142	94	54	1 000
K	478	254	129	83	56	1 000
L	505	274	119	69	33	1 000
M	328	225	192	151	104	1 000
N	445	262	107	141	45	1 000
O	684	172	63	60	21	1 000
P	239	185	164	197	215	1 000
Q	349	250	149	158	94	1 000
Total	449	243	128	104	76	1 000

4. *Complexions.*

TABLE XVII.

Complexions. By States.

State of Enlistment	Volunteers				Recruits			
	Dark	Light	Medium	Totals	Dark	Light	Medium	Totals
Maine . . .	17 002	21 175	1 106	39 283	5 142	13 013	1 173	19 328
New Hampshire	5 900	11 310	898	18 108	3 352	3 744	1 659	8 755
Vermont . .	4 307	7 340	1 052	12 699	2 746	5 368	647	8 761
Massachusetts.	6 171	11 899	608	18 678	8 060	15 882	1 395	25 337
Connecticut .	5 124	10 782	549	16 455	4 793	8 849	1 939	15 581
New York . .	–	–	–	–	13 523	23 879	14 712	52 114
Pennsylvania .	9 061	14 789	2 125	25 975	15 748	24 478	6 292	46 518
West Virginia	4 783	9 498	2	14 283	878	1 907	–	2 785
Kentucky . .	4 584	9 325	–	13 909	1 729	3 984	–	5 713
Ohio	18 310	38 916	44	57 270	1 942	5 195	22	7 159
Indiana . . .	21 165	34 426	2 489	58 080	2 099	3 733	190	6 022
Illinois . . .	22 451	42 105	3 241	67 797	581	1 344	78	2 003
Michigan . .	2 357	6 582	16	8 955	4 557	14 287	16	18 860
Wisconsin . .	8 906	21 515	2	30 423	5 927	13 095	–	19 022
Iowa	4 584	5 388	3 964	13 936	1 376	1 799	1 251	4 426
Missouri . .	8 879	20 138	314	29 331	160	380	3	543
Total . . .	143 584	265 188	16 410	425 182	72 613	140 937	29 377	242 927

TABLE XVIII.

Complexions. By Nativities.

Nativity	Volunteers				Recruits			
	Dark	Light	Medium	Totals	Dark	Light	Medium	Totals
A	34 815	57 375	3 673	95 863	12 217	28 190	3 063	43 470
B	22 945	43 017	3 470	69 432	25 689	47 776	13 492	86 957
C	36 766	68 875	4 098	109 739	4 818	10 634	881	16 333
D	8 434	17 523	911	26 868	2 447	6 058	292	8 797
E	6 753	11 444	428	18 625	2 051	3 243	426	5 720
F	8 247	14 613	488	23 348	1 753	3 795	149	5 697
G_1	369	602	206	1 177	175	291	167	633
G_2	1 935	4 205	80	6 220	219	371	48	638
H	699	1 186	104	1 989	1 238	2 054	363	3 655
I	2 425	3 431	249	6 105	3 929	5 573	1 005	10 507
J	2 732	5 998	352	9 082	2 773	5 325	1 351	9 449
K	645	1 297	88	2 030	663	1 514	435	2 612
L	6 291	11 752	927	18 970	7 423	13 482	4 272	25 177
M	703	769	52	1 524	863	578	222	1 663
N	8 381	19 273	1 147	28 801	4 807	9 804	2 701	17 312
O	447	2 079	61	2 587	338	1 332	140	1 810
P	25	14	–	39	193	48	48	289
Q	972	1 735	76	2 783	1 017	869	322	2 208
Total	143 584	265 188	16 410	425 182	72 613	140 937	29 377	242 927

TABLE XIX.

Complexions.
U. S. Soldiers by States.

State of Enlistment	Absolute				Relative			
	Dark	Light	Medium	Total	Dark	Light	Medium	Total
Maine . . .	22 144	34 188	2 279	58 611	378	583	39	1 000
New Hampshire	9 252	15 054	2 557	26 863	345	560	95	1 000
Vermont . .	7 053	12 708	1 699	21 460	329	592	79	1 000
Massachusetts	14 231	27 781	2 003	44 015	323	631	46	1 000
Connecticut .	9 917	19 631	2 488	32 036	309	613	78	1 000
New York . .	13 523	23 879	14 712	52 114	260	458	282	1 000
Pennsylvania .	24 809	39 267	8 417	72 493	342	542	116	1 000
West Virginia	5 661	11 405	2	17 068	332	668	0	1 000
Kentucky . .	6 313	13 309	0	19 622	322	678	0	1 000
Ohio	20 252	44 111	66	64 429	314	685	1	1 000
Indiana . . .	23 264	38 159	2 679	64 102	363	595	42	1 000
Illinois . . .	23 032	43 449	3 319	69 800	330	622	48	1 000
Michigan . .	6 914	20 869	32	27 815	249	750	1	1 000
Wisconsin . .	14 833	34 610	2	49 445	300	700	0	1 000
Iowa	5 960	7 187	5 215	18 362	325	391	284	1 000
Missouri . .	9 039	20 518	317	29 874	303	686	11	1 000
Total . . .	216 197	406 125	45 787	668 109	324	608	68	1 000

TABLE XX.

Complexions.
U. S. Soldiers by Nativities.

Nativity	Absolute				Relative			
	Dark	Light	Medium	Total	Dark	Light	Medium	Total
A	47 032	85 565	6 736	139 333	338	614	48	1 000
B	48 634	90 793	16 962	156 389	311	581	108	1 000
C	41 584	79 509	4 979	126 072	330	631	39	1 000
D	10 881	23 581	1 203	35 665	305	661	34	1 000
E	8 804	14 687	854	24 345	362	603	35	1 000
F	10 000	18 408	637	29 045	344	634	22	1 000
G_1	544	893	373	1 810	301	493	206	1 000
G_2	2 154	4 576	128	6 858	314	667	19	1 000
H	1 937	3 240	467	5 644	343	574	83	1 000
I	6 354	9 004	1 254	16 612	383	542	75	1 000
J	5 505	11 323	1 703	18 531	297	611	92	1 000
K	1 308	2 811	523	4 642	282	605	113	1 000
L	13 714	25 234	5 199	44 147	311	571	118	1 000
M	1 566	1 347	274	3 187	491	423	86	1 000
N	13 188	29 077	3 848	46 113	286	631	83	1 000
O	785	3 411	201	4 397	178	776	46	1 000
P	218	62	48	328	665	189	146	1 000
Q	1 989	2 604	398	4 991	398	522	80	1 000
Total	216 197	406 125	45 787	668 109	324	608	68	1 000

5. *Inferences.*

It will not require any very close scrutiny of these tables to perceive that deductions must be drawn with caution. They present simply the official records, as reported by a large number of mustering officers, no one of whom probably aimed at anything more than a rough description, sufficient to aid in the identification of the soldier, should this ever become necessary. These records seem indeed to have been regarded by most of the mustering officers as a mere formality, upon which it was needless to expend much attention. If not in clear contradiction to the truth, the entries were considered satisfactory. Thus, for example, while out of 49 445 soldiers from Wisconsin the complexion of only 2 was recorded as "medium," there were 14 712 out of 52 114 from New York, and 5215 out of 18 362 from Iowa, whose complexion was thus noted. Similarly, among the Pennsylvania troops the proportion of "dark" eyes to "black" ones was as 150 to 33; while this proportion for the Kentucky soldiers was as 97 to 126. These discordances are, of course, not to be attributed to any real difference existing, to such an extent, but to the habitudes and peculiarities of the mustering officers.

Yet a proper caution will prevent any serious error in our deductions here, arising from influences of this sort, which cannot have produced the great difference manifested by our tables between the complexions prevailing in most of the Western States on the one hand, where the light complexions overwhelmingly predominate, and those in the Eastern States on the other, where this predominance is by no means so great. So, too, while of every thousand men 58 in Indiana, 54 in Illinois, and 44 in Ohio had red hair, the corresponding number was but 6 in Maine, and 8 in New Hampshire and Vermont. This can no more be due to any carelessness of recruiting officers than can the fact that but 32 men from Pennsylvania for each 56 from Vermont had blue eyes; or that the dark eyes, including black, formed nearly 23 per cent. of the whole number in Kentucky and West Virginia, while they were scarcely 14 per cent. in New Hampshire and Massachusetts. How far these differences are to be attributed to climate, how far to ancestry, and how far to looseness of record, it is not our province to inquire. So far as the army records can throw light upon the subject, the materials are here presented.

When the comparison is made, not between troops from different States, but between men of different nativities, the variations become more manifest and are more easy of interpretation. And we have thus a means of fixing an outer limit, at least, for the inaccuracies of the original records. A comparison of the records for the two nativities O and P illustrates the difference of national characteristics most forcibly, although the descriptions of but 330 individuals belonging to the latter class are among our data. For the first, comprising natives of Denmark, Sweden, and Norway, the ratio of light complexions to dark ones is as 78 to 18; while for the second, which includes natives of Spain, Portugal, and Spanish America, this ratio is as 19 to 66. The cases where the hair was black or dark number 16 per cent. in the former and 75 per cent. in the latter case; while on the other hand those recorded as light, sandy, or red, are in the first instance 51 per cent., and in the second only one tenth part as numerous. The proportion of blue eyes in the two cases is as 68 to 24; that of dark or black eyes as 8 to 41.

CHAPTER VII.

PREVIOUS OCCUPATIONS.

THE occupations of our soldiers before the war are given upon the descriptive muster-rolls, and have been tabulated by the agents of the Commission at the same time with the physical descriptions given on the same rolls. The principles followed in our classification will be most easily set forth by giving the following extract from the instructions to clerks engaged in the work.

"A certain amount of judgement must be used in assorting the 'occupations.' All whose pursuits were mechanical, implying any skill whatever, are to be entered as 'mechanics,' with the single exception of printers, who have a column for themselves. All who depended on their strength, merely, for livelihood, should be classed as 'laborers,' unless their pursuits were purely agricultural. Under 'professional' put those whose occupations are essentially intellectual. In the absence of other clews, a man's rank may sometimes be a guide. As 'engineer,' for instance, the fireman, or the constructor, or the designer of an engine might be recorded, as well as the brakeman and the driver of a railroad train, or the man who laid out the road; yet we should have here laborer, mechanic, and professional, all recorded under one title. So, too, a teacher of music, a maker of instruments, and a drummer or fifer, might all be recorded as musicians; yet the occupation of the first would be professional, of the second mechanical, and the third would have to be classed as miscellaneous. It will be seen that no general rule can be given, but much must be left to judgement. A hostler might be recorded as 'miscellaneous'; an ordinary sailor as 'laborer'; a grocer and a peddler as 'commercial'; a butcher or a baker as a 'mechanic.'"

The class of "printers" was kept distinct from those engaged in other mechanic arts because a considerable number of descriptions had been collected in the year 1863 in which this special occupation was made a class by itself. Although the collection alluded to was subsequently superseded, yet it was not thought amiss to continue the usage thus commenced.

The previous occupations of 666 530 men are thus assorted, among whom it is estimated that about 3330 commissioned officers are included, who had never served as private soldiers, as also some men who enlisted as sailors. To the remaining enlisted men, about 660 000 in all, must have belonged somewhat more than 16 000 other commissioned officers (not here included), besides those who were promoted from the ranks and are consequently registered on the descriptive muster-rolls as enlisted men.

A large proportion of the original commissioned officers, probably four fifths, went from the "professional" class; indeed it is certainly not too much to say, that of the soldiers from this class at least eight out of eleven joined the army as commissioned officers. Yet our records give 158 in each 10 000 enlisted men as taken from professional pursuits, which would at first seem to imply that the proportion of our defenders belonging to this class reached the enormous proportion of 579 in each 10 000; an estimate altogether inadmissible when we bear in mind that, according to the census of 1860, the proportion of the white male population of the loyal States above 18 years of age, who were engaged in professional avocations, was but 336 in each 10 000. It will, however, be manifest that the muster-rolls of enlisted men alone would fall far short of doing justice to the patriotism and self-sacrifice of this portion of our people.

The disproportion of the figures appears to be due to the circumstance that the descriptions here collected include some organizations composed almost entirely of educated men. In several cases companies were composed exclusively of professors and students of colleges; and the inclusion of these exceptional organizations with the rest tends to vitiate the averages, so as to render them inapplicable to the whole army. Deducting the estimated number in these organizations, or about 1700, both from the total number of enlisted men described, and from that of occupations of a professional character, we may attain a better estimate of the general constitution of the army in this respect; and careful study leads to the belief that the true proportion of men from professional pursuits among the private soldiers of our army was about 94, and for recruits alone 102, in each 10 000. For officers and men taken together it was about 321 in each 10 000.

Those who know the extent to which our colleges and universities were drained of pupils and teachers, need no reminder of the fact that the proportionate numbers for the most highly educated class are inadequately given in the appended tables, for the reasons just stated; yet it may not be amiss to place here upon record the fact that many of our seminaries of learning were compelled for

14

a season to suspend their activity and close their doors, in consequence of the departure of instructers and students for scenes of higher and nobler duty. Even the most frequented seminaries, such as Harvard, Yale, and Princeton, found their sphere of usefulness contracted during the war to an extent almost incredible, and the long "rolls of honor," on which it has been their pride to commemorate the beloved sons whom they have offered on their country's altar, bear witness to the unsurpassed zeal with which the most educated classes of the community bore their part in defense of their native land, its nationality, and freedom.

The annexed tabular statements present the statistics collected for the enlisted men (subject to the qualifications already made); but it will not be forgotten that of these men 29½ per cent. were under the age of 21 years, and twice as many were under 25 years, so that the larger portion of them had not yet become definitely wedded to any especial occupation, — a fact which the peculiar versatility of the American people renders especially noticeable.

TABLE I.

Occupations of Volunteers, by States.

State of Enlistment	Agricultural	Mechanic	Commercial	Professional	Printers	Laborers	Miscellaneous	Totals
Maine . . .	11 862	13 235	1 062	856	201	10 455	1 620	39 291
New Hampshire	7 273	7 142	523	221	187	2 177	588	18 111
Vermont . .	8 419	2 275	523	475	58	890	54	12 694
Massachusetts	2 394	10 230	1 881	178	175	2 317	1 513	18 688
Connecticut .	5 427	7 535	710	171	88	1 599	933	16 463
Pennsylvania .	7 142	8 051	398	206	129	8 664	1 386	25 976
West Virginia	8 983	3 213	285	201	47	1 396	125	14 250
Kentucky . .	9 718	2 035	300	117	42	1 014	227	13 453
Ohio	32 076	14 005	3 525	1 824	361	4 812	666	57 269
Indiana . . .	41 127	10 142	1 371	981	319	2 593	1 341	57 874
Illinois . . .	44 937	11 027	2 266	1 565	491	3 514	3 359	67 159
Michigan . .	4 928	1 717	175	120	50	1 217	779	8 986
Wisconsin . .	19 649	4 483	164	329	226	5 471	101	30 423
Iowa	10 445	2 065	159	421	90	413	343	13 936
Missouri . .	16 895	6 553	1 172	386	200	2 932	861	28 999
Total . . .	231 275	103 708	14 514	8 051	2 664	49 464	13 896	423 572

TABLE II.

Occupations of Recruits,
by States.

State of Enlistment	Agricultural	Mechanic	Commercial	Professional	Printers	Laborers	Miscellaneous	Totals
Maine . . .	6 648	3 890	617	306	55	3 695	4 122	19 333
New Hampshire	1 108	2 364	347	78	68	4 407	389	8 761
Vermont . .	5 487	1 348	232	127	30	1 481	90	8 795
Massachusetts	3 771	11 861	1 377	251	219	5 862	1 994	25 335
Connecticut .	2 582	5 656	765	170	139	4 896	1 381	15 589
New York . .	18 090	13 817	3 815	684	476	13 516	1 727	52 125
Pennsylvania .	11 201	14 658	760	191	284	16 678	2 723	46 495
West Virginia	2 042	437	27	18	6	241	14	2 785
Kentucky . .	4 278	676	92	38	12	435	182	5 713
Ohio	4 109	1 564	208	140	46	1 010	80	7 157
Indiana . . .	4 547	812	64	56	14	390	146	6 029
Illinois . . .	1 365	276	56	14	6	176	114	2 007
Michigan . .	12 059	3 663	323	187	63	2 365	199	18 859
Wisconsin . .	12 450	2 461	55	134	49	3 786	87	19 022
Iowa	3 393	618	25	82	32	160	111	4 421
Missouri . .	298	120	19	4	–	63	28	532
Total . . .	93 428	64 221	8 782	2 480	1 499	59 161	13 387	242 958

TABLE III.

Occupations of U. S. Soldiers, by States.

State of Enlistment	Agricultural	Mechanic	Commercial	Professional	Printers	Laborers	Miscellaneous	Totals
Maine . . .	18 510	17 125	1 679	1 162	256	14 150	5 742	58 624
New Hampshire	8 381	9 506	870	299	255	6 584	977	26 872
Vermont . .	13 906	3 623	755	602	88	2 371	144	21 489
Massachusetts	6 165	22 091	3 258	429	394	8 179	3 507	44 023
Connecticut .	8 009	13 191	1 475	341	227	6 495	2 314	32 052
New York . .	18 090	13 817	3 815	684	476	13 516	1 727	52 125
Pennsylvania .	18 343	22 709	1 158	397	413	25 342	4 109	72 471
West Virginia	11 025	3 650	312	219	53	1 637	139	17 035
Kentucky . .	13 996	2 711	392	155	54	1 449	409	19 166
Ohio	36 185	15 569	3 733	1 964	407	5 822	746	64 426
Indiana . . .	45 674	10 954	1 435	1 037	333	2 983	1 487	63 903
Illinois . . .	46 302	11 303	2 322	1 579	497	3 690	3 473	69 166
Michigan . .	16 987	5 380	498	307	113	3 582	978	27 845
Wisconsin . .	32 099	6 944	219	463	275	9 257	188	49 445
Iowa	13 838	2 683	184	503	122	573	454	18 357
Missouri . .	17 193	6 673	1 191	390	200	2 995	889	29 531
Total . . .	324 703	167 929	23 296	10 531	4 163	108 625	27 283	666 530

TABLE IV.

Occupations of Volunteers,
by Nativities.

Nativity	Agricultural	Mechanic	Commercial	Professional	Printers	Laborers	Miscellaneous	Totals
A	35 540	34 815	4 599	2 093	684	14 056	4 034	95 821
B	33 228	18 313	2 202	1 521	543	10 466	2 963	69 236
C	78 426	17 063	3 734	2 701	639	4 940	1 979	109 482
D	20 839	2 383	617	413	193	1 409	893	26 747
E	12 899	3 437	384	313	86	1 165	312	18 596
F	18 558	2 545	330	299	63	692	410	22 897
G_1	924	99	14	18	21	52	37	1 165
G_2	4 737	687	203	49	46	270	139	6 131
H	529	603	39	22	20	665	112	1 990
I	3 131	1 469	135	70	32	1 052	211	6 100
J	3 564	3 251	249	103	59	1 336	500	9 062
K	670	797	57	26	31	304	145	2 030
L	4 926	4 775	421	96	67	7 642	960	18 887
M	544	557	61	17	7	242	76	1 504
N	10 212	11 430	1 268	253	143	4 352	895	28 553
O	1 620	503	60	15	4	325	50	2 577
P	7	16	3	–	1	5	6	38
Q	921	965	138	42	25	491	174	2 756
Total	231 275	103 708	14 514	8 051	2 664	49 464	13 896	423 572

TABLE V.

Occupations of Recruits, by Nativities.

Nativity	Agricultural	Mechanic	Commercial	Professional	Printers	Laborers	Miscellaneous	Totals
A	16 930	13 596	1 826	641	244	6 284	3 978	43 499
B	35 075	23 402	3 231	830	656	20 141	3 618	86 953
C	11 606	2 379	300	215	78	1 457	296	16 331
D	6 165	1 047	176	82	38	1 148	150	8 806
E	3 168	1 249	131	42	31	915	185	5 721
F	4 555	539	97	31	13	311	149	5 695
G_1	474	57	6	5	6	53	32	633
G_2	289	145	26	10	4	102	61	637
H	582	895	117	28	30	1 506	494	3 652
I	3 425	2 503	301	82	76	3 589	530	10 506
J	1 861	2 877	422	104	94	3 369	720	9 447
K	589	914	154	23	23	761	145	2 609
L	2 568	6 858	639	80	134	13 216	1 682	25 177
M	214	449	97	31	10	660	200	1 661
N	4 905	6 345	1 010	207	46	4 007	798	17 318
O	811	261	49	10	2	606	72	1 811
P	8	69	32	4	–	150	28	291
Q	203	636	168	55	14	886	249	2 211
Total	93 428	64 221	8 782	2 480	1 499	59 161	13 387	242 958

TABLE VI.

Occupations of U. S. Soldiers, by Nativities.

Nativity	Agricultural	Mechanic	Commercial	Professional	Printers	Laborers	Miscellaneous	Totals
A	52 470	48 411	6 425	2 734	928	20 340	8 012	139 320
B	68 303	41 715	5 433	2 351	1 199	30 607	6 581	156 189
C	90 032	19 442	4 034	2 916	717	6 397	2 275	125 813
D	27 004	3 430	793	495	231	2 557	1 043	35 553
E	16 067	4 686	515	355	117	2 080	497	24 317
F	23 113	3 084	427	330	76	1 003	599	28 592
G_1	1 398	156	20	23	27	105	69	1 798
G_2	5 026	832	229	59	50	372	200	6 768
H	1 111	1 498	156	50	50	2 171	606	5 642
I	6 556	3 972	436	152	108	4 641	741	16 606
J	5 425	6 128	671	207	153	4 705	1 220	18 509
K	1 259	1 711	211	49	54	1 065	290	4 639
L	7 494	11 663	1 060	176	201	20 858	2 642	44 064
M	758	1 006	158	48	17	902	276	3 165
N	15 117	17 775	2 278	460	189	8 359	1 693	45 871
O	2 431	764	109	25	6	931	122	4 388
P	15	85	35	4	1	155	34	329
Q	1 124	1 601	306	97	39	1 377	423	4 967
Total	324 703	167 929	23 296	10 531	4 163	108 625	27 283	666 530

TABLE VII.

Occupations.
Proportionate Numbers for Different States.

State of Enlistment	Agricultural	Mechanic	Commercial	Professional	Printers	Laborers	Miscellaneous	Totals
Maine . . .	316	292	29	20	4	241	98	1 000
New Hampshire	312	354	32	11	10	245	36	1 000
Vermont . .	647	169	35	28	4	110	7	1 000
Massachusetts	140	502	74	10	9	186	79	1 000
Connecticut .	250	411	46	11	7	203	72	1 000
New York . .	347	265	73	13	9	260	33	1 000
Pennsylvania .	253	313	16	5	6	350	57	1 000
West Virginia	647	214	19	13	3	96	8	1 000
Kentucky . .	730	142	20	8	3	76	21	1 000
Ohio	562	242	58	30	6	90	12	1 000
Indiana . . .	715	171	23	16	5	47	23	1 000
Illinois . . .	670	163	34	23	7	53	50	1 000
Michigan . .	610	193	18	11	4	129	35	1 000
Wisconsin . .	649	141	4	9	6	187	4	1 000
Iowa	754	146	10	27	7	31	25	1 000
Missouri . .	582	226	40	13	7	102	30	1 000
Total . . .	487	252	35	16	6	163	41	1 000

TABLE VIII.

Occupations.

Proportionate Numbers for Different Nativities.

Nativity	Agricultural	Mechanic	Commercial	Professional	Printers	Laborers	Miscellaneous	Totals
A	377	347	46	20	7	146	57	1 000
B	437	267	35	15	8	196	42	1 000
C	716	154	32	23	6	51	18	1 000
D	760	96	22	14	7	72	29	1 000
E	661	193	21	15	5	85	20	1 000
F	808	108	15	11	3	35	20	1 000
G_1	778	87	11	13	15	58	38	1 000
G_2	743	123	34	9	7	55	29	1 000
H	197	265	28	9	9	385	107	1 000
I	395	239	26	9	7	279	45	1 000
J	293	331	36	11	9	254	66	1 000
K	271	369	45	11	12	230	62	1 000
L	170	264	24	4	5	473	60	1 000
M	240	318	50	15	5	285	87	1 000
N	330	387	50	10	4	182	37	1 000
O	554	174	25	6	1	212	28	1 000
P	46	258	107	12	3	471	103	1 000
Q	226	322	62	20	8	277	85	1 000
Total	487	252	35	16	6	163	41	1 000

CHAPTER VIII.

MEAN DIMENSIONS OF BODY.

1. *History of the Investigation.*

In the early part of the year 1863, an extensive series of inquiries as to the physical and social condition of our soldiers was prepared by Mr. Olmsted, the General Secretary of the Commission, and Mr. Elliott, the Actuary. These were intended to include the most important physical dimensions and personal characteristics, and the necessary apparatus was procured without delay. Similar investigations had already been undertaken, to some extent, by Professor Henry, in behalf of the Smithsonian Institution, who had caused apparatus to be constructed for the purpose; and new instruments for measuring were made at the Coast Survey office, under the supervision of the Vice President of the Commission and Superintendent of the Coast Survey, the late Professor Bache. Two inspectors were appointed, and charged with the duty of obtaining the desired measurements and information for as many men as possible. One of these, Dr. S. B. Buckley, was assigned to the army of the Potomac, while the other, Mr. Risler, measured soldiers in Washington City. The latter was, after a month's service, relieved by Mr. E. B. Fairchild, who was stationed first at a camp on one of the islands in New York harbor, and subsequently at that for rebel prisoners at Point Lookout in Maryland.

The schedule to be filled out by the examiner was in two parts, one pertaining solely to physical characteristics, and such other questions as might be supposed to be of importance in connection with these, and the other having only a bearing on the purely moral and social condition of the same men. The former series only is here discussed, the blank schedule containing them, and known as Form E, having been as follows: —

1. Number of soldier in order of examination?

2. Name of soldier?

Rank?

3. Regiment?
4. Entire height (in stockings — inches and tenths)?
5. Height from ground to lower part of neck (7th cervical vertebra)?
6. Height to perinæum?
7. Breadth of neck?
8. Breadth of shoulders?
9. Breadth of pelvis?
10. Circumference of chest over the nipple (under the coat and vest — inches and tenths)?
11. Circumference of waist?
12. Length of arm — from arm-pit to tip of middle finger?
13. Capacity of chest (cubic inches)?
14. Weight (lbs. and half lbs.) without coat, hat, arms, or accoutrements?
15. Dynamometer?
16. In the opinion of Inspector, from appearance and statements of subject, is he of American stock of three or more generations? (In cases where this question cannot be answered with confidence, affirmatively or negatively, it will be best not to pursue the examination.)
17. If so, period of immigration of ancestry? (Detail of both sides desirable.)
18. Where born — country or State?
    " county?
    " parish or town?
19. If foreign born, year of arrival in this country?
    Supposed about?
20. Country of birth — of father?
    " " of mother?
    " " of grandparents?
21. Enlisted — when?
    where?
    for what period?
22. Conjugal relation (as single, married, or widower)?
23. Age (last birthday)?
24. Former occupation?
25. Hair — color?
    Bald?
    " slightly?
    If so, at what age did baldness become distinct?
26. Eyes — color?
    " distance between pupils?
    " prominent?
27. Complexion?
28. Pulse (regular), beats per minute?
29. Respiration (number of inspirations per minute)?

30. Muscular development?
31. State if in usual vigor?
    if reduced by disease?
    " wounds?
    " recent exertion?
    " hardship?
    " poor fare?
32. Is he, when ordinarily well, a tougher and more vigorous man than before he entered the army?
    Less so?
33. Condition of teeth?
    Number lost?
    Number decayed?
    Number filled?
34. Head — circumference about frontal eminence and greatest projection of occiput?
    Distance between the condyloid process of lower jaw over *os frontis* — longest measurement?
    Distance between condyloid processes over parietal bones?
    Distance from frontal eminence to protuberance of occiput?
35. Facial angle?

The questions of which the numbers are omitted here belonged to the social series.

Of examinations and measurements made in conformity with his schedule, there are existing very nearly 8000, which will be specified in detail hereafter.

In June 1864 the author of this treatise was appointed Actuary of the Commission, and the following passage is quoted from his first report, made after an examination into the statistical materials of the Commission, and their condition, and dated 1864, July 12.

"Of the reports of physical and social condition of soldiers not quite 7200 have been received, namely, about 5200 for national, and 1970 for rebel soldiers. . . . The results of the physical inspections are tabulated for all the 1970 rebel prisoners, and for 3277 of the United States soldiers; also for about 760 returns from the convalescent camp.

"A cursory examination of these returns has impressed me forcibly not only with the great value of the work, but also with the importance of some more distinct understanding and interchange of ideas between different inspectors, if their results are to be combined or compared with one another. Those questions which are necessarily general in their nature have been answered by the inspectors according to their individual interpretation of somewhat vague words, and it appears to me essential that some arbitrary directions be prescribed for their guidance, or better still, agreed upon by the inspectors themselves after personal conference.

"In view of the slowness with which these valuable data can be collected, I would strongly recommend as large an increase of the number of inspectors as may appear feasible to the Commission. Twenty inspectors could furnish but about 7500 to 8000 returns a month, and the best exertions of the Commission can only obtain a comparatively small number. No examinations of the negro troops seem to have yet been made, and the importance of such inspections needs no comment. The blank forms might perhaps be somewhat modified with advantage.

"Should it accord with the views of the Commission to organize a large force of inspectors of physical condition at least, I would farther suggest the desirableness of some official chief of the corps, a part of whose duty it should be to insure uniformity in the interpretation of the questions, and in the signification attributed to the phraseology of answers."

The Commission, with the ready aid and confidence which they have never failed to accord their Actuary, and which will always remain among his most gratifying recollections of an agreeable personal intercourse of nearly four years, adopted the suggestions of this report, and authorized the construction of twelve sets of measuring apparatus, as well as the employment of twelve examiners, who should devote their attention to these investigations and measurements exclusively, — and a sufficient number of clerks to tabulate the results as fast as received.

Considerable modifications were introduced into the apparatus, already excellent, and the schedule of questions was enlarged and revised, with the view of introducing as much precision as possible regarding the points of the body which should serve as bases for measurement. It has always been a source of regret to the writer, that the preparation of this series of questions had not fallen to more competent and experienced hands, since his previous studies had been in totally different departments of research. But the circumstances of the case rendered this impossible, and he endeavored to render the consequent disadvantages a minimum by consultation with friends whose pursuits are of an anthropological or physiological nature. Among those whom he would especially mention with gratitude, as having aided with useful counsel, are Professors Agassiz, J. Wyman, and Holmes, as well as Dr. J. H. Douglas, till that time Chief Inspector and Assistant Secretary of the Commission. Many points of the present inquiry would have been more judiciously ordered, and many of the measurements more effectively conducted, had the knowledge and experience which have necessarily followed this work been available at its commencement; but the author ventures to hope that the materials obtained, and the elaboration which has been found possible for them, may be regarded as contributions to human knowledge, sufficient to palliate the want of the ampler results which these opportunities would have yielded to abler and more experienced inquirers. It was only after the measurements were completed that he first saw the learned and instructive "*Vorlesungen über den Menschen*," by Professor Vogt, which would have given most valuable guidance.

The apparatus employed will be described hereafter. Unfortunately the difficulties under which all mechanic arts were suffering at that period of the war, frcm lack of men and materials, prevented the prompt completion of the apparatus, and it was not till after four months that all the instruments were ready for use. The fact that all the previous measurements had been made in inches seemed to render it advisable that the new ones should be likewise recorded in inches as the units, which was accordingly done, instead of employing the metric system. This has since been a subject of regret, on several accounts, not the least of which is the almost insuperable tendency of all measurers to record their results in some full number of units whenever possible, so that the degree of accuracy is increased to a marked extent as the magnitude of the unit is decreased. Had the dimensions been taken in centimeters instead of inches, not only would the results have been more universally apprehended, but they would really have gained in precision.

The new form prescribed for the examinations received the title "Form EE." To avoid confusion, the same numbers were retained for the questions as had been given in Form E, the new questions being interpolated with fractional numbers or discriminated by small letters affixed.

The following was the schedule, in which the nature of the modifications introduced will be recognized at once.

[Form EE.]

SANITARY COMMISSION.

INDIVIDUAL INSPECTION.

1. Number of soldier in order of examination?
2. Name of soldier?
   Rank?
3. Regiment?
4. Entire height (in stockings — inches and tenths)?

4½. Distance from tip of middle finger to level of upper margin of patella (in "attitude of the soldier")?

5. Height to lower part of neck (spine of the prominent, *i. e.*, 7th cervical vertebra)?

5½. Height to knee (middle of patella)?

6. Height to perinæum?

6½. Perinæum to most prominent part of pubes?

7. Breadth of neck?

7½. Girth of neck?

8. Breadth of shoulders between acromion processes?
9. Breadth of pelvis between crests of ilia?
10. Circumference of chest across the nipples —
    a. Full inspiration?
    b. After expiration?

10½. Distance between nipples?

11. Circumference of waist above hips?

11½. Circumference around hips on level with trochanters?

12 *a.* Length of arm — from tip of acromion to tip of middle finger?
  b. Distance from middle of top of sternum to tip of middle finger, arm extended?
  c. Distance from tip of acromion to extremity of elbow?

13. Capacity of chest in cubic inches (*i. e.*, amount exhaled after full inhalation)?
14. Weight (lbs. and half lbs.) without coat, hat, arms, or accoutrements?

14½. Weight (from memory) at enlistment?

15. Dynamometer?
16. In the opinion of the Inspector, from appearance and statements of subject, is he of American stock of three or more generations?
17. If so, period of immigration of ancestry? (Detail of both sides desirable.)
18. Where born — country or State?
    " county?
    " parish or town?

19. If foreign born, year of arrival in this country?
    Supposed about?
20. Country of birth — of father?
    " of mother?
    " of grandparents?
21. Enlisted — when?
    where?
    for what period?
22. Conjugal relation (as single, married, or widower)?
23. Age (last birthday)?
24. Former occupation or occupations?
25. Hair — color?
    amount?
    texture?
    If bald, at what age did baldness become distinct?
26. Eyes — color?
    distance between outer angles?
    " " inner angles?
    prominent?
27. Complexion?
28. Pulse (regular) beats per minute?
29. Respiration (number of inspirations per minute, when quiet)?
30. Muscular development?
31. Is he in usual vigor?
    reduced by disease?
    " wounds?
    " recent exertion?
    " hardship?
    " poor fare?
32. Is he, when ordinarily well, a tougher and more vigorous man than before he entered the army?
33. Condition of teeth?
    Number lost?
34. Head — *a.* Circumference about frontal eminence, and greatest projection of occiput?
    b. Distance between the condyloid processes of lower jaw over *os frontis*, longest measurement?
    c. Distance between condyloid processes over parietal bones?
    d. Distance between condyloid processes over occipital protuberance?
    e. Distance from frontal eminence to protuberance of occiput?
    f. Width between angles of jaws?
    g. Width between condyloid processes?

35. Facial angle?
36. Foot — *a.* Length from tip of great toe to extremity of heel?
b. Length from tip of great toe to hollow above heel?
c. Thickness at instep?
d. Circumference around heel and anterior ligament?
51. Was he, before the war, given to athletic recreations, and if so, what kind?
55. Education — Limited common school?
Good common school?
High school?
Professional?
57. Distance of distinct vision for small pica double-leaded type?
58. Does he distinguish colors correctly?
If not, describe the irregularity?

To secure uniformity in the mode of measurement by different examiners, Dr. Buckley, whose experience and scientific attainments had already proved serviceable in the examinations under Form E, was appointed Chief Examiner, and all the other gentlemen engaged upon the work went through some days' practice in measuring with him. The following printed instructions were also furnished to each examiner.

INSTRUCTIONS FOR EXAMINATION OF INDIVIDUALS. — [FORM EE.]

The persons examined should not be selected, but should be taken indiscriminately, — by companies and regiments, when possible.

The object of Question 4½, is to determine the point on the outer side of the thigh corresponding with the tip of the middle finger, in the "attitude of the soldier." It is best measured with the calipers.

Question 6½ cannot be answered by means of the andrometer, but may be omitted, as also may Question 10½, when no opportunity is found for examination of the individual without clothing. Such opportunities are never to be lost; although the ordinary examination requires merely the removal of hat, coat, waistcoat, and boots, and loosening the shirt at the breast.

The Girth of neck (Question 7½) is to be taken around the *pomum Adami*.

The Circumference of chest (10) is to be measured under all the clothing; the Distance between nipples (10½), taken with calipers.

For ascertaining the Capacity of the chest (13), the lungs are to be fully inflated, and then as completely emptied as may be, by breathing through the tube of the spirometer. The results of three consecutive trials are to be recorded.

The Questions 28 and 29, as to the number of pulsations and inspirations in a minute, must both be answered before the trial of the Dynamometer (15), which would derange the normal condition. The respirations are of course to be counted without the knowledge of the individual. It is recommended that they be noted immediately after the arm-measurements (13), when the person examined is not suspecting a change in the order of questions as printed; and before the trials with the Spirometer. The precautions for insuring accurate answers are self-evident.

In answer to Question 16, state the *stock*, if possible (as English, Irish, French, etc.); if not, state the race, unless Caucasian, (as African, Malay, etc.); or if of mixed races, and what.

In Trades (Question 24), the journeyman is to be distinguished from the master in all cases — as, Baker (journeyman); Carpenter (master). Laborers are to be described according to the nature of their employment — as Agricultural Laborer, Railway Laborer. The term Farmer should be applied only to those who have themselves owned or rented land. The sons of farmers, living on the farm and working on it, may be returned "Farmers' sons." Descriptions of occupation should be precise — they are too often incomplete: for example, *engine* feeder, *engine* driver, not engineer; *brass* founder, *iron* founder, not founder simply; *commercial* clerk, *lawyer's* clerk, not clerk, simply. If a Mechanic, state the Branch of manufacture; if a Shopkeeper or Salesman, state the kind of business.

The Color of the Hair (25), may be described as Black, Dark-Brown, Brown, Light-Brown, Sandy, Red, Gray (if gray, the original color should also be ascertained and recorded); its Amount, as Thick, Medium, Scanty, or the degree of baldness indicated; its Texture, as Straight, Wavy, or Curly, and as Coarse, Medium, or Fine.

The Color of the Eyes (26), — as Blue, Gray, Hazel, Light-Brown, Dark-Brown, Black.

The Complexion (27), — as Fair, Ruddy, Medium, or Dark.

The Muscular Development (30), — as Large, Moderate, or Deficient.

In the Measurements of Head (34), — the lengths under the hair are desired. The measures *a* and *b* refer to the "frontal eminence," or most prominent part of the forehead above the superciliary ridge. But the distance *e* should be measured from the angle of the skull between the eyebrows to that at the base behind. The widths *f* and *g* are to be taken with calipers; the other measures with the tape.

The Length and Thickness of Foot (36), are to be measured with calipers.

In answering Question 55, record the apparent degree of actual culture or intelligence, rather than the mode in which it was obtained.

The Facial Angle (35), has its center at the alveolar process, and the angle desired is included between lines drawn to the orifice of the ear, and to the "frontal eminence" as above defined.

The lines entitled "Objects of the Examination" are printed on the back of the Forms EE in small-pica double-leaded, and may be used for Question 57.

The object of Question 58 is to determine the comparative frequency of what is called color-blindness, by ascertaining whether green can be distinguished easily from red, yellow from blue, etc.

All measurements are to be noted in inches and tenths, so far as possible; and if for any reason it should not be found practicable to obtain satisfactory and accurate answers, it is better to make a dash against the question, omitting the answer entirely, than to record an uncertain result.

In examining negro troops, give, as answer to Question 30, an estimate of the proportion of black blood, such as Full Black, Mulatto, Quadroon, Octroon; as well as of the negro race, if this can be discriminated. In answer to Question 55, a statement of the apparent intelligence may be given, such as Very low, Low, Average, Quick, etc.; — the ordinary white private soldier being taken as the standard of comparison. Also state whether he can read or write, or both, well or imperfectly; and when this was learned.

The blanks, when filled, are to be sent to the Statistical Department of the Commission, at Washington, — weekly, if possible. Not more than one hundred sets of measures should ever remain in the hands of the examiner at a time.

CAMBRIDGE, *March* 1, 1865.

The close of the war happily deprived us of the opportunities for measuring, by dispersing the citizen soldiery to their homes; but all means of obtaining the desired data were actively improved, so that our total number of men measured according to the new form nearly reaches the number of 15 900. Some of these it has seemed desirable not to incorporate with our results, but the measurements of 15 781 men seem entitled to full confidence, as honestly, carefully, and intelligently made.

In arranging the stations of the different examiners, and giving instructions as to the special duties of each, efforts were made to provide so far as possible that the measurements by each person should be confined to no one class of men, and that the measurements of no class should be restricted to a single examiner. The various exigencies of the work, and a proper regard to economy, prevented entire compliance with this rule; yet it was never overlooked, and in those cases where the physical examination of any class of men was conducted by one person only, the duty was assigned to the most experienced and careful person available, and to some one moreover whose other duties had, when possible, been such as to permit his work to be easily compared with that of more than one other examiner.

The military officers at the various camps and stations afforded all needful opportunities for these examinations with unfailing readiness, no obstacles having been encountered in any instance from want of coöperation on the part of commanding officers. By the Navy Department here, as in all other cases, facilities were accorded with cordiality, and both the late Chief of the Medical Bureau, Dr. Whelan, and the present Chief of Bureau, Dr. Horwitz, issued orders which greatly aided our endeavors. To Admiral Stringham, then commanding the Charlestown Navy Yard, as also to Admiral Thatcher, and to the officers of the Naval Recruiting Station, in New York city, our thanks are also due. In those cases where application to the Secretary of War became necessary, we were less fortunate, all such applications being refused without exception. This has unfortunately precluded us from repeating the measurements of prisoners of war, in order to test the correctness of the differences found by comparison of the results of examinations according to the earlier form. Farther permission was refused, nor could appeals or explanations to the Surgeon-General or the Secretary avail to obtain permission for the agents of the Commission to measure any of the large number of full-blooded Indians, who were held for a considerable time as prisoners of war near Rock Island, on the Upper Mississippi.

A detailed exhibit of the materials collected will be presented in the next section.

The reports from the examiners were sent in weekly, whenever possible, and were immediately tabulated upon sheets prepared for the purpose. Those data which seemed capable of influence by ethnological agencies, were then assorted according to the nativities of the men; those who were in their ordinary health being kept distinct from those who were not, and different classes of men being separately tabulated, so far as was possible. Subsequently a minute comparison was made between the original report and the tabulated copy, for the detection of errors; those of the copyist were corrected; and the examiner was called upon without delay for information as to any measurements or statements which seemed probably erroneous in his reports. At a later period a different scrutiny was also applied, as will be described in its proper order.

In the distribution by nativities, the same classification was employed for the later measurements, which was adopted in the discussion of the Statures, and has been described in Chapter V. But for the earlier measurements and examinations, the arrangement is different, the subdivision being only into ten classes.

Careful discussion of the earlier measures soon made manifest the great importance, not to say necessity, of the precautions, fortunately already taken, to provide that methods of measurement should be the same with different examiners. Differences of the most marked and peculiar kind appeared to exist between the United States soldiers and the rebel prisoners, natives of Southern States. So, too, a comparison of the physical conformation of soldiers measured at the Convalescent Camp, with that of men in active service, seemed to point to very remarkable inferences; yet subsequent measurements of other men of the same classes do not appear to confirm these deductions, and it is more than probable that the discordances arose from different modes of measurement to a much greater extent than from real differences between the classes of men. No pains have been spared in the arrangement of the later measurements [EE], to avoid and to eliminate errors of this kind, yet it would be vain to suppose that they have been entirely obviated; and indeed their influence can be made perceptible by minute discussion in almost every one of the measures prescribed by the schedule. This is especially the case with the head-measurements, but the phenomenon is well known to anthropologists; and there is ground to hope that the employment of the results obtained by many examiners, each of whom aimed at the same object, may afford a means for final deductions comparatively free from individual error. For some questions, such as the facial angle, special determinations of personal difference have been made, and applied as a correction to the result. Accidental errors of measurements follow a general law, and are absolutely eliminated when the mean value is deduced from a sufficiently large number of cases; but no amount of repetition by the same individual can eliminate these constant personal peculiarities. Their elimination implies measurements of the same quantity by a number of different persons.

After the tabulation, classification by nativities, and verification of the numbers by a new comparison with the original reports, had been completed, the mean values for each dimension were computed, and the individual cases assorted by magnitude.

A system of groups was arranged, each group corresponding to certain limits of variation from the mean value for that particular dimension, and the number of cases was counted which belonged within each group. Several desirable ends were attained by this process, but its principal object was to determine the extent to which the distribution of the individual values, around their mean, conformed to the Law of Error, and thus to decide whether the mean already determined truly represented a type; in which case it would not be essentially changed by any increase in the number of equally good measurements; while, on the other hand, any different system of distribution would indicate that the true type had not been attained, so that our mean would require an increase of measurements for its proper determination. An opportunity was also thus afforded and improved for discovering and investigating cases of excessive discordance from the mean.

At a later period of the investigation, when from study of the Law of Growth, it became manifest that the dimensions of the body are very dependent upon the age of the individual, and that the increase of stature generally continues for more than ten years after the age at which most enlistments took place, the full importance of considering the age, as an element of the inquiry, was first appreciated. This would require a classification of the men of each nativity according to age, and a comparative discussion of their dimensions at different ages. Three of the nativities appear to include a sufficient number of individuals to permit some inferences to be obtained in this manner, especially since the statistics of stature are so thoroughly deduced from a large number of cases. Financial considerations, only, have prevented this investigation, which is among the many of which the prosecution was most reluctantly foregone. The materials, however, exist, available for any future inquirer, and in a form which will require a minimum amount of labor for attaining the desired results. Whether the several dimensions which depend upon the development of the bony structure increase according to the same or similar laws, or in the same proportions, during the years between the ages of eighteen and forty-five, is the question to be determined.

One important part of the discussion of our materials it has happily been found possible to complete, namely, the reduction of all the measured dimensions to decimals of the stature. Thus the proportions, as well as actual dimensions, are determined for nearly twenty-four thousand men; and if we are justified in the assumption that the osseous system is symmetrically developed after eighteen years, all our data for each nativity may be combined, without fear of affecting the mean results by the aggregation of the individual dimensions of men of different age. And on the other hand, since any variation in the relative dimensions, for different classes, must be on a scale much smaller than the variations of the actual dimensions, our mean results are entitled to greater confidence, the peculiarity of abnormal cases is more distinctly manifested, and the materials for farther investigation of the modification of bodily proportions by age, stature, nativity, place of residence, occupation, class of society, etc., as well as by race, are brought into the form most favorable for use.

The excessively laborious character of the processes to which these measurements have already been subjected, will be palpable upon the most cursory examination, and will doubtless lead to as full an appreciation of what has been accomplished, as of what has been omitted. Still, it may be well to record that the omissions are not altogether the result of neglect, or of want of desire to continue the inquiries for which these measurements afford a fuller scope than has before been available for anthropologists or statisticians; but it is in great part due to the limits of pecuniary outlay, and of time, to which the Sanitary Commission has felt bound to restrict their researches.

The results of the measurements so carefully planned and carried out by Drs. Schultz and Scherzer of the Exploring Expedition in the Austrian steam-frigate "Novara," would doubtless have aided in the discussion of the materials here presented, by affording the guidance which the inquiries of scholars learned and trained in anthropological researches could not fail to offer; but although anxiously awaited, these results have not yet been published, so far as the author of this volume is aware.

To give as wide usefulness as possible to these researches in their ethnological relations, the Commission has distributed the apparatus with which the measurements were made, among various institutions of learning in the United States; and has disseminated the blank forms [EE] and the instructions to examiners as widely as possible among scientific travellers. Governor MacTavish, of the Red River Territory of British North America, has cordially undertaken to obtain similar measurements of Indians of that region, and to send them to the Smithsonian Institution; and analogous measurements of Indians of the Pacific Coast, both in North and South America, have been promised, and are probably now making. Although this schedule is doubtless defective, the large number of men who have been measured according to its provisions, will probably render it more useful now than a better one would be, as a guide for ethnological determinations.

2. *Measurements obtained.*

It has been stated that about 8000 men were examined according to the original Form E. Of these examinations, by far the greater portion were made before the present Actuary assumed the charge of the work. Some of the results, based upon measures of 776 volunteers made by Dr. Buckley at the Convalescent Camp near Alexandria, and those of 916 men made by the same examiner at the camp at Aquia Creek Landing, were communicated in behalf of the Commission by the former Actuary, Mr. Elliott, to the Statistical Congress at Berlin in September 1863, and subsequently elaborated, and published in a paper, "On the Military Statistics of the United States," with the Proceedings of that Congress. Mr. Elliott's well known ability and learning render this document one of high interest. Until the new apparatus was completed for use in the examinations according to the Schedule [EE], the former system was continued, and the total number of the earlier physical examinations now in our possession is as follows.[1]

Examiner	No. and Class of Men	Place	Date
Dr. S. B. Buckley	776 U. S. soldiers	Conval. Camp, Va.	Jan.–Apr. 1863
"	916 " "	Aquia Creek, Va.	Apr.–June 1863
"	4045 " "	Camps in D. C.	July 1863–Sept. 1864
H. Risler	234 " "	Washington	May and June 1863
E. B. Fairchild	32 " "	David's Island, N. Y.	Sept. 1863
"	75 Rebel pris'rs		
"	1915 " "	Pt. Lookout, Md.	Oct. 1863–Feb. 1864
"	11 U. S. soldiers		
	8004		

The uncertainties which may arise, and the possible errors incurred by comparing or combining these several sets of measures by different examiners, have been already alluded to. The mean dimensions deduced from measurements by any one examiner, for men of different classes or nativities, may legitimately be compared; but it is not so for the mean values obtained for one class by one examiner, and for another class by another examiner, unless a sufficient number of some one class has been measured by both examiners, to permit a trustworthy determination of the mean difference of their results. The effect of the want of some good method

[1] The whole number of these returns considered worthy of tabulation and incorporation with our results was 7904. Subsequently the reports for 252 men, measured by Mr. Fairchild at Chattanooga in April 1864, were discovered after being long supposed lost. They were received, however, too late for incorporation with the present results.

of determining this mean difference, for the earlier measures, will seriously impair the reliance to be placed upon any comparative inference from these. Thus, for example, for natives of the New England States, the mean breadth of the pelvis appears to be 12.96 inches, and the distance over the top of the head between the frontal and occipital eminences 14.44 inches; while for natives of the Slave States, the corresponding mean values are found to be 13.41 and 13.57 inches. Or, if we consider relative dimensions only, expressed in terms of the height as a unit, the average length of the legs is 0.459 for natives of Pennsylvania, and 0.473 for rebel prisoners; and the head measure already cited gives 0.215 for New Englanders, and 0.199 for Southerners. Or, yet again, if we compare men in perfect health with men not in their usual vigor, we shall find the heads of the former to be, on the average, above three tenths of an inch larger in circumference. These differences do not exist in the men measured, but in the usages and judgements of the men measuring — the different class of soldiers being chiefly examined by different persons.

Ineffectual efforts have been made to deduce the personal differences between Messrs. Buckley and Fairchild, so as to permit a safer comparison of their respective results. In the absence of this important means of referring one system of measures to the other, the results of these earlier measures have been classified by nativities only, and directly combined. Therefore, in those nativities which include measurements by both of these gentlemen, the results are intermediate between those which would have been derived from the measurements by each examiner separately.

The mean values of the Actual and Relative dimensions, or as we will designate them, the Dimensions and the Proportions, which are deducible from this series of physical examinations, will be given in their appropriate place, with the other values which result from the subsequent series of measurements with improved apparatus, and according to the new schedule. Where marked differences are found to exist between the two determinations purporting to be of the same dimensions, the explanation will generally suggest itself upon comparison of the language of the question in the two blank forms.

The instruments employed consisted of an andrometer, spirometer, dynamometer, facial-angle instrument, platform-balance, calipers, and measuring tape.

The andrometer is said to have been originally devised by a tailor in Edinburgh, named McDonald, who used it to determine the proper size for soldiers' clothing, for which he had undertaken a considerable contract with the military authorities. Ballingall has given [1] some account, as well as a representation of it; and states that the instrument is deposited in the Museum of the Edinburgh University. It enables the total height, breadth of neck, of shoulders, and of pelvis, the length of legs and height to the knee to be measured with greater accuracy and rapidity than otherwise would be possible, since when the man to be measured has taken his position, gauges are quickly set for the measures of all these dimensions, and the numerical values read off after the man has left the instrument. Instruments of this kind were constructed for the Sanitary Commission in 1863, at the office of the U. S. Coast Survey, under the special supervision of the late Professor Bache, the lamented Superintendent of the Survey, and Vice President of the Commission. These contained some improvements upon the original instrument, especially such as permitted more accurate adjustment to the person, as well as an additional gauge for measuring the height of the body proper, of which the seventh cervical vertebra was taken as the limit. When in August and September, 1864, the new instruments were ordered, Dr. Douglas kindly charged himself with the supervision of the work, which was executed with great care and fidelity by Mr. William Belcher of New York. In the new instruments many addi-

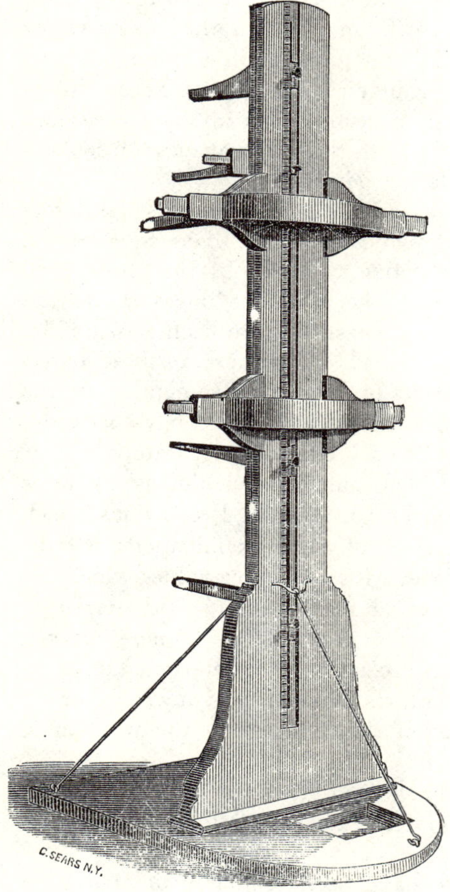

1 *Outlines of Military Surgery*, 1855, pp. 35, 36.

tional improvements were introduced, a considerable part of them being suggested by the experience obtained by the use of the two former ones, which were themselves correspondingly modified as soon as they could be spared for the purpose. The annexed figures will indicate the general construction of the andrometer, and the manner of use.

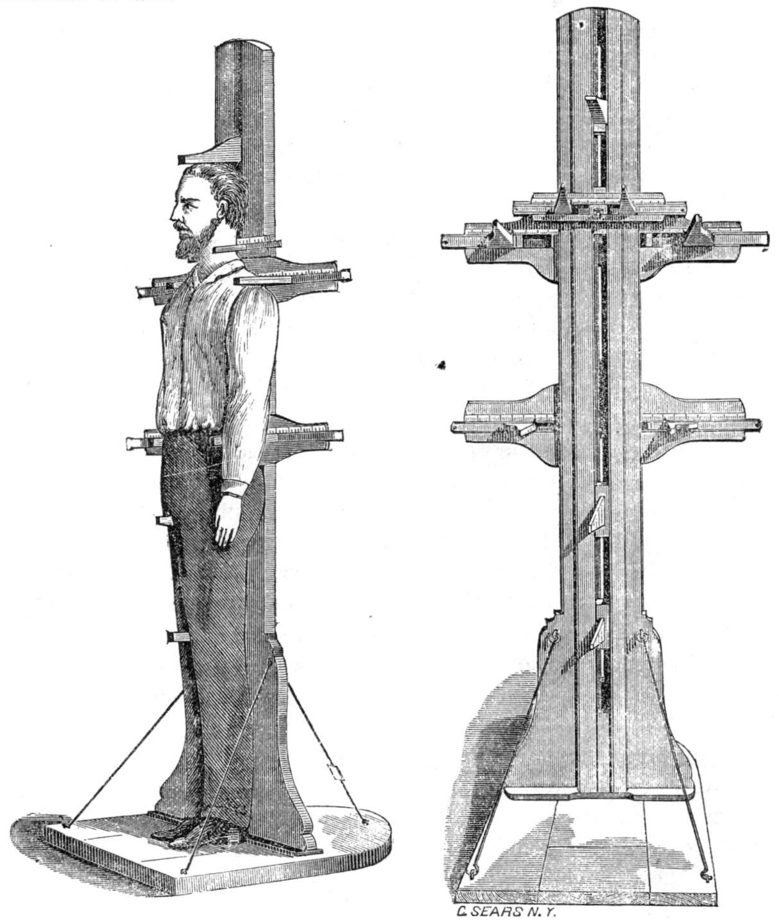

The graduations of this instrument, and of all our implements for linear measure, are in inches and tenths, all danger of error from the use of divisions not decimal being thus avoided. It is a source of regret to the author that he did not employ the metric system for all these measurements, not only as attended with less uncertainty on account of the smaller unit employed when centimeters are substituted for inches, and for the more obvious reason of greater facility in comparing them with other similar measurements, but also as a means of contributing in some small degree towards the important and philanthropic work, now going on among civilized nations, of promoting a uniform decimal international system of weights and measures.

The great deficiency of skillful mechanics in the country during the last years of the war delayed the completion of the apparatus, the first set of which was not ready until the middle of December, and but one hundred and eighty men had been examined according to the new programme, at the beginning of the year 1865. The overthrow of the rebellion was finished early in April, and the disbandment of the army soon commenced, so that more than five sixths of our data in this series were collected during the first eight months of 1865.

Examiners were appointed as rapidly as the sets of apparatus were completed, and each examiner practised a day or two with Dr. Buckley before commencing his own independent series of measurements. The first examinations attempted were at Elmira, N. Y., where was a large camp of rebel prisoners. A set of apparatus was provisionally made up, by the use of some of the old and some of the new instruments, and taken by Dr. Buckley to Elmira, where he instructed Mr. William S. Baker in their use, and remained for some time in the expectation of permission to commence the desired measurements. Every courtesy and assistance possible was afforded by the officers in command, but access to the prisoners could only be obtained by permission of the Secretary of War, and our application was refused by him. This camp was, however, found to be a very favorable position for obtaining measurements of our own soldiers, and about a thousand men were measured there by Mr. Baker.

During the month of December, 1864, five more examiners were appointed, instructed, and assigned to duty. Mr. Arthur Phinney was stationed at the Naval Rendezvous in New York City, where he was able to measure the men while entirely unclothed, immediately after their examination by the medical officer of the station. Here he measured more than eight hundred men at the time of their acceptance into the navy, thus obtaining a peculiarly valuable collection of data, to which his scrupulous accuracy has given additional worth. Dr. W. B. Wells was assigned to the Marine Barracks at the Brooklyn Navy Yard, and Messrs. F. H. Smith and G. F. Murray to Fort McHenry and another of the military stations near Baltimore, where quarters and all desired assistance were readily afforded them by General Morris, then commanding the defenses of Baltimore. Arrangements had also been made for the examination of uncivilized Indians, a large number of whom were held as prisoners of war near Rock Island in Illinois, but these were rendered futile by the failure of repeated attempts on the part of various officers of the Commission to obtain the needed authority from the War Department, the Surgeon-General reporting officially "that the scientific results did not promise to be of sufficient value to warrant the introduction of irresponsible persons into our large prison camps."

In January 1865, Messrs. C. D. Lewis, Horatio T. Myers, and James Russell, together with Dr. Buckley, commenced the examination of soldiers of Western regiments and of the First Army Corps near Washington. In February Mr. Russell established himself at City Point, Va., where he commenced the measurement of colored soldiers; and Dr. B. G. Wilder, a naturalist of distinction, then Assistant Surgeon of a Massachusetts negro regiment, and Major Sigourney Wales measured sailors on board the receiving ship at the Charlestown Navy Yard with Dr. Buckley, as preliminary to a series of examinations of black troops in South Carolina, whither they returned in the month following. In March, Dr. John Elsner relieved the last named gentleman at the Charlestown Navy Yard; Mr. Lewis was transferred to Detroit, where was a large camp; and Mr. Myers to New Orleans, to measure Southern white men. This last undertaking, however, proved unsuccessful. Mr. Myers's health gave way under the climatic influences; and he was able to reach his home in New York State but a few weeks before he fell a victim to the debility resulting from malarial fever.

The collapse of the rebellion in April, and the extensive military movements which preceded and followed this event, together with the cessation of recruiting for the navy, interrupted or restricted most of the work of the examiners; while the approaching concentration of the Armies of the Potomac and of the West, around Washington, indicated that a very short-lived but abundant opportunity for the collection of materials was near at hand. Another examiner, Mr. James M. Stark, was accordingly added to the corps; and measures were taken to transfer to Washington or vicinity all of our examiners whose supply of men did not promise to be abundant for two or three months to come, excepting Mr. Russell, who accompanied the Twenty-fifth Army Corps to the Rio Grande, in order to increase the number of measurements of colored troops. The interval was improved to obtain similar measurements, by Dr. Elsner, of the older students of the universities at Cambridge and New Haven, of whom two hundred and ninety-one were examined, as has been already stated in Chapter V., where their statures are discussed.

With the disbandment of the grand armies around Washington, and the mustering out of service, which so promptly followed for other soldiers, our opportunities for obtaining men were greatly diminished, and the examinations were discontinued wherever the supply of subjects became insufficient to furnish measures of eighty men a week.

At a later period, a considerable number of examinations, both of white and colored men, were made at New Orleans, by Dr. George W. Avery, Surgeon of the 1st Louisiana Infantry; and Mr. Thomas Furniss and Dr. Buckley measured somewhat more than five hundred Indians, belonging to the Iroquois or Six Nations, including all the full-grown men of unmixed race accessible on the Iroquois reservations in Western New York.

The total number of the men of different classes whose measurements have been made and tabulated according to Schedule [EE], will be most readily seen from the accompanying tabular view, in which the work of each examiner is indicated.

Examiners	White Soldiers		Sail-ors	Ma-rines	Stu-dents	Full Blood Negroes		Mulattoes		Indians		Total
	In Vigor	Not in Vigor				In Vigor	Not in Vigor	In Vigor	Not in Vigor	In Vigor	Not in Vigor	
Buckley	1 498	549	–	–	–	–	–	7	–	507	6	2 567
Baker	1 754	69	–	–	–	305	22	57	3	–	–	2 210
Phinney	747	250	822	–	–	45	1	20	1	1	–	1 887
Lewis	2 455	169	–	–	–	1	–	–	–	–	–	2 625
Smith	1 340	256	1	–	–	–	–	–	–	–	–	1 597
Russell	149	24	–	–	–	601	53	148	34	–	–	1 009
Myers	168	54	–	–	–	116	31	34	17	–	–	420
Wells	–	13	–	68	–	–	–	–	–	–	–	81
Murray	68	–	–	–	–	–	–	–	–	–	–	68
Elsner	607	170	295	–	291	29	1	3	–	–	–	1 396
Wales	–	–	28	–	–	504	118	103	40	–	2	795
Wilder	1	–	–	–	–	3	–	30	11	–	–	45
Stark	225	29	–	–	–	2	2	1	1	–	1	261
Avery	50	2	–	–	–	48	–	300	35	–	–	435
Furniss	209	20	–	–	–	–	–	–	2	–	–	231
Marcy	–	–	–	–	–	138	–	16	–	–	–	154
Total	9 271	1 605	1 146	68	291	1 792	228	719	144	508	9	15 781

In making these examinations the usual course was to cause the man to take off shoes, coat, and waistcoat, the trousers and under-clothing remaining; but the girth of the chest was measured under the shirt. Men thus measured are recorded as "clothed." In many cases all clothing was removed, except trousers and drawers; and men thus measured are recorded as "half-naked." Others still were measured while entirely divested of clothing.

Our materials, assorted on this basis, are as follows: —

	White Soldiers	White Sailors	Marines	Students	Negroes	Mixed Races	Indians	Total
Clothed . . .	10 876	–	–	291	1 196	607	517	13 487
Half-naked . .	–	85	68	–	147	47	–	347
Naked	–	1 061	–	–	677	209	–	1 947
Total . . .	10 876	1 146	68	291	2 020	863	517	15 781

Of these there are some belonging to each of the classes into which the nativities have been divided, as already described, although to some, such as the 'Free States west of the Mississippi,' or 'Spain and Spanish Colonies,' there belong but few. About one ninth of the total number of white soldiers were born in the New England States, about one third in New York, Pennsylvania, or New Jersey, and nearly one sixth in Ohio and Indiana, while between one fifth and one sixth were born on the other continent.

A very considerable number of measurements of certain dimensions were erroneously made, in spite of all efforts to the contrary. This was especially the case with the width of shoulders, where, not the distance between the acromion processes, but the full width, was measured for a while by some examiners, giving results analogous to those obtained in the early series according to Form E. Similar misconceptions took place in some of the head measurements, especially 34*e*, and in the facial angles. In all these instances, however, the erroneous methods were soon detected, investigated, and remedied; while the results, though valueless as regards the answer to the real question, are yet not without their use as affording some measurement, other than the one demanded.

To guard against dangers of this sort, the tabulation of the returns was made to keep pace as far as possible with the examinations made; and the mean dimensions resulting from the measurements by each examiner were frequently computed and collated. Any indication of systematic discordance was followed up without delay, and traced either to some peculiarity of individual method, or to some characteristic of the class of men involved.

The value of the earlier measurements (Form E) is of course incommensurate with that of the later ones (Form EE), apart from the much larger number of these latter. The relative trustworthiness of the two series can be estimated from the details already given, and the results from each have been independently elaborated, by similar methods. It has been already stated, however, that the classification by nativities is not the same for the two series; that which was finally employed for the discussion of the later measurements and of the statures having been adopted after considerable progress had already been made in the reduction of the earlier ones.

In the present chapter, only the linear dimensions of the body will be considered; while the proportions deducible from these, as well as the measures of the head, will form the subjects of subsequent chapters, the latter being followed in their turn by some discussion of the other points regarding which information is afforded by our physical examinations.

A few remarks on the nature of the inferences legitimately deducible from our results will perhaps be appropriate here; after which they will be presented in as condensed and concise a form as the nature of the case seems properly to admit. It will be remembered by the considerate student of the facts which we have gathered, and striven to offer in this compact form, that the present investigation does not aspire to, and may not even aim at, any thorough discussion of the large mass of data which have been collected. The means of the Commission and the pursuits of the author alike forbid such an undertaking; but it is hoped and believed that the means for such researches have been collected and arranged in a form well adapted for the use of the anthropological inquirer, and that such facts as are deducible from our materials, though not from their printed results, may be obtained with comparative ease from the manuscript archives of the Statistical Department, which it is the desire of the Commission to preserve in a form convenient for access.

3. *Averages, Types, etc.*

The value of the results of these measurements will depend chiefly upon the degree of approximation with which their mean represents the normal dimensions of the classes of men under consideration. These normal dimensions would, for any one class of persons, be afforded by the arithmetical mean, or average value, of the corresponding dimensions of all men of the same class, provided an indefinitely large number could be obtained; and it becomes an important problem to ascertain the limits within which our finally adopted determinations would probably be varied by an indefinite increase in the number of men measured, — or, in other words, to obtain some numerical expression of the degree of reliance which should be placed on the mean values derived from our respective measurements, as indicating the normal dimensions.

It seems, therefore, not amiss to offer here a few words concerning the true significance of averages, and the nature of typical forms. The subject has been so thoroughly elaborated, both in its mathematical and its philosophical bearings, that few, if any, remarks on its elementary principles may claim the credit of originality. Even the mode of presenting the ideas involved in a popular form offers little unoccupied ground, since the elegant and learned treatises by Quetelet, De Morgan, and others. And the only endeavor in this place will be to present such considerations as are requisite for proper criticism of our materials.

If after a marksman has fired a large number of times at a distant target, we examine the several shots, measuring their distances and directions from the center, we shall soon be able to discover in this experimental way a number of theorems, which hold good, not merely for all similar cases, but for all human efforts in science or art, and for all phenomena in which those complex influences are involved which are implied in such words as accident, fortune, hazard, chance, or random. Among these theorems, two are especially important.

We shall find that there is a mean or average point from which the sum of the distances of all the individual shots is a minimum. This point may not have been struck by a single ball, yet it represents the average of all the shots, and is in fact the point more likely than any one other to have been hit by each individual ball. If it coincide with the central point of the target, this is the highest testimony to the accuracy of the marksman, since it is thus made evident that his aim was affected by no vicious habit in pointing or in firing; but that the divergence of the several shots from their central or average point was exclusively due to errors which may be classed as fortuitous.

Practically, however, such accordance will seldom, and strictly speaking, it will probably never, be found; but it will be seen that this mean or central point of all the shots fired deviates from the center of the target by a certain amount, and in a certain direction. This amount and direction measure the constant or personal error of aim, which will usually be found a very decided and well marked quantity, both in its character (*i. e.* the direction) and in its intensity (*i. e.* the distance). Under the same circumstances it will be essentially the same for the same individual; but it is only partially dependent either upon the person or the circumstances. The amount and direction of the wind, the position of the sun, the rifle used, and other influences, will modify the error due to the individual.

We shall also find that the shots are systematically grouped about their central point, being more numerous in its immediate vicinity, and their number decreasing with the distance, in conformity with some regular law. This law is known; it is deducible from abstract mathematical investigation; its sway is supreme throughout the whole domain of chance or hazard, wherever this may extend. And the precise proportion of the shots which belong to each successive interval of distance from the mean of all, may be computed either before or after the event. This proportion is not necessarily that which will be found there, but it will closely approximate thereto; the degree of accordance will be greater, the greater the number; and if the number be indefinitely increased, the accordance will be absolute. The scale of application of this law, as exhibited by the magnitude of the successive equal intervals of distance, will vary with different individuals, and must be deduced by experiment before the actual numbers can be assigned for each inch or centimeter, or other definite linear dimension. This depends upon a numerical value easily deduced, and known as the "measure of precision," and in the case supposed indicates, not the accuracy of the aim, but its regularity; the former being measured by the uniform or constant, and the latter by the accidental or variable, error. Now the degree of accordance between the theoretical distribution of the distances of the several shots about their central point, on the one hand, — as computed by the mathematical formula, when the measure of precision is known, — and the distribution actually observed, on the other hand, affords a criterion as to how far the central point found represents the true point which it is desired to find, and which would be shown after an indefinite number of shots. A close accordance between the computed and predicted series shows that the true point has been so well determined by observation, that no considerable increase in accuracy would probably be attained by a considerable increase in the number of trials. But a marked discordance between the two series implies an inadequate number of trials, and consequently an untrustworthy determination of the desired mean.

Let us now suppose the same marksman to make similar trials on a large number of different occasions, under varying physical conditions, at various hours of the day, in various states of the weather, and, in short, under circumstances as diverse as possible; and let us consider the several resulting determinations of the point at which he actually does aim, while intending to aim at the center of the target. Here the positions deduced for the central point of his shots on different days will also be grouped about a mean position, and in accordance with the same law of error, and under the same conditions as already described. And this group of points will give us the measure and direction of that portion of the several errors (constant under certain circumstances), which belongs to the individual alone, and is constant for him under all circumstances. Moreover we may here deduce a "measure of precision" which indicates the average effect of extraneous influences, and by its aid may determine the accordance between theory and observation, — thus measuring the degree of accuracy with which the true point of individual aim has been determined.

Taking yet another step, we may similarly combine the points of aim, thus found, for a large number of individual marksmen, and shall find the same laws to prevail. Different individuals will be found affected with tendencies to constant errors varying in magnitude and in direction; and, unless some overruling influence exist, common to all or nearly all, we shall find that the central point of aim for a large corps of marksmen coincides with the center of the target, their individual points of aim being grouped around this center, according to the same law of error. Should any agency affect all to such an extent as to prevent a coincidence between their average aim and the true center of the target, this want of coincidence would disclose the existence, and lead to the detection, of the disturbing influence.

It is manifest that the steps here considered in succession need not be successively taken, but that a considerable number of men, practising together on various occasions, would enable us, by finding the mean of all the shots, and their several divergences therefrom, to arrive at a close approximation to the central point of the target, after all other means of recognition had been effaced or destroyed. We should, moreover, attain a knowledge of the average skill displayed, as affected by the average circumstances.

Now we may regard the laws of Nature, to which the Supreme Being has assigned the duty of carrying out his creative mandates, as occupying, in the almost infinitely varied circumstances under which they find application, a position analogous to that of marksmen aiming at a target. There exists, for plant and beast and man, a type, — not necessarily clothed with a material body, yet none the less a real entity. And as, among hundreds of thousands of shots, no single one may centrally strike the target, while their grouping may indicate its center, with a precision greater than our senses permit us to appreciate ; so, by a sufficient number of measurements, under circumstances sufficiently varied, upon a sufficient number of subjects, we may arrive at a knowledge of the form and dimensions of the ideal, typical plant, or animal, or man,— to which all individuals are approximations, although no one of them may ever have attained, or hoped to attain, its accurate impersonation. Varieties and individual dissimilarities here occupy positions relatively analogous to the constant and variable errors of aim on the part of the marksman ; and possibly in the exalted scheme of Nature, even species and genera, to go no higher, may in their turn occupy the same relative stations, when our field of view is adequately magnified.

Applying these principles to the present investigation, we see that there is a human type to be sought, though attainable only by the combination of results from many races ; a type of race, attainable through the study of many nationalities ; a type of nationality, and a type of each class within its bounds. Our measurements pertain almost exclusively to American soldiers, and these not of the same age, nor all of them of mature growth ; yet they are from wide-spread regions of the continent, and many of them belonged by birth to other nations. Our aim has been to deduce the types for as many as may be of these various classes of men, and to test the trustworthiness of the results by the accordance between the series of observed and theoretical deviations of the several measurements from their mean.

The existence of types for man, and for the races and classes of men, was first demonstrated by Quetelet, who has done more than any one else to study and discuss the average man, in his various relations, physical, social, and moral. He has illustrated the relation of the theoretical laws of chance to investigations like the present so happily, that, even at the risk of prolixity, it seems well to reproduce the illustration here. It must first be premised that, by the mean or average result of measurement, two distinct kinds of inference may be denoted. The mean result may be the mean of many measurements of a single object, — and thus afford the closest attainable representation of a material thing, — or it may be a mean of the measurements of many different, although similar objects, and thus represent no particular thing. In the first instance, the individual measures, and in the second, the measures of individuals, group themselves about the mean in conformity with the law of error; but there is this wide distinction, that while in the former case the several values are closely connected, varying only by the errors of the measurer, they are in the latter case devoid of all mutual connection of a material kind; and the existence of any mutual connection must be determined by the degree and nature of the accordance of the measures. When such connection exists, the accordance or discordance of the several measures follows precisely the same laws in the two instances; and the adoption of the idea of a type, in approximate conformity to which all individuals of a class are fashioned, abolishes the practical distinction between the two sorts of means.

To borrow Quetelet's illustration, let us suppose that it is desired to obtain by measurement the dimensions of a statue. Measuring any portion ten or twelve times successively, with all possible care, it is improbable that any two of the results would be identical; and in a thousand repetitions of the process we should obtain a series of numerical values, the mean of which would differ very little from the true one, while the amount of discordance in individual cases would be inversely proportional to the precision of the measures. And assorting the results by order of discordance from the mean, we should find their distribution to follow the law of probability, since the only deviations would be those due to want of skill, or care, or to imperfection of the senses.

If, instead of a statue, a living person be taken as the subject of measurement, the chances of error are much more numerous, and the magnitude of the errors would be increased by the absence of rigidity of the flesh, and by the real fluctuations of the dimensions in consequence of respiration and other involuntary motions, and unconscious changes of attitude by the subject. Yet the mean of a thousand measurements of each dimension would afford an approximation to the true average dimensions of the living person, nearly as close as to those of the statue in the former instance, and the variations of the several results would follow a similar law.

Modifying the supposition, imagine a thousand sculptors em ployed to copy the statue or the person, with all possible precision, and their copies measured in the place of the original. Then, to the original sources and chances of error would be added the inaccuracies of the copyists ; still from the mean of all we should derive essentially the same value, and the discordances would be similarly grouped about this mean.

Finally, suppose that while the number of the copyists is adequately increased, many of them are hampered by the prejudices or prepossessions of their several schools of art ; that their material varies in character, both for the different copies and for the different portions of the same copy ; that many are supplied with improper tools ; that some are partially blind, others crippled in their hands and arms ; and that their degrees of skill are very diverse ; still the mean of all the results would enable the archetype to be reproduced with much accuracy, and the agreement, in number and amount, of the variations with those prescribed by the law of error, would establish the fact that such a common model had actually existed.

Thus it is that we may hope to discover the type of humanity, as well as the types of the several classes and races of man. In the present research we are dealing only with some of his external physical manifestations, but we aim at the deduction of the numerical exprèssions of these as a step toward constructing the typical or average man, who, though probably never clad in flesh, is yet a reality, not merely existing in the Divine mind, but capable of perception and recognition by human sense. Indeed the external form of this average man may legitimately be adopted as a standard of beauty and a model for art. The eminent scientist already named has shown that we may discover not merely the outward semblance of this abstract being, but his needs, capacities, intellect, judgement, and tendencies ; and Quetelet may thus be regarded as the founder of statistical anthropology, indeed of social science, in the true significance of the word, according to which science depends upon the investigation of laws, not upon the consideration of isolated facts, nor the dissemination of correct principles.

It is only when statistical research conducts to the discovery of types, or when the inferences drawn from it may be tested, and confirmed by detection of some systematic subordination to law in their variations, that statistics afford a safe guidance. The discredit in which this mode of investigation is held by many able men, and the errors in which it has frequently involved candid inquirers, may thus be accounted for. To hold any means of research in disrepute is unphilosophical; to regard any process as responsible for the results of its misapplication is absurd. Many moral, social, political, and physical laws seem only deducible, and are certainly only demonstrable, by statistical investigation, although no methods in the whole range of science require more caution and skill in their employment, or can more easily delude the unwary.

"The average man," says Quetelet, "is for a nation what the center of gravity is for a body; to the consideration of this are referred all the phenomena of equilibrium." The full discussion of many of the data collected in these examinations, and preserved in the archives of the Sanitary Commission, would doubtless bring many important facts clearly to light. But various considerations, especially that of financial means, restrict the present discussion to some of the more important physical characteristics.

The mathematical presentation of the subject is needless here; for the several quantities involved have been abundantly investigated by analysts, and are well understood. Special tables have been computed for most of the more important dimensions, showing not only the actual distribution of the variations, but also that distribution which would be indicated by the theoretical law of error, on the assumption that the number of cases is sufficient to allow the full application of the doctrine of probability. A very few words will suffice to indicate the mode of computation and the significance of the auxiliary quantities.

In the formula —

$$y = \frac{h}{\sqrt{\pi}} e^{-h^2\Delta^2} d\Delta$$

y represents the probability that the error of an observation, or the variation of a single case from a type, will fall between the limits Δ and $d\Delta$; and the integral of this equation, between the definite limits $\Delta = 0$ and $\Delta = a$, will express the probability that such error will be found between 0 and a, or that it will be found between 0 and $-a$. The quantities π, e, and h are constants, the two former denoting, as usual, the ratio of the circumference of a circle to its diameter and the base of the Neperian system of logarithms, while the latter is the "measure of precision."[1]

Effecting the integration of this formula, after putting for con-

[1] See Chauvenet's *Manual of Spherical and Practical Astronomy*, II. 478–493, the notation of which is here retained.

venience $h\Delta = t$, we find the probability that any discordance from the mean is less than a, or, in other words, the proportional number of cases where the variation is less than a, to be

$$P = \frac{2}{\sqrt{\pi}} \int_0^{ah} e^{-t^2} dt$$

one half this number corresponding to positive, and one half to negative discordances.

Since, in tabulating the number of instances found at each specific dimension x, we record all those which are nearer to this value than to either of the adjacent ones $x \pm \Delta x$, the corresponding theoretical values are best found by computing $\frac{1}{2}P$ for the interval between the mean, x_0, and the value $x + \frac{1}{2}\Delta x$, for successive values of x. The difference of the corresponding successive values of $\frac{1}{2}P$ thus gives that theoretical proportion of all the instances recorded, which belongs to the interval between $x + \frac{1}{2}\Delta x$ and $x - \frac{1}{2}\Delta x$.

Tables for P are given in most works upon probability, based upon numerical values given by Kramp in a treatise[1] on Refractions. They have been largely expanded for the purposes of the present investigation.

Denoting by η the average discordance from the mean, the measure of precision will be approximately

$$h = \frac{\Delta x}{\eta\sqrt{\pi}} = 0.56419 \frac{\Delta x}{\eta}$$

The so-called "probable error" (probable discordance from the type), in any series of measurements, is the amount of variation from the mean for which it may be asserted that in the case of any single measurement, the probabilities are equal that the discordance will be greater or less than this amount. It is generally denoted by r, and we may use $r = 0.8453\ \eta$

The "mean error" (mean discordance from the type) is that amount of variation from the mean, of which the square is the mean of the squares of the individual discordances. It is denoted by e, and $e = 1.4826\ r = 1.2533\ \eta$

When the circumstances are such that the law of error may be strictly applied, the precision of the mean of any number of observations increases as the square root of their number, so that the probable error of the mean of any series of measurements is equal to the probable error of a single measurement divided by the square root of their total number. Hence we may estimate the accuracy with which the typical value of any dimension has been

[1] *Analyse des Refractions astronomiques et terrestres.* Strasbourg, l'an vii. (1799.)

attained, by dividing the probable discordance, r, of an isolated measurement, by the square root of the number of measurements, to obtain r_0, the probable error of the result.

In all this investigation, however, it must not be forgotten that our results are dependent upon the assumption that the number of men measured, and the number of measurers, and the precision of their implements, are all sufficient to give full scope for the application of the law of error. This assumption is, of course, not conformable with fact; still, until the work can be repeated upon a more extended and elaborate scale, the present results must necessarily suffice.

The numerical values of some of the quantities here described are given, with some of the mean results of measures of the several dimensions, in order to aid the student in estimating the degree of reliance to which the results are entitled. But he must remember that the average discordances, being deduced from the variations of individual measures from their mean, show the numerical values, not of the tendency to error in the measurements, but of the tendency of single members of a class to vary from the mean or type corresponding to that class. So, too, the quantity which we call the Probable Error of the Mean denotes the value of this probable error, as deduced from intrinsic evidence alone, this same degree of variation in individual results furnishing the basis. Whether the value obtained is a typical value or not, must be inferred from the degree of accordance between the system of computed and the system of observed variations. This degree of accordance between the two systems is itself capable of expression in a concise numerical form, by deducing its modulus from the series of differences between the theoretical and actual values, after each difference has been affected with its proper weight; but such computation is somewhat laborious, and it has appeared unadvisable to undertake it here.

4. *White Soldiers.*

The total number of white soldiers of whom we possess measures tabulated according to the later schedule is 10 876; thirteen different persons having been engaged in measuring them, as will be seen by the tabular view given in the second section of this chapter. These and all the other classes of men measured, have been discussed in two divisions, those who were in possession of ordinary health being considered separately from those who were not in usual vigor, in order to determine whether any of the results might be sufficiently different for these two divisions to afford any clews to the hygienic tendencies of physical proportions. The number of men reported as not in usual vigor is 1605, leaving 9271 as the number in ordinary health.

The men have also, as heretofore stated, been classed according to nativities, upon the same basis as was adopted in Chapter V. for the discussion of the statures, with the additional separation of the natives of Wales and the Isle of Man, 20 in number, from the 306 natives of England proper. Various causes have slightly modified the number of the measurements for different dimensions, but the numbers given in the General Table of Results (p. 238), have not been essentially changed except for the Question 8, "Breadth of shoulders between acromion processes"; for which about one fifth of the answers give the simple "breadth of shoulders" at the widest part, like the measurements according to the first schedule. These two sorts of measures have been carefully kept distinct, and in some cases both have intentionally been taken for the same man. Question 10½ is answered for only 2068 soldiers; Question 6½ for none of the soldiers, and for only 1013 white men.

The measurements by the earlier schedule were all for white soldiers; 5736 being of men who were, and 2168 of men who were not in their ordinary health, — the whole number of cases in our tabulation being 7904.

Thus for the entire number of white soldiers included in the two series, we have 15 007 in usual vigor, and 3773 others, 18 780 in all.

The heights of white soldiers specially measured are given in the appended table, which may possess some interest in connection with the researches of Chapter V. The number and amount of variations from the mean, and the trustworthiness of that mean, were not there discussed for the several nativities; since the labor thus entailed, though perhaps not very great, in the present condition of our records, would yet be needless, — inasmuch as the large number of our data, and their mutually confirmatory results, make manifest the correctness of our inferences, and the limited financial means available for our researches preclude many desirable computations.

The mean value of the height of our soldiers, here deduced, can make no claim to precision, since no account is taken of their ages, although an overwhelming proportion of the whole number had not attained their full growth; and in this table men of all nativities are indiscriminately combined. The number given for each inch of height comprises all whose stature was between a half inch below, and a half inch above the height named.

Distribution by Height of White Soldiers measured.

Height Inches	Actual Number	Proportional Number in 10 000		
		Observed	Calculated	Calc.-Obs.
61	197	105	100	- 5
62	317	169	171	+ 2
63	692	369	368	- 1
64	1 289	686	675	- 11
65	1 961	1 044	1 051	+ 7
66	2 613	1 391	1 399	+ 8
67	2 974	1 584	1 584	0
68	3 017	1 607	1 531	- 76
69	2 287	1 218	1 260	+ 42
70	1 599	852	884	+ 32
71	878	467	531	+ 64
72	520	277	267	- 10
73	262	139	118	- 21
74 etc.	174	92	61	- 31

The excess of men of 73 inches and upwards, is probably due to an unconscious bias of the examiners in selecting their subjects for measurement; although it was carefully endeavored to avoid any principle of selection, and, whenever possible, to have the men detailed for measurement without any choice on the part of the examiner. The average and probable discordances are thus enlarged.

The average age of the men was 25.76 years, and their mean height 67.240 inches, which would (roughly) correspond to a full stature of 67.33 inches.[1]

The average discordance, η, is 1.983 inches; the probable discordance of a single determination, r, is 1.676; and the probable error of the final result is 0.012 inches.

The distribution of the statures of men of different classes, examined according to Form [EE] has been specially studied. This was, however, not with the expectation of deducing any valuable result for their mean heights, since the aggregation of all ages in one class would preclude this, and the numbers, likewise, are inadequate; but for the sake of thoroughly scrutinizing the individual results, which were to be adopted as units of measure for all

[1] Since the growth was more rapid at ages below, than at those above the mean, the full stature would actually be larger than that here obtained by adding the average growth between the mean age and that of maximum height.

the other dimensions. It seems, therefore, unadvisable to present the assortments for special classes, although the accordance between their computed and recorded numbers for the several dimensions is much better than that found in the preceding table; yet it may be worth while to give a few of the results. The following were found, among others, for men in usual vigor:—

Nativity	Number of Men	Mean Age	Mean Height	Probable Variation for an Individual	Probable Error of Mean	Corresponding Full Stature [1]
			in.	in.		in.
A.—New England . .	978	25.30	67.202	1.625	0.052	67.40
New York . . .	2 098	25.84	67.150	1.666	0.036	67.31
B.—N. Y., N. J., Penn.	3 125	25.67	67.132	1.648	0.029	67.29
N. Jersey & Penn.	1 036	25.33	67.097	1.635	0.051	67.27
C.—Ohio and Indiana	1 418	24.43	67.687	1.566	0.042	67.98
D.—Mich., Wisc., Ill. .	938	24.44	67.223	1.542	0.050	67.51
L.—Ireland	559	28.09	66.703	1.492	0.063	66.74

Distance from tip of middle finger to level of upper margin of patella (in "attitude of the soldier").—The object of this question, which was originally suggested by Dr. Wm. H. Van Buren, was to expose, if possible, any ethnological differences or peculiarities in the relative proportions of arms, legs, and body, which might, in their combined influence, be more conspicuous than when severally considered; and the results seem to show its aptitude for this purpose.

Comparisons of the actual and theoretical discordances from the mean for men in usual vigor, have been made separately for the three nativities, A, B, and D, comprising about 5000 men, as also for the men from New York State by themselves. The results are satisfactory, the chief want of accordance being due to the unconquerable tendency of examiners to record their measurements in inches or half inches when the true quantity differs slightly from such values. The means are manifestly typical for the nativities specially tested, and probably for all those nativities or classes which comprised so many as 500 men. The total range of the means is between 4.70 inches for Canadians, and 6.07 inches for natives of Kentucky and Tennessee; but this difference is very largely due to the maintenance of the same proportional value among men differing in stature. The amounts of probable variation of a single individual from the mean of all of the same nativity, and of this

[1] See note on preceding page.

mean from its true value, are as follows in the four classes mentioned: —

Nativity	Number	Mean Value	Probable Variation	
			Individual r	Mean r_0
		in.	in.	in.
New England States .	977	4.862	0.856	0.027
New York	2 087	4.883	0.825	0.018
N. Y., N. J., and Penn.	3 122	4.891	0.827	0.015
Mich., Wis., and Illinois	938	4.806	0.767	0.025

Height to the spine of the seventh cervical vertebra. — This point, the highest distinctly recognizable one which is not moved by flexure of the head and neck, was taken as the limit of the body proper, which may be regarded as extending from the seventh cervical vertebra, to the perinæum.

Deducting the height to this point from the total height, we obtain the measure of *Head and Neck*, which is in general a very little short of ten inches for the white race, or 0.148 of the average height of the men measured. The ordinary value is about 9.95 inches, varying from this amount by scarcely more than half an inch for the extreme groups, and by so much as one inch in very few individual cases. The variation is by no means proportional to that of the stature, and it would seem that its greater part is due to differences in the length of the neck, rather than to the height of the head itself, which seems to be more uniform than almost any other physical dimension. The greatest deviation in the mean value for any of our nativity-groups, is for the small group G_2, which comprises natives of the Slave States west of the Mississippi. It contains but 51 cases, 19 of which are in a series measured by Dr. Avery, at New Orleans, and in which I suspect some error. Omitting these, the remaining 32 cases give an average of 9.95 inches, quite in conformity with the results for other nativities.

The most marked discordance in the length of head and neck, among those nativities of which an adequate number of men were examined, is for Germans, for whom this dimension averaged 9.76 inches, from 562 cases. Omitting all measurements made by Dr. Avery and Mr. Furniss, the two examiners whose average measures of this dimension are smallest, the average is still but 9.81 inches. The results for those nativities for which the height to the seventh cervical vertebra has been specially assorted, are here appended. They apply only to men in usual vigor. For all of them the theoretical distribution of individual cases has been carefully computed, and its accordance with the observed distribution found satisfactory.

Nativity	Number	Mean	r	r_o	Height	Head and Neck
					in.	in.
New England States .	977	57.241	1.525	0.049	67.202	9.961
New York	2 088	57.230	1.642	0.036	67.150	9.920
New Jersey and Penn. .	1 034	57.080	1.515	0.047	67.097	10.017
Ohio and Indiana . .	1 414	57.692	1.452	0.039	67.687	9.995
Mich., Wisc., & Illinois	936	57.288	1.510	0.049	67.223	9.935
Ireland	558	56.738	1.395	0.059	66.703	9.965

Length of Body. — Deducting, from this height to the seventh cervical vertebra, the height to the perinæum as recorded in answer to Question 6, we have the length of the body. This has not been investigated according to nativities, but in the discussion of the spirometer results (Qu. 13) it appeared desirable to classify them with reference to the length of the body; so that we have the number of cases for each half inch of length as derived from the aggregate of all in usual vigor, who were examined with reference to their pulmonary capacity. These are as follows; the number for each half inch being the sum of those recorded for the five consecutive tenths of which this is the mean.

Length of Body	Later Measures			Earlier Measures		
	No. in usual Vigor	Others	Total	No. in usual Vigor	Others	Total
in.						
22 or less	55	7	62	41	14	55
22½	36	4	40	32	3	35
23	72	21	93	68	19	87
23½	183	38	221	140	43	183
24	381	67	448	238	67	305
24½	617	109	726	415	117	532
25	1 007	194	1 201	542	180	722
25½	1 221	190	1 411	634	187	821
26	1 400	246	1 646	641	231	872
26½	1 233	216	1 449	500	212	712
27	1 027	156	1 183	422	203	625
27½	723	106	829	328	155	483
28	470	65	535	201	112	313
28½	316	43	359	150	67	217
29	180	28	208	107	55	162
29½	93	19	112	58	41	99
30	46	15	61	43	23	66
30½	57	8	65	45	35	80
Total . .	9 117	1 532	10 649	4 605	1 764	6 369

The mean of all gives for the average length of body of white soldiers —

			inches.
Form EE,	by measures of	9 243 men in usual vigor	26.149
		1 598 " not in " "	26.091
		10 841 men in all	26.140
Form E,	by measures of	5 569 men in usual vigor	26.011
		2 102 " not in " "	26.331
		7 671 men in all	26.100

The discordance of the results in the measurements by the earlier schedule between those who were, and those who were not, in ordinary health, is without question chiefly due to the circumstance that a very large proportion of the latter class were men at the convalescent camp, measured by Dr. Buckley, whose measures differed somewhat from those of Mr. Fairchild in consequence of want of an accordant method of measuring, and possibly also of a peculiarity in one of the earlier instruments. The total mean from the earlier measures may be regarded as corroborating that from the more careful later ones, and it seems clear that no relation between the length of body and liability to disease is deducible from these later statistics.

If we assort the length of body by Nativities, we find —

Nativity	Later Measures		Earlier Measures	
	Number	Length	Number	Length
		in.		in.
A. New England States.	1 208	26.14	914	26.31
B. N. Y., N. J., and Penn.	3 758	26.13	3 133	26.20
C. Ohio and Indiana . .	1 657	26.28	463 (C, D)	26.75
D. Mich., Wis., and Illinois	1 012	26.27		
E. Coast Slave States . .	365	26.00	2 009 (E, F)	25.78
F. Kentucky and Tenn. .	266	26.95		
H. I. British Provinces . .	556	26.25	177	25.94
J. England, Wales, etc. .	324	25.89	205 (J, K)	25.86
K. Scotland	81	26.12		
L. Ireland	821	25.98	440	25.93
M. France	98	25.52		
N. Germany	561	25.70	251	25.86
O. P. Q. All others . . .	73	26.37	79	25.54
Total	10 780	26.14	7 671	26.10

The inferences warrantable from this exhibit are not very manifest, so far as they pertain to any characteristic difference in the length of body between men of different nativities, since many of the distinctions most marked in the later measures are contradicted by the earlier ones. The trustworthiness of the means from the later series is probably four times greater than that of the others, still no deduction is entitled to much reliance which the earlier series does not corroborate.

Nevertheless, it would seem probable that the length of the body is somewhat greater for Americans in general than for Europeans, although perhaps not more than is required for maintaining the same proportion to the stature ; as also that it is greater for natives of the Northern and Western, than for those of the extreme Southern, States.

Height to Perinæum. — The length of the legs is clearly that dimension upon which the differences in stature of the white soldiers chiefly depend. In this the distinctions between the different nativities are clearly marked, and the inferences deduced in the chapter upon Statures seem corroborated in general by the results of our independent measurements of the height to the perinæum made upon soldiers in the field.

The results for those nativities for which the theoretical distribution of the individual cases has been computed, and found satisfactorily accordant with the distribution observed, are these : —[1]

Nativity	Number of Men	Mean Age	Mean Value	r	r_o
			in.	in.	in.
New England States	976	25.30	31.088	1.075	0.034
New York	2 087	25.84	31.078	1.075	0.023
New York, New Jersey, and Penn.	3 120	25.67	31.052	1.055	0.919
Ohio and Indiana	1 415	24.43	31.462	1.025	0.027
Ireland	558	28.09	30.650	1.018	0.043

The maximum values of the means for other nativities are —

Nativity	Number of Men	Mean Age	Mean Value
			in.
Kentucky and Tennessee	266	26.0	31.68
Coast Slave States	366	26.9	31.57
Scandinavia	34	29.2	31.45
States west of Mississippi River .	61	24.1	31.12
Michigan, Wisconsin, and Illinois	1 012	24.4	31.05

and by the earlier measures —

Nativity	No. of Men	Mean Age	Mean Value
			in.
Late Slave States	2 015	25.43	32.38
Western States (C and D) . . .	479	23.54	31.15

while the well established minima are —

Nativity	Later Measures			Earlier Measures		
	No. of Men	Mean Age	Mean Value	No. of Men	Mean Age	Mean Value
			in.			in.
France, Belgium, etc.	98	27.7	30.20	–	–	–
Ireland	824	29.2	30.67	466	27.15	30.76
Germany	562	29.8	30.71	256	27.65	30.72
British American Provinces . .	556	25.5	30.82	184	24.72	30.93

[1] All these tables of distribution for white soldiers are deduced from men in actual vigor only.

There is no one of the eight nativities within the United States for which the mean value is below 31 inches, according to the later series of measures; for the earlier series the averages are generally smaller, owing probably to want of sufficient care in measuring.

It will be remembered that all the white soldiers measured were partially clothed.

Height to Middle of Patella. — The typical value of the height of the knee has been tested, and found satisfactory for the soldiers in usual vigor of the nativities following: —

Nativity	No. of Men	Value	r	r_0
		in.	in.	in.
New England States	978	18.753	0.735	0.023
New York State, alone	2 084	18.610	0.772	0.017
New York, New Jersey, and Penn.	3 119	18.635	0.764	0.014
Michigan, Wisconsin, and Illinois	936	17.836	0.706	0.023

We may compare the height of the knee with that of the thigh, by subtracting the former from the total height to the perinæum, and thus obtain relative values for the different nativities. The appended table presents these values for all the soldiers measured.

Nativity	Number of Men	Height to Knee	Knee to Perinæum	Ratio
		in.	in.	
New England States	1 208	18.75	12.34	1.52
New York, New Jersey, and Penn.	3 758	18.64	12.41	1.50
Ohio, Indiana	1 659	18.76	12.70	1.48
Michigan, Wisconsin, and Illinois	1 012	18.09	12.96	1.40
Coast Slave States	366	19.06	12.51	1.52
Kentucky and Tennessee . . .	266	19.19	12.49	1.54
States West of Mississippi River .	61	18.90	12.22	1.55
British Amer. Prov., excl. Canada	38	18.69	12.09	1.55
Canada	518	18.43	12.39	1.49
England	304	18.30	12.15	1.51
Wales and Isle of Man	20	18.63	11.98	1.55
Scotland	81	18.36	12.47	1.47
Ireland	824	18.54	12.13	1.53
France, Belgium, etc.	98	18.19	12.01	1.51
Germany	562	18.52	12.19	1.52
Scandinavia	34	18.97	12.48	1.52
Spain, etc.	7	18.04	11.65	1.55
Miscellaneous	32	18.65	12.13	1.54
Total	10 848	18.609	12.456	1.494

The normal ratio between these two dimensions would thus appear to be very nearly as three to two, the extreme deviations[1] from this ratio being 1.396 for nativity D, and 1.555 for Wales, etc., the latter depending on only 20 men. The extreme variation in the mean values of the height to the knee, in any of the above-named groups, is 1.15 inches, or .062 of the mean of all. The variation in the mean distance from knee to perinæum is comprised within 1.31 inches, or .105 of the total mean.

Perinæum to the most prominent part of Pubes. — The position of the *symphysis pubis* renders it a prominent point for any series of measurements based on the structure of the skeleton, and this has been frequently stated to indicate the medial point as regards stature : an assumption approximately, but not strictly true. Any determination of this point through clothing is difficult and uncertain ; and no attempts were made at measuring it excepting when the subjects could be examined while perfectly naked.

This was not the case for any white soldiers ; but 1013 white sailors were thus measured, mostly by Mr. Phinney, as will be hereafter described, giving the mean value of this distance as 1.891 inches, their mean stature being 65.99, and the mean height to the perinæum 31.37.

Breadth of Neck. — The mean breadth of neck for all the white soldiers examined is 4.22 inches; the maximum for any nativity being 4.31 inches, for 1014 natives of Michigan, Wisconsin, and Illinois, and the minimum for any, which comprised an adequate number of men, being for the two groups of natives of Southern States ; for each of which it is 4.15 inches. Comparisons between the theoretical and observed distribution for individuals have been made for only four groups, namely, the men of nativities A, B, D, and L, who were in usual vigor. These give —

Nativity	No. of Men	Mean Breadth	r	r_0
		in.	in.	
New England States . .	976	4.177	0.160	0.005
New York, New Jersey, and Penn.	3 122	4.244	0.178	0.003
Michigan, Wisconsin, and Illinois	937	4.326	0.143	0.005
Ireland	558	4.206	0.153	0.006

1 The small value of this dimension in nativity D appears, after careful examination, to be owing to a systematic personal error in the measurements made by Mr. Lewis, who examined a large proportion of these men, and whose records of this dimension appear uniformly too small. Excluding his measurements, we have for natives of Michigan, Wisconsin, and Illinois —

No. of Men	Height to Knee	Knee to Perinæum	Ratio
	in.	in.	
254	18.85	12.34	1.528

The values for men not in usual vigor are markedly and universally less, the average difference being about one thirty-second part. The results of the earlier measures are not altogether in accord with these; the mean value deduced from them being 4.098 for men in usual vigor, and 4.053 for others. The natives of the Southern States surpassed this maximum value, almost all of them having been measured by Mr. Fairchild.

Girth of Neck. — The mean girth of neck, from nearly 9300 men in usual vigor, is 13.633 inches, and for 1600 not in usual vigor it is 13.521 inches, there being but a single nativity-group containing so many as a hundred representatives, in which a similar difference is not manifest. It is also to be observed that the periphery, being measured around the *pomum Adami*, is larger than the circumference of a circle of which the breadth of the neck constitutes the diameter. The smallest observed mean value in any of the large groups is for New Englanders, 13.44 inches, from 1210 men; the largest (excluding groups of less than 40 men) is for natives of Germany, 13.79 inches, from 562 men.

The assortment for five groups of men in usual vigor gives the following results:—

Nativity	No. of Men	Mean Girth	r	r_o
		in.	in.	in.
New England States	978	13.436	0.442	0.014
New York, New Jersey, and Penn.	3 123	13.629	0.466	0.008
New York State, alone	2 089	13.593	0.460	0.010
Ohio and Indiana	1 416	13.699	0.459	0.012
Michigan, Wisconsin, and Illinois	939	13.526	0.414	0.013

Breadth of Shoulders. — It has been already stated that the earlier measurements gave simply the maximum breadth of the shoulders, whereas it was specially provided in the schedule for the later series that this measure should be taken between the tips of the acromion processes; the purpose being, both to select distinctly marked points of the bony structure, and to furnish a control and test for the dimensions 12*a* and 12*b*. These two dimensions are from the tip of the middle finger to the acromion, and to the middle of the sternum respectively, so that they should differ by one half the distance between the acromia.

Through some misapprehension, the old method of measuring was retained by Dr. Buckley for a time, and the new examiners instructed accordingly; so that nearly one fifth part of the measures of white soldiers were thus made, before the fact was discovered and special instructions given. Consequently we have from the series of examinations by Form [EE] 8796 measures of the distance between the tips of the acromia, and 2072 of the full breadth of shoulders. The former have been tabulated as 8*a*; and the latter, which are strictly comparable with the results of the earlier series, have been classified as 8*b*.

The mean of these last named measures, 8*b*, is 16.350 inches by the later series, and 16.359 by the earlier, which are nearly four times as numerous. The differences of the dimensions for different nativities do not seem to be characteristic, nor to correspond in the two series of measurements. The means for the several nativities are quite accordant in both series, wherever the number of men is sufficiently great to render the results at all worthy of confidence. For individual men, this dimension ranges between 13 and 19 inches.

The mean distance between the tips of the acromion processes, as given by the 8796 measures of this dimension, is 12.731 inches, the individual cases ranging between the limits 9½ and 16½ inches. Among natives of this country, the mean value is decidedly largest for natives of Kentucky and Tennessee, being 13.51; but the assortment-tabulation shows such discordance from the theoretical distribution that this inference is entitled to but small reliance. Nativities A, B, and C give mean values not diverse from that of the grand total, but for D this value is but 12.34, while for G it rises to 13.21 inches. The computation for 878 New England men in usual vigor gives 12.790, with a probable variation of 0.646 for an individual, and a probable error of 0.022 for the mean; but one half of this quantity exceeds the difference between 12*a* and 12*b* by half an inch, and it is to be feared that our determination of this dimension is not entitled to much confidence. The identification of this apophysis is not easy, and some of our examiners seem to have succeeded here but ill. The results deduced by others appear, however, to be very trustworthy, and will be specially considered hereafter when the arm-measurements are described.

A thorough scrutiny into the mean results obtained from the returns of different examiners, with a view to determining their personal equations, shows a gradual improvement in many cases, and leads to the belief that inaccuracies are mostly eliminated from the mean of all. Yet the tendency has unquestionably been to record this dimension as larger than its true value.

Breadth of Pelvis between Crests of Ilia. — For this dimension, which was apparently determined with care, we have 11.916 inches as the mean value; the mean result for men in usual vigor being greater by 0.14 than for men not in full health. This dimension is not one of those which seem to show the most characteristic differences for different nativities, although the corresponding dimension deducible from the earlier series exhibits very marked distinctions.

The latter, which was taken under the title of "Breadth of Pelvis," is on the average an inch and a quarter greater than the dimension here considered, and seems, so far as now discoverable, to have been the breadth between the trochanters, — the breadth of hips, rather than of pelvis. The earlier measures are accordant among themselves, and are much larger for Southern than for Northern men; the difference between the values for natives of the Slave States and of New England amounting to half an inch. The mean value is 12.96 inches for New England men; 13.15 for Western men; 13.41 for Southerners; 13.153 for the whole 7905 men measured.

The assortments of the later series for men in usual vigor, give the following values: —

Nativity	No. of Men	Mean Value	r	r_0
		in.	in.	in.
New England	976	11.890	0.675	0.022
New York alone	2 085	12.046	0.628	0.012
New York, New Jersey, and Penn.	3 119	12.014	0.523	0.009
Ohio and Indiana	1 417	11.890	0.474	0.013
Ireland	556	12.036	0.525	0.022

Circumference of Thorax. — This measurement was directed to be made in the later series "under all the clothing" and "across the nipples"; also both while the lungs were fully inflated and after exhalation. We thus have two measurements of actual dimensions, whence the mean circumference and the mobility of the chest may each be deduced.

In the earlier series [E] the "circumference of the chest" was required, without any farther instruction than that it should be measured "over the nipples," and under the coat and waistcoat.

It may perhaps be assumed that, in the absence of any instruction as to the state of expansion in which the thorax should be measured, the mean deduced from the 7907 returns according to Form E would represent an average condition of the lungs. How far this is correct would be difficult to determine at present, but the circumstance that these measures were taken around the flannel shirt, and yet with results smaller than those of the later series, which are made directly around the body without the intervention of clothing, suggests either that such an average condition is not represented by the mean value from the earlier series, or that in the slightly ambiguous phrase "over the nipples," the word over may have been sometimes construed in the sense of "higher than," instead of its intended signification of "across." These earlier measures give as the mean circumference of chest over the nipples —

35.424 inches, for 5 734 soldiers in usual vigor.
35.166 inches, for 2 173 soldiers not in usual vigor.

35.353 inches, for 7 907 soldiers in all.

The later series of examinations gives the mean circumference of the chest across the nipples and under all the clothing —

	Full Inspiration	After Expiration	Mean of Both
	in.	in.	in.
From 9 270 men in usual vigor .	37.195	34.476	35.836
1 604 men not in usual vigor	36.846	34.604	35.725
10 874 men in all	37.143	34.494	35.818

It is thus seen that for men in ordinary health the circumference was not merely greater than for the others, while the lungs were inflated, but was also less after expiration, owing without doubt to the superior muscular force in the thorax exerted by the stronger men. Also that the mean value of the two measurements was only the ninth part of an inch, or about three tenths of one per cent. less for the feebler class of men.

From the measures of circumference of the chest of 5738 Scotch soldiers, — given [1] by an anonymous author in the Edinburgh "Medical and Surgical Journal," and used [2] by Quetelet, in illustration of the application of the law of error, and of the typical character of the mean deduced from an adequate number of such measures, — the mean circumference of the chest is found to be 39.8 inches, or more than two inches and a half greater than the mean here found for men in usual vigor during full inspiration. The 80 natives of Scotland examined by us, measured 37.45 inches when the lungs were fully inflated and 34.67 after expiration. Of these 80 there were but 11 cases in which the circumference at full inspiration was found so large as the mean value resulting from the Edin-

[1] Vol. XIII. p. 263. [2] *Theorie des Probabilités*, p. 136.

burgh measures, which ranged from 33 to 48 inches. Unless these measures were made upon men very much larger than the average, our present results would almost lead to the suspicion that some considerable amount of clothing was included in the dimension published as "circumference of the chest."

The mean circumference of chest for 343 764 drafted men, recruits and substitutes, examined by the military boards of enrollment, are given[1] by Dr. Baxter, chief Medical Officer of the late Provost Marshal General's Bureau, in the Report of the medical branch of that bureau. He has published the results of measurements at inspiration and expiration, arranged by nations of birth, and, for natives of the United States, by States. His totals give as the mean circumference —

	At Inspiration	At Expiration	Mean
	in.	in.	in.
From 273 391 natives of the U. S. .	35.61	33.11	34.36
343 764 of all nativities . .	35.59	33.12	34.36

these values being less than ours by nearly an inch and a half, and less than the Edinburgh values by nearly five and a half inches. Among the men measured were 2127 natives of Scotland, for whom the mean circumference was 35.97 inches at inspiration, and 33.14 at expiration (or 1.48 inches in the one case and 1.53 in the other less than our values); the results for Scotchmen thus differing by essentially the same amount as the total means from those here found.

In these examinations by the medical officers of the Provost Marshal General's Bureau, it is not stated at what part of the chest the measurement was made. Of course a very considerable number of the men examined were those whose physical condition excluded them from acceptance for military duty, and for these a smaller girth of chest should be expected.

In all these cases the mean circumference of the chest exceeds half the height. Other deductions from these chest-measurements will be considered hereafter.

The distribution of the individual variations in our returns is so symmetrical as to produce great confidence in the trustworthiness of the results deduced. For the aggregate of white soldiers, in usual vigor, we have, moreover, the following values of individual discordance, and probable error of mean —

[1] *Final Report of the Provost Marshal General*, pp. 698, 699.

Circumference of Chest.

	No. of Men	Circumference	r	r_o
		in.	in.	in.
At inspiration . .	9 271	37.195	1.469	0.015
At expiration . .	9 270	34.476	1.428	0.015
Mean		35.836		0.021

It will be remembered that the measurements were made with out the intervention of any clothing. The mean stature being 67.150 inches, it will be seen that the circumference of chest exceeded half the height even after full expiration.

Distance between Nipples. — This dimension seemed entitled to some importance on account of the belief, which obtains very generally, that in a normally proportioned body it is equal to one fourth of the entire circumference of the chest. Thus Dr. Hammond, in his "Military Hygiene," after citing sundry proportions given by Brent as holding good for all cases in which there is no positive deformity, says:[1] "A more convenient method, however, is to measure the distance between the nipples with a pair of dividers, or a graduated rule, and to multiply the result by four. As we have seen, this gives us the entire circumference of the chest." Regarding the correctness of the inferences as to such simple relations between different dimensions of the human body, we shall have something to say in Chapter IX. At present it will suffice to say, that our results do not appear to confirm the theory of Brent, but indicate that this dimension is uniformly less than one fourth the circumference. Thus we have the following mean values: —

	Height	Mean Circumference of Chest	Distance between Nipples	Ratio to Circumference
	in.	in.	in.	
From 1 771 soldiers in usual vigor. .	67.185	35.973	8.142	0.2263
From 297 soldiers not in usual vigor	67.124	35.646	8.101	0.2273
From 2 068 soldiers in all.	67.176	35.926	8.136	0.2265

The minimum and maximum values of this distance which occur upon our records are: —

[1] Page 38.

Distance	Mean Circumference of Chest	Nativity	Height	Ratio to Circumference
in.	in.		in.	
5.4	25.3	Indiana	58.3	0.213
10.3	38.7	New York	69.6	0.266

Circumference of Waist. — In the later series of measurements, the "circumference of the waist above the hips" was required, and the examiners were instructed to measure below the ribs. In the earlier series, the question asked simply the "circumference of the waist." The means of the two series are —

	In usual Vigor		Not in usual Vigor		Total	
	No. of Men	Inches	No. of Men	Inches	No. of Men	Inches
Earlier Series .	5 729	32.059	2 173	32.166	7 902	32.089
Later Series .	9 271	31.483	1 605	31.377	10 876	31 467

the values of the earlier series being larger on the average by about six tenths of an inch.

Using the later measures only, we find the mean circumference of the waist for 9271 men in usual vigor, at the mean age 25.7 years, to have been less than that of the chest at inspiration by 5.712 inches, and at expiration by 2.993 inches, and less than the mean circumference of the chest across the nipples by 4.353 inches. If we compare the mean value of these dimensions for the 1605 men not in their ordinary health. and averaging 29.2 years of age, we find the difference to be 4.348 inches, or practically the same as for the others.

The values of this dimension differ somewhat with the different nativities, but the distribution of the discordances is in general quite satisfactory. The three following nativities will suffice to exhibit the range of individual discordances.

	No. of Men	Circumference	r	r_0
		in.	in.	in.
New England States . . .	977	31.809	1.517	0.048
New York, New Jersey, Penn.	3 124	31.431	1.508	0.027
Ohio and Indiana	1 417	32.031	1.469	0.039

Circumference around Hips. — This dimension was taken on the level of the trochanters, and the mean values, for all those nativities which comprise more than 51 individual cases, vary between

36.51 and 37.77 inches; the former being deduced from 1211 New England men, the latter from 267 natives of Kentucky and Tennessee, and the diversity being clearly typical. The mean from the entire series of nearly eleven thousand men is 36.930 inches.

The assortment of the results shows a very satisfactory accordance with law in the distribution of the errors for most of the several nativities. The range of variation for these nativities is shown in the appended table, deduced from men in usual vigor only.

Nativity	No. of Men	Circumference	r	r_0
		in.	in.	in.
New England	978	36.523	1.298	0.041
New York, New Jersey, Penn.	3 124	37.037	1.250	0.022
Ohio and Indiana	1 417	37.280	1.365	0.036

Length of Arm. — The measurement taken in the earlier series was from the armpit to the tip of the middle finger. The mean values were —

From 5721 men in usual vigor . 29.284 inches.
From 2168 men not in usual vigor, 28.973 inches.
From 7889 men in all . . . . 29.200 inches.

In the later series this dimension was measured from the tip of the acromion to the tip of the middle finger, and we have the mean values.

From 9198 men in usual vigor . 29.139 inches.
From 1605 men not in usual vigor, 29.235 inches.
From 10 803 men in all . . . . 29.153 inches.

The extreme values for nativities comprising an adequate number of men are 30.02 inches from 267 natives of Kentucky and Tennessee, and 28.52 from 100 Frenchmen, etc. The range of error may be seen by the results for men in usual vigor, for four nativities.

Nativity	No. of Men	Length	r	r_0
		in.	in.	in.
New England States . . .	978	29.253	0.969	0.031
New York, New Jersey, Penn.	3 123	29.096	0.963	0.017
Ohio and Indiana	1 417	29.503	0.948	0.025
Ireland	559	28.922	0.987	0.042

A second measurement was made from the *middle of the tip of the breast-bone to the tip of the middle finger*, this length being, according to some writers on the fine arts, just one half the height in a well-formed man, — a supposition which our results do not corroborate.

Of the 10 865 white soldiers for whom this distance was measured, there were found but 625 men, being $5\frac{3}{4}$ per cent., whose height was equal to twice this dimension. These were distributed among the several nativities as follows: —

Nativity	Total Number Examined	No. of Cases Found	Proportion
New England States	1 211	98	.081
New York, New Jersey, and Pennsylvania .	3 761	263	.070
Ohio and Indiana	1 660	35	.021
Michigan, Wisconsin, and Illinois	1 014	42	.041
Coast Slave States	365	23	.063
Kentucky and Tennessee	267	11	.041
West of Mississippi River	61	13	.213
British American Provinces	558	44	.079
England	326	22	.067
Scotland	81	8	.099
Ireland	826	36	.044
Germany	562	19	.034
All others	173	11	.064
Total	10 865	625	.0575

The mean value of this dimension was: —

	Mean Height in.	Mean Value in.
From 9263 men in usual vigor,	67.150	35.040
1605 men not in usual vigor,	67.148	35.055
10 868 men in all, averaging	67.149	35.042

The mean for nativity C gives 35.47 inches, from 1660 men, that for Kentucky and Tennessee gives 35.99 inches, from 267 men. For Germans the mean from 562 men is 34.78. These differences appear to be characteristic, and we have for men in health: —

Nativity	No. of Men	Length	r	r_o
		in.	in.	in.
New England States . . .	978	35.087	1.055	0.034
New York, New Jersey, Pa. .	3 122	35.011	1.071	0.019
Ohio, Indiana	1 416	35.473	1.022	0.027
Ireland	558	34.891	1.043	0.044

Length of Upper Arm. — The mean distance from tip of acromion to extremity of elbow was found —

From 9253 men in usual vigor, 13.604 inches,
making the lower arm and hand 15.535 inches.
From 1603 men not in usual vigor, 13.609 inches,
making the lower arm and hand 15.626 inches.
From 10 856 men in all, 13 605 inches,
making the lower arm and hand, 15.548 inches.

It is a source of regret that the length of the hand was not determined, and a means thus afforded for comparing the length of the humerus and radius, from which comparison valuable ethnological inferences might have been deduced; but this measurement was not provided for in the schedule. A comparison of our results for different nativities gives: —

Nativity	No. of Men	Upper Arm	Lower Arm and Hand	Ratio
		in.	in.	
New England States	1 199	13.76	15.47	1.12
New York, New Jersey, and Penn.	3 742	13.62	15.50	1.14
Ohio and Indiana	1 646	13.72	15.81	1.15
Michigan, Wisconsin, and Illinois .	1 012	13.39	15.42	1.15
Coast Slave States	364	13.75	15.65	1.14
Kentucky and Tennessee . . .	267	13.63	15.39	1.20
British American Provinces . .	557	13.61	15.38	1.13
England, Wales, etc.	323	13.39	15.29	1.14
Scotland	81	13.53	15.43	1.14
Ireland	826	13.46	15.53	1.15
France, etc.	99	13 22	15.30	1.16
Germany	554	13.54	15.43	1.14
Scandinavia	34	13.86	16.03	1.16
All others	39	13.40	15.42	1.15

The range of individual variation from the mean for the corresponding nativity, may be seen from the appended results, for men in usual vigor, belonging to three nativities which exhibit a satisfactory distribution of these variations.

Nativity	No. of Men	Length	r	r_o
		in.	in.	in.
New England States	978	13.865	0.708	0.023
New York, New Jersey, and Penn.	3 117	13.617	0.639	0.011
Michigan, Wisconsin, and Illinois	938	13.365	0.488	0.016

It has already been remarked that an estimate may be made of the correctness of the mode of measuring adopted, by comparing half the measured distance between the acromia with the difference between the two dimensions from the tip of the middle finger, 12*a* to the acromion, and 12*b* to the middle of the breastbone, respectively; as also that the measurements have not in many cases borne this test satisfactorily. The errors committed seem however to have been not so much in the length of the arm as in the breadth of the shoulders; and a word of comment here may be advisable.

The examiners were severally instructed by Dr. Buckley, and only commenced independent operations after he considered them well versed, and warned against all probable dangers of error. As a precaution, however, the results deduced from the returns of the several examiners were compared as frequently as the progress of the tabulation permitted, and whenever the values for any dimension, resulting from the measures by any one person appeared to be systematically different from those given by the others, this examiner was informed of the discordance, and cautions were impressed upon him if they seemed called for. Thus, the first quarter of the measurements by most of the examiners differed, in some one or more respects, from the subsequent ones. The breadth of shoulders and the head-measurements were those in which such criticisms were found chiefly necessary; and it may therefore not be amiss to give the results as derived from those examinations only, in which such discordances were not so large, or which were subsequent to special caution upon the subject.

The following results are derived from such data only as appear to have been made with the greatest care; their number being not quite nine sixteenths of the full number purporting to have been made between the acromia. They do not comprise all those which seem beyond question, but merely those which it has been found convenient to aggregate without too large an expenditure of labor.

The table presents the mean values for the stature, and for the three arm-measurements of the same men, together with a final column exhibiting the difference between one half the mean breadth of shoulders between the acromia, as obtained from the direct measurements, and the value deduced by subtracting the mean distance "acromion to finger-tip" from the mean distance "from middle of top of sternum to finger-tip."

The values in this last column are, with a single exception, positive, and suggest that even here the recorded width of shoulders may have exceeded the true value. But the discrepancy may not improbably arise from a slight deficiency in the recorded distance from the middle of the breast-bone to the finger-tip. The former of these dimensions is gauged between the arms of the andrometer, so that the errors can arise only from an incorrect determination of the points to be measured; but in the latter it may well be that the graduated tape was made to form a chord between the two extremities of the line, and that it thus gave lengths short of the truth by an amount averaging nearly the tenth of an inch. It will be seen in the next chapter that the negative value here obtained for the nativity D disappears when proportions only, and not actual dimensions, are considered.

Means of Arm and Shoulder Measures

(including only the most trustworthy returns).

Nativity	No.	Mean Stature	Breadth between Acromia, 8a	Acromion to Finger-tip, 12a	Middle of Sternum to Finger-Tip, 12b	Acromion to Elbow, 12c	$\frac{1}{2}$ 8a—(12b—12a)
		in.	in.	in.	in.	in.	
New England States .	322	67.168	12.377	28.926	35.004	13.440	0.090
N. Y., N. J., and Penn.	1 866	67.891	12.351	29.043	35.085	13.743	0.134
Ohio and Indiana . .	840	67.701	12.248	29.389	35.402	13.677	0.111
Mich., Wisc., and Ill. .	842	67.229	12.231	28 679	34.820	13.325	− 0.026
Coast Slave States . .	44	67.366	12.027	29.327	35.332	13.702	0.008
Kentucky and Tennessee	32	68.916	12.700	29.884	36.178	13.744	0.056
States W. Miss. River	18	67.861	12.549	29.400	35.539	13.650	0.135
British Amer. Provinces	273	67.074	12.338	28.900	34.949	13.485	0.120
England	153	66.548	12.436	28.601	34.686	13.288	0.133
Scotland	50	66.653	12.241	28.667	34.685	13.320	0.103
Ireland	205	66.736	12.459	28.868	35.035	13.241	0.062
France, etc.	17	65.929	12.288	28.417	34.429	13.100	0.132
Germany	175	66.413	12.308	28.828	34.887	13.394	0.095
Miscellaneous	18	67.028	12.361	28.956	35.078	13.511	0.058
Total	4 855	67.484	12.316	28.998	35.061	13.566	0.095

Distance between Eyes. — In the later series, the distances between the outer and the inner angles of the eyes were measured with calipers. Half the sum of these measures gives the distance between the centers of the eyeballs; half their distance is the width of the eye. The resultant mean values of these quantities, assorted by nativities, are as follows: —

Nativity	No. of Men	Distance of Centers	Width of Eye
		in.	in.
New England States	1 211	2.508	1.288
N. Y., N. J., and Penn. . . .	3 765	2.496	1.266
Ohio and Indiana	1 662	2.466	1.272
Michigan, Wisconsin, Illinois .	1 016	2.425	1.201
Coast Slave States	367	2.457	1.280
Kentucky and Tennessee . . .	267	2.520	1.296
States W. of Mississippi River .	61	2.486	1.242
British American Provinces . .	558	2.579	1.325
England, Wales, etc.	326	2.474	1.249
Scotland	81	2.475	1.256
Ireland	827	2.512	1.262
France, Belgium, Switzerland .	100	2.498	1.254
Germany	562	2.526	1.276
Scandinavia	34	2.520	1.286
All others	39	2.523	1.285
Total	10 876	2.492	1.267

The probable discordance of the individual variations in the measured dimensions, from the mean, is found by a discussion of results for four nativities to be less than 0.15 inch. For the nativity B the probable variation of individuals from the mean, derived from 3121 cases, is 0.157 inch for the distance between the outer angles, and 0.110 inch for that between the inner angles. Other nativities give less average variations for the larger dimension. The extreme values found for the distance between outer angles were 2.4 inches and 5.1 inches; for the interval between the inner angles they were 0.6 inch and 1.9 inch. The probable error of the mean varies for the larger nativities, between 0.002 inch and 0.004 inch.

The mean "distance between the pupils," as given by the Earlier Series, is also appended, assorted in the same manner. This measurement appears to have been taken by holding a graduated tape or foot-rule in front of the eyes, and thus estimating the distance. The uncertainty of this method is obvious, and it will be seen that the interval is, for all nativities, about one tenth of an inch larger than that deduced from the later series.

Nativity	No. of Men	Distance of Pupils
New England States	880	2.605
N. Y., N. J., and Penn. . . .	3 072	2.606
Ohio and Indiana	268	2.604
Michigan, Wisconsin, Illinois .	130	2.601
Coast Slave States	218	2.596
Kentucky and Tennessee . . .	10	2.587
States W. of Mississippi River .	8	2.547
British American Provinces . .	168	2.601
England, Wales, etc.	158	2.614
Scotland	39	2.641
Ireland	387	2.612
France, Belgium, Switzerland .	44	2.602
Germany	211	2.608
Scandinavia	9	2.681
All others	17	2.581
Total	5 619	2.606

Dimensions of Foot. — These were measured only in those examinations which were made according to Form [EE].

The mean length was found for no nativity to exceed 10.24 inches, and for none to fall below 9.89 inches; the value for the total being 10.058 inches. These differences, moreover, correspond closely with differences in the mean stature, and it would appear that, considerable as is the variation in this respect between individuals, the mean value is very well marked; its ratio to the stature differing but very slightly in the different nativities, and being very close to 0.15.

The range of variation may be inferred from the results for men in usual vigor, of four nativities.

Nativity	No. of Men	Length	r	r_o
		in.	in.	in.
New England States	976	10.092	0.330	0.011
New York, New Jersey, and Penn.	3 115	10.072	0.326	0.006
Ohio and Indiana	1 416	10.106	0.316	0.008
Michigan, Wisconsin, and Illinois	938	10.035	0.328	0.011

The largest value on our record was 12.1 inches, and belonged to a native of New York 71.8 inches in height, and aged 30 years, thus measuring 0.169 of the stature. The shortest foot measured was 7.8 inches in length, and belonged to a native of Scotland, who was 59.2 inches in height and 17 years old. This foot was 0.132 of the height.

The dimension 36*b* was taken for comparison with the length of the foot proper. It was measured from the tip of the great toe to the hollow above the heel, and the difference between these two dimensions thus gives a close approximation to the length of the heel itself, by the addition of 0.3 inch as a correction, upon the assumption that the angle at the toe subtended by the height of the heel is about 14°. The average variation, and the probable error of the mean were found for the nativities examined, to be between two and three per cent. smaller than for the length of the foot, as measured to the extremity of the heel; the difference being probably due to the greater facility with which the measures can be correctly made, in consequence of the less compressible character of the tendon.

The mean length of the heel, thus measured, is 0.485 inch for the aggregate of white soldiers, and very constant for the several nativities.

The mean thickness of the foot at instep varies in our results for different nativities from 2.844 inches (0.041 of the stature) for 267 natives of Kentucky and Tennessee, to 2.438 inches (0.036 of the stature) for 520 Canadians.

Uncertainty as to the precise point at which the calipers were applied renders comparisons of this dimension unsatisfactory at the best; still the differences deduced for the several nativities would appear to be not altogether due to peculiarities or errors of the examiners. The mean value is 2.572 inches for white soldiers. All these measures are proved to have an important ethnological bearing, as will be seen hereafter.

A satisfactory distribution of the individual measurements was found only in the two nativities B and C, which give —

Nativity	No. of Men	Thickness	r	r_0
		in.	in.	in.
New York, New Jersey, and Penn.	3 115	2.495	0.237	0.004
Ohio and Indiana	1 415	2.684	0.204	0.005

The extreme values of this dimension upon our record are 1.6 inch for a native of Canada, and 4.0 inches for a native of New York. The former corresponds to 0.025, and the latter to 0.055 of the stature.

The fourth foot-measurement prescribed by our schedule is the circumference around the extremity of the heel and the anterior ligament; and was, like the second, designed to permit ethnological comparisons, without affecting the sense of caste of the newly enfranchised colored troops by any odious suggestions; and the results have been found entirely satisfactory. The mean values for those different nativities which comprise more than 60 men range from 13.023 to 13.675 inches, corresponding to 0.197 and 0.200 of the stature. The mean of all gives 13.201.

The probable variations for men in actual vigor belonging to three nativities are —

Nativity	No. of Men	Circumference	r	r_o
		in.	in.	in.
New York, New Jersey, and Penn.	3 110	13.210	0.375	0.007
Ohio and Indiana	1 415	13.412	0.439	0.012
Michigan, Wisconsin, and Illinois	939	13.219	0.368	0.012

The largest and smallest values upon our records are —

17.1 inches for a native of Germany, aged 31 and 73.4 inches high, being 0.233 of the stature,

and 10.0 inches for a native of England, aged 31 and 60.0 inches high, being 0.167 of the stature.

The results thus found for white soldiers are appended in tabular form, the mean values deduced from men not in their usual health and strength being also given, separately from the others.[1] Of the six pages of which this Table I. consists, the first three pertain to the first ten nativities, and the last three contain the remaining eight nativities, which have been separately considered, together with a "miscellaneous," class comprising all not included in the preceding eighteen, and finally the means derived from the aggregate of all. It is probably needless to call attention to the fact that the trustworthiness of the mean dimensions for any nativity depends largely upon the number of men from which these mean dimensions were deduced. The mean age of the men at the time of measurement, is also given for every group.

[1] The means given in Table I. differ slightly from those already cited for soldiers in their usual vigor, from the tables of actual and theoretical distribution. This variance is owing to the incorporation, with the materials for Table I., of some additional measurements which were received after the assortment-tables had been completed.

TABLE I.

Mean Dimensions of White Soldiers.

Nativity	Number of Men	Actual Mean Age	4 Height	4½ Tip of Finger to Margin of Patella	5 Height to 7th Cervical Vertebra	5½ Height to Knee	6 Height to Perinæum	7 Breadth of Neck
A. New England States			in.	in.	in.	in.	in.	in.
In usual vigor	1 000	25.36	67.21	4.90	57.25	18.75	31.10	4.18
Others . .	211	27.67	67.15	5.06	57.15	18.73	31.02	4.11
Total . . .	1 211	25.76	67.20	4.93	57.23	18.75	31.09	4.17
B. N. Y., N. J., and Penn.								
In usual vigor	3 177	25.71	67.13	4.92	57.18	18.64	31.06	4.25
Others . .	588	28.71	67.20	4.96	57.16	18.65	31.04	4.11
Total . . .	3 765	26.18	67.14	4.92	57.18	18.64	31.05	4.23
C. Ohio and Indiana								
In usual vigor	1 443	24.44	67.68	5.37	57.69	18.74	31.43	4.18
Others . . .	219	26.46	68.12	5.37	58.08	18.87	31.64	4.10
Total . . .	1 662	24.70	67.74	5.37	57.74	18.76	31.46	4.17
D. Mich., Wisc., and Ill.								
In usual vigor	945	24.44	67.22	4.82	57.29	18.06	31.02	4.32
Others . . .	71	23.54	67.60	5.13	57.57	18.44	31.30	4.16
Total . . .	1 016	24.38	67.26	4.84	57.32	18.09	31.05	4.31
E. Coast Slave States								
In usual vigor	315	25.89	67.62	5.25	57.62	19.08	31.60	4.18
Others . . .	52	32.80	67.19	5.21	57.28	18.91	31.41	3.99
Total . . .	367	26.88	67.56	5.24	57.57	19.06	31.57	4.15
F. Kentucky and Tenn.								
In usual vigor	223	25.19	68.57	6.07	58.68	19.20	31.68	4.16
Others . . .	44	30.13	68.31	5.69	58.35	19.16	31.67	4.13
Total . . .	267	26.00	68.53	6.01	58.63	19.19	31.68	4.15
G_1. W. of Miss. R. — Free .								
In usual vigor	10	22.28	67.89	5.83	58.00	18.90	31.32	4.10
G_2. W. of Miss. R. — Slave								
In usual vigor	46	24.50	66.29	5.52	56.66	18.88	31.06	4.25
Others . . .	5	25.09	66.56	5.52	56.62	19.06	31.16	3.94
Total . . .	51	24.56	66.32	5.52	56.65	18.90	31.07	4.22
H. Brit. Prov. excl. Canada								
In usual vigor	36	27.16	67.31	5.25	57.45	18.74	30.85	4.22
Others . . .	2	23.48	66.40	5.90	56.30	17.70	29.58	4.00
Total . . .	38	26.96	67.26	5.28	57.39	18.69	30.78	4.21
I. Canada								
In usual vigor	474	24.91	66.85	4.70	57.05	18.43	30.82	4.30
Others . . .	46	30.64	67.20	5.04	57.02	18.43	30.84	4.18
Total . . .	520	25.43	66.88	4.73	57.04	18.43	30.82	4.29

TABLE I. — (*Continued.*)

Mean Dimensions of White Soldiers.

Nativity	7½ Girth of Neck	8a Breadth of Shoulders between Acromia	8b Breadth of Shoulders	9 Breadth of Pelvis	10a Circumference of Chest: Full Inspiration	10b Circumference of Chest: After Expiration.	11 Circumference of Waist	11½ Circumference around Hips
	in.	in.	in.	in.	in.	in.	in.	in.
A. New England States								
In usual vigor	13.44	12.77	16.28	11.91	36.74	34.06	31.08	36.50
Others . . .	13.42	12.71	16.26	11.76	36.58	34.33	30.98	36.52
Total . .	13.44	12.76	16.28	11.88	36.71	34.11	31.06	36.51
B. N. Y., N. J., and Penn.								
In usual vigor	13.63	12.69	16.38	12.02	37.09	34.33	31.42	37.03
Others . . .	13.51	12.69	16.18	11.85	86.88	34.65	31.35	36.91
Total . .	13.61	12.69	16.36	11.99	37.06	34.38	31.41	37.01
C. Ohio and Indiana								
In usual vigor	13.70	12.74	16.40	11.90	37.60	34.98	32.01	37.27
Others . . .	13.57	12.61	16.28	11.77	37.07	34.76	31.81	36.95
Total . .	13.68	12.72	16.38	11.88	37.53	34.95	31.98	37.22
D. Mich., Wisc., and Ill.								
In usual vigor	13.52	12.33	16.21	11.68	37.35	34.01	31.07	36.78
Others . . .	13.50	12.47	16.48	11.80	36.78	34.42	31.20	36.93
Total . .	13.52	12.34	16.23	11.69	37.29	34.04	31.08	36.79
E. Coast Slave States								
In usual vigor	13.64	12.75	15.85	11.73	36.68	34.27	31.30	36.67
Others . . .	13.40	12.27	15.64	11.61	36.39	34.00	30.92	36.24
Total . .	13.61	12.68	15.82	11.71	36.64	34.23	31.25	36.61
F. Kentucky and Tenn.								
In usual vigor	13.72	13.59	16.70	12.03	37.87	35.31	32.69	37.82
Others . . .	13.83	13.17	16.22	11.80	37.61	35.23	32.31	37.51
Total . .	13.73	13.51	16.65	11.99	37.83	35.30	32.63	37.77
G_1. W. of Miss. R. — Free								
In usual vigor	14.01	13.12	17.30	11.84	37.53	34.84	31.83	38.09
G_2. W. of Miss. R. — Slave								
In usual vigor	13.32	13.34	15.83	11.65	35.64	33.38	29.89	35.40
Others . . .	13.48	12.38	–	11.47	34.60	32.70	29.32	36.00
Total . .	13.33	13.23	15.83	11.64	35.54	33.31	29.83	35.46
H. Brit. Prov. excl. Canada								
In usual vigor	13.87	12.90	16.77	11.84	37.24	34.91	31.25	36.60
Others . . .	13.05	13.00	–	11.50	35.05	33.10	30.50	35.55
Total . -	13.83	12.91	16.77	11.82	37.13	34.81	31.21	36.54
I. Canada								
In usual vigor	13.60	12.64	16.30	12.05	37.13	34.30	31.38	37.00
Others . . .	13.57	12.78	15.90	11.79	37.26	34.90	32.17	37.07
Total . .	13.60	12.65	16.29	12.03	37.14	34.35	31.45	37.00

TABLE I.—(*Continued.*)

Mean Dimensions of White Soldiers.

Nativity	12a	12b	12c	26b	26c	36a	36b	36c	36d
	Length of Arm	Middle of Breast-bone to Tip of Finger	Acromion to Elbow	Distance between Angles of Eyes		Length of Foot	Length to Hollow above Heel	Thickness at Instep	Circumf. around Heel and Anterior Ligament
				Outer	Inner				
A. New England States	in.	in.	in.	in.	in.	in.	in.	in.	in.
In usual vigor .	29.26	35.09	13.80	3.805	1.224	10.092	9.912	2.53	13.07
Others	29.08	34.85	13.58	3.760	1.202	9.931	9.749	2.65	13.05
Total . . .	29.23	35.05	13.76	3.797	1.220	10.065	9.883	2.55	13.06
B. N. Y., N. J., Penn.									
In usual vigor .	29.10	35.01	13.62	3.765	1.237	10.071	9.878	2.50	13.20
Others	29.25	35.13	13.62	3.744	1.196	9.970	9.793	2.67	13.16
Total . . .	29.12	35.03	13.62	3.761	1.230	10.055	9.864	2.53	13.20
C. Ohio and Indiana									
In usual vigor .	29.50	35.47	13.70	3.744	1.199	10.105	9.918	2.68	13.40
Others	29.72	35.50	13.83	3.695	1.157	10.112	9.949	2.76	13.30
Total . . .	29.53	35.47	13.72	3.738	1.194	10.106	9.922	2.69	13.39
D. Mich., Wisc., and Ill.									
In usual vigor .	28.74	34.74	13.37	3.622	1.225	10.036	9.854	2.47	13.21
Others	29.33	35.26	13.67	3.680	1.213	10.070	9.886	2.69	13.30
Total . . .	28.81	34.77	13.39	3.626	1.224	10.039	9.856	2.49	13.22
E. Coast Slave States									
In usual vigor .	29.40	35.08	13.74	3.747	1.188	10.108	9.926	2.67	13.20
Others	29.42	35.02	13.84	3.679	1.110	9.979	9.798	2.72	13.14
Total . . .	29.40	35.07	13.75	3.737	1.177	10.089	9.908	2.67	13.19
F. Kentucky and Tenn.									
In usual vigor .	30.01	36.00	13.61	3.828	1.231	10.270	10.077	2.85	13.68
Others	30.10	35.94	13.74	3.763	1.188	10.123	9.957	2.80	13.67
Total . . .	30.02	35.99	13.63	3.817	1.224	10.245	10.057	2.84	13.67
G_1. W. of Miss. R.—Free									
In usual vigor .	29.19	35.09	13.30	3.860	1.230	10.000	9.840	2.84	13.42
G_2. W. of Miss. R.—Sl.									
In usual vigor .	29.10	34.36	13.43	3.700	1.254	9.891	9.678	2.65	12 90
Others	29.16	34.66	13.52	3.720	1.180	9.880	9.600	2.64	12.90
Total . . .	29.11	34.39	13.44	3.702	1.247	9.890	9.671	2.65	12.90
H. Brit. Prov. excl. Can.									
In usual vigor .	29.28	35.11	13.88	3.800	1.225	10.075	9.908	2.56	13.17
Others	28.20	33.50	12.80	3.600	1.200	10.150	9.900	2.80	13.80
Total . . .	29.22	35.03	13.82	3.789	1.224	10.079	9.908	2.57	13.20
I. Canada									
In usual vigor .	28.93	34.82	13.57	3.926	1.265	10.082	9.889	2.41	13.19
Others	29.38	35.10	13.90	3.772	1.169	9.989	9.843	2.72	13.21
Total . . .	28.97	34.83	13.60	3.912	1.256	10.074	9.885	2.44	13.19

TABLE I.—(*Continued.*)

Mean Dimensions of White Soldiers.

Nativity	Number of Men	Actual Mean Age	4 Height	4½ Tip of Finger to Margin of Patella	5 Height to 7th Cervical Vertebra	5½ Height to Knee	6 Height to Perinæum	7 Breadth of Neck
J_1. England			in.	in.	in.	in.	in.	in.
In usual vigor	261	26.16	66.17	4.90	56.27	18.28	30.39	4.23
Others . . .	45	31.33	66.75	4.84	56.62	18.41	30.76	4.12
Total . . .	306	27.08	66.25	4.90	56.32	18.30	30.45	4.21
J_2. Wales & I. of Man								
In usual vigor	18	30.10	66.83	5.45	56.78	18.58	30.59	4.19
Others . . .	2	40.49	67.25	5.20	56.95	19.10	30.80	4.00
Total . . .	20	31.14	66.87	5.42	56.80	18.63	30.61	4.17
K. Scotland								
In usual vigor	70	28.48	66.83	4.89	56.87	18.34	30.75	4.23
Others . . .	11	31.67	67.59	5.25	57.51	18.52	31.30	4.16
Total . . .	81	28.91	66.94	4.94	56.95	18.36	30.83	4.22
L. Ireland								
In usual vigor	648	28.36	66.68	5.08	56.75	18.57	30.71	4.24
Others . . .	179	32.42	66.29	5.07	56.28	18.42	30.51	4.09
Total . . .	827	29.24	66.59	5.08	56.65	18.54	30.67	4.21
M. France, etc.								
In usual vigor	84	27.38	65.73	5.01	55.77	18.22	30.24	4.23
Others . . .	16	29.62	65.31	4.97	55.48	18.03	29.99	4.10
Total . . .	100	27.74	65.66	5.00	55.72	18.19	30.20	4.22
N. Germany								
In usual vigor	462	28.88	66.22	5.00	56.49	18.54	30.76	4.31
Others . . .	100	33.85	65.96	4.88	56.06	18.44	30.51	4.14
Total . . .	562	29.76	66.17	4.98	56.41	18.52	30.71	4.28
O. Scandinavia								
In usual vigor	28	27.92	68.06	5.14	58.20	19.04	31.63	4.34
Others . . .	6	34.99	66.37	5.30	56.40	18.67	30.63	3.98
Total . . .	34	29.17	67.76	5.17	57.88	18.97	31.45	4.27
P. Spain, Portugal, etc.								
In usual vigor	6	31.99	65.52	5.70	55.93	18.15	29.72	4.22
Others . . .	1	29.49	63.90	5.30	54.80	17.40	29.50	4.30
Total . . .	7	31.63	65.29	5.64	55.77	18.04	29.69	4.23
Q. Miscellaneous								
In usual vigor	25	26.07	67.07	5.15	57.17	18.68	30.82	4.24
Others . . .	7	32.49	66.43	5.73	57.04	18.56	30.64	3.91
Total . . .	32	27.48	66.93	5.27	57.14	18.65	30.78	4.17
All Nativities								
In usual vigor	9 271	25.705	67.150	5.028	57.218	18.603	31.069	4.238
Others . . .	1 605	29.165	67.148	5.081	57.131	18.644	31.040	4.108
Total . . .	10 876	26.215	67.149	5.036	57.205	18.609	31.065	4.219

TABLE I. — (*Continued.*)

Mean Dimensions of White Soldiers.

Nativity	7½ Girth of Neck	8a Breadth of Shoulders between Acromia	8b Breadth of Shoulders.	9 Breadth of Pelvis	10a Circumference of Chest. Full Inspiration	10b Circumference of Chest. After Expiration	11 Circumference of Waist	11½ Circumference around Hips
J_1. England	in.	in.	in.	in.	in.	in.	in.	in.
In usual vigor .	13.65	12.80	16 21	11.85	36.92	34.24	31.25	36.72
Others . . .	13.44	12.77	16.17	11.80	36.89	34.69	31.36	36.50
Total . . .	13.62	12.80	16.21	11.84	36.91	34.30	31.26	36.68
J_2. Wales & I. of Man								
In usual vigor .	13.69	12.42	16.35	11.80	36.42	33.94	31.08	36.60
Others . . .	14.30	14.55	–	12.20	38.25	36.50	33.50	38.50
Total . . .	13.75	12.69	16.35	11.84	36.60	34.19	31.32	36.79
K. Scotland								
In usual vigor .	13.61	12.46	16.62	11.70	37.57	34.69	31.24	36.67
Others . . .	13.46	12.47	16.70	11.66	36.74	34.56	31.44	36.80
Total . . .	13.59	12.46	16.64	11.69	37.45	34.67	31.26	36.69
L. Ireland								
In usual vigor .	13.76	13.07	16.52	12.05	37.54	35.27	31.67	36.89
Others . . .	13.54	12.71	15.92	11.74	36.87	34.74	31.27	36.41
Total . . .	13.71	12.98	16.47	11.98	37.39	35.15	31.59	36.79
M. France, etc.								
In usual vigor .	13.82	12.90	16.70	12.02	36.91	34.37	31.53	36.99
Others . . .	13.59	12.91	16.60	11.69	36.29	33.92	31.39	36.76
Total . . .	13.78	12.90	16.69	11.97	36.81	34.30	31.51	36.96
N. Germany								
In usual vigor .	13.83	12.97	16.49	11.98	37.20	34.74	31.67	36.98
Others . . .	13.65	12.78	15.47	11.91	36.74	34.60	31.35	36.65
Total . . .	13.79	12.93	16.44	11.97	37.12	34.72	31.62	36.92
O. Scandinavia								
In usual vigor .	14.06	13.19	16.30	11.94	38.44	35.36	32.39	37.74
Others . . .	13.50	12.82	–	12.23	38.17	35.42	32.48	37.15
Total . . .	13.96	13.12	16.30	11.99	38.39	35.37	32.41	37.63
P. Spain, etc.								
In usual vigor .	13.83	13.05	–	11.40	35.20	32.93	30.75	36.13
Others . . .	13.00	–	14.80	11.10	36.00	34.20	31.40	35.90
Total . . .	13.71	13.05	14.80	11.36	35.31	33.11	30.84	36.10
Q. Miscellaneous								
In usual vigor .	13.90	12.87	16.62	12.11	37.15	34.32	31.59	36.77
Others . . .	13.14	13.30	15.30	11.57	34.39	32.31	29.46	35.56
Total . .	13.73	12.97	16.43	11.99	36.54	33.99	31.12	36.51
All nativities								
In usual vigor .	13.633	12.738	16.370	11.936	37.195	34.476	31.483	36.957
Others . . .	13.521	12.693	16.151	11.800	36.846	34.604	31.377	36.770
Total . . .	13.617	12.731	16.350	11.916	37.143	34.494	31.467	36.930

TABLE I.—(*Continued.*)

Mean Dimensions of White Soldiers.

Nativity	12a Length of Arm	12b Middle of Breast-bone to Tip of Finger	12c Acromion to Elbow	26b Distance between Angles of Eyes: Outer	26c Distance between Angles of Eyes: Inner	36a Length of Foot	36b Length to Hollow above Heel	36c Thickness at Instep	36d Circumf. around Heel & Anterior Ligament
J_1. England	in.	in.	in.	in.	in.	in.	in.	in.	in.
In usual vigor	28.62	34.52	13.35	3.720	1.232	10.051	9.841	2.55	13.03
Others . . .	28.84	34.72	13.45	3.744	1.198	9.857	9.700	2.63	12.20
Total . . .	28.66	34.55	13.37	3.724	1.227	10.023	9.821	2.56	13.02
J_2. Wales, I. of Man									
In usual vigor	29.09	35.09	13.82	3.711	1.183	9.933	9.761	2.48	12.79
Others . . .	28.85	35.10	13.25	3.900	1.050	10.150	9.900	2.70	12.20
Total . . .	29.07	35.09	13.76	3.730	1.170	9.955	9.775	2.50	12.73
K. Scotland									
In usual vigor	28.87	34.76	13.48	3.721	1.226	10.066	9.871	2.54	13.15
Others . . .	29.51	35.34	13.86	3.791	1.173	10.000	9.818	2.70	13.60
Total . . .	28.96	34.84	13.53	3.731	1.219	10.057	9.864	2.56	13.21
L. Ireland									
In usual vigor	29.03	34.90	13.51	3.771	1.262	9.965	9.789	2.64	13.08
Others . . .	28.84	34.62	13.30	3.783	1.213	9.781	9.621	2.67	13.02
Total . . .	28.99	34.84	13.46	3.774	1.251	9.925	9.752	2.65	13.07
M. France, etc.									
In usual vigor	28.58	34.49	13.29	3.764	1.263	10.100	9.898	2.58	13.12
Others . . .	28.21	34.02	12.87	3.687	1.144	10.024	9.812	2.74	13.05
Total . . .	28.52	34.42	13.22	3.752	1.244	10.087	9.884	2.61	13.11
N. Germany									
In usual vigor	28.98	34.80	13.53	3.806	1.258	10.087	9.905	2.46	13.15
Others	28.92	34.70	13.56	3.788	1.219	9.978	9.796	2.66	12.72
Total . . .	28.97	34.78	13.54	3.802	1.251	10.068	9.886	2.49	13.07
O. Scandinavia									
In usual vigor	30.02	35.94	13.92	3.807	1.239	10.261	10.075	2.75	13.35
Others . . .	29.27	35.22	13.55	3.800	1.050	10.000	9.867	2.82	13.20
Total . . .	29.89	35.81	13.86	3.806	1.235	10.216	10.038	2.76	13.32
P. Spain, etc.									
In usual vigor	28.60	34.63	13.57	3.817	1.200	10.067	9.850	2.65	13.47
Others . . .	26.10	32.70	12.10	3.500	1.300	9.300	9.100	2.30	12.40
Total . . .	28.24	34.36	13.36	3.771	1.214	9.957	9.743	2.60	13.31
Q. Miscellaneous									
In usual vigor	29.03	34.70	13.50	3.863	1.258	10.124	9.920	2.53	13.19
Others . . .	28.69	34.51	13.10	3.671	1.200	10.043	9.829	2.77	13.07
Total . . .	28.95	34.66	13.41	3.819	1.245	10.106	9.900	2.58	13.16
All Nativities									
In usual vigor	29.139	35.040	13.604	3.761	1.231	10.073	9.886	2.552	13.312
Others . . .	29.235	35.055	13.609	3.743	1.191	9.970	9.797	2.689	13.140
Total . . .	29.153	35.042	13.605	3.759	1.225	10.058	9.873	2.572	13.201

Although, for most of the dimensions, differences of value corresponding to the different states of health are not so strongly marked as to appear attributable to any other source than the inadequacy of the number of men belonging to the smaller class, this is not everywhere the case.

The most prominent difference between the classes is in their age, the class "not in usual vigor" having a mean age greater by some years than the other. There is but one exception to this rule, in any nativity for which the class not in usual health consists of more than two persons. The mean age for the aggregate in the two classes differs by nearly 3½ years; that of the men in full vigor being 25.7, and of the others 29.2 years. We have here a clew of great importance for arriving at the relative power of endurance at different ages, and a most useful investigation might be made from our materials did time and means permit, by excluding from the comparison all those who were enfeebled by wounds, and classifying the remaining cases by age. Then the proportions of men of each age found in the two classes, or even the relative number in each class for the several ages, would afford very suggestive indications. When we bear in mind the very large proportion of the total number who were at the earlier military ages, as has been fully developed in Chapters III. and IV., we cannot fail to perceive at once how much greater must have been the proportion of invalids at the more advanced ages, in order to produce such an effect upon the mean of all. Without having entered upon this desirable research, which the present circumstances forbid, it may be allowable to express an opinion that the results of this inquiry would probably indicate a decided decrease of capacity for enduring the hardship of military life, after the age of thirty-five years.

In the breadth of the neck a difference between the two classes is well marked, the feebler men measuring in the average about one thirtieth less in this dimension. In the girth of the neck an analogous difference of course exists, although not so conspicuous, probably because the measures were taken around the *pomum Adami*, the prominence of which, being the same for the two classes, masks the other phenomenon.

In the full breadth of shoulders, 8*b*, the distinction between the classes is manifest, as also to some extent in the circumference of the waist and hips (11 and 11½).

The breadth of pelvis seems also systematically less for the feebler men, and the difference in the circumference of the chest has been already commented upon; this circumference being greater at full inhalation, and somewhat less at exhalation, for the stronger class of men.

The differences above mentioned are not so well manifest in the earlier series of measures [Form E]. This is probably due to the circumstance already narrated, that the respective classes of men were measured by different persons, between whom a large personal equation existed, and who were governed by no distinct rules in ambiguous cases. The inferences, too, which are deducible from these earlier measurements regarding characteristic differences for the several nativities, have not been corroborated in general by the later and more elaborate measures, of which the results are given in Table I. Still they form a valuable collection of materials, and their mean results are here presented.

TABLE II.

Mean Dimensions of White Soldiers, from Earlier Measures.

Nativity and Class		Number of Men	Actual Mean Age	Height	5 Height to 7th Cervical Vertebra	6 Height to Perinæum
				in.	in.	in.
New England.	In usual vigor	588	24.91	67.15	57.10	30.96
	Not in usual vigor	355	27.26	67.46	57.62	31.03
	In all	943	25.79	67.27	57.30	30.98
New York.	In usual vigor	1 506	23.71	67.06	57.06	31.02
	Not in usual vigor	550	26.11	67.09	57.18	30.80
	In all	2 056	24.35	67.07	57.09	30.96
N. Jersey, Penn.	In usual vigor	833	23.83	67.19	57.23	30.87
	Not in usual vigor	363	25.74	67.11	57.02	30.76
	In all	1 196	24.42	67.17	57.17	30.84
Western States.	In usual vigor	293	23.04	67.88	57.92	31.21
	Not in usual vigor	185	24.32	67.50	57.86	31.05
	In all	478	23.54	67.73	57.89	31.15
Slave States.	In usual vigor	1 650	25.11	68.11	58.03	32.31
	Not in usual vigor	374	26.86	68.68	58.64	32.61
	In all	2 024	25.43	68.22	58.17	32.38
Canada.	In usual vigor	134	23.95	66.97	56.85	30.94
	Not in usual vigor	51	26.74	66.84	56 93	30.93
	In all	185	24.72	66.93	56.87	30.93
Eng. & Scot.	In usual vigor	145	26.01	66.54	56.69	30.83
	Not in usual vigor	71	27.15	66.05	56.09	30.21
	In all	216	26.37	66.38	56.49	30.62
Ireland.	In usual vigor	345	25.96	66.52	56.59	30.78
	Not in usual vigor	122	30.50	66.99	56.94	30.70
	In all	467	27.15	66.65	56.69	30.76
Germany.	In usual vigor	179	26.49	66.39	56.47	30.71
	Not in usual vigor	77	30.34	66.58	56.82	30.74
	In all	256	27.65	66.44	56.58	30.72
All others.	In usual vigor	63	27.75	66.10	55.93	30.56
	Not in usual vigor	20	27.44	66.59	56.74	30.70
	In all	83	27.66	66.22	56.14	30.60
Total.	In usual vigor	5 736	24.542	67.354	57.354	31.343
	Not in usual vigor	2 168	26.669	67.398	57.468	31.137
	In all	7 904	25.127	67.366	57.385	31.286

TABLE II. — (*Continued.*)

Mean Dimensions of White Soldiers, from Earlier Measures.

Nativity and Class		7 Breadth of Neck	8 Breadth of Shoulders	9 Breadth of Pelvis	10 Circumference of Chest	11 Circumference of Waist	12 Length of Arm
		in.	in.	in.	in.	in.	in.
New England.	In usual vigor	4.07	16.17	12.87	35.29	32.08	29.26
	Not in usual vigor	4.04	16.32	13.11	35.31	32.54	28.96
	In all	4.06	16.23	12.96	35.30	32.25	29.14
New York.	In usual vigor	4.07	16.36	13.05	35.44	32.25	29.41
	Not in usual vigor	4.02	16.35	13.07	35.20	32.12	29.19
	In all	4.05	16.35	13.06	35.38	32.22	29.35
N. Jersey, Penn.	In usual vigor	4.08	16.41	13.06	35.64	32.29	29.86
	Not in usual vigor	4.02	16.45	13.23	35.21	32.64	28.67
	In all	4.06	16.42	13.11	35.51	32.40	29.50
Western States.	In usual vigor	4.11	16.53	13.13	35.74	32.30	29.84
	Not in usual vigor	4.05	16.31	13.18	35.09	32.43	29.03
	In all	4.09	16.44	13.15	35.49	32.35	29.53
Slave States.	In usual vigor	4.14	16.33	13.41	35.14	31.67	28.88
	Not in usual vigor	4.13	16.31	13.40	34.82	31.45	29.19
	In all	4.14	16.32	13.41	35.08	31.63	28.94
Canada.	In usual vigor	4.08	16.33	13.00	35.50	32.17	29.40
	Not in usual vigor	4.10	16.46	13.13	35.31	32.15	28.90
	In all	4.09	16.37	13.03	35.45	32.16	29.26
Eng. & Scot.	In usual vigor	4.09	16.28	13.07	35.37	31.94	28.75
	Not in usual vigor	4.02	16.09	12.93	34.62	31.38	28.21
	In all	4.07	16.22	13.02	35.12	31.76	28.57
Ireland.	In usual vigor	4.10,	16.38	13.09	35.97	32.25	29.20
	Not in usual vigor	4.09	16.52	13.14	36.04	32.43	28.81
	In all	4.09	16.63	13.11	35.98	32.29	29.10
Germany.	In usual vigor	4.13	16.34	13.10	35.66	32.20	28.95
	Not in usual vigor	4.09	16.34	13.05	35.13	31.85	28.98
	In all	4.12	16.34	13.09	35.50	32.10	28.96
All others.	In usual vigor	4.10	16.45	13.14	35.56	31.89	28 58
	Not in usual vigor	4.08	16.24	13.15	34.38	31.56	28 20
	In all	4.10	16.36	13.14	35.28	31.80	28.49
Total.	In usual vigor	4.098	16.342	13.146	35.424	32.059	29.281
	Not in usual vigor	4.053	16.400	13.174	35.166	32.166	28 975
	In all	4.085	16 359	13.153	35.353	32.089	29 200

5. *Sailors.*

Of the 1146 sailors whose physical characteristics have been collected, 822 examined by Mr. Phinney at the Naval Recruiting Station in New York, and 239 examined by Dr. Elsner and Major Wales at the Receiving Ship at the Charlestown Navy Yard, were entirely unclothed, so that no impediment existed to the facility of the measurements. In addition to these, 85 others were examined at Charlestown while wearing only trowsers and drawers, and 68 marines at the Brooklyn Navy Yard by Dr. Wells in the same way. No one of our examiners was more scrupulously exact and thorough than Mr. Phinney, and this series of results seems the most accurate and trustworthy of all that we have collected, especially since the personal error of the examiners appears to be remarkably small. The 1061 men who were examined without clothes have been assorted by nativities, like the soldiers of Table I., and the 85 others who were partially clad, as well as the 68 marines, have been tabulated by themselves, without assortment according to nativity. Most of them were examined at the time of their enlistment, and almost all were in full health; so that no classification depending upon their state of health seemed desirable, especially since all that such classification would suggest has been attained on a larger scale, in the discussion of the results from soldiers.

The *mean age* of the sailors examined differs by just a month from that of the soldiers in Table I., and their *height* is less by 1.14 inch, thus corroborating the results obtained in Chapter V. for the difference in stature between soldiers and sailors. The average height of the 68 marines was precisely midway between that of the sailors and the soldiers. But here, as indeed for sailors of the several nativities, the numbers are in general altogether too small to permit any safe inductions from a comparison of the mean results.

A few brief remarks as to the comparison of some of the dimensions with those of soldiers, may perhaps be appropriate.

The values of the dimension 4½ are decidedly larger for sailors, owing in part to the greater length of their thighs. The *height to perinæum* seems, notwithstanding the inferior stature, to be absolutely greater for the seamen. There are, to be sure, two considerations which should qualify any inference from direct comparison of our mean values, namely, that the soldiers wore trowsers and drawers while subjected to measurement, so that the thickness of their clothing was practically deducted from the true height to perinæum; and that the distribution of nativities is very different in the two cases.

The first-named consideration is apparently borne out by a comparison of the mean length of legs for the partially clothed sailors and marines, since for the 85 sailors this average comes out 1.3 inch less, and for the 68 marines 0.88 inch less, than for those who were measured while naked; yet only a portion of these differences can be due to the presence or absence of clothing. For the marines, the mean value of the dimension 4½ appears actually more than an inch greater than for the sailors without clothing, in consequence of their short arms and greater length of body. But all these measures of marines were made by Dr. Wells, who made but few others; and too great stress ought not to be laid upon them.

The second consideration is more serious. But each of the four nativities A, B, J, and L, comprises more than one hundred sailors, so that we may collate the mean values for these special nativities, and thus obtain comparisons free from this source of error.

Mean Values of Dimension 4½.

(Distance from Tip of Middle Finger to Level of Upper Margin of Knee-pan.)

	New England States		New York, New Jersey, Penn.		England		Ireland	
	No. of Men	Distance	No. of Men	Distance	No. of Men	Distance	No. of Men	Distance
		in.		in.		in.		in.
Soldiers . .	1 208	4.93	3 761	4.92	306	4.90	876	5.08
Sailors . .	129	5.57	155	6.06	102	5.55	335	6.07
Excess . .		0.64		1.14		0 65		0.99

Thus the original inference as to the excess of this dimension in the sailors is thoroughly justified, and the difference of 0.70 inch between the mean values for soldiers and sailors is seen to be probably due neither to the clothing, nor to any error in the mode of measurement, nor to the different proportions of men of the several nativities.

From a similar comparison it will become manifest whence this difference arises. The following tables present the mean values of the height to perinæum (*Qu.* 6), and of the length of arm as measured from the central line of the body (12*b*) for soldiers and sailors of the same four nativities.

Mean Height to Perinæum.

	New England States		New York, New Jersey, Penn.		England		Ireland	
	No. of Men	Height	No. of Men	Height	No. of Men	Height	No. of Men	Height
		in.		in.		in.		in.
Soldiers . .	1 208	31.09	3 759	31.05	304	30.45	824	30.67
Sailors. . .	129	31.44	155	31.75	102	30.69	335	31.52
Excess . .		0.35		0.70		0.24		0.85

Mean Values of Dimension 12*b.*

(*Distance from Middle of Top of Sternum to Tip of Middle Finger, Arm extended.*)

	New England States		New York, New Jersey, Penn.		England		Ireland	
	No. of Men	Distance	No. of Men	Distance	No. of Men	Distance	No. of Men	Distance
		in.		in.		in.		in.
Soldiers . .	1 211	35.05	3 762	35.03	306	34.55	826	34.84
Sailors . .	129	34.10	155	33.79	102	33.32	335	33.82
Defect . .		0.95		1.24		1.23		1.02

It is thus palpable that, notwithstanding a superiority of stature on the part of the soldiers over the sailors measured, amounting to 0.73 inch for the New Englanders, 0.87 for the natives of the Middle States, 1.14 for the Englishmen, and 0.37 for the Irishmen, the legs of the sailors are all longer, the excess amounting to 0.217 for the aggregate averages; and their arms all shorter, by an amount averaging 1.09 inch for the men whose measures are here given, and entirely disproportionate to the difference in height.

The mean height to the knee for the aggregate of the sailors is 18.47 inches, or 0.14 less than for the aggregate of the soldiers, although the height to the perinæum is greater; thus showing that the chief difference is in the length of the thigh. If from the height to the perinæum we subtract the height to the knee, we find the values of the dimension for each of the four nativities before compared.

Mean Distance from Knee to Perinæum.

	N. E. States		N. Y., N. J., Pa.		England		Ireland	
	No. of Men	Distance	No. of Men	Distance	No. of Men	Distance	No. of Men	Distance
		in.		in.		in.		in.
Soldiers	1 208	12.34	3 758	12.41	304	12.15	824	12.13
Sailors	129	12.98	155	13.05	102	12.50	335	12.95
Excess		0.64		0.64		0.35		0.82

The ratio of the height of knee to the distance between knee and perinæum, which we found to be 1.494 for the aggregate of the soldiers, is 1.442 for the aggregate of the sailors.

The breadth and girth of the neck appears to be systematically greater for sailors, by nearly 3 per cent.; the breadth of pelvis, the circumference of chest, of waist, and of hips, to be severally less by almost as much.

The length of arm and hand has been already seen, by a comparison of the dimension 12*b*, to be relatively, as well as actually, less for sailors than soldiers. And if we compare, not the distance from the medial line of the body to the tip of the middle finger, but the distances from the acromion process to the elbow and to the tip of the middle finger, we arrive at the same result, as the annexed comparisons make evident.

Length of Arm and Hand,

from Acromion to Tip of Middle Finger.

	N. E. States		N. Y., N. J., Penn.		England		Ireland		Aggregate	
	No. of Men	Length	No. of Men	Length	No. of Men	Length	No. of Men	Length	No. of Men	Length
		in.		in.		in.		in.		in.
Soldiers . . .	1 199	29.23	3 742	29.12	303	28.66	826	28.99	10 803	29.153
Sailors . . .	129	28.83	155	28.49	102	28.09	335	28.47	1 061	28.538
Defect . . .		0.40		0.63		0.57		0.52		0.615

Length of Upper Arm

from Acromion to Elbow.

	N. E. States		N. Y., N. J., Penn.		England		Ireland		Aggregate	
	No. of Men	Length	No. of Men	Length	No. of Men	Length	No. of Men	Length	No. of Men	Length
		in.		in.		in.		in.		in.
Soldiers . . .	1 210	13.76	3 755	13.62	305	13.37	827	13.46	10 856	13.605
Sailors . . .	129	13.28	155	13.19	102	12.97	335	13.14	1 061	13.171
Defect . . .		0.48		0.43		0.40		0.32		0.434

The distance between perinæum and pubes was measured for no white men excepting sailors; but this dimension has been already given with the measurement of the soldiers, since the general discussion of dimensions there given appeared to render that a more appropriate place than this, for such measurements as are not presented for the sake of comparison. From 1013 cases we find —

Mean Height	Mean Distance	Ratio to Height	Minimum	Maximum
in.	in.		in.	in.
65.99	1.891	.0287	1.2	3.7

The distance between nipples was measured for not quite three fourths of the sailors; for whom the following mean dimensions were found —

No. of Men	Height	Circum. of Chest	Dist. betw. Nipples	Ratio to Circumf.
	in.	in.	in.	
753	65.836	35.141	8.304	0.2363

The ratio of this distance to the mean circumference of thorax is thus seen to be decidedly greater than for the soldiers.

The foot dimensions obtained for sailors and soldiers are not essentially different, with the exception of the thickness at the instep, which appears to be much larger for sailors. For the marines this is not the case, and it is not improbable that this greater thickness may be due to the habit of climbing shrouds, and standing upon ropes.

Table III. presents, in three pages, the mean dimensions of the sailors measured, classified as already described.

TABLE III.

Mean Dimensions of Sailors.

Nativity	Number of Men	Actual Mean Age	4 Height	4½ Tip of Finger to Margin of Patella	5 Height to 7th Cervical Vertebra	5½ Height to Knee	6 Height to Perinæum	7 Breadth of Neck
			in.	in.	in.	in.	in.	in.
A. N. E. States . .	129	25.81	66.47	5.57	56.30	18.46	31.44	4.16
B. N. Y., N. J., Penn.	155	26.30	66.27	6.06	56.22	18.70	31.75	4.35
C. Ohio and Indiana	2	31.49	64.87	5.73	54.97	17.60	30.30	4.23
D. Mich., Wisc., Ill.	6	25.49	68.21	6.09	57.96	19.83	32.71	4.46
E. Coast Slave States	19	27.53	65.89	5.66	55.80	18.77	31.23	4.30
F, G_2. Other Sl. States	2	24.49	70.50	6.35	60.10	19.00	31.70	4.00
H. Br. Prov. ex. Can.	50	25.70	66.96	5.83	56.78	18.74	31.79	4.38
I. Canada	16	25.65	66.62	5.47	56.27	18.48	31.16	4.25
J_1. England . . .	102	25.40	65.11	5.55	55.05	18.19	30.69	4.31
J_2. Wales, Isle of Man	6	28.32	64.42	4.92	54.38	18.30	31.10	4.62
K. Scotland . . .	27	29.19	64.79	5.53	54.85	17.96	30.30	4.25
L. Ireland	335	25.90	66.22	6.07	56.09	18.57	31.52	4.41
M. France, etc. . .	20	26.84	65.35	5.14	55.55	18.30	31.23	4.20
N. Germany . . .	62	25.83	66.09	6.01	56.13	18.65	31.58	4.40
O. Scandinavia . .	82	26.19	65.55	5.21	55.49	18.19	31.15	4.30
P. Spain, etc. . . .	18	27.54	64.94	5.06	54.89	18.49	31.02	4.28
Q. Miscellaneous . .	30	27.68	64.77	5.12	54.75	18.26	30.80	4.40
Total without clothes	1 061	26.132	66.018	5.778	55.927	18.498	31.378	4.336
Sailors partly clothed	85	26.12	65.95	5.27	55.64	18.15	30.08	4.03
Marines, " "	68	26.270	66.58	6.86	56.62	18.32	30.50	4.29

TABLE III. — (*Continued.*)

Mean Dimensions of Sailors.

Nativity	7½ Girth of Neck	8a Breadth of Shoulders	8b Breadth of Shoulders	9 Breadth of Pelvis	10a Circumference of Chest: Full Insp.	10b Circumference of Chest: After Exp.	11 Circumference of Waist	11½ Circumference around Hips
	in.	in.	in.	in.	in.	in.	in.	in.
A. N. E. States . .	13.99	12.70	16.01	11.24	35.47	33.63	30.15	34.91
B. N. Y., N. J., Penn.	13.79	12.51	16.12	11.74	35.51	33.35	29.94	34.67
C. Ohio and Indiana	13.57	11.50	16.45	11.30	35.50	32.63	29.77	34.80
D. Mich., Wisc., Ill.	14.06	13.30	16.17	13.47	36.33	34.27	30.01	36.00
E. Coast Slave States	13.63	12 40	16.09	11.61	35.50	33.45	29.95	34.51
F, G_2. Other Sl. States	14.10	13.05	–	11.60	38.65	37.90	33.15	36.80
H. Br. Prov. ex. Can.	14.21	13.40	16.41	11.63	36.79	34.80	31.02	35.52
I. Canada	14.08	12.82	16.55	11.39	36.69	34.79	31.04	35.55
J_1. England . . .	13.98	12.89	16.26	11.49	35.76	33.71	30.31	34.69
J_2. Wales, Isle of Man	14.05	–	16.42	11.78	36.00	33.67	30.00	33.92
K. Scotland . . .	14.07	12.82	16.44	11.50	37.19	35.22	30.58	34.76
L. Ireland	14.05	13.10	16.40	11.74	36.41	34.26	30.68	34.92
M. France, etc. . .	14.15	12.92	16.26	11.25	36.39	34.46	30.79	34.77
N. Germany . . .	13.97	13.12	16.39	12.00	36.42	34.22	30.36	35.57
O. Scandinavia . .	14.06	12.85	16.59	11.63	37.06	34.91	31.03	35.40
P. Spain, etc. . . .	13.99	13.01	16.33	11.22	36.07	34.28	30.09	34.48
Q. Miscellaneous . .	14.26	12.39	16.57	11.63	36.07	33.96	30.10	34.46
Total without clothes	14.001	12.879	16.310	11.625	36.162	34.085	30.457	34.942
Sailors partly clothed	14.08	12.44	–	10.92	38.44	35.42	31.53	35.68
Marines, " "	13.96	–	15.42	11.64	36.45	34.55	30.42	36.56

TABLE III. — (*Continued.*)

Mean Dimensions of Sailors.

Nativity	12a Length of Arm	12b Middle of Breast-bone to Tip of Finger	12c Acromion to Elbow	26b Distance between Angles of Eyes: Outer	26c Distance between Angles of Eyes: Inner	36a Length of Foot	36b Length to Hollow above Heel	36c Thickness at Instep	36d Circumf. around Heel and Anterior Ligament
	in.	in.	in.	in.	in.	in.	in.	in.	in.
A. N. E. States . .	28.83	34.10	13.28	3.831	1.153	10.025	9.866	2.90	13.13
B. N. Y., N. J., Pa.	28.49	33.79	13.19	3.693	1.195	10.129	9.934	2.89	13.07
C. Ohio and Ind.	27.70	32.63	13.47	3.600	1.167	9.567	9.467	2.60	12.53
D. Mich., Wisc., Ill.	29.96	35.27	13.66	3.843	1.329	10.500	10.314	2.99	13.47
E. Coast Slave St.	28.67	33.89	13.29	3.654	1.162	10.100	9.896	2.97	13.06
F, G. Other Sl. St.	30.10	37.20	13.85	3.950	1.050	10.900	10.900	2.50	14.20
H. Br. Pr. ex. Can.	28.90	34.43	13.27	3.842	1.187	10.096	9.908	2.98	13.11
I. Canada . . .	28.81	34.43	13.47	3.863	1.174	10.084	9.942	2.96	13.17
J_1. England . . .	28.09	33.32	12.97	3.712	1 202	10.033	9.845	2.90	12.99
J_2. Wales, I. of Man	28.25	32.83	13.03	3.617	1.300	10.017	9.567	2.83	12.93
K. Scotland . . .	28.07	33.29	12.92	3.690	1.197	10.003	9.827	2.87	12.98
L. Ireland . . .	28.47	33.82	13.14	3.713	1.189	10.095	9.912	2.94	13.09
M. France, etc. . .	28.66	34.01	13.17	3.870	1.205	10.130	10.005	2.90	13.17
N. Germany . . .	28.72	33.92	13.40	3.764	1.259	10.342	10.108	2,95	13.19
O. Scandinavia . .	28.85	34.00	13.28	3.836	1.206	10.173	10.014	2.95	13.23
P. Spain, etc. . .	27.98	33.89	12.96	3.828	1.189	9.994	9.811	2.92	13.13
Q. Miscellaneous .	28.16	33.44	12.70	3.827	1.263	10.071	9.894	2.89	12.96
Total with't clothes	28.538	33.848	13.171	3.752	1.194	10.114	9.920	2.921	13.098
Sailors part. cloth'd	29.04	35.08	13.50	3.931	1.115	10.036	9.975	2.84	13.34
Marines " "	28.66	35.02	13.22	4.253	1.056	10.065	9.881	2.41	13.05

6. *Students.*

It has already been stated that the temporary suspension of opportunities for measuring soldiers in the field, was made the occasion for obtaining similar data for the elder students at Cambridge and New Haven. The members of the Senior and Junior classes being at the same age as a large portion of the soldiers who had been examined, afforded an excellent opportunity for comparing the physical characteristics of the two classes of men. Accordingly the students of the two higher classes and of the Scientific Schools were requested to permit themselves to be measured, and all who complied with the request were examined in the same manner as the soldiers. The materials presented in Table IV. are derived from these examinations, 291 in number, all of which were made by Dr. Elsner.

A column has been inserted, giving the full stature which corresponds with the mean height found at the mean age. These values can however make no claim to accuracy. Were the individuals classified by ages at half-year intervals, then the mean height found for each half year could be reduced, with a tolerable approximation to correctness, to the corresponding full stature; and the mean of the values for full statures thus obtained would represent quite closely that mean height which would be found for the same young men after their full development in stature had been attained. The values here given are simply those which would be correct were all the students at their mean age, and are intended only as a rough estimate. Since the rate of growth at ages prior to this mean was greater than at those subsequent, the "corresponding full statures" as given fall short of those which would have been attained by the more accurate process. In the reduction it has been assumed that the nativities of the students in each class were distributed in the same proportion as the aggregate of those examined at the same university.

The actual nativities were as follows: —

	N. E. States	Middle States	Others	Total
Harvard	94	17	13	124
Yale	62	78	27	167
Total	156	95	40	291

The statures of the students are seen to be nearly an inch greater than those of the soldiers of the same nativities; the dimension 4½ is more than an inch greater, in consequence both of the shorter fore-arm and of the longer thigh. In four instances this dimension attained the limit of 9.2 inches, and in three it did not exceed 3.4 inches. The mean distance from knee to perinæum is 12.65 inches, and the mean height of knee 19.24, the variations ranging from 16.3 to 24.0, these values for soldiers of the nativities A and B being 12.39 and 18.67 respectively.

The breadth and girth of neck are less for the students, as also is the breadth of the pelvis; the length of body and circumference of chest are about the same.

The mean distance between the nipples and its relative magnitude were found to be —

	No. of Men	Height	Mean Circ. of Chest	Dist. betw'n Nipples	Ratio to Circumf.
		in.	in.	in.	
Harvard	124	68.601	35.290	8.115	0.2300
Yale	167	67.726	35.329	8.038	0.2275
Total	291	68.099	35.313	8.071	0.2286

From acromion to elbow we have the mean distance 13.71 inches, and from elbow to finger-tip 15.31; the corresponding values for soldiers having been found 13.66 and 15.49 respectively.

The Yale students measured were in general shorter than those of Harvard; this difference is conspicuously manifest in the height to the perinæum, and many of the dimensions are clearly affected by this circumstance, being relatively about the same for the New Haven men, though absolutely smaller. It would seem that the inequality of ages is greater among the latter, so that the mean development of size for the same mean age is not quite so great as for Cambridge students.

TABLE IV.

Mean Dimensions of Students of Harvard and Yale Colleges.

Class	No. of Men	Actual Mean Age	4 Height	5 Corresponding Full Stature	4½ Tip of Finger to Margin of Patella	Height to 7th Cervical Vertebra	5½ Height to Knee	6 Height to Perinæum
			in.	in.	in.	in.	in.	in.
Harvard, Seniors .	69	21.93	68.76	69.12	6.17	58.26	19.35	32.08
Juniors .	51	21.03	68.29	69.08	6.00	57.79	19.57	32.04
Scientific	4	21.73	69.82	70.17	6.77	59.70	20.60	33.27
Total	124	21.555	68.601	69.00	6.121	58.117	19.482	32.098
Yale, Seniors .	92	22.70	67.82	68.13	6.73	57.78	19.15	31.72
Juniors .	63	21.10	67.73	68.19	6.74	58.23	19.00	31.77
Scientific	12	19.15	66.99	68.24	6.71	57.27	18.69	31.77
Total	167	21.841	67.726	68.10	6.735	57.916	19.060	31.740
Aggregate . . .	291	21.719	68.099	68.49	6.473	58.001	19.240	31.892

Class	7 Breadth of Neck	7½ Girth of Neck	8a Breadth of Shoulders	9 Breadth of Pelvis	10a Circ. of Chest: Full Inspiration	10b Circ. of Chest: After Expiration	11 Circumference of Waist	11½ Circumference around Hips
	in.	in.	in.	in.	in.	in.	in.	in.
Harvard, Seniors .	4.02	13.28	12.38	11.18	36.75	33.73	31.13	35.68
Juniors .	3.97	13.25	13.30	11.49	36.86	33.98	30.77	36.21
Scientific	4.00	12.80	12.95	11.45	35.92	32.95	29.77	34.42
Total	4.002	13.247	12.781	11.314	36.772	33.809	30.943	35.854
Yale, Seniors .	3.96	13.28	13.15	11.06	37.12	33.93	31.58	36.93
Juniors .	4.11	13.34	13.49	11.20	36.73	33.59	31.57	37.25
Scientific	4.02	12.95	13.59	10.77	36.20	33.27	30.02	37.07
Total	4.026	13.281	13.311	11.093	36.902	33.756	31.460	37.065
Aggregate . . .	4.015	13.267	13.085	11.187	36.847	33.779	31.240	36.549

TABLE IV. — (*Continued.*)

Mean Dimensions of Students of Harvard and Yale Colleges.

Class		12a	12b	12c	26b	26c	36a	36b	36c	36d
		Length of Arm	Middle of Breast-bone to Tip of Finger	Acromion to Elbow	Dist. between Angles of Eyes		Length of Foot	Length to Hollow above Heel	Thickness at Instep	Circum. around Heel and Anterior Ligament
					Outer	Inner				
		in.	in.	in.	in.	in.	in.	in.	n.	in.
Harvard,	Seniors .	29.36	35.19	13.76	3.84	1.11	10.10	9.97	2.73	13.05
	Juniors .	29.07	34.97	13.56	3.83	1.12	10.15	9.98	2.62	13.30
	Scientific	29.50	35.55	13.65	3.85	1.17	10.05	9.92	2.42	12.95
Total		29.244	35.113	13.673	3.837	1.117	10.120	9.975	2.675	13.150
Yale,	Seniors .	28.83	34.80	13.49	3.85	1.12	9.84	9.67	2.83	13.06
	Juniors .	28.96	34.84	14.09	3.91	1.10	9.85	9.67	2.92	13.06
	Scientific	28.45	34.24	13.83	3.83	1.03	9.72	9.55	2.90	12.83
Total		28.854	34.776	13.741	3.872	1.107	9.837	9.664	2.868	13.043
Aggregate .		29.021	34.920	13.712	3.857	1.111	9.957	9.797	2.786	13.088

7. *Colored Soldiers.*

Our measurements of colored men have already been described in § 2, and the number specified which were made by the several examiners, as well as the number of men measured in the different conditions as regards clothing.

Strenuous endeavors have been made to assort them with more nicety than has been found practicable, using various bases of classification. Three or more distinct races of negroes are to be found in the Southern States, and these present themselves in every degree and mode of admixture with one another and with the Indian and white races. The investigation of the effect of climate and soil upon the blacks is a research of interest and importance, yet all attempts to prosecute our inquiries in this direction have proved unavailing. The impossibility of discriminating among the numerous classes, sufficiently to obtain an adequate number of cases belonging without doubt to any one class, made itself felt at an early stage of our work; and it soon became evident that even the different African races could not be habitually distinguished from one another by our examiners. The colored men measured have therefore been divided into two classes; one containing, under the title of "Full Blacks," all in whom no admixture of white or red ancestry was perceptible, and the other giving as "Mixed Races" all other colored men. Our records contain all information that could be collected regarding the ancestry of each individual, so that they are capable of combination in whatever manner future study or discovery may render desirable. Each of the classes has been subdivided into natives of the Free States, and natives of the [late] Slave States; those who were in their usual vigor have been treated separately from those who were not; and those who were partially clothed when measured have also been kept distinct from the rest.

The average *height* of the colored men examined was less than the mean height of those obtained from the records which furnished the materials for Chapter V. This discrepancy is not surprising, when we consider the limited extent of our materials, as well as the fact that the men whose statures are discussed in the chapter on that subject were only those for whom the descriptive musters are on file in the State archives. Had the Commission been allowed to consult the large store of materials on file at the War Department in Washington, it is probable that our results regarding the growth and development of the negro races would have been comparable with those obtained for the whites. Much information on this subject may be expected from the forthcoming report of Dr. Baxter upon the medical statistics of the Provost Marshal General's Bureau.

The dimension 4½ is, as would have been anticipated by ethnologists, one which manifests the most striking contrast with the white race. We find the mean value to be as follows: —

	No. of Men	Distance	Minimum	Maximum	Range
		in.	in.	in	in.
Full Blacks . .	2 020	2.884	− 0.5	7.6	8.1
Mixed Races . .	863	4.125	+ 0.2	7.2	7.0

For the full blacks the smaller value of this dimension among natives of the Slave States is also quite noticeable, although for the mixed races the results of this mode of classification are variant and contradictory. Thus for the full blacks we have the mean value —

	Naked.		Half Clothed		Clothed		Total	
	No. of Men	Dist.	No. of Men	Dist.	No. of Men.	Dist.	No. of Men	Dist.
		in.		in.		in.		in.
Natives of Free States	123	3.094	2	3.000	101	3.551	226	3.298
" " Slave States	554	2.590	145	2.449	1 095	3.006	1 794	2.832

The mean length of *head and neck*, obtained by subtracting the height to the seventh cervical vertebra from the total height, is 9.62 inches for the full blacks, and 9.56 for the mixed races, the corresponding value for whites being 9.94 inches. This length is markedly less for natives of the Slave States than for those born the Free States.

The *length of body*, too, is less for the colored race than for the white, and for mixed races somewhat greater than for the full blacks. This quantity, which we have found to be 26.14 inches for the average white soldier, is by our measurements of colored men —

	Born in Free States		Born in Slave States		Total	
	No. of Men	Length	No. of Men	Length	No. of Men	Length
		in.		in.		in.
Full Blacks	226	24.20	1 794	24.52	2 020	24.487
Mixed Races	169	24.37	694	24.76	863	24.680

Among the colored troops, natives of the Southern States, are incorporated a considerable number of men measured in New Orleans after the close of the war. These are 385 in number, and appear to have been so much less accurate than the rest that it is a source of regret that they have been incorporated with the means. They were no doubt conscientiously made, but both of the examiners appear to have been habitually and unconsciously biased, to some extent, in their measures for certain dimensions, especially in their estimates of the position of the seventh cervical vertebra, of the center and upper margin of the patella, in questions $4\frac{1}{2}$ and $5\frac{1}{2}$, and of the elbow. The mean results are probably not largely affected by the incorporation of these measurements, but the range of individual variation is considerably extended thereby.

The *height to perinæum* appears greater for colored men than for whites, the excess being both above and below the knee. Thus we find: —

Class of Men		No. of Men	Height to Perinæum	Height to Knee	Knee to Perinæum	Ratio
			in.	in.	in.	in.
Full Blacks. —	Free States . . .	226	32.289	18.870	13.419	1.406
	Slave States . .	1 794	32.076	19.169	12.907	1.485
	Aggregate . . .	2 020	32.100	19.136	12.964	1.476
Mixed Races. —	Free States . . .	169	31.993	18.787	13.206	1.423
	Slave States . .	694	32.015	19.446	12 569	1.547
	Aggregate . . .	863	32.010	19.318	12.692	1.522

The distance from perinæum to pubes is clearly greater for blacks than for whites. We have this dimension for only 89 colored men, but it was taken by our most exact examiners, and any effect of personal equation is mostly eliminated by the large proportion of both classes which was measured by Mr. Phinney.

FULL BLACKS.

Examiner	No. of Men	Mean Distance	Mean Height	Mean Height to Perinæum
		in.	in.	in.
A. Phinney	45	2.169	65.784	31.662
B. G. Wilder . . .	3	2.700	63.533	31.167
	48	2.202	65.644	31.631

MIXED RACES.

Examiner	No. of Men	Mean Distance	Mean Height	Mean Height to Perinæum
		in.	in.	in.
A. Phinney	12	1.633	66.742	32.983
B. G. Wilder	29	2.893	66.683	32.303
	41	2.524	66.700	32.502

The colored men measured by Mr. Phinney were sailors, enlisting at the New York rendezvous, and mostly natives of the Northern States. Those measured by Dr. Wilder were mostly members of the Fifty-fifth Massachusetts Regiment, serving in South Carolina; about one half of them having been born in the Slave States, and a considerable proportion of the remainder in Indiana.

The mean *girth of neck*, which was 13.62 inches for the white soldiers, is 13.92 for the full blacks, and 13.83 for the mixed races.

The *breadth of shoulders* appears also decidedly greater when measured between the acromia, and slightly greater when the full breadth is taken.

The *circumference of thorax* at full inspiration is less than for whites by an inch and a quarter for the full blacks, and an inch and four tenths for the mixed races. The difference after exhalation is somewhat less than a quarter-inch for the former, and somewhat greater for the latter class. The play of chest in breathing appears to be not much more than three fifths as great as for white men.

The *distance between nipples* has been found as follows: —

Class	No. of Men	Mean Height	Mean Circ. of Chest	Distance between Nipples	Ratio to Circ. of Chest
		in.	in.	in.	in.
Full Blacks. — In usual vigor . .	617	65.661	35.368	7.970	0.2253
Not in usual vigor .	129	65.748	35.595	7.971	0.2239
Total	746	65.676	35.407	7.970	0.2251
Mixed Races. — In usual vigor . .	510	65.821	34.798	7.878	0.2264
Not in usual vigor .	94	66.152	34.952	7.963	0.2278
Total	604	65.873	34.822	7.891	0.2266

The smallest value found for this dimension was 6.2 inches, being 0.196 of the mean circumference of chest; the largest was 10 inches or 0.274.

The circumference of *waist* and *hips* are less than for whites; the mean value of the former being larger by a quarter inch, and that of the latter smaller by not quite so much, for the mulattoes than for the full blacks.

The *arms* of the black men are relatively longer than in the white races, the excess being principally in the fore-arm. This will be best perceived by means of a tabular view.

Class	No. of Men	Height	12*b* Middle of Body to Finger-Tip	12*a* Acromion to Tip of Finger	12*c* Acromion to Elbow	Lower Arm and Hand	Ratio
		in.	in.	in.	in.	in.	
Full Blacks . .	2 020	66.210	35.808	29.405	13.302	16.103	1.211
Mixed Races . .	863	66.251	35.822	30.271	13.856	16.415	1.185
Whites	10 803	67.149	35.042	29.153	13.605	15.548	1.143

The ratio given in the last column is that obtaining between the two preceding ones, or the proportion which the distance, from elbow to tip of middle finger, bears to the distance from the acromion process to the elbow. The preeminent excess of the lower arm for the full blacks and the intermediate value for the mixed races are as conspicuous as the increased length of the arm.

If we compare the lengths of arms and legs for the same classes of men, we find the proportional differences less conspicuous.

	Height to Perinæum	Distance from Acromion to Finger-Tip	Ratio
	in.	in.	
Full Blacks	32.100	29.405	1.092
Mixed Races	32.010	30.271	1.057
Whites	31.065	29.153	1.066

The eyes of the black man seem in general wider, and more distant from each other, than those of the white man. Our measures give the mean values: —

	Distance between		Distance of Centers	Width of Eye
	Outer Angles	Inner Angles		
	in.	in.	in.	in.
Full Blacks	4.090	1.338	2.714	1.376
Mixed Races	3.981	1 360	2.670	1.310
Whites	3.759	1.225	2.492	1.267

The well known difference between the two races, in the size and shape of the foot, will be recognized by a glance at our numerical results.

We find, namely, —

	Length of Foot	Length to Hollow above Heel	Circ. around Heel and Anterior Lig't	Heel	Thickness at Instep
	in.	in.	in.	in.	in.
Full Blacks	10.600	10.079	13.643	0.821	2.672
Mixed Races . . .	10.439	10.172	13.463	0.567	2.770
Whites	10.058	9.873	13.201	0.485	2.572

The largest foot measured belonged to a full blooded negro, 72.7 inches tall. The length was 12.4 inches, the heel was 0.7 inch long, and the thickness at instep, 3 inches.

No measures of the breadth of the foot, and none of any dimension of the hand, were recorded.

In the annexed table, the mean results of these measurements of colored men are given, classified in as large a variety of ways as seems worth the while.

TABLE V.

Mean Dimensions of Full Blacks.

Class	Number of Men	Actual Mean Age	4 Height	4½ Tip of Finger to Margin of Patella	5 Height to 7th Cervical Vertebra	5½ Height to Knee	6 Height to Perinæum	7 Breadth of Neck
			in.	in.	in.	in.	in.	in.
Naked, Free States	123	26.08	65.93	3.09	55.85	18.35	32.21	4.12
Slave States	554	24.75	65.80	2.59	56.05	18.45	32.12	4.14
All . .	677	24.993	65.821	2.682	56.012	18.429	32.140	4.137
Half Naked								
Free States	2	22.98	66.65	3.00	57.15	19.90	31.20	4.35
Slave States	145	28.18	65.15	2.45	55.98	19.35	30.49	4.23
All . .	147	28.112	65.169	2.456	55.998	19.359	30.501	4.233
Clothed								
Free States	101	24.20	66.86	3.55	57.24	19.48	32.40	4.30
Slave States	1095	25.89	66.53	3.01	56.96	19.51	32.26	4.22
All . .	1196	25.750	66.558	3.053	56.984	19.509	32.275	4.227
In usual vigor								
Free States	194	24.88	66.35	3.37	56.49	18.91	32.32	4.21
Slave States	1598	25.42	66.22	2.86	56.62	19.18	32.10	4.20
All . .	1792	25.364	66.237	2.914	56.610	19.148	32.123	4.202
Not in usual vigor								
Free States	32	27.21	66.39	2.86	56.48	18.63	32.08	4.14
Slave States	196	28.25	65.94	2.62	56.39	19.11	31.89	4.16
All . .	228	28.104	66.003	2.655	56.405	19.043	31.917	4.160
Total born in								
Free States	226	25.212	66.354	3.298	56.487	18.870	32.289	4.212
Slave States	1794	25.727	66.192	2.832	56.599	19.169	32.076	4.196
Grand Total . . .	2020	25.668	66.210	2.884	56.587	19.136	32.100	4.197

TABLE V. — (*Continued.*)

Mean Dimensions of Full Blacks.

Class	7½	8a	8b	9	10a	10b	11	11½
	Girth of Neck	Breadth of Shoulders between Acromia	Breadth of Shoulders	Breadth of Pelvis	Circumference of Chest: Full Inspiration	Circumference of Chest: After Expiration	Circumference of Waist	Circumference around Hips
	in.	in.	in.	in.	in.	in.	in.	in.
Naked, Free States	13.98	14.72	16.33	10.56	36.05	34.18	29.81	34.94
Slave States	13.89	15.06	16.13	10.34	36.28	34.87	29.51	34.53
All . .	13.907	15.003	16.271	10.378	36.240	34.745	29.568	34.606
Half Naked								
Free States	13.75	15.00	–	10.85	38.15	36.20	29.75	36.85
Slave States	13.61	14.00	–	10.77	35.99	34.50	29.81	36.64
All . .	13.615	14.010	–	10.775	36.018	34.524	29.812	36.639
Clothed								
Free States	14.07	13.55	16.25	11.44	35.66	33.92	30.91	36.44
Slave States	13.96	13.56	16.44	11.29	35.69	33.98	30.75	35.94
All . .	13.966	13.556	16.378	11.300	35.691	33.979	30.767	35.983
In usual vigor								
Free States	14.05	14.12	16.35	10.99	35.80	33.99	30.32	35.64
Slave States	13.92	13.99	16.40	10.97	35.88	34.28	30.32	35.59
All . .	13.933	14.000	16.390	10.969	35.870	34.248	30.320	35.598
Not in usual vigor								
Free States	13.85	15.18	15.72	10.75	36.45	34.61	30.20	35.58
Slave States	13.82	14.70	–	10.83	36.07	34.47	30.09	35.31
All . .	13.826	14.759	15.717	10.819	36.123	34.487	30.103	35.346
Total born in								
Free States	14.018	14.276	16.276	10.954	35.893	34.082	30.303	35.630
Slave States	13.909	14.070	16.414	10.952	35.890	34.300	30.295	35.562
Grand Total . . .	13.921	14.089	16.358	10.952	35.899	34.275	30.296	35.569

TABLE V.—(*Continued.*)

Mean Dimensions of Full Blacks.

Class	12a Length of Arm	12b Middle of Breast-Bone to Tip of Finger	12c Acromion to Elbow	26b Distance between Angles of Eyes: Outer	26c Distance between Angles of Eyes: Inner	36a Length of Foot	36b Length to Hollow above Heel	36c Thickness at Instep	36d Circumf. around Heel and Anterior Ligament
	in.	in.	in.	in.	in.	in.	in.	in.	in.
Naked, Free States	29.32	35.50	13.14	3.92	1.26	10.44	10.19	2.60	13.54
Slave States	29.20	35.54	12.99	4.03	1.32	10.61	10.27	2.44	13.82
All . .	29.222	35.573	13.014	4.009	1.310	10.583	10.252	2.471	13.766
Half Naked									
Free States	28.95	36.45	14.00	3.65	1.25	10.75	10.70	2.65	13.85
Slave States	29.07	35.99	14.30	3.73	1.37	10.53	10.17	2.69	13.80
All . .	29.067	35.997	14.292	3.727	1.366	10.534	10.180	2.695	13.803
Clothed									
Free States	30.10	35.54	14.32	4.24	1.41	10.61	10.32	2.90	13.55
Slave States	29.50	35.98	13.27	4.17	1.34	10.62	9.94	2.77	13.56
All . .	29.549	35.939	13.346	4.181	1.350	10.618	9.969	2.783	13.555
In usual vigor									
Free States	29.69	35.49	13.62	4.07	1.33	10.52	10.24	2.76	13.54
Slave States	29.32	35.84	13.21	4.10	1.34	10.61	10.03	2.67	13.64
All . .	29.362	35.801	13.247	4.101	1.337	10.596	10.053	2.683	13.631
Not in usual vigor									
Free States	29.55	35.77	13.54	4.00	1.32	10.55	10.33	2.57	13.58
Slave States	29.77	35.87	13.76	4.00	1.35	10.65	10.28	2.59	13.76
All . .	29.740	35.861	13.732	4.004	1.345	10.633	10.289	2.586	13.735
Total born in									
Free States	29.669	35.525	13.604	4.061	1.329	10.522	10.253	2.734	13.550
Slave States	29.371	35.843	13.267	4.094	1.339	10.610	10.058	2.664	13.655
Grand Total . .	29.405	35.808	13.302	4.090	1.338	10.600	10.079	2.672	13.643

TABLE VI.

Mean Dimensions of Mixed Races.

Class	Number of Men	Actual Mean Age	4 Height	4½ Tip of Finger to Margin of Patella	5 Height to 7th Cervical Vertebra.	5½ Height to Knee	6 Height to Perinæum	7 Breadth of Neck
			in.	in.	in.	in.	in.	in.
Naked, Free States	98	27.08	66.38	3.71	56.11	18.44	32.34	4.09
Slave States	111	26.41	66.43	3.60	56.46	18.63	32.23	4.04
All . .	209	26.726	66.408	3.652	56.300	18.544	32.281	4.065
Half Naked								
Slave States	47	27.423	65.794	3.474	56.660	19.170	30.296	4.215
Clothed								
Free States	71	24.47	66.25	4.36	56.70	19.25	31.52	4.22
Slave States	536	26.18	66.23	4.33	56.84	19.64	32.12	4.44
All . .	607	25.942	66.232	4.337	56.826	19.594	32.050	4.416
In usual vigor								
Free States	127	25.56	66.16	4.09	56.20	18.76	31.90	4.16
Slave States	592	25.93	66.25	4.16	56.88	19.48	32.03	4.38
All . .	719	25.864	66.235	4.147	56.760	19.355	32.003	4.340
Not in usual vigor								
Free States	42	27.25	66.85	3.68	56.88	18.88	32.30	4.10
Slave States	102	28.49	66.12	4.15	56.13	19.23	31.94	4.27
All . .	144	28.126	66.330	4.014	56.339	19.132	32.045	4.221
Total born in								
Free States	169	25.983	66.324	3.990	56.362	18.787	31.993	4.146
Slave States	694	26.305	66.233	4.157	56.770	19.446	32.015	4.362
Grand Total . . .	863	26.242	66.251	4.125	56.690	19.318	32.010	4.320

TABLE VI. — (*Continued.*)

Mean Dimensions of Mixed Races.

Class	7½ Girth of Neck	8a Breadth of Shoulders between Acromia	8b Breadth of Shoulders	9 Breadth of Pelvis	10a Circumference of Chest: Full Inspiration	10b Circumference of Chest: After Expiration	11 Circumference of Waist	11½ Circumference around Hips
	in.	in.	in.	in.	in.	in.	in.	in.
Naked, Free States	13.81	15.10	16.12	10.69	35.90	33.94	29.94	34.76
Slave States	13.65	14.83	16.47	10.50	35.90	34.13	29.69	34.48
All . .	13.725	14.913	16.184	10.588	35.903	34.040	29.808	34.609
Half Naked								
Slave States	13.602	13.632	–	10.957	35.772	34.111	29.585	36.232
Clothed								
Free States	13.83	13.40	16.53	11.61	35.97	34.39	31.22	36.51
Slave States	13.90	14.84	16.73	11.51	35.66	34.21	30.83	35.42
All . .	13.889	14.772	16.601	11.525	35.700	34.234	30.874	35.548
In usual vigor								
Free States	13.82	14.49	16.40	11.15	35.86	34.04	30.54	35.47
Slave States	13.86	14.79	15.95	11.31	35.71	34.18	30.57	35.29
All . .	13.851	14.755	16.343	11.285	35.736	34.157	30.568	35.322
Not in usual vigor								
Free States	13.82	15.05	16.31	10.85	36.16	34.39	30.29	35.56
Slave States	13.72	14.52	16.93	11.31	35.70	34.26	30.50	35.52
All . .	13.748	14.663	16.708	11.175	35.836	34.299	30.436	35.533
Total born in								
Free States	13.818	14.652	16.381	11.077	35.933	34.127	30.480	35.494
Slave States	13.838	14.755	16.681	11.313	35.709	34.193	30.562	35.324
Grand Total . .	13.834	14.742	16.473	11.267	35.753	34.180	30.546	35.357

TABLE VI. — (*Continued.*)

Mean Dimensions of Mixed Races.

Class	12a Length of Arm	12b Middle of Breast-Bone to Tip of Finger	12c Acromion to Elbow	26b Distance between Angles of Eyes: Outer	26c Distance between Angles of Eyes: Inner	36a Length of Foot	36b Length to Hollow above Heel	36c Thickness of Instep	36d Circumf. around Heel & Anterior Ligament
	in.	in.	in.	in.	in.	in.	in.	in.	in.
Naked, Free States	29.19	35.28	12.98	3.89	1.29	10.40	10.09	2.57	13.38
Slave States	28.98	34.62	12.86	3.86	1.29	10.43	10.13	2.49	13.55
All . .	29.080	34.928	12.912	3.879	1.288	10.415	10.109	2.531	13.464
Half Naked									
Slave States	28.730	35.345	14.002	3.696	1.326	10.428	10.185	2.689	13.755
Clothed									
Free States	29.95	35.46	13.74	3.95	1.38	10.37	10.09	2.78	13.38
Slave States	30.91	36.13	14.23	4.05	1.39	10.46	10.21	2.87	13.45
All . .	30.797	36.049	14.176	4.038	1.387	10.447	10.193	2.859	13.439
In usual vigor									
Free States	29.38	35.15	13.23	3.93	1.32	10.36	10.06	2.69	13.36
Slave States	30.49	35.99	14.01	4.01	1.37	10.46	10.20	2.81	13.46
All . .	30.296	35.838	13.869	3.996	1.359	10.438	10.173	2.786	13.445
Not in usual vigor									
Free States	29.89	35.97	13.49	3.89	1.34	10.47	10.16	2.56	13.44
Slave States	30.26	35.65	13.91	3.92	1.37	10.43	10.17	2.74	13.33
All . .	30.148	35.744	13.793	3.909	1.364	10.443	10.167	2.687	13.365
Total born in									
Free States	29.508	35.353	13.298	3.917	1.329	10.386	10.089	2.659	13.379
Slave States	30.458	35.937	13.944	3.997	1.367	10.451	10.193	2.797	13.484
Grand Total . .	30.271	35.822	13.856	3.981	1.360	10.439	10.172	2.770	13.463

8. *Indians.*

Of the 517 Indians who have been physically examined by the agents of the Commission, 503 were measured by Dr. Buckley at the Reservations belonging to the Iroquois, or Six Nations, near Buffalo, and comprise all the full-grown males of unmixed blood who were accessible there. Ten of the remaining 14 cases were measured by the same examiner in the Army of the Potomac, where they were enlisted in the First Regiment of Michigan Sharp-shooters.

Only 9 of them were not in ordinary health. For the other 508, comparative tables of actual and theoretical distribution of the variations in the several dimensions have been computed, analogous to those for white soldiers of certain nativities.

The mean *stature* of these men was greater than that for any nativity of white soldiers examined, with the exception of Kentucky and Tennessee, and 1.075 inch greater than the mean for the white soldiers born in the same State. But on the other hand, the proportion of men who have attained their full stature is unquestionably much larger in these Indian measurements than in those of any group of enlisted men, so that while the average full stature of white men born in New York probably reaches 68.13 inches, it appears improbable that for these Indians it can surpass the limit of 68.40. The lowest stature recorded is 61.4 inches, being for a man of South American descent; the lowest for an Iroquois was 64.0 inches, and the highest, 75.7. The amount of probable variation of any individual from the mean is $r = 0.898$, and the probable error of the mean value $r_o = 0.040$.

The length of *head* and *neck* is small, like that of the negro, averaging but 9.55 inches, or 0.4 less than for white soldiers. The probable variations of the height to the seventh cervical vertebra are $r = 0.875$, $r_o = 0.039$, or almost identical with the analogous values for the total height.

The length of *body* is 26.87 inches, being greater than for the white soldiers measured; and although some allowance should be made for the difference of stature, the body is decidedly longer than in the white race.

The dimension 4½, which for white soldiers averaged 5.04 inches, for blacks 2.88, and for mulattoes 4.12, is for the Indians 3.65 inches, being thus short in consequence of the excessive length of the arm, notwithstanding that the body and the thigh are also longer than for whites. The probable variation in this dimension in an individual case is 0.55 inch, and the probable error of the mean 0.024 inch. The maximum value found was 7.0 inches, and the minimum 1.6 inch.

As regards the length of *legs*, both above and below the knee, the structure of the red man appears to be intermediate between the white and the black. Thus we find —

	No. of Men	Height to Perinæum	Height to Knee	Knee to Perinæum	Ratio
		in.	in.	in.	
White Soldiers . . .	10 848	31.06	18.61	12.46	1.494
Indians	517	31.81	19.01	12.80	1.485
Full Blacks	2 020	32.10	19.14	12.96	1.476

For the height to perinæum, $r = 0.931$ in. $r_o = 0.041$ in.
For the height to knee, $r = 0.631$ in. $r_o = 0.028$ in.

But it is in the length of the *arm* that the difference in proportions between the Indians and the other races manifests itself most prominently, and seems most characteristic. It would appear that the arm of the red man is certainly longer by more than an inch and a half on the average than that of the white. For the distance from acromion to the tip of middle finger we find the average to be 30.792 inches, with a probable error of 0.035 for this mean, and a probable variation of 0.799 for individuals; the maximum value being 33.1, and the minimum value 27.3. For the distance from acromion to elbow, the mean result is 13.757 inches, the probable error of this mean being 0.022, the probable variation for an individual 0.486, the maximum record 16.4, and the minimum 12.1.

The comparison of these mean dimensions with those of the two other races gives —

	Medial Line to Finger Tip	Acromion to Finger Tip	Ratio of Leg to Arm	Acromion to Elbow	Lower Arm and Hand	Ratio
	in.	in.		in.	in.	
White Soldiers	35.042	29.153	1.066	13.605	15.548	1.143
Full Blacks .	35.808	29.405	1.092	13.302	16.103	1.211
Indians . . .	37.198	30.792	1.033	13.757	17.035	1.238

The third column of numbers shows the proportion which the height to perinæum bears to the total distance from the tip of the acromion to the tip of middle finger; and the last column shows the ratio existing between the lower arm, including the hand, and the upper arm. It is noteworthy that this also is much greater for the Indian than for the Caucasian; while the corresponding ratio for the inferior limbs of the Indian is intermediate between those which hold for the two other races.

For the *breadth of neck* $r = 0.081$ in.; $r_o = 0.004$ in. and for the *girth of neck* $r = 0.228$ in.; $r_o = 0.010$ in.

The mean *breadth of pelvis* is greater for the Indian than for the white man by nearly one twelfth part, and greater than for the black man by more than twice that amount. For the *waist*, too, the circumference is about one tenth part larger than for the white, and one seventh larger than for the black man. The probable variations of this dimension are $r = 0.836$ in. and $r_o = 0.037$ in. So too in the circumference *around hips*, a similar, though somewhat less predominance is manifest, and we have $r = 0.961$, $r_o = 0.043$.

The *circumference of thorax* is much greater than in the whites, although its play during respiration appears not to be so wide. We find, namely, for the mean circumference —

	At Inspiration	At Expiration	Play	Mean
	in.	in.	in.	in.
Whites	37.143	34.494	2.649	35.818
Blacks	35.899	34.275	1.624	35.087
Red	38.920	37.082	1.838	38.001

The measures during inspiration ranged from 50.2 inches to 34.6; those after expiration from 48 inches to 32.

For the *distance between the eyes*, the mean value is 2.715 inches, the same as for the full blacks; but the mean *width of the eye* is 1.312 inch, being the same as for the mixed races, and nearly midway between the values for whites and blacks.

Lastly we find the mean *length of foot* but slightly greater than for whites; although the distribution of the values indicates that we have not a number of measures sufficient to give this mean a typical character. The heel is no longer than for white men, but the foot appears somewhat thicker.

Our means derived from measurements of Indians are given in Table VII., in which the nine men who were not in their usual vigor have been separately classified.

TABLE VII.

Mean Dimensions of Indians.

Class	Number of Men	Actual Mean Age	4 Height	4½ Tip of Finger to Margin of Patella	5 Height to 7th Cervical Vertebra	5½ Height to Knee	6 Height to Perinæum	7 Breadth of Neck
			in.	in.	in.	in.	in.	in.
In usual vigor . .	508	30.59	68.22	3.65	58.68	19.01	31.81	4.13
Others	9	38.82	68.38	4.06	58.68	18.91	31.71	4.20
Total	517	30.73	68.225	3.653	58.678	19.009	31.808	4.128

Class	7½ Girth of Neck	8a Breadth of Shoulders be-tw'n Acromia	8b Breadth of Shoulders	9 Breadth of Pelvis	10a Circumference of Chest: Full Inspiration	10b Circumference of Chest: After Expiration	11 Circumference of Waist	11½ Circumference around Hips
	in.	in.	in.	in.	in.	in.	in.	in.
In usual vigor . .	13.67	12.82	17.00	12.90	38.94	37.10	34.63	38.99
Others	13.64	13.58	–	12.18	37.96	36.16	32.53	37.40
Total	13.665	12.830	17.000	12.889	38.920	37.082	34.593	38.962

TABLE VII.—(*Continued.*)

Mean Dimensions of Indians.

Class	12a Length of Arm	12b Middle of Breast-Bone to Tip of Finger	12c Acromion to Elbow	26b Dist. between Angles of Eyes — Outer	26c Dist. between Angles of Eyes — Inner	36a Length of Foot	36b Length to Hollow above Heel	36c Thickness of Instep	36d Circum. around Heel & Anterior Ligament
	in.	in.	in.	in.	in.	in.	in.	in.	in.
In usual vigor . .	30.80	37.21	13.76	4.028	1.406	10.120	9.938	2.69	13.45
Others	30.23	36.47	13.63	3.988	1.312	10.278	9.989	2.67	13.69
Total	30.792	37.198	13.757	4.027	1.404	10.123	9.939	2.687	13.457

9. *Abnormal Cases.*

The presence in Washington of three dwarves, who were on exhibition there while Dr. Buckley was engaged in the measurement of soldiers, suggested their measurement in the same manner ; especially since their dimensions and proportions might thus be compared with those of the noted dwarf Stratton, *alias* "Tom Thumb," whom Quetelet measured in 1845, and whose dimensions[1] may be found in his "*Théorie des Probabilités*," p. 404. Stratton was at that time but 27.56 inches high, but since his age was only 13½ years, his subsequent growth was doubtless quite considerable.

The three dwarves here considered were all of German parentage, their ages were 23, 17, and 15 years, and the full reports of their examination are here presented.

To these may also be added the corresponding data regarding the so-called Australian children, exhibited in various American cities in the years 1864 and 1865, and measured in New York by Dr. Buckley in December 1864.

[1] For the sake of more convenient comparison, those of Mr. Quetelet's measurements which represent dimensions also determined for these dwarves, are here copied, with their equivalents in American inches.

	m.	in.
Height	0.700	27.6
Head and neck	0.173	6.8
Height to knee	0.175	6.9
Height to perinæum	0.265	10.4
Breadth of shoulders between acromia	0.202	8.0
Circumference around hips	0.478	18.8
Length of arm from acromion	0.245	9.6
Half span of extended arms	0.330	13.0
Length of foot	0.105	4.1

TABLE VIII.

Results of Physical Examination of Three Dwarves and the two "Australian Children."

	Joseph Hunter *alias* Col. Small	Chas. W. Nestel *alias* Com. Foote	Eliza Nestel	Hoomio (Tom)	Iola (Hetty)
2. Name ?					
4. Height ?	40.4	37.4	31.4	62.6	49.5
23. Age (last birthday) ?	17	23	15	21[a]	16[b]
4½. Distance from tip of middle finger to patella	2.4	3.3	3.8	5.1	7.
5. Height to 7th cerv. vertebra ?	33.2	31.4	25.2	54.9	43.1
5½. Height to middle of patella ?	11.2	10.1	8	21	15.5
6. Height to perinæum ?	18	18.5	12.3	31.2	23.1
7. Breadth of neck ?	3.4	3	2.7	3.6	3.1
7½. Girth of neck ?	11.8	9.3	9	13.2	11
8*a*. Breadth of shoulders ?	9.5	9.4	8	13.6[c]	12.1[c]
9. Breadth of pelvis ?	8	8.2	8.6	11.3	9.2
10. Circumference of chest —					
a. Full inspiration ?	21.9	23.2	19.1	40.4	32.1
b. After expiration ?	21	21	18.1	37.2	29.9
10½. Distance between nipples ?	–	–	–	9.2	–
11. Circumference of waist ?	20.0	20.0	16.0	26.2	24.0
11½. Circumference around hips ?	22.7	23.4	20.1	33.2	28.2
12*a*. Length of arm — from tip of acromion ?	17.3	14.8	12	30.2	27.3
b. Distance from middle of sternum to tip of finger ?	21.9	19.1	15.8	35.0	30.6
c. Distance fr. acromion to elbow ?	8	6.4	5.1	13.3	11.0
14. Weight (estimated) ?	40 lbs.	40 lbs.	25 lbs.	105 lbs.	80 lbs.
18. Where born ?	Germany	Indiana	Indiana	Australia	
19. Arrival in this country ?	1849	–	–	1862	1862
20. Country of father ?	Germany	Germany	Germany	–	–
of mother ?	"	"	"	–	–
of grandparents ?	"	"	"	–	–
25. Hair — color ?	Brown	Brown	Brown	Dark brown	
amount ?	Average	Average	Average	Very short	
texture ?	Straight	Straight	Straight	Rather coarse	
26. Eyes — color ?	Gray	Gray	Blue	D'k hazel	Black
distance outer angles ?	2.5	2.8	2.5	4.1	3.2
" inner angles ?	1.0	1.0	0.9	1.5	1.2
prominent ?	No	No	No	No	No
27. Complexion ?	Fair	Fair	Fair	Dark; a little lighter than the American Indian	
28. Pulse per minute ?	90	90	90	60	61
29. Inspirations per minute ?	17	17	17	–	–
30. Muscular development ?	Small	Small	Small	Moderate	Small

[a] Supposed.

[b] Said to have attained age of puberty two years previous.

[c] Full breadth (not between acromia).

TABLE VIII. — (*Continued.*)

Results of Physical Examination of Three Dwarves and the two "Australian Children."

33. Teeth, condition ?	Good	Poor	Good	Sound	Sound
number lost ?	None	Several	None	None	None
34. Head — *a.* Frontal eminence and occiput ?	20.3	20.3	19.3	15.0	14.9
b. Distance between condyloid processes over *os frontis* ?	10.5	9.8	9.0	7.8	7.4
c. Dist. over parietal bones ? .	12.6	12.1	12.4	6.5	7.2
d. Distance over occipital protuberance ?	11.7	11.4	10.1	7.2	7.8
e. Distance from frontal eminence to protuberance of occiput ?	13.1	13.3	13	9.1[a]	8.4[b]
f. Width betw. angles of jaws ?	4.1	3	3.2	4.2	3.6
g. Width between condyloid processes ?	4.7	4.4	3.9	4.3	4.2
35. Facial angle ?	76°	77.°5	80°	–	–
36. Foot — *a.* Length to heel ? . .	5.3	5.4	4.2	8.8	7.4
b. Length to hollow above heel ?	5.1	5.3	4.1	8.6	7.3
c. Thickness at instep ? . .	1.6	1.5	0.9	2.3	2.1
d. Circumference around heel and anterior ligament ? .	8.7	7.3	7.1	13.0	10.0
57. Distance of distinct vision for adopted type ?	44	50	38	–	–
58. Does he distinguish colors correctly ?	Yes	Yes	Yes	–	–
31. In usual vigor ?	Yes	Yes	Yes	Yes	Yes
Date of examination	1865 June 9	1865 June 9	1865 June 9	1864 Dec. 7	1864 Dec. 7

NOTE. — The curious beings known as the Australian children were exhibited by Capt. J. Reid, who professes to have captured them in the interior of Australia while he was, in company with two other New Yorkers, conducting an exploring party. He states that when among the mountains in the interior, they discovered three children drinking from a spring at the bottom of a deep gorge, and captured them with lassoes; that they were naked, and at first "wild and fierce," but were soon tamed by kindness. They were carried first to California, and exhibited in the principal cities of that State, after which they were brought to the Atlantic seaboard, arriving in New York in November 1863.

They appear certainly not to belong to the Malay race, their color being entirely different. Their gait is stooping, and their arms crooked, and incapable of being straightened at the elbows beyond the ordinary posture of the arm of our own race when standing at ease. The development of the chest is large; the pelvis comparatively small, elongated and circular. The female is entirely different from the white race in this respect. Dr. Buckley had excellent opportunities for the examination, through the courtesy of Capt. Reid. Their legs are spare, with small calves.

[a] 5.6 by calipers. [b] 5.0 by calipers.

But their heads are the most remarkable part. The faces are large, and the crania small; the superciliary ridge very prominent, nose and lips large. The other marked peculiarities will be seen in the table of dimensions.

Their eyes are bright and sparkling, and Capt. Reid says that they show a good deal of intelligence. The male speaks a few words of English, and they have a peculiar "gibberish," by which they communicate with each other.

Regarding the real origin and character of these very peculiar specimens of the human family, the author of this volume is unable to express an opinion. A pair of singular children were exhibited several years since in this country and in Europe in 1855–56, under the name of the Aztec children, who seemed to be idiotic, and apparently dwarfish specimens of some Central American race of Indians, but whether of mixed blood or not it would be difficult to say. No measurements[1] of these are accessible to the writer; if there are any such, a comparison of their relative dimensions with those deduced from this examination of the pair here referred to might be interesting. At any rate the present measurements appear worth placing upon record, and not out of place here. Certainly their microcephalous character is extremely analogous to that of the so-called Aztecs, although their stature is not so much below that of many adult whites. Their hair was so closely shorn that its characteristics could not well be recognized. The proportions are certainly quite different from those deduced by Vogt[2] from measures of the Aztec children in 1856.

10. *General Inferences.*

It will now be useful to bring into juxtaposition some of the principal mean dimensions and ratios, already deduced from our measurements of the several classes of men, and thus to facilitate their comparison.

[1] Vogt, in his *Vorlesungen über den Menschen*, I. p. 247, cites the measures of Leubuscher, which we have vainly endeavored to obtain. Carus, in the *Bericht der Königl. Sächsischen Gesellschaft*, VIII. 13, 14, gives some cranial measures, and their statures in 1856. The papers of Saussure, *Comptes Rendus Acad. Paris*, vol. XXXVII., and of Serres, *id.* vol. XLI. contain no measurements.

[2] *Vorlesungen*, I. 252.

TABLE IX.

Comparison of Mean Dimensions.

	White Soldiers		Sailors	Students	Full Blacks	Mixed Races	Indians
	Later Series	Earlier Series					
Number of Men . .	10 876	7 904	1 061	291	2 020	863	517
	y	y	y	y	y	y	y
Mean Age	26.2	25.1	26.1	21.7	25.7	26.2	30.7
	in.	in.	in.	in.	in.	in.	in.
Length Head & Neck	9.944	9.981	10.091	10.098	9.623	9.561	9.547
Length of Body . .	26.140	26.099	24.549	26.109	24.487	24.680	26.870
Knee to Perinæum .	12.456	–	12.880	12.652	12.964	12.692	12.799
Height to Knee . .	18.609	–	18.498	19.240	19.136	19.318	19.009
Stature	67.149	67.366	66.018	68.099	66.210	66.251	68.225
Acromion to Elbow .	13.605	–	13.171	13.712	13.302	13.856	13.757
Elbow to Finger-tip .	15.548	–	15.367	15.309	16.103	16.415	17.035
Dist. betw. Acromia	12.731	16.359[a]	12.879	13.085	14.089	14.742	12.830
Ratio of parts of Arm	1.143	–	1.167	1.116	1.211	1.185	1.238
" " Leg	1.494	–	1.436	1.521	1.476	1.522	1.485
Med. line to Finger-tip	35.042	–	33.848	34.920	35.808	35.822	37.198
Acromion " "	29.153	29.200[b]	28.538	29.021	29.405	30.271	30.792
Height to Perinæum	31.065	31.286	31.378	31.892	32.100	32.010	31.808
Ratio of Leg to Arm	1.066	1.071	1.100	1.099	1.092	1.058	1.033
Height to Pubes . .	–	–	33.269	–	34.302	34.534	–
Finger-tip to Patella	5.036	–	5.778	6.473	2.884	4.125	3.653
Circumf. of Waist .	31.467	32.089	30.457	31.240	30.296	30.546	34.593
Circumf. of Hips .	36.930	–	34.942	36.549	35.569	35.357	38.962
Circumf. of Chest .	35.818	35.353[c]	35.124	35.313	35.087	34.966	38.001
Play of Chest . . .	2.65	–	2.08	3.07	1.62	1.57	1.84
Dist. between Nipples	8.136	–	8.304	8.071	7.970	7.891	–
Ratio to circum. Chest	0.226	–	0.236	0.229	0.225	0.227	–
Dist. between Eyes .	2.492	2.606	2.473	2.484	2.714	2.670	2.716
Breadth of Pelvis .	11.916	13.153[d]	11.625	11.187	10.952	11.267	12.889
Length of Foot . .	10.058	–	10.114	9.957	10.600	10.439	10.123
Thickness of Foot .	2.572	–	2.921	2.786	2.672	2.770	2.687
Length of Heel[e] . .	0.48	–	0.49	0.46	0.82	0.57	0.48

[a] Full breadth of shoulders. [b] Measured from arm-pit.

[c] Not the half-sum of circumferences at inspiration and expiration, as the others are.

[d] Probably the breadth of hips. See page 262.

[e] These values are obtained by adding 0.3 to the difference between the dimensious 36*a* and 36*b*. See page 274.

Inspection of this table discloses many curious and interesting facts, full of significance to the physiologist and ethnologist, and possibly not without some bearing upon doubtful points of theory. Upon these it seems more proper to leave the discussion to experts, trusting that the results may have been so elaborated and presented, as to be available for them in a convenient form.

The ratio between the lower and upper parts of the arm seems one of the most characteristic numerical values.[1] The average values found for the several races are: —

Whites, Students	1.116	
Soldiers	1.143	
Sailors	1.167	
Total		1.144
Mulattoes		1.185
Full Blacks		1.211
Indians		1.238

This is, however, the only respect in which so marked differences between the different classes of men have been observed to follow this order of sequence. In the ratio between the two parts of the leg, no such relation is manifest. Nor does any ethnological significance show itself in our results for the relative length of the arm and leg. The distance between the eyes follows the same order of races; but when it is considered with reference to the stature, the order of the relative dimensions is modified.

Some other ratios between parts of the frame seem to possess an ethnological significance; especially those between the lengths of the body and of the arm, between the upper arm and the length of body and width of shoulders respectively, and between the width of shoulders and the length of body.[2] The latter proportion is affected with sundry elements of uncertainty; both in consequence of the difficulties, already described,[3] in obtaining an accu-

1 The length of the hand was not specially determined. According to Vogt (*Vorlesungen*, I. 193), this is in white men about 0.53 of the length of the humerus.

2 "In the orang the clavicle decidedly exceeds one fourth of the length of the spine (as measured from the atlas to the coccygeal end of the sacrum), while in man and the *troglodytes* it always, as far as I have observed, falls short of that proportion. The clavicle of the orang also more nearly equals the length of the scapula than in the higher forms." Mivart, "On the Skeleton of the Primates," *Trans. Zool. Soc. Lond.*, VI. 179.

"As in the gorilla, the humerus exceeds three fifths the length of the spine measured from the atlas to the lower end of the sacrum — a proportion decidedly exceeding that existing in the chimpanzee, and greatly so that found in man. It is nearly twice the length of the scapula, which is less than in man, though more than in troglodytes." *Ibid.* pp. 180, 181.

3 See pp. 48, 59, 60.

rate determination of the mean distance between the acromia for any class of men, and still more by reason of the actual change which this dimension undergoes in persons of the same class, according to their mode of life. Still its results are interesting.

The proportion of the length of the body to that of the arm is found, from our mean results, to be as follows: —

White Students	0.8997	
Soldiers, Later Series	0.8966	
" Earlier "	0.8938	
Sailors	0.8601	
Total		0.8936
Indians		0.8727
Full Blacks		0.8328
Mixed Races		0.8153

Between the upper arm (acromion to elbow) and the length of body, we find the average proportion to be —

Indians		0.512
White Soldiers	0.520	
Students	0.525	
Sailors	0.537	
Total		0.522
Full Blacks		0.543
Mixed Races		0.561

The proportion between the length of upper arm and the distance of the acromia, as deduced from our table of mean dimensions, is found to be —

Indians		1.072
White Students	1.048	
Sailors	1.022	
Soldiers	1.069	
Total		1.065
Full Blacks		0.944
Mixed Races		0.940

Finally, the ratio of the mean distance between the acromia to the mean length of body is: —

Indians		0.4775
White Soldiers	0.4870	
Students	0.5012	
Sailors	0.5246	
Total		0.4906
Full Blacks		0.5754
Mixed Races		0.5973

The curious and important fact that the mulattoes, or men of mixed race, occupy so frequently in the scale of progression a place outside of, rather than intermediate between, those races from the combination of which they have sprung, cannot fail to attract attention. The well-known phenomenon of their inferior vitality may stand, possibly, in some connection with the fact thus brought to light.

In the length of head and neck, and in the distance from the middle of the sternum to the tip of the middle finger, the order by races is the same as that deduced from the ratio between the upper and the lower arm, except that the men of mixed race come after the full blacks.

As regards the breadth of pelvis, the red men come first, then the whites, mulattoes, and blacks, in order; and the same holds true for the circumference of hips, excepting that here also the mulattoes follow the pure negroes.

The most marked characteristics of the races, here manifested, appear to be — for the whites, the length of head and neck and the short fore-arms; for the reds, the long fore-arms and the large lateral dimensions, excepting at the shoulders; for the blacks, the wide shoulders, long feet, and protruding heels.

Among the whites, the sailors are conspicuous for their shortness of body, which is clearly the chief element of their defect in stature, while the students are remarkable for their height to the knee.

It will be seen that the simple numerical ratios popularly supposed to exist between the normal dimensions of different parts of the body do not here exhibit themselves, otherwise than as coarse approximations. Thus the average[1] span of the extended arms uniformly exceeds the height; the height to the pubes surpasses half the stature; the mean[2] distance between the nipples is always

[1] The full span was found as small as the height in about two cases of every thirty-five.

[2] This distance attained the magnitude of one fourth the circumference in about one individual of every fourteen.

less than one fourth the circumference of the chest; and similarly for the other dimensions. These supposed simple numerical proportions seem to be the offspring of fancy and conjecture rather than of accurate observation; and, while they always represent a near approach to the true typical ratio, they are demonstrably removed from it in the cases here investigated. The predisposition to believe in the existence of such harmonic relations as may accord with preconceived ideas of symmetry, and to assume that a near approach to commensurability implies an organic tendency toward its absolute attainment, seems to furnish all needful explanation of this general belief, which appears to be almost universally adopted by artists, and has been inculcated by many eminent and learned men. A striking analogy to this hypothesis is afforded by the doctrine, — so long cherished by astronomers, and even now retained in some of the books, — regarding supposed simple numerical ratios in the planetary distances. The proportionate dimensions of the several parts, discussed in the ensuing chapter, will afford means of considering these questions yet more understandingly.

Farther discussion of the results of the present chapter belongs apparently so fully within the realms of physiology and ethnology, with which the author is too little acquainted to venture upon any special inquiries, that it seems most advisable to leave the materials for the scrutiny of others. In the different mean values of the several dimensions and ratios for men of different nativities here grouped in the same class; in the determination of typical or characteristic ratios, not mentioned here, between the various dimensions; in the pursuit of the clew which is afforded by the constant excess of the mean age of men not in usual vigor; in the comparison of the varying proportions of the respective classes and races with the corresponding ones of anthropoid quadrupeds, there seems to be opportunity for extensive and valuable research. And for those points elicited by the schedule of examination, but unavoidably left undiscussed and untabulated in the present volume, the records, which have been tabulated with care and which will be preserved in the form permitting the most convenient consultation, afford copious material, as yet unused.

CHAPTER IX.

MEAN PROPORTIONS OF BODY.

1. *Preliminary*

THE mean results obtained for the several dimensions, in the preceding chapter, will doubtless be regarded as, in general, highly satisfactory. Yet the variations between the values deduced for those nativities in which the number of men is small are much greater than those between the larger groups. And, although for these larger groups, as indeed for all those which comprise more than three or four hundred men in usual vigor, the test applied, by comparing the observed distribution of individual cases around their mean with that distribution which the law of probability would prescribe, indicates this mean to be typical, still the average variation in individual cases is so large as to excite a wish that the number of men examined had been greater yet.

The mean age of the men examined falls, for most of the nativity-groups, much below that of full stature; and since the mean rate of growth during the years immediately preceding this mean age is very different from that which corresponds to the years immediately following, the probability is strong that we have not attained, for any group, precisely the mean dimensions belonging to the mean age of that group, but that the deduced values are smaller than the true ones.

Beside the influence of the different degrees of immaturity in the physical development, that of difference in the full stature also makes itself strongly manifest, in the wide range of the difference of value for the same dimension. And could we assume that the growth of all parts of the frame is proportionate as the period of full development in size is approached, we might, by referring all the dimensions to the actual height as a unit of length, greatly increase the precision of our determinations; while the range of individual discordance would be diminished. The assumption that the same normal type of form holds good for men differing in stature, but otherwise strictly belonging to the same class, seems warrantable, and is certainly susceptible of test by such a procedure. If warrantable, we are justified in regarding the typical or normal man, of any class, in his two distinct relations of normal stature and normal proportions separately, and no error will result from the fact that these two relations are separated in their respective discussions. If not warrantable, the character and distribution of the discordances from the mean would betray the error of our assumption. And it therefore seemed well worth consideration, whether the labor of reducing the several actual dimensions of each individual to their corresponding relative or proportionate dimensions, in decimal fractions of the stature taken as unity, would not be fully repaid, in spite of the immense labor which it would entail.

The characteristic differences between the races are in general shown by the relative dimensions more distinctly than by the actual ones; those dissimilarities which are due to differences in general size disappearing, while those which actually exist in the type are rendered more prominent. The only exception to this remark, if indeed it be an exception, is formed by those parts of the body, such as the head for instance, which do not appear to vary to the same extent as the general dimensions of the physical frame. The normal variations of the stature, arms, feet, etc., are as distinctly a part of the fundamental scheme as are their normal mean dimensions; and the present computations show that the range of these variations is relatively not very diverse for most of the dimensions; and that the development by growth is also at a rate not far from the same. Not so with the head, the general size of which varies less with individual differences of stature, and increases less with the growth, than most other portions of the physical structure, as we have already seen in the last chapter. On this account it might perhaps have been satisfactory had the proportionate dimensions been computed relatively to the height to the last cervical vertebra. Yet the present form of computation will probably answer all reasonable demands.

Our materials for determining the normal stature, for different classes and nativities of men, promised to be so ample as to leave little to be desired on this point, could they be properly collected and discussed. Thus the investigation regarding statures and the law of growth, the results of which have been presented in Chapter V., seemed to derive a new importance from their applicability to the investigation of the normal dimensions of the average man, by means of a determination of his proportions as expressed in a relative instead of an absolute unit; and the increased value, which each of these researches would derive from the other, was a strong incentive to the prosecution of both.

The results presented in this chapter are deduced from the reduction of the individual measurements of each of our 23 685 men to the form of thousandths of his height, and the mean results for any group are of course applicable to the mean stature for that group. And the application of the relative dimension or proportional number, obtained for any class or nativity of men, to the normal stature of the same class or nativity as derived from more ample sources, is but another form of application of the very hypothesis which we must necessarily adopt in this investigation, namely, that the proportions of the body remain practically unchanged for men of the different ages comprised in our examinations. These ages are chiefly between 19 and 30 years for white soldiers; and for the other classes and races of men examined the great majority of cases is included within the same limits. That this hypothesis is correct, the writer is far from being disposed to maintain, but he is equally indisposed to believe that any serious error will result in the present case from its incorrectness. Even the error to which this incorrectness may give rise will, from the nature of the case, be in great measure eliminated from the mean result as applied to the mean age. It is a source of much regret that the limits of the present investigation preclude the prosecution of the inquiry as to the extent to which the proportions of the bodily frame vary during the years of military age.

These Relative Dimensions for each man are tabulated and preserved in the archives of the Sanitary Commission with the same care as the Actual Dimensions, the mean values of which for given nativities have been presented in Chapter VIII. The same man is designated by the same number in the two series of records, and the documents containing the computations have been made, so far as possible, to correspond with each other, for the greater facility of reference.

Tables exhibiting, for each class, the distribution of the values observed for each proportionate dimension, — and for many classes the corresponding theoretical distribution according to the law of error, — have also been computed in the same manner as for the actual dimensions.

Regarding the amount of labor involved in the execution, verification, and discussion of these computations, there is small need of speaking, since the case will speak for itself after the slightest consideration. The principal hesitation in carrying out the plan has arisen, not from the labor and time which it has entailed, but from anxiety lest this labor and time might be better bestowed in other directions. The event appears to justify the course taken; the results are even more satisfactory than we had ventured to anticipate; and by combining the typical proportions, thus attained, with the typical unit of dimension, as resulting from the discussion of statures, it would seem that close approximation may be made to a knowledge of the normal man, in the different ages, and places, and belonging to the different races and classes, for whom our data have been collected.

The present chapter makes no claim to the character of an exhaustive research; indeed it disclaims such an object. Only the more obvious results of the investigation are here collected and presented, since our resources permit no more than this. But the materials available for the anthropologist in the tabulated results for individuals are large; and by a proper determination of the personal errors of the several examiners, by classification according to ages, according to previous pursuits, according to parentage as well as nativity, and in numerous other ways, there is small room for doubt that results of great value may be deduced with minimum labor.

The various classes of men will be considered in this chapter, in the same order as in the chapter upon the Mean Dimensions of the body.

Attention has already been asked to the fact, that in arranging the schedule of questions adopted for the later series, and known as Form [EE], it was a leading principle to require the measurements to be made when possible between points corresponding to prominent points in the bony frame. It is hoped that this may render the comparison or combination of the present results with those of the skeleton itself less embarrassing than would otherwise be the case; and that the comparatively exact measures which may be instituted in a museum may be found susceptible of employment in connection with the proportionate numbers here deduced.

Since the results of the present chapter have been prepared for the press, the author has seen for the first time the magnificent work of Bougery and Jacob, upon human anatomy. In this the dimensions of the human frame are similarly reduced to decimals of the stature — a form of expression which the authors state that they have borrowed from Montabert. Their results are derived from measures of "a great number of individuals," and, so far as they can be tested by the present materials, appear to be closely approximate to the truth; the relative dimensions given by them, for men, rarely differing from those here deduced from the white soldiers, by much more than one hundredth of the stature.[1]

2. *White Soldiers.*

The extreme range of the *height to the 7th cervical vertebra,*— or of its converse, the length of *head and neck,*—among any of the nineteen mean values by nativity in the later series, is but 0.006; corresponding, for the average stature, to four tenths of an inch; whereas the corresponding variation in the mean actual dimensions for this height was 2.91 inches.

The aggregate mean value for length of *head and neck* is 0.1481, nor does the mean for any nativity which comprises more than 306 men differ from this aggregate by more than 0.001. The largest value is 0.151 for the group of 100 French; the smallest 0.145 for 267 natives of Kentucky and Tennessee. From the assortment tables we find:—

Nativity	Number	Head and Neck	r	r_o
New England States	977	0.1482	0.0052	0.0002
New York, New Jersey, and Penn.	3 123	0.1484	0.0056	0.0001

showing that the probable error of the mean cannot amount to so much as 0.014 inch, and indicating that it would be quite needless to push the test for other nativities.

Even for the Germans, among whom the wide discordance of this dimension from that found for the other large nativity-groups was noticeable in the dimension-tables, we here find the same value 0.148 as its proportion to the stature, thus conclusively showing that the type for this nativity was identical with that for the other large groups, and that the discordance arose solely from the smaller stature.

In the Earlier Series the variation in this mean height for the several nativity-groups is but 0.005, corresponding to only one third of an inch for the average stature; the corresponding variation in the mean actual dimensions being 2.03 inches. The mean value for head and neck is 0.148; as in the series [EE]. The largest value is 0.1508 for 204 British; the smallest are 0.1458 for the Western, and 0.1471 for the Southern men.

In the *length of body*, of which the proportional mean value is

[1] *Iconographie d'Anatomie Chirurgicale*, etc., I. pp. 26–29, and Plate I.

0.3893 by the later, and 0.3876 by the earlier series of measurements, the different nativities appear to present some characteristic differences. We find for this dimension the proportions following: —

Nativity	Later Measures		Earlier Measures	
	Number	Length of Body	Number	Length of Body
New England States . . .	1 208	0.390	912	0.391
N. Y., N. J., and Penn. . .	3 758	.389	3 128	.390
Ohio and Indiana	1 657	.387	458	.394
Mich., Wisc., and Illinois .	1 012	.391		
Coast Slave States . . .	365	.384	2 007	.380
Kentucky and Tennessee .	266	.394		
Slave States W. of Miss. R.	51	.385	–	–
British American Provinces	556	.393	177	.389
England, Wales, etc. . .	324	.391	204	.388
Scotland	81	.391		
Ireland	821	.391	440	.389
France, Belgium, etc. . .	98	.390	–	–
Germany	561	.388	251	.389
All others	73	0.394	79	0.387
Total	10 831	0.3893	7 656	0.3876

From this table it is manifest that the superior length of body, which appeared, from the figures of the last chapter, to belong to natives of this country, is attributable to their greater stature, and that in several nativities the mean length, while actually greater, is relatively smaller, in consequence of the much greater length of the legs for the men of those nativities. In other words, a higher stature seems in general to imply a longer, but not a proportionally longer, trunk.

The mean distance from *middle finger to top of knee-pan* is 0.075 for the aggregate of all measured, but is seen to be especially variable, ranging from 0.070 to 0.087 even in groups containing more than 250 men, the smallest value being for Canadians, and the largest for natives of Kentucky and Tennessee. The explanation of this large fluctuation is readily seen by comparing the variations in the lengths of body, arms, and legs, for the several nativities involved.

The variations and probable errors deduced for Nativities A and B are appended: —

Nativity	Number	Dim. 4½	r	r_o
New England States	977	0.0721	0.0120	0.0004
New York, New Jersey, and Penn.	3 123	0.0725	0.0118	0.0002

The mean *height to perinæum* for the small group of 7 Spaniards is but 0.455 of the stature, but this of course is an untrustworthy determination. For each of two groups comprising 326 English, Welsh, etc., and 100 French, we find the mean value 0.459, while for natives of the Southern States (excluding Kentucky and Tennessee), we find the large value 0.468, and this for each of the two groups, both for those in, and those not in, their usual health. The tables of probable distribution are computed for two nativities only.

Nativity	Number	Height	r	r_o
New England States . . .	976	0.4625	0.0096	0.0003
Ohio and Indiana	1 415	0.4646	0.0095	0.0003

The mean of the earlier measures accords with that of the later within 0.0015, and these measures also agree with the other in assigning a low value 0.461 to natives of Great Britain, and the maximum value 0.473 to natives of the Slave States. But the minimum value here belongs to the natives of New Jersey and Pennsylvania, for whom it is 0.459.

The distance from *perinæum to the symphysis pubis* was not measured in any of the examinations of soldiers. From 1013 measurements of sailors the mean value of this distance was found to be 0.0287 of the height. This would make the total height to the symphysis 0.4913 of the stature, for soldiers.

Height to Knee. — The average proportion for this dimension varies in the large groups from 0.269, for 1015 Northwestern men, to 0.282, for 367 Southerners. The range of variation is sufficiently manifest from the assortment of the first two nativities, which give —

Nativity	Number	Height	r	r_o
New England States . . .	978	0.2788	0.0073	0.0002
New York, New Jersey, Penn.	3 119	0.2776	0.0081	0.0001

Comparing the average proportionate numbers representing the height to the knee, with those representing the length of the thigh, we find —

Nativity	Number of Men	Height to Knee	Knee to Perinæum	Ratio
New England States	1 208	0.279	0.183	1.52
New York, New Jersey, and Penn.	3 757	.278	.185	1.50
Ohio and Indiana	1 659	.277	.188	1.47
Michigan, Wisconsin, and Illinois	1 012	.269	.192	1.40[a]
Coast Slave States	365	.282	.186	1.52
Kentucky and Tennessee . . .	266	.280	.181	1.55
States West of Mississippi River .	61	.283	.185	1.53
British Amer. Prov., excl. Canada	38	.277	.180	1.54
Canada	518	.275	.186	1.48
England	304	.276	.183	1.51
Wales and Isle of Man	20	.278	.179	1.55
Scotland	81	.275	.186	1.48
Ireland	824	.278	.182	1.53
France, Belgium, etc.	98	.277	.182	1.52
Germany	562	.280	.184	1.52
Scandinavia	34	.280	.184	1.52
Spain, etc.	7	.276	.179	1.54
Miscellaneous	32	0.279	0.181	1.54
Total	10 846	0.2771	0.1855	1.494

The ratios given in the last column differ somewhat from the corresponding ones deduced from the actual dimensions, although the range of the variation is not much restricted, and the ratio for the total is identical.

The mean *breadth of neck* is 0.063, and varies from this value by more than 0.002 for no nativity of any importance. We have

Nativity	Number	Breadth	r	r_o
New England States	976	0.0623	0.0027	0.00009
New York, New Jersey, and Penn.	3 122	0.0633	0.0027	0.00005

The measures by Form E give only 0.060, and the mean for no nativity-group reaches so high as 0.0620 if we carry it to four decimals. The explanation of this difference must apparently be sought either in the examiners, or, what is equally possible, in the andrometers, the gauges of which, as first constructed, were liable to become loosened by the rough treatment inseparable from military transportation.

The *girth of neck* varies from its mean value 0.203 by more than 0.003 for only two nativities comprising over 10 men. These

[a] See note page 259.

are the 100 French and 562 Germans, for whom the resultant values are 0.210 and 0.209 respectively.

Nativity	Number	Girth	r	r_0
New England States . . .	978	0.1998	0.0066	0.0002
New York, New Jersey, Penn.	3 123	0.2032	0.0066	0.0001
Ohio and Indiana	1 416	0.2025	0.0068	0.0002

The mean *breadth of shoulders*, between the acromia, fluctuates in the large nativity-groups from 0.182 for the Northwestern men, to 0.195 for the Irish. The probable variation for a single individual among New Englanders was not quite 0.010.

If however we consider only those measurements which appear to be entitled to the fullest reliance, as given on page 271, we find 0.1828 as the total mean, — the several mean values for particular nativities varying between the limits 0.179, for 44 natives of the seaboard Slave States, and 0.187, which value is given alike by the English, the Irish, and the French group, numbering 375 in the aggregate.

For the following table the same returns have been used which were employed for the analogous table in the last chapter, on page 271. It will be seen that the average discordance between the half-width of shoulders, as measured by the half-span of extended arms diminished by the length of the arm from acromion to finger-tip, and the same dimension directly observed, is here always positive, and amounts to less on the average than 0.002.

Results of Arm and Shoulder Measurements.

(*Excluding all Unsatisfactory Returns.*)

Nativity	No.	Mean Stat-ure	Breadth between Acro-mia, 8a	Middle of Ster-num to Finger-Tip, 12a	Acro-mion to Fin-ger-tip, 12b	Acro-mion to El-bow, 12c	½ 8a—(12b—12a)
New England States .	322	67.17	.184	.431	.521	.200	+.002
N. Y., N. J., and Penn.	1 866	67.89	.183	.428	.517	.202	.0025
Ohio and Indiana . .	840	67.70	.181	.434	.523	.202	.0015
Mich., Wisc., and Ill. .	842	67.23	.181	.427	.517	.198	.0005
Coast Slave States . .	44	67.37	.179	.435	.524	.204	.0005
Kentucky and Tenn. .	32	68.92	.185	.434	.526	.199	.0005
States W. Miss. River	18	67.86	.185	.433	.524	.201	.0015
British Amer. Provinces	273	67.07	.184	.432	.521	.201	.0025
England	153	66.55	.187	.429	.520	.200	.0025
Scotland	50	66.65	.184	.431	.521	.200	.002
Ireland	205	66.74	.187	.433	.525	.199	.0015
France, etc.	17	65.93	.187	.432	.523	.199	.0025
Germany	175	66.41	.185	.434	.526	.201	.0005
Miscellaneous	18	67.03	.185	.432	.524	.201	+.0005
Total	4 855	67.48	.1828	.4299	.5195	.2008	+.0018

Where the *full breadth* was measured, we find it to vary among those nativity-groups which number not less than 40 cases, between the limits 0.235 for Southerners, and 0.250 for Germans, in the later series of measurements; the mean value being 0.2435. The mode of life and previous occupation doubtless influence this dimension in a large degree. In the earlier series, the mean value of the full breadth comes out as 0.2432 for the aggregate, thus closely agreeing with the other determination. Here, too, it is a minimum for men born in the Slave States.

The average proportionate *breadth of pelvis*, for the several nativities, seems to have varied from its mean value 0.1775 for the aggregate of all, by more than 0.003 for the French only, for whom it is 0.182. It certainly seems less for Western than for Eastern men, among Americans. Our distribution tables give —

Nativity	Number	Breadth	r	r_o
New England States . . .	976	0.1770	0.0057	0.0002
New York, New Jersey, Penn.	3 119	0.1790	0.0077	0.0001
Ohio and Indiana	1 417	0.1752	0.0061	0.0002

The series E, regarding the measurements of which we would refer to the statements made in the last chapter, gives the mean value 0.1951. This is probably the width of the hips at the trochanters.

The *circumference of chest* (under the clothes) was found to be as follows: —

	Inspiration	Expiration	Play	Mean Value
From 9 270 men in usual vigor . .	0.5539	0.5134	0.4405	0.5336
From 1 604 men not in usual vigor .	0.5485	0.5153	0.0332	0.5319
From 10 874 men in all	0.5531	0.5137	0.0394	0.5334

thus corroborating the inferences deduced in Chapter VIII.

The distribution tables give us —

Nativity	No. of Men	Circ. at Insp'n	r	r_o	Circ. at Exp'n	r	r_o
New England States	978	0.5473	0.0210	0.0007	0.5074	0.0221	0.0007
N. Y., N. J., and Penn.	3 125	0.5527	0.0198	0.0004	0.5115	0.0203	0.0004

From the earlier series, we obtain the mean values for the circumference of chest —

For 5722 men in usual vigor		0.5257
2163 " not " "		0.5220
7885 " in all		0.5247

No rules existed in the schedule for this series, either as to the part of the chest, or regarding the degree of inflation at which the measurement was to be taken.

The mean *girth of waist*, for the soldiers measured in the later series, varied between 0.463 and 0.480, excepting for nativity G_2, but was of course dependent upon the mean age of the men, which it has not been possible to discuss in this connection, although ample material exists for determining its average variation with the age, for men between 18 and 35. The degree of accuracy of the measures may be inferred from the results for two nativity-groups.

Nativity	No. of Men	Waist	r	r_o
New England States	977	0.4635	0.0203	0.0007
New York, New Jersey, and Penn.	3 124	0.4687	0.0215	0.0004

The mean of all examined by Form EE is 0.4685 ; but for those of the earlier series it is 0.4767.

The mean *distance between nipples* was found to be —

For 1 771 soldiers in usual vigor	0.1212
297 " not " " "	0.1207

being very nearly one eighth part of the height, but measurably diverse therefrom. The extreme values found were 0.090 and 0.152.

The mean *circumference around hips* for the aggregate of all is found to be 0.550 ; it varies, however, with the nativity, from 0.541 for 367 natives of the Slave States, to 0.563 for 100 Frenchmen, if we omit the value for nativity G_2, which appears discordant in many respects. We also find —

Nativity	No. of Men	Circumference	r	r_o
New England States	978	0.5440	0.0222	0.0007

but the distribution of the individual discordances for this dimension seems to be far from conformable with theory.

The distance, from the middle of the top of the *breast-bone to the tip of the middle finger*, is for the aggregate of all the soldiers 0.5218. This dimension, so often alleged to be equal to half the height in a well formed man, is thus seen to be nominally much greater, its minimum being 0.517 for the group composed of natives of Michigan, Wisconsin, and Illinois, and its maximum 0.529 for Swedes and Norwegians. The confidence to be placed in the results may be inferred from the fact that, for the only two nativities for which the distribution of discordances has been investigated, the probable variation, r, of an individual from the mean was found to be but 0.010, and the probable error, r_o, of the mean was but 0.0003 in the one case, and 0.0002 in the other.

From the *acromion to the end of the middle finger* the average distance was 0.4341, and the variations of individual cases, being tested for the same nativities as the last-named dimension, gave results almost identical, thus furnishing satisfactory indications of equal precision in the measurements, and in the mean results.

The measures from *acromion to elbow* prove even more accordant ; the mean value for the aggregate of all nativities being 0.2025, and the probable individual variations from the mean, in the first two nativities, being respectively 0.0087 and 0.0076, which correspond to the probable errors of the mean 0.0003 and 0.0001.

From these values we find the ratios between the two parts of the arm, and between the height to perinæum and the length from acromion to finger-tip, to be as follows:—

Nativity	No. of Men	Acromion to Elbow	Elbow to Finger-tip	Ratio of Lower to Upper Arm	Ratio of Leg to Arm
New England States	1 199	0.205	0.230	1.12	1.06
N. Y., N. J., and Penn. . . .	3 741	.203	.231	1.14	1.07
Ohio and Indiana	1 646	.202	.234	1.16	1.07
Michigan, Wisconsin, Illinois .	1 011	.199	.230	1.16	1.07
Coast Slave States	363	.203	.233	1.15	1.07
Kentucky and Tennessee . . .	266	.199	.239	1.20	1.05
Free States W. of Miss. River .	10	.196	.234	1.19	1.07
Slave States W. of Miss. River .	50	.203	.236	1.16	1.07
Br. Provinces excluding Canada	37	.205	.229	1.12	1.05
Canada	518	.203	.230	1.13	1.06
England	303	.202	.230	1.14	1.06
Wales, and Isle of Man . . .	20	.206	.229	1.11	1.05
Scotland	81	.202	.231	1.14	1.06
Ireland	824	.202	.234	1.16	1.05
France, Belgium, etc.	98	.202	.231	1.14	1.06
Germany	554	.205	.233	1.14	1.06
Scandinavia	34	.205	.236	1.15	1.05
Spain, Portugal, etc.	7	.204	.229	1.12	1.05
Miscellaneous	32	0.200	0.232	1.16	1.06
Total	10 794	0.2025	0.2316	1.144	1.066

It has already been seen that the length of the arm, as measured from the armpit, in the earlier series was closely accordant with the length as measured from the tip of the acromion process, in the later series. In the actual dimensions, the mean value of the former was found to be 29.200 inches, and that of the latter 29.153 In the comparison of relative dimensions, this accordance is seen to be closer yet, the resultant from the aggregate of all being 0.4339 for the mean length from armpit, for 7865 men measured by Form E, and 0.4341 for the mean length from the acromion, for 10 800 men in the later series.

Computing the ratio between the height to the perinæum and the length of arm with hand, as deduced from the relative dimensions in the earlier series, we have —

Nativity	No. of Men	Ratio of Leg to Arm
New England States	936	1.06
New York	2 048	1.05
New Jersey and Pennsylvania .	1 191	1.04
Western States	474	1.05
Slave States	2 010	1.11
Canada	184	1 06
Great Britain	214	1.08
Ireland	466	1.05
Germany	256	1.06
All others	81	1.07
Total	7 860	1.070

The caution with which inferences must be drawn from the collation of the results for different classes of men, when determined by different examiners, need scarcely be mentioned here. In the present instance, this is especially noticeable in the large proportionate value obtained for the length of legs of natives of the Slave States, a result not corroborated by the subsequent series of measurements. Yet the close accordance of the ratios deduced from the two series is noteworthy.

The proportionate *length of foot* as deduced from 10 851 measures in the later series is 0.1498, this dimension varying for the several nativity-groups between the limits 0.147 and 0.153, and being largest for French and Germans.

The distribution-tables give, for the men in usual vigor —

Nativity	No.	Length	r	r_o
New England States	976	0.15022	0.0039	0.0001
New York, New Jersey, and Penn.	3 117	0.15005	0.0038	0.0001
Ohio and Indiana	1 416	0.14933	0.0036	0.0001

and show the close precision with which this length is relatively determined, as well as the comparatively small individual variation from the normal proportion.

The longest foot in proportion to the stature which was measured, was that of an Englishman, and amounted to 0.181; the shortest was 0.114 in length and belonged to a native of New York aged 43 years.

Tables I. and II. present the mean proportions for white soldiers, assorted and combined in the same manner as the actual dimensions of the same men in Chapter VIII., but with the omission of some of the smaller measurements, for which this mode of discussion seemed unnecessary.

TABLE I.

Mean Proportional Dimensions of White Soldiers.

(*Later Series.*)

Nativity	Number of Men	4½ Tip of Finger to Margin of Patella	5 Height to 7th Cervical Vertebra	5½ Height to Knee	6 Height to Perinæum	7 Breadth of Neck	7½ Girth of Neck	8a Breadth of Shoulders between Acromia	8b Breadth of Shoulders
A. New England States									
In usual vigor	1 000	.073	.852	.279	.463	.062	.200	.190	.243
Others . . .	211	.075	.850	.279	.462	.061	.200	.189	.241
Total . .	1 211	.073	.852	.279	.462	.062	.200	.190	.243
B. N. Y., N. J., & Penn.									
In usual vigor	3 177	.073	.852	.278	.463	.063	.203	.189	.245
Others . .	588	.074	.851	.278	.463	.061	.201	.188	.242
Total . . .	3 765	.073	.852	.278	.463	.063	.203	.189	.244
C. Ohio and Indiana									
In usual vigor	1 443	.079	.852	.277	.465	.062	.203	.188	.242
Others . . .	219	.079	.852	.276	.465	.060	.199	.186	.237
Total . . .	1 662	.079	.852	.277	.465	.062	.202	.188	.241
D. Mich., Wisc., and Ill.									
In usual vigor	945	.072	.852	.269	.461	.064	.201	.182	.241
Others . . .	71	.076	.851	.273	.463	.062	.200	.184	.245
Total . . .	1 016	.072	.852	.269	.461	.064	.201	.182	.241
E. Coast Slave States									
In usual vigor	315	.078	.852	.283	.468	.062	.202	.188	.236
Others . . .	52	.077	.852	.281	.468	.059	.200	.183	.231
Total . . .	367	.078	.852	.282	.468	.061	.201	.188	.235
F. Kentucky and Tenn.									
In usual vigor	223	.088	.855	.280	.461	.061	.201	.198	.239
Others . . .	44	.083	.855	.281	.464	.061	.203	.193	.232
Total . . .	267	.087	.855	.280	.461	.061	.201	.198	.239
G_1. W. of Miss. R. — Free									
In usual vigor	10	.085	.854	.278	.461	.060	.207	.194	.244
G_2. W. of Miss. R. — Sl.									
In usual vigor	46	.083	.854	.284	.469	.064	.201	.203	.234
Others . . .	5	.084	.851	.286	.468	.059	.201	.186	–
Total . . .	51	.083	.854	.284	.469	.064	.201	.201	.234
H. Brit. Prov. excl. Can.									
In usual vigor	36	.078	.853	.278	.458	.063	.206	.193	.245
Others . . .	2	.088	.848	.267	.444	.060	.196	.195	–
Total . . .	38	.078	.853	.277	.457	.063	.206	.193	.245
I. Canada									
In usual vigor	474	.070	.853	.276	.461	.064	.204	.189	.244
Others . . .	46	.076	.849	.275	.459	.062	.202	.190	.236
Total . . .	520	.070	.853	.275	.461	.064	.203	.189	.244

TABLE I. — (*Continued.*)

Mean Proportional Dimensions of White Soldiers.

(*Later Series.*)

Nativity	9	10a	10b	11	11½	12a	12b	12c	36a
		Circumference of Chest							
	Breadth of Pelvis	Full Inspiration	After Expiration	Circumference of Waist	Circumference around Hips	Length of Arm	Middle of Breast-bone to Tip of Finger	Acromion to Elbow	Length of Foot
A. New England States									
In usual vigor	.177	.547	.507	.463	.544	.435	.522	.205	.150
Others . . .	.175	.545	.511	.461	.544	.433	.519	.202	.148
Total . .	.177	.547	.508	.463	.544	.435	.521	.205	.150
B. N. Y., N. J., & Penn.									
In usual vigor	.179	.553	.511	.469	.552	.434	.521	.203	.150
Others . . .	.176	.549	.516	.466	.550	.436	.523	.203	.149
Total . .	.179	.552	.512	.468	.551	.434	.522	.203	.150
C. Ohio and Indiana									
In usual vigor	.175	.556	.517	.473	.551	.436	.524	.202	.149
Others . . .	.173	.544	.510	.467	.543	.436	.521	.203	.148
Total . .	.175	.554	.516	.472	.549	.436	.524	.202	.149
D. Mich., Wisc., and Ill.									
In usual vigor	.174	.556	.506	.463	.547	.428	.517	.199	.149
Others . . .	.175	.544	.509	.461	.546	.434	.522	.202	.149
Total . .	.174	.555	.506	.463	.547	.429	.517	.199	.149
E. Coast Slave States									
In usual vigor	.174	.541	.507	.463	.542	.435	.517	.203	.149
Others . . .	.173	.542	.506	.460	.539	.438	.521	.206	.148
Total . .	.174	.541	.507	.463	.541	.436	.518	.203	.149
F. Kentucky and Tenn.									
In usual vigor	.175	.552	.515	.477	.551	.437	.525	.198	.150
Others . . .	.173	.551	.516	.473	.550	.441	.527	.201	.148
Total . .	.175	.552	.515	.476	.551	.438	.525	.199	.150
G_1. W. of Miss. R. — Free									
In usual vigor	.174	.553	.513	.469	.561	.430	.517	.196	.147
G_2. W. of Miss. R. — Sl.									
In usual vigor	.176	.538	.504	.451	.534	.439	.519	.203	.149
Others . . .	.176	.519	.491	.441	.542	.438	.521	.204	.148
Total . .	.176	.536	.503	.450	.535	.434	.519	.203	.149
H. Brit. Prov. excl. Can.									
In usual vigor	.176	.554	.519	.464	.544	.435	.521	.206	.150
Others . . .	.173	.527	.498	.458	.535	.425	.505	.193	.153
Total . .	.176	.553	.517	.464	.544	.434	.521	.205	.150
I. Canada									
In usual vigor	.180	.555	.513	.470	.554	.433	.521	.203	.151
Others . . .	.175	.555	.520	.479	.552	.436	.523	.207	.149
Total . .	.180	.555	.514	.470	.554	.433	.521	.203	.151

TABLE I. — (*Continued.*)

Mean Proportional Dimensions of White Soldiers.

(*Later Series.*)

Nativity	Number of Men	4½ Tip of Finger to Margin of Patella	5 Height to 7th Cervical Vertebra	5½ Height to Knee	6 Height to Perinæum	7 Breadth of Neck	7½ Girth of Neck	8a Breadth of Shoulders betw'n Acromia	8b Breadth of Shoulders
J_1. England									
In usual vigor	261	.074	.850	.276	.459	.064	.207	.193	.246
Others . . .	45	.072	.848	.276	.461	.062	.201	.191	.250
Total . . .	306	.073	.850	.276	.459	.064	.206	.193	.246
J_2. Wales & I. of Man									
In usual vigor	18	.082	.849	.278	.457	.063	.205	.186	.246
Others . . .	2	.077	.846	.284	.458	.059	.212	.216	–
Total . . .	20	.081	.849	.278	.457	.062	.206	.190	.246
K. Scotland									
In usual vigor	70	.073	.853	.275	.460	.063	.204	.187	.246
Others . . .	11	.077	.850	.274	.463	.061	.199	.184	.241
Total . . .	81	.074	.852	.275	.461	.063	.203	.186	.246
L. Ireland									
In usual vigor	648	.076	.851	.278	.461	.064	.206	.196	.248
Others . . .	179	.076	.849	.279	.460	.062	.204	.192	.241
Total . . .	827	.076	.851	.278	.460	.063	.206	.195	.248
M. France, etc.									
In usual vigor	84	.076	.850	.277	.459	.065	.211	.196	.255
Others . . .	16	.076	.849	.276	.459	.063	.208	.199	.245
Total . .	100	.076	.849	.277	.459	.064	.210	.197	.255
N. Germany									
In usual vigor	462	.076	.852	.280	.464	.065	.209	.196	.251
Others . . .	100	.074	.849	.280	.462	.063	.207	.194	.236
Total . . .	562	.075	.852	.280	.464	.064	.209	.195	.250
O. Scandinavia									
In usual vigor	28	.075	.855	.280	.465	.064	.207	.193	.244
Others . . .	6	.079	.850	.281	.462	.060	.204	.193	–
Total . . .	34	.076	.854	.280	.464	.064	.206	.193	.244
P. Spain, Portugal, etc.									
In usual vigor	6	.086	.854	.276	.454	.064	.211	.200	–
Others . . .	1	.083	.858	.272	.462	.067	.203	–	.232
Total . . .	7	.086	.854	.276	.455	.065	.210	.200	.232
Q. Miscellaneous									
In usual vigor	25	.077	.853	.280	.459	.063	.207	.192	.249
Others . . .	7	.086	.859	.279	.461	.059	.198	.201	.227
Total . . .	32	.079	.854	.279	.460	.062	.205	.194	.246
All Nativities									
In usual vigor	9 271	.0748	.8521	.2770	.4627	.0631	.2031	.1894	.2440
Others . . .	1 605	.0758	.8507	.2777	.4623	.0612	.2014	.1890	.2406
Total . . .	10 876	.0749	.8519	.2771	.4626	.0628	.2028	.1893	.2435

TABLE I. — (*Continued.*)

Mean Proportional Dimensions of White Soldiers.

(*Later Series.*)

Nativity	9 Breadth of Pelvis	10a Circumference of Chest Full Inspiration	10b After Expiration	11 Circumference of Waist	11½ Circumference around Hips	12a Length of Arm	12b Middle of Breast-bone to Tip of Finger	12c Acromion to Elbow	36a Length of Foot
J_1. England									
In usual vigor .	.179	.558	.518	.472	.555	.433	.522	.202	.152
Others . . .	.177	.553	.519	.470	.547	.432	.520	.201	.148
Total . . .	.179	.557	.518	.472	.554	.432	.522	.202	.152
J_2. Wales & I. of Man									
In usual vigor .	.177	.545	.508	.466	.548	.435	.525	.207	.149
Others . . .	.181	.569	.543	.498	.572	.429	.522	.197	.151
Total . . .	.177	.548	.512	.469	.550	.435	.525	.206	.149
K. Scotland									
In usual vigor .	.175	.562	.519	.468	.549	.432	.520	.202	.151
Others . . .	.171	.544	.512	.465	.545	.436	.522	.205	.148
Total . . .	.175	.560	.518	.467	.548	.433	.520	.202	.150
L. Ireland									
In usual vigor .	.181	.563	.529	.475	.554	.436	.523	.202	.149
Others . . .	.177	.556	.524	.473	.550	.435	.522	.201	.148
Total . . .	.180	.562	.528	.475	.553	.436	.523	.202	.149
M. France, etc.									
In usual vigor .	.183	.562	.523	.480	.563	.433	.524	.202	.154
Others . . .	.179	.556	.520	.481	.563	.433	.521	.197	.153
Total . . .	.182	.561	.523	.480	.563	.433	.523	.202	.153
N. Germany									
In usual vigor .	.181	.563	.524	.478	.558	.438	.526	.204	.152
Others . . .	.179	.557	.525	.475	.556	.439	.526	.206	.151
Total . . .	.181	.561	.525	.478	.557	.438	.526	.205	.152
O. Scandinavia									
In usual vigor .	.176	.565	.520	.476	.555	.441	.528	.205	.151
Others . . .	.184	.575	.534	.489	.560	.441	.531	.204	.151
Total . . .	.177	.567	.522	.479	.556	.441	.529	.205	.151
P. Spain, etc.									
In usual vigor .	.174	.538	.503	.470	.552	.437	.530	.207	.153
Others . . .	.175	.563	.535	.491	.562	.408	.512	.189	.146
Total . . .	.174	.541	.508	.473	.554	.433	.527	.204	.152
Q. Miscellaneous									
In usual vigor .	.180	.554	.512	.471	.549	.432	.517	.201	.151
Others . . .	.175	.517	.494	.444	.536	.432	.520	.197	.151
Total . . .	.179	.546	.508	.465	.546	.432	.518	.200	.151
All Nativities									
In usual vigor .	.1777	.5539	.5134	.4687	.5504	.4339	.5218	.2025	.1500
Others . . .	.1757	.5485	.5153	.4673	.5476	.4356	.5220	.2026	.1487
Total . . .	.1775	.5531	.5137	.4685	.5500	.4341	.5218	.2025	.1498

TABLE II.

Mean Proportional Dimensions of White Soldiers.

(*Earlier Series.*)

Nativity		Number of Men	5 Height to 7th Cervical Vertebra	6 Height to Perinæum	7 Breadth of Neck	8 Breadth of Shoulders
New England.	In usual vigor . .	588	.850	.461	.060	.241
	Others	355	.854	.460	.060	.242
	Total	943	.852	.461	.060	.241
New York.	In usual vigor . .	1 506	.851	.463	.061	.244
	Others	550	.852	.459	.060	.246
	Total	2 056	.851	.462	.060	.245
N. Jersey, Penn.	In usual vigor . .	833	.852	.459	.060	.244
	Others	363	.852	.459	.060	.245
	Total	1 196	.852	.459	.060	.244
Western States.	In usual vigor . .	293	.853	.459	.060	.243
	Others	185	.856	.461	.059	.241
	Total	478	.854	.460	.060	.243
Slave States.	In usual vigor . .	1 650	.853	.473	.060	.241
	Others	374	.853	.474	.060	.238
	Total	2 024	.853	.473	.060	.240
Canada.	In usual vigor . .	134	.850	.462	.061	.244
	Others	51	.853	.463	.061	.246
	Total	185	.851	.462	.061	.245
Eng. & Scot.	In usual vigor . .	145	.849	.463	061	.244
	Others	71	.848	.457	.061	.244
	Total	216	.849	.461	.061	.244
Ireland.	In usual vigor . .	345	.850	.462	.061	.246
	Others	122	.851	.458	.061	.246
	Total	467	.850	.461	.061	.246
Germany.	In usual vigor . .	179	.850	.463	.062	.246
	Others	77	.853	.461	.061	.245
	Total	256	.851	.462	.062	.246
Miscellaneous.	In usual vigor . .	63	.848	.462	.062	.249
	Others	20	.852	.461	.061	.244
	Total	83	.849	.462	.062	.248
All Nativities.	In usual vigor . .	5 736	.8513	.4649	.0606	.2431
	Others	2 168	.8527	.4619	.0599	.2433
	Total	7 904	.8517	.4641	.0604	.2432

TABLE II. — (*Continued.*)

Mean Proportional Dimensions of White Soldiers.

(*Earlier Series.*)

Nativity		9 Breadth of Pelvis	10 Circumference of Chest	11 Circumference of Waist	12 Length of Arm
New England.	In usual vigor	.192	.526	.478	.436
	Others	.195	.524	.482	.429
	Total	.193	.525	.479	.433
New York.	In usual vigor	.195	.527	.482	.439
	Others	.193	.524	.484	.435
	Total	.194	.526	.482	.438
N. Jersey, Penn.	In usual vigor	.194	.530	.479	.445
	Others	.197	.526	.485	.428
	Total	.195	.529	.481	.440
Western States.	In usual vigor	.193	.526	.476	.439
	Others	.195	.520	.481	.430
	Total	.194	.524	.478	.436
Slave States.	In usual vigor	.197	.516	.465	.426
	Others	.196	.507	.458	.424
	Total	.197	.514	.464	.426
Canada.	In usual vigor	.194	.530	481	.437
	Others	.196	.528	.481	.433
	Total	.195	.530	.481	.436
Eng. & Scot.	In usual vigor	.196	.533	.481	.425
	Others	.196	.525	.476	.427
	Total	.196	.530	.479	.426
Ireland.	In usual vigor	.196	.542	.483	.438
	Others	.189	.537	.484	.437
	Total	.194	.541	.483	.438
Germany.	In usual vigor	.197	.537	.485	.436
	Others	.196	.526	.479	.436
	Total	.197	.534	.483	.436
Miscellaneous.	In usual vigor	.199	.538	.483	.434
	Others	.197	.517	.474	.424
	Total	.198	.533	.481	.432
All Nativities.	In usual vigor	.1952	.5257	.4760	.4351
	Others	.1948	.5220	.4785	.4304
	Total	.1951	.5247	.4767	.4339

3. *Sailors.*

In Table III. the mean proportional dimensions are given for sailors and marines, arranged as in the corresponding table of the last chapter.

The dimension $4\frac{1}{2}$ is seen to be relatively larger than for soldiers, thus confirming the corresponding inference deduced from the actual dimensions. Notwithstanding the inferior length of body, which would diminish the interval in question by .017, this interval is greater by .012, making a difference of .029 to be accounted for. About one third of this difference is referable to the superior length from knee to perinæum, and since the arms are only shorter by .002, the remainder of the difference must be accounted for by a less slope of the shoulders in the sailors.

The greater length of thigh will become manifest upon comparison of the annexed table with the similar one given for soldiers in the last section. The table includes all the nativity-groups which comprise more than 30 men. It should be repeated that all these sailors were measured while naked, excepting the group of 85 who are separately classed, and who were mostly measured by Dr. Elsner, while the marines were examined by Dr. Wells, who made but few measurements of any other class, in consequence of the brevity of his connection with our work. The results for the marines accord closely with those for white soldiers.

Nativity	No. of Men	Height to Knee	Knee to Perinæum	Ratio
New England States	129	0.278	0.194	1.43
New York, New Jersey, and Penn.	155	.283	.196	1.44
British Provinces	66	.279	.194	1.44
England	102	.279	.192	1.45
Ireland	335	.280	.195	1.43
Germany	62	.282	.196	1.44
Scandinavia	82	0.277	0.198	1.40
Total Sailors naked	1 061	0.2802	0.1948	1.438
Sailors clothed	85	.275	.181	1.52
Marines	68	0.275	0.183	1.51

These mean relative dimensions corroborate the inferences drawn from the actual ones, with regard to the greater size of the neck, and the smaller girth of chest, waist, and hips.

The mean distance from perinæum to the prominent bone of the pubes being 0.0287, we have the mean height to the symphysis 0.5037, or very slightly more than half the total height, while for the soldiers it was found decidedly less than half the stature.

For the distance between nipples, the mean value from 753 sailors was 0.1258, being also greater than for the soldiers by nearly four per centum.

The arm-measures give us, as the average distance from the middle of the breast to the tip of the middle finger, 0.5143, a value somewhat less than that found for the soldiers; and the proportion between the different members as follows: —

Nativity	No. of Men	Acromion to Elbow	Elbow to Finger-tip	Ratio of Lower to Upper Arm	Ratio of Leg to Arm
New England States	129	0.200	0.234	1.17	1.09
N. Y., N. J., and Penn.	155	.199	.231	1.16	1.11
British Provinces	66	.199	.233	1.17	1.09
England	102	.199	.232	1.17	1.09
Ireland	335	.198	.232	1.17	1.11
Germany	62	.203	.231	1.14	1.10
Scandinavia	82	0.202	0.238	1.18	1.08
Total Sailors naked	1 061	0.1995	0.2328	1.17	1.10
Sailors clothed	85	.205	.236	1.15	1.03
Marines	68	0.198	0.232	1.17	1.07

The ratio between the two parts of the arm is here modified, unlike that between the two parts of the leg, by the relative elongation of the lower portion. But the excess of relative length in the leg is very marked, while the arm is relatively shorter.

Finally, the relative length of foot is seen to be about two per cent. greater than in the case of the soldiers.

TABLE III.

Mean Proportional Dimensions of Sailors.

Nativity	Number of Men	4½ Tip of Finger to Margin of Patella	5 Height to 7th Cervical Vertebra	5½ Height to Knee	6 Height to Perinæum	7 Breadth of Neck	7½ Girth of Neck	8a Breadth of Shoulders between Acromia	8b Breadth of Shoulders
A. New Eng. States	129	.084	.847	.278	.472	.062	.210	.191	.241
B. N. Y., N. J., Pa.	155	.091	.849	.283	.479	.066	.208	.192	.242
C. Ohio and Indiana	2	.088	.848	.272	.467	.065	.209	.174	.256
D. Mich., Wisc., Ill.	6	.089	.850	.290	.480	.065	.206	.188	.238
E. Coast Sl. States	19	.086	.847	.285	.474	.065	.207	.185	.245
F, G. Other S. States	2	.090	.852	.271	.457	.057	.200	.186	–
H. Br. Pr. excl. Can.	50	.087	.848	.280	.475	.066	.212	.200	.246
I. Canada . . .	16	.082	.845	.277	.467	.064	.211	.195	.245
J_1. England . . .	102	.085	.846	.279	.471	.066	.215	.199	.249
J_2. Wales, I. of Man	6	.077	.844	.284	.483	.072	.218	–	.255
K. Scotland . . .	27	.085	.847	.277	.467	.066	.217	.198	.254
L. Ireland . . .	335	.091	.847	.280	.476	.077	.212	.199	.247
M. France, etc. . .	20	.079	.850	.280	.478	064	.217	.197	.250
N. Germany . . .	62	.091	.849	.282	.478	.067	.211	.198	.248
O. Scandinavia . .	82	.079	.847	.277	.475	.066	.215	.198	.252
P. Spain, etc . . .	18	.078	.845	.284	.477	.066	.216	.200	.252
Q. Miscellaneous .	30	.079	.845	.282	.476	.068	.221	.196	.253
Total with't clothes	1 061	.0873	.8472	.2802	.4750	.0657	.2122	.1960	.2470
Sailors part. clothed	85	.0798	.8434	.2753	.4563	.0611	.2136	.1890	–
Marines " "	68	.1029	.8510	.2750	.4576	.0649	.2095	–	.2316

4. *Students.*

Discussion of the mean proportions deduced from the Student-measures shows that the relative length of the body is smaller than for soldiers, by nearly .006 of the stature, and the height to the knee greater by nearly the same amount. The length of head and neck appears the same, and the length of thigh scarcely different. The lower arm (with the hand) is decidedly shorter, and the humerus slightly so.

TABLE III. — (*Continued.*)

Mean Proportional Dimensions of Sailors.

Nativity	9 Breadth of Pelvis	10a Circumf. of Chest Full Inspiration	10b Circumf. of Chest After Expiration	11 Circumference of Waist	11½ Circumference around Hips	12a Length of Arm	12b Middle of Breast-bone to Tip of Finger	12c Acromion to Elbow	36a Length of Foot
A. New England States	.169	.534	.506	.454	.525	.434	.513	.200	.151
B. N. Y., N. J., and Pa.	.177	.536	.503	.452	.523	.430	.510	.199	.153
C. Ohio and Indiana .	.174	.548	.504	.459	.536	.427	.503	.208	.147
D. Mich., Wisc., & Ill.	.183	.532	.502	.440	.528	.439	.517	.200	.154
E. Coast Slave States	.176	.539	.508	.455	.524	.435	.515	.202	.153
F, G. Other Sl. States	.165	.548	.537	.470	.522	.427	.528	.197	.155
H. Brit. Pr. excl. Can.	.174	.550	.520	.464	.531	.432	.514	.198	.151
I. Canada	.171	.551	.523	.466	.534	.432	.517	.202	.151
J¹. England	.176	.550	.518	.466	.533	.431	.513	.199	.154
J_2. Wales, Isle of Man	.183	.559	.523	.466	.526	.438	.510	.202	.155
K. Scotland	.178	.575	.544	.473	.537	.433	.514	.199	.154
L. Ireland	.177	.550	.518	.463	.527	.430	.511	.198	.153
M. France, etc. . . .	.172	.557	.528	.476	.533	.438	.521	.201	.155
N. Germany	.182	.551	.518	.460	.537	.434	.513	.203	.156
O. Scandinavia . . .	.178	.566	.534	.475	.541	.440	.519	.202	.155
P. Spain, etc. . . .	.173	.556	.528	.464	.531	.431	.522	.199	.154
Q. Miscellaneous . .	.179	.557	.524	.465	.532	.435	.517	.196	.154
Total without clothes .	.1761	.5481	.5167	.4617	.5295	.4323	.5129	.1995	.1531
Sailors partly clothed .	.1662	.5575	.5361	.4782	.5415	.4414	.5317	.2051	.1534
Marines " "	.1748	.5475	.5186	.4584	.5495	.4296	.5249	.1984	.1509

The shoulders are very slightly broader; the play of chest too is greater, but this may perhaps arise from the superior and better directed effort to inflate and collapse the lungs, which might be expected from a more highly educated class.

All other measures of breadth and girth are smaller. The neck is narrower by 6 per cent., and less in girth by 4 per cent.; the pelvis narrower by 7½ per cent.; the waist and hips smaller. The mean age of the students examined was, however, less than that of the soldiers. Few of either class were below 19 years of age, but while few of the students had passed the age of 25, many of the soldiers measured were above the age of 30 years; so that a fuller development in breadth was to be expected. The average weight[1] of the soldiers was 144.8 lbs., that of the students on the other hand but 139.7.

The mean values of the relative dimensions for the several groups of students, and their aggregate, are presented in the following table: —

TABLE IV.

Mean Proportional Dimensions of Harvard and Yale Students.

Class	Number of Men	4½ Tip of Finger to Margin of Patella	5 Height to 7th Cervical Vertebra	5½ Height to Knee	6 Height to Perinæum	7 Breadth of Neck	7½ Girth of Neck	8a Breadth of Shoulders betw'n Acromia
Harvard, Seniors .	69	.090	.847	.281	.466	.059	.193	.180
Juniors .	51	.088	.846	.287	.469	.058	.194	.195
Scientific	4	.097	.855	.294	.476	.057	.183	.186
Total	124	.0893	.8472	.2840	.4679	.0584	.1933	.1864
Yale, Seniors .	92	.099	.852	.282	.468	.059	.196	.194
Juniors .	63	.100	.860	.280	.469	.061	.197	.199
Scientific	12	.101	.855	.279	.474	.060	.193	.203
Total	167	.0995	.8551	.2813	.4688	.0596	.1963	.1965
Aggregate . . .	291	.0951	.8518	.2825	.4684	.0591	.1950	.1922

[1] These values include about 3.2 lbs. of clothing.

TABLE IV. — (*Continued.*)

Mean Proportional Dimensions of Harvard and Yale Students.

Class	9	10a	10b	11	11½	12a	12b	12c	36a
		Circ. of Chest							
	Breadth of Pelvis	Full Inspiration	After Expiration	Circumference of Waist	Circumference around Hips	Length of Arm	Middle of Breast-bone to Tip of Finger	Acromion to Elbow	Length of Foot
Harvard, Seniors .	.263	.535	.491	.453	.519	.427	.512	.200	.147
Juniors .	.168	.540	.498	.450	.530	.426	.513	.198	.149
Scientific	.164	.516	.473	.427	.493	.422	.508	.196	.144
Total. . . .	.1649	.5363	.4930	.4511	.5228	.4263	.5121	.1993	.1476
Yale, Seniors .	.163	.547	.500	.466	.545	.425	.513	.199	.145
Juniors .	.165	.543	.497	.466	.550	.428	.514	.208	.145
Scientific	.161	.541	.497	.448	.554	.424	.511	206	.145
Total. . . .	.1638	.5452	.4989	.4648	.5477	.4260	.5135	.2029	.1454
Aggregate . .	.1643	.5414	.4964	.4589	.5371	.4261	.5129	.2014	.1464

5. *Colored Troops.*

The characteristic differences between the colored troops and the whites, as manifested by the computation of their proportional dimensions, differ little from those previously deduced by the study of the means from actual measurements. But the range of variation is so much restricted, that their characteristic nature becomes more evident, and the inferences to be drawn from them become more trustworthy.

Regarding these differences little need be added to the comments in the last chapter, which may not readily be gathered from the Tables V. and VI., where are presented the relative dimensions of the full blacks, and the men of mixed races, respectively.

The distance from finger-tip to knee-pan (dimension 4½) shows probably the greatest diversity; the mean values being for the full blacks less than three fifths, and for the mixed races only five sixths, as large as for white soldiers. This is due to the greater length of the arms, and less length of body. We have, namely: —

Class	Finger-tip to Knee-pan	Length of Body	Length of Arm	Length of Thigh
Full Blacks	0.0437	0.3698	0.4516	0.1957
Mixed Races	0.0623	0.3735	0.4569	0.1915
White Soldiers	0.0749	0.3893	0.4341	0.1855

The length of the legs is greater than in white soldiers by two hundredths of the entire stature ; and the mean value for men of mixed race is almost as large as that for the full blacks. The excess appears to be divided nearly equally between the thigh and the part below the knee, being however a little greater in the latter.

The length of head and neck is decidedly less. This dimension, of which the mean value was 0.1481 for white soldiers, is found to average .1455 in the blacks, and .1433 in the mixed races. Those who were naked when measured give a mean value most nearly approaching that of the whites. About three fourths of this class were natives of the Southeastern States, and were measured by Major Wales.

The arms are longer than in whites, both above and below the elbow, very much so in the forearm. Thus we find as mean values —

Class	Medial Line to Finger-tip	Acromion to Elbow	Elbow to Finger-tip
Full Blacks	0.5408	0.2101	0.2415
Mixed Races	.5406	.2095	.2474
White Soldiers	0.5218	0.2025	0.2316

The average ratios between the two parts of the arm, the two parts of the leg, and the whole arm and leg are —

Class	Lower Arm and Hand to Upper Arm	Height below Knee to Thigh	Leg to Arm
Full Blacks	1.15	1.48	1.07
Mixed Races	1.18	1.52	1.06
White Soldiers	1.14	1.49	1.07

Comparing the black with the white soldiers, we find the mean circumference of waist and breadth of pelvis to be decidedly smaller, and these dimensions in the men of mixed race to be generally intermediate between the two.

The distance between the nipples is about the same as in white soldiers, the mean of our measurements giving —

Class	In Usual Vigor	Not in Vigor	Total
Full Blacks	0.1214	0.1212	0.1213
Mixed Races	.1197	.1204	.1198
White Soldiers	0.1212	0.1207	0.1211

Finally the foot is longer by about 7 per cent. for the full blacks, and about $5\frac{1}{4}$ per cent. for the mulattoes.

The detailed means are given in Tables V. and VI., arranged in the same manner as the actual mean dimensions in the preceding chapter.

TABLE V.

Mean Proportional Dimensions of Full Blacks.

Class	Number of Men	4½ Tip of Finger to Margin of Patella	5 Height to 7th Cerv. Vertebra	5½ Height to Knee	6 Height to Perinæum	7 Breadth of Neck	7½ Girth of Neck	8a Breadth of Shoulders between Acromia	8b Breadth of Shoulders
Naked — Free States .	123	.047	.848	.279	.488	.063	.212	.223	.246
Slave States	554	.040	.852	.281	.488	.063	.211	.229	.242
All . . .	677	.041	.851	.280	.488	.063	.211	.228	.245
Half Naked									
Free States .	2	.046	.857	.298	.467	.065	.206	.226	–
Slave States	145	.038	.860	.297	.468	.065	.209	.215	–
All . . .	147	.038	.860	.297	.468	.065	.209	.215	–
Clothed									
Free States .	101	.053	.856	.291	.484	.064	.210	.202	.245
Slave States	1 095	.045	.856	.293	.485	.064	.210	.204	.247
All . . .	1 196	.046	.856	.293	.485	.064	.210	.204	.246
In usual vigor									
Free States .	194	.051	.851	.285	.487	.064	.212	.213	.246
Slave States	1 598	.043	.855	.290	.485	.064	.210	.211	.246
All . . .	1 792	.044	.854	.289	.485	.064	.210	.211	.246
Not in usual vigor									
Free States .	32	.043	.851	.281	.483	.062	.209	.228	.240
Slave States	196	.040	.855	.290	.484	.063	.210	.223	–
All . . .	228	.040	.855	.288	.483	.063	.210	.224	.240
Total born in									
Free States .	226	.0497	.8513	.2847	.4865	.0634	.2114	.2152	.2454
Slave States	1 794	.0429	.8549	.2896	.4845	.0636	.2103	.2127	.2461
Grand Total . . .	2 020	0437	.8545	.2890	.4847	.0636	.2104	.2130	.2458

TABLE V. — (*Continued.*)

Mean Proportional Dimensions of Full Blacks.

Class	9	10a	10b	11	11½	12a	12b	12c	36a
		Circumf. of Chest							
	Breadth of Pelvis	Full Inspiration	After Expiration	Circumference of Waist	Circumference around Hips	Length of Arm	Middle of Breast-bone to Tip of Finger	Acromion to Elbow	Length of Foot
Naked — Free States .	.160	.547	.517	.452	.530	.445	.539	.199	.158
Slave States	.157	.552	.530	.449	.525	.444	.540	.197	.161
All . . .	.158	.551	.528	.450	.526	.444	.540	.198	.161
Half Naked									
Free States .	.162	.572	.543	446	.553	.434	.547	.209	.161
Slave States	.165	.553	.530	.458	.563	.446	.553	.219	162
All . . .	.165	.553	.530	.458	.563	.446	.552	.219	.162
Clothed									
Free States .	.171	.533	.507	.462	.545	.450	.532	.212	.159
Slave States	.170	.538	.511	.462	.539	.457	.541	.217	.160
All . . .	.170	.537	.511	.462	.539	.457	.540	.217	.160
In usual vigor									
Free States .	.166	.540	.513	.457	.537	.447	.535	.204	.158
Slave States	.166	.543	.518	.458	.537	.452	.541	.211	.160
All . . .	.166	.542	.517	458	.537	.452	.540	.210	.160
Not in usual vigor									
Free States .	.162	.549	.517	.455	.537	.446	.540	.204	.159
Slave States	.164	.547	.522	.456	.536	.451	.544	.209	.161
All . . .	.164	.548	.521	.456	.536	.451	.544	.208	.161
Total born in									
Free States .	.1652	.5412	.5132	.4569	.5370	.4471	.5356	.2044	.1586
Slave States	.1655	.5433	.5184	.4580	.5365	.4521	.5414	.2109	.1603
Grand Total . . .	.1654	.5431	.5179	.4579	.5366	.4516	.5408	.2101	.1601

TABLE VI.

Mean Proportional Dimensions of Mulattoes.

Class	Number of Men	4½ Tip of Finger to Margin of Patella	5 Height to 7th Cerv. Vertebra	5½ Height to Knee	6 Height to Perinæum	7 Breadth of Neck	7½ Girth of Neck	8a Breadth of Shoulders between Acromia	8b Breadth of Shoulders
Naked — Free States .	96	.055	.846	.278	.487	.062	.208	.229	.241
Slave States	111	.054	.849	.280	.485	.061	.206	.223	.242
All . . .	207	.055	.848	.279	.486	.061	.207	.226	.241
Half Naked									
Slave States	47	.053	.858	.291	.461	.064	.207	.207	–
Clothed.									
Free States .	71	.066	.856	.291	.476	.064	.209	.203	.249
Slave States	536	.065	.860	.297	.485	.067	.210	.224	.250
All . . .	607	.066	.860	.296	.484	.067	.210	.223	.250
In usual vigor									
Free States .	127	.062	.850	.284	.482	.063	.209	.220	.247
Slave States	592	.063	.858	.294	.483	.066	.209	.223	.236
All . . .	719	.063	.857	.292	.483	.066	.209	.223	.246
Not in usual vigor									
Free States .	42	.054	.851	.282	.483	.062	.207	.227	.243
Slave States	102	.063	.857	.291	.483	.064	.208	.220	.253
All . . .	144	.060	.856	.288	.483	.063	.207	.222	.250
Total born in									
Free States .	169	.0599	.8500	.2836	.4823	.0627	.2086	.2219	.2463
Slave States	694	.0629	.8583	.2937	.4834	.0659	.2091	.2230	.2489
Grand Total . . .	863	.0623	.8567	.2917	.4832	.0653	.2090	.2228	.2471

TABLE VI. — (*Continued.*)

Mean Proportional Dimensions of Mulattoes.

Class	9 Breadth of Pelvis	10a Circumf. of Chest: Full Inspiration	10b Circumf. of Chest: After Expiration	11 Circumference of Waist	11½ Circumference around Hips	12a Length of Arm	12b Middle of Breast-bone to Tip of Finger	12c Acromion to Elbow	86a Length of Foot
Naked — Free States .	.161	.542	.512	.451	.525	.440	.531	.196	.157
Slave States	.158	.541	.516	.447	.518	.436	.530	.193	.157
All . . .	.160	.541	.514	.449	.521	.438	.531	.194	.157
Half Naked									
Slave States	.166	.544	.518	.450	.551	.436	.537	.212	.159
Clothed									
Free States .	.175	.543	.519	.472	.551	.452	.536	.210	.157
Slave States	.174	.536	.518	.466	.537	.467	.545	.215	.158
All . . .	.174	.537	.518	.466	.539	.465	.544	.214	.158
In usual vigor									
Free States .	.168	.542	.515	.462	.537	.444	.532	.202	.157
Slave States	.171	.537	.517	.462	.535	.460	.543	.211	.158
All . . .	.170	.538	.517	.462	.535	.457	.541	.210	.158
Not in usual vigor									
Free States .	.163	.542	.516	.454	.533	.448	.538	.202	.156
Slave States	.171	.540	.520	.461	.537	.457	.539	.211	.158
All . . .	.169	.541	.519	.459	.536	.454	.539	.208	.157
Total born in									
Free States .	.1673	.5423	.5151	.4600	.5363	.4451	.5334	.2019	.1566
Slave States	.1710	.5373	.5175	.4616	.5350	.4598	.5424	.2113	.1580
Grand Total . . .	.1702	.5382	.5170	.4613	.5352	.4569	.5406	.2095	.1577

6. *Indians.*

The relative distance from the finger-tip to the patella, which we have seen to be so small for the negro race, is also small for the Indian, the mean value being not far from midway between those of the full blacks and of the mulattoes. This is owing to the length of his arm.

The length of head and neck is apparently less, and that of the body greater, than for any other class of men measured. This effect would, it is true, be produced by an erroneous habit on the part of the examiner in deciding on the common terminal point of both dimensions, namely, the protuberant spine of the vertebra; and it is not to be overlooked that all our measurements of Indians, excepting four, were made by one and the same examiner. The difference in question seems altogether too large to be satisfactorily explained by any such hypothesis; still it is desirable to test the question, by comparing these means with those obtained by Dr. Buckley alone for men of other races.

The height to perinæum, the size of neck and length of foot, are not essentially different from the corresponding dimensions as found for white soldiers. In the lateral dimensions of the body, however, a marked diversity is exhibited. The mean circumference of the thorax and the hips exceeds that of the whites by about 4 per cent.; that of the waist is greater by twice this ratio, and the breadth of the pelvis by $6\frac{1}{2}$ per cent.

But it is in the length of the fore-arm that the most characteristic difference seems to be manifest. Here the excess for the Indians, above the full blacks, is nearly as great as that of the latter class above the white soldiers or sailors. The difference between the mean values for the Indians and the whites is nearly 0.02, or eight per cent. of the whole amount, if we deduce it from the dimension 12*a* and 12*c*; and if we deduce it from 12*b* it will amount to yet more than this.

No corresponding excess is manifest in the height to the knee.

These peculiarities of the Indian type are so marked, that it has seemed well worth the while to compare, not only the lengths of head and body, but some of the other measurements, with the results deduced from those white soldiers only, who had been measured by the same examiner. All influence of personal error in observation will then be eliminated from the differences.

We thus find from Dr. Buckley's examinations alone, taking at random such of the white soldiers in usual vigor as were most readily separated from the aggregate, the following mean values for the two races of men: —

Measures by Dr. Buckley.

	Indians	White Soldiers
Number of Men	517	840
Length of Head and Neck	0.140	0.151
Length of Body	.394	.390
Circumference of Chest	.556	.549
Circumference of Hips	.571	.556
Breadth of Pelvis	.189	.180
Medial Line to Finger-Tip	.545	.523
Acromion to Elbow	.201	.199
Elbow to Finger-Tip	.250	.236
Height to Knee	.278	.273
Knee to Perinæum	0.188	0.186
Ratio to Upper Arm of Fore-Arm and Hand	1.24	1.19
Ratio of Leg to Arm	1.03	1.06

A comparison of these values certainly warrants us in referring the characteristic differences observed to peculiarities in the respective classes of men, and not to any idiosyncrasy of the examiner.

The mean relative dimensions for the Indians here follow, together with the probable variation for individuals, and the probable error of the mean, for some of the dimensions of those in usual vigor. It has been deemed unnecessary to compute these subsidiary quantities for all the dimensions; and those here given will afford a fair criterion for the range of individual discordance, and the probable error of the results in general.

TABLE VII.

Mean Proportional Dimensions of Iroquois Indians.

Class	Number of Men	4½ Tip of Finger to Margin of Patella	5 Height to 7th Cervical Vertebra	5½ Height to Knee	6 Height to Perinæum	7 Breadth of Neck	7½ Girth of Neck	8a Breadth of Shoulders between Acromia	8b Breadth of Shoulders
In usual vigor . .	508	.053	.860	.278	.466	.061	.200	.188	.272
r			.0038		.0088	.0010			
r_o			.0002		.0004	.0000			
Not in usual vigor	9	.059	.858	.277	.464	.061	.200	.199	–
Total	517	.0536	.8601	.2784	.4663	.0606	.2004	.1882	.272

Class	9 Breadth of Pelvis	10a Circumference of Chest: Full Inspiration	10b Circumference of Chest: After Expiration	11 Circumference of Waist	11½ Circumference around Hips	12a Length of Arm	12b Middle of Breastbone to Tip of Finger	12c Acromion to Elbow	36a Length of Foot
In usual vigor . .	.189	.569	.543	.507	.572	.452	.545	.201	.148
r	.0044	.0143							
r_o	.0002	.0006							
Not in usual vigor	.178	.555	.529	.477	.547	.443	.534	.199	.150
Total	.1890	.5689	.5427	.5068	.5712	.4516	.5449	.2015	.1484

7. *Abnormal Cases.*

For the sake of completeness, and to facilitate any comparisons which may be found desirable, the dimensions of the dwarves, etc., given in the last chapter, are here reproduced in the form of proportionate numbers. They require no additional comment.

TABLE VIII.

Proportional Dimensions of Certain Dwarves, etc.

	Joseph Hunter	Charles W. Nestel	Charles S. Stratton	Eliza Nestel	"Hoomio"	"Iola"
	in.	in.	in.	in.	in.	in.
Actual Height	40.4	37.4	27.6	31.4	62.6	49.5
Age	17	23	13½	15	21	16
4½. Finger-Tip to Patella	0.059	0.088	–	0.121	0.081	0.144
5. Height to 7th Cervical Vertebra . .	.822	.840	0.754	.803	.877	.871
5½. Height to Knee	.277	.270	.250	.255	.335	.313
6. Height to Perinæum	.446	.495	.377	.392	.498	.467
7. Breadth of Neck	.084	.080	–	.086	.058	.063
7½. Girth of Neck	.292	249	–	.287	.211	.222
8*a*. Breadth of Shoulders betw'n Acromia	.235	.251	.290	.255	.217[a]	.245[a]
9. Breadth of Pelvis	.198	.219	–	.274	.181	.186
10. Circumference of Chest						
a. Full Inspiration	.542	.620	–	.608	.645	.649
b. After Expiration	.520	.562	–	.577	.594	.604
10½. Distance between Nipples	–	–	–	–	.147	–
11. Circumference of Waist	.495	.535	–	.510	.419	.485
11½. Circumference around Hips	.562	.626	.681	.640	.530	.570
12*a*. Length of Arm & Hand, fr. Acromion	.428	.396	.348	.382	.482	.552
12*b*. From Medial Line to Finger-Tip . .	.542	.511	.471	.503	.559	.618
12*c*. Acromion to Elbow	.198	.171	–	.163	.212	.222
36*a*. Length of Foot	0.131	0.144	0.149	0.134	0.141	0.149

8. *Deductions and General Remarks.*

Some of the mean values of the proportionate dimensions here deduced, are collected and arranged in the appended table, which presents most of the principal results in a compendious form, entirely analogous to the corresponding Table IX. of the last chapter.

[a] Full Breadth (not between acromia).

TABLE IX.

Comparison of Proportional Dimensions.

	White Soldiers		Sailors	Students	Full Blacks	Mixed Races	Indians
	Later Series	Earlier Series					
Number of Men . .	10 876	7 904	1 061	291	2 020	863	517
Length Head and Neck	0.1481	0.1483	0.1528	0.1482	0.1455	0.1433	.01399
Length of Body . .	.3893	.3876	.3722	.3834	.3698	.3735	.3938
Knee to Perinæum .	.1855	–	.1948	.1859	.1957	.1915	.1879
Height to Knee . . .	.2771	–	.2802	.2825	.2890	.2917	.2784
Acromion to Elbow .	.2025	–	.1995	.2014	.2101	.2095	.2015
Elbow to Finger-tip .	.2316	–	.2328	.2247	.2415	.2474	.2501
Med. Line to Finger-tip	.5218	–	.5129	.5129	.5408	.5406	.5449
Acromion to " "	.4341	.4339[a]	.4323	.4261	.4516	.4569	.4516
Height to Perinæum .	.4626	.4641	.4750	.4684	.4847	.4832	.4663
Height to Pubes . .	–	–	.5037	–	.5183	.5210	–
Finger-tip to Patella .	.0749	–	.0873	.0951	.0437	.0623	.0536
Circumf. of Waist . .	.4685	.4767	.4617	.4589	.4579	.4613	.5068
Circumf. of Hips . .	.5500	–	.5295	.5371	.5366	.5352	.5712
Circumf. of Chest . .	.5334	.5247[b]	.5324	.5189	.5305	.5276	.5558
Play of Chest . . .	.0394	–	.0314	.0450	.0252	.0212	.0262
Distance betw. Nipples	.1211	–	.1258	.1185	.1213	.1198	–
Distance between Eyes	0371	.0387	.0375	.0365	.0410	.0403	.0398
Breadth of Pelvis . .	.1775	.1951[c]	.1761	.1643	.1654	.1702	.1890
Length of Foot . . .	.1498	–	.1531	.1464	.1601	.1577	.1484
Thickness of Foot . .	0.0383	–	0.0442	0.0409	0.0404	0.0418	0.0394

The absolute elimination here of all influences resulting from the scale of magnitude, either as varying with individuals or as normal for classes or races, enables us to form much more definite

[a] Measured from arm-pit.
[b] Not, as in the other classes, the mean between inflated and exhausted thorax.
[c] Probably the breadth of hips.

ideas concerning the order of the various classes, as arranged according to the proportionate value of any physical dimension.

Thus we see that the distance between the eyes, so very large in the embryonic condition, increases in the order — 1, student; 2, sailor; 3, soldier; 4, Indian; 5, mulatto; 6, negro.

For the length of the foot, we have the sequence — 1, student; 2, Indian; 3, soldier; 4, sailor; 5, mulatto; 6, negro.

In length of body the red man is preeminent; in the length of legs, the negro; and in both these races the arms are longer than in the white.

Notwithstanding their small play of chest, the difference between the mulattoes and the full blacks is here very conspicuous, whether the actual or the proportional values are considered; the blacks in their turn falling below the Indians, and these vastly below the whites, of whatever class.

By comparing the values obtained for the average interval, between the tip of the middle finger and the upper margin of the patella, with the difference between the length of arms and the combined length of body and thigh, we find among the whites a wide diversity, between the soldiers on the one hand, and the sailors and students on the other. The soldiers, however, represent the great mass of the population, unaffected by special training or peculiar avocations, since their military character arose from the emergency of the period and not from personal habitudes; while on the other hand the sailors and students may be assumed to represent particular classes, to which most of the individuals had probably belonged from a comparatively early age. The peculiarities implied in the difference ought therefore to be referred to the latter classes.

The mean difference, between the dimension $4\frac{1}{2}$, and the height from the knee to the 7th cervical less the length of arm, comes out as .066 for soldiers, and .048 for both sailors and students. The agreement in value for the latter classes is fortuitous, being produced by a concurrence of different circumstances, the shorter bodies of the sailors being nearly compensated by the longer thighs. The difference in question is the sum of half the diameter of the patella, the amount of curvature of the arms and the slope of the shoulders, the last-named constituting the principal source of diversity. The amount of slope appears to be a minimum for the sailors, and for the students intermediate between the sailors and soldiers.

The mean values obtained, and presented in this and the preceding chapter, may be regarded as typical within very restricted limits of possible error, for the great majority of all the dimensions and ratios. Where they do not possess this degree of accuracy the fact has been indicated in the special discussion. With these values the scientific anthropologist may safely compare his measurements of individuals, classes, or races; the ethnologist may determine the position of any race of men relatively to those here considered; and the artist may calculate the proportions and dimensions of his statue or drawing, emancipated from the dictum of any human authority, or from the prejudice of any conventional school. Is it too much to hope that the time may come when measurements, for the twofold object of determining the type and the limits of normal variation, may be made to furnish a criterion for the discrimination of varieties, and even species, in other departments of biology? Not only in animate, but in inanimate nature, opportunity seems to be afforded for what may be termed the statistical method of investigation. For the naturalist to determine by the inspection of a single specimen what are the characteristics of a species, or even of a genus, might lead to consequences as absurd as those which would follow the determination of a human type from the Australian children, or of the characteristics of the Caucasian type from the measurement of Tom Thumb. Not only must typical characteristics be recognized, but the fact that they are typical must be rendered probable, before the system of classification attains its perfect development.

The demonstration, which the actual mean dimensions in the last chapter afforded, regarding the purely approximative character of the simple numerical ratios which artists and speculative theorists have supposed to obtain, between different parts of the normally proportioned body, is repeated yet more forcibly by the typical proportionate dimensions elicited. And we have here a new illustration of the freedom of the creative energy, which, whether in the organic or the inorganic creation, shows itself untrammeled in its numerical and geometrical relations; using in physical laws the closest harmony, the sharpest rhythm, and the most perfect geometric symmetry, wherever these possess a physical significance and importance, — yet dispensing with these relations quite as freely where they are not requisite for the end in view, — and finding equal simplicity and adaptation in those proportions which to human perception appear complicated or incommensurate. A few illustrations of this principle may not be inappropriate here.

Carus, in an elaborate investigation founded on measurements of his own, takes the length of the hand as a unit, or "modulus," and, dividing this unit into twenty-four parts, finds the normal relations between the several parts to be capable of simple expression in terms of these measures. The stature he regards as 9½ times the length of the hand, or in his system of notation 9..12; the height of the vertebral column is 3..0, as is also the circumference of the head; the length of the foot is 1..12, etc., etc. Dividing all the dimensions, as given by him, by 9½, his expression for the height, we may easily convert his results into decimals of the stature, and compare them with our own.

We thus find the several proportions according to Carus —

	Moduli	Proportion
Height	9..12	1.000
Length of Foot	1..12	0.158
" " Thigh	2..12	0.263
" " Leg below Knee	2.. 0	0.210
" " Arm	3.. 0	0.316
" " Upper Arm	1..15	0.171
" " Fore-arm	1.. 9	0.145
" " Hand	1.. 0	0.105
Distance between Ilia	1..16	0.175
Length of Vertebral Column	3.. 0	0.316
" " Head	1.. 0	0.105
Circumference of Head	3.. 0	0.316

It will be seen that these proportions are near approximations to the truth, and that the smallness of his actual unit, which is less than 4½ thousandths of the stature, permits an expression of most of the proportions within the limits of their probable error, where the number of observations is not very large.

Yet with the greatest deference for this eminent investigator, we venture to express the conviction that had the number of cases from which he drew his inferences been larger, his faith in the existence of such simple numerical relations between the normal dimensions of the human body as he has indicated, would have been much impaired.

So also Schadow, in the well-known and important work already cited, speaks of the stature[1] as consisting of "7½ times the height of the head, which agrees with the proportions of most of the ancient statues." Unfortunately we have not the height of the head; since our point of measure was neither the base of the occiput nor the chin, but the spine of the highest vertebra which does not belong to the neck. Yet the relative height of the head and neck to-

[1] *Polyklet*, p. 61.

gether, which we find to vary from the mean of all by only a single unit in the 4th decimal, either in the earlier series of 8000, or the later series of nearly 11 000 soldiers, — agreeing also with this mean for the students, and discordant for the sailors only, among the Caucasians (a discordance entirely explained by the stunting of this class already commented upon), — is 0.1482, a quantity standing in no simple relation to unity. But since this illustration may be fairly objected to, we will cite the next paragraph.[1]

"More accurately than the human head, the foot would serve. This is according to Vitruvius the sixth part of the whole stature, and therefore 11 inches,[2] which agrees tolerably well with living nature. Nevertheless I found the well-proportioned natural size to be but 10 inches."

This acknowledgement practically concedes the whole point. Still, if we investigate thoroughly, we find the mean length for our 11 000 soldiers to be 0.1498; varying somewhat with the nationality, yet not surpassing the limit of 0.003 in the variation for any nativity; while the error of the mean values (always between 0.149 and 0.150 for those groups in which the values are typical) does not attain the limit of 0.00015. Yet one sixth is 0.1667, one seventh is 0.1429, and two thirteenths is 0.1538; all of which are far beyond our limits.

Again, Zeising in a most learned and elaborate treatise[3] on the Proportions of the Human Body, and later in a very ingenious and thorough memoir on the metamorphoses in the Proportions of the Human Form, from birth until the completion of the growth in height,[4] published in 1857, has with great ability maintained, and undertaken to demonstrate, that the proportions of the human form depend upon a consistent division and subdivision of the total stature, in the ratio of the "*goldener Schnitt*," or in what in geometry is termed "extreme and mean ratio," the proportion 1 : 1.618 being dominant. This gives an infinite series, identical with one of those known as the phyllotactic, to which there certainly seems to be an approximation in the arrangement of leaves on many plants, and in the structure of some of the *foraminiferæ*. This scale of progress manifests itself, according to Zeising, in the growth of man and in other natural developments, giving a gradual transition from the ratio of equality to that of doubleness. The argument is supported by many æsthetic consid-

1 *Polyklet*, p. 62.

2 Rhenish measure, = 11.327 American inches.

3 *Neue Lehre von den Proportionen des menschlichen Körpers*, Leipzig, R. Weigel, 1854.

4 *Nova Acta Acad. Naturæ Curiosorum*, XXVI., 781.

erations and inferences from analogy, and by comparisons with the measurements of Carus, Schadow, and others.

This scale gives the universal relation 1 : 1.618, with its major and minor modifications 3 : 5 and 5 : 8 ; but the author only claims that his theory applies to the dimensions as determined by the contours of the muscles, and not necessarily to those of the bony structure.

Among the proportions which follow from Zeising's theory, and are comparable with our results, are the following : —

Head (Crown to Adam's Apple) . . .	0.1458
Body (Adam's Apple to Crest of Ilium)	0.2360
Thigh (Ilium to beginning of Calf) . .	0.3819
Lower Leg (beginning of Calf to Sole) .	0.2360
Height to Perinæum	0.4722
Length of Arm (Acromion to Finger-tip)	0.4377
Finger-tip to beginning of Knee . . .	0.0557
Breadth of Neck	0.0688
Length of Foot	0.1458

The values given in our Table IX. have been, it is true, deduced so far as possible from dimensions bearing a close relation to the bony structure, but several of our dimensions are legitimately comparable with the foregoing, and do not seem to confirm them. It is but fair, however, to add the comment which Zeising appends to his computation of the theoretical dimensions. "It is to be understood of course that all these measures are to be regarded only as ideal-normal, and as such they undergo in actual forms very manifold modifications, by differences of sex, nationality, age, etc. But if we compare these modifications it will be found that they all oscillate about the normal measures here laid down, as about a center."

The careful and earnest spirit manifested in these interesting memoirs can but lead to a more thorough scrutiny of the subject from the now greatly enlarged materials, and if any harmonic law exist in these dimensions, it will surely soon be brought to light. Yet the indications seem very decided to the author of these pages, that the harmonious and æsthetic influences which unquestionably pervade all the material creation, are not here exhibited in the form of simple numerical ratios.

Still more recently Liharžik in Vienna has been led, in the prosecution of similar inquiries,[1] to the enunciation of yet another harmonic theory. After repeatedly measuring the dimensions of each

[1] *Das Gesetz des menschlichen Wachsthums*, etc., Vienna, 1858.

one of 300 individuals, a work in which he was engaged for seven years, he arrived[1] at the conclusion that the form of the human body can be constructed by means of seven quantities, of which the length of the clavicle is one, and the six others are portions of the length of the body. This doctrine is elaborated in detail. Among his results are these: —

The heights above and below the *symphysis pubis* are as 81 to 94;

The lengths of the lower arm, with hand, and the upper arm are as 91 to 63;

The length from the medial line to the finger-tip is one half the height;

The half-breadth of the shoulders is one tenth the height;

The lengths of the hand and clavicle are equal;

They are also equal to six sevenths of the forearm, or two thirds the humerus;

The length of head and neck together is to the stature as 33 to 175;

The length of foot is equal to that of the forearm, also to $\frac{7}{12}$ that of fore-arm and hand together.

These ingenious inferences form but a portion of his results, which apply also to the law of growth. It is painful to see the disproval of an elaborate and conscientiously developed theory, especially when it is supposed to be deduced from observation. But most assuredly this is not confirmed for any of the classes or races of men here discussed, as will be shown by a very cursory inspection.

In a yet later publication[2] of great ingenuity and laborious algebraic research, the same author develops the more elaborate theory that all the proportions of the human frame are derived from the square of the number 7. But the numerical values here employed for the proportions now under consideration, are identical with those already cited.

Again Brent[3] has promulgated sundry curious statements regarding numerical ratios in the human form, which seem to have been generally accepted. Thus he thought that he had discovered the following relations: —

The distance between the nipples is one half the breadth of shoulders.

The breadth of shoulders is one half the circumference of the thorax.

The circumference of the chest (degrees of inflation not stated) is

[1] *Der Bau und das Wachsthum des Menschen.— Sitzungsb. der Wiener Akad.* XLIV., 2, pp. 631–36.

[2] *Das Quadrat die Grundlage aller Proportionalität in der Natur, und das Quadrat aus der Zahl* 7 *die Uridee des menschlichen Körperbaues.* — Vienna, 1865.

[3] Cited by Hutchinson, *Medico-Chirurgical Journal*, Vol. XXIX., etc.

$\frac{1}{2} - \frac{1}{61}$ of the stature, in minimum size, or 0.4836
$\frac{1}{2} + \frac{1}{15}$ " " " " medium " " 0.5667
$\frac{1}{2} + \frac{1}{6}$ " " " " maximum " " 0.6667

But we find that the corresponding values deduced from our measurements give —

For the mean distance of nipples in no case so much as one fourth the circumference of thorax:

For the mean breadth of shoulders in no case so much as one half the circumference of thorax:

For the mean circumference of thorax in no case so much as $\frac{1}{2} + \frac{1}{15}$ the stature:

This circumference itself —

for Soldiers	
at expiration	0.5137
at inspiration	0.5531
measured at random	0.5247
for Sailors	
at expiration	0.5167
at inspiration	0.5481
for Students	
at expiration	0.4964
at inspiration	0.5414

The largest value found for a white man in good health was 0.670, and the smallest 0.410; so that these fancied ratios of Brent also fail of confirmation.

Analogous statements are made[1] by Silbermann, who puts the symphysis pubis at one half the height, etc., etc., and by others. But no farther illustrations on this point seem needed.

That the highest beauty in organized form should imply simple numerical relations, seems as little demanded by æsthetic as by philosophical considerations, and certainly the hypothesis finds no support from these observations.

[1] *Proportions physiques du corps humain*, Comptes Rendus, XLII., 454.

CHAPTER X.

DIMENSIONS AND PROPORTIONS OF HEAD.

1. *Statistics Collected.*

THE measurements required by the programmes, both of the earlier and later series, have already been given in detail, yet, notwithstanding much effort to secure uniformity of method, this was not thoroughly attained. The additional material derived from other measures than those required may, however, possibly be regarded as compensating for the diminution of the number made according to the programme.

At the commencement of our inquiries, the dimensions directed to be taken over the frontal eminence, and from this to the protuberant ridge of the occiput, were so recorded by several examiners, who did nevertheless in fact use the superciliary ridge instead of the frontal eminence, making their measures over the frontal sinuses. The remoteness of the places at which these examiners were stationed, prevented the discovery of these errors for some time; but the instructions were then so explained and amended, that those measures of circumference which were made across the forehead should always be made around that part, above the superciliary ridge, which would give the largest value, while the distance from the front to the back of the head should be measured from the angle between the eyebrows, both its extremities being thus well marked positions. The distance "over parietal bones" has been interpreted to signify the distance over the top of the head, as far back as can conveniently be measured by the tape without bringing it into contact with the ears.

We have thus the following dimensions derived from the later series of measurements:—

a. Circumference around frontal eminence and occipital protuberance.

(*a.*) Circumference around ridge above eyebrows and occipital protuberance.

b. Distance between condyloid processes of lower jaw, over frontal eminence.

(*b.*) Distance between the same points, around the ridge above eyebrows.

c. Distance between the same points, over the top of the head.

d. Distance between the same points, around the occipital protuberance.

e. Distance over the head from angle of brow to occipital protuberance.

f. Width between the angles of the lower jaw, gauged by calipers.

g. Width between condyloid processes, similarly determined.

In the earlier series the measurements appear in fact to have been also chiefly made in accordance with the rules as subsequently explained for the dimensions *a* and (*b*), although the latter seems to have been somewhat too far above the brow, at the base of the superciliary ridge rather than upon it. The dimension *c* was, it would appear, measured a little farther forward upon the head than in the later series, the tape lying flat upon the top of the head. But instead of *e*, a distance e' was taken from the frontal eminence, or from what was regarded as such.

None will be so indulgent and considerate in judging of these cranial measures as those who have attempted investigations of the same kind, and who have thus become acquainted by experience with the great difficulties of the problem. Even when the simple denuded skull is subjected to repeated measurement by the same person, the variations between the successive results are quite considerable. When different persons undertake the same measurements, even in each others' presence, the discordances become greater still; and when the process is independently undertaken, without mutual understanding or explanation, the paucity of well-marked points introduces a new obstacle to agreement of the results, by the difference of judgement regarding the terminal points of the dimension and the position of the line along which it is to be measured.

When, now, to the difficulties mentioned are superadded those occasioned by the fleshy integument and the hair, which is often so abundant as seriously to interfere with the process of measuring, it will not be expected that our resultant values should claim any high precision. Indeed we are disposed to prefix an avowal that the fruit of this research is less abundant and less satisfactory than we had ventured to anticipate; yet with this avowal we would join the expression of a sincere conviction that the several measures have been carefully and conscientiously made, and that any incongruities which may seem to exist are due neither to carelessness nor to systematic error, but are fairly to be regarded as inseparable from the circumstances and conditions of the case.

The author regrets not having added to this series of head-measures two more, — the length and the height from the chin, both gauged by calipers with parallel arms, — and he would urgently recommend the incorporation of these or some analogous dimensions in any future programme of the kind. To scientific anthropologists or comparative anatomists he would of course presume to offer no advice on such a subject, being too well aware of the very serious deficiencies and errors in the system here adopted, to suppose that it is likely to be followed by experts to any considerable extent. Yet it may again happen that large opportunities, too valuable for any scientist conscientiously to leave unimproved, may be suddenly opened to those who, like the author, have had small previous training in this field; and to such, any suggestions will be useful. And the assumption is perhaps not too bold, that the present large mass of measurements and computations may give to the particular dimensions here determined a value to which they would independently not be entitled.

2. *Linear Measures of White Soldiers.*

The first tabular view of the mean results of these measures contains those derived from the later series of examinations. These have been kept distinct from those of the earlier series, both on account of the larger number of dimensions which they comprise, and because the want of mutual understanding between the several examiners may have rendered the measurements less congruous. The same assortment according to nativity is here retained which has been employed in Chapters V., VIII., and IX.

It will be perceived that the dimensions (*a*) and (*b*), which were taken immediately over the brows, differ but slightly from *a* and *b*, which were measured around the frontal eminence. For these soldiers the mean value of (*a*), measured in the first-named way, exceeds that of *a* by not quite one seventh of an inch, or about six thousandths of the whole amount; while that of (*b*) falls short of the mean for *b* by less than one eighth of an inch, or one per cent. The measures over the brow were among the earliest made by the several examiners, and, other things being equal, they would seem entitled to less reliance than the subsequent ones; this, too, apart from the consideration that they were not made as intended by our programme, so that the methods adopted by different examiners may have varied slightly. A very slight difference in the part of the superciliary ridge over which the measuring tape was passed, would account for variations greater than are found to exist between the measures over the brows and those over the most prominent portion of the forehead proper. The smallness of the differences between the results of the two modes of measurement may thus be accounted for, although these differences might reasonably have been expected to be manifold larger than here recorded.

In the table the results from each mode of measurement are given by nativities.

TABLE I.

Mean Dimensions of Heads of White Soldiers.

(*Later Series.*)

Nativity	Number of Men	Circumference around Forehead and Occiput *a*	Between Condyloid Processes over Forehead *b*	Number of Men	Circumference around Forehead and Occiput (*a*)	Between Condyloid Processes over Forehead (*b*)
		in.	in.		in.	in.
A. New England States	1 122	22.02	11.42	84	22.29	11.17
B. N. Y., N. J., Penn. .	3 183	22.10	11.32	551	22.22	11.20
C. Ohio and Indiana .	1 420	22.17	11.34	194	22.41	11.11
D. Mich., Wisc., and Ill.	959	22.19	10.76	55	22.15	11.16
E. Seaboard Slave States	335	21.93	11.55	25	22.43	11.18
F. Kentucky and Tenn.	226	22.32	11.26	37	22.39	11.08
G. States W. of Miss. R.	55	21.97	11.59	4	22.15	10.93
H. Brit. Prov. excl. Cañ.	35	22.13	11.58	3	22.20	11.23
I. Canada	417	22.11	11.18	100	22.17	11.26
J. England, etc. . . .	293	22.16	11.35	33	21.95	11.10
K. Scotland	72	22.23	11.19	8	22.54	11.70
L. Ireland	731	22.30	11.59	92	22.38	11.27
M. France, etc. . . .	80	22.10	11.46	16	22.43	11.26
N. Germany	502	22.09	11.47	49	22.38	11.38
O. Scandinavia . . .	33	22.37	11.63	1	22.80	11.40
P. Spain, etc.	7	21.83	11.43	–	–	–
Q. All others	25	22.14	11.51	7	21.94	11.03
Total	9 495	22.131	11.313	1 259	22.269	11.190

TABLE I. — (*Continued.*)

Mean Dimensions of Heads of White Soldiers.

(*Later Series.*)

Nativity	Number of Men	Between Condyloid Processes: Over Top of Head *c*	Between Condyloid Processes: Over Protuberance of Occiput *d*	From between Eyebrows to Occiput *e*	Width between Angles of Lower Jaw *f*	Width between Condyloid Processes *g*
		in.	in.	in.	in.	in.
A. New England States	1 211	13.42	11.62	14.36	4.56	5.40
B. N. Y., N. J., Penn. .	3 765	13.55	11.72	14.45	4.61	5.44
C. Ohio and Indiana .	1 662	13.45	11.97	14.64	4.68	5.48
D. Mich., Wisc., and Ill.	1 016	13.70	12.01	14.64	4.67	5.50
E. Seaboard Slave States	367	13.57	11.92	14.40	4.72	5.46
F. Kentucky and Tenn.	267	13.08	11.93	14.76	4.60	5.49
G. States W. of Miss. R.	61	13.43	12.25	14.21	4.64	5.41
H. Brit. Prov. excl. Can.	38	13.50	11.62	14.46	4.57	5.46
I. Canada	520	13.59	11.65	14.43	4.60	5.45
J. England, etc. . . .	326	13.50	11.80	14.45	4.61	5.41
K. Scotland	81	13.51	11.87	14.61	4.64	5.44
L. Ireland	827	13.40	11.95	14.39	4.73	5.48
M. France, etc. . . .	100	13.71	11.96	14.47	4.72	5.56
N. Germany	562	13.52	11.96	14.27	4.77	5.58
O. Scandinavia . . .	34	13.38	12.04	14.56	4.69	5.61
P. Spain, etc.	7	13.28	12.00	14.45	4.33	5.43
Q. All others	32	13.51	11.76	14.26	4.68	5.53
Total . . .	10 876	13.511	11.823	14.478	4.642	5.462

The differences in the general size of the head between men of the several nativities seem greater than is fairly attributable to the influence of accidental error in determining the typical size for any one group; and we have here an excellent opportunity for investigating the question whether the magnitude of the head is influenced by that of the body in general, or remains approximately the same for men of all statures.

In the foregoing table, it is manifest that the circumference *a* is largest for the Scandinavian group, the natives of Kentucky and Tennessee coming next in order; these two nativity-groups containing, as has already been found, men of stature superior to the average. So too the groups F, C, D, and K, which surpass the rest in length of the vertical longitudinal periphery, *e*, have all of them large mean statures. This may fairly excite some suspicion that any observed superiority in the size of head for particular nativities may be due to superior magnitude of the body in general, — the proportions of the head to the rest of the frame remaining constant, or nearly so.

To decide this question Table II. has been computed. It contains the dimensions *a*, *c*, *d*, and *e*, corresponding to those of Table I., but expressed in decimals of the stature like the proportional dimensions in the last chapter. From its indications the influence appears warrantable, that the dimensions of the head do vary with the stature, although by no means to an equal relative amount. The consequence of this principle would be that for the largest men, the heads would be absolutely the largest, and so inversely; while, if the size of the head be considered only in its relation to the stature, it would be smallest for the tallest men. Thus for example, the mean horizontal circumference of the head in the Scandinavian group actually exceeds that of the Spaniards by 0.54 inch, or about one fortieth part; but it falls below that of the same men by .003, or nine one thousandths of its whole amount, when the relative magnitude of the same dimension is considered. A similar phenomenon will be observed on comparison of the actual and relative values of the same dimension in the groups F and G; and so too in other cases.

TABLE II.

Mean Relative Dimensions of Heads of White Soldiers.

(*Later Series.*)

Nativity	Circumference around Forehead and Occip. Protub.	Distance between Condyloid Processes		Distance from Brow to Occip. Protub.
		Over Top of Head	Over Occip. Protub.	
	a	*c*	*d*	*e*
New England States	.328	.200	.173	.214
New York, New Jersey, and Penn.	.330	.202	.175	.216
Ohio and Indiana	.328	.199	.177	.216
Michigan, Wisconsin, and Illinois	.330	.204	.179	.218
Seaboard Slave States	.325	.201	.176	.214
Kentucky and Tennessee	.327	.191	.174	.216
States West of Mississippi River	.330	.202	.184	.212
British Provinces excl. Canada	.330	.201	.173	.214
Canada	.331	.203	.174	.216
England, etc.	.334	.204	.178	.218
Scotland	.333	.202	.177	.218
Ireland	.335	.201	.179	.216
France, etc.	.337	.209	.182	.220
Germany	.335	.204	.181	.215
Scandinavia	.331	.197	.178	.215
Spain, etc.	.334	.203	.184	.221
All others	.330	.202	.176	.212
Total	.3299	.2012	.1761	.2156

The results from the earlier series of measurements are, as will be remembered, assorted by nativities somewhat differently from those just presented. From the best information attainable, it would seem that the circumference *a* was generally measured around the frontal eminence, but not infrequently somewhat lower down the forehead; that *b* was usually measured above the edge of the brow; *c*, generally in a plane not quite so far back as in the later measures, although over the top of the head; but *e′* from the point regarded as the vertex of the frontal eminence — not from between the eyebrows, as in the later series. It is at present nearly, if not quite, impossible to obtain accurate information on these points, and it is strongly probable that the three persons engaged in the measurements made them in as many, somewhat different, ways. Yet it may apparently be taken for granted, without risk of large error, that the dimensions *a* and *b* in this series belong to a region[1] slightly below the frontal eminence, *c* to a plane passing just back of the fontanelle, and *e′* to the frontal eminence proper. The protuberance of the occiput is ordinarily so well defined, that there can be small danger of uncertainty in its recognition.

With these preliminary cautions we will give in Table III. the mean values, both actual and relative, of the four head-dimensions observed in the earlier series.

TABLE III.

Mean Dimensions of Heads of White Soldiers, Actual and Proportional.

(Earlier Series.)

	Number	Actual Dimensions				Proportional Dimensions			
		a	(*b*)	*c*	*e′*	*a*	(*b*)	*c*	*e′*
		in.	in.	in.	in.				
New Eng. States	941	22.18	11.13	12.95	14.44	0.330	0.165	0.193	0.215
New York . .	2 058	22.15	11.13	13.01	14.36	.332	.166	.194	.214
N. J. and Penn.	1 196	21.97	11.13	13.01	14.28	.331	.165	.191	.213
Western States	478	22.20	11.33	13.06	14.37	.328	.167	.193	.212
Slave States . .	2 024	22.05	11.08	13.14	13.57	.324	.162	.194	.199
Brit. Provinces .	183	22.28	11.22	13.06	14.41	.333	.168	.195	.215
Eng. and Scot. .	217	22.25	11.17	12.97	14.19	.336	.168	.196	.214
Ireland . . .	466	22.42	11.28	13.01	14.21	.336	.169	.195	.215
Germany . . .	254	22.25	11.20	13.02	14.11	.335	.169	.196	.213
All others . .	83	22.30	11.26	13.01	14.17	0.337	0.171	0.197	0.215
Total . . .	7 900	22.129	11.144	13.042	14.134	0.3300	0.1654	0.1936	0.2102

It will be seen that by an accidental coincidence the mean values of the circumference *a*, derived from the two series, are practically identical, and that those of (*b*) differ by less than one twentieth of an inch. The mean values of *c* are less accordant, their difference amounting to nearly half an inch, or three and a half per cent. Yet the values afforded by the later series for the other classes of

[1] See pages 368, 369.

white men resemble those furnished for soldiers by the earlier series; so that it would seem most proper, under the circumstances, to consolidate all the values of these three dimensions for white soldiers, as if they belonged to a single group of men, and thus for *a* we have 22.13 from about 17 400 men, for (*b*) 11.15 from about 9000 men, and for *c* 13.31 from about 18 700 men.

The distance of the frontal eminence from the angle of the brow is certainly more than thirty-five hundredths of an inch, but the mean values of *e* in the two series differ by only this amount. This incongruity is probably due to inaccuracy in the earlier series, and to error in estimating the position of a point which in many individuals scarcely exists.

3. *Linear Measures of Heads of other White Men.*

After the remarks already made, few additional comments seem requisite in presenting the mean results deduced for the other classes of white men. For somewhat more than half the sailors, the first two measurements were made in the erroneous form (*a*) and (*b*); and the total mean from these is for each dimension about one fifth of an inch smaller than that from the prescribed dimensions *a* and *b*.

The next following series of tables, IV. to IX., contain the actual mean dimensions, and the same expressed in terms of the stature as unit, for the sailors, the students, and the five abnormal specimens of humanity whose other dimensions are given in the two preceding chapters.

TABLE IV.

Mean Dimensions of Heads of Sailors.

Nativity	No.	*a*	*b*	No.	(*a*)	(*b*)
A. New England States .	80	22.06	11.06	49	21.72	10.92
B. N. Y., N. J., and Penn.	43	22.52	11.38	112	21.80	10.92
C. Ohio and Indiana . .	1	22.66	11.27	1	22.00	11.00
D. Mich., Wisc., and Ill.	–	–	–	6	21.80	11.04
E. Seaboard Sl. States .	3	22.79	11.62	16	21.59	10.73
F. Kentucky and Tenn.	1	23.40	12.10	–	–	–
G. States W. of Miss. R.	1	23.00	11.00	–	–	–
H. Brit. Prov. excl. Can.	29	22.23	11.34	21	21.73	11.01
I. Canada	10	22.14	11.32	6	21.87	10.70
J. England, etc. . . .	49	22.11	11.11	59	21.82	10.85
K. Scotland	14	22.36	11.14	13	21.90	10.90
L. Ireland	132	21.99	11.27	203	22.19	11.13
M. France, etc. . . .	12	22.02	11.03	8	22.39	11.27
N. Germany	26	22.25	11.34	36	21.94	10.84
O. Scandinavia . . .	44	22.37	11.37	38	22.09	11.09
P. Spain, etc.	9	22.21	11.09	9	21.83	11.13
Q. All others	12	22.09	11.52	18	21.87	11.02
Total	466	22.161	11.236	595	21.961	10.997
Other Sailors & Marines	153	22.25	11.213	–	–	–

TABLE IV. — (*Continued.*)

Mean Dimensions of Heads of Sailors.

Nativity	No.	*c*	*d*	*e*	*f*	*g*
A. New England States .	129	13.20	12.05	14.54	4.31	5.40
B. N. Y., N. J., and Penn.	155	13.04	11.53	14.12	4.52	5.40
C. Ohio and Indiana . .	2	13.20	11.30	14.37	4.50	5.63
D. Mich., Wisc., and Ill.	6	12.33	11.60	13.74	4.61	5.47
E. Seaboard Sl. States .	19	13.02	11.43	14.15	4.56	5.38
F. Kentucky and Tenn.	1	14.30	12.20	16.10	4.10	5.80
G. States W. of Miss. R.	1	13.00	12.40	15.30	3.80	5.70
H. Brit. Prov. excl. Can.	50	13.30	11.82	14.40	4.50	5.56
I. Canada	16	13.10	11.94	14.57	4.36	5.44
J. England, etc. . . .	108	12.99	11.67	14.26	4.48	5.39
K. Scotland	27	13.17	11.83	14.36	4.42	5.44
L. Ireland	335	13.17	11.77	14.27	4.60	5.45
M. France, etc. . . .	20	13.23	12.04	14.59	4.46	5.50
N. Germany	62	12.95	11.65	13.94	4.62	5.54
O. Scandinavia . . .	82	13.29	11.99	14.47	4.50	5.57
P. Spain, etc.	18	13.42	11.83	14.66	4.48	5.38
Q. All others	30	13.12	11.70	14.40	4.57	5.51
Total	1 061	13.133	11.773	14.304	4.510	5.449
Other Sailors & Marines	153	13.48	12.34	14.50	4.35	5.29

TABLE V.

Mean Relative Dimensions of Heads of Sailors.

Nativity	*a*	*c*	*d*	*e*
A. New England States	.332	.199	.181	.219
B. New York, New Jersey, Penn.	.340	.197	.174	.213
C. Ohio and Indiana	.349	.203	.174	.221
D. Michigan, Wisc., and Illinois .	–	.181	.170	.202
E. Seaboard Slave States . . .	.346	.198	.173	.215
H. British Provinces excl. Canada	.332	.199	.177	.215
I. Canada	.332	.197	.179	.219
J. England, etc.	.340	.200	.179	.219
K. Scotland	.345	.203	.183	.222
L. Ireland	.332	.199	.178	.216
M. France, etc.	.337	.202	.184	.224
N. Germany	.337	.196	.176	.211
O. Scandinavia	.341	.203	.183	.221
P. Spain, etc.	.342	.207	.182	.226
Q. All others	.341	.202	.180	.223
Total	.3357	.1989	.1783	.2171
Other Sailors and Marines . . .	.336	.204	.186	.219

The sailors who are assorted by their nativities in Tables IV. and V., are those who were measured throughout without clothing, and have formed a class by themselves. The other sailors, 85 in number, and the 68 marines, are retained in a separate group, partly because some labor was thus avoided, but principally because they formed the first subjects of several of the examiners, whose earlier measures were not so well made, for want of experience.

TABLE VI.

Mean Dimensions of Heads of Students.

	No.	a	b	c	d	e	f	g
		in.	in.	in.	in.	in.	in.	in.
Harvard . .	124	22.41	11.00	13.03	12.38	14.91	3.73	5.28
Yale	167	22.49	11.22	13.00	12.48	15.26	3.82	5.28
Total . . .	291	22.456	11.129	13.015	12.433	15.110	3.781	5.278

TABLE VII.

Mean Relative Dimensions of Heads of Students.

	a	b	c	d	e	f	g
Harvard	.327	.160	.190	.180	.217	.054	.077
Yale	.332	.166	.192	.184	.226	.056	.078
Total	.3298	.1634	.1911	.1826	.2222	.0555	.0775

TABLE VIII.

Mean Dimensions of Heads of Dwarves, etc.

	a	b	c	d	e	f	g
	in.	in.	in.	in.	in.	in.	in.
Joseph Hunter . .	20.3	10.5	12.6	11.7	13.1	4.1	4.7
Charles W. Nestel .	20.3	9.8	12.1	11.4	13.3	4.0	4.4
Eliza Nestel . . .	19.3	9.0	12.4	10.1	13.0	3.2	3.9
"Hoomio" . . .	15.0	7.8	6.5	7.2	9.1	4.2	4.3
"Iola"	14.9	7.4	7.2	7.8	8.4	3.6	4.2

TABLE IX.

Mean Relative Dimensions of Heads of Dwarves, etc.

	a	*b*	*c*	*d*	*e*	*f*	*g*
Joseph Hunter . .	.502	.260	.312	.290	.324	.101	.116
Charles W. Nestel .	.543	.262	.324	.305	.356	.107	.118
Eliza Nestel . . .	.615	.287	.395	.322	.414	.102	.124
"Hoomio". . . .	.240	.125	.104	.115	.145	.067	.069
"Iola"	.301	.149	.145	.158	.170	.073	.085

As regards the length and height of the heads of the abnormal specimens of humanity included in Tables VIII. and IX., it will be seen that the principle already deduced, concerning the relative sizes of head and body, holds good for the dwarves; since their heads, though relatively so much larger, are actually smaller than usual; while probably the most striking feature of the abnormality of the two other cases consists in their microcephalous character.

But notwithstanding the inordinate diversity of these heads, both in their actual and their relative magnitude, it is remarkable how slightly the two dimensions *f* and *g*, which depend upon the breadth, vary from the normal values.

The Table IX. probably presents as wide a range of relative cranial dimension as can easily be found; the three dwarves possessing heads not very much smaller than the full size for adults, so that the dimensions become enormous, in proportion to the stature, — while the statures of the microcephalous Australian children are not much below those of many full grown men and women. The relative horizontal circumference of Hoomio's head is less than two fifths, and the relative length of the periphery over the top of the head is but little more than one third, of the length of the same dimensions in Eliza Nestel.

4. *Linear Measures of Heads of Other Races.*

The mean actual dimensions of head for the full blacks, for the mulattoes, and for the Indians, are given in Table X., natives of the Free States and of the Slave States being distinguished in the assortment. Similarly the mean relative dimensions of the same men are included in Table XI.

TABLE X.

Mean Dimensions of Heads of Blacks and Indians.

Class of Men	Number	Circumference around Forehead and Occiput	Distance between Condyloid Processes			Distance of Eyebrows to Occiput	Width between	
			Over Forehead	Over Top of Head	Over Occipital Protub.		Angles of Lower Jaw	Condyloid Processes
		a	*b*	*c*	*d*	*e*	*f*	*g*
Full Blacks								
Natives of Free States	226	21.88	11.90	13.97	11.44	14.57	4.61	5.20
Natives of Sl. States .	1 794	21.91	12.00	13.95	11.57	14.38	4.67	5.22
Total	2 020	21.909	11.985	13.950	11.552	14.397	4.664	5.219
Mulattoes								
Natives of Free States	169	21.87	11.94	14.12	11.61	14.40	4.77	5.24
Natives of Sl. States .	694	22.03	12.44	14.11	12.40	13.28	4.85	5.23
Total	863	22.003	12.345	14.109	12.244	13.548	4.837	5.231
Iroquois Indians . .	517	22.482	12.083	13.707	11.584	14.447	5.177	5.839

TABLE XI.

Mean Relative Dimensions of Heads of Blacks and Indians.

Class	No.	*a*	*b*	*c*	*d*	*e*	*f*	*g*
Full Blacks								
Natives of Free States	226	.330	.179	.210	.172	.220	.069	.078
Natives of Sl. States .	1 794	332	.181	.211	.175	.217	.070	.079
Total	2 020	.3314	.1810	.2106	.1745	.2177	.0704	.0788
Mixed Races								
Natives of Free States	169	.330	.180	.213	.175	.217	.072	.079
Natives of Sl. States .	694	.332	.187	.213	.187	.218	.073	.079
Total	863	.3319	.1863	.2129	.1848	.2176	.0730	.0789
Iroquois Indians . .	517	.3296	.1771	.2009	.1698	.2117	.0759	.0856

5. *General Inferences from the Linear Measures.*

Commencing with the linear measurements, our principal mean results may be usefully arranged in compact form, for comparison, as in the following table: —

TABLE XII.

Comparison of Mean Dimensions of Head.

Class of Men	Circumference around Forehead and Occiput	Distance between Condyloid Processes			Periphery from Eyebrows to Occipital Protub.	Width between	
		Over Forehead	Over Top of Head	Over Occiput		Angles of Jaws	Condyloid Processes
	a	*b*	*c*	*d*	*e*	*f*	*g*
Students	22.46	11.13	13.02	12.43	15.11	3.78	5.28
White Soldiers . .	22.13	11.31	13.31	11.82	14.48	4.64	5.46
Sailors	22.16	11.24	13.13	11.77	14.30	4.51	5.45
Indians	22.48	12.08	13.71	11.58	14.45	5.18	5.84
Mulattoes	22.00	12.34	14.11	12.24	13.55	4.84	5.23
Negroes	21.91	11.98	13.95	11.55	14.40	4.66	5.22

In this table the values of *a* and *c* for white soldiers are deduced from the aggregate material afforded by the two series of measures, which contain about 18 700 men in all. For the first of these dimensions the two series give mean values, identical to the hundredth of an inch; but for the latter their difference is considerable, as has already been commented upon.

The dimension *a* represents the circumference of the head in a plane approximately parallel to the base of the skull, and may, perhaps, not improperly be termed the horizontal circumference. It may be considered the largest measurement attainable in this direction; since those taken around the brow gave on the average results nearly identical with those taken around the frontal eminence, as has been already stated, while measurements over regions of the forehead intermediate between these yield smaller values, as is well known.

A brief examination of the comparative table just presented will disclose some interesting facts, the chief of which may be briefly stated.

It is noticeable that the mean value of the horizontal circumference *a* varies within comparatively restricted limits; the maximum for any one of the six groups differing from the minimum by only one fortieth of its whole amount. The largest value belongs to the Indians; the students fall but little below these; and the other white men, the mulattoes, and the full blacks follow in the order named.

The Indian breadth of face is especially manifest from the foregoing table, from which it is seen that the mean width exceeds that found for students by more than four elevenths of its whole amount at the angles of the jaw,[1] and by nearly one ninth part at the condyloid processes.

It is also noticeable that, while the width at the angles of the jaw is smallest for whites, that at the hinge is smallest for blacks; the mean value for mulattoes lying between those of the black and red men in the former case, but differing only slightly from that for black men in the latter. These apparently complicate relations become nevertheless quite simple and clear when we consider the width of the jaw at the angles, not independently, but with regard to its difference from the width at the condyloid processes, as will be seen in the next following table.

The comparatively small values of the frontal semi-circumference, *b*, and the large values of the occipital one *d*, in all the groups of white men, and especially in the students, seem somewhat opposed to the views hitherto prevailing; and the large values of the three lateral semi-circumferences *b*, *c*, *d*, in connection with the very small longitudinal one, *e*, in the mulattoes cannot fail to attract attention.

These facts seem to indicate that in the white race that part of the skull to which the lower jaw is attached, is farther forward, and higher than in the black or red race; thus producing a decrease of the frontal and an increase of the occipital semi-circumference as measured from these points, as well as a diminution of the transverse periphery over the top of the head. The form of the postero-superior portion of the head apparently more than compensates for the loss of cerebral space thus occasioned.

An accurate comparison of some of the mutual relations of the quantities given in the last table may be both instructive and sug-

[1] The singularly small width found for students at the angles of the jaw is apparently the result of a personal error on the part of Dr. Elsner, all whose measurements of this dimension are small, in consequence of a habit of measuring somewhat in front of the true "angle of jaw." This is not the case, of course, with the width between the condyloid processes.

gestive; and the next table has been prepared with a view to affording the most convenient oversight, and recognition of ethnological distinctions.

TABLE XIII.

Comparison of Proportional Dimensions of Head.

Class of Men	$b+d-a$	$2b-a$	$g-f$	$\frac{b}{d}$	$\frac{b}{g}$	$\frac{c}{g}$	$\frac{d}{g}$	$\frac{e}{c}$	$\frac{a}{2c}$
Students . . .	1.10	-0.20	1.50[a]	0.90	2.11	2.47	2.35	1.16	0.86
White Soldiers .	1.00	0.49	0.82	0.96	2.07	2.44	2.16	1.09	0.83
Sailors	0.85	0.32	0.94	0.96	2.06	2.41	2.16	1.09	0.84
Indians	1.18	1.68	0.66	1.04	2.07	2.35	1.98	1.05	0.82
Mulattoes . . .	2.58	2.68	0.39	1.01	2.36	2.70	2.34	0.96	0.78
Negroes	1.62	2.05	0.56	1.04	2.29	2.67	2.21	1.03	0.79

The first column gives the excess of the sum of the two semi-circumferences from the condyloid processes, around the frontal eminence and the occipital protuberance respectively, above the full horizontal circumference measured around the same parts, and therefore in a plane which passes above the condyloid processes. The excess in question affords a rude means of estimating the distance between this plane and the line joining the condyloid processes. The sharp contrast to the others, in this respect, which the white race exhibits, will attract immediate attention, as will also the curious fact, already more than once mentioned in previous chapters, that in those features in which the black and white races present marked differences of conformation, the mulattoes, sprung from the mixture of these two, frequently differ from the whites yet more widely than do the full negroes themselves. The red man, for whom the mean value of the horizontal circumference, *a*, was found to be larger than for either the white or black race, occupies in this column a position intermediate between these two.

The second column shows the excess of twice the semi-circumference around the forehead, over the full circumference around forehead and occiput; and here too the contrasts between the races are strong, and our comments upon the first column find application in a yet higher degree.

In the third column is the difference between the width at the

[a] See note page 382.

angles of the jaws and at the condyloid processes; characteristic ethnical differences being also manifest in these numbers.

The six remaining columns contain ratios, and seem likewise well deserving of attentive consideration in their ethnological bearings.

Column four exhibits the proportion between the frontal and the occipital semi-circumferences; and discloses the curious and suggestive fact that the occipital is the larger for all the classes of white men, being a maximum for the most intellectual class, while the frontal is larger for Indians, full blacks, and men of mixed race, in the order named.

The fifth, sixth, and seventh columns show the ratios which the three peripheries, — measured from the condyloid processes, around the forehead, the top of the head, and the occiput, — bear to the width of the head between these points. In a crude way they indicate the extent to which these peripheries vary from semicircular arcs described about this width as a diameter; the ratio of the semi-circumference to the diameter of a circle being 1.571. In all of these ratios, ethnical differences are clearly manifest; the order of races being in each case, — Indians, whites, negroes, mulattoes. The order of the three classes of whites does not appear to be that of their intellectual development.

In the eighth column is the ratio which the periphery from brow to occiput over the top of the head bears to that from side to side, in a plane nearly vertical and at right angles to the former. This ratio is seen to be the largest for the students, and successively smaller for the other white men, the Indians, the blacks, and last of all the mulattoes; for which last named class the lateral dimension is actually larger than the longitudinal.

Finally, the last column exhibits the magnitude of the semi-circumference parallel to the base of the skull relatively to the transverse lateral one; and in these ratios the order of races is essentially the same as in the column preceding.

The ratio of e to $\frac{1}{2}a$, — that is, of the two longitudinal peripheries in perpendicular planes, — shows no marked ethnical distinctions.

6. *Facial Angles.*

The measurements of the Facial Angle have yielded a less satisfactory return for the labor expended upon them, than almost any portion of our materials or computations. The large individual diversity, — the inordinate differences between the results obtained by different examiners, notwithstanding great efforts to secure uniformity of method, — and the erroneous mode of measurement adopted by some, and not immediately detected, — have combined to make the assortment and reduction of the results very onerous, and at first bid fair to render it a thankless task. But the personal differences of the several observers, after their methods had become professedly identical, have been found tolerably constant; and the determination and application of these differences have ultimately afforded results which seem fairly entitled to confidence.

The mode of measurement will probably be understood from the annexed representation of the instrument devised for the purpose. The original instrument was constructed, under Professor Bache's authority, at the United States office of Weights and Measures, having been contrived by Mr. Saxton, of that Bureau, and Dr. Buckley. Those subsequently made have been but slightly modified, and their form and arrangement may be easily understood from the representation here given. A fixed peg, at

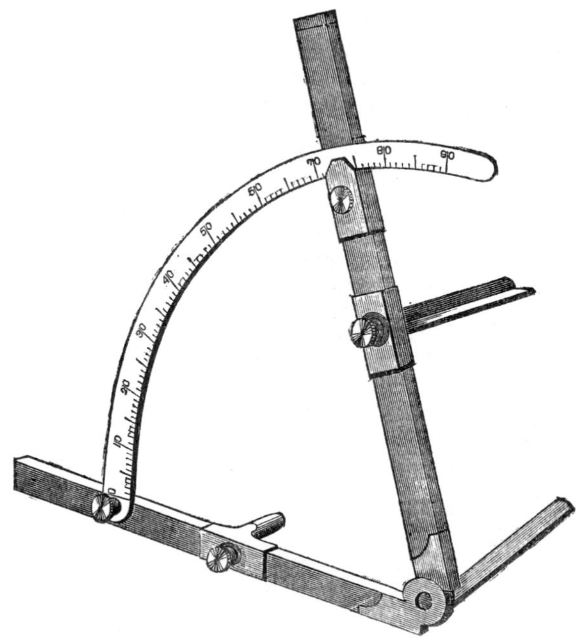

the extremity of one arm, fits the external orifice of the ear, the center of angular motion being pressed firmly against the bone of the jaw as far above the upper lip as the septum of the nose allows, while the extremity of the second arm (which is so constructed as not to interfere with the nose) is applied closely to the most prominent part of the forehead; the angle being read off from the graduated arc to the nearest half degree. By these practical directions it was believed that a good determination would be obtained for the angle, of which the center is at the alveolar margin, and the two sides are the lines drawn to the aural aperture and the frontal eminence respectively.

From the earlier series of measurements the observations are so discordant and unsatisfactory, that our attempts to deduce satisfactory results were soon abandoned as hopeless. The discrepancy between the average values obtained for white soldiers by two of the three inspectors, actually amounts to nearly thirteen and a half degrees, or more than one fifth of the smaller value. And although subsequent measurements have rendered it not improbable that the arithmetical mean between these two values would not differ very widely from the truth, yet no real reliance could be placed upon numbers deduced in such a way. In the annexed Table XIV. the results of this first series are given, rather as a historical and curious record than for any other purpose. It would seem that the large values obtained by Dr. Buckley are chiefly owing to his use, at that time, of the superciliary ridge as the frontal plane of tangency; and that the small values given by Messrs. Fairchild and Risler are in great part due to their having habitually placed the center of angular motion too far down upon the lip — against the upper incisors, in fact, rather than the alveolar margin; also, partly, to an insufficient pressure of this center against the face.

TABLE XIV.

Mean Facial Angles according to the Earlier Series.

Nativity	Dr. Buckley		Mr. Fairchild		Mr. Risler	
	No. of Men	Angle	No. of Men	Angle	No. of Men	Angle
		°		°		°
A	459	78.64	7	65.94	153	64.85
B	2 204	78.71	10	66.10	23	67.83
C	166	78.73	8	66.5	2	62.00
D	61	78.47	2	67.25	1	61.0
E	137	79.34	1 322	66.98	1	53.0
F	3	79.33	115	67.52	2	58.00
G_2	3	73.67	73	67.15	–	–
H	7	79.57	1	69.0	3	67.17
I	108	78.56	4	66.75	–	–
J	111	78.19	18	65.22	3	66.67
K	26	77.54	1	61.5	2	66.00
L	258	78.37	50	66.81	6	62.50
M	17	78.82	4	66.25	3	65.33
N	126	78.46	13	65.54	22	66.14
O	5	79.1	1	64.5	–	–
Q	57	78.68	6	65.67	5	70.20
Total . .	3 748	78.66	1 635	66.97	226	65.25

Passing to the later series of measures, these are of two classes. In the first the superciliary ridge was used to fix the direction of one side of the angle; while the second consists of those made after this usage was changed and the angle was determined by means of the frontal eminence, or most projecting portion of the forehead proper. This latter class is much the more numerous for the white soldiers and sailors, and it includes nearly all the other men.

Taking then the latter measurements only, our first problem is, to deduce values for the personal differences of the several examiners in measuring the facial angle.

For this purpose those seven examiners were selected who had measured the largest number of white soldiers and sailors; the men examined by each were assorted according to nativity; and for each nativity the average discordance was determined between the results of the several examiners and the mean from the measures of all. The series of discordances, thus obtained, was combined according to the weights of their several mean values for each of the seven examiners, and the correction thus deduced for each person, which should be applied to all his results. These values of the personal errors were regarded as a first approximation, and after their application to the original measures the process was repeated, until the repetition produced no farther change.

The weights are best determined according to the method given by the author in Vol. III. of the "United States Astronomical Expedition to Chile," Chapter on Weights and Mean Errors.

The trustworthiness of the values thus deduced was tested by a similar computation in which the total numbers of men were used without assortment according to nativities. To accomplish this, however, the differences of the means for the several nativities were first determined, and corrections then applied to the mean aggregate results from each examiner, in order to render them comparable by eliminating the effect of the different proportions of the various nativities examined by them.

The values for the totals obtained by these different methods were entirely accordant to the hundredths of a degree, and the following series of corrections was thus found. They are to be applied to any measurement of the facial angle to render the results of the different examiners homogeneous.

Corrections for Personal Error, of Seven Examiners,

from Measures of White Men.

Nativity	Buckley		Baker		Phinney		Lewis	
	No. Men	Correction	No. Men	Correction	No. Men	Correction	No. Men	Correction
		°		°		°		°
A	278	− 3.88	323	+ 2.25	94	+ 0.10	117	+ 2.11
B	716	− 3.69	220	+ 1.39	326	+ 0.47	832	+ 2.51
C	356	− 4.03	1	+ 1.14	297	+ 0.17	251	+ 2.11
D	68	− 3.73	3	+ 1.83	33	+ 0.97	745	+ 2.93
E	55	− 3.51	38	+ 2.17	80	+ 0.23	33	+ 1.83
F	27	− 4.40	1	+ 5.49	24	− 0.18	23	+ 0.99
I	36	− 3.75	33	+ 1.10	22	+ 0.20	189	+ 2.89
J	52	− 3.33	13	+ 3.93	47	− 0.34	78	+ 2.17
L	224	− 3.91	36	+ 2.13	145	− 0.97	69	+ 2.28
N	115	− 3.36	14	+ 0.59	83	+ 0.32	71	+ 1.99
Q, P, etc.	8	− 3.36	6	− 0.01	25	+ 0.10	16	+ 2.39
Total . . .	1935	− 3.780	688	+ 1.888	1176	+ 0.152	2 424	+ 2.550

Corrections for Personal Error, of Seven Examiners.—(Continued.)

Nativity	Smith		Elsner		Stark	
	No. of Men	Correction	No. of Men	Correction	No. of Men	Correction
		°		°		°
A	171	−2.14	127	+1.45	16	+0.11
B	510	−2.35	178	+1.58	18	+0.08
C	170	−2.56	226	+1.60	78	+0.96
D	39	−3.42	33	+0.86	6	−0.17
E	66	−3.22	18	+1.85	–	
F	34	−1.30	54	+2.54	59	+0.63
I	43	−3.21	21	+2.14	1	−3.10
J	46	−2.13	52	+1.24	1	+12.43
L	133	−3.06	116	+2.58	10	+1.34
N	92	−2.18	74	+2.01	5	−3.30
Q, P, etc.	23	−2.70	29	+1.70	3	−2.68
Total . . .	1 327	−2.482	928	+1.760	197	+0.570

The almost uniform agreement in the sign, and the accordance in amount also, for those groups where the number of cases is sufficient to give significance to the determinations, furnish a manifest corroboration of the general correctness of our values.

If we now discuss the results obtained for colored men, in the same manner, we similarly obtain the correction requisite for reducing the measures made by any one person to those corresponding with the mean of all. But it is clear that this correction for any individual will not be the same as that deduced from the results for white men, inasmuch as the standard of comparison is derived from independent and dissimilar materials. And in comparing tne values for white and black men, it becomes necessary to adopt some one standard of reference, which we may assume to be free from error.

The corrections for personal error thus derived from the measures of facial angles of colored men only, by the process heretofore explained, and referred to the average value obtained from colored men only, are given in the next tabular view, the full blacks being as heretofore discriminated from the mulattoes, and natives of the Free States from those born in Slave States. The great inferiority of their numbers to those of the whites whose measures we possess gives of course a corresponding inferiority to the value of the determination, and the non-accordance of the numbers shows the importance of resorting to some other method, for establishing the personal equation between those examiners who measured chiefly white men, and those whose examinations were mostly confined to the black race. The values of the several corrections are those which will reduce the mean value, for the particular examiner and class of men, to the mean value deduced from all the angles measured, by all the examiners included in the table, for the aggregate of all the colored men, whether full blacks or mulattoes.

Corrections for Personal Difference of Examiners,

as deduced from Measures of Colored Men.

Examiner	Full Blacks				Mixed Races			
	Natives of Free Sts.		Natives of Sl. States		Natives of Free Sts.		Natives of Sl. States	
	Number	Correction	Number	Correction	Number	Correction	Number	Correction
		°		°		°		°
Baker . .	4	+ 2.88	322	+ 3.18	3	+ 1.75	53	+ 3.21
Phinney .	4	− 0.37	7	− 1.24	4	− 0.58	3	− 3.30
Russell .	28	− 3.33	162	− 3.53	48	− 4.43	88	− 3.40
Myers . .	3	− 1.32	144	− 2.52	2	− 2.58	44	− 2.11
Elsner . .	23	− 1.43	7	− 0.96	–	–	–	–
Wales . .	82	− 3.14	539	− 4.11	60	− 3.11	80	− 3.39
Wilder .	1	− 4.99	1	+ 2.04	20	− 1.20	18	− 1.55
Avery . .	–	–	19	+ 10.62	2	+ 12.42	198	+ 9.27

The great influence which the 219 very abnormal values, obtained by Dr. Avery, exert upon the mean of all, and thus upon the other individual corrections, is palpable. Even rejecting these, moreover, the comparatively small number of blacks measured by Messrs. Phinney and Elsner, and the small number of whites measured by Messrs. Myers, Russell, and Wales, would throw some doubt on the trustworthiness of the remaining values. We must therefore resort to some entirely different means of obtaining the desired comparison.

If from the observations of each of those ten examiners, who measured both white and black men, we deduce the differences of facial angle in these classes, and, in combining these differences, use weights proportional to the number of cases in the smaller of the two groups from which they have been severally determined, we shall find the facial angles for the colored men smaller than for the whites by the following amounts: —

Class	Number	Difference
		°
Full Blacks born in Free States . .	82	1.027
" " " " Slave "	473	3.011
Total Full Blacks . . .	504	2.826
Mulattoes born in Free States . .	59	1.199
" " " Slave "	160	2.392
Total Mulattoes	169	2.248
Aggregate Natives of Free States .	93	1.035
" " " Slave "	531	2.953
Aggregate of all Negroes	569	2.768

The reason why the numbers of men from which the totals are derived, are not the sums of the numbers corresponding to the component groups, will be evident on consideration of the mode of computation, which assigns to the differences obtained from the observations of each examiner the number of men in the smaller of the two groups compared.

The remarkable superiority here visible in the value of the facial angle for colored natives of the Free States is very striking, — greatly surpassing, as it does, the excess of the angle in mulattoes over that in full blacks. Yet although this cannot be entirely attributed to the influence of personal equation between the examiners, it may be considerably affected by this disturbing element; and in comparing the measurements by different examiners, it seems unadvisable to use the foregoing determinations as a means of reduction.

Assorting the results obtained by each examiner according to the class of men to which they belong, we have the next table, in which the number of cases from which each mean is computed is indicated by figures in smaller type immediately above the corresponding angle.

TABLE XV.

Mean Facial Angles, as determined by each Examiner.

(*Later Series.*)

	Phinney	Baker	Russell	Myers	Wales
White Men	1 228 72°.048	702 70°.355	143 77°.868	78 75°.000	28 74°.138
Full Blacks — Free States	4 70.375	4 67.125	28 73.339	3 71.333	82 73.152
" " Slave States	7 71.286	322 66.861	162 73.571	144 72.566	539 74.153
Mulattoes — Free States .	4 71.500	3 69.167	48 75.354	2 73.500	60 74.033
" Slave States	3 73.833	53 67.330	88 73.932	44 72.648	80 73.905
Total Free States .	8 70.937	7 68.000	76 74.612	5 72.200	142 73.525
" Slave States .	10 72.050	375 66.927	250 73.698	188 72.585	619 74.121
Aggregate Negroes . . .	18 71.556	382 66.947	326 73.911	193 72.575	761 74.010

	Elsner	Lewis	Wilder	Avery	Furniss
White Men	1 029 70°.410	2 469 69°.722	1 70°.000	10 65°.200	229 67°.333
Full Blacks — Free States	23 71.435	–	1 75.000	–	–
" " Slave States	7 71.000	1 63.000	1 68.000	19 59.421	–
Mulattoes — Free States .	–	–	20 72.125	2 58.500	–
" Slave States .	–	–	18 72.083	198 61.270	2 64.500
Total Free States .	23 71.435	–	21 72.262	2 58.500	–
" Slave States .	7 71.000	1 63.000	19 71.868	217 61.108	2 64.500
Aggregate Negroes . . .	30 71.333	1 63.000	40 72.075	219 61.084	2 64.500

	Buckley	Smith	Stark	Wells	
White Men	1 970 75°.967	1 357 74°.701	200 71°.445	73 74°.185	

A very slight comparison of these results suffices to elicit the curious fact that the personal equation between any two examiners seems to vary with the class of men examined, so that the results deduced from the examinations of white and of black men are quite diverse in most cases, and in some are actually discordant. This may in some instances be accounted for, by supposing a gradual change in the habitude of the examiner, — in consequence of which his personal error, at the period when he measured whites, was actually different from that when at a later date he measured negroes. But these sources of error seem inseparable from the problem, and our aim must be to detect and eliminate them where this is possible, and to exclude from our discussion those materials which clearly forbid the possibility of such elimination.

For this purpose the mean value obtained from the measurements by each examiner, was compared with that resulting from those of every examiner, for each of five classes of men separately, namely, whites, full blacks, and mulattoes, born in the Free States, full blacks, and mulattoes, born in the Slave States. The determinations from these five classes were then combined by weight, where the groups were sufficiently large to make this worth while, and preliminary values of the differences were thus obtained. But no determinations were employed except those obtained by comparing results from the same class of men.

Without entering upon prolix and tedious details of the investigation, which proved laborious in the extreme, it may be stated at once that it was found necessary to exclude the measures by Major Wales on account of the great discrepancy between his personal errors as deduced from the different classes of men measured, no matter what other examiner might be taken for comparison. The measures by Messrs. Stark and Wells were also provisionally omitted, on account of the small number of men which they comprised; as also those of Messrs. Avery and Furniss in consequence of their great deviation from the others.

The mean results of the remaining nine examiners thus afford twenty-three determinations of personal difference in the measurement of facial angles, yet these several observed values are by no means mutually consistent. The true values must be subject to the restrictions imposed by thirty-six absolute equations of condition. Thus, denoting the several personal differences by the letters of the alphabet, and putting the true values —

Buckley — Phinney $= a$; Phinney — Baker $= h$; etc.
Buckley — Baker $= b$; Phinney — Russell $= i$; etc.
Buckley — Russell $= c$; Phinney — Myers $= k$; etc.

we must have —

$$a + h = b, \quad a + i = c, \text{ etc.}$$

The observed values therefore require such modification as will bring about an absolute conformity to these rigorous conditions, by some process which shall make the sum of the squares of the amounts of change a minimum, after the amount of each change has been multiplied by its appropriate weight. In other words, that system of interdependent values must be found, which best accords with the observed system of twenty-three approximate values, taken as a whole, while it perfectly satisfies the twenty-six rigorous conditional equations.

This is accomplished by means of what Gauss has named the "correlatives" of the equations of condition.

Denoting the several observed values of the personal differences by the capital letters

$$A, B, C, D, \text{ etc.},$$

the corresponding probable values, which we desire to obtain, by

$$a, b, c, d, \text{ etc.},$$

and the corrections needed by the former by the Greek letters

$$\alpha, \beta, \gamma, \delta, \text{ etc.},$$

we have twenty-three observed equations of the form

$$a = A + \alpha, \quad b = B + \beta, \quad c = C + \gamma, \text{ etc.},$$

and thirty-six rigorous equations of the form

$$a - b + h = 0, \quad a - c + i = 0, \quad b - c + 0 = 0, \text{ etc.},$$

in all fifty-nine equations from which the most probable values of the twenty-three unknown quantities α, β, γ, etc., are to be deduced.

For this end, the weights p', p'', p''', etc., or measures of the relative trustworthiness, of the several mean values A, B, C, etc., are to be determined, from considerations both of the number of cases upon which these means depend, and of the mutual accordance of the individual results. Then substituting in the rigorous equations of condition, the values of a, b, c, etc., derived from the observed quantities, we obtain thirty-six equations of the form

$$\text{(I.)} \qquad \begin{array}{c} n' + \alpha - \beta + h = 0 \\ n'' + \alpha - \gamma + i = 0 \\ \text{etc., etc.,} \\ n^{\text{vii}} + \beta - \gamma + o = 0 \\ \text{etc., etc.} \end{array}$$

And introducing the correlatives (1), (2), (3), (4), etc., so as to satisfy the conditions of "least squares," we form twenty-three new conditional equations containing only these correlatives, the weights p', p'', p''', etc., and the unknown quantities α, β, γ, etc., in the form

$$\text{(II.)}\quad \begin{array}{l} (1)+(2)+(3)+(4)+(5)+(6)-p'\,\alpha=0 \\ -(1)+(7)+(8)+(9)+(10)+(11)-p''\,\beta=0 \\ -(2)-(7)-(12)+(13)+(14)+(15)-p'''\,\gamma=0 \\ -(3)-(8)+(12)+(16)+(17)+(18)-p''''\,\delta=0 \\ \text{etc., etc.} \end{array}$$

Substituting now in the equations I. the values of α, β, γ, etc., as derived from the series II., we obtain thirty-six normal equations containing only the known quantities n', n'', n''', etc., together with the thirty-six unknown correlatives (1), (2), (3), etc.; and thus affording the most probable values of these correlatives for determining the desired corrections α, β, γ, from the series of equations II.[1]

Even this simple process necessarily becomes exceedingly onerous in such a case as the present, which demands the numerical solution of thirty-six equations containing an equal number of unknown quantities. Still we have not shrunk from this labor, even when the incorporation of Major Wales's observations raised the number of equations to 62. After it became evident that these must be excluded from the series and the work repeated, the rigorous solution was not reattempted, but closely approximate values were deduced by sundry devices of numerical computation. Thus we obtain the following results, which are entitled to full confidence. Mr. Phinney's measures are selected as the basis of comparison, both because they are near the mean of all, and on account of the very satisfactory character of their mutual accordance.

Phinney	— Buckley	=	— 3°.873
"	— Baker	=	+ 1.743
"	— Russell	=	— 5.387
"	— Myers	=	— 2.989
"	— Elsner	=	+ 1.667
"	— Lewis	=	+ 2.381
"	— Smith	=	— 2.635
"	— Wilder	=	— 2.579
"	— Stark	=	+ 0.632
"	— Wells	=	— 2.114
"	— Avery		+ 7.858
"	— Furniss	=	+ 4.687

[1] For the details of this method in its general form, see Gauss, *Supplem. Theoriæ Combinationis*, pp. 16 *et seqq.* and Chauvenet, *Spher. and Pract. Astron.*, II. pp. 552–57.

The last four of these values have been deduced on the assumption that the preceding eight were absolutely correct, and probably differ by entirely unimportant amounts from those which would have been obtained had they been included in the original solution.

In the entire series of nearly eighty personal differences, only four, of those which depend upon so many as twenty comparisons, are found to require a change of their observed values by so much as four tenths of a degree, to produce the entire accordance and consistency which has been attained. The greatest change was 0°.800, required by the difference "Russell — Myers," which depended upon only 266 comparisons as follows: —

	No.	Difference
White Men	78	+ 2°.868
Mulattoes born in Slave States . . .	44	+ 1.284
Full Blacks born in Slave States . .	144	+ 1.005
Mean	266	+ 1.598
Adopted value		+ 2.398

The rejection of Major Wales's facial angles will be justified by a tabular view showing the nature of the discrepancy.

	Wales — Baker		Wales — Russell		Wales — Myers		Wales — Elsner	
	No. of Men	Difference	No. of Men	Difference	No. of Men	Difference	No. of Men	Difference
White Men	28	+ 3°.783	28	- 3°.730	28	- 0°.862	28	+ 3°.728
Mulattoes Free States	–	–	48	- 1.321	–	–	–	–
Mulattoes Sl. States	53	+ 6.575	80	- 0.027	44	+ 1.257	–	–
Full Blacks Fr. States	–	–	28	- 0.187	–	–	23	+ 1.717
Full Blacks Sl. States	322	+ 7.292	162	+ 0.582	144	+ 1.587	–	–

The impossibility of deducing trustworthy results from these data needs no comment, and no entirely satisfactory explanation of the discordance has been found. A gradual unrecognized change in the manner of measuring seems to offer the most plausible solution of the difficulty.

The values of personal equation now deduced must be applied to all the facial angles excepting those measured by Major Wales. The results will then be essentially such as they would have been had all been measured by Mr. Phinney, and the work of the various examiners may be aggregated without hesitation. Thus we obtain the following table of results: —

TABLE XVI.

Mean Facial Angles of Different Classes of Men,

corrected for Personal Equation.

Class	Number of Examiners	Number of Cases	Facial Angle
			°
White Soldiers and Sailors	13	9365	72.082
Students	1	290	73.874
Full Blacks born in Free States	6	63	70.133
Full Blacks born in Slave States	8	663	68.736
Total Full Blacks	8	726	68.857
Mulattoes born in Free States	6	79	69.897
Mulattoes born in Slave States	7	406	69.104
Total Mulattoes	7	485	69.233
Indians	1	505	72.864

The values given in this table are probably entitled to full reliance, at least to the first decimal figure inclusive.

Of the facts thus brought to light, the most noticeable are the large mean values for students and Indians, surpassing those for all the other classes, — the marked superiority in the mean facial angle of natives of the Free States over natives of the Slave States; and the comparatively low values for the black race. The preeminent values found for students and for Indians do not seem referable in any degree to personal equation, although but one examiner was employed for each of these groups; since in both cases the correction for personal difference is well established, and has already been applied.

Considering next the white men by themselves (excluding students), and classifying them according to their nativities, we obtain the results following: —

TABLE XVII.

Mean Facial Angles of White Soldiers and Sailors,

corrected for Personal Equation.

Nativity	Soldiers			Sailors			Aggregate		
	No. of Exam-iners	No. of Men	Facial Angle	No. of Exam-iners	No. of Men	Facial Angle	No. of Exam-iners	No. of Men	Facial Angle
A	11	1 049	72.09°	2	94	72.63°	11	1 143	72.139°
B	12	2 829	72.09	2	50	73.00	12	2 879	72.102
C	9	1 406	72.18	2	2	68.08	9	1 408	72.169
D	9	929	72.08	1	1	76.67	9	930	72.081
E	11	321	71.98	2	8	71.85	11	329	71.978
F	9	225	71.32	1	1	67.17	9	226	71.301
G_1	5	12	71.53	1	1	66.67	5	13	71.156
G_2	8	30	72.93	–	–	–	8	30	72.934
H	11	32	72.86	2	23	72.67	11	55	72.782
I	9	343	71.75	2	12	70.25	9	355	71.700
J	10	271	72.09	2	53	73.51	10	324	72.320
K	9	65	71.82	2	17	71.65	9	82	71.785
L	11	732	71.93	2	132	72.72	11	864	72.055
M	9	69	72.41	2	12	74.46	9	81	72.714
N	11	479	72.06	2	23	72.30	11	502	72.075
O	8	33	72.12	2	47	72.09	8	80	72.103
P	4	6	72.57	2	10	70.92	5	16	71.538
Q	9	35	71.81	2	13	71.37	9	48	71.699
Total	13	8 866	72.055	2	499	72.561	13	9 365	72.082

Here there appears to be no sufficient ground for inferring any decided difference in the facial angle, connected with the nativity. Those nativity-groups for which the mean values vary most from the mean of all are composed of the least numbers of men, and it is noteworthy that of the first six groups of the aggregate column in order of magnitude, including all those which consist of so many as four hundred men, the maximum variation from the mean of all is but 5′.

The absolute values, here given, are of course dependent to a certain extent upon the correctness of Mr. Phinney's work, since all the measurements have been referred to him as the standard. But it will be borne in mind that his mean value is closely accord ant with the mean of the aggregate of those other examiners whose experience was greatest, and whose accuracy is best established by the character of their results.

The diversity of the mean values found for soldiers and for sailors seems unimportant, in view of the small number in the latter class ; and we may be justified in inferring that the average facial angle among white men, as represented in the American army and navy, does not vary by one fifth of a degree, or 12′, from our final value 72°.1, — while for the negroes, whether of pure blood or mulattoes, it is below 70°.

Our next table exhibits the range of variation found in the several classes of men examined.

TABLE XVIII.

Greatest and Least Facial Angles observed.

Nativity	Largest Value		Smallest Value	
	Angle	Remarks	Angle	Remarks
	°		°	
White Soldiers . .	85.7	Ohio or Ind. ; Elsner, Ex.	55.0	Ireland ; Phinney Ex.
Sailors	86.7	Eng. and Ireland, 1 each	56.7	Middle Sts. ; Elsner "
Students	81.7	1 each of 5 diff'nt nations	61.7	New England States
Full Blacks, Fr. Sts.	85.7	No other above 74.6 .	61.7	Elsner, Examiner
Full Blacks, Sl. Sts.	84.7	Two others of 80° . .	56.7	Baker, "
Mulattoes, Fr. Sts.	75.6	Russell, Examiner . .	63.6	Russell, "
Mulattoes, Sl. Sts.	79.0	Myers, " . .	59.0	Myers, "
Indians	76.6	Buckley, " (2 cases)	66.6	Buckley, "

When the facial angle was measured by using the superciliary ridge instead of the frontal eminence, the mean value was greater, by the following amounts : —

Examiner	Excess	No. Obs.
	°	
Buckley	4.853	50
Baker	7.516	333
Phinney	3.883	508
Lewis	8.662	144
Myers	2.841	78
Smith	2.744	256
	5.028	1 369

The "number of observations" in the last column is the number made in the erroneous manner, which was always less than that made in the manner prescribed. The great variation in the mean values found by different examiners is probably due, to some extent, to actual differences in the classes of men chiefly measured; but a very small amount of experience will show how easily slight differences of personal habitude in measuring will produce large differences in the determination of the angle.

The final mean shows that 5° is a reasonable estimate for the excess of the angle when the superciliary ridge is used. For negroes this excess is probably a little greater, but will hardly reach the limit of 6°.

CHAPTER XI.

WEIGHT AND STRENGTH.

1. *Determination of Weight, and its Relation to Stature.*

EACH examiner was specially provided with Fairbanks's platform scales, of the best construction. The scales are graduated[1] to quarters of a pound, but the weight was generally recorded only to the nearest half-pound.

In the discussion of our results, the estimated weight of the clothing has in all cases been subtracted. Very accordant weighings of 24 suits of clothing such as was worn by most of the men during their examination, different sizes being employed in the proportions issued by the Quartermaster's department, as nearly as could be estimated, gave the results: —

24 pairs trowsers .	37 lbs. 10 oz.,	Mean 1.57 lbs.
24 sets underclothing	39 " 5 "	Mean 1.64 "
Total . . .	76 " 15 "	Mean 3.21 "

The underclothing consisted of woolen shirts, drawers, and stockings.

The mean weights, for the total of all the men measured, are given in the first of our tables, together with the number of men from which each mean has been deduced.

[1] The author's regret has been already expressed that the measures and weights throughout these investigations were not taken and recorded in units of the metric system. A table for the reciprocal conversion of kilograms and pounds, as well as of centimeters and inches, is given at the end of this volume. The pounds used are the legal pounds ("avoirdupois") of 453.59 grams each. [1 kilogram = 2.2046 lbs.]

TABLE I.

Average Weight of Men examined.

Class of Men	In usual Vigor		Not in usual Vigor		Total	
	Number	Pounds	Number	Pounds	Number	Pounds
White Soldiers, Earlier Series	5 936	143.49	2 162	140.99	8 098	142.83
White Soldiers, Later Series .	9 157	142.08	1 600	137.35	10 757	141.38
Sailors	1 144	138.92	–	–	1 144	138.92
Students	288	136.51	–	–	288	136.51
Full Blacks	1 775	143.83	226	142.62	2 001	144.58
Mulattoes	680	145.12	140	143.15	820	144.78
Indians	507	162.82	9	148.01	516	162.56

Assorting the weights according to the nativities of the men, we find the means to be as given in the next two tables, in which the results of the earlier and the later series of examinations are kept distinct from each other.

TABLE II.

Average Weight of White Soldiers by Nativities.

(*Earlier Series.*)

Nativity	In usual Vigor		Not in usual Vigor		Total	
	Number	Weight	Number	Weight	Number	Weight
		lbs.		lbs.		lbs.
New England	589	142.60	350	142.89	939	142.71
New York	1 521	145.15	546	142.58	2 067	144.47
New Jersey and Penn. .	849	144.64	364	140.32	1 213	143.35
Ohio & other West. States	413	148.73	187	144.26	600	147.34
Slave States	1 659	140.64	375	137.16	2 034	140.00
Canada	135	144.73	50	141.70	185	143.91
England and Scotland .	159	140.96	72	134.82	231	139.04
Ireland	350	142.99	122	141.11	472	142.50
Germany	191	143.77	76	140.39	267	142.81
Miscellaneous	70	143.59	20	139.59	90	142.70
Total	5 936	143.49	2 162	140.99	8 098	142.83

TABLE III.

Average Weight of White Soldiers, by Nativities.

(*Later Series.*)

Nativity	In usual Vigor		Not in usual Vigor		Total	
	Number	Weight	Number	Weight	Number	Weight
		lbs.		lbs.		lbs.
New England	974	140.05	211	136.11	1 185	139.39
N. Y., N. J., and Penn. .	3 139	141.39	588	137.43	3 727	140.83
Ohio and Indiana . . .	1 442	145.99	218	141.24	1 660	145.37
Mich., Wisc., and Illinois	944	141.78	71	139.72	1 015	141.78
Coast Slave States . .	301	142.08	52	134.68	353	140.99
Kentucky and Tennessee	223	150.58	44	146.10	267	149.85
Free Sts. west Miss. River	10	145.09	–	–	10	145.09
Sl. Sts. west Miss. River	38	135.76	5	128.59	43	134.95
Br. Am. Pr. excl. Canada	35	143.82	2	139.54	37	143.59
Canada	474	141.26	45	142.28	519	141.35
England	258	138.15	45	134.58	303	137.61
Wales and Isle of Man .	18	138.05	2	148.09	20	139.13
Scotland	70	138.71	11	132.38	81	137.85
Ireland	644	141.08	177	132.26	821	139.18
France, Belgium, etc. . .	80	138.76	16	133.35	96	137.85
Germany	448	141.06	99	137.27	547	140.37
Scandinavia	28	150.28	6	138.12	34	148.14
Spain, etc.	6	138.16	1	109.79	7	134.15
Miscellaneous	25	140.31	7	126.58	32	137.31
Total	9 157	142.08	1 600	137.35	10 757	141.38

The degree of trustworthiness of the mean weights as tested by the accordance between the actual and theoretical distribution of the individual weights is very satisfactory, and the range of variation in all appears analogous to that in the nativities A and C, which are [1] as follows : —

[1] See foot-note to page 275.

Nativity	Mean Weight	Number of Men	r	r_0
	lbs.		lbs.	lbs.
New England States	140.06	953	10.853	0.351
Ohio and Indiana	145.99	1 417	11.383	0.302

TABLE IV.

Average Weight of Colored Men.

Class	In usual Vigor		Not in usual Vigor		Total	
	Number	Weight	Number	Weight	Number	Weight
		lbs.		lbs.		lbs.
Full Blacks, Natives of Fr. Sts.	192	144.60	32	144.93	224	144.65
" " " " Sl. "	1 583	144.86	194	142.24	1 777	144.58
Mulattoes, Natives of Free Sts.	125	141.51[a]	40	145.04	165	142.37
" " " Sl. "	555	145.93	100	142.40	655	145.39
Total Full Blacks . . .	1 775	144.83	226	142.62	2 001	144.58
Total Mulattoes	680	145.12	140	143.15	820	144.78

It is manifest that the variations of the mean weight with the nativity must be closely commensurate with those of the mean stature ; and, in order to determine the degree to which these elements are independent of one another, the Tables V., VI., and VII. have been prepared, exhibiting for each nativity-group the ratio of weight to stature, or in other words the weight in pounds corresponding to each inch of stature. These have not been prepared by dividing the mean weights by the mean heights, but have been computed for each individual case ; and the accuracy of the results here also tested where the numbers are sufficiently large, by the character of the distribution of individual weights around their mean. They apply to men in full vigor, exclusively.

[a] If we omit the forty-five members of the two Massachusetts colored infantry regiments, which appear to have been composed of men much lighter than the average of their class, the mean weight of the remaining eighty men is 143 lbs. The average age of these forty-five men was a year and a half less than that of the other colored soldiers measured.

TABLE V.

Ratio of Weight to Stature for White Soldiers.

(*Earlier Series.*)

Nativity	No. of Men	Pounds to Inch	Nativity	No. of Men	Pounds to Inch
		lbs.			lbs.
New England . . .	589	2.121	England & Scotland	159	2.118
New York	1 521	2.161	Ireland	350	2.144
New Jersey & Penn.	849	2.146	Germany	191	2.168
Ohio & other W. Sts.	413	2.185	Miscellaneous . . .	70	2.167
Slave States . . .	1 659	2.010			
Canada	135	2.161			
			Total	5 936	2.1110

TABLE VI.

Ratio of Weight to Stature for White Soldiers and Sailors.

(*Later Series.*)

Nativity	Soldiers		Sailors		Total	
	Number	Pounds to Inch	Number	Pounds to Inch	Number	Pounds to Inch
New England	974	2.082	129	2.018	1 103	2.075
N. Y., N. J., and Penn. .	3 139	2.107	155	2.003	3 294	2.102
Ohio and Indiana . . .	1 442	2.153	2	1.984	1 444	2 153
Mich., Wisc., & Illinois .	944	2.106	6	2.122	950	2.106
Coast Slave States . . .	301	2.099	19	2.021	320	2.094
Kentucky and Tennessee	223	2.190	1	2.620	224	2.192
Free Sts. west Miss. River	10	2.136	–	–	10	2.136
Sl. Sts. west Miss. River	38	2.025	1	1.827	39	2.020
Br. Am. Pr. excl. Canada	35	2.133	50	2.121	85	2.126
Canada	474	2.110	16	2.242	490	2.114
England	258	2.083	102	2.024	360	2.066
Wales, and Isle of Man .	18	2.064	6	2.000	24	2.048
Scotland	70	2.090	27	2.075	97	2.086
Ireland	644	2.114	335	2.060	979	2.096
France, Belgium, etc. . .	80	2.106	20	2.082	100	2.101
Germany	448	2.126	62	2.104	510	2.123
Scandinavia	28	2.203	82	2.143	110	2.158
Spain, etc.	6	2.114	18	2.034	24	2.054
Miscellaneous	25	2.081	30	2.049	55	2.064
Total	9 157	2.0432	1 061	2.0547	10 218	2.0444

For the ratio between weight and stature we find —

Nativity	Average Ratio	Number of Men	r	r_0
New England States . . .	2.083	953	0.135	0.0044
New York, New Jersey, Penn.	2.106	3 088	0.142	0.0026
Ohio and Indiana	2.152	1 417	0.139	0.0037

TABLE VII.

Ratio of Weight to Stature for other Classes of Men.

Class	Number of Men	Pounds to the Inch
Students	288	2.001
Full Blacks, Natives of Free States	192	2.176
" " " " Slave "	1 583	2.184
" " Total	1 775	2.183
Mulattoes, Natives of Free States .	125	2.127
" " " Slave "	555	2.198
" Total	680	2.185
Indians	507	2.384

Could we assume that the ratio of weight to stature remains the same for all heights, the foregoing values would enable us easily to construct tables giving closely approximate values of the weight of our soldiers and sailors in usual vigor, during the war ; the former well representing the average of the male population of military age, taken in the proportions in which they enlisted, as developed in Chapters III. and IV. But this assumption is far from correct, as will be seen when the men are assorted according to their height, and the mean weights determined for the several statures. This is done in Table VIII., which contains the mean weight for each half inch of height, for each class of white men (in usual vigor) examined.

The next subsequent table, IX., exhibits the mean height of the aggregate of these men for each half-inch of stature, and the corresponding ratios of weight to height. It will be seen that in this latter respect the increase is progressive, throughout the limits of stature included in our collection of materials. To some extent this may be attributed to the influence of age, since the lower statures manifestly belong in greater proportion to youths whose

TABLE VIII.

Mean Weights of White Men, by Height.

Height	Soldiers						Sailors		Students	
	Earlier Series		Later Series		Total		Number	Weight	Number	Weight
	No.	Weight	No.	Weight	No.	Weight				
in.		lbs.		lbs.		lbs.		lbs.		lbs.
Under 60	11	94.34	22	97.22	33	96.26	3	98.26	–	–
60	4	115.91	11	107.58	15	109.80	9	115.11	–	–
60½	11	114.11	23	114.70	34	114.51	10	120.08	–	–
61	25	119.03	26	119.13	51	119.08	6	118.33	–	–
61½	24	122.19	40	117.48	64	119.24	22	120.97	–	–
62	50	123.62	88	119.24	138	120.83	34	123.28	–	–
62½	70	123.45	117	119.52	187	120.99	30	120.94	–	–
63	99	124.31	159	124.30	258	124.30	35	125.57	1	108.79
63½	161	126.52	236	126.60	397	126.57	51	127.93	7	118.15
64	182	129.67	315	129.61	497	129.63	76	131.89	3	119.62
64½	255	133.29	469	130.42	724	131.43	81	132.68	11	121.93
65	260	134.11	463	132.01	723	132.77	85	134.11	12	126.46
65½	383	135.59	664	135.06	1 047	135.25	104	136.40	21	123.18
66	363	136.86	521	137.55	884	137.27	76	137.16	16	131.13
66½	446	139.80	810	139.04	1 256	139.31	81	141.41	21	131.60
67	419	142.80	763	141.96	1 182	142.26	88	144.67	13	130.44
67½	526	144.98	853	144.16	1 379	144.47	81	145.40	23	128.54
68	464	146.22	701	145.78	1 165	145.95	55	146.91	26	132.25
68½	481	148.99	688	147.69	1 169	148.22	61	152.88	18	139.43
69	378	150.03	473	150.49	851	150.28	42	148.97	24	142.54
69½	312	151.53	457	153.35	769	152.61	45	151.52	22	140.24
70	273	154.81	323	154.54	596	154.66	18	157.54	19	145.32
70½	212	157.39	250	157.44	462	157.42	20	157.99	15	150.59
71	148	159.58	183	160.12	331	159.88	8	152.25	9	155.85
71½	110	159.85	135	164.70	245	162.52	11	162.37	13	154.10
72	76	159.43	118	165.84	194	163.33	4	157.00	2	139.79
72½	55	164.37	80	165.56	135	165.08	1	168.00	4	163.16
73	39	170.35	47	168.41	86	169.29	3	165.00	3	148.12
73½	20	164.06	34	170.82	54	168.32	1	175.00	1	149.79
74	17	164.76	25	171.14	42	168.56	2	191.64	1	190.79
74½	10	170.79	6	178.21	16	173.57	–	–	1	171.79
75	8	164.79	4	165.79	12	165.12	1	204.00	1	147.79
Over 75	4	176.29	18	174.90	22	175.15	–	–	1	142.79

full stature is not yet attained, and in whom the lateral development of the body, which is normally completed at a still later date, has by no means kept pace with the longitudinal growth. But a very slight additional study of the numbers will suffice to show the inadequacy of this explanation.

TABLE IX.

Aggregate Mean Weight of White Men, by Height, and Ratio to Stature.

Height	Number of Men	Weight	Pounds to Inch	Height	Number of Men	Weight	Pounds to Inch
in.		lbs.		in.		lbs.	
60	24	111.79	1.863	68	1 246	145.71	2.143
60½	44	115.78	1.914	68½	1 248	148.32	2.165
61	57	119.00	1.951	69	917	150.02	2.174
61½	86	119.68	1.946	69½	836	152.23	2.190
62	172	121.31	1.957	70	633	154.46	2.207
62½	217	120.98	1.936	70½	497	157.24	2.230
63	294	124.40	1.975	71	348	159.60	2.248
63½	455	126.59	1.994	71½	269	162.11	2.267
64	576	129.88	2.029	72	200	162.97	2.263
64½	816	131.43	2.038	72½	140	165.04	2.276
65	820	132.81	2.043	73	92	168.46	2.308
65½	1 172	135.14	2.063	73½	56	168.11	2.287
66	976	137.16	2.078	74	45	170.08	2.298
66½	1 358	139.32	2.095	74½	17	173.47	2.328
67	1 283	142.31	2.124	75	14	166.66	2.222
67½	1 483	144.27	2.137	Over 75	23	173.75	2.286

It is clear that in similar bodies, of the same material, the masses must vary as the cubes of any dimension; so that, did the average proportions remain unchanged in men of different stature, we might expect their weights to be to one another as the third powers of their heights. Very slight investigation, however, is required to show that this is by no means the case. The differences of stature among the men weighed are in great part due to differences in their degree of physical development, and in great part also to differences in their normal dimensions at maturity; so that the only mode of discriminating between the effects of these two influences is by a classification of the individuals on the twofold basis of age and stature. This has been done, and the results will be found in the ensuing section; but we are here considering the statures only, and — notwithstanding the irregularities which might reasonably have been anticipated from the unequal combination of the two sources of variation at the different statures — we are irresistibly led to the singular and interesting discovery that the mean weights, at least within the limits of the present researches, appear to vary strictly as the squares of the statures. This is made manifest by Table X., which gives for each stature the hypothetical weight based on this assumption (using the modulus 0.03156), and in the next column the difference between this hypothetical, or as we may fairly say, theoretical, weight, and the mean weights actually obtained by observation, and presented in Table IX. No reasonable doubt seems admissible that this is the true law of normal variation in weight for statures within our limits, and we are thus led to the inference that the product of the ratios of increase in the breadth and thickness of the body is on the average equal to the simple ratio of the increase in length.

TABLE X.

Theoretical Weight for different Statures, and Comparison with Observation.

Height	Computed Weight	Difference Comp.— Obs.	Height	Computed Weight	Difference Comp.— Obs.
in.	lbs.	lbs.	in.	lbs.	lbs.
60	113.62	+ 1.83	68	145.94	+ 0.23
60½	115.52	- 0.26	68½	148.09	- 0.23
61	117.44	- 1.56	69	150.26	+ 0.24
61½	119.37	- 0.31	69½	152.45	+ 0.22
62	121.32	+ 0.01	70	154.65	+ 0.19
62½	123.28	+ 2.30	70½	156.87	- 0.37
63	125.27	+ 0.87	71	159.10	- 0.50
63½	127.26	+ 0.67	71½	161.35	- 0.76
64	129.27	+ 0.61	72	163.61	+ 0.64
64½	131.30	- 0.13	72½	165.89	+ 0.85
65	133.34	+ 0.53	73	163.19	- 5.27
65½	135.40	+ 0.26	73½	170.50	+ 2.39
66	137.48	+ 0.32	74	172.83	+ 2.75
66½	139.57	+ 0.25	74½	175.17	+ 1.70
67	141.68	- 0.63	75	177.53	–
67½	143.80	- 0.47	Over 75	–	–

The fact here elicited was observed by Quetelet, who says,[1]

[1] *Sur l'Homme*, II. 53, 61.

"During the period of development, the squares of the weights at different ages are as the fifth powers of the stature," but "the weights of individuals of different heights who have attained their full development are approximately as the squares of their statures."

It is remarkable that with the limited number of cases upon which his generalizations were necessarily based, he should have been able to detect the actual law,[1] which, however, seems to be much more rigorously true than he suspected. Even during the period of growth subsequent to the age of about 16 years, the increase in weight appears nearer to the 2nd than to the $2\frac{1}{2}$th power of the stature, although when extended to the earliest years of life it evidently requires modification. The corresponding results for the weight of boys would be, according to the formula —

Height	Weight
inches	lbs.
15	7.10
20	12.62
25	19.72
30	28.40
35	38.66
40	50.50
45	63.91
50	78.90
55	95.47

which manifestly give weights too large. The circumstance to which Quetelet himself calls attention, that his statistics for children were collected from classes of society less favored, and in less easy circumstances, than those which furnished the statistics for the more advanced ages, may account for the apparent deviation of his own results in the other direction. The facts now available for testing the question are altogether too meager to warrant any definite conclusions as to the inferior limit to which the ratio between weight and the square of height, remains constant.

The results obtained by Quetelet we will here reproduce for the sake of comparison, both in their original form. and as reduced to the units of weight and measure employed in the present investigation.

1 *Systême Sociale*, p. 43.

Mean Weight of Belgian Males, by Stature, according to Quetelet.

Stature	Weight	Stature	Weight
centimeters	kilograms	in.	lbs.
50	3.20	19.69	7.06
60	6.20	23.62	13.67
70	9.30	27.56	20.51
80	11.36	31.50	25.06
90	13.50	35.44	29.78
100	15.90	39.37	35.07
110	18.50	43.31	40.80
120	21.72	47.24	47.91
130	26.63	51.18	58.74
140	34.48	51.12	76.05
150	46.29	59.06	102.10
160	57.15	62.99	126.05
170	63.28	66.93	139.57
180	70.61	70.87	155.74
190	75.56	74.80	166.66

It may not be without interest also to compare our results with those deduced by still other investigators.

Hutchinson,[1] from the weights of 2648 men "at the middle period of life" taken from all classes of society, deduced the values given in the second column of the following table. Since the weight of the clothing was included in these results, we add a third column for the supposed true weight, determined according to the rule of Quetelet, approvingly cited by Hutchinson, which makes the average weight of men's clothing to be one eighteenth part of the weight of the body.[2]

[1] *Medico-Chirurgical Transactions*, XXIX. 165, 166.

[2] *Sur l'Homme*, II. 44.

Observed Mean Weight of Englishmen according to Hutchinson.

Stature	Recorded Weight	True Weight
in.	lbs.	lbs.
61	119.9	113.6
62	126.1	119.5
63	132.9	125.9
64	138.6	131.3
65	142.1	134.6
66	144.6	137.0
67	148.4	140.6
68	155.2	147.0
69	162.1	153.6
70	168.6	159.7
71	174.2	165.0

From these observations Hutchinson concluded[1] that the weights increased in the ratio of the $2\frac{3}{4}$th powers of the height, and that the average increment of weight for each inch of height, within the limits of ordinary stature, was about 5.43 pounds.

Our own statistics make this increment about $4\frac{1}{4}$ pounds for each inch — the value deduced from statures between five and six feet being 4.265, and that from a somewhat wider range, 4.253 pounds.

Mr. Elliott, in his learned paper presented to the Statistical Congress of 1863, cites[2] the mean weight of the 27 853 recruits to the British army in 1860, from the official statistical report[3] of that year, as 128 pounds, their mean age being 21.4 years and their mean stature 66.2 inches; and that of 12 191 recruits in the year 1861 as 131 pounds, corresponding to the mean age 21.0 years, and the stature 66.8 inches. The statures are not comparable with those of the American army, on account of the minimum limit for enlistments, which varied from 64 to 68 inches during these two years; but the mean weights corresponding to the mean statures are fairly comparable, on the assumption that the men were weighed without clothing and measured without their shoes.

Boudin, in the very able and comprehensive article already alluded to, which the writer has only succeeded in obtaining since

1 *Medico-Chirurgical Transactions*, XXIX., 168.

2 *On the Military Statistics of the United States of America*, pp. 17, 21.

3 *Statistical, Sanitary, and Medical Reports for the year* 1860. — *Army Medical Department.* 1862.

the completion of the present treatise, gives[1] the statistics of weight and height of the French regiment of mounted *chasseurs* of the guard, which had been determined for him by Mr. Allaire, the regimental surgeon. In this regiment of picked men, 705 were examined; their mean height being found to be 167.9 centimeters [66.10 in.], and their mean weight 64.5 kilograms [142.26 lbs.]. Mr. Elliott states[2] that the mean age of these men was 30 years.

M. Boudin farther quotes[3] from the Report of a British official commission "On the Sanitary Condition of Large Cities," the following statistics of the mean stature and weight of men of four European countries. Neither the sources of information are given, nor any account of the classes of men, nor any of the conditions or circumstances of the measurement. For England, at least, there is room for very strong suspicion that the weight of the clothing is included in the given weight of the men, and the height of the average of their boot-heels added to their mean stature.

Nation	Stature	Weight
	in.	lbs.
Belgium . . .	66½	140½
Sweden . . .	67	141
Russia. . . .	68	143
England . . .	69	151

In these data the relations of weight to stature are not dissimilar to those which would be inferred from our Table VIII., except for the Russians, whose weight would according to that table be two or three pounds greater, or their stature three quarters of an inch less. Possibly the stature may include their shoes, while the weight of their clothing has been deducted from their total weight.

Considering next the variation in weight for different men of the same height, and still confining ourselves to the white race and to men in full vigor, we obtain the two following tables, which present the maxima and minima observed at each half-inch of stature; the ages of the individuals being also given, together with the total number of men among whom these extreme values were found.

[1] *Recueil de Mémoires de Médecine, de Chirurgie, et de Pharmacie Militaires*, IX., 194.
[2] *Military Statistics of the United States of America*, p. 17.
[3] *Recueil*, etc., IX., 195.

TABLE XI.

Limits of Weight observed at Different Statures.
White Soldiers.

(*Earlier Series.*)

Height	No. of Men	Maximum		Minimum		Range
		Weight	Age	Weight	Age	
		lbs.		lbs.		lbs.
Under 60	11	116.8	22	72.8	14	44.0
60	4	136.8	35	98.8	24	38.0
60½	11	132.3	22	99.3	14	33.0
61	25	159.8	27	89.3	14	70.5
61½	24	140.3	23	95.3	15	45.0
62	50	153.8	25	98.8	17	55.0
62½	70	155.8	22	94.8	16	61.0
63	99	153.8	20	101.8	23	52.0
63½	161	162.3	19	87.3	15	75.0
64	182	163.8	27	100.8	20	63.0
64½	255	178.8	37	96.3	22	82.5
65	260	175.8	44	98.3	18	77.5
65½	383	174.8	25	102.3	19	72.5
66	363	175.3	19	101.8	19	73.5
66½	446	224.3	30	99.8	20	124.5
67	419	202.3	18	101.8	31	100.5
67½	526	205.3	25	107.3	24	98.0
68	464	188.8	25	99.3	20	89.5
68½	481	197.8	21	102.8	19	95.0
69	378	200.8	44	107.8	18	80.0
69½	312	191.8	28	102.8	23	89.0
70	273	193.3	18	110.8	18	82.5
70½	212	194.8	27	121.3	19	73.5
71	148	195.8	23	127.8	27	68.0
71½	110	228.3	37	119.3	17	109.0
72	76	196.8	31	112.3	36	84.5
72½	55	191.8	38	138.8	19	53.0
73	39	206.8	29	137.3	22	69.5
73½	20	206.8	22	118.8	24	88.0
74	17	184.8	23	136.3	28	48.5
74½	10	209.8	38	158.8	21	51.0
75	8	205.8	26	145.3	29	60.5
Over 75	4	205.3	20	155.8	25	49.5

TABLE XII.

Limits of Weight observed at Different Statures.
White Soldiers.

(*Later Series.*)

Height	No. of Men	Maximum		Minimum		Range
		Weight	Age	Weight	Age	
		lbs.		lbs.		lbs.
Under 60	22	125.8	25	64.8	19	61.0
60	11	137.3	26	91.8	17	45.5
60½	23	136.8	21	96.8	16	40.0
61	26	144.3	21	91.8	16	52.5
61½	40	158.8	38	94.8	21	64.0
62	88	154.8	25	90.8	17	64.0
62½	117	151.8	27	96.8	21	55.0
63	159	146.8	23	98.8	16	48.0
63½	236	169.8	24	91.8	16	78.0
64	315	163.3	36	95.8	22	67.5
64½	469	166.8	43	98.8	17	68.0
65	463	175.3	18	98.3	18	77.0
65½	664	173.8	41	101.3	19	72.5
66	521	184.8	33	107.3	18	77.5
66½	810	194.8	36	104.8	17	90.0
67	763	196.8	25	110.3	21	86.5
67½	853	206.8	25	99.8	17	107.0
68	701	213.8	27	111.3	23	102.5
68½	688	213.8	24	107.8	16	106.0
69	473	219.8	30	115.8	17	104.0
69½	457	196.8	54	113.8	27	83.0
70	323	196.8	43	107.8	18	89.0
70½	250	207.8	42	127.8	22	80.0
71	183	213.8	53	123.8	27	90.0
71½	135	209.8	24	116.8	29	93.0
72	118	202.8	25	133.8	26	69.0
72½	80	200.8	28	137.3	21	63.5
73	47	200.8	35	138.8	24	62.0
73½	34	201.8	38	144.8	21	57.0
74	25	209.8	44	145.8	27	64.0
74½	6	191.8	21	150.8	35	41.0
75	4	172.8	19	157.8	36	15.0
Over 75	18	192.8	29	150.8	23	42.0

When we subject the weights of the negroes and Indians to a similar discussion, we find the numbers of men in the several height-groups insufficient for establishing any definite law for weight as dependent upon stature, although the indications are decided that a relation holds good for these other races similar to that which we have found to exist in the white race.

Our statistics for the full blacks, mulattoes, and Indians, in usual vigor, are assorted by height in the following table.

TABLE XIII.

Mean Weights of Negroes and Indians, by Height.

Height	Full Blacks		Mulattoes		Aggregate		Indians	
	No.	Weight	No.	Weight	No.	Weight	No.	Weight
		lbs.		lbs.		lbs.		lbs.
Under 60	9	116.83	2	117.11	11	116.88	–	–
60	5	118.10	3	121.12	8	119.23	–	–
60½	13	124.51	5	123.87	18	124.33	–	–
61	12	122.52	4	128.66	16	124.05	–	–
61½	19	126.85	10	123.52	29	125.70	–	–
62	33	128.68	3	139.89	36	129.61	–	–
62½	43	130.38	25	130.56	68	130.45	1	133.79
63	48	131.84	35	131.22	83	131.58	–	–
63½	73	130.31	30	136.71	103	132.17	–	–
64	74	136.46	46	136.65	120	136.53	1	132.29
64½	102	138.63	47	138.89	149	138.71	2	164.04
65	105	140.71	41	144.21	146	141.69	4	140.04
65½	110	139.94	54	142.49	164	140.78	22	143.36
66	137	140.75	57	143.30	194	141.50	9	146.79
66½	122	144.01	62	149.96	184	146.01	25	143.13
67	135	146.52	44	147.94	179	146.87	25	153.39
67½	116	150.65	60	150.32	176	150.54	116	154.44
68	102	151.81	32	150.99	134	151.61	54	157.84
68½	93	153.74	33	152.70	126	153.47	111	167.12
69	74	156.24	30	158.70	104	156.95	21	168.26
69½	57	159.07	23	157.39	80	158.59	50	174.38
70	32	162.83	21	156.56	53	160.35	17	176.82
70½	32	162.89	8	157.52	40	161.82	22	185.24
71	15	166.50	11	157.32	26	162.62	5	188.19
71½	22	170.02	9	171.56	31	170.47	8	186.29
72	14	167.10	6	163.31	20	165.96	2	209.29
72½	8	170.28	4	180.29	12	173.62	8	198.04
73	3	166.46	–	–	3	166.46	1	197.79
73½	1	164.79	–	–	1	164.79	1	166.79
74	1	212.00	–	–	1	212.00	1	196.79
74½	–	–	1	170.79	1	170.79	–	–
75	–	–	–	–	–	–	–	–
Over 75	3	173.53	2	163.11	5	169.36	1	190.29

Assuming the law of increase according to the square of the height to hold for the weights of the full blacks, the most probable modulus deducible from our materials is 0.03296, with which the theoretical weights for this race of men have been computed for each half-inch of stature. These and their discordances from the observed mean weights are given in Table XIV.

TABLE XIV.

Theoretical Weights of Full Blacks at Different Statures.

Height	Weight	Comp.—Obs.	Height	Weight	Comp.—Obs.
in.	lbs.	lbs.	in.	lbs.	lbs.
60	118.7	+0.6	66½	145.8	+1.8
60½	120.6	−3.9	67	148.0	+1.5
61	122.7	+0.2	67½	150.2	−0.5
61½	124.7	−2.2	68	152.4	+0.6
62	126.7	−2.0	68½	154.7	+1.0
62½	128.8	−1.6	69	156.9	+0.7
63	130.8	−1.0	69½	159.2	+0.1
63½	132.9	+2.6	70	161.5	−1.3
64	135.0	−1.5	70½	163.8	+0.9
64½	137.1	−1.5	71	166.2	−0.3
65	139.3	−1.4	71½	168.5	−1.5
65½	141.4	+1.5	72	170.9	+3.8
66	143.6	+2.8	72½	173.3	+3.0

Although the accordances here are neither so close as those exhibited in Table X., nor the distribution of their signs so equable, there seems to be small room for doubt that more copious statistics would afford a more perfect agreement between the observed mean weights and those afforded by the law of the squares of the height.

For the mulattoes and the Indians our observations are not numerous enough to render similar investigations valuable. So far as we can form any good opinion, it is in favor of the existence of the same law, though with a different modulus for each class of men.

The observed limits of weight, among the individuals examined in the several classes of men, are shown by the appended table.

TABLE XV.

Limits of Weight observed in each Class of Men examined.

Class	In usual Vigor			Not in usual Vigor		
	No. Men	Max'm	Min'm	No. Men	Max'm	Min'm
		lbs.	lbs.		lbs.	lbs.
White Soldiers, Earlier Series	5 936	228.3	72.8	2 162	229.8	78.3
White Soldiers, Later Series	9 157	219.8	64.8	1 600	230.8	90.3
Sailors	1 144	204.0	58.0	–	–	–
Students	288	190.8	103.8	–	–	–
Full Blacks	1 775	212.0	95.0	226	182.8	96.0
Mulattoes	680	206.0	96.8	140	198.3	74.4
Indians	507	276.8	123.8	9	172.3	128.8

2. *Relations of Weight to Age.*

The variation of weight of the human body with the age was carefully investigated by Quetelet, from the largest collection of materials available at the time. He obtained approximately typical numbers, representing this change and its rate; and the alterations in the ratio of weight to stature gave the corresponding measure of the lateral expansion of the body, or its development in weight irrespective of increase in height.

For carrying out a similar investigation upon the extended scale which the present collection of materials permits, the weights of the various classes of men here examined have been assorted with regard both to age and stature, and the means taken for each group. These are presented in the next series of tables, in which, following the fundamental principle which has governed the arrangement and preparation of the present volume, the aim has been to furnish trustworthy facts and materials ready for use, rather than to attempt any thorough discussion. Inevitable restrictions of time in preparing the work for the press preclude our deduction of inferences to any adequate extent; but the very simple process of converting these tables of actual weight into corresponding ones for the ratio between weight and stature will exhibit the average lateral growth for each stature during the years of military age. The amount of this lateral development will be found somewhat less than Quetelet's statistics imply, as may be inferred from a very slight inspection of the mean weights found for the same stature at different ages; and also, crudely but clearly, from the Table XXV., which exhibits the mean weights at each year of age for the several classes of white men and for their total, irrespective of their height. It will be seen that after deducting one eighteenth part of the total weight, as a crude estimate of the weight of the clothing, the weights found by Forbes for Irish students at the Edinburgh University between the ages of 16 and 26, will accord closely with the results here deduced, for white soldiers, in Tables XXV. and XXVII.

The next nine tables (XVI. to XXIV.) contain the mean weights for each year of age (last birthday) and for each successive height, for men in vigorous health only; the assortment being by half-inches of stature for the white soldiers, and by whole inches for the other classes of men. Table XVI. gives the results from the men examined in the earlier series, all of whom were white soldiers; Table XVII. similarly contains the means for the white soldiers of the later series; and Table XVIII. those deduced from the aggregate of these two series, including a few men of the earlier series, for whom the returns were received, after the completion of Table XVI. In Table XIX. are given the values found for sailors; in Table XX. those for students; and in Tables XXI. to XXIV. those for the negroes and Iroquois Indians. In the last-named four tables, the observed weights at the several half-inches of stature have been aggregated with those for the full inch next preceding, and the means deduced from the sum of the two groups are entered as belonging to the stature represented by the intermediate quarter-inch. The close agreement between the results deduced for full blacks and for mulattoes seemed to make it advisable to consolidate the separate Tables XXI. and XXII. into one, and Table XXIII. was thus formed, comprising all the black men, whether of pure blood or not. To this series of tables are subjoined two others, showing the mean weights of the men at each year of age, their stature being disregarded; Table XXV. comprising the results for white men, and Table XXVI. those for the other races to which our observations have extended.

TABLE XVI.

Mean Weights of White Soldiers, by Age and Height.

(*Earlier Series.*)

Age	64 Inches		64½ Inches		65 Inches		65½ Inches		66 Inches	
	No.	Weight	No.	Weight	No.	Weight	No.	Weight	No.	Weight
		lbs.		lbs.		lbs.		lbs.		lbs.
15	1	112.8	3	119.8	4	128.5	2	114.8	6	121.8
16	10	125.6	8	119.4	5	140.0	8	118.7	6	126.3
17	12	129.0	18	124.0	10	138.6	17	129.9	14	130.5
18	26	122.4	26	133.1	17	126.2	40	132.3	31	133.2
19	16	126.3	28	134.7	37	129.0	32	129.6	43	137.5
20	15	127.9	30	131.4	28	133.0	40	136.6	29	137.1
21	25	131.9	16	137.0	27	132.9	39	138.9	36	134.4
22	14	129.8	22	131.1	17	133.9	35	136.8	25	139.0
23	12	132.4	19	133.6	23	136.0	20	133.1	35	134.9
24	8	127.7	13	137.7	13	136.3	32	138.8	15	139.2
25	3	126.6	7	133.7	9	137.9	12	141.5	18	141.5
26	8	136.4	6	140.5	4	139.4	11	133.3	16	139.4
27	3	127.0	7	134.7	12	139.5	14	137.6	8	136.5
28	4	138.3	5	148.6	8	140.7	10	138.4	16	141.5
29	1	111.8	8	130.2	6	134.5	8	136.8	10	134.1
30	2	136.8	7	141.6	3	140.3	7	137.0	7	146.9
31	1	144.3	1	145.3	3	130.8	5	134.4	2	137.0
32	–	–	2	118.3	3	120.6	10	139.2	5	133.2
33	2	129.3	1	118.3	2	152.8	4	144.2	4	140.3
34	1	138.8	2	126.8	3	133.3	1	138.8	4	141.6
35	2	118.0	3	130.6	3	143.1	3	149.5	2	153.0
36	1	145.8	4	142.3	3	132.1	7	150.2	4	134.8
37	1	137.8	3	148.5	–	–	3	143.1	1	131.8
38	2	144.5	1	128.8	1	171.3	3	132.0	4	139.0
39	–	–	1	169.3	2	124.8	1	135.3	4	144.3
40	–	–	1	138.3	–	–	1	111.8	–	–
41	1	117.3	–	–	–	–	–	–	–	–
42	1	152.3	–	–	1	139.8	1	166.8	2	154.0
43	–	–	1	150.3	–	–	–	–	–	–
44	–	–	1	140.3	1	175.8	1	131.8	–	–
45	4	148.4	2	137.5	–	–	–	–	2	142.5
46	1	140.3	1	167.8	–	–	–	–	–	–
47	–	–	–	–	–	–	–	–	–	–
48	1	142.3	–	–	–	–	–	–	–	–
49	–	–	–	–	–	–	–	–	–	–
50	–	–	1	117.3	1	166.3	1	128.8	–	–
51	–	–	1	114.8	–	–	1	123.8	–	–
52	–	–	–	–	–	–	–	–	–	–
53	–	–	–	–	1	119.8	–	–	–	–
54	–	–	–	–	–	–	–	–	–	–
55	–	–	–	–	–	–	–	–	–	–

TABLE XVI. — (*Continued.*)

Mean Weights of White Soldiers, by Age and Height.

(*Earlier Series.*)

Age	66½ Inches		67 Inches		67½ Inches		68 Inches		68½ Inches	
	No.	Weight	No.	Weight	No.	Weight	No.	Weight	No.	Weight
		lbs.		lbs.		lbs.		lbs.		lbs.
15	2	119.0	–	–	–	–	1	120.3	–	–
16	4	123.4	2	137.3	3	142.1	5	132.0	–	–
17	17	128.4	14	134.4	16	135.6	8	136.5	13	142.8
18	31	131.6	38	137.6	34	142.3	27	138.9	24	143.6
19	42	135.7	38	141.2	53	139.2	37	139.2	32	139.7
20	60	139.8	52	138.7	51	143.5	47	147.1	54	148.6
21	41	142.3	43	143.1	55	141.9	45	145.9	55	147.4
22	39	141.8	42	143.9	51	146.1	40	148.6	35	148.0
23	22	138.4	30	142.7	42	145.3	32	142.9	45	146.5
24	26	137.0	17	148.0	40	149.0	41	147.2	32	151.3
25	26	141.9	15	148.9	22	147.7	24	154.0	29	152.0
26	17	145.5	17	147.4	18	143.6	18	148.5	22	154.8
27	12	140.9	16	141.0	19	152.9	15	148.4	21	150.5
28	14	141.5	12	144.0	9	147.8	16	149.9	19	148.7
29	6	138.6	6	142.3	9	148.5	20	150.3	14	150.3
30	10	155.9	10	147.3	15	151.4	18	146.1	11	162.5
31	4	134.7	7	138.6	5	149.6	8	147.6	7	146.6
32	7	142.3	9	149.1	7	142.4	8	152.6	4	158.2
33	9	158.9	1	151.8	5	141.6	7	147.9	7	150.2
34	4	144.5	5	151.7	7	151.9	7	154.1	7	155.1
35	3	150.0	12	146.5	9	148.1	4	156.8	8	153.0
36	8	139.7	3	153.0	4	141.5	1	149.8	5	155.7
37	3	144.8	3	137.6	6	147.5	3	133.8	5	150.8
38	4	134.3	3	140.8	2	139.0	1	144.3	1	149.8
39	4	136.9	1	126.3	3	146.0	–	–	1	124.3
40	1	160.8	2	171.3	3	173.0	2	147.8	2	154.0
41	4	140.7	–	–	3	148.6	–	–	1	153.3
42	1	147.3	–	–	6	150.9	–	–	2	139.0
43	–	–	1	152.3	1	154.3	3	140.6	4	156.9
44	1	150.8	2	154.3	3	141.6	2	133.5	3	155.8
45	2	153.8	2	161.0	–	–	1	139.8	–	–
46	3	143.5	2	139.3	1	143.8	–	–	2	163.5
47	1	143.3	–	–	–	–	1	158.8	–	–
48	2	150.3	–	–	1	140.8	–	–	1	164.3
49	1	160.8	–	–	–	–	–	–	–	–
50	–	–	1	156.8	–	–	1	143.5	–	–
51	1	123.8	1	147.3	–	–	–	–	–	–
52	–	–	–	–	–	–	1	144.8	–	–
53	–	–	–	–	1	144.8	–	–	–	–
54	–	–	–	–	–	–	–	–	–	–
55	–	–	–	–	–	–	–	–	–	–

TABLE XVI. — (*Continued.*)

Mean Weights of White Soldiers, by Age and Height.

(*Earlier Series.*)

Age	69 Inches		69½ Inches		70 Inches		70½ Inches	
	No.	Weight	No.	Weight	No.	Weight	No.	Weight
		lbs.		lbs.		lbs.		lbs.
15	–	–	–	–	–	–	–	–
16	2	125.5	1	113.3	–	–	–	–
17	3	142.6	3	135.6	3	150.5	4	140.3
18	27	141.1	13	149.9	12	150.3	10	145.7
19	30	146.1	22	147.0	21	146.6	10	152.8
20	37	150.2	27	144.8	24	153.4	14	152.7
21	37	146.6	34	153.0	29	156.2	26	154.8
22	36	151.5	29	147.6	32	158.3	18	152.9
23	29	150.8	18	146.4	23	153.9	20	150.4
24	23	150.6	20	150.4	19	152.7	19	162.6
25	20	154.3	22	154.3	19	155.5	12	162.8
26	11	151.4	17	153.4	6	156.5	15	158.2
27	16	149.8	16	155.3	10	152.1	8	159.2
28	20	150.6	15	156.5	12	156.4	7	160.4
29	7	147.2	9	156.9	8	159.2	8	166.0
30	7	160.4	5	152.8	8	158.4	2	154.5
31	7	152.3	8	162.2	5	149.1	3	162.5
32	5	156.2	4	148.7	7	163.9	4	174.5
33	3	160.5	6	155.8	1	175.8	5	161.9
34	3	146.3	2	170.0	2	151.5	3	179.1
35	10	143.6	5	139.5	4	141.8	2	161.8
36	4	156.5	–	–	1	161.3	2	160.3
37	5	152.5	4	152.4	1	160.3	–	–
38	3	156.3	2	163.8	3	154.8	1	151.3
39	–	–	1	148.8	4	158.9	4	153.3
40	1	136.8	2	173.0	–	–	2	177.3
41	–	–	1	166.8	1	138.8	2	161.5
42	5	165.7	4	148.8	2	177.0	1	181.8
43	4	143.6	2	161.3	–	–	–	–
44	2	186.0	2	158.5	1	140.8	1	159.8
45	1	152.8	2	146.8	2	154.3	–	–
46	1	160.8	–	–	1	172.8	–	–
47	1	162.8	–	–	–	–	–	–
48	2	154.5	2	158.8	–	–	–	–
49	–	–	–	–	–	–	–	–
50	1	146.8	–	–	–	–	–	–
51	–	–	–	–	1	150.3	–	–
52	–	–	–	–	–	–	–	–
53	–	–	1	150.3	2	164.3	–	–
54	–	–	–	–	–	–	–	–
55	–	–	–	–	–	–	–	–

TABLE XVII.

Mean Weights of White Soldiers, by Age and Height.

(Later Series.)

Age	64 Inches		64½ Inches		65 Inches		65½ Inches		66 Inches	
	No.	Weight	No.	Weight	No.	Weight	No.	Weight	No.	Weight
		lbs.		lbs.		lbs.		lbs.		lbs.
15	2	116.8	–	–	4	127.8	–	–	3	117.8
16	9	123.6	9	119.7	9	114.1	10	129.1	7	125.4
17	17	124.5	22	118.4	17	122.7	19	131.2	18	130.7
18	33	122.0	50	127.1	40	127.0	53	128.2	53	130.2
19	36	122.8	37	127.0	43	128.0	50	131.0	41	133.2
20	14	128.4	43	129.7	42	133.6	58	131.8	42	135.9
21	32	131.7	37	130.1	37	134.2	51	134.7	47	136.5
22	23	129.1	44	133.5	46	135.2	67	133.6	38	139.6
23	20	137.7	38	133.1	31	135.6	48	136.8	27	139.6
24	17	132.7	22	133.0	26	133.9	48	137.2	38	141.7
25	19	134.0	20	127.1	24	131.3	22	136.5	28	137.7
26	7	136.9	14	135.4	14	133.1	32	139.7	17	141.6
27	6	126.9	17	134.9	17	134.6	17	135.7	15	144.5
28	8	129.3	14	137.6	13	137.7	18	138.5	19	136.2
29	9	130.4	18	135.3	10	134.7	18	135.7	6	135.9
30	5	139.3	10	130.4	8	130.3	22	136.2	20	141.5
31	7	132.6	7	133.9	7	125.5	15	137.7	7	147.6
32	6	136.0	9	128.8	15	133.8	17	138.0	12	140.6
33	9	132.0	8	130.7	5	138.3	6	143.0	14	150.7
34	3	137.8	7	131.1	6	131.3	15	135.3	6	139.7
35	5	131.4	10	131.8	9	131.3	4	133.9	8	139.0
36	5	141.6	4	146.6	6	130.7	9	141.5	6	137.0
37	–	–	3	131.5	3	138.8	8	136.8	9	138.9
38	6	133.6	7	128.4	5	132.9	7	139.0	5	145.3
39	4	137.2	3	130.5	4	137.9	5	134.2	7	138.7
40	2	127.5	2	120.5	3	129.0	9	141.9	4	148.0
41	1	150.8	–	–	3	127.1	4	153.8	2	125.5
42	2	128.8	3	142.8	3	137.7	4	136.8	6	137.2
43	2	127.3	4	138.5	3	138.8	4	143.0	2	132.3
44	1	140.8	2	137.3	3	145.1	2	139.8	5	141.2
45	3	132.1	1	128.8	2	150.3	6	143.7	2	150.8
46	–	–	1	111.8	–	–	5	135.6	2	143.8
47	1	115.8	–	–	1	118.8	1	138.8	–	–
48	–	–	1	124.8	2	129.3	1	131.8	2	135.8
49	–	–	–	–	–	–	–	–	–	–
50	1	124.8	–	–	–	–	4	136.9	–	–
51	–	–	1	148.8	–	–	2	139.8	–	–
52	–	–	–	–	–	–	1	142.8	1	137.8
53	–	–	–	–	–	–	–	–	–	–
54	–	–	–	–	–	–	1	160.3	–	–
55	–	–	–	–	–	–	1	143.8	2	138.8

TABLE XVII. — (*Continued.*)

Mean Weights of White Soldiers, by Age and Height.

(*Later Series.*)

Age	66½ Inches		67 Inches		67½ Inches		68 Inches		68½ Inches	
	No.	Weight	No.	Weight	No.	Weight	No.	Weight	No.	Weight
		lbs.		lbs.		lbs.		lbs.		lbs.
15	2	133.8	1	115.8	–	–	–	–	–	–
16	10	128.3	11	130.9	7	129.3	5	132.1	4	124.9
17	18	126.4	20	136.7	10	133.1	11	132.2	5	138.0
18	52	131.0	40	133.2	50	137.9	47	139.4	48	141.7
19	53	136.5	51	136.5	52	141.0	54	143.6	48	145.1
20	87	137.3	69	141.4	77	142.3	64	145.0	55	146.0
21	72	137.9	64	138.7	85	143.3	59	146.2	61	146.7
22	92	137.7	74	141.4	84	142.4	73	143.8	57	146.2
23	50	139.8	48	140.6	61	143.8	59	148.0	51	148.1
24	65	141.8	59	145.2	70	146.9	51	147.5	58	149.4
25	41	143.2	31	148.1	36	145.1	35	148.0	41	148.1
26	32	139.4	39	145.1	37	145.4	24	151.0	37	150.1
27	19	144.3	27	145.2	23	149.6	27	150.3	28	152.7
28	21	137.4	27	144.9	40	147.9	29	143.9	30	153.4
29	25	139.8	20	147.2	20	144.5	18	147.9	23	152.4
30	19	142.2	30	146.1	24	146.1	24	149.2	20	147.3
31	13	140.0	18	143.2	14	142.6	11	147.9	8	150.2
32	20	140.1	11	138.5	19	146.3	17	146.3	19	146.4
33	9	149.0	11	144.1	18	150.3	9	151.6	9	152.6
34	5	147.4	14	146.2	24	146.3	10	147.0	19	148.3
35	20	146.6	16	143.9	17	149.9	7	147.4	18	151.3
36	11	153.8	11	144.6	12	147.6	4	154.4	9	148.7
37	9	135.5	9	142.0	9	151.7	8	148.9	3	145.8
38	17	138.9	8	151.8	9	151.5	6	143.6	6	151.3
39	5	144.9	6	148.0	8	146.6	11	149.1	4	138.4
40	3	161.6	10	146.2	9	148.2	8	143.7	6	150.5
41	4	140.9	6	144.0	2	136.0	5	139.9	2	144.3
42	4	146.0	5	137.6	5	135.4	3	149.1	10	149.3
43	7	149.8	4	151.0	8	141.5	1	122.8	5	150.7
44	7	149.5	7	149.9	4	145.9	4	152.3	1	142.3
45	3	151.5	2	133.5	6	145.9	9	149.2	–	–
46	4	143.8	2	154.5	1	146.3	2	152.0	–	–
47	1	138.3	3	142.8	2	157.8	–	–	–	–
48	2	115.4	4	137.8	2	160.0	1	173.8	1	135.8
49	1	141.8	–	–	1	144.8	–	–	–	–
50	4	132.5	1	150.8	1	156.8	–	–	–	–
51	–	–	1	163.3	–	–	1	127.8	–	–
52	–	–	–	–	1	131.8	–	–	–	–
53	1	133.8	–	–	1	128.3	2	142.3	1	159.8
54	1	143.8	1	156.8	1	139.8	–	–	1	157.8
55	–	–	–	–	–	–	–	–	–	–

TABLE XVII. — (*Continued.*)

Mean Weights of White Soldiers, by Age and Height.

(*Later Series.*)

Age	69 Inches		69½ Inches		70 Inches		70½ Inches	
	No.	Weight	No.	Weight	No.	Weight	No.	Weight
		lbs.		lbs.		lbs.		lbs.
15	–	–	1	156.8	1	146.8	–	–
16	2	167.0	–	–	–	–	–	–
17	9	136.2	6	138.5	3	134.5	3	147.7
18	43	143.8	23	148.9	20	147.7	8	148.7
19	27	141.8	21	151.3	15	149.5	16	152.5
20	38	148.4	30	149.6	23	150.5	18	156.2
21	43	153.9	51	150.7	35	151.4	30	158.0
22	33	150.5	38	150.9	23	160.8	18	157.7
23	40	150.6	38	155.8	27	151.3	16	154.4
24	32	149.6	42	157.6	22	156.1	15	156.8
25	29	149.9	19	160.9	22	150.8	13	159.5
26	17	154.1	26	150.9	12	161.5	16	157.5
27	24	153.8	22	151.5	18	158.0	14	159.2
28	23	150.4	18	155.8	11	159.0	10	162.0
29	14	146.9	14	152.3	8	158.0	7	156.9
30	14	152.1	12	161.6	14	162.8	9	156.9
31	6	149.8	8	160.1	7	159.5	3	162.5
32	5	164.0	9	152.6	10	152.8	7	162.4
33	7	159.7	14	154.0	5	152.2	6	156.0
34	7	156.2	14	155.0	10	159.4	7	152.9
35	2	157.0	9	148.6	7	148.8	4	154.9
36	6	151.5	2	147.3	6	167.5	2	160.3
37	13	162.6	10	148.0	3	164.4	4	163.8
38	6	155.5	9	154.8	4	154.0	5	161.3
39	2	152.5	1	175.8	5	148.9	7	166.5
40	4	161.8	4	162.2	–	–	1	160.8
41	2	141.5	3	153.5	5	146.2	1	183.3
42	8	145.3	1	146.3	2	163.5	2	193.8
43	2	153.5	2	153.8	3	164.6	2	155.5
44	9	158.8	3	150.5	1	177.8	2	140.8
45	2	152.3	2	149.8	–	–	2	151.5
46	–	–	–	–	–	–	1	151.8
47	–	–	–	–	–	–	1	141.3
48	–	–	1	161.8	–	–	–	–
49	2	146.3	1	155.8	1	164.3	–	–
50	–	–	–	–	–	–	–	–
51	1	174.8	–	–	–	–	–	–
52	1	164.8	–	–	–	–	–	–
53	–	–	–	–	–	–	–	–
54	–	–	2	196.8	–	–	–	–
55	–	–	1	161.3	–	–	–	–

TABLE XVIII.

Mean Weights of White Soldiers, by Age and Height.

(*Both Series.*)

Age	64 Inches		64½ Inches		65 Inches		65½ Inches		66 Inches	
	No.	Weight	No.	Weight	No.	Weight	No.	Weight	No.	Weight
		lbs.		lbs.		lbs.		lbs.		lbs.
15	3	115.5	3	119.8	8	128.2	2	114.8	9	120.5
16	19	124.7	18	119.7	14	123.4	18	124.5	13	125.8
17	29	126.4	40	121.0	27	128.6	36	130.6	32	130.6
18	59	122.2	77	129.1	58	127.0	93	130.0	86	131.4
19	52	123.9	65	130.3	81	128.4	82	130.4	84	135.4
20	29	128.1	73	130.4	70	133.4	98	133.8	74	136.4
21	57	131.8	54	132.4	67	133.6	92	136.4	85	135.8
22	37	129.4	66	132.7	63	134.9	105	134.8	64	139.6
23	32	135.7	58	133.3	56	135.4	70	135.7	64	137.3
24	25	131.1	35	134.7	42	135.3	81	137.9	56	140.8
25	22	133.0	27	128.8	33	133.1	35	137.7	46	139.2
26	16	136.1	21	137.6	19	134.6	43	138.0	33	140.6
27	10	130.6	24	134.8	29	136.6	31	136.6	23	141.7
28	12	132.3	19	140.5	21	138.9	29	138.5	35	138.6
29	11	128.2	27	133.6	16	134.6	28	136.2	16	134.8
30	7	138.6	17	135.0	11	133.1	29	136.4	27	142.9
31	8	134.0	8	135.4	10	127.1	20	136.8	9	145.3
32	6	136.0	11	126.9	18	131.6	28	139.0	17	138.4
33	11	131.5	9	129.3	7	142.4	10	143.4	18	148.4
34	4	138.0	9	130.1	9	132.0	16	135.6	10	140.5
35	7	127.6	13	131.5	12	134.3	7	140.6	10	141.8
36	6	142.3	8	144.4	10	133.0	16	145.3	10	136.1
37	1	137.8	6	140.0	3	138.8	11	138.5	10	138.2
38	8	136.4	8	128.5	6	139.3	10	136.9	9	142.5
39	4	137.2	4	140.2	6	133.5	6	134.4	12	140.5
40	2	127.5	3	126.5	3	129.0	10	138.9	4	148.0
41	2	134.0	–	–	3	127.1	4	153.8	2	125.5
42	4	136.2	3	142.8	4	138.2	5	142.8	8	141.4
43	2	127.3	5	140.9	3	138.8	4	143.0	2	132.3
44	1	140.8	3	138.5	4	152.8	3	137.1	5	141.2
45	7	141.4	3	134.6	2	150.3	6	143.7	4	146.7
46	1	140.3	2	139.8	–	–	5	135.6	2	143.8
47	1	115.8	–	–	1	118.8	1	138.8	–	–
48	1	142.3	1	124.8	2	129.3	1	131.8	2	135.8
49	–	–	–	–	–	–	–	–	–	–
50	1	124.8	1	117.3	1	166.3	5	135.3	–	–
51	–	–	2	131.8	–	–	3	134.5	–	–
52	–	–	–	–	–	–	1	142.8	1	137.8
53	–	–	–	–	1	119.8	–	–	–	–
54	–	–	–	–	–	–	1	160.3	–	–
55	–	–	–	–	–	–	1	143.8	2	138.8

TABLE XVIII. — (*Continued.*)

Mean Weights of White Soldiers, by Age and Height.

(*Both Series.*)

Age	66½ Inches		67 Inches		67½ Inches		68 Inches		68½ Inches	
	No.	Weight	No.	Weight	No.	Weight	No.	Weight	No.	Weight
		lbs.		lbs.		lbs.		lbs.		lbs.
15	4	126.4	1	115.8	–	–	1	120.3	–	–
16	14	126.9	13	131.9	10	133.2	10	132.0	4	124.9
17	36	127.5	35	135.4	26	134.6	20	134.8	18	141.5
18	83	131.2	78	135.3	86	139.4	75	139.5	72	142.3
19	95	136.1	90	138.6	108	140.0	91	141.8	83	143.1
20	149	138.5	121	140.2	130	142.8	112	146.0	110	147.3
21	116	139.6	110	140.2	141	142.9	108	146.2	120	147.5
22	134	138.9	117	142.3	137	144.1	114	145.5	93	147.0
23	74	139.7	80	141.5	104	144.5	92	146.3	96	147.3
24	91	140.4	78	145.9	112	147.9	96	147.4	91	150.1
25	67	142.7	46	148.4	61	146.2	62	150.4	72	149.8
26	49	141.6	56	145.8	57	145.1	42	149.9	60	152.4
27	31	143.0	44	143.6	43	151.4	42	149.6	50	151.5
28	35	139.0	39	144.6	49	147.9	45	146.1	49	151.5
29	31	139.6	26	146.1	29	145.7	39	149.0	38	151.2
30	29	147.0	41	147.0	39	148.2	42	147.9	31	152.7
31	17	138.7	25	141.9	19	144.5	19	147.8	15	148.5
32	27	140.7	20	143.3	27	145.4	25	148.3	23	148.4
33	18	149.0	12	144.8	23	148.4	17	149.8	16	151.5
34	9	146.1	19	147.7	31	147.6	17	149.9	26	150.1
35	23	147.0	28	145.0	26	149.3	11	150.8	26	151.9
36	19	147.8	14	146.4	16	146.1	5	153.5	14	151.2
37	13	139.8	12	140.9	15	150.0	12	145.0	8	148.9
38	21	138.1	11	148.8	11	149.2	7	143.7	7	151.1
39	9	141.4	7	144.9	11	146.4	11	149.1	5	135.6
40	5	156.9	12	150.4	12	154.4	11	145.8	8	151.4
41	9	142.1	6	144.0	5	143.6	5	139.9	3	147.3
42	5	146.3	5	137.6	12	143.1	3	149.1	12	147.6
43	7	149.8	5	151.3	9	142.9	4	136.2	9	153.5
44	8	149.7	9	150.9	7	144.1	6	146.0	4	152.4
45	5	152.4	4	147.3	6	145.9	10	148.3	–	–
46	7	143.7	4	146.9	2	145.0	2	152.0	2	163.5
47	2	140.8	3	142.8	2	157.8	1	158.8	–	–
48	4	132.8	4	137.8	3	153.6	1	173.8	2	150.0
49	2	151.3	–	–	1	144.8	–	–	–	–
50	4	132.5	2	153.8	1	156.8	1	143.5	–	–
51	1	123.8	2	155.3	–	–	1	127.8	–	–
52	–	–	–	–	1	131.8	1	144.8	–	–
53	1	133.8	–	–	2	136.5	2	142.3	1	159.8
54	1	143.8	1	156.8	2	132.3	–	–	1	157.8
55	–	–	–	–	–	–	–	–	–	–

TABLE XVIII. — (*Continued.*)

Mean Weights of White Soldiers, by Age and Height.

(*Both Series.*)

Age	69 Inches		69½ Inches		70 Inches		70½ Inches	
	No.	Weight	No.	Weight	No.	Weight	No.	Weight
		lbs.		lbs.		lbs.		lbs.
15	–	–	1	156.8	1	146.8	–	–
16	4	146.3	1	113.3	–	–	–	–
17	12	137.8	9	137.5	6	142.5	7	143.9
18	70	142.7	36	149.3	32	148.7	18	147.1
19	58	144.2	43	149.1	36	147.8	26	152.6
20	77	149.3	58	147.4	47	152.0	33	154.7
21	81	150.8	87	152.0	65	153.8	56	156.5
22	70	150.9	69	149.5	58	159.3	36	155.3
23	72	151.3	56	152.8	52	152.4	38	151.9
24	58	150.0	63	155.4	43	154.8	37	160.0
25	50	151.9	42	157.6	41	153.0	26	161.8
26	29	152.9	45	152.6	18	159.8	31	157.8
27	40	152.2	38	153.1	28	155.9	24	161.9
28	43	150.5	33	156.2	23	157.6	17	161.4
29	21	147.0	25	153.9	16	158.6	15	161.8
30	22	155.3	17	159.0	22	161.2	11	156.5
31	13	151.1	17	161.1	12	155.2	6	162.5
32	10	160.1	13	151.4	17	157.4	11	166.8
33	10	159.9	20	154.6	6	156.1	11	158.7
34	10	153.2	16	156.9	12	158.1	10	160.8
35	12	145.9	14	145.4	11	146.2	6	157.2
36	10	153.5	2	147.3	7	166.7	4	160.3
37	18	159.8	14	149.3	4	163.4	4	163.8
38	9	155.7	11	156.4	7	154.4	6	159.6
39	2	152.5	2	162.3	9	153.3	11	161.7
40	5	156.8	6	165.8	–	–	3	171.8
41	2	141.5	4	156.8	6	145.0	3	168.8
42	13	153.1	5	148.3	4	170.3	3	189.8
43	6	146.9	4	157.5	3	164.6	2	155.5
44	11	163.7	5	153.7	2	159.3	3	147.1
45	3	152.5	4	148.3	2	154.3	2	151.5
46	1	160.8	–	–	1	172.8	1	151.8
47	1	162.8	–	–	–	–	1	141.3
48	2	154.5	3	159.8	–	–	–	–
49	2	146.3	1	155.8	1	164.3	–	–
50	1	146.8	–	–	–	–	–	–
51	1	174.8	–	–	1	150.3	–	–
52	1	164.8	–	–	–	–	–	–
53	–	–	1	150.3	2	164.3	–	–
54	–	–	2	196.8	–	–	–	–
55	–	–	1	161.3	–	–	–	–

TABLE XIX.

Mean Weights of Sailors, by Age and Height.

Age	64¼ Inches		65¼ Inches		66¼ Inches		67¼ Inches		68¼ Inches		69¼ Inches		70¼ Inches	
	No.	Wt.	No.	Wt.	No.	Wt.	No.	Wt.	No.	Wt.	No.	Wt.	No.	Wt.
		lbs.		lbs.		lbs.		lbs.		lbs.		lbs.		lbs.
16	1	116.0	–	–	–	–	–	–	–	–	–	–	–	–
17	1	121.3	–	–	2	116.0	–	–	–	–	–	–	–	–
18	4	110.2	2	143.3	2	135.6	3	141.6	2	141.5	1	151.0	–	–
19	8	122.5	10	124.6	5	131.0	2	145.0	1	125.0	2	174.0	–	–
20	11	121.4	12	127.1	11	133.9	10	143.9	5	140.2	5	138.6	2	143.4
21	15	131.4	20	129.1	15	137.6	16	137.7	13	143.9	12	143.4	4	157.0
22	14	132.6	24	142.0	16	135.0	17	143.9	11	158.5	8	147.9	4	159.0
23	5	129.2	11	132.8	12	145.8	13	144.4	7	148.8	5	152.8	1	159.0
24	16	139.5	16	134.6	10	142.1	13	146.3	17	157.8	7	154.3	5	158.3
25	14	135 5	15	142.7	10	147.2	15	138.3	13	154.6	9	156.4	5	156.8
26	9	134.1	11	135.6	2	140.0	12	146.7	7	153.2	5	153.0	3	157.8
27	3	130.7	6	132.7	8	142.7	3	149.3	5	142.3	5	152.6	3	154.0
28	8	132.6	4	139.8	6	146.0	14	151.3	6	151.8	4	154.5	2	161.4
29	8	130.2	11	136.9	9	142.0	4	137.3	3	151.0	2	137.0	1	149.0
30	2	131.0	7	131.4	4	146.1	5	145.2	6	140.7	1	128.0	–	–
31	5	130.8	6	142.5	2	136.9	2	150.9	3	138.3	–	–	2	164.5
32	4	138.8	7	135.8	1	153.0	8	145.9	3	144.3	3	155.3	1	150.0
33	2	139.8	2	133.5	2	142.5	2	142.5	–	–	–	–	1	149.0
34	5	137.8	–	–	3	142.1	2	141.0	2	155.8	1	160.0	–	–
35	2	147.0	3	142.7	4	146.2	2	145.9	2	146.0	4	152.9	–	–
36	3	147.0	5	141.7	–	–	2	143.8	–	–	2	155.0	3	157.3
37	–	–	–	–	1	143.0	2	136.5	1	158.0	–	–	–	–
38	–	–	1	146.8	2	150.1	1	123.0	–	–	1	140.0	–	–
39	2	131.0	1	124.0	2	145.5	2	159.9	1	184.0	–	–	–	–
40	1	137.0	1	133.0	1	135.0	–	–	1	173.8	1	148.0	–	–
41	–	–	1	133.0	–	–	–	–	–	–	1	133.0	–	–
42	–	–	1	148.0	1	129.0	1	168.0	–	–	–	–	–	–
43	1	137.0	–	–	–	–	–	–	1	134.0	–	–	–	–
44	–	–	–	–	–	–	1	164.0	–	–	–	–	–	–
45	2	128.9	–	–	2	144.5	–	–	–	–	–	–	–	–
Over 45	2	150.5	1	139.0	1	115.0	2	167.6	–	–	3	149.3	–	–

TABLE XX.

Mean Weights of Students, by Age and Height.

Age	64¼ Inches		65¼ Inches		66¼ Inches		67¼ Inches		68¼ Inches		69¼ Inches		70¼ Inches	
	No.	Wt.	No.	Wt.	No.	Wt.	No.	Wt.	No.	Wt.	No.	Wt.	No.	Wt.
		lbs.		lbs.		lbs.		lbs.		lbs.		lbs.		lbs.
17	–	–	–	–	1	127.8	1	120.8	1	133.8	–	–	–	–
18	2	112.8	1	111.8	1	139.8	–	–	–	–	2	127.5	–	–
19	3	132.1	8	124.5	5	121.8	5	124.5	6	130.0	7	145.3	1	150.8
20	1	114.8	7	126.5	7	136.5	8	130.3	13	132.4	15	138.8	8	147.4
21	3	123.0	7	126.4	11	130.1	11	128.5	10	138.5	9	143.3	16	145.0
22	1	113.8	6	121.6	5	131.8	7	131.9	6	136.5	6	147.5	6	152.5
23	1	105.8	–	–	1	142.3	1	133.3	1	131.8	4	142.3	–	–
24	2	125.8	–	–	1	142.8	2	125.8	4	136.2	2	132.3	–	–
25	1	123.3	–	–	3	134.8	1	144.8	2	146.3	1	143.8	1	153.8
26	–	–	1	134.8	2	125.3	–	–	–	–	–	–	–	–
27	–	–	1	119.8	–	–	–	–	1	139.8	–	–	2	150.3
Over 27	–	–	2	120.6	–	–	–	–	–	–	–	–	–	–

TABLE XXI.

Mean Weights of Full Blacks, by Age and Height.

Age	64¼ Inches		65¼ Inches		66¼ Inches		67¼ Inches		68¼ Inches		69¼ Inches		70¼ Inches	
	No.	Wt.	No.	Wt.	No.	Wt.	No.	Wt.	No.	Wt.	No.	Wt.	No.	Wt.
		lbs.		lbs.		lbs.		lbs.		lbs.		lbs.		lbs.
15 & und.	1	137.7	1	102.8	–	–	1	131.0	–	–	–	–	–	–
16	1	145.0	8	128.3	4	120.8	1	129.3	1	146.8	1	153.8	–	–
17	5	128.5	6	131.5	4	133.2	9	128.8	2	143.8	2	151.1	–	–
18	9	126.4	10	130.5	13	134.9	7	136.4	7	144.7	3	152.2	2	148.8
19	12	136.0	7	131.1	11	133.2	12	139.8	11	144.9	6	149.3	3	154.9
20	19	140.7	26	139.1	26	142.8	23	147.4	17	149.2	7	156.3	2	143.5
21	19	139.8	20	143.9	19	142.5	21	146.4	15	155.6	8	152.4	2	160.0
22	23	137.7	24	143.5	28	140.9	20	151.9	18	152.4	11	157.4	5	162.3
23	16	137.1	23	140.9	29	143.5	24	149.7	23	151.6	14	156.5	–	–
24	8	139.9	9	144.0	26	144.1	30	151.9	21	157.5	16	159.0	11	160.4
25	8	131.8	14	143.4	18	145.4	17	151.4	16	156.9	10	150.9	12	166.4
26	8	133.9	9	150.9	10	146.5	20	151.0	9	150.4	4	151.5	4	172.3
27	9	135.8	4	149.0	8	144.7	14	151.6	10	153.9	4	164.5	1	134.0
28	5	138.2	10	142.8	12	147.7	9	145.8	12	155.3	8	156.4	6	164.8
29	3	146.0	3	135.4	8	143.7	7	155.4	4	148.9	7	163.4	1	166.8
30	5	140.5	8	140.4	9	141.1	4	150.1	7	156.6	5	162.4	3	162.1
31	2	145.2	3	137.9	3	131.3	4	154.8	3	155.7	3	150.2	1	173.0
32	2	124.3	4	135.8	5	149.7	3	148.5	1	174.8	3	196.5	2	163.8
33	1	135.0	3	140.7	2	143.4	3	147.2	2	146.9	1	152.5	–	–
34	2	143.3	3	149.9	3	156.0	2	159.8	1	168.3	4	151.3	1	174.8
35	3	141.9	4	135.6	4	144.6	1	170.0	2	153.4	1	161.8	–	–
36	1	137.0	3	151.9	1	152.8	3	151.5	1	140.8	–	–	1	170.8
37	2	151.5	2	129.4	3	142.9	1	165.0	3	159.6	3	162.0	1	170.8
38	1	137.8	4	139.4	1	131.8	2	141.8	1	119.3	–	–	1	159.8
39	2	150.0	2	140.9	–	–	3	139.3	–	–	1	150.0	–	–
40	3	144.9	1	153.0	7	142.2	1	156.0	2	146.1	1	184.8	1	177.8
41	–	–	–	–	–	–	1	174.3	–	–	–	–	–	–
42	–	–	–	–	2	151.4	1	156.8	1	156.8	–	–	2	165.0
43	3	142.9	–	–	–	–	1	134.8	1	126.8	–	–	1	145.4
44	–	–	–	–	–	–	–	–	1	154.8	–	–	–	–
45	1	132.4	–	–	–	–	–	–	–	–	3	160.7	–	–
46	1	146.8	–	–	1	153.4	–	–	–	–	1	179.8	–	–
47	–	–	–	–	–	–	1	138.3	1	173.8	–	–	1	186.5
48	1	151.4	1	130.8	–	–	1	144.3	2	160.3	2	146.9	–	–
49	–	–	–	–	–	–	2	152.8	–	–	–	–	–	–
50	–	–	–	–	2	145.9	–	–	–	–	–	–	–	–
Over 50	–	–	3	144.8	–	–	2	152.3	–	–	2	164.9	–	–

TABLE XXII.

Mean Weights of Mulattoes, by Age and Height.

Age	64¼ Inches		65¼ Inches		66¼ Inches		67¼ Inches		68¼ Inches		69¼ Inches		70¼ Inches	
	No.	Wt.	No.	Wt.	No.	Wt.	No.	Wt.	No.	Wt.	No.	Wt.	No.	Wt.
		lbs.		lbs.		lbs.		lbs.		lbs.		lbs.		lbs.
15 & und.	–	–	2	116.8	–	–	1	139.8	–	–	–	–	–	–
16	4	117.6	–	–	2	123.1	–	–	1	112.0	–	–	–	–
17	6	130.9	1	121.8	2	136.8	–	–	–	–	–	–	–	–
18	4	119.1	2	165.8	3	125.5	5	138.8	5	138.0	1	132.8	1	144.8
19	7	124.5	4	139.8	11	136.0	4	136.9	2	134.8	3	151.9	–	–
20	9	134.9	12	135.2	7	137.4	10	139.5	9	154.2	2	155.3	5	145.3
21	6	138.0	5	134.4	11	150.8	9	145.2	–	–	3	149.0	3	154.1
22	10	147.0	8	141.0	9	147.0	7	149.6	10	156.8	4	158.1	2	164.8
23	6	137.2	5	140.5	13	146.4	10	150.0	6	148.1	6	164.6	3	159.5
24	7	139.5	10	150.2	9	152.6	11	147.2	2	171.3	5	162.8	3	163.2
25	4	146.5	6	140.3	6	153.3	12	154.1	4	156.8	5	155.7	–	–
26	–	–	5	150.8	9	154.0	4	157.6	3	151.0	5	151.7	1	149.8
27	2	145.9	4	156.4	4	162.1	2	167.8	1	157.8	6	157.1	1	181.8
28	5	131.0	–	–	4	144.5	3	151.5	2	153.5	1	132.0	2	170.3
29	2	151.5	7	152.9	4	154.4	1	147.8	–	–	–	–	4	164.8
30	3	148.5	4	147.0	2	146.2	8	151.2	3	147.9	4	157.8	2	144.0
31	2	148.3	–	–	2	137.8	1	156.8	1	162.4	1	175.0	–	–
32	–	–	2	139.2	2	150.8	5	153.5	2	161.8	1	141.8	1	123.0
33	–	–	–	–	3	149.2	–	–	1	164.8	–	–	–	–
34	–	–	2	141.6	–	–	2	154.4	2	142.0	–	–	–	–
35	5	144.6	2	142.0	2	149.8	–	–	3	144.5	–	–	–	–
36	–	–	1	141.8	2	148.6	–	–	3	163.5	1	164.8	–	–
37	3	147.5	3	139.5	1	154.0	1	157.8	1	146.8	1	201.8	–	–
38	–	–	2	154.8	2	139.8	–	–	–	–	1	163.8	–	–
39	3	140.7	1	150.8	1	147.8	3	157.0	–	–	1	173.8	–	–
40	1	155.8	3	146.5	1	146.8	–	–	–	–	–	–	1	179.0
41	–	–	–	–	–	–	–	–	–	–	–	–	–	–
42	–	–	1	147.8	–	–	–	–	1	142.4	1	181.8	–	–
43	2	131.4	–	–	2	151.4	1	167.8	–	–	1	154.8	–	–
44	1	131.0	1	140.8	–	–	1	162.0	–	–	–	–	–	–
45	–	–	2	131.9	1	156.8	–	–	1	152.8	–	–	–	–
46	–	–	–	–	2	150.3	–	–	1	159.8	–	–	–	–
47	–	–	–	–	–	–	–	–	–	–	–	–	–	–
48	1	144.4	–	–	1	142.8	1	159.8	–	–	–	–	–	–
49	–	–	–	–	–	–	–	–	–	–	–	–	–	–
50	–	–	–	–	–	–	2	150.6	1	161.8	–	–	–	–
Over 50	–	–	–	–	–	–	–	–	–	–	–	–	–	–

TABLE XXIII.

Mean Weights of all Negroes, by Age and Height.

Age	64¼ Inches		65¼ Inches		66¼ Inches		67¼ Inches		68¼ Inches		69¼ Inches		70¼ Inches	
	No.	Wt.	No.	Wt.	No.	Wt.	No.	Wt.	No.	Wt.	No.	Wt.	No.	Wt.
		lbs.		lbs.		lbs.		lbs.		lbs.		lbs.		lbs.
Under 16	1	137.8	3	112.1	–	–	2	135.4	–	–	–	–	–	–
16	5	123.1	8	128.3	6	121.6	1	129.3	2	129.4	1	153.8	–	–
17	11	129.8	7	130.1	6	134.4	9	128.8	2	143.8	2	151.1	–	–
18	13	124.2	12	136.4	16	133.1	12	137.4	12	141.9	4	147.3	3	147.5
19	19	131.8	11	134.2	22	134.6	16	139.1	13	143.4	9	150.2	3	154.9
20	28	138.8	38	137.9	33	141.7	33	145.0	26	150.9	9	156.0	7	144.8
21	25	139.4	25	142.0	30	145.6	30	146.0	15	155.6	11	151.5	5	156.5
22	33	140.8	32	142.9	37	142.4	27	152.3	28	153.9	15	157.6	7	163.0
23	22	137.1	28	140.8	42	144.4	34	149.8	29	150.9	20	158.9	3	159.5
24	15	139.7	19	147.3	35	146.2	41	150.6	23	158.7	21	159.9	14	161.0
25	12	136.7	20	142.5	24	147.1	29	152.5	20	156.9	15	152.5	12	166.4
26	8	138.2	14	150.9	19	150.1	24	152.1	12	150.6	9	151.6	5	167.8
27	11	137.7	8	152.7	12	150.5	16	153.6	11	154.2	10	160.1	2	157.9
28	10	134.6	10	142.9	16	146.9	12	147.2	14	155.0	9	153.7	8	166.2
29	5	148.2	10	147.6	12	147.3	8	154.4	4	148.9	7	163.4	5	165.2
30	8	143.5	12	142.6	11	142.0	12	150.8	10	153.9	9	160.4	5	154.9
31	4	146.8	3	137.9	5	133.9	5	155.2	4	157.4	4	156.4	1	173.0
32	2	124.3	6	137.0	7	150.0	8	151.6	3	166.1	4	182.8	3	150.2
33	1	135.0	3	140.7	5	146.9	3	147.2	3	152.9	1	152.5	–	–
34	2	143.3	5	146.6	3	156.0	4	157.1	3	150.8	4	151.3	1	174.8
35	8	143.6	6	137.7	6	146.4	1	170.0	5	148.1	1	161.8	–	–
36	1	137.0	4	149.4	3	150.0	3	151.5	4	157.8	1	164.8	1	170.8
37	5	149.1	5	135.5	4	145.6	2	161.4	4	156.4	4	172.0	1	170.8
38	1	137.8	6	144.6	3	137.1	2	141.4	1	119.3	1	163.8	1	159.8
39	5	144.4	3	144.2	1	147.8	6	148.2	–	–	2	161.9	–	–
40	4	147.6	4	148.1	8	142.7	1	156.0	2	146.1	1	184.8	2	178.4
41	–	–	–	–	–	–	1	174.3	–	–	–	–	–	–
42	–	–	1	147.8	2	151.4	1	156.8	2	149.6	1	181.8	2	165.0
43	5	138.3	–	–	2	151.4	2	151.3	1	126.8	1	154.8	1	145.4
44	1	131.0	1	140.8	–	–	1	162.0	1	154.8	–	–	–	–
45	1	132.4	2	131.9	1	156.8	–	–	1	152.8	3	160.7	–	–
46	1	146.8	–	–	3	151.3	–	–	1	159.8	1	179.8	–	–
47	–	–	–	–	–	–	1	138.3	1	173.8	–	–	1	186.5
48	2	147.9	1	130.8	1	142.8	2	152.0	2	160.3	2	146.9	–	–
49	–	–	–	–	–	–	2	152.8	–	–	–	–	–	–
50	–	–	–	–	2	145.9	2	150.6	1	161.8	–	–	–	–
Over 50	–	–	3	144.8	–	–	2	152.3	–	–	2	164.9	–	–

TABLE XXIV.

Mean Weights of Iroquois Indians, by Age and Height.

Age	64¼ Inches		65¼ Inches		66¼ Inches		67¼ Inches		68¼ inches		69¼ Inches		70¼ Inches	
	No.	Wt.	No.	Wt.	No.	Wt.	No.	Wt.	No.	Wt.	No.	Wt.	No.	Wt.
		lbs.		lbs.		lbs.		lbs.		lbs.		lbs.		lbs.
Under 18	–	–	–	–	–	–	–	–	1	136.3	–	–	–	–
18	–	–	–	–	2	141.8	–	–	–	–	–	–	–	–
19	–	–	–	–	1	133.3	1	147.3	–	–	–	–	2	147.8
20	–	–	3	128.9	1	128.8	2	155.5	2	154.3	–	–	–	–
21	–	–	2	129.8	3	138.5	3	150.3	5	161.3	–	–	–	–
22	–	–	6	139.4	6	132.0	11	141.0	4	158.2	2	159.8	–	–
23	–	–	4	147.2	1	133.8	11	152.2	9	157.4	4	171.8	1	190.8
24	–	–	1	139.3	1	155.8	17	154.4	12	161.6	4	161.9	2	172.8
25	–	–	1	149.8	1	131.8	5	157 1	3	167.8	1	159.8	3	171.0
26	–	–	4	143.0	7	147.6	11	155.5	13	164.5	7	172.5	1	183.8
27	–	–	–	–	1	130.8	7	150.4	11	163.9	3	167.4	3	180.8
28	1	132.3	2	166.5	2	145.3	16	159.5	12	167.8	3	171.1	2	176.8
29	–	–	–	–	2	152.3	12	155.3	14	163.4	5	176.2	4	184.0
30	–	–	–	–	–	–	5	161.4	6	168.5	7	176.4	3	180.8
31	–	–	–	–	–	–	4	151.8	3	165.5	–	–	2	175.0
32	–	–	–	–	–	–	1	144.8	6	163.4	1	170.8	–	–
33	–	–	–	–	1	181.8	4	154.3	2	159.8	1	180.8	–	–
34	–	–	–	–	–	–	10	152.7	15	165.8	8	175.7	4	175.0
35	–	–	1	142.8	–	–	1	156.8	3	171.3	1	170.8	1	170.8
36	–	–	–	–	1	156.8	4	165.0	15	161.5	5	175.0	–	–
37	–	–	–	–	2	142.8	2	160.8	8	165.8	–	–	4	189.9
38	1	166.3	–	–	–	–	–	–	2	176.8	6	178.3	2	188.3
39	–	–	–	–	1	168.8	1	190.8	2	161.5	1	166.8	–	–
40	–	–	–	–	–	–	3	157.8	6	172.0	2	161.8	2	195.3
41	1	161.8	–	–	–	–	1	151.8	1	166.8	2	178.8	–	–
42	–	–	1	169.3	–	–	5	156.5	1	182.8	–	–	1	141.8
43	–	–	–	–	–	–	2	144.8	5	160.8	1	158.8	–	–
44	–	–	–	–	–	–	–	–	–	–	–	–	–	–
45	–	–	–	–	–	–	1	131.3	–	–	–	–	–	–
46	–	–	–	–	–	–	–	–	2	170.8	2	180.3	1	211.8
47	–	–	–	–	–	–	–	–	1	164.8	–	–	1	276.8
48	–	–	–	–	–	–	–	–	1	162.8	–	–	–	–
49	–	–	–	–	–	–	–	–	–	–	–	–	–	–
50	–	–	–	–	–	–	–	–	–	–	1	182.8	–	–
Over 50	–	–	1	135.8	1	172.8	1	165.8	–	–	4	169.3	–	–

TABLE XXV.

Mean Weights of White Men, by Age.

Age	Soldiers					
	Earlier Series		Later Series		Total	
	No.	Weight	No.	Weight	No.	Weight
		lbs.		lbs.		lbs.
Under 16	43	110.94	31	114.82	74	112.56
16	87	121.62	129	120.72	216	121.03
17	204	130.01	242	126.35	446	128.02
18	433	135.32	667	133.02	1 100	133.93
19	515	137.87	635	136.38	1 150	137.05
20	590	142.35	767	140.64	1 357	141.38
21	617	144.52	829	141.99	1 446	143.06
22	530	145.29	821	142.51	1 351	143.60
23	467	143.50	641	144.93	1 108	144.31
24	413	146.75	646	146.02	1 059	146.31
25	302	149.16	443	145.26	745	146.84
26	224	148.35	375	146.27	599	147.05
27	221	147.50	330	146.54	551	146.93
28	193	147.65	319	146.95	512	147.21
29	145	146.55	241	144.89	386	145.51
30	133	151.46	262	145.67	395	147.62
31	87	151.53	155	145.46	242	147.65
32	93	147.81	205	145.17	298	146.00
33	68	150.53	157	147.66	225	148.53
34	63	151.59	162	147.00	225	148.29
35	80	145.95	159	145.38	239	145.57
36	60	147.49	124	150.16	184	149.29
37	55	151.09	112	147.69	167	148.81
38	40	148.48	113	146.77	153	147.22
39	36	145.92	87	146.57	123	146.38
40	24	160.17	74	146.71	98	150.01
41	17	149.44	44	145.09	61	146.30
42	32	152.95	70	144.24	102	146.97
43	17	151.25	56	143.91	73	145.62
44	26	155.89	57	151.38	83	152.75
45	19	149.24	48	146.20	67	147.06
46	13	150.79	24	144.89	37	146.97
47	4	155.41	15	142.29	19	145.05
48	13	153.94	22	142.61	35	146.82
49	3	139.62	7	147.58	10	145.19
50	7	139.68	14	137.25	21	138.06
51	5	131.99	7	153.00	12	144.25
52	4	142.79	6	137.29	10	139.49
53	5	148.69	6	153.21	11	151.15
54	1	124.79	7	164.58	8	159.60
Over 54	7	148.72	13	140.67	20	143.49

TABLE XXV. — (*Continued.*)

Mean Weights of White Men, by Age.

Age	Sailors		Students		Total White Men	
	No.	Weight	No.	Weight	No.	Weight
		lbs.		lbs.		lbs.
Under 16	2	81.15	–	–	76	111.73
16	4	107.82	–	–	220	120.84
17	5	111.12	3	127.46	454	127.83
18	26	124.93	7	123.58	1 133	133.65
19	46	126.02	39	133.06	1 235	136.51
20	71	131.03	72	137.82	1 500	140.72
21	124	135.53	69	136.69	1 639	142.23
22	132	140.16	44	137.00	1 527	143.11
23	75	139.15	13	136.02	1 196	143.90
24	105	143.99	16	137.45	1 180	145.98
25	97	145.09	11	140.20	853	146.55
26	82	142.31	5	147.19	686	146.48
27	47	138.61	5	146.39	603	146.27
28	56	145.15	1	114.79	569	146.95
29	53	138.49	2	129.29	441	144.59
30	36	138.23	–	–	431	146.84
31	24	138.99	1	144.29	267	146.85
32	36	139.19	–	–	334	145.26
33	12	138.50	–	–	237	148.02
34	16	141.59	–	–	241	147.84
35	23	144.17		–	262	145.45
36	18	147.40		–	202	149.12
37	4	143.50	–	–	171	148.69
38	5	142.02	–	–	158	147.05
39	11	146.18	–	–	134	146.37
40	7	139.18	–	–	105	149.29
41	3	131.00		–	64	145.58
42	3	148.33		–	105	147.01
43	2	135.50		–	75	145.35
44	3	137.67		–	86	152.26
45	4	136.70	–	–	71	146.47
46	1	156.00	–	–	38	147.20
47	1	175.00	–	–	20	146.55
48	4	147.07	–	–	39	146.85
49	1	125.00	–	–	11	143.35
50	2	143.40	–	–	23	138.53
51	–	–	–	–	12	144.25
52	–		–	–	10	139.49
53	–	–	–	–	11	151.15
54	1	145.00	–	–	9	157.98
Over 54	–	–	–	–	20	143.49

TABLE XXVI.

Mean Weights of Negroes and Indians, by Age.

Age	Negroes						Indians	
	Full Blacks		Mulattoes		Aggregate			
	No.	Weight	No.	Weight	No.	Weight	No.	Weight
		lbs.		lbs.		lbs.		lbs.
Under 16	10	111.51	6	118.97	16	114.32	–	–
16	27	121.68	13	117.08	40	120.18	1	136.29
17	45	127.08	11	127.57	56	127.18	–	–
18	78	132.92	25	134.34	103	133.26	2	141.79
19	87	136.62	36	134.90	123	136.12	6	162.12
20	144	141.91	60	142.03	204	141.95	9	148.12
21	133	145.70	53	142.42	186	144.77	14	149.93
22	151	145.33	64	147.48	215	145.97	29	142.48
23	158	146.20	61	147.37	219	146.52	32	159.18
24	139	149.80	54	150.97	193	150.13	39	159.85
25	118	148.37	46	149.88	164	148.79	14	160.22
26	75	149.52	38	149.61	113	149.55	45	159.97
27	70	148.95	26	155.04	96	150.60	28	165.36
28	68	149.72	24	143.74	92	148.16	38	162.87
29	41	150.88	23	152.48	64	151.45	39	165.39
30	43	147.35	33	146.30	76	146.89	21	171.17
31	22	148.60	8	158.65	30	151.28	13	172.21
32	25	151.35	19	151.16	44	151.27	8	161.98
33	13	143.55	4	153.09	17	145.79	8	162.41
34	20	156.08	7	145.55	27	153.35	38	166.17
35	23	144.69	13	145.26	36	144.90	8	168.16
36	11	150.18	10	149.48	21	149.85	26	165.29
37	16	150.87	10	152.15	26	151.36	17	166.29
38	16	143.08	8	145.79	24	143.98	11	178.74
39	10	149.78	11	146.83	21	148.23	6	180.37
40	19	146.26	12	151.44	31	148.27	14	171.79
41	1	174.29	–	–	1	174.29	5	167.59
42	6	157.73	3	157.33	9	157.60	8	159.54
43	7	137.52	6	148.03	13	142.37	8	156.54
44	3	146.61	2	144.60	5	145.81	–	–
45	5	144.89	6	147.16	11	146.13	1	131.29
46	3	160.00	4	152.29	7	155.60	5	182.79
47	3	166.19	–	–	3	166.19	2	220.79
48	9	147.87	3	149.00	12	148.16	1	162.79
49	3	147.46	–	–	3	147.46	–	–
50	3	143.41	4	151.95	7	148.29	1	182.79
51	1	163.00	–	–	1	163.00	2	166.79
52	2	133.79	–	–	2	133.79	1	135.79
53	–	–	2	138.86	2	138.86	1	161.79
54	1	152.79	–	–	1	152.79	–	–
Over 54	4	154.54	3	143.59	7	149.85	6	176.46

The comparatively small size of the groups for ages above 45 years, precludes any reliance upon the mean values deduced from them; but for the ages from 15 to 45 inclusive, our results cannot be far wrong. An empirical determination of the mean weight belonging to each age, as derived from Table XXV., shows that the increase between the ages 21 and 45 cannot well exceed five pounds, great as is the change in many individual cases. The appended Table XXVII., gives the most probable values for the mean weight at each year of age; the data upon which it is based

TABLE XXVII.

Empirical Table of Weight by Age, from White Soldiers.

Age	No. of Men	Weight	Difference Comp. — Obs'd.
		lbs.	lbs.
17	446	128.8	+ 0.8
18	1 100	133.5	− 0.4
19	1 150	137.7	+ 0.6
20	1 357	140.8	− 0.6
21	1 446	142.7	− 0.4
22	1 351	143.9	+ 0.3
23	1 108	145.0	+ 0.7
24	1 059	145.9	− 0.4
25	745	146.6	− 0.2
26	599	146.8	− 0.2
27	551	146.9	0.0
28	512	147.0	0.2
29	386	147.0	+ 1.5
30	395	147.1	− 0.5
31	242	147.1	− 0.5
32	298	147.2	+ 1.2
33	225	147.3	− 1.2
34	225	147.4	− 0.9
35	239	147.5	+ 1.9
36	184	147.6	− 1.7
37	167	147.6	− 1.2
38	153	147.7	+ 0.5
39	123	147.7	+ 1.3
40	98	147.7	− 2.3
41	61	147.7	+ 1.4
42	102	147.8	+ 0.8
43	73	147.8	+ 2.2
44	83	147.8	− 5.0
45	67	147.8	+ 0.7

including all our statistics of white soldiers, but excluding the sailors and students, partly on account of the decidedly inferior weight of the former, but especially since these classes comprise but a portion of the ages under consideration.

Finally, we add in Tables XXVIII. and XXIX. a summary of the maximum and minimum weight observed among the men at each successive year of age, arranged in the same way as our Tables XI. and XII., which showed the extreme values observed at each stature.

TABLE XXVIII.

Limits of Weight observed at Different Ages.

White Soldiers — Earlier Series.

Age	Number of Men	Maximum		Minimum		Range
		Weight	Height	Weight	Height	
		lbs.	in.	lbs.	in.	lbs.
Under 18	334	186.8	72½	72.8	56½	14.0
18	433	202.3	67	98.3	65	104.0
19	515	176.8	70	96.8	62½	80.0
20	590	205.3	76	99.3	68	106.0
21	617	197.8	68½	105.8	63	92.0
22	530	206.8	73½	96.3	64½	110.5
23	467	195.8	71	101.8	63	94.0
24	413	191.8	73	98.8	60	93.0
25	302	205.3	67½	107.3	62½	90.5
26	224	205.8	75	106.8	66	99.0
27	221	195.8	72	116.8	65	79.0
28	193	191.8	69½	110.8	64	81.0
29	145	206.8	73	108.8	66	98.0
30	133	224.3	66½	103.8	66	110.5
31	87	198.3	71½	101.8	67	96.5
32	93	188.8	70½	106.3	65½	82.5
33	68	195.3	73	114.8	67½	80.5
34	63	195.3	71	118.8	63½	76.5
35	80	188.8	68½	112.8	63½	76.0
36	60	189.3	71½	112.3	72	77.0
37	55	228.3	71½	119.8	67	108.5
38	40	209.8	74½	115.8	65½	94.5
39	36	178.8	72	118.8	65	60.0
40	24	197.8	67½	111.8	65½	86.0
Over 40	173	206.8	73	114.8	64½	92.0

TABLE XXIX.

Limits of Weight observed at Different Ages.

White Soldiers — Later Series.

Age	Number of Men	Maximum		Minimum		Range
		Weight	Height	Weight	Height	
		lbs.	in.	lbs.	in.	lbs.
Under 18	402	166.8	67	79.8	58	87.0
18	667	175.3	65	95.8	61½	79.5
19	635	191.3	74½	64.8	58½	126.5
20	767	193.8	68½	96.8	62	97.0
21	829	131.4	66½	94.8	61½	86.6
22	821	191.8	76	95.8	64	96.0
23	641	193.8	72½	102.8	60	91.0
24	646	213.8	68½	101.8	65½	112.0
25	443	206.8	67½	98.8	64	108.0
26	375	186.8	67½	100.8	60½	86.0
27	330	213.8	68	103.8	60	110.0
28	319	200.8	72½	107.8	63	93.0
29	241	192.8	76	106.8	63½	86.0
30	262	219.8	69	106.8	64½	113.0
31	155	207.8	71	91.8	60	116.0
32	205	196.8	73½	111.8	64½	85.0
33	157	184.8	66	98.3	61½	86.5
34	162	198.8	73½	104.8	63½	94.0
35	159	200.8	73	108.8	65	92.0
36	124	194.8	66½	111.8	63½	83.0
37	112	192.8	69	118.3	65½	74.5
38	113	201.8	73½	115.8	65	86.0
39	87	191.3	70½	103.8	62	87.5
40	74	195.8	67½	107.8	61½	88.0
Over 40	396	212.8	71	93.8	63½	119.0

3. *Relation of Weight to Circumference of Chest.*

In the last section, our materials were arranged in such a form as to exhibit the relation of Weight to Age and Stature, without regard to any other influences. By studying the mean weights of men having the same stature, though of different ages, — those of men of different statures, but the same age, — and especially those of groups at successive years of age and of mean statures corresponding to their normal growth as elicited in Chapter V., the law of average lateral expansion, as affected by increase in age, may be investigated with thoroughness and doubtless with success. And its study may be facilitated, as has been already mentioned, by converting the mean weights for each height and age irto ratios between weight and stature.

The present section contains the same materials, grouped according to a different system; namely, by Height and Girth of Chest, without regard to age; and the tables now offered are analogous in arrangement and number to those of the former series, with the substitution of the Circumference of Chest, in the place of Age, as their vertical argument.

In the earlier series of examinations, no rule was prescribed for measuring the circumference of the chest, except that it should be taken over the nipples; and it has already been stated, in our chapter upon Dimensions of Body, that it is impossible to determine what was the usual degree of inflation of the thorax at the time of measurement. Still it may fairly be assumed that the mean of a large number of measures will closely correspond with an average condition of the lungs.

In the later examinations, — comprising all the Sailors, Students, and men of other races than the white, as well as a large preponderance of the volunteer soldiers measured, — the girth was taken both after full inspiration, and after expiration, and the mean between these two values has been employed in our tabulations.

The series of tabular results of our weighings is closed by the Tables XXXIX. and XL., which exhibit the consolidated results, arranged by circumference of chest, as their sole argument, — and analogous to the Tables VIII., XIII., XXV., and XXVI. These tables show so marked a conformity to law that the empirical Table XLI. has been prepared, showing the average weight for white men corresponding to each half-inch of circumference of chest, — the height and the age both being disregarded. The column of differences between the observed and computed values bears witness to the correctness of this determination.

TABLE XXX.

Mean Weights, by Height and Circumference of Chest.

White Soldiers — Earlier Series.

Circ. of Chest	64 Inches		64½ Inches		65 Inches		65½ Inches		66 Inches		66½ Inches		67 Inches	
	No.	Wt.	No.	Wt.	No.	Wt.	No.	Wt.	No.	Wt.	No.	Wt.	No.	Wt.
in.		lbs.		lbs.		lbs.		lbs.		lbs.		lbs.		lbs.
28	–	–	–	–	–	–	–	–	1	165.8	–	–	–	–
28½	–	–	–	–	–	–	–	–	–	–	–	–	–	–
29	–	–	–	–	–	–	–	–	–	–	1	132.3	–	–
29½	1	115.8	2	108.0	–	–	–	–	–	–	–	–	–	–
30	1	109.8	–	–	1	116.8	5	110.8	1	107.8	5	115.8	1	110.8
30½	4	113.4	5	127.3	4	112.9	–	–	2	116.0	1	109.8	8	117.5
31	5	115.7	6	120.5	7	133.2	3	110.6	8	118.9	10	117.7	2	126.0
31½	5	114.7	8	117.2	5	118.7	8	119.0	5	117.9	7	124.4	8	125.2
32	9	116.1	11	116.5	22	121.6	18	121.7	11	121.0	10	122.5	10	118.1
32½	16	118.0	12	120.0	19	122.6	16	126.0	15	128.5	21	125.5	12	127.6
33	12	124.8	21	128.6	11	124.4	20	129.0	26	120.7	23	128.9	16	132.4
33½	17	124.2	23	129.2	13	125.8	31	128.2	29	131.9	18	129.3	18	130.8
34	26	129.5	23	132.2	37	133.9	38	135.4	35	131.3	43	135.4	30	136.1
34½	13	129.3	38	134.0	36	133.0	40	134.6	35	134.2	36	137.1	32	135.3
35	25	135.2	22	133.6	20	134.5	39	136.0	39	137.6	45	139.1	47	141.0
35½	12	135.5	18	137.7	24	141.0	45	137.8	45	140.5	44	140.3	46	142.8
36	12	141.0	17	139.0	18	144.1	37	139.9	28	142.2	54	144.4	40	146.7
36½	8	137.0	18	143.0	15	139.4	23	145.1	20	146.3	30	142.1	31	149.0
37	2	153.0	5	146.3	6	147.4	21	144.4	13	143.4	23	150.5	32	150.8
37½	5	143.4	3	145.1	9	147.7	11	147.8	17	151.1	20	153.2	23	154.6
38	2	143.8	8	144.6	3	145.1	7	141.8	12	152.4	14	148.5	26	156.8
38½	1	153.3	6	148.5	2	156.5	7	151.2	3	158.5	13	154.6	13	153.9
39	2	162.3	3	159.5	3	160.6	3	152.1	3	161.8	4	158.9	10	155.1
39½	2	149.3	1	152.8	2	161.3	1	158.8	3	158.5	6	154.5	3	150.0
40	–	–	1	165.8	1	171.3	2	163.8	1	162.8	2	162.5	4	152.5
40½	–	–	–	–	1	143.8	–	–	–	–	1	183.8	2	155.3
41	–	–	–	–	1	145.3	1	160.3	1	146.3	2	161.8	–	–
41½	–	–	–	–	–	–	–	–	–	–	–	–	1	186.8
42	–	–	1	167.8	–	–	–	–	–	–	2	177.5	–	–
42½	–	–	–	–	–	–	–	–	–	–	–	–	–	–
43	–	–	–	–	–	–	–	–	–	–	–	–	–	–
43½	–	–	–	–	–	–	–	–	–	–	1	224.3	–	–
44	–	–	–	–	–	–	–	–	–	–	–	–	–	–
44½	–	–	–	–	–	–	–	–	–	–	–	–	–	–

TABLE XXX. — (*Continued.*)

Mean Weights, by Height and Circumference of Chest.

White Soldiers — Earlier Series.

Circ. of Chest	67½ Inches		68 Inches		68½ Inches		69 Inches		69½ Inches		70 Inches		70½ Inches	
	No.	Wt.	No.	Wt.	No.	Wt.	No.	Wt.	No.	Wt.	No.	Wt.	No.	Wt.
in.		lbs.		lbs.		lbs.		lbs.		lbs.		lbs.		lbs.
28	–	–	–	–	–	–	–	–	–	–	–	–	–	–
28½	–	–	–	–	–	–	–	–	–	–	–	–	–	–
29	1	111.8	–	–	–	–	1	164.8	–	–	–	–	–	–
29½	–	–	–	–	–	–	–	–	–	–	–	–	–	–
30	–	–	1	99.3	1	156.8	–	–	–	–	1	136.8	–	–
30½	2	128.0	1	125.8	3	126.1	2	116.0	1	113.3	–	–	–	–
31	2	130.5	9	119.0	–	–	2	116.5	1	138.3	–	–	–	–
31½	7	125.8	2	119.8	5	124.4	7	126.8	2	122.5	1	123.3	–	–
32	9	127.5	11	127.4	12	132.2	6	135.8	3	128.1	–	–	2	134.3
32½	12	129.2	4	130.2	12	126.4	8	131.4	8	134.0	6	139.5	4	138.4
33	30	131.1	27	131.0	22	133.5	11	134.4	8	139.0	7	131.2	6	135.2
33½	29	133.7	25	135.8	29	136.6	10	139.8	11	139.9	8	138.7	7	136.0
34	46	138.2	42	135.3	27	141.3	28	142.5	20	138.8	15	138.5	7	148.6
34½	53	136.9	32	141.2	33	140.5	21	141.9	22	140.4	15	143.0	14	147.4
35	40	142.9	39	143.6	35	144.9	37	144.6	27	146.8	17	151.7	21	143.7
35½	46	146.9	31	145.1	38	146.3	41	147.9	26	147.6	27	147.3	19	152.5
36	55	147.3	48	149.1	45	149.4	39	150.8	25	152.4	26	151.7	15	156.1
36½	45	148.7	29	151.7	42	152.1	37	152.4	30	155.5	22	153.5	19	157.9
37	44	154.9	37	153.0	36	157.6	31	153.2	31	154.8	28	158.0	17	156.4
37½	35	153.8	36	156.4	49	159.1	21	155.8	22	153.3	29	162.7	13	163.7
38	17	157.9	31	158.9	34	159.4	18	160.9	18	160.5	14	160.3	15	165.9
38½	13	160.5	14	155.4	22	158.5	15	163.3	22	164.3	14	160.9	14	168.8
39	9	162.9	13	163.2	9	163.0	19	165.0	8	163.4	18	173.4	12	170.1
39½	2	162.8	5	161.4	11	165.8	3	171.3	8	166.7	7	172.4	6	178.0
40	4	164.5	6	159.1	3	167.8	3	167.1	5	170.8	3	182.8	7	175.2
40½	2	168.5	4	170.8	2	174.0	2	176.8	4	167.8	1	161.8	2	177.0
41	1	140.8	1	182.8	–	–	1	177.8	3	178.6	3	172.0	1	174.0
41½	–	–	–	–	–	–	1	170.3	1	176.8	–	–	2	178.5
42	3	164.6	–	–	–	–	2	186.3	–	–	1	174.3	1	175.3
42½	–	–	–	–	–	–	1	200.8	–	–	2	177.3	1	181.8
43	–	–	–	–	–	–	–	–	–	–	1	192.8	–	–
43½	1	174.3	–	–	–	–	–	–	–	–	–	–	–	–
44	1	197.8	–	–	–	–	–	–	–	–	–	–	–	–
44½	–	–	–	–	–	–	–	–	–	–	–	–	–	–

TABLE XXXI.

Mean Weights, by Height and Circumference of Chest.

White Soldiers — Later Series.

Circ. of Chest	64 Inches		64½ Inches		65 Inches		65½ Inches		66 Inches		66½ Inches		67 Inches	
	No.	Wt.	No.	Wt	No.	Wt.	No.	Wt.	No.	Wt.	No.	Wt.	No.	Wt.
in.		lbs.		lbs.		lbs.		lbs.		lbs.		lbs.		lbs.
28	–	–	–	–	–	–	–	–	1	110.8	–	–	–	–
28½	1	101.8	–	–	–	–	–	–	–	–	–	–	–	–
29	1	101.8	–	–	–	–	–	–	–	–	–	–	–	–
29½	–	–	1	98.8	–	–	–	–	–	–	–	–	1	116.8
30	1	110.8	2	109.8	2	101.8	1	121.3	2	111.8	2	120.3	–	–
30½	3	110.6	5	110.3	2	121.3	2	113.3	3	125.8	1	116.8	1	113.8
31	7	106.9	4	119.0	8	112.2	5	116.5	3	113.5	4	114.9	2	129.8
31½	10	111.2	11	112.1	6	118.9	6	118.8	5	113.0	10	115.1	8	119.0
32	12	114.4	21	120.0	21	119.6	13	121.6	8	117.4	15	122.1	12	122.7
32½	13	118.9	21	118.6	21	121.1	21	122.3	17	122.7	19	121.4	19	126.0
33	27	120.7	42	121.3	28	125.9	34	127.3	34	127.5	28	128.5	31	127.8
33½	22	128.6	34	123.6	32	124.9	55	124.5	21	129.3	31	126.8	36	132.5
34	29	127.4	44	126 3	59	128.6	52	127.5	37	129.7	75	131.2	49	132.2
34½	34	126.8	39	128.1	48	129.3	59	131.1	54	131.8	72	133.7	48	134.0
35	29	129.8	42	131.6	51	133.0	78	135.3	52	136.2	79	134.8	57	137.2
35½	26	134.9	43	136.6	38	134.2	66	136.4	57	137.4	82	137.0	74	139.4
36	30	138.4	40	137.3	31	135.0	60	138.9	50	138.1	92	141.3	87	142.2
36½	18	140.0	31	136.1	27	141.4	52	139.0	44	145.9	64	143.2	72	146.1
37	16	140.7	25	146.3	29	142.9	36	143.1	33	147.9	58	145.9	79	146.9
37½	11	137.9	21	140.4	15	144.0	33	143.7	24	146.1	55	145.7	56	151.7
38	6	144.9	11	140.9	15	148.1	22	151.2	20	151.5	34	152.5	38	150.7
38½	4	138.3	1	155.8	7	154.2	19	150.5	13	153.2	17	153.5	33	157.8
39	1	151.3	7	142.4	6	152.6	12	150.8	12	156.1	20	160.9	17	157.9
39½	2	153.5	4	145.8	3	165.5	6	157.3	8	151.0	9	156.5	9	163.0
40	–	–	1	166.8	2	161.0	4	154.2	4	153.2	7	157.0	7	164.8
40½	1	151.8	–	–	–	–	–	–	2	165.3	4	162.5	2	164.3
41	1	159.8	1	151.3	–	–	1	142.8	–	–	4	163.7	–	–
41½	–	–	–	–	–	–	–	–	–	–	3	174.6	1	181.8
42	–	–	–	–	–	–	–	–	1	183.8	–	–	3	165.6
42½	–	–	–	–	–	–	1	152.8	1	184.8	1	159.8	–	–
43	–	–	–	–	–	–	–	–	–	–	–	–	–	–
43½	–	–	–	–	–	–	–	–	–	–	–	–	1	180.8
44	–	–	–	–	–	–	–	–	–	–	–	–	–	–
44½	–	–	–	–	–	–	–	–	–	–	–	–	–	–

TABLE XXXI. – (*Continued.*)

Mean Weights, by Height and Circumference of Chest.

White Soldiers — Later Series.

Circ. of Chest	67½ Inches		68 Inches		68½ Inches		69 Inches		69½ Inches		70 Inches		70½ Inches	
	No.	Wt.	No.	Wt.	No.	Wt.	No.	Wt.	No.	Wt.	No.	Wt.	No.	Wt.
in.		lbs.		lbs.		lbs.		lbs.		lbs.		lbs.		lbs.
28	–	–	–	–	–	–	–	–	–	–	–	–	–	–
28½	–	–	–	–	–	–	–	–	–	–	–	–	–	–
29	–	–	–	–	–	–	–	–	–	–	–	–	–	–
29½	–	–	–	–	–	–	–	–	–	–	–	–	–	–
30	1	105.8	–	–	–	–	1	118.8	–	–	1	134.8	–	–
30½	2	116.8	1	119.8	–	–	–	–	–	–	–	–	–	–
31	4	113.3	1	136.8	1	108.8	2	109.0	–	–	1	107.8	–	–
31½	2	123.8	2	122.5	3	129.6	2	128.8	1	127.3	–	–	–	–
32	8	123.4	6	129.5	6	132.3	3	129.1	3	125.6	–	–	2	137.3
32½	16	129.8	12	133.5	13	130.8	12	127.6	6	134.7	5	135.9	–	–
33	18	131.6	21	130.4	12	132.1	7	135.5	9	132.4	2	134.3	4	140.4
33½	29	132.9	22	135.5	24	133.4	9	132.7	9	141.2	3	131.5	6	147.1
34	44	136.0	35	135.7	37	140.1	29	142.9	25	139.7	10	140.0	6	141.5
34½	49	137.5	32	139.3	47	138.8	31	141.1	17	145.1	12	142.9	9	151.8
35	77	138.9	56	141.1	40	140.4	45	143.8	29	143.7	30	144.9	21	149 5
35½	85	141.4	69	145.2	68	143.1	47	145.7	45	147.2	33	148.7	18	149.7
36	114	142.8	109	144.4	49	145.2	49	147.2	43	148.4	37	152.8	24	151.5
36½	82	145.0	74	147.2	78	148.3	45	148.8	49	152.3	35	152.1	18	155.7
37	82	148.7	71	148.0	65	151.3	51	155.0	44	155.5	29	155.8	27	158.2
37½	62	147.5	49	150.5	57	153.0	25	154.2	32	159.2	26	158.2	27	156.2
38	47	153.3	45	155.9	55	153.5	30	161.2	40	158.4	30	161.7	24	162.4
38½	45	155.2	23	153.6	43	156.5	23	164.4	24	163.4	22	163.3	15	159.6
39	26	156.8	18	161.7	16	158.3	16	162.3	28	161.6	15	163.7	16	168.0
39½	15	156.3	14	158.7	21	163.5	10	163.3	9	169.8	7	169.0	6	168.8
40	12	164.6	7	162.4	8	164.9	14	167.7	11	164.8	8	172.1	8	178.6
40½	7	168.3	2	168.8	7	167.9	3	181.1	5	172.7	–	–	4	177.4
41	1	173.3	–	–	5	171.4	2	173.3	4	181.8	3	178.5	5	176.3
41½	–	–	3	172.5	1	158.3	3	170.1	4	180.4	3	183.5	2	183.0
42	1	186.8	–	–	1	180.8	2	171.8	1	183.8	2	175.0	–	–
42½	1	195.8	1	213.8	–	–	–	–	1	184.5	–	–	–	–
43	1	163.4	–	–	1	213.8	–	–	1	196.8	1	192.8	–	–
43½	–	–	–	–	–	–	–	–	–	–	–	–	–	–
44	–	–	–	–	–	–	1	218.8	–	–	–	–	–	–
44½	–	–	–	–	–	–	1	214.8	–	–	–	–	–	–

TABLE XXXII.

Mean Weights, by Height and Circumference of Chest.

White Soldiers — Both Series.[1]

Circ. of Chest	64 Inches		64½ Inches		65 Inches		65½ Inches		66 Inches		66½ Inches		67 Inches	
	No.	Wt.	No.	Wt.	No.	Wt.	No.	Wt.	No.	Wt.	No.	Wt.	No.	Wt.
		lbs.		lbs.		lbs.		lbs.		lbs.		lbs.		lbs.
28	–	–	–	–	–	–	–	–	2	138.3	–	–	–	–
28½	1	101.8	–	–	–	–	–	–	–	–	–	–	–	–
29	1	101.8	–	–	–	–	–	–	–	–	1	132.3	–	–
29½	1	115.8	3	105.0	–	–	–	–	–	–	–	–	1	116.8
30	2	110.3	3	108.1	3	106.8	6	112.5	3	110.5	7	117.1	1	110.8
30½	7	112.2	10	118.8	6	115.7	2	113.3	5	121.9	3	113.0	9	117.1
31	12	110.6	11	118.9	15	122.0	8	114.3	11	117.4	14	116.9	4	127.9
31½	15	112.4	19	114.2	11	118.8	14	118.9	10	115.4	18	119.5	17	122.0
32	21	115.1	33	118.8	45	120.6	31	121.7	19	119.5	25	122.3	22	120.6
32½	29	118.4	34	119.0	41	121.7	38	124.4	32	125.5	40	123.6	32	126.4
33	39	122.0	64	123.7	39	125.5	56	128.0	60	124.5	51	128.7	48	129.2
33½	39	126.7	61	125.7	46	125.4	87	125.8	57	130.9	49	127.8	55	132.0
34	56	128.5	68	128.3	91	130.3	92	130.6	75	130.5	121	132.9	81	133.3
34½	50	127.7	79	131.1	87	131.0	101	132.4	91	132.7	114	135.0	85	134.6
35	58	132.0	65	132.3	74	133.3	119	135.5	94	136.9	126	136.4	108	139.1
35½	40	134.2	67	136.5	64	136.6	117	136.9	109	138.7	131	138.5	125	140.9
36	43	139.0	61	137.9	51	138.3	102	139.2	80	139.5	150	142.6	131	143.5
36½	27	138.8	50	138.6	47	140.6	81	140.6	66	146.0	98	143.1	106	147.0
37	19	142.2	31	146.2	35	143.7	58	143.4	50	146.6	84	147.2	113	148.1
37½	17	140.1	25	141.1	26	145.6	46	144.8	44	148.7	78	147.8	81	152.5
38	8	144.6	19	142.5	19	147.7	30	148.6	34	152.0	50	151.7	66	153.8
38½	5	141.3	8	149.7	9	155.5	26	150.7	17	154.3	32	154.0	49	154.3
39	3	158.6	10	147.5	9	155.3	15	151.0	15	157.4	24	160.6	28	156.9
39½	5	153.9	5	147.2	5	163.8	8	155.4	11	153.1	15	155.7	12	159.7
40	–	–	2	166.3	3	164.5	6	157.4	5	155.1	9	158.3	12	161.1
40½	1	151.8	–	–	1	143.8	–	–	2	165.3	5	166.8	4	159.8
41	1	159.8	1	151.3	1	145.3	2	151.5	1	146.3	7	163.0	–	–
41½	–	–	–	–	–	–	–	–	–	–	3	174.6	2	184.3
42	–	–	1	167.8	–	–	–	–	1	183.8	2	177.5	3	165.6
42½	–	–	–	–	–	–	–	152.8	1	184.8	1	159.8	–	–
43	–	–	–	–	–	–	–	–	–	–	–	–	–	–
43½	–	–	–	–	–	–	–	–	–	–	1	224.3	1	180.8
44	–	–	–	–	–	–	–	–	–	–	–	–	–	–
44½	–	–	–	–	–	–	–	–	–	–	–	–	–	–

[1] A few men are included in this table, for whom the returns were received too late for incorporation in the tables immediately preceding.

TABLE XXXII. — (*Continued.*)

Mean Weights, by Height and Circumference of Chest.

White Soldiers — Both Series.

Circ. of Chest	67½ Inches		68 Inches		68½ Inches		69 Inches		69½ Inches		70 Inches		70½ Inches	
	No.	Wt.	No.	Wt.	No.	Wt.	No.	Wt.	No.	Wt.	No.	Wt.	No.	Wt.
in.		lbs.		lbs.		lbs.		lbs.		lbs.		lbs.		lbs.
28	–	–	–	–	–	–	–	–	–	–	–	–	–	–
28½	–	–	–	–	–	–	–	–	–	–	–	–	–	–
29	1	111.8	–	–	–	–	1	164.8	–	–	–	–	–	–
29½	–	–	–	–	–	–	–	–	–	–	–	–	–	–
30	1	105.8	1	99.3	1	156.8	1	118.8	–	–	2	274.8	–	–
30½	4	122.4	2	122.8	3	126.1	2	116.0	1	113.3	–	–	–	–
31	6	115.7	10	120.8	1	108.8	4	112.8	1	138.3	1	107.8	–	–
31½	9	125.4	4	121.2	9	127.3	9	127.2	3	124.1	1	123.3	–	–
32	18	125.0	18	129.1	18	132.2	9	133.6	6	126.9	–	–	4	135.8
32½	28	129.5	18	132.9	25	128.7	20	129.1	14	134.3	12	137.9	4	138.4
33	48	131.3	48	130.7	35	133.2	18	134.8	17	135.5	9	131.9	10	137.3
33½	60	133.3	47	135.7	53	135.2	19	136.4	20	140.5	11	136.7	13	141.2
34	91	137.0	80	135.7	65	140.4	58	142.8	46	139.5	27	138.9	14	144.9
34½	106	137.3	65	140.4	82	139.5	52	141.4	40	142.7	27	142.9	23	149.1
35	119	140.1	98	142.0	75	142.5	85	144.3	57	145.2	48	147.1	43	146.5
35½	138	143.2	105	145.3	108	144.3	90	146.9	72	147.4	61	148.1	37	151.1
36	174	144.3	163	146.0	101	146.9	90	148.8	69	149.6	64	152.3	42	153.5
36½	131	146.6	111	148.9	121	149.6	88	150.4	85	153.2	57	152.6	43	158.0
37	131	150.6	113	149.7	105	153.5	83	154.3	79	155.4	59	157.0	45	157.4
37½	99	150.0	86	152.9	109	155.8	51	155.5	56	157.1	57	160.6	40	158.6
38	66	154.5	78	157.1	90	155.8	50	161.2	62	159.2	44	161.3	39	163.8
38½	59	156.6	41	154.1	66	157.1	40	163 6	49	163.8	37	162.5	30	163.7
39	41	159.0	32	162.1	29	161.2	37	164.2	36	162.0	34	168.7	28	168.9
39½	17	157.1	19	159.4	33	164.0	14	166.7	17	168.3	14	170.7	14	173.6
40	17	164.2	13	160.9	12	165.4	17	167.6	17	167.4	13	175.2	17	176.7
40½	9	168.4	7	168.5	9	169.3	5	179.4	9	170.5	1	161.8	6	177.3
41	2	157.0	1	182.8	6	173.2	3	174.8	7	180.4	7	174.7	8	178.0
41½	1	200.8	3	172.5	1	158.3	4	170.2	5	179.7	3	183 5	4	180.8
42	4	170.2	–	–	1	180.8	4	179.0	1	183.8	3	174.8	1	175.3
42½	1	195.8	1	213.8	–	–	1	200.8	1	178.5	2	177.3	1	181.8
43	1	163.3	–	–	1	213.8	–	–	1	196.8	2	192.8	–	–
43½	1	174.3	–	–	–	–	–	–	–	–	–	–	–	–
44	1	197.8	–	–	–	–	1	218.8	–	–	–	–	–	–
44½	–	–	–	–	–	–	1	214.8	–	–	–	–	–	–

TABLE XXXIII.

Mean Weights of Sailors,
by Height and Circumference of Chest.

Circ. of Chest	64¼ Inches		65¼ Inches		66¼ Inches		67¼ Inches		68¼ Inches		69¼ Inches		70¼ Inches	
	No.	Wt.	No.	Wt.	No.	Wt.	No.	Wt.	No.	Wt.	No.	Wt.	No.	Wt.
in.		lbs.		lbs.		lbs.		lbs.		lbs.		lbs.		lbs.
Under 30	1	112.0	1	103.0	2	108.5	–	–	–	–	–	–	–	–
30	1	119.0	2	108.0	–	–	–	–	–	–	–	–	–	–
30½	3	115.3	–	–	–	–	–	–	–	–	–	–	–	–
31	1	103.0	2	115.0	–	–	2	123.5	1	125.0	1	126.0	–	–
31½	4	117.5	2	123.0	1	114.0	3	122.3	–	–	–	–	–	–
32	10	116.2	9	121.9	4	130.1	3	121.0	1	124.0	2	126.5	–	–
32½	6	125.8	9	122.9	5	122.9	5	127.5	–	–	1	134.0	1	145.0
33	18	124.1	17	130.1	17	129.9	6	134.0	8	135.3	3	134.0	–	–
33½	7	124.4	14	125.6	7	132.0	8	131.6	7	139.5	3	137.3	3	148.1
34	20	129.2	17	132.0	22	136.9	13	138.6	9	146.6	8	142.3	4	145.8
34½	10	135.0	13	134.2	10	137.9	14	143.6	4	143.5	6	144.5	3	149.3
35	21	135.9	19	140.5	19	138.2	28	140.9	18	146.7	11	148.2	5	145.6
35½	9	134.6	13	136.1	10	142.9	10	145.3	8	147.2	10	151.8	1	140.0
36	14	142.6	18	137.0	17	140.4	19	145.6	12	149.8	14	157.7	–	–
36½	8	139.4	15	141.4	10	140.8	13	148.2	10	147.8	4	153.2	6	156.3
37	8	136.8	12	145.1	18	150.6	16	158.0	15	151.4	9	155.4	3	163.3
37½	4	149.3	8	144.9	4	146.4	12	154.8	3	159.5	5	154.8	2	172.5
38	6	145.3	12	146.8	5	154.7	4	157.0	9	163.2	5	158.0	3	165.3
38½	–	–	3	150.3	2	162.5	6	162.4	1	161.0	3	157.5	1	172.0
39	3	148.6	1	168.0	1	144.0	5	161.2	2	169.5	1	175.0	3	177.0
39½	1	151.3	1	155.3	2	168.0	–	–	3	174.3	1	164.0	–	–
40	–	–	–	–	–	–	–	–	2	171.5	–	–	1	171.8
40½	2	163.5	1	166.0	–	–	–	–	1	178.0	–	–	–	–
41	–	–	–	–	–	–	2	169.8	2	174.5	–	–	–	–
41½	–	–	–	–	–	–	–	–	–	–	–	–	1	175.0
42	–	–	–	–	1	163.0	–	–	–	–	–		–	–
42½	–	–	–	–	–	–	–	–	–	–	–	–	1	189.0

TABLE XXXIV.

Mean Weights of Students,
by Height and Circumference of Chest.

Circ. of Chest	64¼ Inches		65¼ Inches		66¼ Inches		67¼ Inches		68¼ Inches		69¼ Inches		70¼ Inches	
	No.	Wt.	No.	Wt.	No.	Wt.	No.	Wt.	No.	Wt.	No.	Wt.	No.	Wt.
in.		lbs.		lbs.		lbs.		lbs.		lbs.		lbs.		lbs.
31½	1	114.8	–	–	1	121.8	3	112.0	–	–	–	–	–	–
32	–	–	2	113.3	–	–	2	121.8	–	–	–	–	–	–
32½	4	114.3	4	121.9	1	120.8	–	–	–	–	3	125.6	1	129.8
33	–	–	1	122.1	2	116.8	–	–	1	120.8	2	130.1	–	–
33½	1	116.8	8	119.7	4	120.1	7	121.0	2	123.1	6	126.1	–	–
34	–	–	–	–	3	134.5	1	123.3	2	126.8	3	139.0	1	141.8
34½	4	127.8	8	123.4	11	129.5	5	125.9	11	131.8	5	134.3	5	140.0
35	2	131.1	1	114.8	3	127.1	2	130.4	12	133.6	1	152.8	1	141.3
35½	2	125.1	2	133.8	6	135.1	4	135.2	7	134.7	6	143.6	6	145.1
36	–	–	4	130.7	1	142.3	7	139.5	1	133.8	3	142.1	3	148.1
36½	–	–	3	139.4	3	144.6	3	137.3	4	152.3	5	147.4	4	137.8
37	–	–	–	–	–	–	2	141.6	–	–	4	149.9	2	142.5
37½	–	–	–	–	1	142.8	–	–	3	142.8	3	148.0	5	153.0
38	–	–	–	–	–	–	–	–	–	–	1	146.8	–	–
38½	–	–	–	–	–	–	–	–	1	160.8	3	160.5	6	164.6
Over 38½	–	–	–	–	1	166.8	–	–	–	–	1	174.8	–	–

TABLE XXXV.

Mean Weights of Full Blacks, by Height and Circumference of Chest.

Circ. of Chest	64¼ Inches		65 Inches		66¼ Inches		67¼ Inches		68¼ Inches		69¼ Inches		70¼ Inches	
	No.	Wt.	No.	Wt.	No.	Wt.	No.	Wt.	No.	Wt.	No.	Wt.	No.	Wt.
in.		lbs.		lbs.		lbs.		lbs.		lbs.		lbs.		lbs.
32	6	127.8	6	131.2	9	128.6	6	126.2	3	133.9	1	123.0	–	–
32½	15	130.4	6	129.9	12	131.0	10	132.2	3	137.5	3	133.1	–	–
33	12	129.9	20	132.9	18	134.4	12	138.5	4	136.6	1	159.8	3	138.6
33½	21	133.6	27	134.4	27	136.5	16	142.5	7	144.3	6	147.6	–	–
34	15	135.9	19	138.8	29	139.1	22	143.2	15	142.0	9	144.8	4	157.3
34½	16	138.6	24	135.9	28	144.9	28	147.0	24	147.8	12	146.2	3	166.9
35	15	141.7	20	140.8	23	143.6	36	147.1	27	153.2	12	154.3	8	149.9
35½	21	139.7	23	143.3	30	145.0	22	147.6	28	151.0	15	163.6	2	160.9
36	14	145.7	17	143.1	20	146.6	23	150.0	14	156.5	16	158.8	11	160.0
36½	6	144.2	13	150.2	16	148.2	24	151.1	23	156.7	14	158.7	8	161.2
37	8	142.6	16	150.0	19	151.7	15	159.0	14	159.4	6	161.7	4	168.2
37½	8	150.2	7	155.6	6	160.4	8	159.7	10	166.1	9	164.6	4	170.8
38	4	156.8	7	154.3	5	153.1	11	162.0	8	166.6	7	164.4	11	169.6
38½	1	153.0	4	150.9	6	156.8	5	157.3	2	165.2	7	175.4	1	187.1
39	–	–	–	–	2	163.2	5	175.0	2	163.3	3	177.7	4	179.0
39½	–	–	–	–	1	161.8	1	162.0	2	170.3	3	168.2	–	–
40	1	161.0	2	137.6	–	–	1	185.8	3	151.9	1	167.0	1	183.6

TABLE XXXVI.

Mean Weights of Mulattoes,
by Height and Circumference of Chest.

Circ. of Chest	64¼ Inches		65¼ Inches		66¼ Inches		67¼ Inches		68¼ Inches		69¼ Inches		70¼ Inches	
	No.	Wt.	No.	Wt.	No.	Wt.	No.	Wt.	No.	Wt.	No.	Wt.	No.	Wt.
in.		lbs.		lbs.		lbs.		lbs.		lbs.		lbs.		lbs.
32	4	122.0	5	132.4	5	140.9	1	145.2	–	–	–	–	–	–
32½	9	130.4	3	121.8	6	134.7	5	141.9	2	144.0	–	–	–	–
33	3	135.9	10	140.7	11	137.5	3	131.1	3	135.8	1	140.5	–	–
33½	11	134.2	13	138.2	3	135.4	10	138.6	3	137.3	5	149.7	2	136.6
34	8	139.1	9	139.0	14	140.7	7	145.1	4	143.5	3	141.5	2	149.1
34½	8	136.5	8	141.1	24	147.1	16	150.7	9	146.6	3	151.7	4	146.3
35	11	136.0	10	146.6	7	154.0	10	148.0	10	153.4	7	152.4	3	159.7
35½	10	149.0	8	145.3	13	153.4	16	150.6	8	154.7	7	156.2	3	150.8
36	4	152.0	6	150.1	9	153.3	9	153.9	6	159.0	7	157.7	3	163.5
36½	8	140.0	7	152.1	3	153.2	10	151.6	4	157.4	5	168.1	2	156.3
37	2	150.1	–	–	4	144.4	3	163.6	2	152.0	3	173.5	2	157.6
37½	5	152.3	4	152.1	7	154.6	2	171.9	–	–	5	168.6	–	–
38	–	–	4	151.7	3	166.1	1	167.6	3	164.0	3	165.9	–	–
38½	–	–	1	167.5	2	175.9	2	167.2	4	164.1	3	176.9	5	171.2
39	–	–	–	–	1	147.5	1	163.7	–	–	–	–	–	–
39½	–	–	1	168.1	1	182.5	2	159.4	–	–	–	–	1	185.2
40	–	–	–	–	–	–	–	–	1	171.6	–	–	–	–

TABLE XXXVII.

Mean Weights of Negroes,
by Height and Circumference of Chest.

Circ. of Chest	64¼ Inches		65¼ Inches		66¼ Inches		67¼ Inches		68¼ Inches		69¼ Inches		70¼ Inches	
	No.	Wt.	No.	Wt.	No.	Wt.	No.	Wt.	No.	Wt.	No.	Wt.	No.	Wt.
inches		lbs.		lbs.		lbs.		lbs.		lbs.		lbs.		lbs.
32	10	125.5	11	131.7	14	133.0	7	128.9	3	133.9	1	123.0	–	–
32½	24	130.4	9	127.2	18	132.2	15	135.4	5	140.1	3	133.1	–	–
33	15	131.1	30	135.5	29	135.6	15	137.0	7	136.3	2	150.2	3	138.6
33½	32	133.8	40	135.6	30	136.4	26	141.0	10	142.2	11	148.5	2	136.6
34	23	137.0	28	138.9	43	139.6	29	143.7	19	142.3	12	144.0	6	154.6
34½	24	137.9	32	137.2	52	145.9	44	148.3	33	147.5	15	147.3	7	155.1
35	26	139.3	30	142.7	30	146.0	46	147.3	37	153.3	19	153.6	11	152.6
35½	31	142.7	31	143.8	43	147.5	38	148.9	36	151.8	22	161.2	5	154.8
36	18	147.1	23	144.9	29	148.7	32	151.1	20	157.2	23	158.5	14	160.7
36½	14	141.8	20	150.9	19	149.0	34	151.2	27	156.8	19	161.2	10	160.2
37	10	144.1	16	150.0	23	150.4	18	159.8	16	158.5	9	165.6	6	164.7
37½	13	151.0	11	154.3	13	157.3	10	162.1	10	166.1	14	166.0	4	170.8
38	4	156.8	11	153.4	8	158.0	12	162.5	11	165.9	10	164.8	11	169.6
38½	1	153.0	5	154.2	8	161.6	7	160.1	6	164.5	10	175.8	6	173.8
39	–	–	–	–	3	158.0	6	173.1	2	163.3	3	177.7	4	179.0
39½	–	–	1	168.1	2	172.1	3	160.3	2	170.3	3	168.2	1	185.2
40	1	161.1	2	137.6	–	–	1	185.8	4	156.8	1	167.0	1	183.6

TABLE XXXVIII.

Mean Weights of Iroquois Indians, by Height and Circumference of Chest.

Circ. of Chest	64¼ Inches		65¼ Inches		66¼ Inches		67¼ Inches		68¼ Inches		69¼ Inches		70¼ Inches	
	No.	Wt.	No.	Wt.	No.	Wt.	No.	Wt.	No.	Wt.	No.	Wt.	No.	Wt.
inches		lbs.		lbs.		lbs.		lbs.		lbs.		lbs.		lbs.
35 & less	–	–	4	129.8	6	135.0	3	138.0	2	142.0	–	–	2	144.8
35½	–	–	7	138.7	5	137.2	4	138.8	2	137.8	–	–	1	141.8
36	–	–	2	131.3	7	145.0	6	143.5	6	154.3	–	–	1	141.8
36½	–	–	4	146.8	8	141.4	16	149.5	16	153.8	9	165.9	1	151.8
37	–	–	1	154.8	4	148.3	31	155.1	35	158.6	6	157.6	2	167.8
37½	1	132.3	4	144.3	1	140.8	24	156.2	34	165.3	13	170.4	1	174.8
38	–	–	–	–	–	–	5	162.3	7	169.3	3	165.5	2	169.3
38½	–	–	1	164.8	–	–	12	165.5	28	167.6	14	174.8	8	181.7
39	–	–	2	154.0	–	–	2	161.8	7	173.2	7	176.7	4	176.6
39½	1	161.8	1	169.3	1	168.8	6	166.2	13	170.9	3	177.8	2	177.3
40	–	–	–	–	–	–	1	156.8	2	167.8	3	177.8	–	–
40½	–	–	–	–	–	–	2	168.3	2	181.8	1	190.8	2	188.3
41	1	166.3	–	–	1	181.8	2	158.3	2	176.8	4	184.3	3	192.1
41½	–	–	–	–	1	172.8	2	178.3	4	178.3	2	180.8	4	189.9
42	–	–	–	–	–	–	1	159.3	3	173.0	1	164.8	2	198.8
42½	–	–	–	–	–	–	–	–	–	–	5	179.4	1	193.8
43 & over	–	–	–	–	–	–	–	–	3	176.5	–	–	3	204.4

TABLE XXXIX.

Mean Weights of White Men, by Circumference of Chest.

Circumf. of Chest	Soldiers					
	Earlier Series		Later Series		Total	
	No.	Weight	No.	Weight	No.	Weight
inches		lbs.		lbs.		lbs.
Under 26	–	–	1	64.79	1	64.79
26	–	–	1	86.79	1	86.79
26½	2	77.29	–	–	2	77.29
27	3	96.96	1	79.79	4	92.66
27½	–	–	1	81.79	1	81.79
28	5	120.99	4	89.29	9	106.90
28½	1	95.29	1	101.79	2	98.54
29	9	109.46	7	102.36	16	106.35
29½	3	110.62	11	100.33	14	102.54
30	34	110.61	31	111.21	65	110 90
30½	44	116.39	32	112.92	76	114.93
31	70	118.91	81	112.39	151	115.41
31½	92	121.38	104	115.38	196	118.20
32	169	121.83	192	118.93	361	120.29
32½	197	125.60	249	123.31	446	124.32
33	291	128.54	364	126.25	655	127.27
33½	334	131.13	411	128.12	745	129.47
34	495	135.11	645	132.03	1 140	133.37
34½	493	137.14	656	134.18	1 149	135.45
35	540	140.93	797	137.93	1 337	139.14
35½	544	144.03	879	140.69	1 423	141.96
36	553	147.16	935	143.33	1 488	144.76
36½	465	149.42	803	147.18	1 268	148.00
37	392	153.43	750	150.01	1 142	151.18
37½	360	156.68	601	152.04	961	153.77
38	274	158.09	495	156.27	769	156.92
38½	206	159.83	357	158.78	563	159.17
39	146	165.93	269	161.24	415	162.89
39½	80	165.86	167	163.76	247	164.44
40	62	168.15	122	168.30	184	168.25
40½	36	175.03	51	174.71	87	174.84
41	25	172.10	41	173.86	66	173.19
41½	9	182.73	25	178.85	34	179.88
42	13	180.67	16	179.65	29	180.11
42½	4	184.29	9	185.48	13	185.12
43	3	192.96	4	191.66	7	192.22
43½	3	201.29	3	200.46	6	200.87
44	3	196.45	1	218.79	4	202.04
44½	–		2	214.29	2	214.29
45	–		1	184.79	1	184.79

TABLE XXXIX. — (*Continued.*)

Mean Weights of White Men, by Circumference of Chest.

Circumf. of Chest	Sailors		Students		Total White Men	
	No.	Weight	No.	Weight	No.	Weight
inches		lbs.		lbs.		lbs.
Under 26	1	58.00	–	–	2	61.39
26	–	–	–	–	1	86.79
26½	–	–	–	–	2	77.29
27	–	–	–	–	4	92.66
27½	–	–	–	–	1	81.79
28	–		–	–	9	106.90
28½	5	106.66	–	–	7	104.34
29	2	94.75	–		18	105.06
29½	6	106.25	–		20	103.65
30	6	113.33	–	–	71	111.10
30½	4	112.29	–	–	80	114.80
31	17	112.59	–	–	168	115.13
31½	15	117.57	5	114.49	216	118.07
32	44	119.13	4	117.54	409	120.14
32½	37	121.57	14	119.22	497	123.97
33	89	127.54	7	120.33	751	127.23
33½	65	130.07	32	122.57	842	129.25
34	125	133.62	11	131.88	1 276	133.38
34½	77	136.44	53	129.81	1 279	135.28
35	149	140.00	29	136.25	1 515	139.17
35½	76	140.69	40	137.95	1 539	141.80
36	112	144.39	21	139.91	1 621	144.67
36½	73	145.10	25	146.71	1 366	147.83
37	87	151.28	9	147.07	1 238	151.16
37½	40	152.41	17	152.52	1 018	153.70
38	50	155.22	2	159.29	821	156.82
38½	18	156.67	15	166.59	596	159.28
39	21	166.14	1	166.79	437	163.06
39½	8	166.17	1	174.79	256	164.53
40	5	177.36	–	–	189	168.49
40½	5	172.86	–	–	92	174.73
41	4	172.14	2	183.29	72	173.41
41½	1	175.00	–	–	35	179.74
42	1	163.00	–	–	30	179.54
42½	1	189.00	–	–	14	185.39
43	–	–	–	–	7	192.22
43½	–	–	–	–	6	200.87
44	–	–	–	–	4	202.04
44½	–	–	–	–	2	214.29
45	–	–	–	–	1	184.79

TABLE XL.

Mean Weights of Negroes and Indians, by Circumference of Chest.

Circumf. of Chest	Negroes						Indians	
	Full Blacks		Mulattoes		Aggregate			
	No.	Weight	No.	Weight	No.	Weight	No.	Weight
inches		lbs.		lbs.		lbs.		lbs.
Under 26	–	–	1	157.79	1	157.79	–	–
26	–	–	1	169.79	1	169.79	–	–
26½	–	–	1	152.29	1	152.29	–	–
27	–	–	–	–	–	–	–	–
27½	1	170.00	–	–	1	170.00	–	–
28	–	–	1	96.79	1	96.79	–	–
28½	1	102.00	2	115.39	3	110.93	–	–
29	2	97.50	2	138.39	4	117.94	–	–
29½	6	106.22	2	139.29	8	114.49	–	–
30	11	109.51	8	135.54	19	120.47	–	–
30½	7	127.68	4	113.55	11	122.55	–	–
31	22	116.52	17	129.18	39	122.04	–	–
31½	19	120.50	12	121.32	31	120.82	–	–
32	44	127.47	23	132.07	67	129.05	–	–
32½	65	130.28	32	132.54	97	131.02	–	–
33	94	132.91	44	135.60	138	133.76	–	–
33½	132	135.18	58	136.50	190	135.58	–	–
34	133	138.61	56	140.16	189	139.07	1	123.79
34½	159	142.66	89	144.33	248	143.25	5	139.49
35	165	145.71	72	147.37	237	146.21	11	135.93
35½	168	146.75	75	150.29	243	147.84	19	138.37
36	138	149.82	53	152.92	191	150.68	32	145.01
36½	131	152.35	48	153.69	179	152.71	68	151.61
37	93	154.42	22	154.45	115	154.43	81	156.65
37½	67	162.21	29	156.86	96	160.59	81	162.58
38	62	162.01	20	161.71	82	161.94	18	168.07
38½	36	165.07	17	170.43	53	166.79	64	170.53
39	19	175.92	2	155.79	21	174.00	24	173.64
39½	8	164.92	6	168.73	14	166.55	30	172.42
40	13	164.84	3	184.40	16	168.51	7	173.79
40½	2	183.39	–	–	2	183.39	8	182.29
41	1	190.50	1	155.79	2	173.14	16	179.54
41½	–	–	–	–	–	–	15	184.02
42	–	–	–	–	–	–	11	186.70
42½	–	–	–	–	–	–	6	181.79
43	–	–	–	–	–	–	4	183.29
43½	–	–	–	–	–	–	3	201.12
44	–	–	–	–	–	–	–	–
44½	–	–	–	–	–	–	–	–
45	–	–	–	–	–	–	–	–

TABLE XLI.

Empirical Table for Weight, by Circumference of Chest.

Total White Men.

Circumference of Chest	No. of Men	Weight	Difference Comp. — Obs'd.
in.		lbs.	lbs.
28	9	99.8	−7.1
28½	7	102.3	−2.0
29	18	104.8	−0.3
29½	20	107.4	+3.8
30	71	110.0	−1.1
30½	80	112.7	−2.1
31	168	115.4	+0.3
31½	216	118.2	+0.1
32	409	121.0	+0.9
32½	497	123.9	−0.1
33	751	126.8	−0.4
33½	842	129.8	+0.6
34	1 276	132.8	−0.6
34½	1 279	135.8	+0.5
35	1 515	138.8	−0.4
35½	1 539	141.8	0.0
36	1 621	144.8	+0.1
36½	1 366	147.8	0.0
37	1 238	150.8	−0.4
37½	1 018	153.8	+0.1
38	821	156.8	0.0
38½	596	159.8	+0.5
39	437	162.8	−0.3
39½	256	165.0	+1.3
40	189	168.8	+0.3
40½	92	171.8	−2.9
41	72	174.9	+1.5
41½	35	178.2	−1.5
42	30	181.7	+2.2
42½	14	185.4	0.0

4. *Determinations of Muscular Strength.*

The dynamometers employed were devised for measuring the strength in pulling upward, and are represented in the annexed figures, which will render detailed verbal description needless. One of them represents the general aspect of the instrument, and the other shows the internal arrangement as disclosed by the removal of the dial-plate. The man stands upon the movable lid of the wooden packing box, to which the apparatus is firmly attached, and grasps with both hands the rounded extremities of a wooden bar, of convenient shape and adjustable in height. Although this apparatus is less compact and portable than the well known dynamometer of Regnier,[1] and lacks the incontestable advantage of testing the force of pressure as well as that of traction, yet the form of construction here employed seems to avoid the objections urged[2] against that instrument, and to be well fitted for practical use. The handle is conveniently shaped for firm and easy grasp, its height well suited for application of the full muscular power, and the mechanism such as to afford results which are to all appearance very trustworthy.

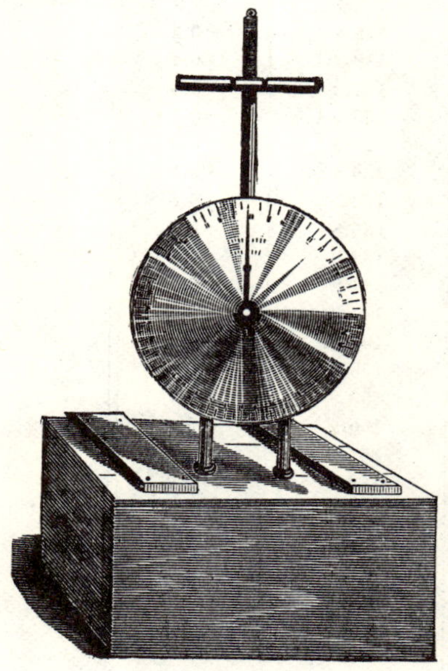

The first two of our instruments were made by Mr. Thomas, of New York, under the direction of Messrs. Olmsted and Elliott; the subsequent ones by Mr. Thomas Morton.

Any comparison of our results with those of the renal [lifting] force, as determined by others, is unsatisfactory, without a careful comparison of the structure of the instruments employed and the manner of their use. Very few sets of such measurements are on record, and these generally comprise too few individual cases to afford results at all satisfactory.

Regnier, in the memoir already cited, gives[3] as the result of his

[1] *Journal de l'École Polytechnique*, II. 160. [2] Quetelet, *Sur l'Homme*, II. 64, 68, 73.
[3] Page 168.

experiments, 130 kilograms (287 lbs.) for the weight which a man of from 25 to 30 years can generally lift with both hands, and says that this degree of strength continues until about the age of 50 years.

Péron was the first[1] to carry a dynamometer as part of the apparatus of a scientific expedition, and to attempt its employment for ethnological purposes. Although he evidently took much pains with his observations, the results proved quite discordant from those of other observers, until the source of the error was detected[2] by Mr. Freycinet, his companion on the Southern Exploring Expedition, who after Péron's death edited the second volume of his narrative. The dynamometer had been provided with two graduated scales, one for showing the force of pressure, the other for the force of traction; and its indications had been transcribed from the wrong scale. This discovery rendered it easy to reproduce the true values, which Mr. Freycinet has given.[3]

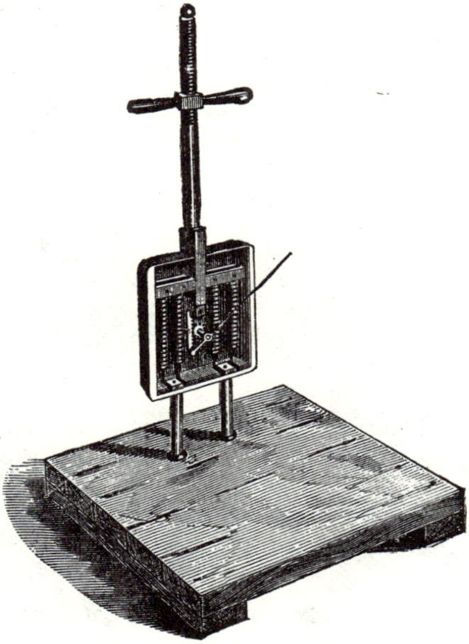

The measures of Péron thus afford the following mean results for the lifting, or renal, force: —

		No.	Kilograms	Lbs.
Savage natives of New Holland above	18 years old	13	102	225
Malays of the Island of Timor, from	18 to 20 years	4	96	212
	20 to 30	15	118	260
	30 to 40	7	119	262
	40 to 50	8	106	234
	50 to 60	4	109	240
French members of the Expl. Exp., from	20 to 50	17	152	335
English residents of Port Jackson, from	20 to 50	14	163	359

His dynamometer was left[4] with the government physician at Mauritius, Mr. Chapotin, in the hope that extensive observations might be made upon the strength of men of different races.

[1] *Voyage aux terres Australes*, I. 447.
[2] *Ibid.* II. 461.
[3] *Ibid.* II. 463, 464.
[4] *Ibid.* I. 457.

Mr. Ransonnet, also a member of the same expedition, and whose determinations of the renal strength of sailors at Havre led to the discovery of the error in Péron's records, found the average lifting power of 345 French sailors to be 142 kilograms, or 313 lbs.[1]

Quetelet's measures in Brussels, gave [2] the mean values for men at different ages as follows, the number of individuals in each group being not less than ten; but he regarded his values as probably less than the truth.[3]

Age	Renal Strength	
	kilograms	lbs.
15	88	194
16	102	225
17	126	278
18	130	287
19	132	291
20	138	304
21	146	322
25	155	342
30	154	340
40	122	269
50	101	223
60	93	205

The mean lifting strength for the various classes of men examined during the present investigations is shown in the appended table.

TABLE XLII.

Average Lifting Strength of Men examined.

Class of Men	In usual Vigor		Not in usual Vigor		Total	
	No.	Strength	No.	Strength	No.	Strength
		lbs.		lbs.		lbs.
White Soldiers, Earlier Series	5 776	314.46	2 082	266.25	7 858	301.69
" " Later Series	6 381	343.20	1 025	280.89	7 406	334.58
Sailors	1 141	307.36	–	–	1 141	307.36
Students	208	308.41	–	–	208	308.41
Full Blacks	1 600	323.51	195	276.15	1 795	318.36
Mulattoes	704	348.90	128	293.69	832	340.41
Indians	503	419.31	5	290.00	508	418.04

[1] *Voyage aux terres Australes*, II. 461; Quetelet, *Sur l'Homme*, II. 66.

[2] *Sur l'Homme*, II. 70.

[3] *Ibid.* II. 74.

The marked inferiority of the mean strength of soldiers in the earlier series cannot fail to attract attention; and the explanation is afforded by the fact that a large number of these men were rebel prisoners, whose lifting power was about 50 lbs. less than that of soldiers in our own army.

Assorting the men in usual vigor according to their ages (last birthday), we obtain the mean values in the following table: —

TABLE XLIII.

Mean Lifting Strength of White Soldiers, in usual Vigor.

Age	Earlier Series		Later Series	
	No. of Men	Strength	No. of Men	Strength
		lbs.		lbs.
Under 17 [a]	126	238.4	92	250.4
17	210	273.8	171	292.8
18	440	286.7	502	312.6
19	508	298.9	454	320.7
20	588	307.7	542	331.2
21	613	319.2	610	337.4
22	503	325.9	606	343.3
23	444	317.2	476	358.4
24	405	325.9	464	355.8
25	286	333.2	296	365.1
26	230	325.3	254	363.0
27	212	326.0	212	350.1
28	190	323.8	236	367.6
29	135	333.8	158	365.9
30	133	338.5	171	351.2
31-34	315	330.2	467	361.9
35-39	253	325.6	371	366.0
40-44	113	324.7	199	347.0
45-49	44	311.4	66	325.7
50 & over	28	291.7	34	321.2

The inadequacy of the number of men of each age in the preceding table may be easily remedied, and the series of means rounded into a curve of satisfactory continuity, by combining the aggregate results for each consecutive three years after the age of twenty, and using their mean to represent the value for the middle year of the three. And by charting the series of values thus obtained, the curious fact is developed that the curve within the lim-

[a] The mean age of this group was 15.7 years, at last birthday.

its of military age is not very dissimilar from a hyperbola of which the apex corresponds to about 24½ years last birthday, or the actual age of 25 years, and a strength of 359 lbs.; the maximum strength being about 362 lbs., and belonging to an actual age of 31 years.

The empirical values of the strength of white soldiers, given in the next succeeding table, are computed from the statistics of the later series, using the actual mean ages, not those corresponding to the last birthday.

TABLE XLIV.

Empirical Table for Strength of White Soldiers.

Actual Age	Lifting Strength	Comp. — Obs.	Actual Age	Lifting Strength	Comp. — Obs.
	lbs.	lbs.		lbs.	lbs.
17	282.0	− 0.8	29	361.8	− 4.0
18	300.6	− 4.3	30	361.9	+ 10.7
19	315.2	− 0.4	31	362.0	}
20	325.4	− 1.0	32	361.8	}
21	334.3	+ 1.0	33	361.5	} − 0.3
22	342.5	+ 3.1	34	361.0	}
23	350.0	− 5.2	35	360.6	− 6.4
24	355.9	+ 2.2	36	360.0	− 9.0
25	359.5	− 4.9	37	359.3	− 15.7
26	360.7	− 1.9	38	350.3	+ 5.5
27	361.4	+ 11.5	39	357.3	− 11.5
28	361.7	− 5.8	40	355.7	+ 3.6

If we compare these values with those found by Forbes[1] for British and Irish students, the differences are seen to be very large, reaching a maximum apparently at about 22 years when the comparison is made with Scotch students only, and remaining constant thereafter. The small number of individuals, from which Forbes deduced his value for the English and Irish, precludes any great reliance upon these results, which are in general yet more diverse from our own, — to an extent indeed not well explicable by any difference in the dynamometers employed. On the other hand our results somewhat exceed those found for the lifting, or renal, force by other investigators; they are considerablv larger than those already cited, which Quetelet obtained from trials on Belgians, up to the age of 30 years; and for ages above 30 they are largely in excess.

[1] *London and Edinburgh Philos. Journal*, X. 197-200.

Forbes's values were purely empirical ones, deduced from observations of 523 Scotch, 178 English, and 72 Irish, — 773 in all, besides 56 from British colonies. To the tabular values deduced graphically he adds what seems to be a similar series of empirical values as derived from the actual observations given by Quetelet, and reproduced in the present chapter. A comparison of these results with our own may not be inappropriate here.

Comparison of Determinations of Lifting Strength, according to Forbes, with those of U. S. Soldiers.

Age	Scotch above English	Irish above Scotch	Scotch above Americans	Amer. above Belgians
	lbs.	lbs.	lbs.	lbs.
17	− 12	29	58	22
18	− 4	29	59	21
19	0	26	63	19
20	7	24	67	15
21	10	21	68	12
22	13	17	68	12
23	16	13	67	15
24	19	10	65	19
25	20	9	64	20

The maximum strength being at about 31 years, according to our data, the mean value falls slowly, and has been diminished by a little more than six pounds at the age of 40 years, after which our results scarcely warrant any safe induction. Quetelet, however, from his Belgians, having not less than ten men at each age, found a maximum at about 25 years, at which epoch the mean strength was 342 lbs., according to his observations, and 339 lbs. according to Forbes's curve, — that for American soldiers at the same age being 360 lbs. But Quetelet's values for subsequent ages fall with much greater rapidity than our own, and for the age of 40 years he found the mean strength to be but 269 lbs., or 73 lbs. below his maximum value, and nearly 87 lbs. below that of American soldiers at the same age.

The mean values given by Forbes for Irish students, surpass those found by ourselves for any class of men, even for the Indians; and we cannot avoid the conviction that a repetition of his experiments with sharp determination of the index-error and errors of graduation would yield smaller numerical values.

For sailors, the dynamometer has indicated a development of strength decidedly less than for soldiers, as the appended table shows, the ages here being for last birthday. This result is in conformity with that of Ransonnet.

TABLE XLV.

Mean Lifting Strength of Sailors, in usual Vigor.

Age	No. Men	Strength	Age	No. Men	Strength
		lbs.			lbs.
Under 17	6	193.8	26	82	323.8
17	5	220.0	27	47	307.3
18	25	266.3	28	56	312.7
19	46	267.9	29	53	318.0
20	71	287.1	30	36	304.9
21	124	304.7	31–34	88	319.1
22	132	307.8	35–39	61	303.3
23	75	312.1	40–44	18	315.1
24	105	321.6	45–49	11	279.0
25	97	318.8	50 & over	3	298.0

For the students our numbers are too small to afford very satisfactory means for the individual years, but the statistics afford the following mean values; showing their average strength to be generally less than that of soldiers of the same age, who represent the average of the American population; but perhaps slightly greater than that of sailors.

TABLE XLVI.

Mean Lifting Strength of Students, in usual vigor.

Age	No. of Men	Strength
		lbs.
18	2	195.0
19	17	295.8
20	58	315.9
21	51	300.7
22	37	319.3
23	10	323.8
24	14	276.2
25	8	331.1
26	3	293.3
27	5	319.0
28	1	283.0
29	1	350.0
30	–	–
31	1	390.0

The strength found for men of other races than the white is shown in the next two tables, in which it will be seen that the full blacks proved weaker than the white men, and the mulattoes somewhat stronger, while the Indians far surpassed all the others in the strength exhibited. The ages are for last birthday, as before.

TABLE XLVII.

Mean Lifting Strength of Negroes, in usual Vigor.

Age	Full Blacks		Mulattoes		Aggregate	
	No. of Men	Strength	No. of Men	Strength	No. of Men	Strength
		lbs.		lbs.		lbs.
Under 17	36	265.6	19	246.3	55	258.9
17	44	289.4	11	317.0	55	295.0
18	73	287.1	25	282.0	98	285.8
19	91	290.1	35	315.3	126	297.1
20	142	309.1	60	332.9	202	316.2
21	128	325.7	54	331.4	182	327.4
22	145	319.8	65	351.6	210	329.6
23	157	329.1	55	351.1	212	334.8
24	143	335.4	54	378.5	197	347.2
25	124	342.0	47	369.3	171	349.5
26	77	330.6	38	355.8	115	338.9
27	73	329.5	27	380.1	100	343.2
28	67	354.1	24	354.1	91	354.1
29	41	337.1	24	390.7	65	356.9
30	39	337.8	33	363.9	72	349.8
31-34	81	363.2	36	374.9	117	366.8
35-39	72	328.3	52	354.3	124	339.2
40-44	34	306.3	23	381.5	57	336.6
45-49	22	321.3	13	341.2	35	328.7
50 & over	11	290.7	9	304.6	20	297.0

TABLE XLVIII.

Mean Lifting Strength of Iroquois Indians.

Age	No. of Men	Strength	Age	No. of Men	Strength
		lbs.			lbs.
Under 17	1	340.0	26	45	407.2
17	–	–	27	28	436.0
18	2	430.0	28	38	425.2
19	6	529.7	29	38	406.6
20	8	362.2	30	20	428.4
21	14	393.3	31–34	67	428.2
22	29	373.4	35–39	68	441.1
23	32	419.0	40 44	35	430.2
24	39	411.9	45–49	8	425.5
25	14	417.1	50 & over	11	377.9

It was comprised in the plan of this investigation, to institute some inquiry into the relations between the observed strength and the stature, and also into the mutual relations of strength and weight. But the large amount of labor bestowed upon other inquiries unfortunately precludes a farther extension of the present research. The materials for such inquiries will however remain easily available for future investigators.

It only remains, in the present chapter, to give the maximum strength recorded for any individual, in each of our classes, with such other facts regarding the person as may possess interest in this connection. These data we will arrange in tabular form.

TABLE XLIX.

Greatest Lifting Strength Observed.

Class	Previous Occupation	Pounds Lifted	Nativity	Height	Age
White Soldiers, Earlier Series	Cooper . .	650	Germany .	68.3	26
White Soldiers, Later Series .	Blacksmith	840	Ohio . . .	71.8	35
Sailors		640	Nova Scotia	70.0	31
Students		662	Maine . .	66.4	20
Full Blacks	Field Hand	624	Alabama .	64.3	25
Mulattoes	" "	695	N. Carolina	68.6	23
Indians	Farmer . .	741	W. N. York	67.7	33

The greatest strength here exerted by a white soldier, 840 lbs. or 381 kilograms, is somewhat in excess of the maximum lifting force observed[1] by Regnier, which was 370 kilograms or 816 lbs.

And it will be seen that the mean lifting strength varies from about 2¼ to about 2½ times the weight, so that in general a man can lift considerably more than twice his own weight.

[1] *Journal de l'École Polytechnique*, II. p. 168.

CHAPTER XII.

PULMONARY CAPACITY.

1. *Preliminary.*

THE Spirometers employed are simply dry meters, agreeing in their general construction with the most approved form of those used for illuminating gas, and were made for the Sanitary Commission by the American Meter Company, of Philadelphia. Their structure and general appearance are shown in the accompanying

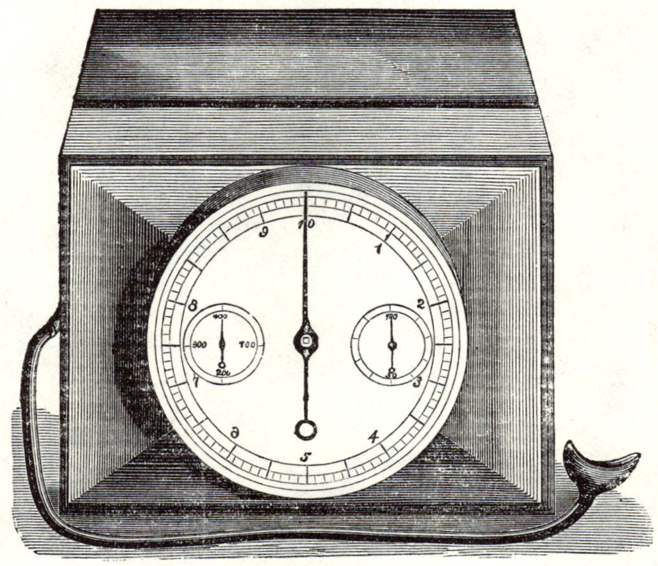

figures. Those metallic portions which are exposed to the breath are of copper, or some alloy which does not corrode by moisture at ordinary temperatures; and they are provided with special contrivances for removing the vapor as it condenses. They were tested from time to time, and so far as experience warrants a judgement they appear far superior to the cumbrous and complicated apparatus hitherto employed for the same purpose. It must not be forgotten that our aim was not to introduce such apparatus as would permit the highest degree of precision absolutely, but such as would, under the circumstances of the case, afford the best results. For instruments which are to undergo the rough usage inseparable from transportation by army trains or on military railroads, which are in danger of being handled roughly at some unguarded moment by rude men, and which must be employed at posts remote from facilities for repairing injuries or maladjustments, the conditions to be consulted are widely different from those which

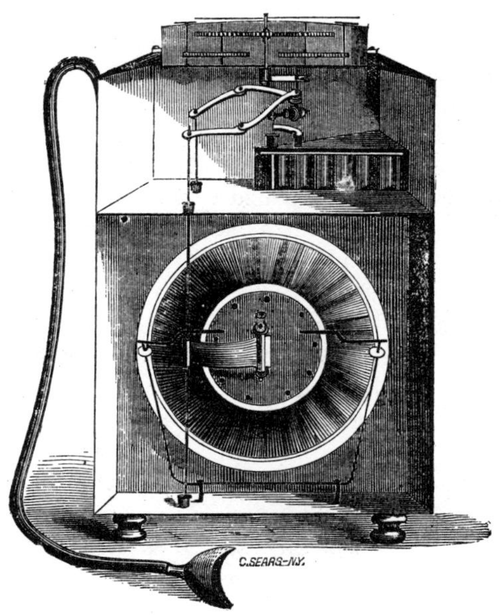

would be imposed under other circumstances. And although there are of course many respects in which the experience now obtained would indicate important modifications of method, inquiries, and precautions, were this work to be repeated or continued, yet the instruments employed have given entire satisfaction and very few points have suggested themselves in which the apparatus could clearly be changed for the better. The spirometers are graduated to indicate cubic inches (although cubic centimeters would be preferable for any future occasions), and are furnished with a mouthpiece of convenient form, connected with the instrument by flexible tubing.

It was directed that, in each case, the results of three consecutive trials be recorded for the maximum amount which could be expelled from the lungs after a full inflation. The second trial was almost uniformly found to give a value decidedly larger than the first, and somewhat larger than the third; but it is the mean of all three, and not the strict maximum value, which has been used in our tabulations.

The volume of air thus exhaled is, of course, not the full capacity of the lungs. Such an effort can rarely be supposed to measure the highest value possibly attainable by the individual, but simply affords a near approximation to it. And this value itself shows not the full capacity of the lungs, but rather what Hutchinson has called the "vital capacity," being the amount of air used in breathing. This author classifies the various supplies of air in the chest as — 1. Residual air, or that which remains after all possible effort at expulsion has been made; 2. Reserve air, or that which remains after ordinary expiration, but which may nevertheless be expelled by voluntary effort; 3. Breathing air, which is inhaled and exhaled alternately under ordinary circumstances; 4. Complemental air, which the lungs may be made to contain by vigorous effort in inhalation. And the sum of these three latter quantities, which he denotes by the name of "vital capacity," is the amount exhaled by the maximum effort after the deepest possible inspiration.

In the present chapter the phrases, "Pulmonary Capacity" and "Capacity of Lungs," are employed solely as a convenient form of expression, and used to denote the results afforded by the spirometer.

The average amount of air exhaled after a full inhalation was thus found to be, in cubic inches, as follows: —

TABLE I.

Average Capacity of Lungs.

	In usual Vigor		Not in usual Vigor		Total	
	No. Men	Cubic Inches	No. Men	Cubic Inches	No. Men	Cubic Inches
White Soldiers, Earlier Series	4 837	175.655	1 915	155.699	6 752	169.995
White Soldiers, Later Series	8 895	187.868	1 541	166.321	10 436	184.686
Sailors	1 104	179.217	–	–	1 104	179.217
Students	288	204.382	–	–	288	204.382
Full Blacks	1 631	165.319	221	149.697	1 852	163.455
Mulattoes	671	161.635	138	145.428	809	158.870
Indians	504	185.058	7	179.286	511	184.978

The extreme values recorded for any individual in the several classes were, in cubic inches: —

	In usual Vigor		Not in usual Vigor	
	Greatest	Smallest	Greatest	Smallest
White Soldiers, Earlier Series	360	50	353	10
White Soldiers, Later Series	358	40	325	36
Sailors	387	50	–	–
Students	312	100	–	–
Full Blacks	360	70	246	55
Mulattoes	359	43	262	33
Indians	310	60	283	110

The great difference of the mean volume found for the black race from that which seems to belong to the whites, cannot fail to attract attention at the first glance. Its bearings are perhaps better manifested by the more detailed tabulations which will follow.

The volume of air expelled from the lungs, as related to the size and mobility of the thorax, and to the other physical dimensions of the individuals, has been made the subject of careful and extensive study by many able men. The present discussion aims only at the proper presentation and classification of the results, obtained at the same time as the physical dimensions in our examinations. The tabulation has been arranged with a view to the acquisition of evidence upon theories heretofore suggested, and with hope and confidence that the numerical results thus attained may prove valuable for professional investigators of this important subject.

Hutchinson's results are concisely summed up [1] by himself; the following being among the chief of those regarding which our measurements are capable of furnishing evidence: —

"The vital capacity differs in man according to height, weight, age, and disease.

"By *height*, in the arithmetical relation of 8 cubic inches for every inch of height between five and six feet.

"By *weight*, at five feet six inches it decreases 1 cubic inch per lb. between $11\frac{1}{2}$ and 14 stone.[2] At other heights 7 per cent. must be added to the weight. The weight increases in a certain relation with the height in 3000 cases examined. The weight may be calculated from the height.

"By *age*. Age after a certain time decreases the vital capacity. The decrease is nearly $1\frac{1}{2}$ inch per year between 30 and 60 years of age.

"By *disease*, the vital capacity decreases from 10 to 70 per cent.

"The size of the chest and the quantity of air a man can breathe have no direct relation with each other. The circumference of the chest also has no relation to the vital capacity; but it has an exact relation to the weight, increasing an inch for every 10 lbs.

"A stout man may have large lungs, and a spare man may have small lungs; there appears no relation between the cubic space in the thorax and the weight.

"The size of the chest and its mobility bear a strict relation to the quantity of air we breathe; a 40 inch chest with 3 inches mobility, will breathe less in a deep inspiration than a 40 inch chest with 4 inches mobility.

"There appears no relation between the sitting and standing height."

These measurements are evidently made with great care and deserving of full confidence; while the results deduced from them are entitled to all respect, and seem to have been generally accepted by physiologists. Yet the present investigations appear to indicate that some of the inferences must be considerably modified. And while it is very probable that, in spite of all endeavors, many of our examiners may have devoted less punctilious care to the measurements than was bestowed by Dr. Hutchinson, who appears to have personally conducted more than three fifths of the examinations upon which his memoir is based, this circumstance must be

1 *Medico-Chirurgical Transactions*, XXIX. p. 248.

2 The British "stone" is 14 lbs. avoirdupois, or about $6\frac{1}{3}$ kilograms.

far more than counter-balanced by the copious material here collected, which is about twelve fold greater.

2. *Relation to Stature.*

Tables exhibiting the mean pulmonary capacity of men in usual vigor for each successive tenth of an inch in stature, have been prepared, in the belief that the results for an adequate number of the arguments, would represent the normal average for these statures, and that a regularly progressive increase would thus be exhibited. But although the number of men comprised in many of the groups was quite considerable, amounting for two of the arguments to more than 225, the fluctuations in the corresponding mean capacity observed were very large, altogether too large in deed to indicate any regular curve. Subsequent tabulations indicate that no real increase in accuracy can be expected by reducing the groups to smaller intervals of stature than single inches; and only the results of a tabulation by inches of height are here presented. The several groups in the appended table are deduced from those cases respectively for which the stature was found to be between half an inch below and half an inch above the round number; and the actual mean stature is given for each group in a special column.

TABLE II.

Pulmonary Capacity of White Soldiers, in usual vigor, by Height.

Earlier Series			Later Series			Total		
No. Men	Mean Height	Cubic In.	No. Men	Mean Height	Cubic In.	No. Men	Mean Height	Cubic In.
	in.			in.			in.	
1	56.30	90.0	2	56.65	143.0	3	56.53	125.3
2	58.00	95.0	2	58.30	102.0	4	58.15	98.5
7	58.93	113.3	9	59.07	137.4	16	59.01	126.9
10	60.09	159.6	27	60.11	148.1	37	60.10	151.2
30	60.99	136.4	54	61.11	146.2	84	61.07	142.7
85	62.03	143.9	138	62.04	156.8	223	62.04	151.9
168	63.01	144.1	312	62.99	161.2	480	62.99	155.2
312	63.99	153.3	612	63.99	167.4	924	63.99	162.6
489	64.97	158.4	981	64.97	174.6	1 470	64.97	169.3
643	65.98	166.2	1 239	65.96	181.4	1 882	65.97	176.2
722	66.96	176.0	1 491	66.94	185.4	2 213	66.94	182.3
834	67.95	181.9	1 466	67.92	192.2	2 300	67.93	188.5
618	68.91	184.9	1 027	68.88	200.4	1 645	68.89	194.6
437	69.91	193.8	721	69.89	205.9	1 158	69.90	201.3
250	70.87	196.1	385	70.86	207.0	635	70.87	202.7
129	71.85	206.9	244	71.86	217.6	373	71.85	213.9
62	72.87	202.3	112	72.86	220.7	174	72.86	214.2
27	73.89	217.2	49	73.85	233.9	76	73.87	228.0
9	74.91	207.1	10	74.88	242.6	19	74.89	225.8
1	76.40	211.0	9	75.88	242.0	10	75.93	238.9
1	77.40	335.0	4	76.78	206.2	5	76.90	232.0
–	–	–	1	77.50	263.0	1	77.50	263.0
4 837	67.296	175.65	8 895	67.164	187.87	13 732	67.211	183.57

The mean capacity is thus seen to increase with the height according to some general law, as would naturally be expected; but neither so regularly for individuals as has been alleged, nor at so high a rate as 8 cubic inches for each inch of height. About 6¼ cubic inches seems to be the normal increase with each inch of stature.

A similar examination of the results for sailors and for students leads to similar inferences; and it can scarcely admit of doubt that the pulmonary capacity, corresponding to any given stature, is subject to individual variations relatively as great as those for any of the other physical dimensions or characteristics, and that the number of cases requisite for affording a normal mean value for any height is decidedly larger than can be found in our groups for these classes.

The degree of reliance, to which the determinations of pulmonary capacity in the preceding tables are entitled, may be tested by assorting the several individual determinations for men of any given stature, and comparing the distribution thus found with that corresponding to the law of error as explained in the third section of Chapter VIII. The degree of accordance between the two systems of distribution will then afford a criterion as to the extent to which the mean of the determinations ought to be regarded as typical. The result of such an assortment for white soldiers 67 inches in height, who were in usual vigor, is here given.

TABLE III.

Assortment by Pulmonary Capacity, between the limits 66.5 *and* 67.5 *inches in Height, of White Soldiers in usual vigor.*

(*Mean Height* = 66.936 *Inches.*)

Cubic Inches	No. of Men	Theoretical Proportion		Difference
		For 10 000 Cases	For 1491 Cases	c. — o.
Below 96	19	75	11	− 8
96-115	52	219	33	− 19
116-135	81	592	88	+ 7
136-155	136	1 210	180	+ 44
156-175	271	1 853	276	+ 5
176-195	319	2 132	319	0
196 215	330	1 845	275	+ 55
216-235	160	1 201	179	+ 19
236-255	85	585	87	+ 2
256 275	22	214	32	+ 10
Above 275	16	74	11	− 5
	1 491	10 000	1 491	+ 87 − 87

	in.
Mean Pulmonary Capacity . .	185.36
Probable Individual Variation .	24.92
Probable Error of Mean . . .	0.65

Table IV. shows the mean pulmonary capacity for each inch of height, as derived from our measurements of sailors and of students, both in usual health, and also the results for the aggregate of all white men of this class examined; the measurements for soldiers, sailors, and students being combined in this Grand Total result for white men in ordinary vigor.

TABLE IV.

Pulmonary Capacity of White Men, in usual Vigor, by Height.

Sailors			Students			Total of White Men		
No. Men	Mean H't	Cubic In.	No. Men	Mean H't	Cubic In.	No. Men	Mean H't	Cubic In.
	in.			in.			in.	
1	48.40	70.0	–	–	–	4	54.50	111.5
–	–	–	–	–	–	4	58.15	98.5
1	59.40	80.0	–	–	–	17	59.03	124.1
12	60.03	177.7	–	–	–	49	60.09	157.7
25	61.05	157.0	–	–	–	109	61.07	146.0
49	62.01	159.1	–	–	–	272	62.03	153.2
78	63.02	158.6	3	63.27	196.7	561	63.00	155.9
132	63.98	167.5	8	63.79	192.6	1 064	63.99	163.5
165	64.96	174.8	32	64.97	179.5	1 667	64.97	170.0
161	65.90	180.0	37	66.01	189.8	2 080	65.96	176.7
162	66.93	192.4	34	66.93	194.3	2 409	66.94	183.1
121	67.90	186.1	49	67.98	196.5	2 470	67.93	188.5
102	68.90	191.5	42	69.02	210.8	1 789	68.90	194.8
49	69.79	192.1	36	69.90	222.7	1 243	69.89	201.5
28	70.81	188.7	24	70.92	223.5	687	70.87	202.8
12	71.82	204.3	14	71.86	237.1	399	71.85	214.4
4	72.87	207.2	5	72.98	251.0	183	72.87	215.0
1	74.20	151.0	1	74.10	273.0	78	73.87	227.5
1	75.00	200.0	1	74.70	120.0	21	74.89	219.5
–	–	–	1	75.60	261.0	11	75.90	240.9
–	–	–	1	77.40	265.0	6	76.98	237.5
–	–	–	–	–	–	1	77.50	263.0
1 104	66.009	179.22	288	68.119	204.38	15 124	67.140	183.64

For the men not in usual vigor the corresponding results are neither so interesting nor so important, at least so long as the cause or degree of their enfeebled condition does not appear as an element in the classification. The material for such a classification exists to some extent in the answers to Question 31, which assort the occasions of the loss of vigor into the five classes, disease, wounds, recent exertion, hardship, and poor fare; but it has not appeared probable, in view of the large variations in the values deduced for men in health, that the results thus attained would reward the labor of such a classification.

In Table V. are condensed the mean values obtained for those white men who were not included in the last table, because not in their usual vigor. All of these men were in the volunteer army, — a considerable portion being examined at the Convalescent Camp.

TABLE V.

Pulmonary Capacity of White Men not in usual Vigor, by Height.

Number of Men	Mean Height	Cubic Inches
	in.	
16	59.02	124.2
25	61.02	132.8
56	61.95	132.8
125	62.97	135.6
253	64.00	140.9
357	64.99	152.2
504	65.95	152.2
530	66.96	160.3
513	67.94	164.2
429	68.89	165.5
291	69.91	179.0
165	70.92	180.6
101	71.91	189.6
49	72.91	175.9
29	73.92	196.3
13	75.84	194.8
3 456	67.230	160.43

Comparing the pulmonary capacity of the black race with that of the white, the difference is very striking. The results presented for the blacks are deduced from those men only who were apparently in full health and strength, and the excess of average capacity in whites of the same stature is added in a special column.

TABLE VI.

Pulmonary Capacity of Negroes, in usual Vigor, by Height.

Full Blacks			Mulattoes			Total			Mean Difference from Whites
No. Men	Mean H't	Cubic In.	No. Men	Mean H't	Cubic In.	No. Men	Mean H't	Cubic In.	
	in.			in.			in.		
6	58.70	150.2	–	–	–	6	58.70	150.2	–
14	60.10	131.5	5	59.80	101.8	19	60.02	123.7	34.05
29	60.96	146.0	10	60.88	117.0	39	60.94	138.6	7.41
55	61.99	140.4	18	61.89	141.5	73	61.97	140.7	12.50
112	62.94	144.6	58	62.95	148.8	170	62.95	146.0	9.85
173	63.97	155.4	72	63.95	144.8	245	63.97	152.3	11.17
209	64.91	160.5	100	64.95	158.1	309	64.92	159.7	10.26
258	65.97	162.6	112	65.96	156.9	370	65.97	160.9	15.81
258	66.97	166.5	94	66.95	168.4	352	66.96	167.0	16.12
220	67.95	172.7	67	67.83	160.7	287	67.92	169.9	18.68
142	68.98	183.2	65	68.92	180.5	207	68.96	182.3	12.44
72	69.86	176.7	33	69.87	189.8	105	69.86	180.8	20.72
48	70.92	196.7	19	70.97	186.7	67	70.94	193.9	8.96
26	71.97	203.7	13	71.86	203.1	39	71.93	203.5	10.90
5	72.86	184.0	2	72.50	190.5	7	72.76	185.9	29.16
2	73.85	256.0	1	74.40	131.0	3	74.03	214.3	13.22
2	76.60	240.0	2	76.30	253.5	4	76.45	246.7	–
1 631	66.257	165.32	671	66.229	161.63	2 302	66.249	164.24	.

Since the number of Indians examined was not sufficient to ensure a symmetrical distribution of the proportion at different heights, this fact is manifested in our mean difference between their average pulmonary capacity and that of white men ; this difference indicating an excess for the total of the Indians examined, while for every individual inch of stature, except one, the capacity is greater for the whites.

TABLE VII.

Pulmonary Capacity of Indians, in usual vigor, by Height.

No. of Men	Mean Height	Cubic Inches	Less than for Whites	Greater than for Blacks
	in.			
1	62.50	130.0	–	–
1	64.00	162.0	–	–
13	65.09	177.3	– 7.31	+ 17.57
33	65.92	162.8	+ 13.96	1.85
88	67.14	173.8	9.31	6.81
178	67.93	185.3	3.23	15.45
102	68.87	194.4	0.36	12.08
50	69.88	199.6	1.95	+ 18.77
17	70.76	192.9	9.96	– 1.00
13	71.93	191.2	23.21	– 12.31
5	72.72	178.6	36.42	– 7.26
2	73.75	167.0	+ 60.55	– 47.33
1	75.70	214.0	–	–
504	68.238	185.06		

If from the means of the actually observed numbers, as above recorded, we endeavor by graphical methods to construct normal curves showing the best value empirically deducible for men in good health, of any given stature, without regard to other elements than the mere height, we shall find: — 1st that the mean increase of pulmonary capacity appears closely proportional to the increase of height, and 2d, that among white men this mean increase is at the very nearly constant rate of a little more than six cubic inches for each inch of stature.

The results in Table VIII. have been deduced by graphical means exclusively, the values already given being carefully charted, and a line drawn through the series of points to represent the system as closely as possible. The columns headed c. — o. (Calculation *minus* Observation) show the discordance between the empirical and the observed values, for each inch of mean stature. In judging of the weight to be attributed to these discordances, the number of observed cases, as shown by the preceding tables, should be kept in mind. The similarity of the values for full blacks and mulattoes, as shown by Table VI., warrants their consolidation into a single class.

TABLE VIII.

Empirical Determination of Pulmonary Capacity, by Stature.

Height	White Soldiers Earlier Series		White Soldiers Later Series		Total White Men		Negroes	
	Cubic In.	c. — o.	Cubic In.	c. — o.	Cubic In.	c. — o.	Cubic In.	c. — o.
inches								
59	120	+ 6.3	136½	− 0.5	132	+ 8.1	–	–
60	126½	− 32.5	142½	− 5.0	138½	18.6	130½	+ 6.9
61	133	− 3.4	149	+ 3.4	145	− 0.6	136	− 2.9
62	139½	− 4.2	155	− 1.5	151	− 2.0	141	+ 0.2
63	146½	+ 2.5	161½	+ 0.3	157½	+ 1.7	146	− 0.3
64	153	− 0.4	167½	+ 0.0	163½	− 0.0	151½	− 1.0
65	160	+ 1.4	174	− 0.8	170	− 0.2	156½	− 3.6
66	166½	+ 0.2	180	− 1.6	176	− 1.0	162	+ 0.9
67	173½	− 2.7	186½	+ 0.7	182½	− 1.0	167½	+ 0.2
68	180	− 2.3	192½	− 0.2	188½	− 0.5	173½	+ 3.2
69	186½	+ 1.0	199	− 2.1	194½	− 0.9	179	− 3.6
70	192½	− 1.8	205	− 1.5	200½	− 1.7	185	+ 3.3
71	198½	+ 1.6	211½	+ 3.6	206½	+ 2.9	191	− 3.2
72	204	− 3.7	218	− 0.5	212	− 3.3	197½	− 6.5
73	209½	+ 6.5	224	+ 2.4	218	+ 2.2	–	–
74	214½	− 3.2	230½	− 4.4	223½	− 4.8	–	–
75	–	–	237	− 6.4	229½	+ 9.3		–

The close accordance of this empirical and very simple law with the observed facts, within the limits of manly stature, is very striking. That there must be an inferior limit to the application of the law is equally manifest, but our materials furnish no clew for its detection. There would seem to be ground for suspecting this limit to be at about the mean stature corresponding to the age of 16 or 17 years.

3. *Relation to Length of Body.*

Since the variations in height of different persons depend so largely upon the length of the legs, it would appear probable that the size of the thorax, or at least its depth, would be found to occupy some much more definite and manifest relation to the capacity of the lungs, than would be the case for the stature. The examination of this question was naturally not omitted by Dr. Hutchinson in his elaborate and able memoir, but his inferences after the investigation were strongly adverse to this natural supposition; and he states that he was forced to the conclusion, already cited, that "the size of the chest and the quantity of air a man can breath, have no direct relation with each other;[1] although he also says: "I am quite at a loss to explain why height governs, or why a relation exists between the amount of air expelled and the stature. It is well known that the difference of height is chiefly regulated by the length of the legs; I found by direct experiments upon men (between 5 and 6 feet) that whatever be their standing height, their sitting height is on an average 3 feet."[2]

In yet other places he says, "Contrary to what I ever expected (and agreeable to the opinion of others) I do not find there exists any direct relation between the circumference of the chest and the vital capacity,"[3] and "I have frequently been asked if the depth of the chest did not increase with the height of the individual. I find this not to be the case."[4]

The investigation of this relation to the circumference of the thorax has of course been repeated here, as the largely increased number of cases at our disposal demanded, and the results of this inquiry will be presented in the next section; but it seemed also advisable to tabulate the results according to the Length of Body, *i. e.* the height between the perinæum and the 7th cervical vertebra. This dimension is recorded for all our cases; and the results given in Chapter VIII. show that although varying within much narrower limits than the height, the length of body is by no means so constant as Dr. Hutchinson seems to have supposed.

From this tabulation it becomes unmistakably evident that the pulmonary capacity does not stand in a relation to the length of body, at all comparable for distinctness or regularity with that which it appears to occupy toward the stature. The best graphical representation of the series gives a slightly curved line, and falls far short of a satisfactory accordance with individual determinations. The capacity seems however to increase with the length of body, which doubtless generally increases with the stature. In the appended tables the results of this mode of tabulation are given, but *for men in good health, only.*

[1] *Medico-Chirurgical Transactions*, XXIX. p. 248. [2] *Ibid.* p. 183.
[3] *Ibid.* p. 172. [4] *Ibid.* p. 179.

TABLE IX.

Pulmonary Capacity of White Soldiers, by Length of Body.

Earlier Series			Later Series			Total		
No.	Mean Length	Cubic In.	No.	Mean Length	Cubic In.	No.	Mean Length	Cubic In.
	in.			in.			in.	
3	18.90	197.7	5	16.88	141.0	8	17.64	162.2
5	20.02	139.4	6	20.08	171.0	11	20.05	156.6
7	20.54	138.6	10	20.50	162.7	17	20.52	152.8
4	20.97	163.7	4	21.00	156.0	8	20.99	159.9
4	21.60	138.2	8	21.50	140.1	12	21.53	139.5
19	21.96	134.9	22	22.06	163.1	41	22.01	150.0
41	22.51	140.3	36	22.52	158.0	77	22.51	148.6
76	23.03	137.9	72	23.03	158.3	148	23.03	147.9
155	23.54	154.1	183	23.46	173.1	338	23.50	164.4
264	24.00	154.6	381	24.02	165.6	645	24.01	161.1
451	24.50	160.3	617	24.51	172.1	1 068	24.51	167.1
578	25.01	165.3	1 007	25.01	179.9	1 585	25.01	174.6
667	25.50	174.0	1 221	25.51	181.2	1 888	25.51	178.6
667	26.00	177.2	1 400	26.00	188.7	2 067	26.00	185.0
512	26.49	186.5	1 233	26.49	190.8	1 745	26.49	189.5
431	26.99	194.3	1 027	26.99	195.6	1 458	26.99	195.2
332	27.49	190.2	723	27.48	201.6	1 055	27.48	198 0
202	28.00	200.3	470	27.99	203.1	672	27.99	202.3
151	28.47	204.3	316	28.48	198.5	467	28.48	200.4
107	28.97	204.4	180	28.98	202.4	287	28.98	203.2
58	29.49	200.5	93	29.47	212.3	151	29.48	207.8
44	30.00	218.0	46	29.99	211.9	90	29.99	214.9
15	30.45	232.1	19	30.48	193.3	34	30.47	210.4
14	30.96	221.1	14	30.96	208.1	28	30.96	214.6
7	31.39	231.3	3	31.37	230.3	10	31.38	231.0
4	31.97	270.7	3	32.07	177.7	7	32.01	230.9
2	32.65	144.0	6	32.53	177.8	8	32.56	169.4
3	33.33	235.0	12	36.29	162.7	15	35.70	177.1

TABLE X.

Pulmonary Capacity of White Men, by Length of Body.

Sailors			Students			Total White Men		
No.	Mean Length	Cubic In.	No.	Mean Length	Cubic In.	No.	Mean Length	Cubic In.
	in.			in.			in.	
–	–	–	–	–	–	8	17.64	162.2
–	–	–	–	–	–	11	20.05	156.6
1	20.40	151.0	–	–	–	18	20.51	152.7
2	21.05	132.0	–	–	–	10	21.00	154.3
5	21.62	143.6	–	–	–	17	21.56	140.7
9	22.07	183.6	2	22.20	252.5	52	22.03	159.8
40	22.54	155.7	–	–	–	117	22.52	151.0
86	23.02	164.0	2	23.10	139.0	236	23.03	153.6
139	23.51	172.8	7	23.46	202.6	484	23.50	167.4
196	24.01	174.4	13	23.97	176.5	854	24.01	164.4
204	24.50	179.4	28	24.49	187.5	1 300	24.51	169.5
175	25.00	187.5	37	25.00	192.2	1 797	25.01	176.2
106	25.48	183.6	38	25.51	193.5	2 032	25.51	179.2
69	25.97	186.1	42	26.01	201.1	2 178	26.00	185.3
47	26.47	202.6	36	26.50	215.4	1 828	26.49	190.4
29	26.99	196.5	28	27.03	212.4	1 515	26.99	195.5
10	27.47	183.7	21	27.46	221.9	1 086	27.48	198.4
5	28.14	192.2	11	28.08	243.9	688	27.99	202.8
7	28.49	182.9	7	28.50	194.7	481	28.48	200.1
2	29.05	224.5	6	29.08	231.8	295	28.98	203.9
4	29.45	211.2	4	29.45	251.7	159	29.48	209.0
–	–	–	4	29.92	228.2	94	29.99	215.5
1	30.60	288.0	1	30.50	215.0	36	30.47	212.7
–	–	–	1	30.90	218.0	29	30.96	214.8
–	–	–	1	31.50	340.0	11	31.39	240.9
–	–	–	1	31.90	265.0	8	32.00	235.1
–	–	–	–	–	–	8	32.56	169.4
–	–	–	–	–	–	15	35.70	177.1

TABLE XI.

Pulmonary Capacity of Negroes, by Length of Body.

Full Blacks			Mulattoes			Total			Mean Difference from Whites
No. Men	Mean Length	Cubic Inches	No. Men	Mean Length	Cubic Inches	No. Men	Mean Length	Cubic Inches	
	in.			in.			in.		
8	19.75	141.9	3	19.47	131.3	11	19.67	139.0	–
10	21.00	144.5	6	21.02	134.0	16	21.01	140.6	13.74
21	21.50	145.0	7	21.41	139.9	28	21.48	143.7	– 3.04
47	22.03	155.4	13	22.00	151.7	.60	22.03	154.6	5.17
92	22.52	158.3	25	22.52	143.5	117	22.52	155.1	– 4.09
162	23.00	153.3	48	23.02	149.6	210	23.01	152.5	1.18
185	23.51	159.1	81	23.50	154.3	266	23.50	157.7	9.72
231	24.00	162.9	70	23.98	156.2	301	23.99	161.3	3.11
211	24.50	170.7	121	24.51	156.8	332	24.51	165.6	3.87
187	25.01	171.0	98	24.99	162.6	285	25.01	168.1	8.07
152	25.51	167.2	67	25.51	162.7	219	25.51	165.8	13.38
100	26.00	171.9	62	25.97	162.1	162	25.99	168.2	17.13
72	26.48	178.1	39	26.49	175.8	111	26.49	177.3	13.09
52	26.98	170.7	35	26.95	169.0	87	26.97	170.0	25.51
29	27.49	186.7	17	27.46	190.7	46	27.48	188.2	10.20
23	28.00	171.9	13	27.88	177.6	36	27.96	174.0	28.88
6	28.37	154.5	6	28.40	157.3	12	28.38	155.9	44.15
3	28.80	181.3	2	29.20	108.5	5	28.96	152.2	51.69
3	29.43	157.3	1	29.30	171.0	4	29.40	160.7	48.26
1	29.90	78.0	1	30.10	133.0	2	30.00	105.5	109.96
15	32.87	177.5	3	33.87	217.7	18	34.98	195.0	–

TABLE XII.

Pulmonary Capacity of Indians, by Length of Body.

No. of Men	Mean Length	Cubic Inches	Less than for Whites	Greater than for Blacks
	in.			
2	22.10	166.0	–	–
4	24.47	147.7	24.74	−17.87
8	25.06	165.1	11.10	−3.03
26	25.58	186.0	−6.79	20.17
76	26.03	185.8	−0.45	17.58
122	26.51	189.6	0.76	12.33
116	26.95	188.1	7.43	18.08
84	27.51	182.1	16.23	−6.03
33	27.92	177.5	25.33	3.55
23	28.46	185.7	14.33	29.82
5	28.98	200.0	3.89	47.80
5	29.44	186.6	22.41	25.85
3	30.00	166.0	49.46	60.50

TABLE XIII.

Empirical Determination of Pulmonary Capacity, by Length of Body.

Length of Body	White Soldiers Earlier Series		White Soldiers Later Series		Total White Men		Negroes	
	Cubic In.	c. — o.	Cubic In.	c. — o.	Cubic In.	c. — o.	Cubic In.	c. — o.
inches								
21	–	–	148½	− 7.5	143½	− 10.8	143½	+ 3.0
21½	132	− 5.1	152	+ 11.9	147	+ 6.8	146	+ 2.1
22	137½	+ 2.1	155½	− 7.2	151	− 8.5	148½	− 6.0
22½	142½	+ 2.3	159	+ 1.2	155	+ 4.1	151	− 4.0
23	147½	+ 9.9	163	+ 4.9	159	+ 5.6	154	+ 1.6
23½	153	− 0.7	166½	− 6.9	163	− 4.4	156½	− 1.2
24	158	+ 3.4	170½	+ 5.0	167½	+ 3.2	159½	− 1.9
24½	163	+ 2.7	174½	+ 2.5	171½	+ 2.1	162	− 3.6
25	168	+ 2.8	179	− 0.9	176	− 0.1	165	− 3.1
25½	173	− 1.0	183½	+ 2.5	180½	+ 1.4	168	+ 2.3
26	177½	+ 0.3	188	− 0.7	185	− 0.3	171	+ 2.8
26½	182½	− 4.1	192	+ 1.1	189½	− 1.0	173½	− 3.8
27	187½	− 6.9	195½	− 0.1	194	− 1.6	175½	+ 5.4
27½	192	+ 1.7	199	− 2.8	198	− 0.5	177	− 11.2
28	197	− 3.3	202	− 1.1	201½	− 1.4	178	+ 3.9
28½	201½	− 3.1	204½	+ 5.9	205	+ 4.8	–	–
29	206	+ 1.3	206½	+ 4.0	208	+ 4.0	–	–
29½	210½	+ 9.9	208½	− 4.0	211½	+ 2.4	–	–
30	214½	− 3.5	210½	− 1.4	214½	− 1.0	–	–
30½	219	− 13.6	212	+ 18.7	217½	+ 4.6	–	–
31	223½	+ 2.0	213½	+ 5.2	220	+ 5.0	–	–

That the lung-capacity stands in a closer relation to the stature than to the length of body, and that the latter is apparently available as a criterion only in so far as it represents the average stature to which it corresponds, may easily be made evident. Taking only men of the same stature, and assorting them by their length of body, we find for each group nearly the same value, being an approximation to that which corresponds to the stature. If, however, we take only men of the same length of body and assort them by their stature, we find for each group a different mean value; the capacity increasing with the height.

The appended table will suffice to illustrate this fact.

TABLE XIV.

Pulmonary Capacity by Length of Body, for White Soldiers 67 *Inches high.*

Length of Body	No. of Men	Cubic Inches
inches		
Under 24	13	184.77
24	35	185.54
$24\frac{1}{2}$	73	186.82
25	201	188.93
$25\frac{1}{2}$	250	184.88
26	326	184.94
$26\frac{1}{2}$	255	183.45
27	181	185.65
$27\frac{1}{2}$	92	183.17
28	42	189.71
$28\frac{1}{2}$	14	187.36
29	9	168.78

4. *Relation to Circumference of Chest.*

We have already seen that the mean circumference of the chest across the nipples, for white men in ordinary health, is about 0.55 of the height at full inspiration, and 0.51 at expiration. At first thought it might be supposed, since the mean proportion between the length of body, or the circumference of thorax, and the height possesses a definite and normal value, that the same results would be approximately indicated by a tabulation according to any one of these dimensions provided the number of cases were sufficient. The figures presented in the last section, however, will have made it manifest that such is not the fact; and very slight examination suffices to show that the variations of many individual dimensions, for a given stature, considerably exceed in amplitude the changes of the mean dimension with the stature, when within the ordinary limits. This is especially the case for the girth of the chest; and the indirect influence of the height as shown in the scale of magnitude for all dimensions is thus masked to a greater extent.

The curious deduction of Hutchinson, that the girth of the chest exerts but a comparatively small influence upon the pulmonary capacity, was explained by him through the fact that adipose deposits along the walls of the thorax would tend both to increase the circumference and to diminish the space available for expansion of the lungs. Our results, while confirming his other inference, that the mean increase in the volume of air breathed is closely proportional to the increase in the mean stature, do not appear to corroborate so fully his deductions regarding the limits of individual variation from this rule, or regarding the unimportance of any other relation between the dimensions of the chest and this respiratory capacity.

This will be manifest by inspection of the Tables XV. to XIX., which show the relation between the pulmonary capacity and the circumference of chest, for men in health, and are analogous to the similar tables already given for the relation to height and length of body. In this present tabulation the increase in the mean capacity is seen not to be as strictly and clearly proportional to the increase in the dimension, as was the case in the tabulation by height, where the line which represents this ratio upon the chart is very nearly straight for the whites; still this line is here but slightly curved, and the discordances of the several mean values are by no means so large or irregular.

TABLE XV.

Pulmonary Capacity of White Soldiers, by Circumference of Chest.

Earlier Series			Later Series			Total		
No.	Mean Circ.	Cubic In.	No.	Mean Circ.	Cubic In.	No.	Mean Circ.	Cubic In.
	in.			in.			in.	
8	27.12	134.1	10	27.13	143.0	18	27.13	139.1
6	29.05	136.0	9	29.12	147.3	15	29.09	142.8
5	29.46	124.6	12	29.52	134.3	17	29.50	131.5
22	30.04	145.2	26	30.10	158.0	48	30.07	152.1
27	30.51	144.9	33	30.59	149.6	60	30.55	147.5
51	31.00	153.1	82	31.10	163.2	133	31.06	159.3
70	31.52	151.3	100	31.59	168.1	170	31.56	161.1
127	32.02	151.5	191	32.09	164.6	318	32.07	159.4
137	32 52	163.2	253	32.57	174.4	390	32.55	170.5
240	33.01	156.2	361	33.08	178.1	601	33.05	169.3
249	33.51	165.4	408	33.58	176.6	657	33.56	172.4
422	34.00	166.4	637	34.07	179.5	1 059	34.04	174.3
353	34.52	168.3	666	34.57	182.5	1 019	34.56	177.6
447	34.99	178.5	807	35.07	184.6	1 254	35.04	182.4
386	35.50	178.3	880	35.57	186.0	1 266	35.55	183.6
486	35.99	178.9	906	36.07	189.5	1 392	36.03	185.8
349	36.50	183.1	846	36.56	191.2	1 195	36.53	188.8
370	36.99	186.5	725	37.06	192.9	1 095	37.04	190.8
295	37.49	199.4	583	37.55	196.8	878	37.53	197.7
232	38.00	192.7	478	38.03	200.5	710	38.02	198.0
176	38.49	192.0	382	38.53	204.5	558	38.52	200.6
138	39.00	195.9	258	39.03	201.1	396	39.02	199.3
68	39.48	199.1	170	39.53	195.6	238	39.51	196.6
64	39.99	199.6	118	40.03	204.2	182	40.02	202.6
28	40.49	213.8	50	40.52	202.1	78	40.51	206.3
23	41.01	213.3	38	41.04	223.9	61	41.03	219.9
9	41.50	223.8	24	41.46	206.2	33	41.47	211.0
11	41.99	195.6	18	42.01	201.0	29	42.00	199.0
4	42.52	214.7	10	42.48	210.0	14	42.49	211.4
3	43.00	218.3	4	42.96	200.2	7	42.98	208.0
2	43.55	212.5	4	43.56	175.0	6	43.56	187.5
2	44.40	296.5	3	44.68	157.3	5	44.57	213.0

TABLE XVI.

*Pulmonary Capacity of White Men,
by Circumference of Chest.*

Sailors			Students			Total White Men		
No.	Mean Circ.	Cubic In.	No.	Mean Circ.	Cubic In.	No.	Mean Circ.	Cubic In.
	in.			in.			in.	
5	28.12	178.6	1	26.20	220.0	24	27.30	150.7
1	29.00	100.0	–	–	–	16	29.08	140.1
5	29.57	150.0	–	–	–	22	29.52	135.7
6	30.07	159.2	–	–	–	54	30.07	152.9
4	30.65	167.0	–	–	–	64	30.56	148.7
16	31.07	151.0	–	–	–	149	31.06	158.4
13	31.57	166.5	5	31.64	144.8	188	31.51	161.1
45	32.05	160.7	3	32.10	167.3	366	32.06	159.6
36	32.56	169.1	15	32.65	173.5	441	32.55	170.5
91	33.07	161.2	8	33.18	183.7	700	33.06	168.4
64	33.57	183.1	32	33.63	180.4	753	33.56	173.6
122	34.07	173.6	11	34.12	170.8	1 192	34.06	174.2
73	34.57	182.8	52	34.63	196.2	1 144	34.56	178.7
154	35.06	172.4	29	35.07	210.1	1 437	35.04	181.9
71	35.55	187.1	41	35.64	218.9	1 378	35.55	184.9
114	36.05	177.9	20	36.05	235.3	1 526	36.04	185.8
77	36.55	188.8	26	36.58	213.7	1 298	36.54	189.3
84	37.06	191.4	8	36.97	222.6	1 187	37.04	191.0
41	37.58	198.6	19	37.59	223.7	938	37.54	198.2
48	38.04	190.3	1	38.20	299.0	759	38.02	197.6
18	38.54	205.5	15	38.63	223.2	591	38.52	201.3
21	39.01	210.7	1	39.20	200.0	418	39.02	199.9
7	39.55	199.4	1	39.30	244.0	246	39.51	196.9
6	40.02	203.3	–	–	–	188	40.02	202.6
4	40.69	227.7	–	–	–	82	40.52	207.4
4	40.92	193.5	2	41.20	292.5	67	41.03	220.5
1	41.35	263.0	–		–	34	41.47	212.5
1	42.00	199.0	–	–	–	30	42.00	199.0
–	–	–	–	–	–	14	42.49	211.4
–	–	–	–	–	–	7	42.98	208.0
–	–	–	–	–	–	6	43.56	187.5
1	46.70	186.0	–	–	–	6	44.92	208.5

TABLE XVII.

Pulmonary Capacity of Negroes, by Circumference of Chest.

Full Blacks			Mulattoes			Total			Mean Difference from Whites
No.	Mean Circ.	Cubic In.	No.	Mean Circ.	Cubic In.	No.	Mean Circ.	Cubic In.	
	in.			in.			in.		
5	28.57	151.2	3	27.87	164.0	8	28.31	156.0	–
6	29.53	124.7	2	29.65	133.0	8	29.56	126.7	8.93
13	30.09	133.1	6	30.07	96.3	19	30.08	121.5	31.36
8	30.54	128.2	4	30.69	139.2	12	30.59	131.9	16.81
24	31.07	129.6	15	31.04	144.9	39	31.06	135.5	22.94
21	31.58	130.3	11	31.58	134.9	32	31.58	131.9	29.22
47	32.09	144.2	24	32.04	128.5	71	32.07	138.9	20.70
65	32.55	144.7	35	32.59	146.0	100	32.56	145.2	25.29
97	33.04	152.4	38	33.08	153.3	135	33.05	152.6	15.80
133	33.55	153.8	62	33.58	144.5	195	33.56	150.8	22.82
135	34.07	159.8	61	34.07	149.7	196	34.07	156.6	17.55
155	34.54	159.6	93	34.60	156.6	248	34.56	158.5	20.29
168	35.05	171.0	71	35.04	168.5	239	35.05	170.2	11.68
163	35.55	162.7	77	35.56	158.4	240	35.55	161.4	23.50
139	36.03	172.5	54	36.08	167.2	193	36.05	171.0	14.87
128	36.53	171.8	53	36.53	169.6	181	36.53	171.1	18.15
94	37.05	179.4	25	37.06	168.5	119	37.05	177.1	13.88
71	37.54	182.5	32	37.54	185.9	103	37.54	183.6	14.67
65	38.01	187.3	20	38.03	194.1	85	38.02	188.9	8.73
36	38.51	196.8	15	38.56	213.4	51	38.52	201.7	-0.38
17	39.13	189.6	1	38.90	230.0	18	39.11	191.8	8.06
8	39.47	187.2	6	39.44	189.3	14	39.46	188.1	8.74
11	40.03	230.7	4	39.97	158.7	15	40.02	211.5	-8.93
3	40.72	200.0	2	42.12	145.0	5	41.28	178.0	–

TABLE XVIII.

Pulmonary Capacity of Indians, by Circumference of Chest.

No.	Mean Circumf.	Cubic Inches	Less than Whites	Greater than Blacks
	in.			
1	33.90	148.0	26.18	-8.63
5	34.53	170.2	8.55	11.74
10	35.00	165.4	16.53	-4.85
20	35.66	156.7	28.11	-4.61
32	36.04	165.9	19.91	-5.04
70	36.55	175.7	13.59	4.56
80	36.99	180.2	10.79	3.08
81	37.46	189.2	8.99	5.68
18	37.96	186.6	11.06	-2.33
63	38.47	191.4	9.88	10.26
23	39.[illegible]	199.9	-0.02	8.08
30	39.49	201.0	-4.08	12.82
7	39.93	237.0	-34.40	25.47
8	40.51	207.5	-0.13	0.00
17	41.07	193.1	27.40	-
14	41.37	203.6	8.95	-
10	42.03	190.1	8.87	-
7	42.40	217.0	-5.64	-
4	43.07	185.2	22.75	-
3	43.43	185.0	2.50	-
3	47.95	147.0	-	-

TABLE XIX.

Empirical Determinations of Pulmonary Capacity, by Circumference of Chest.

Circ. of Chest	White Soldiers Earlier Series		White Soldiers Later Series		Total White Men		Negroes	
	Cubic In.	c. — o.	Cubic In.	c. — o.	Cubic In.	c. — o.	Cubic In.	c. — o.
inches								
29	134½	- 1.1	143½	- 2.7	142	+ 2.4	–	–
29½	138	+ 13.1	148	+ 13.8	145½	+ 10.0	–	–
30	141	- 3.9	152	- 5.1	149½	- 2.9	124	+ 3.1
30½	144½	- 0.4	156½	+ 7.6	153	+ 4.7	128	- 3.1
31	148	- 5.1	160½	- 1.8	156½	- 1.5	132½	- 2.4
31½	151	- 0.1	165	- 2.4	160	- 1.0	137	+ 5.8
32	154½	+ 3.1	168½	+ 4.5	163	+ 3.8	141	+ 2.6
32½	157½	- 5.6	172	- 2.0	166½	- 3.7	144½	- 0.2
33	161	+ 4.9	175	- 2.7	169½	+ 1.4	148½	- 3.7
33½	164	- 1.4	177½	+ 1.3	172½	- 0.8	152½	+ 2.1
34	167	+ 0.6	180	+ 0.7	175½	+ 1.6	156	- 0.1
34½	170½	+ 2.3	182	- 0.1	178	- 0.4	159½	+ 1.5
35	173½	- 5.1	184½	+ 0.2	181	- 0.7	163	- 6.8
35½	176½	- 1.8	186½	+ 0.8	184	- 0.6	167	+ 6.0
36	180	+ 1.0	188½	- 0.6	186½	+ 0.9	170½	- 0.1
36½	183	- 0.1	191	+ 0.1	189½	+ 0.4	174	+ 3.1
37	186	- 0.6	193½	+ 0.8	192	+ 1.2	178	+ 1.2
37½	189	- 10.5	195½	- 1.0	194½	- 3.5	181½	- 1.7
38	192	- 0.7	198	- 2.4	196½	- 1.0	185½	- 3.2
38½	194½	+ 2.4	200	- 4.4	198½	- 2.7	189½	- 12.0
39	197	+ 1.1	201½	+ 0.5	200½	+ 0.7	194	+ 3.0
39½	199½	+ 0.3	203	+ 7.4	202½	+ 5.6	198	+ 9.5
40	202	+ 2.3	204	- 0.1	204	+ 1.5	202	- 9.4
40½	204½	- 9.4	204½	+ 2.4	206	- 1.3	–	–
41	206½	- 6.7	204½	- 19.4	207½	- 12.9	–	–

5. *Relation to Play of Chest.*

Before presenting our tabulations made with reference to this element, it may be well to remind the reader of the wide distinction between what we here call the Play of the Chest (namely, the difference in the girth of the thorax across the nipples at full inspiration and at full expiration) and the ordinary expansion and contraction of the thorax in breathing. The amount of air which enters and leaves the lungs every three or four seconds in ordinary unconscious breathing, and which corresponds to the ordinary expansion of the thorax in respiration, differs only in quantity from the volume which is measured by the spirometer in these observations, and which produces the lateral expansion of the thorax here measured. But the motion of the thorax itself in men is very different in the two cases. In the ordinary breathing motion the expansion of the thorax is downward, and the expansion of the body abdominal in consequence of the pressure of the diaphragm against the viscera. The motion of the ribs in men was found[1] by Hutchinson to be so small as to preclude the possibility of counting the respirations, unknown to the subject, by resting the hand either against the ribs or the sternum. It was necessary to let the hand rest in contact with the abdomen; and the costal movement in health was found not to surpass the limit of one thirtieth of an inch.

But the deep inspiratory movement, as occurring in the cases here under consideration, is a process different from ordinary breathing in character as well as in amount. Here the abdomen recedes, and the sternum advances, while the circumference of the thorax is in general largely increased. And while, in consequence of this enlargement of circumference, the diaphragm must in like manner be laterally expanded, this expansion does not necessarily imply a descent of the arch to any great extent. Nor yet does it imply an increase of thoracic area, in any section, commensurate with an equal enlargement of the circumference in a circle; since the expansion and contraction are almost entirely in the anterior part of the body, being produced by the motion of the extremities of the ribs and the sternum, while the lateral diameter of the thorax is relatively but slightly increased.

It is therefore to be remembered that the results of this chapter hold good only for a mode of respiration not employed in ordinary breathing, as well as for volumes of air only attainable by special exertion. Still they are not without an intimate relation to many interesting hygienic and physiological questions which it would be excessively difficult, if indeed it be possible, to approach in any other way.

The next series of tables (XX. to XXII.) exhibit for the respective classes of men considered, all being in usual vigor, the number of cases and the mean pulmonary capacity corresponding to each three tenths of an inch in the play of the thorax, as measured by its variation in girth across the nipples. The tabulation has been made for each tenth of an inch, but the more compen-

[1] *Medico-Chirurgical Transactions*, XXIX., p. 187.

dious form here presented will probably give all desired detail; the values given for each argument being those belonging to the group of three successive numbers of which the argument itself is the middle one.

TABLE XX.

Pulmonary Capacity of White Men, by Play of Chest.

Play of Chest	White Soldiers		Sailors		Students		Total	
	No.	Cubic In.	No.	Cubic In.	No.	Cubic In.	No.	Cubic In.
in.								
Below 0.5	27	159.7	6	179.0	–	–	33	164.0
0.6	83	169.2	11	228.9	–	–	94	176.2
0.9	296	167.3	57	180.9	–	–	353	169.5
1.2	323	174.8	91	184.2	3	244.0	417	177.4
1.5	608	179.0	38	196.9	–	–	646	180.0
1.8	459	179.8	29	184.0	6	185.8	494	180.1
2.1	1 650	185.3	555	173.8	22	206.3	2 227	182.6
2.4	1 089	191.2	178	180.6	5	200.8	1 272	189.8
2.7	438	186.2	10	201.6	22	189.3	470	186.6
3.0	1 565	190.3	136	180.8	135	200.2	1 836	190.3
3.3	318	190.1	10	209.6	45	205.7	373	192.5
3.6	576	193.5	7	176.4	7	228.6	590	193.7
3.9	774	193.0	7	206.7	31	216.7	812	194.1
4.2	144	191.4	–	–	13	223.6	157	194.1
4.5	267	195.5	–	–	–	–	267	195.5
4.8	51	193.5	–	–	–	–	51	193.5
5.1	275	198.4	1	186.0	–	–	276	198.3
5.4	65	204.8	–	–	–	–	65	204.8
5.7	6	158.2	–	–	–	–	6	158.2
6.0	34	215.7	–	–	–	–	34	215.7
6.3	8	231.2	–	–	–	–	8	231.2
6.6	10	217.5	–	–	–	–	10	217.5
6.9	11	213.4	1	176.0	–	–	12	210.2
Over 7.0	6	197.8	–	–	–	–	6	197.8

TABLE XXI.

Pulmonary Capacity of Negroes, by Play of Chest.

Play of Chest	Full Blacks		Mulattoes	
	No. of Men	Cubic Inches	No. of Men	Cubic Inches
Below 0.5	54	145.3	39	127.3
0.6	100	146.6	105	137.4
0.9	165	146.4	170	152.3
1.2	172	150.1	67	157.8
1.5	250	159.0	109	166.6
1.8	204	168.2	50	165.2
2.1	244	175.2	77	168.7
2.4	174	182.2	42	176.5
2.7	67	174.4	23	199.4
3.0	93	180.8	21	188.1
3.3	21	187.5	4	174.5
3.6	28	188.7	7	218.3
3.9	20	190.1	6	243.5
4.2	3	187.3	1	163.0
4.5	7	190.7	1	162.0
4.8	1	150.0	–	–
5.1	1	200.0	1	317.0
5.4	–	–	–	–
5.7	1	140.0	–	–
6.0	–	–	–	–
6.3	1	120.0	–	–
6.6	–	–	–	–
6.9	2	207.5	–	–
Over 7.0	–	–	–	–

TABLE XXII.

Pulmonary Capacity of Indians, by Play of Chest.

Play of Chest	No. of Men	Cubic Inches
Below 0.5	–	–
0.6	2	103.5
0.9	3	168.3
1.2	72	178.0
1.5	106	182.6
1.8	103	186.3
2.1	118	187.6
2.4	66	189.6
2.7	28	191.7
3.0	4	206.2
3.3	2	211.5
3.6	2	210.0
3.9	1	194.0
4.2	1	234.0

The mean difference between the girths of the inflated and of the collapsed thorax, is thus found to be : —

2.72 cub. in. for the White Soldiers,
2.09 " for the Sailors,
3.07 " for the Students,
1.62 " for the Full Blacks,
1.58 " for the Mulattoes,
1.84 " for the Indians.

These numbers are by no means proportional to the average pulmonary capacity of the same classes of men, whence we may obtain an independent confirmation of the small extent to which the lateral mobility of the chest may serve as an index to its real degree of inflation, which is probably quite as dependent, if indeed not much more so, upon the motion of the diaphragm.

6. *Relation to Age.*

The pulmonary capacity was found by Hutchinson [1] to increase with the age of the individual until about the 30th year, after which he observed a decided decrease. The results of our own tabulation excited therefore no small surprise, for the

[1] *Medico-Chirurgical Transactions*, XXIX. pp. 171, 172.

mean capacity, in the soldiers here investigated, after rising at a very rapid rate until the mean age of about 20½ at last birthday, or 21 years actually, attains then a maximum value of nearly 200 cubic inches; and then, receding at once, appears to diminish with the age in a well formed asymptotic curve. Our values are inadequate for any study of the subject as related to ages outside of the military limits; but that the curve of pulmonary capacity as determined by our measurements exhibits this very sharply marked maximum at the age of 21, is as distinctly manifested as is possible for any phenomenon of the sort. How far this may result from the superior strength of the thoracic muscles, manifested in an unusual manner, we cannot presume to decide; but since the epoch of greatest lifting strength seems, by the investigations of the last chapter, not to be attained before the age of 25 years, this would to a considerable extent conflict with any hypothesis which should attribute the results here obtained rather to the muscular power of the thorax than to the pulmonary capacity, in any proper sense of the term.

Our mean values given in Table XXIII. are deduced solely from the later series of examinations of white soldiers, and from these the empirical Table XXIV. has been constructed by the graphical method.

TABLE XXIII.

Pulmonary Capacity of White Soldiers, in usual Vigor, by Age.

(*Later Series.*)

Age last Birthday	Number of Men	Cubic Inches	Age last Birthday	Number of Men	Cubic Inches
Under 17	160	171.0	30	231	178.1
17	243	181.7	31	152	176.9
18	683	187.8	32	198	181.3
19	626	193.5	33	138	177.1
20	765	199.2	34	163	177.8
21	827	198.2	35	153	177.1
22	800	194.9	36	110	169.8
23	627	194.4	37	107	179.0
24	628	189.5	38	108	171.3
25	433	195.4	39	89	170.3
26	359	190.5	40	67	167.4
27	289	188.0	41-44	204	166.6
28	310	185.9	45-49	116	162.4
29	227	178.8	50 & over	49	143.4

TABLE XXIV.

Empirical Table for Pulmonary Capacity of White Men, by Age.

Age last Birthday	Cubic Inches	Comp. — Obs.	Age last Birthday	Cubic Inches	Comp. — Obs.
16	174.1	+ 0.5	34	175.6	- 2.2
17	181.6	- 0.1	35	174.3	- 2.8
18	188.1	+ 0.3	36	173.1	+ 3.3
19	193.9	+ 0.4	37	171.9	- 7.1
20	199.2	+ 0.0	38	170.8	- 0.5
21	198.2	+ 0.0	39	169.7	- 0.6
22	196.1	+ 1.2	40	168.6	+ 1.2
23	194.0	- 0.4	41	167.5	- 0.7 (41–44)
24	192.0	+ 2.5	42	166.5	
25	190.0	- 5.4	43	165.5	
26	188.1	- 2.4	44	164.5	
27	186.3	- 1.7	45	163.5	+ 0.1 (45–50)
28	184.6	- 1.3	46	162.5	
29	182.9	+ 4.1	47	161.5	
30	181.3	+ 3.2	48	160.6	
31	179.8	+ 2.	49	159.7	
32	178.3	- 3.0	50	158.8	
33	176.9	- 0.2			

CHAPTER XIII.

RESPIRATION AND PULSE.

1. *Preliminary.*

Any attempt at determining the frequency of the act of respiration, and of the pulsation of the heart, must inevitably be attended with a considerable degree of uncertainty. Not merely are these functions largely influenced by very transient conditions of the body, especially by slight unusual excitement or embarrassment, but the very consciousness that such observations are making will frequently suffice to modify the phenomena under investigation, without any perception, on the part of the subject, that such modification takes place. The great extent to which the frequency of respiration may be affected by the unconscious will, or by the involuntary result of consciousness, is well known; and such precautions were enjoined upon our examiners as would obviate this disturbing influence so far as possible. Soldiers detailed for examination would frequently run at full speed to the examiner's tent, or would amuse themselves by feats of agility, by wrestling, or by other physical exertion, previous to their examination; and other disturbances of their normal nervous condition not unfrequently occurred. For this reason the men were detained, when possible, for some little time after their arrival before they were examined, remaining meanwhile in a comfortable position. The pulse was noted before the trials were made with spirometer and dynamometer, and the respirations were counted without the subject's knowledge, while the wrist was held as if to feel the pulse.

Yet, although these precautions must have essentially diminished the liability to error, they cannot be supposed to have precluded it altogether, and indeed there seems to be some indication of constant personal differences between several of the examiners. The explanation of such constant differences is in general not easy. Perhaps a constant error by a single unit in counting the respirations or the pulse during any given interval ought sometimes to be expected; but any constant mistake on the part of the examiner, larger than this, appears unwarrantable; so that whatever other errors peculiar to the examiner may exist, seem referable to the condition in which his subjects may have been at the time. That constant differences between the results obtained by the several examiners may be due to some such influence as this, appears highly probable. The easy manners of one man put his subjects at ease, while the less kindly or more reserved demeanor of another excites anxieties or apprehensions which, though trivial in themselves, may yet quicken the pulse, or accelerate the breathing of a nervous or excitable person.

Had the limits of time and means permitted, within which it has been found important to restrict this discussion, efforts would have been made to determine the personal differences of the respective examiners, and to apply corresponding corrections to their results before combining them in the general means. Circumstances have rendered this course unadvisable, and it appears improbable, after some little scrutiny, that our final inferences will be essentially affected by the omission. The materials from which our results are derived, and all the details of tabulation and computation for the discussions of the present volume, are preserved in the archives of the Sanitary Commission, where they will be available for future investigators, and the shortcomings of the present researches may be supplemented hereafter as easily as at present.

That the frequency of pulse and respiration varies with the time of day and with the posture is undoubted, but in researches like these it must be assumed that the effects of such variations are entirely eliminated from the final averages. The pulse and breathing were generally counted while the men were standing, and it was intended that this should be the uniform rule; but the deviations prove to have been not infrequent, and our records do not admit of any thorough discrimination between the different cases.

2. *Respiration by Age.*

The fact, that the respirations during infancy and childhood are much more frequent than at more advanced ages, is well known, and our own tabulations would suggest that the mean numbers for the ages under eighteen are in general larger than the average for subsequent ages. So far as the data at our command, combined with those of Quetelet, Vierordt, Hutchinson, Hooker, and others, warrant an inference, it would seem that the number of respirations under the same circumstances, in a given interval, decreases from birth until the age of puberty, after which it appears to remain essentially constant, at least during the years of military age.

In the first and third of the appended tables are given the numbers of white soldiers in usual vigor, for the earlier and the later series respectively, assorted by ages, according to the number of respirations observed in a minute. We cannot avoid a strong suspicion that those instances, in the later series at least ($1\frac{1}{8}$ per cent. of the whole number), in which the observed respirations exceeded twenty to the minute, were in great measure due to some abnormal acceleration of a temporary kind, occasioned by recent exercise or by agitation of some sort. The proportion of such cases in the second and fourth tables, which comprise the white soldiers not in usual vigor, in the two series respectively, is about threefold larger, yet even here the distribution of the number cannot fail to suggest a similar suspicion. It is noteworthy that in each of these classes of men (in the later series) the great preponderance of such abnormal cases belongs to the group in which the inspirations were twenty-four to the minute, which may possibly indicate this rate as being the most usual for accelerated breathing of the kind referred to. The circumstance, however, that 24 is a multiple of both 2 and 3, has undoubtedly increased the number of cases for which twenty-four respirations to the minute was recorded, and the relatively large number recorded in the group having 18 to the minute is probably attributable in a good degree to a similar cause. But the injunctions were strict, for the later series, that the counting should be continued during an entire minute, and that the recorded numbers should not be inferred from observations during a shorter interval. And the general fidelity of our examiners, tested in many ways, forbids the reference of the unsymmetrical distribution of the numbers to this source alone.

The differences between the results of the earlier and of the later series are so wide, that these are separately presented. And Mr. Fairchild's observations, confined as they were almost exclusively to prisoners, made only during the winter months, and evidently deduced from counting during half a minute only, are kept distinct from those of Dr. Buckley and Mr. Risler, who examined only our own soldiers, and whose work was prosecuted through all seasons of the year.

The distribution tables for students and sailors are not here given, since these were found on scrutiny to be less trustworthy.

The students were all examined by Dr. Elsner, whose results, as regards the counting, appear to have been affected with systematic error. Not a single case was recorded in which the respirations numbered 17 to the minute; but one in which there were 15, and only 35 in which there were 18; all the remaining 254 cases are recorded as 16 to the minute. So, too, with the pulse; about two thirds of all the students being recorded as having exactly 60 beats in a minute, a constancy of proportion not corroborated by the results of any other examiner in any other class. Hence, although Dr. Elsner's measurements seem in other respects entitled to full confidence, his records of pulse and respiration should be rejected.

As regards sailors, all but 324 were measured by Mr. Phinney, as has been heretofore stated, immediately after their examination by the surgeon at the recruiting office. They consequently came to Mr. Phinney's inspection under some nervous excitement, so that it was deemed unadvisable to attempt any determination of the rate of breathing or of pulse. The greater portion of the remainder were examined by Dr. Elsner.

The number of negroes not in usual vigor whose respirations were observed is but 294; the full blacks and mulattoes having been aggregated in the tabulation. Our results differ so decidedly for the men of these two classes, that any inferences from data in which they are combined without discrimination would seem worth but little, even were the number of cases manifold larger.

TABLE I.

Distribution of White Soldiers in usual Vigor, by Age and Number of Respirations.

Earlier Series. A.—Observations by Buckley and Risler.

Respirations in a Minute	Under 17[a]	17	18	19	20	21	22	23	24
10	–	–	–	–	–	1	–	–	–
13	–	–	–	1	–	–	–	–	–
14	–	–	3	2	1	–	–	–	–
15	12	16	40	62	68	63	57	42	27
16	47	73	132	120	130	131	104	84	73
17	14	17	40	34	55	43	35	33	39
18	7	6	23	30	17	23	20	17	10
19	–	–	–	–	–	–	1	–	–
20	–	–	3	–	2	3	1	2	1
21	–	–	–	–	–	–	–	–	–
22	–	–	–	–	1	–	–	–	–
Total .	80	112	241	249	274	264	218	178	150
B.—Observations by Fairchild.									
12	–	–	–	–	2	2	–	2	1
13	–	–	–	–	–	1	–	–	–
14	–	1	5	5	4	8	10	13	6
15	1	–	3	4	3	4	4	8	7
16	5	6	17	32	26	42	30	33	28
17	1	2	2	3	11	6	4	8	7
18	2	10	12	20	27	37	26	38	23
19	–	1	2	4	4	13	5	5	8
20	4	1	7	17	18	25	18	21	17
21	–	–	1	2	1	8	7	4	2
22	1	–	3	8	8	11	9	8	11
23	–	–	–	1	3	–	3	3	5
24	2	1	3	5	5	–	4	6	5
25	–	–	–	1	1	3	1	–	1
26	–	–	1	1	4	2	–	1	2
27	–	–	1	–	–	–	–	–	–
28	–	–	–	–	–	1	1	–	–
29	–	–	–	–	1	–	–	–	–
30	–	–	–	–	–	1	–	–	–
Over 30	–	–	–	–	–	–	–	–	–
Total .	16	22	57	103	118	164	122	150	123

[a] Mean age—15.99.

TABLE I.—(*Continued.*)

Distribution of White Soldiers in usual Vigor, by Age and Number of Respirations.

Earlier Series. A.—Observations by Buckley and Risler.

Respirations in a Minute	25	26	27	28	29	30	31–34	35 and over	Total
10	–	–	–	–	–	–	–	–	1
13	–	–	–	–	–	–	–	–	1
14	–	–	–	–	–	–	–	–	6
15	22	21	18	20	10	8	32	53	571
16	60	31	46	37	17	30	75	95	1 285
17	32	10	12	12	13	12	23	30	454
18	9	5	8	6	8	6	16	19	230
19	–	–	–	–	–	–	–	–	1
20	2	1	1	–	1	–	5	4	26
21	–	–	–	–	–	–	–	–	–
22	–	–	–	1	–	–	1	–	3
Total .	125	68	85	76	49	56	152	201	2 578

B.— Observations by Fairchild.

Respirations in a Minute	25	26	27	28	29	30	31–34	35 and over	Total
12	3	–	1	2	1	–	2	3	19
13	3	–	–	1	–	1	1	2	9
14	3	4	5	7	2	2	6	12	93
15	–	5	2	4	3	1	4	11	64
16	25	22	13	13	10	10	28	27	367
17	2	2	4	4	3	3	5	11	78
18	17	20	21	12	9	10	19	23	326
19	4	3	1	–	–	1	4	4	59
20	10	17	6	5	3	5	9	17	200
21	1	3	4	–	1		1	1	36
22	4	3	2	2	1	3	2	6	82
23	–	1	2	2	–	–	1	4	25
24	4	3	3	1	1	1	–	3	47
25	–	–	–	–	–	–	1	1	9
26	3	–	1	–	1	–	1	1	18
27	–	–	–	–	1	–	–	–	2
28	–	–	1	–	1	–	–	1	5
29	–	–	–	–	–	–	–	–	1
30	–	–	–	–	–	–	–	–	1
Over 30	–	–	–	–	–	–	–	1	1
Total .	79	83	66	53	37	37	84	128	1 442

TABLE II.

Distribution of White Soldiers not in usual Vigor, by Age and Number of Respirations.

Earlier Series. A.— Observations by Buckley and Risler.

Respirations in a Minute	Under 17[a]	17	18	19	20	21	22	23	24
10	–	–	–	–	1	–	–	–	–
12	–	–	–	–	–	–	–	1	–
13	–	–	–	–	1	–	–	–	–
14	1	–	–	–	–	–	–	–	–
15	3	4	12	7	13	18	14	7	9
16	9	11	29	25	30	27	50	27	30
17	4	–	11	2	9	8	11	11	9
18	6	4	13	13	12	15	15	18	18
19	–	–	–	2	1	–	1	1	1
20	9	11	14	23	25	25	23	24	18
21	–	–	–	–	–	–	3	–	1
22	2	1	2	4	5	1	5	5	1
23	–	–	–	1	–	–	1	–	–
24	1	3	7	12	8	10	11	7	5
25	–	–	–	–	–	–	–	–	–
26	–	3	1	4	2	2	5	5	3
27	–	–	–	–		–	–	–	–
28	–	–	–	3	4	2	3	–	3
29	–	–	–	–	–	–	–	–	–
30	–	–	–	2	–	2	–	1	–
Over 30	–	–	–	1	1	1	1	–	–
Total .	35	37	89	99	112	111	143	107	98

[a] Mean age, 15.51.

TABLE II. — (*Continued.*)

Distribution of White Soldiers not in usual Vigor, by Age and Number of Respirations.

Earlier Series. B. — Observations by Fairchild.

Respirations in a Minute	Under 17[a]	17	18	19	20	21	22	23	24
11	–	–	–	–	–		–	–	–
12	–	–	–	–	–	–	–	–	1
13	–	–	–	–	–	–	–	–	–
14	–	–	–	–	–	1	1	–	–
15	–	–	–	–	1	–	–	1	–
16	–	1	–	–	5	2	4	7	10
17	–	1	–	3	–	–	–	–	1
18	–	–	1	4	1	2	2	3	2
19	–	–	–	–	1	1	–	–	–
20	–	1	1	–	–	4	1	3	1
21	–	–	1	–	–	1	2	–	2
22	1	–	–	–	1	–	1	–	2
23	–	–	–	–	–	1	–	–	1
24	–	–	–	2	–	–	–	–	1
25	–	–	–	–	–	–	–	–	–
26	–	–	–	–	–	1	–	–	1
27	–	–	–	–	–	–	–	–	–
Total .	1	3	3	9	9	13	11	14	22

[a] Mean age = 16.00.

TABLE II. — (*Continued.*)

Distribution of White Soldiers not in usual Vigor, by Age and Number of Respirations.

Earlier Series. A. — Observations by Buckley and Risler.

Respirations in a Minute	25	26	27	28	29	30	31–34	35 and over	Total
10	–	–	–	–	–	–	–	–	1
12	–	–	–	–	–	–	–	–	1
13	–	–	–	–	–	–	–	–	1
14	–	–	–	1	–	1	–	–	3
15	7	8	8	8	3	8	6	21	156
16	12	20	20	14	10	10	34	57	415
17	9	4	4	4	3	4	9	18	120
18	17	9	8	13	7	6	24	36	234
19	–	–	1	–	3	1	–	3	14
20	11	8	11	9	4	6	25	36	282
21	–	–	–	–	–	–	–	–	4
22	3	–	1	1	1	–	1	4	37
23	–	–	–	–	–	–	–	–	2
24	3	4	7	8	2	4	8	14	114
25	–	–	–	–	–	–	–	–	–
26	1	2	–	1	–	–	1	6	36
27	–	–	–	–	–	–	–	–	–
28	1	1	–	1	1	1	1	7	28
29	–	1	–	–	–	–	–	–	1
30	–	2	1	–	–	1	1	4	14
Over 30	1	1	2	–	–	–	2	3	13
Total .	65	60	63	60	34	42	112	209	1 476

TABLE II. — (*Continued.*)

Distribution of White Soldiers not in usual Vigor, by Age and Number of Respirations.

Earlier Series. B. — Observations by Fairchild.

Respirations in a Minute	25	26	27	28	29	30	31–34	35 and over	Total
11	–	–	–	–	–	–	–	1	1
12	–	1	–	1	–	–	–	–	3
13	1	–	–	1	–	–	1	–	3
14	–	1	3	2	–	2	–	3	13
15	–	1	–	–	1	–	2	1	7
16	–	4	1	1	2	2	4	12	55
17	2	2	1	1	–	–	1	1	13
18	–	1	2	2	2	–	2	4	28
19	–	2	–	–	–	–	3	2	9
20	1	3	1	1	2	1	–	9	29
21	–	–	–	–	–	–	1	–	7
22	2	–	–	1	–	–	–	2	10
23	–	–	–	–	–	–	–	–	2
24	1	–	–	–	–	–	1	1	6
25	–	–	–	–	–	–	–	–	–
26	–	–	–	–	–	–	–	–	2
27	–	–	–	–	–	–	–	1	1
Total .	7	15	8	10	7	5	15	37	189

TABLE III.

Distribution of White Soldiers, in usual Vigor, by Age and Number of Respirations.

(Later Series.)

Respirations in a Minute	Under 17[a]	17	18	19	20	21	22	23	24
10	–	–	1	–	–	–	–	–	–
11	–	–	–	–	1	1	–	–	–
12	2	1	5	2	2	3	4	2	2
13	–	–	–	–	–	–	–	–	–
14	2	4	8	9	10	10	13	12	7
15	12	10	50	52	53	51	46	32	43
16	86.	147	404	374	460	439	451	357	357
17	17	27	63	61	87	106	85	83	88
18	24	22	82	74	78	110	102	84	72
19	2	–	1	1	–	6	1	–	–
20	3	9	14	13	13	13	13	11	13
21	–	–	1	–	–	1	–	–	1
22	–	–	–	–	–	–	1	–	–
23	–	–	–	–	–	–	1	–	–
24	–	3	4	3	8	8	5	4	6
25	–	–	–	–	–	–	–	–	–
26	–	–	–	–	–	1	–	–	–
27	–	–	–	–	–	–	–	–	–
28	–	–	–	–	–	1	–	1	2
29	–	–	–	–	–	–	–	–	–
30	–	1	–	–	–	–	1	–	–
Over 30	–	–	1	–	1	–	–	–	–
Total	148	224	634	589	713	750	723	586	591

[a] Mean age = 15.76.

TABLE III. — (*Continued.*)

Distribution of White Soldiers, in usual Vigor, by Age and Number of Respirations.

(*Later Series.*)

Respirations in a Minute	25	26	27	28	29	30	31-34	35 and over	Total
10	–	–	–	–	–	–	–	1	2
11	–	–	–	–	–	–	–	–	2
12	1	1	2	2	–	–	3	3	35
13	–	–	1	–	1	–	–	1	3
14	6	6	5	5	2	2	7	10	118
15	33	27	26	26	14	11	39	75	600
16	237	207	168	186	130	150	389	617	5 159
17	57	34	39	39	26	35	93	127	1 067
18	55	41	33	32	33	22	56	102	1 022
19	4	1	–	–	–	–	–	2	18
20	4	6	4	6	8	4	8	23	165
21	–	–	–	2	–	–	–	1	6
22	–	–	–	–	1	–	1	1	4
23	–	–	–	–	–	–	–	–	1
24	–	2	1	1	–	–	4	11	60
25	–	–	–	–	–	–	–	1	1
26	1	–	1	–	–	–	–	1	4
27	–	–	–	–	–	–	–	–	–
28	1	–	–	1	–	1	1	3	11
29	–	–	–	–	–	–	–	–	–
30	1	–	–	–	–	–	–	–	3
Over 30	–	–	–	–	–	–	–	1	3
Total	400	325	280	300	215	225	601	980	8 284

TABLE IV.

Distribution of White Soldiers, not in usual Vigor, by Age and Number of Respirations.

(Later Series.)

Respirations in a Minute	Under 17[a]	17	18	19	20	21	22	23	24
10	–	–	–	–	–	–	1	–	–
12	–	–	–	–	1	1	1	–	–
13	–	–	–	–	–	–	–	–	–
14	–	1	–	1	–	–	–	–	–
15	2	–	4	2	6	5	2	5	5
16	11	10	20	29	38	45	61	31	64
17	1	4	6	11	16	14	26	11	18
18	3	3	11	9	12	17	20	14	9
19	–	1	–	–	–	–	1	–	1
20	–	1	–	1	2	5	3	2	2
21	–	1	–	–	–	–	–	–	–
22	1	–	–	–	–	–	–	–	–
23	–	–	–	–	–	–	–	–	–
24	–	–	1	–	–	1	–	2	1
25	–	–	–	–	–	–	–	–	–
26	–	–	–	–	1	–	–	–	–
27	–	–	–	–	–	–	–	–	–
28		–	–	–	–	–	–	–	–
29		–	–	–	–	–	–	–	–
30	1	–	–	–	–	–	–	–	–
Over 30		–	–	–	–	–	–	–	1
Total .	19	21	42	53	76	88	115	65	101

[a] Mean age = 15.63.

TABLE IV. — (*Continued.*)

Distribution of White Soldiers, not in usual Vigor, by Age and Number of Respirations.

(*Later Series.*)

Respirations in a Minute	25	26	27	28	29	30	31–34	35 and over	Total
10	–	–	–	–	–	–	–	–	1
12	–	1	–	1	–	–	1	1	7
13	–	–	–	–	–	–	–	–	–
14	–	1	–	3	–	2	2	1	11
15	1	5	2	1	3	2	9	15	69
16	38	41	21	26	24	25	68	164	716
17	15	8	5	2	17	8	17	55	234
18	14	5	10	7	8	10	22	54	228
19	–	1	1	–	–	–	–	–	5
20	2	1	3	3	2	–	6	14	47
21	–	–	–	–	–	–	–	–	1
22	–	–	–	–	–	–	1	–	2
23	–	–	–	–	–	–	–	–	–
24	2	1	1	–	–	3	2	9	23
25	–	–	–	–	–	–	–	–	–
26	–	–	–	–	–	–	–	–	1
27	–	–	–	–	–	–	–	–	–
28	–	–	–	–	1	–	–	–	1
29	–	–	–	–	–	1	–	–	1
30	–	–	–	–	–	–	–	–	1
Over 30	–	–	–	–	–	–	–	3	4
Total .	72	64	43	43	55	51	128	316	1 352

TABLE V.

Distribution of Full Blacks, in usual Vigor, by Age and Number of Respirations.

Respirations in a Minute	Under 17[a]	17	18	19	20	21	22	23	24
11	–	–	–	–	–	–	–	1	–
12	–	–	–	–	1	1	4	3	4
13	–	–	–	2	8	10	14	13	16
14	–	1	1	4	8	7	15	21	27
15	2	2	4	2	10	4	17	14	13
16	14	20	26	23	27	30	22	29	16
17	3	–	5	6	6	8	4	7	6
18	9	8	13	7	5	6	11	11	8
19	–	1	2	3	3	3	2	3	5
20	6	6	9	19	41	29	15	26	17
21	–	–	–	1	1	2	1	2	–
22	–	–	3	3	7	2	4	2	2
23	–	–	–	1	1	–	–	1	–
24	–	2	6	11	10	8	11	5	10
25	–	1	–	–	1	–	2	–	–
26	–	1	2	–	2	1	–	3	1
27	–	–	–	–	–	–	–	2	–
28	3	–	2	8	4	5	3	2	4
29	–	–	–	–	1	–	–	–	–
30	1	1	–	–	–	–	1	–	–
Over 30	–	–	–	–	1	–	2	2	–
Total .	38	43	73	90	137	116	128	147	129

[a] Mean age = 15.74.

TABLE V. — (*Continued.*)

Distribution of Full Blacks, in usual Vigor, by Age and Number of Respirations.

Respirations in a Minute	25	26	27	28	29	30	31-34	35 and over	Total
11	–	–	–	–	–	–	–	–	1
12	4	1	2	1	1	2	2	1	27
13	9	8	5	8	3	1	2	4	103
14	24	13	12	6	11	5	12	7	174
15	4	5	5	8	3	5	4	10	112
16	22	18	20	16	6	11	24	48	372
17	7	3	1	2	3	1	2	6	70
18	7	6	6	8	2	2	9	18	136
19	2	–	3		–	–	–	2	29
20	15	8	11	9	1	4	7	22	245
21	1	2	1	–	3	1	–	1	16
22	1	2	–	–	–	3	1	4	34
23	1	1	–	1	–	–	–	–	6
24	6	4	1	1	5	1	3	14	98
25	–	–	–	–	–	–	–	–	4
26	1	–	1	1	–	–	–	–	13
27	1	–	–	1	–	–	–	–	4
28	5	–	2	4	–	1	2	1	46
29	–	–	–	–	–	–	–	–	1
30	–	–	–	–	–	–	–	–	3
Over 30	1	–	–	–	–	–	1	2	9
Total .	111	71	70	66	38	37	69	140	1 503

TABLE VI.

Distribution of Mulattoes, in usual Vigor, by Age and Number of Respirations.

Respirations in a Minute	Under 17[a]	17	18	19	20	21	22	23	24
11	–	–	–	–	–	–	–	–	–
12	–	–	–	-	–	1	–	–	1
13	–	–	–	1	–	1	–	2	1
14	3	–	–	1	1	1	7	2	3
15	–	–	1	2	1	3	2	6	4
16	3	4	10	4	13	12	9	9	4
17	2	1	1	5	4	5	6	6	2
18	1	2	2	4	7	3	8	6	7
19	3	2	2	1	7	6	10	9	2
20	4	2	5	7	10	5	11	12	9
21	1	–	1	2	6	5	2	1	6
22	–	–	2	–	2	4	3	1	2
23	–	–	–	2	2	1	1	2	3
24	2	–	1	5	3	5	4	–	5
25	–	–	–	1	1	–	–	3	1
26	–	–	–	–	–	–	–	–	2
27	–	–	–	–	–	–	–	–	–
28	–	–	–	–	1	1	–	1	–
29	–	–	–	–	–	–	–	–	–
30	–	–	–	–	–	–	–	–	1
Over 30	–	–	–	1	2	–	1	1	1
Total .	19	11	25	36	60	53	64	61	54

[a] Mean age = 15.52.

TABLE VI. — (*Continued.*)

Distribution of Mulattoes, in usual Vigor, by Age and Number of Respirations.

Respirations in a Minute	25	26	27	28	29	30	31-34	35 and over	Total
11	–	–	–	–	–	–	–	–	–
12	–	–	1	–	–	–	–	–	3
13	1	1	1	–	2	1	2	3	16
14	3	3	1	2	1	2	1	3	34
15	1	2	2	2	4	–	3	5	38
16	4	4	3	2	2	6	7	16	112
17	3	3	2	1	–	3	–	5	49
18	6	4	3	2	2	3	5	17	82
19	3	3	4	3	3	5	6	16	85
20	7	8	3	6	3	4	4	12	112
21	8	–	1	1	1	3	–	6	44
22	1	–	1	2	2	–	2	4	26
23	1	3	1	–	2	2	–	1	21
24	3	4	3	2	1	4	5	5	52
25	1	–	–	–	–	–	1	–	8
26	2	1	–	–	–	–	–	2	7
27	–	–	–	–	–	–	–	–	–
28	1	1	–	–	–	–	2	–	7
29	–	–	–	–	–	–	–	–	–
30	–	–	–	1	–	–	–	–	2
Over 30	1	1	–	–	–	–	–	2	10
Total .	46	38	26	24	23	33	38	97	708

TABLE VII.

Distribution of Indians in usual Vigor, by Age and Number of Respirations.

Respirations in a Minute	16	17	18	19	20	21	22	23	24
14	–	–	–	–	–	–	–	–	–
15	–	–	1	–	–	–	2	–	3
16	1	–	1	6	8	14	26	30	35
17	–	–	–	–	–	–	1	–	–
Total .	1	–	2	6	8	14	29	32	38

Respirations in a Minute	25	26	27	28	29	30	31-34	35 and Over	Total
14	–	1	–	–	–	–	–	2	1
15	3	9	6	4	8	5	7	31	81
16	11	34	22	34	31	16	60	90	419
17	–	1	–	–	–	–	–	–	2
Total .	14	45	28	38	39	21	67	121	503

The foregoing tables have been given in this full detail, in order to permit, not only the amplest discussion by other investigators, but also the most thorough criticism. The distribution of the numbers corresponding to the several rates of breathing is far from satisfactory, the great majority of the cases being as we have stated in those groups which correspond to 16, 18, or 20 respirations in a minute, and the group for 18 being very frequently less numerous than that at 20. This would certainly appear to imply that to a great extent the respirations were counted during only one quarter of a minute, and the number thus found then multiplied by 4. The value of our results must be greatly diminished by such a course, and it is difficult for us to believe such to have been the case to the extent apparently indicated. Still the precision of our records must be tested by internal evidence whenever possible ; and it cannot be maintained that these stand the test well. The observations of colored troops seem especially liable to criticism on this account.

Among the white soldiers, of the later series, — whether we take those who were or who were not in vigorous health, — the great preponderance were found to breathe 16 times in a minute, those breathing 15 times numbering less than one eighth part as many; yet the groups whose respirations were 17 and 18 times were found essentially equal to each other, and nearly or quite one fifth part as large as the main group. This mode of distribution appears alike inconsistent with the hypothesis of a typical number, normally constant for white men, and with that which would refer the irregularity simply to a want of care or exactitude on the part of the examiners.

Reducing the tables of distribution, already given, to tables showing the average number of respirations to the minute for each age, we obtain Tables VIII., IX., and X., from which the essential uniformity in the mean frequency of respiration during the years of early manhood and of middle life may fairly be inferred, and in which the greater frequency for the black race is conspicuously manifested. It should be mentioned, however, in this connection, that the black troops were mostly examined in warmer latitudes than the white men; and that several indications suggest a more rapid rate of respiration in warm regions, even for the whites. The writer regrets that here also the inevitable limits of the present investigation preclude him from following up this interesting inquiry.

It has been already stated that Mr. Fairchild's examinations were chiefly confined to rebel prisoners, but the difference between his results and Dr. Buckley's cannot be attributed to this cause alone, but must be due in a great measure to something personal.

TABLE VIII.

Mean Frequency of Respiration by Age.

White Soldiers — Earlier Series.

Age	Buckley and Risler				Fairchild			
	In usual Vigor		Not in usual Vigor		In usual Vigor		Not in usual Vigor	
	No.	Mean	No.	Mean	No.	Mean	No.	Mean
Under 17	80	16.20	35	17.91	16	18.62	1	22.00
17	112	16.12	37	18.92	22	17.59	3	17.67
18	241	16.22	89	17.79	57	18.02	3	19.67
19	249	16.10	99	19.68	103	18.26	9	19.00
20	274	16.12	112	18.59	118	18.59	9	17.11
21	264	16.12	111	18.63	164	18.24	13	19.31
22	218	16.11	143	18.53	122	18.31	11	18.00
23	178	16.18	107	18.66	150	17.92	14	17.21
24	150	16.24	98	18.33	123	18.45	22	18.36
25	125	16.29	65	18.43	79	17.92	7	19.29
26	68	16.04	60	18.75	83	18.05	15	17.00
27	85	16.16	63	18.59	66	18.26	8	16.38
28	76	16.13	60	18.47	53	17.00	10	16.40
29	49	16.47	34	18.15	37	18.00	7	17.57
30	56	16.29	42	18.17	37	17.73	5	16.00
31-34	152	16.32	112	18.54	84	17.27	15	17.47
35-44	169	16.14	156	18.90	109	17.73	27	17.89
45 & over	32	16.22	53	18.79	19	17.74	10	17.90
Total .	2 578	16.173	1 476	18.600	1 442	18.053	189	17.804

TABLE IX.

Mean Frequency of Respiration by Age.

White Men — Later Series.

Age	White Soldiers				Students	
	In usual Vigor		Not in usual Vigor			
	No. Men	Respiration	No. Men	Respiration	No. Men	Respiration
Under 17	148	16.40	19	17.32	–	–
17	224	16.55	21	16.95	3	16.67
18	634	16.39	42	16.76	7	16.33
19	589	16.36	53	16.55	39	16.21
20	713	16.41	76	16.63	73	16.18
21	750	16.53	88	16.76	69	16.12
22	723	16.45	115	16.60	44	16.41
23	586	16.47	65	16.89	13	16.31
24	591	16.50	101	16.69	17	16.35
25	400	16.46	72	16.92	11	16.33
26	325	16.36	64	16.34	5	16.40
27	280	16.33	43	17.07	5	16.00
28	300	16.38	43	16.40	1	16.00
29	215	16.51	55	16.91	2	17.00
30	225	16.41	51	17.16	–	–
31-34	601	16.37	128	16.70	1	16.00
35 & over	980	16.50	316	17.16	–	–
Total	8 284	16.439	1 352	16.838	290	16.238

TABLE X.

Mean Frequency of Respiration by Age.

Other Races than the White.

Age	In usual Vigor				Not in usual Vigor		Indians	
	Full Blacks		Mulattoes		Aggregate			
	No.	Respiration	No.	Respiration	No.	Respiration	No.	Respiration
Under 17	38	18.45	19	18.32	12	20.50	1	16.00
17	43	18.05	11	17.73	2	20.50	–	–
18	73	18.43	25	18.20	8	19.62	2	15.50
19	90	19.37	36	19.50	11	18.54	6	16.00
20	137	18.74	60	19.55	11	19.82	8	16.00
21	116	18.15	53	18.74	17	22.59	14	16.00
22	128	17.59	64	18.55	27	22.78	29	15.97
23	147	17.46	61	18.57	29	21.21	32	15.94
24	129	16.96	54	20.06	22	20.91	38	15.92
25	111	17.54	46	19.91	17	22.65	14	15.79
26	71	16.69	38	19.47	10	19.70	45	15.78
27	70	16.87	26	18.42	11	22.54	28	15.79
28	66	17.36	24	19.29	9	21.00	38	15.89
29	38	16.74	23	18.26	14	21.21	39	15.79
30	37	17.03	33	18.85	10	22.60	21	15.76
31-34	69	17.09	38	19.10	19	20.21	67	15.90
35 & over	140	18.04	97	18.82	65	18.97	121	15.74
	1 503	17.747	708	19.013	294	20.711	503	15.831

The most noteworthy inferences from these tables appear to be — first, the comparative constancy of the mean value for men of the same classes at the different ages within military limits; second, the much greater frequency of respiration in the black race than in the white; third, the inferior frequency in the Indians examined; and fourth, the accelerated respiration in the men not in full health.

If we may suppose that, of the 254 students examined by Dr. Elsner, and recorded as breathing 16 times in a minute, there were in fact 60 for whom the actual number of respirations was 17, although this number was recorded by him for no one student, —

we shall have as the corresponding average rate of breathing 16.445 instead of 16.238, and the result therefore practically accordant with that deduced for white soldiers in vigor, from the observations of the later series.

3. *Pulse.*

Our statistics regarding the frequency of the pulse have been elaborated with considerable detail; and an extended series of tables has been constructed, exhibiting for each class of men examined the maximum, minimum, and mean values found at each year of age, as also the relative frequency of pulse and respiration. The limited range of ages, over which our observations extend, moderates the interest of our results, since these, although more numerous than any preceding determinations, cover only a portion of the ground already well studied by others; and that portion, moreover, which exhibits the least variation of the phenomenon. Our observations were taken during the ordinary hours of daily labor; most of them also in the standing posture, but there were some exceptions to this rule, which our records do not enable us to distinguish from the rest. In view of this uncertainty, and the comparative unimportance of new determinations of the average frequency, it seems hardly worth while to give our series of fourteen tables in this place. They are at the service of any investigator. The mean frequency of pulse deducible from the later series of examinations is greater by 4.84 pulsations in the minute than that indicated by Guy's observations.

Assuming, as our results seem to warrant, that the average pulse remains essentially constant during the period of military age, we have from the total averages —

TABLE XI.

Mean Frequency of Pulse for different Classes of Men.

Class	In usual Vigor		Not in usual Vigor	
	No. of Men	Pulsations	No. of Men	Pulsations
White Soldiers, Earlier Series[1]	2 578	77.67	1 476	79.41
White Soldiers, Later Series	8 284	74.84	1 352	77.21
Full Blacks	1 503	74.02	166	76.91
Mulattoes	708	76.97	128	83.12
Indians	503	76.31	7	74.42

[1] Omitting Mr. Fairchild's observations.

The distribution of the numbers for these classes of men, when tested by the law of error, is not all that could be desired; still the observations appear worthy of much confidence.

These data are entirely confirmatory of the results of previous investigators, in showing the apparent absence of any definite ratio between the number of respirations and that of pulsations, which appear to be normally independent of each other, while the abnormal manifestations of each are more frequently in the form of acceleration than of retardation. The well established facts, that in any individual case, increased frequency of respiration is attended by an increased frequency of the pulse, and that the pulse may be greatly affected by voluntary modification of the respiratory movements, as shown[1] by Mitchell, do not seem at all opposed to this inference regarding the non-existence of a definite normal ratio of frequency.

Confining our inferences, as seems proper, to the examinations of the later series, we find the average number of pulsations during a single respiration to be more than $4\frac{3}{4}$ for the Indians, more than $4\frac{1}{2}$ for the white soldiers, and less than $4\frac{1}{4}$ for full blacks, if only men in full vigor are considered. But if we take the number of pulsations observed in those whose respiration was 16 to the minute, and who constitute the largest group for each of these classes of men, and disregard all other cases, we find the ratio of pulsations to respirations for men in usual vigor to be 4.60 for white soldiers, 4.43 for full blacks, 4.79 for Indians. For mulattoes, the corresponding ratio is 4.2, but this determination is less trustworthy than the others.

It has been definitely stated by Rameaux and Sarrus,[2] and the statement cited by Quetelet with apparent approval,[3] although with the suggestion of some qualifications, that the pulse not only diminishes with the stature, but this according to a law so distinct and well marked that the effect of increase of age upon the frequency of the pulse is only perceptible while the stature increases with the age, and is referable to this influence alone. These gentlemen found, namely, on examining a battalion of French troops and comparing the stature with the pulse, that the frequency of the latter varied just in the inverse ratio of the square of the stature, and they maintained that this law was so strictly applicable that the normal pulse might always be deduced from the stature, and

1 *Amer. Journal of Med. Science*, XXVII., 388–394.

2 *Comptes Rendus de l'Acad. des Sciences*, IX., 275.

3 *Systême Sociale*, p. 48.

vice versa, being 70 to the minute for the stature of 168.4 centimeters.

With this distinct statement before us it appeared clearly our duty to tabulate our results in such a manner as to test the question; and the appended table of Pulse by Stature has been prepared from our statistics for white soldiers in good health, of the later series. A glance will show how totally its indications are at variance with the inferences of Rameaux and Sarrus. Indeed, the relation between the stature and the pulse scarcely appears to follow any general law. To render this more distinct, we give together with the observed mean frequency for each half-inch of stature, an additional column, to show the best empirical value for the same stature which we have been able to deduce by charting the results and drawing a curve, to represent them as nearly as may be.

TABLE XII.

Frequency of Pulse by Stature.
White Soldiers in usual Vigor.

(*Later Series.*)

Stature	No. of Men	Observed Mean	Empirical Mean
Under 60 [a]	18	74.56	–
60	10	76.20	–
60½	23	70.70	73.18
61	22	70.54	73.74
61½	39	77.95	74.49
62	82	74.44	75.08
62½	119	75.62	75.13
63	148	74.82	75.03
63½	222	75.36	74.79
64	301	73.94	74.70
64½	430	74.64	74.68
65	453	74.87	74.74
65½	622	75.14	74.73
66	522	74.22	74.71
66½	748	74.50	74.70
67	687	74.86	74.75
67½	797	75.14	74.77
68	662	74.47	74.74
68½	645	74.61	74.64
69	462	74.74	74.49
69½	417	74.51	74.32
70	310	73.01	74.26
70½	282	75.03	74.23
71	182	74.37	74.22
71½	137	73.97	74.22
72	125	73.52	74.24
72½	81	75.44	74.31
73	54	73.85	74.47
73½	30	74.13	74.45
74	27	76.30	74.79
74½	6	77.67	75.24
75	4	73.25	75.69
Over 75 [b]	16	75.87	–

[a] Mean stature = 58.9 inches.

[b] Mean stature = 76.2 inches.

CHAPTER XIV.

VISION.

1. *Statistics Collected.*

It was not until a considerable number of the examinations of our later series had been made, that the value of this opportunity for obtaining some general information regarding the eye-sight of the soldiers suggested itself. The two questions, numbers 57 and 58, were then added to the schedule;[1] the one, asking the maximum distance at which double-leaded small pica type could be distinctly read, and the other inquiring as to the existence of any tendency to color-blindness, and its character, if found. In the former question, the type named was selected because a paragraph was thus printed upon the back of the examination-blanks and was therefore always at hand during the measurements. This paragraph consisted of twelve lines, entitled "Objects of the Examination," and had been placed there, by way of explanation of our motives, in order to disabuse the minds of the men who entertained, as at first was sometimes the case, apprehensions lest these examinations might be designed to enable the military authorities to select the men of greatest physical capability for employment in some unwelcome service or even for special detention. In all subsequent editions of the blank forms, care was taken to retain the same type and the same distance between the lines. The type was like that in which these pages are printed, and the distance of the lines from each other was about one third part greater than is here the case. The paper was of a bluish tinge. Some careful optical tests which Dr. B. Joy Jeffries has had the goodness to make since our materials were collected, give the value of this test-type as nearly number 11 of Jäger's scale, and between numbers 5 and 6 of Snellen.

Had the writer been then, as he soon afterwards became, acquainted with the tables and type of Snellen, he would of course

[1] Page 225.

have endeavored to employ these. That they were not used is a source of regret; but it will be remembered that the advent of the year 1865 found our examinations scarcely more than begun, while the war was brought to an end during the following April; so that it was only by vigorous effort and constant stimulus that our materials could be collected before the disbandment of the armies. The questions regarding Vision were added to our schedule in February; and when, soon afterward, the advantages of the Snellen type were understood, it seemed better to collect all the observations possible, upon the system already adopted, than to incur risk of an inadequate amount of material in each of two systems, although the second might in itself be much the more desirable. The author was not unaware that these inquiries would probably afford but small contributions, even if any, to ophthalmic science. The nature of the case precluded any discrimination between the two components of the maximum distance of vision, since the distance measured was the sum of the distance to the normal far-point, and of the amount of optical accommodation. Still, adopting the fundamental principle that any facts, however incomplete or crudely gathered, should be welcome to the student of nature, and considering that results possessing small technical value might yet claim a higher importance from the anthropological point of view, it has seemed not amiss to classify and combine such materials as we have collected. Should they neither develop new facts, nor confirm any uncertain inferences, the existence of so large a number of determinations conscientiously made and carefully combined, will certainly not be without some present or future value.

The number of men, for whom our statistics of Vision were collected, was thus less than that of those whose dimensions and other physical characteristics were determined; and it was still farther diminished by various circumstances. Those white soldiers who were unable to read are not included, and in many cases the circumstances under which the examinations were made, rendered the measurement of the distance of the object from the eye difficult, if not impossible. Whenever the examinations were made in a room with a ceiling, or in a tent across the upper part of which a board or wooden bar could be placed, a measuring tape, or some other graduated scale, was fastened at a height of about 75 inches. The men examined were placed under this, and when the greatest distance was found at which the printed words could be clearly read without conscious effort, this could be very easily and accurately noted by the examiner, using a few obvious precautions. Care was always taken to insure ample light.

This procedure offered no difficulty for those white soldiers and sailors, who could read; and the number of others was very inconsiderable. But when similar measurements were undertaken for the colored troops, the large proportion of those who could not read, precluded the method previously employed. Some experiments were therefore made to test the availability of printed characters of the same size as the small pica type, but of shapes more easily recognizable by the unlettered, than those of many characters of the Latin alphabet. The result of these experiments indicated that no perceptible advantage was thus obtained, but that the statements by uneducated persons of moderate intelligence, regarding the positions at which they could distinctly recognize the forms of the letters, afforded results quite as accurate when the men were not, as when they were, able to derive ideas from the juxtaposition of the printed characters. It thus, greatly to our satisfaction, became needless to undertake any modification of the system employed for the whites, and all requisites seemed answered by the expenditure of some additional care on the part of the examiners.

The greatest distance of distinct vision for the same object was thus determined for somewhat more than 10 000 men out of about 15 800 who were examined in the later series.

For testing the perception of colors, the examiners used a number of pieces of paper or cloth of brilliant hues, especially of the primary and principal secondary colors.

2. *Distance of Distinct Vision, for the Test-Object.*

The number of men in each class who were examined in this respect, and the average value of the greatest distance at which the test-object already described could be distinctly seen, are shown in the annexed table.

TABLE I.

Mean Distances for Different Classes of Men.

Class	In usual Vigor		Not in usual Vigor		Aggregate	
	No.	Distance	No.	Distance	No.	Distance
		in.		in.		in.
White Soldiers	6 564	47.77	1 357	45.10	7 921	47.31
Sailors	269	36.57	–	–	269	36.57
Students	281	42.28	–	–	281	42.28
Full Blacks	778	45.33	140	46.13	918	45.45
Mulattoes	186	47.23	67	44.69	253	46.56
Indians	442	51.77	–	–	442	51.77

The small value here found for sailors is the most striking result of the preceding table, and seems the more remarkable since the common opinion unquestionably assigns to sailors a peculiarly keen eye-sight, and long range of vision. Our inferences are derived from a comparatively small number of sailors, since the circumstances under which Mr. Phinney's examinations were made, rendered it almost impracticable for him to measure this distance, and our values for sailors are therefore mostly confined to measurements by others. But with the disadvantage of a small number is combined the almost equal advantage of freedom from personal equation in the comparison of sailors with soldiers, for here as in every other subject of quantitative determination, a field is offered for the action of the personal peculiarities of the individual by whom the determination is made. Internal evidence too, corroborates the correctness of the results, unexpected as they may have been.

A little reflection diminishes our surprise at this result. The sailor's ordinary distance of vision is necessarily restricted to the length of his vessel, and the height of her mast. The cases when his eyes are fixed upon any marine phenomenon are rare in comparison with the many objects which attract the attention of landsmen at equal or superior distances; and since habitual use exerts a very important influence upon the eye-sight, it is but reasonable to infer that the average range of distinct vision would become diminished by a nautical life. The proverbial quickness with which a sailor detects a distant object upon the horizon, before a landsman can perceive it, may be due to habit and training more than to superior eye-sight, and landsmen who have been impressed by personal experience with the keen eye of seafaring men for a distant sail, or the first glimpse of land, will generally also bear witness to the distinctness with which they have themselves been able to perceive and recognize the same object, after it has been once pointed out to them.

It must be conceded that the facts observed may likewise be explained by assuming a normal distance of vision not inferior to that of landsmen, but combined with a very restricted range of accommodation. But whether our view of the case be correct or not, the results obtained for the average distance of vision of the 269 sailors to whom our observations extend, seem worthy of confidence. It will be seen that for the same object this distance is one quarter part less than that found for the soldiers, whereas between the students and soldiers the difference is but one ninth part of the same amount. But the comparison of the numbers in these two classes of men for the successive intervals of distance shows at once that although the number of near-sighted persons is much greater among the students than among the sailors, so also is the number of very far-sighted ones — the mean distance for the students thus becoming much the greater.

In the six tables next following, the results for the six classes of men are assorted by ages, those in usual vigor being discriminated from those who were not.

TABLE II.

Mean Distance for White Soldiers, by Ages.

Age	In usual Vigor		Not in usual Vigor		Aggregate	
	No.	Distance	No.	Distance	No.	Distance
		in.		in		in.
Under 16	28	44.6	6	47.5	34	45.2
16	85	46.6	11	40.7	96	45.9
17	168	49.4	21	46.1	189	49.0
18	428	47.8	49	48.0	477	47.8
19	453	49.2	59	44.9	512	48.7
20	578	49.1	76	46.8	654	48.8
21	616	49.2	88	45.8	704	48.8
22	614	47.1	118	47.1	732	47.1
23	481	49.7	70	45.4	551	49.2
24	466	47.3	103	46.7	569	47.2
25	331	46.3	71	48.9	402	46.8
26	265	47.7	66	46.3	331	47.4
27	219	48.6	43	47.6	262	48.4
28	231	48.7	47	47.3	278	48.4
29	181	47.1	50	44.4	231	46.5
30	183	46.8	51	46.8	234	46.8
31	119	46.3	22	44.5	141	46.0
32	154	47.1	38	45.8	192	46.8
33	98	47.6	25	43.6	123	46.8
34	117	45.9	45	47.4	162	46.3
35	132	46.3	18	42.6	150	45.8
36	92	44.3	31	46.7	123	44.9
37	77	46.7	21	40.6	98	45.4
38	87	47.3	27	40.2	114	45.6
39	59	47.7	25	38.1	84	44.8
40	49	46.4	24	47.5	73	46.8
41	21	43.0	14	48.3	35	45.1
42	38	47.7	11	45.2	49	47.2
43	27	46.1	12	42.1	39	44.9
44	31	46.0	16	38.2	47	43.4
45	44	41.5	10	39.3	54	41.1
46-50	64	42.2	58	37.2	122	39.8
Over 50	28	41.4	31	29.4	59	35.1

TABLE III.

Mean Distance for Sailors, by Ages.

Age	Number	Distance
		in.
Under 18	3	40.3
18	9	34.2
19	11	36.6
20	10	34.8
21	27	38.1
22	41	36.9
23	20	37.7
24	23	39.7
25	19	35.7
26	21	35.8
27	12	39.9
28-29	20	38.5
30-32	21	29.6
33-37	19	36.2
38-45	9	38.1
Over 45	4	29.0

TABLE IV.

Mean Distance for Students, by Ages.

Age	Number	Distance
		in.
Under 19	10	35.4
19	37	41.2
20	69	40.1
21	69	44.1
22	43	43.0
23	11	45.1
24	17	43.5
25	11	40.2
Over 25	14	47.6

TABLE V.

Mean Distance for Full Blacks, by Ages.

Age	In usual Vigor		Not in usual Vigor		Aggregate	
	No.	Distance	No.	Distance	No.	Distance
		in.		in.		in.
Under 17	20	38.3	7	46.3	27	40.4
17	28	44.5	–	–	28	44.5
18	45	42.2	4	55.5	49	43.2
19	59	45.5	4	41.0	63	45.2
20	89	46.5	6	48.5	95	46.7
21	73	47.0	10	43.7	83	46.6
22	66	45.2	11	46.2	77	45.3
23	60	44.7	14	45.8	74	44.9
24	50	49.6	14	47.1	64	49.1
25	52	44.2	7	44.6	59	44.3
26	26	47.4	4	40.0	30	46.4
27	32	43.5	6	35.2	38	42.2
28	26	45.4	4	52.7	30	46.4
29	13	45.0	11	48.2	24	46.5
30	17	47.3	6	44.2	23	46.5
31-32	19	45.7	4	56.0	23	47.5
33-35	27	45.7	8	33.1	35	42.8
36-38	25	44.1	5	49.6	30	45.0
39-41	18	47.8	5	55.2	23	49.4
42-45	17	46.1	5	52.8	22	47.6
Over 45	16	38.7	5	49.0	21	41.1

TABLE VI.

Mean Distance for Mulattoes, by Ages.

Age	In usual Vigor		Not in usual Vigor		Aggregate	
	No.	Distance	No.	Distance	No.	Distance
		in.		in.		in.
Under 17	10	46.4	2	55.0	12	47.8
17	4	39.0		–	4	39.0
18	13	50.1	2	50.0	15	50.1
19	10	46.9	4	42.5	14	45.6
20	18	46.7	2	54.0	20	47.4
21	14	53.9	6	41.0	20	50.0
22	13	49.9	12	47.4	25	48.7
23	9	45.1	6	46.7	15	45.7
24	14	43.5	5	52.8	19	45.9
25	11	48.6	4	50.2	15	49.1
26	8	54.0	3	57.7	11	55.0
27	7	44.9	1	60.0	8	46.8
28	8	47.7	2	39.0	10	46.0
29	3	42.7	2	13.5	5	31.0
30	9	45.7	3	37.7	12	43.7
31-32	10	50.8	1	29.0	11	48.8
33-35	4	44.0	1	54.0	5	46.0
36-38	10	40.9	2	25.5	12	38.3
39-41	4	44.5	2	32.0	6	40.3
42-45	5	45.4	4	50.0	9	47.4
Over 45	2	42.5	3	32.3	5	36.4

TABLE VII.

Mean Distance for Iroquois Indians, by Ages.

Age	Number	Distance
		in.
Under 20	9	55.6
20	6	58.7
21	9	54.4
22	22	54.5
23	29	53.2
24	38	52.6
25	14	52.4
26	38	52.7
27	25	54.8
28	33	51.9
29	31	53.7
30	20	54.8
31	12	53.3
32	7	52.1
33	8	55.7
34	31	52.4
35	8	54.6
36	21	51.0
37	14	51.4
38	11	53.1
39	5	57.6
40	11	48.2
41-45	21	42.9
Over 45	19	32.3

From those of the preceding tables in which the numbers are sufficiently large to permit any inference, namely, from all excepting those for sailors and students, it is evident that the outer limit of distinct vision gradually diminished with advancing years, although we have here no means of learning whether the decrease is greater than would result from the well-known diminution of the power of accommodation. The maximum mean value would seem to be between the ages of 17 and 25, and the subsequent decrease to amount to not less than ten per cent. before the age of 50. The fact that the minimum limit increases with the age is well known, so that it would appear that increasing age brings with it a diminution of the range of vision by curtailment at each of its limits. If we compare the results for soldiers not in usual health with the others, we perceive that the mean distance is less, not only for the aggregate, but for most of the individual years of age. The same holds good for the mulattoes; and although the reverse is indicated in our table for negroes of pure race, it is in a much smaller degree; and an inspection of the results by years of age shows the variations to be so great as to forbid much reliance upon their aggregate. It has already been stated that the ages of the negroes are among the most uncertain of all our data, being in many cases only estimated by the examiner. Entire ignorance as to their age is very frequent among the blacks, as has been heretofore mentioned. If the inference thus suggested is entitled to credence, and the distance of distinct vision is affected by the general condition of the individual, as would seem probable, this distance must be to some extent a variable quantity, fluctuating with the health.

Our next series of tables exhibits the distribution of each class of men according to their distance of vision for the printed text, which has served as our test-object. These are chiefly intended to show the proportionate number of near-sighted and of far-sighted persons. The numbers appear in no instance to follow any regular law. Comparing Tables IX., and X., which show this distribution for sailors and students, respectively, the fact, already mentioned, becomes patent, that the latter furnish a greater proportion at each extreme of range. Thus, there were 11 students out of 281, while out of an almost equal number of sailors, there was but one, for whom the distance of distinct vision was less than ten inches. On the other hand there were 31 students, and only 8 sailors, for whom this limit was as high as 60 inches.

The distribution of the Indians in this respect appears at the first glance unsatisfactory. But although the observations are seen by this searching test not to have been very sharply made, yet an assortment by intervals of two inches exhibits a very good accordance with the law of error,[1] indicating a normal distance not far from 54, and an average distance of about 52, inches.

[1] Page 249.

TABLE VIII.

Distribution of Soldiers according to Distance of Vision.

Distance	In usual Vigor	Not in usual Vigor	Total
inches Under 10	7	6	13
10–19	125	69	194
20–24	122	44	166
25–29	229	56	285
30	111	22	133
31	38	9	47
32	109	26	135
33	32	9	41
34	79	28	107
35	117	31	148
36	91	20	111
37	154	27	181
38	279	31	310
39	115	19	134
40	289	50	339
41	133	22	155
42	292	54	346
43	149	33	182
44	146	46	192
45	144	26	170
46	166	42	208
47	144	33	177
48	242	53	295
49	137	41	178
50	369	60	429
51	142	29	171
52	243	48	291
53	151	32	183
54	249	64	313
55	150	27	177
56	237	40	277
57	160	27	187
58	203	36	239
59	96	15	111
60	316	59	375
61–65	368	76	444
66–70	224	33	257
71–80	154	10	164
Over 80	52	4	56
	6 564	1 357	7 921

TABLE IX.

Distribution of Sailors according to Distance of Vision.

Distance	No. of Men	Distance	No. of Men	Distance	No. of Men
inches		inches		inches	
Under 10	1	35	5	48	6
10 19	24	36	6	49	6
20-24	25	37	6	50	8
25	6	38	10	51	3
26	7	39	4	52	6
27	4	40	10	53	6
28	3	41	9	54	5
29	6	42	11	55	2
30	7	43	5	56	1
31	13	44	6	57	3
32	7	45	5	58	1
33	8	46	4	59	4
34	13	47	5	60	8

TABLE X.

Distribution of Students according to Distance of Vision.

Distance	No. of Men	Distance	No. of Men	Distance	No. of Men
inches		inches		inches	
Under 10	11	35	3	48	19
10-19	16	36	4	49	4
20-24	7	37	6	50	11
25	–	38	11	51	4
26	1	39	6	52	4
27	3	40	16	53	4
28	1	41	7	54	10
29	5	42	16	55	6
30	2	43	4	56	5
31	1	44	15	57	3
32	2	45	9	58	10
33	1	46	2	59	4
34	7	47	10	60	31

TABLE XI.

Distribution of Full Blacks according to Distance of Vision.

Distance	In usual Vigor	Not in usual Vigor	Total
inches Under 10	2	–	2
10-19	14	2	16
20-24	23	6	29
25-29	49	6	55
30	14	4	18
31	14	1	15
32	10	–	10
33	8	–	8
34	10	2	12
35	18	3	21
36	19	2	21
37	18	–	18
38	12	3	15
39	14	3	17
40	32	3	35
41	22		22
42	23	4	27
43	8	4	12
44	18	7	25
45	30	9	39
46	29	8	37
47	27	4	31
48	21	3	24
49	27	5	32
50	28	6	34
51	26	4	30
52	24	5	29
53	15	9	24
54	25	3	28
55	13	3	16
56	27	3	30
57	17	4	21
58	23	5	28
59	14	2	16
60	84	16	100
61-65	8	1	9
66-70	8	–	8
71-80	4	–	4

TABLE XII.

Distribution of Mulattoes according to Distance of Vision.

Distance	In usual Vigor	Not in usual Vigor	Total
inches			
Under 10	–	1	1
10-19	3	2	5
20-24	2	5	7
25-29	8	4	12
30	3	–	3
31	1	1	2
32	3	1	4
33	1	–	1
34	3	3	6
35	2	1	3
36	8	3	11
37	6	–	6
38	8	2	10
39	3	–	3
40	8	2	10
41	3	–	3
42	6	3	9
43	1	1	2
44	3	1	4
45	4	–	4
46	8	–	8
47	12	3	15
48	2	4	6
49	2	1	3
50	7	1	8
51	5	–	5
52	4	3	7
53	3	1	4
54	8	2	10
55	5	2	7
56	3	3	6
57	5		5
58	9	2	11
59	9	1	10
60	20	8	28
61-65	2	2	4
66-70	2	2	4
71-80	4	2	6

TABLE XIII.

Distribution of the Indians according to Distance of Vision.

Distance	No. Men	Distance	No. Men	Distance	No. Men
inches		inches		inches	
12 19	4	39	1	51	–
20 24	7	40	8	52	12
25–29	4	41	–	53	9
30	1	42	6	54	75
31	–	43	3	55	1
32	1	44	14	56	41
33	–	45	1	57	12
34	2	46	26	58	44
35	–	47	8	59	11
36	–	48	38	60	19
37	–	49	49	61 65	18
38	–	50	17	66 76	10

Constructing, from data already given, a table exhibiting for each of the six classes the proportional number of men whose outer limit of distinct vision for our test-object falls within a given range of distance, we obtain at a glance a knowledge of the comparative number of the near-sighted or far-sighted in each class, and may thus compare the classes with one another.

TABLE XIV.

Comparison of the Vision of Different Classes of Men.

Class	Under 10 in.	10 to 20 in.	20 to 40 in.	40 to 60 in.	60 to 70 in.	Over 70 in.
Soldiers	.002	.025	.227	.582	.136	.028
Sailors	.004	.089	.483	.394	.030	.000
Students	.039	.057	.214	.580	.110	.000
Full Blacks . . .	.002	.018	.260	.588	.128	.004
Mulattoes	.004	.020	.269	.541	.142	.024
Indians	.000	.009	.036	.849	.097	.009

3. *Color-blindness.*

Few observant persons, in our own community at least, can have failed to be frequently impressed by the comparatively large number of persons, who are more or less unable to distinguish between colors the most strikingly contrasted. The ordinary intercourse of daily life does not usually attract attention to this peculiarity; but when any accident has brought it to notice, we are surprised at discovering its existence in some familiar acquaintance in whom it had never occurred to us to suspect it. Persons who cannot distinguish ripe cherries upon the tree, or strawberries on the vine, by their color, are far more numerous than would be suspected by those who have given no attention to the subject; and unless some grotesque incongruity in costume, or some remarkably inaccurate description of the color of a well-known object, compels our notice, we remain unaware of the imperfection. Serious misunderstandings or calamities have been reported in the army, resulting from mistakes in the color of green and red lights by officers of the signal corps, themselves not fully aware of their failing in this respect; and cases have occurred where ludicrous, and even disastrous, results have followed the use of a badge of precisely the wrong color.

The number of persons thus affected has been estimated by some as being not less than one in every twenty; and the range of estimates by different authorities is extremely wide. With a view to more accurate determination both of the ratio, and of the most usual form of the phenomenon, as well as the possible detection of some clew to its explanation, our examiners were instructed to test the sight of each individual measured, and, when any abnormality was perceived, to record its nature so far as they could determine it.

We have thus obtained the numbers given in Table XV., from which it would appear that about one in each fifty white men examined was thus affected. This is not improbably a near approximation to the proportionate number of those who are unable to distinguish colors correctly, but it does not include that class, — a large one, so far as our own experience extends, — for whom this recognition is not easy, although their decision is in general correct; in other words, those persons in whom the sense of color does not appear to be well developed. Many acquaintances of the writer, among them more than one medical professor of high eminence, have assured him, that although they could recognize the difference of tint between bright red fruit and the green foliage surrounding it, yet the contrast was not sufficiently vivid to enable them to profit by it to any considerable extent in gathering strawberries, partridge-berries, etc. Such cases are of course not comprised in our table; although under the title of "Color-blind," we have included all those, whose power of discriminating between colors was in any degree incomplete.

TABLE XV.

Number of Color-blind found in each Class of Men.

Class	No. Examined	Color-blind	Proportion
Soldiers . . .	8 089	178	0.022
Sailors . . .	451	2	.004
Students . .	291	1	.003
Full Blacks .	1 508	17	.011
Mulattoes . .	666	2	.003
Indians . . .	512	6	0.012

Classifying the 181 cases found among white men, according to their nativities, we obtain the assortment given in the next table, which likewise exhibits the proportionate number for each nativity.

Assorting these cases by the Color of the Eyes, we find their distribution to be as follows:—

Color	No. Cases	Proportion
Blue	75	0.42
Gray	35	.19
Hazel . . .	33	.18
Dark. . . .	32	.18
Black . . .	6	0.03
	181	1.00

It is difficult to give the corresponding numbers for the men, whose vision was thus tested, assorted according to the colors of their eyes, since many obstacles arise in the details of the numeration. But from a general investigation of this point, as well as from a comparison of these numbers with the tables of Chapter VI., it would seem improbable that the amount of color-blindness varies essentially with the different hues of the iris.

TABLE XVI.

Color-blindness among White Men, by Nativities.

Nativity	No. Examined	Color-blind	Proportion
New England	1 299	12	0.009
New York, New Jersey, and Penn.	2 687	76	.028
Ohio and Indiana	1 329	28	.021
Michigan, Wisconsin, and Illinois	907	8	.009
Coast Slave States	295	13	.044
Kentucky and Tennessee . . .	220	2	.009
Free States West of Miss. River .	10	–	–
Slave States West of Miss. River	27	–	–
British America excl. Canada . .	56	–	–
Canada	349	5	.014
England	239	7	.029
Scotland	82	–	–
Ireland	690	22	.032
France, Belgium, and Switzerland	77	–	–
Germany	418	6	.014
Scandinavia	75	2	.027
Spain, etc.	13	–	–
Miscellaneous . .	58	–	–
	8 831	181	0.020

Assorting by degrees of education, as a crude method of discriminating between the several classes of society to which the men belonged by birth, we find, for the white men —

University	1
High School	7
Good Common School	66
Moderate " "	92
Limited	2
None	13

whence we may infer that although the tendency to color-blindness is certainly to some extent hereditary or constitutional, as shown by its prevalence in particular families, the argument drawn from our data, so far as it has any weight, would be in opposition to

35

theories which should connect this tendency with any educational or social grade.

And although the proportional numbers for the different nativities vary widely, these proportions are deduced from too small a number of cases to warrant any safe inferences regarding this point.

The description of the irregularities manifested in distinguishing colors, are in general neither complete nor adequate, owing probably to insufficiency of the instructions given. Of the 181 cases observed, there are but 57 in which the character of the phenomenon is indicated with any precision, and even in these the description is generally not discriminating. Our instructions should have been so framed as to call for a special statement not only of those primary colors which could not, but also of those which could, be distinguished from each other, an omission of which we only became conscious too late for remedy. The annexed tabular view exhibits a crude assortment of the peculiarities as recorded by the several examiners, for these 57 cases —

Colors confounded	No. Cases
Red and Blue	4
Red, Blue, and Green	2
Red and Green	26
Red and Yellow	4
Yellow and Blue	1
Yellow, Blue, and Green	1
Yellow and Green	1
Green and Blue	9
Red, Blue, and Yellow	2
Red, Green, and Yellow	2
Red, Green, and Blue	1
Blue and Purple	1
Pink and Yellow	1
Green and Brown	1
Yellow and Brown	1

A glance suffices to show the incompleteness of the description, and the consequent inadequacy of the classification ; yet it is clearly not without its value. The well-known fact, that the most usual form of color-blindness is that which fails to distinguish between green and red, is distinctly manifest, as is also the fact that the confusion of colors sometimes embraces the other half of the spectrum, and sometimes its entire range.

The origin of this phenomenon has been the subject of much

curious investigation since the time of Dalton, who was himself unable to distinguish red from green, and attributed this defect of vision to an actual coloration of the vitreous humor of the eye. In conformity with his direction, an examination of his eyes was made after his death to decide the question, but the suspected coloration was not found.[1]

Although it is perhaps not strictly appropriate to offer in this place other inferences than those deduced from the data here presented, it may not be improper to express an opinion regarding the cause of the phenomenon, since it has been long entertained, and has seemed to be supported by numerous observations which we have made within the last fifteen years; namely, that it is the result of a want of sensibility in the retina to rays of certain refrangibility, most frequently at the red end of the spectrum, sometimes however at the violet end, and possibly sometimes for the intermediate rays only.

Reference to the authorities on this subject shows this view to be by no means a new one, but in general conformity with the theory supported by the great names of Seebeck and Helmholtz. It would seem to be corroborated by the well authenticated cases in which the phenomena of color-blindness have accompanied cerebral congestion and disappeared with it.[2] It does not necessarily assume that any elements of the retina are wanting or paralyzed; but it does imply something analogous to incapacity in the whole retina adequately to respond to vibrations of certain velocities; just as we know that the capacity of the tympanum for vibrations is comprised between different limits in different persons, so that some do not hear very high notes, some do not hear very low ones, while others still can only hear certain notes when they are loudly sounded. It implies, furthermore, that the phenomenon is purely functional and not due to any defective power of appreciation; as also that a division of the color-blind into the two categories of red-blind and green-blind is but a crude and imperfect approximation to a just classification.

If this view be correct, green is not seen as red in the majority of cases, but the several colors, yellow, orange, and red, are seen either with a great diminution of their intensity, or as different shades of green; while those greens in which the impression of color is not derived from the true green rays, but from an admixture of blue and yellow, as is the case with foliage, are seen of a strongly

[1] *London Medical Gazette*, 1845, p. 810.

[2] Hays, *Amer. Jour. Med. Science*, 1840, p. 277.

bluish shade. The insensibility seems to extend over a range of refrangibilities varying greatly in different individuals, and of course modifies all composite colors by eliminating or greatly subduing those hues to which it extends. Our view is presented with diffidence, but seems to explain some observations otherwise apparently incompatible, such as the power of distinguishing certain dyes with ease, while the same colors appear not easily distinguishable in some other fabrics or in natural objects. Carefully conducted observations, accompanied by spectroscopic tests, could hardly fail to afford a decisive verdict as to the correctness of this explanation.

It has been seen by Table XV. that the proportionate number of color-blind found among the full blacks, or among the Indians, is not more than one half as great as among the white men. But a more remarkable fact is furnished by the proportion found among those men of mixed black and white race, whose vision was tested in this respect. Of this class, only two men were found whose faculty of distinguishing colors is not recorded as perfect. Both of these were born in the Free States, as were 108 others, whose vision was complete; while of the 556 mulatto natives of Slave States in whom the perception of color were tested, not one is recorded as deficient in this respect. It will be seen, on reference to Chapter VIII.,[1] that several examiners were engaged in measurements of this class of men; yet only future observations can determine how far its apparent immunity from color-blindness may be the result of insufficiency in the number or thoroughness of the examinations.

[1] Page 238.

CHAPTER XV.

MISCELLANEOUS CHARACTERISTICS.

1. *Preliminary.*

Our schedule of questions included many inquiries upon which it has been found impracticable to enter, in the discussions comprised in this volume. Some of these possess intrinsic interest, others are chiefly valuable in their relations to other information elicited concerning the same individuals. Questions of lineage, of conjugal and social relations, of personal appearance, of muscular development, of past history, may be investigated to a considerable extent from the materials in our possession, and the discussion of the topics already considered might be advantageously extended by considering them severally in their relations to the physical or other characteristics which our opportunities preclude us from presenting here in any detail.

There are, however, one or two of these minor subjects concerning which it may be well to present some of the statistics collected, even though only in a general form, and without entering upon their relations to other traits, features, or qualities found in the same individuals.

In this chapter, therefore, we offer some tables containing general facts pertaining to the condition of the Teeth, to the prevalence of Baldness, and to the relative Pilosity of the black and the white races, and to these have added a general view of the degree of Education found among the soldiers examined in the later series, this in its turn entailing some general inquiry as to the Parentage of these men. These topics, although certainly incongruous, seem scarcely better in place elsewhere in the volume, and are therefore here combined in a single chapter by themselves.

2. *Condition of Teeth.*

Two questions concerning the teeth are included in the blank form adopted; one regarding their general condition, which was answered by referring it to one of the five grades, — good, fair, medium, poor, and bad, — and the other as to the number lost, which was answered numerically. The results of these inquiries are here presented in tabular form, and scarcely require comment. The actual and the proportionate numbers are given in separate tables, and all the statistics pertain to white soldiers in usual vigor,

TABLE I.

Classification by Number of Teeth Lost, and by Age.

Age	Number of Teeth Lost							
	0	1	2	3	4	5	6	7
Under 17	105	17	19	7	2	2	4	–
17	158	29	19	13	15	3	1	–
18	400	105	76	36	22	7	4	1
19	367	105	69	45	21	9	4	3
20	397	116	99	59	43	12	11	1
21	354	154	167	70	42	16	8	7
22	329	124	143	70	59	19	9	2
23	244	102	118	64	43	17	10	2
24	222	81	123	85	52	20	14	1
25	129	68	79	57	40	17	13	4
26	109	49	68	34	34	23	13	4
27	88	39	46	43	25	19	6	3
28	89	52	45	39	40	16	10	5
29	71	24	28	31	28	16	10	5
30	52	28	46	43	21	11	5	4
31	36	21	20	19	18	12	7	9
32	41	11	32	30	29	14	11	5
33	32	24	21	13	11	12	7	6
34	29	15	25	24	23	6	7	1
35	21	16	25	17	34	12	8	2
36	22	13	18	7	19	11	6	2
37	15	7	14	13	22	11	8	5
38	16	9	14	16	14	10	5	3
39	15	11	12	15	16	7	1	5
40	21	5	4	2	8	3	4	6
41-44	35	19	32	22	20	16	17	2
45-49	17	14	14	14	12	6	7	1
50 & over	8	2	1	4	3	7	2	–
Total	3 422	1 260	1 377	892	716	334	212	89

of the later series. The aggregate numbers of the several tables differ slightly in consequence of the answers to some of the inquiries being occasionally omitted or illegible. In a few cases answers have been rejected for manifest error.

TABLE I.—(*Continued.*)

Classification by Number of Teeth Lost, and by Age.

Age	Number of Teeth Lost								
	8	9	10	11–15	16–20	Several	Nearly All	All	Total
Under 17	–	–	–	–	–	1	–	–	157
17	–	–	1	–	–	–	–	–	239
18	1	–	4	1	–	1	–	–	658
19	1	–	3	–	1	1	–	–	629
20	4	1	6	–	–	2	–	–	751
21	5	1	–	1	1	3	–	–	829
22	5	1	3	3	–	5	–	–	772
23	4	–	1	1	1	–	–	–	607
24	9	2	5	1	–	3	–	–	618
25	9	1	4	1	1	1	1	–	425
26	4	1	2	2	1	1	–	–	345
27	8	1	1	3	1	4	–	–	287
28	3	1	4	2	–	1	–	–	307
29	4	–	2	–	1	1	1	–	222
30	1	–	3	4	2	–	–	–	220
31	1	–	–	1	2	2	–	–	148
32	6	1	1	4	1	2	–	1	189
33	2	–	1	2	1	1	–	–	133
34	4	4	1	4	1	–	–	2	146
35	8	1	2	4	–	–	–	–	150
36	5	1	1	1	1	3	–	–	110
37	2	–	3	2	1	–	–	–	103
38	8	–	3	–	2	1	–	1	102
39	4	1	–	1	–	–	–	–	88
40	2	–	1	1	–	3	–	–	60
41-44	3	2	4	7	1	9	1	3	193
45-49	11	1	1	–	3	4	–	–	105
50 & over	3	–	2	2	1	3	–	5	43
Total	117	20	59	48	23	52	3	12	8 636

TABLE II.

Proportional Distribution at each Age, by Number of Teeth Lost.

Age	Number of Teeth Lost							
	0	1	2	3	4	5	6	7
Under 17	669	108	121	45	13	13	25	–
17	661	121	80	54	63	13	4	–
18	608	159	115	55	33	10	6	2
19	583	167	110	71	33	14	6	5
20	529	154	132	79	57	16	15	1
21	427	186	201	85	51	19	10	8
22	426	161	185	91	76	25	12	3
23	402	168	194	105	71	28	16	3
24	359	131	199	138	84	32	22	2
25	304	160	186	134	94	40	31	10
26	316	142	197	98	98	66	38	12
27	307	136	160	150	87	66	21	11
28	290	169	147	127	130	52	33	16
29	320	108	126	140	126	72	45	23
30	236	127	209	196	95	50	23	18
31	243	142	135	128	122	81	47	61
32	217	58	169	159	154	74	58	27
33	240	180	158	98	83	90	52	45
34	199	103	171	164	158	41	48	7
35	140	107	167	113	227	80	53	13
36	200	118	164	64	173	100	55	18
37	145	68	136	126	214	107	78	49
38	157	88	137	157	137	98	49	29
39	171	125	136	171	182	80	11	57
40	350	83	67	33	133	50	67	100
41–44	181	98	166	114	104	83	88	10
45–49	161	133	133	133	114	57	67	10
50 & over	186	47	23	93	70	163	47	–
Total	396	146	159	103	83	39	25	10

TABLE II. — (*Continued.*)

Proportional Distribution at each Age, by Number of Teeth Lost.

Age	Number of Teeth Lost							
	8	9	10	11–15	16–20	Several	Nearly all	All
Under 17	–	–	–	–	–	6	–	–
17	–	–	4	–	–	–	–	–
18	2	–	6	2	–	2	–	–
19	2	–	5	–	2	2	–	–
20	5	1	8	–	–	3	–	–
21	6	1	–	1	1	4	–	–
22	6	1	4	4	–	6	–	–
23	7	–	2	2	2	–	–	–
24	15	3	8	2	–	5	–	–
25	21	2	10	2	2	2	2	–
26	12	3	6	6	3	3	–	–
27	28	3	3	11	3	14	–	–
28	10	3	13	7	–	3	–	–
29	18	–	9		4	5	4	–
30	5	–	14	18	9	–	–	–
31	7	–	–	7	14	13	–	–
32	32	5	5	21	5	11	–	5
33	15	–	8	15	8	8	–	–
34	27	27	7	27	7	–	–	14
35	53	7	13	27	–	–	–	–
36	45	9	9	9	9	27	–	–
37	19	–	29	19	10	–	–	–
38	79	–	29	–	20	10	–	10
39	45	11	–	11	–	–	–	–
40	33	–	17	17	–	50	–	–
41-44	16	10	21	36	5	47	5	16
45-49	105	10	10	–	29	38	–	–
50 & over	70	–	46	46	23	70	–	116
Total	14	2	7	6	3	6	–	1

TABLE III.

Classification by Number of Teeth Lost, and by Nativity.

Nativity	Number of Teeth Lost							
	0	1	2	3	4	5	6	7
New England States	388	137	156	98	62	39	24	8
New York, New Jersey, Penn.	1 145	425	445	325	270	140	88	31
Ohio and Indiana	551	212	247	144	97	50	24	11
Michigan, Wisc., and Illinois .	308	125	148	116	96	42	20	14
Coast Slave States	104	46	52	24	28	13	7	5
Kentucky and Tennessee . .	98	33	32	21	12	1	3	2
Free States W. of Miss. River.	8	3	2	–	–	–	–	–
Slave States W. of Miss. River.	8	6	1	2	2	–	–	–
British Provinces excl. Canada	14	6	5	3	4	–	2	–
Canada	184	83	69	46	37	12	8	5
England	98	32	44	25	30	6	9	2
Scotland	25	9	7	12	6	4	3	4
Ireland	268	81	80	44	44	13	8	2
France, Belgium, etc. . . .	33	11	12	7	7	2	1	1
Germany	161	52	70	36	23	15	10	2
Scandinavia	15	2	2	3	–	–	–	1
Spain, etc.	2	3	–	–	–	1	–	–
Miscellaneous	16	3	–	1	1	1	–	–
Total	3 426	1 269	1 372	907	719	339	207	88

TABLE III. — (*Continued.*)

Classification by Number of Teeth Lost, and by Nativity.

Nativity	Number of Teeth Lost.								
	8	9	10	11–15	16–20	Sev-eral	Near-ly all	All	Total
New England	12	3	3	4	4	6	1	2	947
N. Y., N. J., and Penn. .	45	8	22	20	13	31	2	4	3 014
Ohio and Indiana . . .	16	2	10	7	–	3	–	–	1 374
Mich., Wisc., and Illinois	19	2	9	2	–	1	–	–	902
Coast Slave States . .	2	–	2	1	1	4	–	1	290
Kentucky and Tennessee	1	–	1	1	1		–	–	206
Free Sts. West Miss. River	–	–	–	–		–	–	–	13
Sl. Sts. West Miss. River	–	–	–		–	–	–	–	19
Brit. Prov. excl. Canada	–	–	1	–	–	–	–	–	35
Canada	1	1	1	1	2	1	–	–	451
England	4	3	3	1	–	1	1	1	260
Scotland	1	–	–	1	–	–	–	–	72
Ireland	4	–	1	–	–	1	–	1	547
France, Belgium, etc. . .	1	–	–	–	2	–	–	–	77
Germany	9	1	3	4	2	3	–	2	393
Scandinavia	–	–	–	1	–	1	–	1	26
Spain, etc.	–	–	–	–	–	–	–	–	6
Miscellaneous . . .	–	–	–	–	–	–	–	–	22
Total	115	20	56	43	25	52	4	12	8 654

TABLE IV.

Proportional Distribution by Number of Teeth Lost, and by Nativity.

Nativity	Number of Teeth Lost							
	0	1	2	3	4	5	6	7
New England	410	145	165	104	66	41	25	8
N. Y., N. J., and Penn. .	380	141	148	108	89	47	29	10
Ohio and Indiana . . .	401	154	180	105	71	36	18	8
Mich., Wisc., and Illinois	341	139	164	129	106	47	22	16
Coast Slave States . . .	359	159	179	83	97	45	24	17
Kentucky and Tennessee	475	160	155	102	58	5	15	10
Free Sts. West Miss. River	615	231	154	–	–	–	–	–
Slave Sts. West Miss. River	421	316	53	105	105	–	–	–
Brit. Prov. excl. Canada .	400	171	143	86	114	–	57	–
Canada	408	184	153	102	82	27	18	11
England	377	123	169	96	115	23	34	8
Scotland	347	126	97	167	83	55	42	55
Ireland	490	148	146	80	80	24	15	4
France, Belgium, etc. . .	428	143	156	91	91	26	13	13
Germany	410	132	178	92	58	38	25	5
Scandinavia	577	77	77	115	–	–	–	38
Spain, etc.	333	500	–	–	–	167	–	–
Miscellaneous	727	136	–	46	45	46	–	–
Total	396	147	159	105	83	39	24	10

The end-results of our Tables I.–IV. may be concisely exhibited, by showing the average number of teeth lost by the soldiers of each nativity without regard to age, and by those at each age without regard to their nativity. This is done in the next Table V., in which the average number lost is given for each group, to two decimal places. In computing these mean values the answer "several" has been interpreted as meaning on the average 6, and

TABLE IV. — (*Continued.*)

Proportional Distribution by Number of Teeth Lost, and by Nativity.

Nativity	Number of Teeth Lost							
	8	9	10	11-15	16-20	Several	Nearly All	All
New England	13	3	3	4	4	6	1	2
N. Y., N. J., and Penn. .	15	3	7	7	4	10	1	1
Ohio and Indiana . . .	12	1	7	5	–	2	–	–
Mich., Wisc., and Illinois	21	2	10	2	–	1	–	–
Coast Slave States . . .	7	–	7	3	3	14	–	3
Kentucky and Tennessee	5	–	5	5	5	–	–	–
Free Sts. West Miss. River	–	–	–	–	–	–	–	–
Slave Sts. West Miss. River	–	–	–	–	–	–	–	–
Brit. Prov. excl. Canada .	–	–	29	–	–	–	–	–
Canada	2	2	2	2	5	2	–	–
England	15	12	12	4	–	4	4	4
Scotland	14	–	–	14	–	–	–	–
Ireland	7	–	2	–	–	2	–	2
France, Belgium, etc. . .	13	–	–	–	26	–	–	–
Germany	23	3	8	10	5	8	–	5
Scandinavia	–	–	–	39	–	39	–	38
Spain, etc.	–	–	–	–	–	–	–	–
Miscellaneous	–	–	–	–	–	–	–	–
Total	13	2	7	5	3	6	–	1

"nearly all" has been used as 20. These very arbitrary attempts at assigning average numerical values to vague words are of course only justifiable by the imperative necessity of the case; and it is satisfactory to add the statement that a considerable deviation from these numbers would be scarcely perceptible in its influence upon our results. The number of men belonging to each class has been given in Tables I. and III.

TABLE V.

Average Number of Teeth Lost, by Age, and also by Nativity.

Age	Number Lost	Nativity	Number Lost
Under 17	0.79		
17	0.82		
18	0.89		
19	0.98		
20	1.21		
21	1.38	New England	1.88
22	1.51	New York, New Jersey, & Penn.	2.09
23	1.54	Ohio and Indiana	1.71
24	1.86	Michigan, Wisconsin, and Illinois	2.07
25	2.18	Coast Slave States	2.06
26	2.19	Kentucky and Tennessee . . .	1.43
27	2.35	Free States W. of Miss. River .	0.54
28	2.28	Slave States W. of Miss. River .	1.16
29	2.50	British Provinces excl. Canada .	1.80
30	2.60	Canada	1.62
31	2.86	England	2.20
32	3.35	Scotland	2.36
33	2.77	Ireland	1.38
34	3.56	France, Belgium, and Switzerland	2.01
35	3.47	Germany	2.13
36	3.26	Scandinavia	2.81
37	3.79	Spain, etc.	1.33
38	4.02	Miscellaneous	0.68
39	3.11		
40	3.15		
41 44	4.07		
45-49	3.77		
50 & over	7.93		
Total . .	1.924	Total	1.922

Considering next the condition of the teeth, without reference to the number actually lost, this is shown by the four tables next following, which give both the actual and the proportional numbers, assorted by age and by nativity.

TABLE VI.

Classification by Condition of Teeth, and by Age.

Age	Good	Fair	Medium	Poor	Bad	Total
Under 17	151	4	–	8	–	163
17	227	4	–	17	–	248
18	610	12	2	43	–	667
19	583	5	–	47	4	639
20	664	13	4	87	2	770
21	725	21	5	81	3	835
22	665	19	4	103	9	800
23	546	10	9	61	3	629
24	526	13	7	85	7	638
25	352	8	2	66	4	432
26	279	8	2	72	4	365
27	216	5	6	61	10	298
28	228	10	3	68	–	309
29	165	9	1	56	2	233
30	168	5	3	52	4	232
31	108	2	1	37	2	150
32	128	9	–	65	3	205
33	104	4	–	26	4	138
34	102	3	2	44	5	156
35	95	4	2	58	2	161
36	80	2	1	28	2	113
37	63	1	–	37	4	105
38	70	1	–	36	–	107
39	55	3	–	22	–	80
40	46	3	2	11	5	67
41-44	148	4	2	44	13	211
45-49	67	5	–	35	4	111
50 & over	25	–	–	20	–	45
Total	7 196	187	58	1 370	96	8 907

TABLE VII.

Proportional Distribution by Condition of Teeth, and by Age.

Age	Good	Fair	Medium	Poor	Bad
Under 17	926	25	–	49	–
17	915	16	–	69	–
18	915	18	3	64	–
19	912	8	–	74	6
20	862	17	5	113	3
21	868	25	6	97	4
22	831	24	5	129	11
23	868	16	14	97	5
24	825	20	11	133	11
25	815	19	5	152	9
26	764	22	6	197	11
27	725	17	20	205	33
28	738	32	10	220	–
29	708	39	4	240	9
30	724	22	13	224	17
31	720	13	7	247	13
32	625	44	–	317	14
33	754	29	–	188	29
34	654	19	13	282	32
35	591	25	12	360	12
36	708	18	9	248	17
37	600	10	–	352	38
38	654	10	–	336	–
39	687	38	–	275	–
40	687	45	30	163	75
41–44	701	19	10	209	61
45–49	604	45	–	315	36
50 & over	556	–	–	444	–
Total	808	20	7	154	11

TABLE VIII.

Classification by Condition of Teeth, and by Nativity.

Nativity	Good	Fair	Medium	Poor	Bad	Total
New England States	806	26	5	141	6	984
N. Y., N. J., and Penn. . . .	2 483	90	10	474	64	3 121
Ohio and Indiana	1 137	25	14	233	4	1 413
Michigan, Wisconsin, and Ill. .	700	5	3	226	1	935
Coast Slave States	241	7	6	44	4	302
Kentucky and Tennessee . . .	169	3	8	38	1	219
Free States W. of Miss. River .	10	–	1	2	–	13
Slave States W. of Miss. River .	19	–	–	1	–	20
British Provinces excl. Canada .	28	1	–	6	1	36
Canada	401	8	3	50	5	467
England	219	3	-	41	4	267
Scotland	62	1	–	5	1	69
Ireland	491	11	–	57	2	561
France, Belgium, etc.	67	1	2	10	–	80
Germany	351	8	1	44	–	404
Scandinavia	21	–	1	4	–	26
Spain, etc.	5	1	–	–	–	6
Miscellaneous	23	1	–	1	–	25
Total	7 233	191	54	1 377	93	8 948

TABLE IX.

Proportional Distribution,
by Condition of Teeth and by Nativity.

Nativity	Good	Fair	Medium	Poor	Bad
New England States	819	27	5	143	6
N. Y., N. J., and Penn. . . .	795	29	3	152	21
Ohio and Indiana	805	18	10	164	3
Michigan, Wisconsin, Illinois .	749	5	3	242	1
Coast Slave States	798	23	20	145	14
Kentucky and Tennessee . . .	770	12	36	178	4
Free States W. of Miss. River .	769	–	77	154	–
Slave States W. of Miss. River .	950	–	–	50	–
Br. Provinces excluding Canada	777	28	–	167	28
Canada	859	17	6	107	11
England	821	11	–	154	14
Scotland	899	15	–	72	14
Ireland	875	20	–	102	3
France, Belgium, etc.	837	13	25	125	–
Germany	868	20	3	109	–
Scandinavia	808	–	38	154	–
Spain, Portugal, etc.	833	167	–	–	–
Miscellaneous	920	40	–	40	–
Total	808	21	6	154	11

3. *Baldness.*

Question 25 asked the color, amount, and texture of the hair; and, for those who were bald, the age at which their baldness became distinct. For any general deductions concerning its color, the overwhelming mass of statistics subsequently gathered from the enlistment-rolls, supersedes any deductions which might be drawn from the records of the 20 000 white men examined by our agents in the field; and the chief value of the answers to this inquiry recorded on our examination-reports consists in their relation to answers to yet other inquiries.

Thus classifications of the amount of hair according to its texture, to its color, and to the answers to some of the other questions, — tabular views exhibiting the relations of texture to color, those between the tendency to baldness, and the education of the individual, etc., — would in all probability afford results of interest and value. These inquiries, like so many others, must be left for other inquirers whose interest may lead them to obtain the facts from our records. Only a few tabulations are here attempted, showing the relative amount of baldness, which is of course small for a class of men so young as the great majority of those examined. These tabulations we will present as concisely as possible.

TABLE X.

Baldness observed among Soldiers.

Earlier Series, by Nativity.

Nativity	In usual Vigor			Not in usual Vigor		
	No. Examined	No. Bald	Proportion	No. Examined	No. Bald	Proportion
New England	588	5	.009	355	7	.020
New York	1 506	7	.005	550	4	.007
New Jersey and Pennsylvania .	833	3	.004	363	4	.011
Ohio and other Western States .	293	1	.003	185	–	–
Slave States	1 650	18	.011	374	4	.011
Canada	134	1	.007	51	–	–
England and Scotland	145	2	.014	71	–	–
Ireland	345	3	.009	122	–	–
Germany	179	1	.006	77	5	.065
Miscellaneous	63	4	.063	20	–	–
Total	5 736	45	.008	2 168	24	.011

TABLE XI.

Baldness observed among Soldiers.

Later Series, by Nativity.

Nativity	In usual Vigor			Not in usual Vigor		
	No. Examined	No. Bald	Proportion	No. Examined	No. Bald	Proportion
New England	1 000	21	.021	211	4	.019
N. Y., N. J., and Penn.	3 177	31	.010	588	5	.009
Ohio and Indiana	1 443	4	.003	219	2	.009
Mich., Wisc., and Illinois	945	2	.002	71	–	–
Coast Slave States	315	7	.022	52	1	.019
Kentucky and Tennessee	223	2	.009	44	2	.045
States West of Mississippi River	56	–	–	5	–	–
British Provinces	510	3	.006	48	–	–
England	279	5	.018	47	–	–
Scotland	70	2	.029	11	–	–
Ireland	648	7	.011	179	4	.022
France, Belgium, etc.	84	–	–	16	–	–
Germany	462	9	.019	100	1	.010
Other countries	59	1	.017	14	–	–
Total	9 271	94	.010	1 605	19	.012

TABLE XII.

Baldness observed among Sailors and Students, by Nativity.

Nativity	Sailors			Students		
	No Ex-amined	No. Bald	Propor-tion	No. Ex-amined	No. Bald	Propor-tion
New England	129	5	.039	156	3	.019
New York, New Jersey, & Penn.	155	3	.019	95	1	.011
British Am. Prov., excl. Canada	50	1	.020	40 (British Am. Prov. to All others, bracketed)	0	
England	102	2	.020			
Ireland	335	5	.015			
Germany	62	1	.016			
Spain, etc.	18	1	.056			
All others (not assorted)	210	0	–			
Total	1 061	18	.017	291	4	.014

TABLE XIII.

Baldness observed among Negroes, by Nativity.

Class	In usual Vigor			Not in usual Vigor		
	No. Ex-amined	No. Bald	Propor-tion	No. Ex-amined	No. Bald	Propor-tion
Full Blacks						
Natives of Free States	194	1	.005	32	1	.031
Natives of Slave States	1 598	1	.001	196	3	.015
Mulattoes						
Natives of Free States	127	–	–	42	1	.024
Natives of Slave States	592	1	.002	102	2	.020
Total	2 511	3	.001	372	7	.019

Mr. Russell states that among more than 2100 negroes specially observed by him and belonging to the troops of the 25th Army

Corps on the Rio Grande, in addition to those regularly examined, he saw but one bald head.

The assortment by ages is less easy, since sundry difficulties would render the exact determination of the total number examined at each age a matter of considerable labor. It offers, moreover, less promise of valuable results, since what we really want is not the relative amount of baldness corresponding to each age for the men examined, but that corresponding to each age for the time of its occurrence. A tabulation according to the first named principle might not improbably afford the best means of attaining the results corresponding to the second were the numbers dealt with sufficiently large, but this is not the case. Moreover, a large proportion of the cases observed in so young a body of men are probably abnormal, as is shown not only by the irregular sequence of the numbers, but likewise by the circumstance that the baldness was in comparatively few cases of recent occurrence.

The average time during which the baldness had already existed, according to the statements of the men, was as follows:—

Class	No. of Men	Mean Age	Average Time
		y.	y.
Soldiers, Earlier Series . . .	64	37.29	9.70
Soldiers, Later Series . . .	112	37.62	8.51
Sailors	18	35.72	7.72
Students	4	24.25	5.00
Full Blacks	4	42.50	16.50
Mulattoes	4	39.00	13.75
Indians[1]	0	–	–

The abnormal cases which evidently form a large proportion of the total number recorded were certainly in many instances the result of existing or past constitutional disease, and should as such be excluded from an investigation into the general tendency, among any class of men. One negro of unmixed race born in Connecticut, stated that he shed his hair annually.

The next two tables give a classification by age at the time of examination of the white soldiers and of the negroes who are recorded as bald, a vague expression at the best. In the table of soldiers the two series of examinations are combined, and the men not in usual vigor are distinguished from the others and ex-

[1] Not a single case of baldness was observed among the Indians examined. One of the Chippewas examined was said to be 109 years old, and a white missionary whose judgement seemed trustworthy stated that he had no doubt that such was the fact. Dr. Buckley sent a lock of his hair, which was mostly jet black, with a very slight sprinkling of gray. His name was Konjockerty, and although quite active he was classed as "not in usual vigor."

hibit a larger proportion of baldness. In both tables the number of men examined at each age is deduced by careful estimate and not by actual counting.

TABLE XIV.

Baldness observed among Soldiers, by Age when examined.

Age	In usual Vigor			Not in usual Vigor		
	No. of Men	No. Bald	Proportion	No. of Men[1]	No. Bald	Proportion
Under 21	4 339	1	–	1 091	–	–
21-23	3 902	3	.001	980	–	–
24-26	2 401	5	.002	604	2	.003
27-29	1 448	13	.009	364	4	.011
30-32	934	17	.018	236	2	.008
33-35	689	22	.032	173	4	.023
36-38	504	16	.032	127	7	.055
39-41	282	13	.046	71	4	.056
42-44	258	24	.093	65	5	.077
45 & over	250	25	.100	62	15	.242

TABLE XV.

Baldness observed among Negroes, by Age when examined.

Age	Full Blacks			Mulattoes		
	No. of Men	No. Bald	Proportion	No. of Men	No. Bald	Proportion
Under 21	490	–	–	184	–	–
21-26	969	1	.001	385	–	–
27-32	337	–	–	162	2	.012
33-38	124	1	.008	63	–	–
39-44	58	1	.017	42	1	.024
45 & over	42	3	.071	27	1	.037

[1] The total numbers at each age "not in usual vigor" as given in this column have been made proportional to those in usual vigor, since by accident they were not assorted by ages, and this omission was only detected after our documents had been packed away for transportation to New York. But as we have seen, in Chapter VIII., that the mean age of those not in full health exceeded that of those in usual vigor, we may infer that our distribution is not quite correct, and that the proportions in the last column for the advanced ages are somewhat too large.

An attempt to arrange the numbers according to the alleged ages at which baldness first occurred, gives the following result.

TABLE XVI.

Age at which Baldness appeared.

Age	Whites		Blacks
	Earlier Series	Later Series	
Under 18	–	8	–
18–20	11	14	–
21–23	9	15	1
24–26	17	18	3
27–29	5	8	2
30–32	7	19	1
33-35	8	17	–
36 38	3	9	–
39-41	1	11	–
42-45	1	4	–
Over 45	2	11	1

4. *Pilosity of Negroes.*

The question as to the relative amount of pilosity, or general hairiness of body, in the white and black races is one of some anthropological and ethnological interest. In order to obtain if possible some general information on this subject, Mr. Russell, when accompanying the 25th Army Corps to the Texan boundary, was requested to avail himself of any opportunity which might occur, to observe the colored troops when unclothed, and to record the pilosity upon a scale in which a skin apparently perfectly smooth should be denoted by 0, and an amount of general hairiness equal to the maximum which he had ever seen or should see in a white man, should be called 10. This commission Mr. Russell executed by observing the men while bathing, which was an event of almost daily occurrence in the torrid climate near the mouth of the Rio Grande. He thus noted the relative pilosity of 2129 different colored soldiery, full blacks and mulattoes together; and gives the following as the result of his subsequent counting.

Degree of Pilosity	No. of Men
0	9
1	35
2	152
3	290
4	371
5	512
6	357
7	264
8	118
9	21
10	0

The excellent distribution of these numbers is manifest at a glance, as also is the unavoidable inference that there is but little, if any, difference between the white and the black races in this respect.

5. *Education and Parentage.*

The only remaining characteristic of our men which we have undertaken to investigate is the amount of their education. This, as will be seen by reference to the schedule of questions, was classified in five grades, — of which the lowest was represented by a "limited common school education," and the highest by a "professional" training, this presupposing the "collegiate" education which represented the second grade. To these five is of course to be added a sixth, in which the individual was unable either to read or write. Our reports have shown that this division was inadequate, inasmuch as many of the examiners found it necessary to introduce a degree inferior to what would be called a limited common school education, yet not so low as altogether to preclude the individual from reading and writing, consequently we have many men recorded as possessing a "slight" education, while the absence of this grade on our printed blanks has rendered the number referred to it relatively small. From the best estimate we are able to make it would seem that the number properly belonging to this grade is nearly intermediate between those in the grades adjacent, — and that these two grades have generally drawn from this one in our records nearly in the proportion of their respective numbers. This fact must be kept in view in any inferences drawn from our tables.

We will first give, both for the soldiers of the later series and for the sailors, two tables exhibiting respectively the actual and the proportional numbers of the men examined, assorted by nativities and by grades of education.

TABLE XVII.

Distribution of the Soldiers examined in Later Series, according to Education and Nativity.

Nativity	None	Slight	Limited Com. School	Good Com. School	High School	Collegiate	Professional	Total
New England . . .	30	1	403	643	86	8	3	1 174
N. Y., N. J., Penn. .	132	37	1 627	1 698	169	22	14	3 699
Ohio and Indiana .	63	43	857	614	46	7	7	1 637
Mich., Wisc., and Ill.	24	8	656	286	23	4	–	1 001
Coast Slave States .	58	7	139	121	9	2	2	338
Kentucky and Tenn.	53	5	128	78	1	–	1	266
States W. Miss. Riv.	1	1	15	21	3	–	–	41
Brit. Prov. ex. Can.	–	1	10	23	4	–	–	38
Canada	92	10	237	152	13	3	1	508
England	16	3	148	114	4	2	–	287
Scotland . . .	1	2	39	30	7	2	–	81
Ireland	106	10	379	210	12	3	–	720
France, etc.	2	3	22	11	2	1	1	42
Germany	15	13	226	210	24	2	4	494
Scandinavia . . .	1	–	16	14	–	–	–	31
Other Countries . .	12	1	48	44	6	3	1	115
Total	606	145	4 950	4 269	409	59	34	10 472

TABLE XVIII.

Relative Distribution of Soldiers, by Education and Nativity.

Nativity	None	Slight	Limited Common School	Good Common School	High School	Collegiate	Professional
New England . . .	25	1	343	548	73	7	3
N. Y., N. J., Penn. .	36	10	440	459	45	6	4
Ohio and Indiana .	39	26	524	375	28	4	4
Mich., Wisc., and Ill.	24	8	655	286	23	4	–
Coast Slave States .	171	21	411	358	27	6	6
Kentucky and Tenn.	199	19	481	293	4	–	4
States W. Miss. Riv.	24	24	366	513	73	–	–
Brit. Prov. ex. Can.	–	27	263	605	105	–	–
Canada	181	20	466	299	26	6	2
England	56	10	516	397	14	7	–
Scotland	12	25	482	370	86	25	–
Ireland	147	14	526	292	17	4	–
France, etc.	48	71	524	262	47	24	14
Germany	30	26	458	425	49	4	8
Scandinavia . . .	32	–	517	451	–	–	–
Other Countries . .	104	9	417	383	52	26	9
Total	58	14	473	408	39	5	3

TABLE XIX.

Distribution of the Sailors examined,[1] *by Education and Nativity.*

Nativity	None	Slight	Limited Com. School	Good Com. School	High School	Collegi-ate	Profes-sional	Total
New England . . .	5	14	114	15	–	–	–	148
N. Y., N. J., Penn. .	5	16	132	22	–	1	–	176
Ohio and Indiana .	–	–	2	1	–	–	–	3
Mich., Wisc., and Ill.	1	1	3	2	–	–	–	7
Coast Slave States .	3	3	16	5	–	1	–	28
Kentucky and Tenn.	–	–	1	–	–	–	–	1
States W. Miss. Riv.	1	–	1	–	–	–	–	2
Brit. Prov. ex. Can.	9	6	33	3	1	–	–	52
Canada	3	1	16	2	–	–	–	22
England	17	15	80	2	–	–	–	114
Scotland	4	3	23	3	–	–	–	33
Ireland	72	55	255	6	–	–	–	388
France	2	1	4	1	–	–	–	8
Germany	4	5	44	10	1	1	–	65
Scandinavia . . .	11	9	62	1	–	–	–	83
Other Countries . .	16	9	39	2	–	–	–	66
Total	153	138	825	75	2	3	–	1 196

1 The clothed Sailors and the Marines are included in this table.

TABLE XX.

Relative Distribution of Sailors, by Education and Nativity.

Nativity	None	Slight	Limited Common School	Good Common School	High School	Colle- giate	Profes- sional
New England . . .	34	95	770	101	–	–	–
N. Y., N. J., Penn. .	28	91	750	125	–	6	–
Ohio and Indiana .	–	–	667	333	–	–	–
Mich., Wisc., and Ill.	143	143	428	286	–	–	–
Coast Slave States .	107	107	571	179	–	36	–
Kentucky and Tenn.	–	–	1 000	–	–	–	–
States W. Miss. Riv.	500	–	500	–	–	–	–
Brit. Prov. ex. Can.	173	115	635	58	19	–	–
Canada	136	46	727	91	–	–	–
England	149	132	702	17	–	–	–
Scotland	121	91	697	91	–	–	–
Ireland	186	142	657	15	–	–	–
France	250	125	500	125	–	–	–
Germany	62	77	677	154	15	15	–
Scandinavia . . .	133	108	747	12	–	–	–
Other Countries . .	243	136	591	30	–	–	–
Total	128	115	690	63	2	2	–

Of the 10 472 soldiers and 1196 sailors including in the foregoing tables, 8156 soldiers and 365 sailors, 8521 in all, were Americans (*i. e.* citizens of the United States) by birth. For 235 of these, of whom 43 could not read and write, we are not in possession of the nativity of the parents. The parentage of the remainder was as exhibited by the next table.

TABLE XXI.

Parentage of the Native American Soldiers and Sailors examined.

Mother's Nativity	Father's Nativity						Totals
	Native Amer.	British Provinces	English	Irish	German	Other	
Native Amer.	6 826	48	63	66	46	54	7 103
British Prov. .	51	72	1	5	–	6	135
English . . .	46	3	127	6	3	6	191
Irish	55	4	16	398	4	11	488
German . . .	35	1	3	4	161	10	214
Others . . .	36	2	8	7	5	97	155
Totals . .	7 049	130	218	486	219	184	8 286

If now we assort the 333 native Americans who could not read and write, by their parentage in the same manner, we find—

TABLE XXII.

Parentage of Uneducated Native Americans.

Mother's Nativity	Father's Nativity						Totals
	Native Amer.	British Provinces	English	Irish	German	Others	
Native Amer.	275	–	4	5	3	–	287
British Prov. .	3	10	–	1	–	1	15
English . . .	1	–	4	–	–	–	5
Irish	–	1	2	14	–	–	17
German . . .	1	–	–	–	4	–	5
Others . . .	1	–	–	–	–	3	4
Totals . .	281	11	10	20	7	4	333

A comparison of the figures in Table XXII., with those obtained by reducing the numbers of Table XXI. to the same scale, shows a close similarity, the only marked excess in the actual number of the uneducated over that which would correspond to the proportional number of the same class examined, being for men whose parents were natives of the British Provinces. For the sake of comparison we append the proportionate numbers obtained from Table XXI. by reducing it throughout in the ratio of 8286 to 333.

Mother's Nativity	Father's Nativity						Totals
	Native Amer.	British Provinces	English	Irish	German	Others	
Native Amer.	274	2	2	3	2	2	285
British Prov. .	2	3	–	–	–	–	5
English . . .	2	–	5	–	–	1	8
Irish	2	–	1	16	–	1	20
German . . .	1	–	–	–	7	1	9
Others . . .	1	–	1	–	–	4	6
Totals . .	282	5	9	19	9	9	333

CHAPTER XVI.

MILITARY SERVICE.

1. *Statistics collected.*

THE great mass of the statistics which have been collected by the Sanitary Commission belong to the strictly military class, and are more or less directly connected with questions of health or of mortality. From prompt and thorough discussion of these materials, and from investigations to which such discussion would call attention, the Commission anticipated its principal means of usefulness, in discovering the hygienic needs of our soldiers and bringing them to the attention of the proper authorities; as also in furnishing from its own resources such remedies as might demand greater promptitude than could always be attained through official channels in times of special emergency.

For this purpose an elaborate system of camp-inspections was organized, with an efficient corps of inspectors; and blank forms[1] were prepared containing a very large number of questions, designed for the twofold purpose of obtaining information and of impressing indirectly upon commanding officers various considerations of importance to the welfare of their men. An account of these camp inspections and of their effect may be found[2] in Professor Stillé's "History of the U. S. Sanitary Commission." About 1500 reports of the inspections, made between the months of July 1861 and April 1863, and each containing answers to a number of questions varying from 60 to 180, were received by the Commission and have been carefully discussed by its statistical department. The results of more than 1200 reports, comprising about 176 000 answers, are elaborately assorted and tabulated with a view to their consultation with the least possible trouble, and the documents are preserved with our other archives. They contain valuable and interesting information regarding the sanitary history of the army, but are too extensive for convenient publication, and scarcely capa-

[1] *Sanitary Commission Documents*, Nos. 19, 19 *a*.

[2] Pages 96–100; 454–55.

ble of presentation in a condensed form. A few of the inferences, however, will be given in the next section.

The Hospital Directory, so long maintained by the Sanitary Commission, will also be found described[1] in detail in Professor Stillé's history. In connection with this important and laborious undertaking, a very large amount of material, derived from the daily morning reports of the military hospitals throughout the country, was tabulated under the superintendence of Mr. Bowne; and results of high value, both in their sanitary relations and in their scientific bearings, were anticipated, when, at the beginning of July 1864, the War Department issued an order[2] forbidding the communication of any farther information on the subject to the agents of the Commission. This was the first of a series of orders, necessarily alluded to here and in the history of the Commission, by which, as is well known, the hostility of Mr. Stanton[3] greatly abridged its means of usefulness, and, so far as his power extended, curtailed its opportunities alike for prosecuting labors in the field and investigations in the office. Soon after this event, the author of this volume assumed the duties of Actuary, but in the face of these discouragements it seemed wisest to defer all attempts at farther discussion of the materials until a more propitious season. Subsequently, when in June 1865 it appeared that analogous investigations were making in the Surgeon-General's office, under the very able direction of Dr. Woodward, it clearly became needless for the Sanitary Commission to undertake any farther discussion of the subject. The material now in our archives, contains classified and tabulated summaries and comparisons of the daily returns of the general hospitals and of the hospitals for contagious fevers, from nine military departments, extending over periods not exceeding eighteen months.

The most extensive of all the undertakings of the statistical department, and that for which the greatest amount of labor and expense has been incurred, is the collection and discussion of the regimental monthly returns. These were transcribed from the rolls in the Adjutant General's office, first by Mr. O'Connell and subsequently by Mr. Wilson, with assiduity and punctilious care. Both these gentlemen possessed the confidence of the officers in charge of the rolls, both were scrupulously careful to occasion no inconvenience, and both were subsequently offered permanent positions in that office. But in October 1865, — after nearly three

1 *History of the U. S. Sanitary Commission*, pp. 308–310.
2 *Ibid.* p. 457.
3 *Ibid.* pp. 136, 511.

years of labor, during which about 32 000 reports from 1550 regiments had been transcribed, comprising all the monthly returns up to January 1865, which were on file in the War Department, excepting those for the regular army and for the colored troops, — farther access to these rolls also was suddenly forbidden by order of the Secretary, and all efforts to procure a modification of the order proved unavailing.[1] No reason was assigned for this act, which deprived us of our last source of information from the archives of the War Department, nor were any other opportunities subsequently permitted us.

Before Mr. Stanton left office, our work was completed, and the requisite means for farther computation was no longer available. Meanwhile one additional effort had been made by the Commission in the summer of 1867, to procure some unpublished information as to the composition of our armies during the years 1863 and 1864, by which the material already collected could be properly arranged, as will be stated below. But this effort shared the fate of its predecessors; and for the want of historical data, which a single clerk could have transcribed in a few days without inconvenience to the official authorities, our vast store of well classified material lies useless.

Meanwhile, through the unfailing courtesy and cordial assistance of the Adjutant Generals of the several States, we have obtained copies of many returns for dates previous to 1865, which had not been on file at Washington; and thus our statistics for the Volunteer Army are probably as complete as may be, up to the close of 1864. For the remaining three months of the war, we have but 2000 returns transcribed, being probably three fourths of the whole number; yet it has seemed preferable to make no attempt at extending our inferences to these three months, rather than to give results less accurate than might be afforded through other channels. It can scarcely be doubted that the additional records will be hereafter furnished from the War Department itself, under other guidance. The detailed account of the material in our possession is given in the section devoted to this subject.

The only other military question which we have statistically discussed is the effect of forced marches, as indicated by the experience of the regiments which thus hastened to the battle-field of Gettysburg. Just previous to this battle long and rapid marches were made by large bodies of our soldiery, and special inquiries were instituted by Mr. Olmsted, in order to determine the effect

[1] *History of the U. S. Sanitary Commission*, p. 465.

upon the condition of the men. There are 144 reports of regimental inspection according to the blank forms then prepared. Some inferences from these will be found in the final section of this chapter, with which we bring our volume to an end.

2. *Camp Inspections.*

The tabulated and assorted results of camp-inspections are preserved in the archives of the Statistical Bureau, in nine large folio volumes. The positions of the camps were so various, the qualifications of the commanding officers so different, the places where the regiments were raised, the character of their outfit, the classes of men of which they were composed, and the circumstances at different times, all so diverse, that but little instruction can be deduced from any comparison of averages. We will however give a single general table, showing for some of the principal subjects of inquiry the proportionate number of camps belonging to the several grades, in a classification according to relative excellence, which were found in four successive periods of five months each. The inspection-reports contain comparatively few numerical data, since most of the descriptions are verbal, and the answers to the numerous questions frequently indefinite, — given moreover with many qualifications. Still in tabulating them many have been expressed by a numerical scale, and the average values of the answers to many questions upon kindred topics have furnished the relative estimates from which our table is constructed. Twelve of the most important subjects are selected for our table; and for each of these it exhibits the proportionate number of camps, in each thousand, which belongs to each one of nine grades ranging from "extremely good" to "extremely bad."

The four periods and the number of camps reported upon, in each period, are as follows: —

I.	From August to December, 1861, inclusive,	548 camps.
II.	From January to May, 1862, inclusive,	428
III.	From June to October, 1862, inclusive,	56
IV.	From November, 1862, to March, 1863, inclusive,	127

TABLE I.

Results of Camp Inspections, Proportionate Numbers.

Grade	Camp Site				Tents			
	I.	II.	III.	IV.	I.	II.	III.	IV.
Extremely Good . . .	–	–	–	–	–	25	–	–
Very Good	380	315	268	254	–	–	–	–
Good	111	90	94	81	274	176	241	165
Moderately Good . . .	73	96	67	85	–	1	–	–
Indifferent	58	89	94	37	1	–	–	–
Moderately Bad	101	125	129	157	1	–	–	–
Bad	76	76	36	69	672	678	571	528
Very Bad	98	77	103	85	–	–	–	–
Extremely Bad	45	55	40	26	–	–	–	–
Not stated	10	40	125	147	28	113	161	307
Doubtful	48	37	44	59	24	7	27	–

Grade	Bedding				Clothing			
	I.	II.	III.	IV.	I.	II.	III.	IV.
Extremely Good . . .	–	–	–	–	–	–	–	–
Very Good	268	315	369	347	399	419	426	398
Good	432	356	315	420	295	341	310	335
Moderately Good . . .	120	188	42	92	20	3	–	–
Indifferent	–	35	101	10	5	1	–	–
Moderately Bad	23	10	54	13	8	–	–	–
Bad	125	68	30	26	216	207	181	117
Very Bad	–	–	–	–	13	1	–	1
Extremely Bad	–	–	–	–	8	–	–	–
Not stated	8	26	89	92	33	28	80	149
Doubtful	24	2	–	–	3	–	3	–

TABLE I. — (*Continued.*)

Results of Camp Inspections,
Proportional Numbers.

Grade	Cleanliness				Water			
	I.	II.	III.	IV.	I.	II.	III.	IV.
Extremely Good . . .	–	–	–	–	180	156	155	110
Very Good	530	535	581	486	66	81	77	55
Good	70	64	23	64	668	581	500	428
Moderately Good . . .	3	2	–	–	49	62	36	113
Indifferent	1	5	–	–	–	–	–	–
Moderately Bad	–	–	–	–	–	–	6	3
Bad	219	213	107	138	16	37	18	42
Very Bad	110	60	161	60	10	23	24	34
Extremely Bad	–	–	–	–	–	–	–	–
Not stated	46	94	92	251	10	56	107	210
Doubtful	21	27	36	1	1	4	77	5

Grade	Rations and Cookery				Discipline			
	I.	II.	III.	IV	I.	II.	III.	IV.
Extremely Good . . .	9	18	13	15	–	–	–	–
Very Good	716	752	670	659	321	311	299	238
Good	7	13	5	1	429	424	406	419
Moderately Good . . .	4	6	2	5	9	–	–	–
Indifferent	8	11	5	6	–	–	–	–
Moderately Bad	61	53	62	48	–	–	–	–
Bad	73	51	69	62	141	130	121	163
Very Bad	68	56	78	64	45	48	36	26
Extremely Bad	–	–	–	–	–	–	–	–
Not stated	18	25	54	134	46	79	134	152
Doubtful	36	15	42	6	9	8	4	2

TABLE I.—(*Continued.*)

Results of Camp Inspections,
Proportionate Numbers.

Grade	Recreations				Med. Insp. on Enlistment			
	I.	II.	III.	IV.	I.	II.	III.	IV.
Extremely Good	–	–	–	–	–	–	–	–
Very Good	105	197	219	114	129	119	313	149
Good	44	113	85	32	400	414	420	429
Moderately Good	–	–	–	–	–	–	–	–
Indifferent	8	–	–	–	9	–	–	–
Moderately Bad	–	–	–	–	–	4	–	–
Bad	503	491	486	543	266	279	107	209
Very Bad	–	–		–	81	72	62	16
Extremely Bad	–	–	–	–	–	–	–	–
Not stated	340	199	210	311	98	105	62	177
Doubtful	–	–	–	–	17	7	36	20

Grade	Medical Officers				Hospital			
	I.	II.	III.	IV.	I.	II.	III.	IV.
Extremely Good	–	–	–	–	73	89	69	74
Very Good	644	682	571	756	576	555	417	505
Good	28	12	18	16	1	21	6	10
Moderately Good	–	–	–	–	8	3	–	–
Indifferent	–	–	–	–	6	–	–	–
Moderately Bad	–	–	–	–	98	60	80	79
Bad	33	2	–	–	95	98	190	158
Very Bad	257	185	268	86	107	74	36	66
Extremely Bad	–	2	–	–	5	–	–	–
Not stated	38	117	125	142	30	91	137	98
Doubtful	–	–	18	–	1	9	65	10

3. *Sickness, Mortality, Discharges, etc.*

The extent of our collection and tabulation of the Monthly Regimental Returns has been stated, as also the reason why our results are confined to the white volunteer service, and why they do not comprise the last three months of the war. Many discordances were found in the official records, and these have been investigated at the State capitals and corrected.

The data for the nine months ending with February 1862, were specially discussed by Mr. Elliott, and the results published in pamphlet form as No. 46 of the Commission's documents. In this discussion the troops from the Eastern and those from the Western States were separately considered, which was both justifiable and desirable, inasmuch as the soldiers from each of these sections of the country were employed in that section by which they were furnished. The same is true in general for the next following six months, which have been aggregated and computed in a similar manner. A portion of these results was also published by Mr. Elliott in his paper "On the Military Statistics of the United States of America." For subsequent periods of the war the distinction between Eastern and Western soldiers was less significant, since soldiers from both portions of the country served in each. To deduce the best results from our materials, they should be classified by armies, and those regiments of which each of our armies consisted should be aggregated month by month. The results would then form a most valuable contribution to the military history of the war, exhibiting as they would, at a glance, the mortality from different sources, the sanitary condition, the strength, the loss, the desertions, etc., in each army during each successive month, the numbers of officers and men present and absent respectively, etc., etc. In short, a knowledge of the regiments which formed each several army is the key for unlocking the valuable inferences contained in our army statistics and lying ready for employment; without such knowledge they are comparatively useless.

It seemed therefore to the Commission that a final and earnest effort was desirable, and accordingly at the beginning of June, 1867, one more strenuous endeavor was made to obtain from Mr. Stanton the necessary information or permission for transcribing it by clerks selected or approved by him. The application of the Commission was advocated by prominent statesmen and men high in office, but the Secretary could not be induced to yield his consent and the effort was most reluctantly abandoned. The fruit of years of toil has thus been rendered for a season unavailing, and the extensive collection of materials has been deposited with the archives of the Commission, ready for use at some future time. At present the reports have been so aggregated as to present the total returns from the troops of each arm of the service from each State, a form in which the voluminousness of the results forbids their presentation here.

It may not be too much to hope that at some not distant day the tabulated results, now comparatively valueless, but representing enormous labor and needing almost insignificant accessions from official data to kindle them into living usefulness, may be rendered serviceable to the historian of our great struggle for national existence, and to the nation itself for possible future contingency.

Our material thus comprises for all the several regiments of white volunteers for which the returns are on file, up to the beginning of 1865, as well as for the aggregate of all the cavalry, the artillery, and the infantry from each State separately, the monthly returns according to the schedule seen in Tables II. and III.

In order that the results of this huge labor may not be entirely unrepresented in this volume, of which they were designed to form the most prominent, and it was hoped, the most valuable part, we will present in tabular form some of the aggregated summaries. In the Tables II. and III. are given the actual numbers recorded for the Eastern and Western troops respectively, during the fifteen months from June 1861 to August 1862, inclusive ; the materials from the first nine months having been prepared exclusively, and the remainder in great part under the direction of Mr. Elliott. In the two next following Tables, IV. and V., the proportionate numbers in each 10 000 are similarly given, while the Tables VI. and VII. show some of the most important facts relative to the condition of the total armies of the Union for each month of the whole period over which our statistics extend.

In these tables, columns or lines are given to show the number of regiments reporting, and the average regimental strength. There were, however, some bodies of soldiery, not organized into regiments, — this being generally the case in the artillery, and among some of the troops enlisted for comparatively short terms of service. The number of such cases was relatively small, and would exert but little influence on the results, yet the necessity of some general rule became manifest. In Tables II. and III. independent organizations have been enumerated as regiments in the columns of " Regiments reporting," which would more correctly have been entitled " Organizations reporting," while in computing the column of " Average Regimental Strength," for Table VII. a single battery (assuming the normal strength to be about one hundred and fifty men) has been counted as the sixth part of a regiment. In other cases, a similar rule has been observed, each organization being regarded as so many tenths of a regiment, as there were hundreds of men in the number supposed to form its usual strength.

For the Tables VI. and VII., which exhibit the aggregrate monthly statistics on file, as heretofore stated for the total volunteer army, some indication of the probable degree of reliance to which they are entitled may be derived from a comparison of the recorded strength for each month, with the best attainable estimate of the real strength as derived from the first table in this volume.[1] The meagerness of the reports for the first months of the war forms the most noticeable characteristic, but it can surprise no one, who considers the obstacles, with which the department was then contending, and the fact that a prompt supply of able-bodied men, in large numbers, their equipment, maintenance, and transportation were of paramount importance ; that the energies of all the officers at head-quarters were tasked to the utmost by these most imperative duties, and that time was requisite for extending tó an army of many hundred thousand men, commanded mostly by officers taken from civil life, the systematic details of official relations, which had previously been adapted to the nineteen or twenty regiments of which the U. S. regular army consisted at the outbreak of the insurrection.

Comparing thus the total aggregate strength from the regimental reports, month by month, with the total number of volunteers in the field according to our estimates, we find the difference diminishing, until in August 1862, nearly two thirds of the whole number had reported. For October, the proportion whose reports were filed had increased to nearly three fourths, for November, to nearly four fifths, and for December, to nearly five sixths of the whole number. During the year 1863, the number of reports on file seems to have comprised between five sixths and seven eighths of all the volunteer troops. From accurate statistics of so large a proportion of our men, it would seem that very trustworthy inferences might be drawn for the whole volunteer army ; and this we have endeavored to do in a subsequent table.

[1] Pages 7, 8.

TABLE II.

Summary of the Regimental Reports for Eastern Soldiers up to August 1862.

		1861 June	July	August	Sept.	October	Nov.
Number of Regiments reporting		4	8	21	54	68	73
Strength at close of month . . .	Officers . .	157	300	702	1 875	2 367	2 529
	Men . . .	3 187	6 035	16 277	44 226	56 111	61 383
	Total . .	3 334	6 335	16 979	46 101	58 478	63 912
Sick at close of month . .	Officers present	3	15	24	85	97	104
	Officers absent .	0	9	10	31	46	56
	Total officers .	3	24	34	116	143	160
	Men present . .	133	313	905	2 686	3 361	4 516
	Men absent . .	15	89	201	568	776	728
	Total men . .	148	402	1 106	3 254	4 137	5 244
Gain of officers other than by promotion or transfer . .		–	–	–	2	3	8
Men enlisted in regiment . . .		13	60	502	691	766	529
reenlisted		–	2	15	11	22	2
recruits from depots . . .		44	376	50	784	859	504
Officers resigned or disbanded. .		–	6	27	53	46	79
Men discharged by exp. of service		–	–	2	80	28	–
Men discharged for disability . .		38	121	288	284	449	263
Men deserted		38	268	225	275	353	210
Men returned from desertion . .		–	–	10	57	25	16
Officers missing in action . . .		–	6	–	–	17	3
Men missing in action		–	85	10	61	367	12
Men returned fr. missing in action		–	–	–	5	8	5
Men disch. for causes not named		3	77	18	126	104	106
Died in action . .	Officers . .	–	–	1	2	1	1
	Men . . .	2	12	3	12	37	11
	Total . .	2	12	4	14	38	12
Died of disease . .	Officers . .	–	–	1	–	6	6
	Men . . .	–	4	28	79	111	169
	Total . .	–	4	29	79	117	175

TABLE II. — (*Continued.*)

Summary of the Regimental Reports for Eastern Soldiers up to August 1862.

December	1862 January	February	March	April	May	June	July	August
58	42	84	143	154	125	149	150	67
2 056	1 440	2 964	5 053	5 460	4 579	4 867	5 087	2 099
50 447	34 022	69 760	116 887	125 186	104 434	107 582	110 879	47 987
52 503	35 462	72 724	121 940	130 646	109 013	112 449	115 966	50 086
73	59	104	137	223	184	315	433	115
37	23	42	99	122	192	300	282	83
110	82	146	236	345	376	615	715	198
3 215	1 755	4 215	4 402	5 527	4 610	6 945	9 828	2 835
696	731	1 304	4 035	4 977	8 045	10 887	12 407	4 727
3 911	2 486	5 519	8 437	10 504	12 655	17 832	22 235	7 562
1	–	–	5	4	4	10	15	7
146	161	142	685	339	151	286	212	288
6	4	6	17	4	2	2	–	3
684	206	1 304	1 741	1 024	342	300	354	299
62	19	73	92	89	88	103	204	62
–	–	1	–	3	2	5	–	2
433	187	348	816	774	908	1 016	1 491	520
239	50	265	228	417	327	1 082	946	679
15	10	67	78	47	32	67	89	81
–	–	–	–		15	55	8	9
5	4	2	35	10	569	1 827	434	291
–	3	3	103	39	13	89	206	70
71	33	142	262	236	109	210	335	378
–	1	–	2	5	23	37	7	12
14	7	7	27	120	252	755	146	110
14	8	7	29	125	275	792	153	122
1	–	5	7	11	11	18	17	16
159	90	168	257	271	280	367	534	253
160	90	173	264	282	291	385	551	269

TABLE III.

Summary of the Regimental Reports for Western Soldiers up to August 1862.

		1861 July	August	Sept.	October	Nov.	Dec.
Number of Regiments reporting		3	6	15	20	29	43
Strength at close of month . . .	Officers . .	102	219	504	664	1 021	1 507
	Men . . .	2 924	5 733	12 897	16 438	24 516	38 639
	Total . .	3 026	5 952	13 401	17 102	25 537	40 146
Sick at close of month.	Officers present	1	10	38	31	49	105
	Officers absent .	–	2	9	11	24	38
	Total officers .	1	12	47	42	73	143
	Men present . .	177	419	1 338	1 492	2 951	4 777
	Men absent . .	58	119	310	438	959	1 394
	Total men . .	235	538	1 648	1 930	3 910	6 171
Gain of officers other than by promotion or transfer . .		–	1	–	–	–	3
Men enlisted in regiment . . .		49	66	135	85	346	466
reenlisted		2	2	5	–	2	4
recruits from depots . . .		–	–	42	126	127	52
Officers resigned or disbanded . .		2	3	5	12	10	31
Men discharged by exp. of service		–	–	–	–	–	–
Men discharged for disability . .		8	48	97	160	113	231
Men deserted		1	18	39	34	57	128
Men returned from desertion . .		–	–	2	2	5	12
Officers missing in action . . .		–	–	–	–	–	–
Men missing in action		13	1	17	5	4	17
Men returned fr. missing in action			2	–	–	–	–
Men disch. for causes not named		6	13	13	22	17	39
Died in action . .	Officers . .	–	–	–	–	1	2
	Men . . .	5	2	4	9	4	17
	Total . .	5	2	4	9	5	19
Died of disease . .	Officers . .	–	–	2	3	2	3
	Men . . .	–	5	35	51	127	348
	Total . .	–	5	37	54	129	351

TABLE III. — (*Continued.*)

Summary of the Regimental Reports for Western Soldiers up to August 1862.

1862 January	February	March	April	May	June	July	August
52	53	141	147	147	149	141	104
1 756	1 899	4 683	5 005	4 768	4 612	4 356	3 203
42 799	44 440	110 418	116 938	109 481	104 419	94 716	65 451
44 555	46 339	115 101	121 943	114 249	109 031	99 072	68 654
134	99	218	281	294	282	289	223
70	79	267	323	367	356	254	145
204	178	485	604	661	638	543	368
5 738	3 825	7 888	8 537	7 249	7 088	7 640	6 132
2 738	3 149	12 341	16 661	18 365	17 676	13 057	6 483
8 476	6 974	20 229	25 198	25 614	24 764	20 697	12 615
2	1	15	7	3	6	31	15
382	277	508	305	161	242	112	486
5	72	14	4	27	9	22	15
57	227	345	494	217	64	40	164
52	40	145	178	135	197	117	23
–	–	20	11	2	5	1	38
190	438	808	1 130	1 302	1 003	1 379	1 065
86	218	260	411	539	718	739	1 412
43	34	46	33	50	84	98	307
–	2	2	37	8	13	2	9
6	37	33	695	211	371	89	162
–	2	31	33	18	31	33	62
122	107	286	375	419	417	331	397
–	12	18	55	27	12	5	11
21	208	186	855	355	236	95	170
21	220	204	910	382	248	100	181
2	9	22	22	25	20	16	6
406	229	737	740	809	673	718	489
408	238	759	762	834	693	734	495

TABLE IV.

Monthly Condition of the Eastern Forces, up to August 1862.
Rates for each 10 000 *Men.*[1]

		1861 June	July	Aug.	Sept.	Oct.	Nov.
Average Regimental Strength	Officers	39	38	33	35	35	35
	Men	797	754	775	819	825	841
	Total	836	792	808	854	860	876
Sick at close of month	Officers	191	800	484	619	604	633
	Men	464	666	679	736	737	854
Gain of officers other than by promotion or transfer		–	–	–	11	13	32
Men enlisted in regiment		41	99	308	156	137	86
reenlisted		–	3	9	2	4	–
recruits from depots		138	623	31	177	153	82
Officers resigned or disbanded		–	200	385	283	194	312
Men discharged by expiration of service		–	–	1	18	5	–
Men discharged for disability		119	200	177	64	80	43
Men deserted		199	444	138	62	63	34
Men returned from desertion		–	–	6	13	4	3
Officers missing in action		–	200	–	–	72	12
Men missing in action		–	141	6	14	65	2
Men returned from missing in action		–	–	–	1	1	1
Men discharged for causes not named		9	128	11	28	19	17
Died in action	Officers	–	–	14	11	4	4
	Men	6	20	2	3	7	2
	Total	6	19	2	3	6	2
Died of disease	Officers	–	–	14	–	25	24
	Men	–	7	17	18	20	28
	Total	–	6	17	17	20	27

[1] The average Regimental Strength is here given in actual numbers. The other indications of the table are in proportionate numbers.

TABLE IV. — (*Continued.*)

Monthly Condition of the Eastern Forces, up to August, 1862.
Rates for each 10 000 *Men.*

December	1862 January	February	March	April	May	June	July	August
35	34	35	35	35	37	33	34	31
870	810	831	818	813	835	722	739	716
905	844	866	853	848	872	755	773	747
535	569	493	467	632	821	1 264	1 406	943
775	731	791	722	839	1 212	1 658	2 005	1 576
5	–	–	10	7	9	21	29	33
29	47	20	59	27	14	27	19	60
1	1	1	1	–	–	–	–	1
136	61	187	149	82	33	28	32	62
302	132	246	182	163	192	212	401	295
–	–	–	–	–	–	1	–	–
86	55	50	70	62	87	94	134	108
47	15	38	20	33	31	101	85	142
3	3	10	7	4	3	6	8	17
–	–	–	–	–	33	113	16	43
1	1	–	3	1	54	170	39	61
–	1	–	9	3	1	8	19	15
14	10	20	22	19	10	20	30	79
–	7	–	4	9	50	76	14	57
3	2	1	2	10	24	70	13	23
3	2	1	2	10	25	70	13	24
5	–	17	14	20	24	37	33	76
32	26	24	22	22	27	34	48	53
30	25	24	22	22	26	34	48	54

TABLE V.

Monthly Condition of the Western Forces, up to August, 1862.
Rates for each 10 000 *Men.*[1]

		1861 July	Aug.	Sept.	Oct.	Nov.	Dec.
Average Regimental Strength	Officers .	34	36	34	33	35	35
	Men . .	975	956	860	822	845	899
	Total . .	1 009	992	894	855	880	934
Sick at close of month . .	Officers .	98	548	933	633	715	949
	Men . .	804	938	1 278	1 174	1 595	1 597
Gain of officers other than by promotion or transfer		–	46	–	–	–	20
Men enlisted in regiment		168	115	105	52	141	121
reenlisted		7	3	4	–	1	1
recruits from depots		–	–	33	77	52	13
Officers resigned or disbanded		196	137	99	181	98	206
Men discharged by expiration of service		–	–	–	–	–	–
Men discharged for disability . . .		27	84	75	97	46	60
Men deserted		3	31	30	21	23	33
Men returned from desertion		–	–	2	1	2	3
Officers missing in action		–	–	–	–	–	–
Men missing in action		44	2	13	3	2	4
Men returned from missing in action .		–	3	–	–	–	–
Men discharged for causes not named .		21	23	10	13	7	10
Died in action	Officers .	–		–	–	10	13
	Men . .	17	3	3	5	2	4
	Total . .	16	3	3	5	2	4
Died of disease	Officers .	–		40	45	20	20
	Men . .		9	27	31	52	90
	Total . .		8	28	32	50	87

1 The average Regimental Strength is here given in actual numbers. The other indications of the table are in proportionate numbers.

TABLE V. — (*Continued.*)

Monthly Condition of the Western Forces, up to August 1862.
Rates for each 10 000 *Men.*

1862 January	February	March	April	May	June	July	August
34	36	33	34	32	31	31	31
823	838	783	796	745	701	672	629
857	874	816	830	777	732	703	660
1 162	937	1 036	1 207	1 386	1 383	1 247	1 148
1 980	1 569	1 832	2 155	2 340	2 372	2 185	1 927
11	5	32	14	6	13	71	47
89	62	46	26	15	23	12	74
1	16	1	–	2	1	2	2
13	51	31	42	20	6	4	25
296	211	310	356	283	427	269	72
–	–	2	1	–	–	–	6
44	99	73	97	119	96	146	163
20	49	24	35	49	69	78	216
10	8	4	3	5	8	10	47
–	11	4	74	17	28	5	28
1	8	3	59	19	36	9	25
–	–	3	3	2	3	3	9
28	24	26	32	38	40	35	61
–	63	38	110	57	26	11	34
5	47	17	73	32	23	10	26
5	47	17	75	33	23	10	26
11	47	47	44	52	43	37	19
95	51	67	63	74	64	76	75
92	51	66	62	73	64	74	72

38

TABLE VI.

Strength, Sickness, Mortality, Discharges and Desertions, recorded for the United States Volunteers, in each Month.

Month	No. of Reg'ts reporting	Strength at close of Month		Sick at close of Month		Discharged for Disability	Deserted
		Officers	Men	Officers	Men		
1861 — June . .	4	157	3 187	3	148	38	38
July . .	11	402	8 959	25	637	129	269
August .	27	921	22 010	46	1 644	336	233
September	69	2 379	57 123	163	4 902	381	255
October .	87	3 031	72 549	185	6 067	609	360
November	102	3 550	85 899	233	9 154	376	246
December	101	3 563	89 086	253	10 082	664	340
1862 — January .	93	3 196	76 821	286	10 962	377	83
February .	137	4 863	114 200	324	12 493	786	382
March . .	277	10 052	234 272	736	29 294	1 667	500
April . .	297	10 734	248 121	959	36 299	1 924	876
May . .	272	9 605	219 649	1 042	38 753	2 216	814
June . .	283	9 665	215 779	1 263	42 951	2 027	1 690
July . .	276	9 573	208 496	1 261	43 169	2 900	1 556
August .	519	17 746	387 252	2 207	77 945	4 429	3 716
September	655	22 479	502 862	2 891	106 231	4 437	4 156
October .	782	26 967	596 415	2 999	118 544	7 678	8 053
November	896	31 084	679 318	3 109	133 689	8 434	4 236
December	948	32 865	701 448	3 545	143 973	9 056	6 035
1863 — January .	1 016	34 765	727 917	4 061	155 964	11 200	7 238
February .	1 022	35 408	712 560	3 421	140 211	12 661	6 384
March . .	1 030	35 733	696 567	2 939	122 377	15 757	3 399
April . .	1 005	34 971	661 513	3 128	100 396	11 592	2 357
May . .	975	33 404	625 470	2 917	104 752	5 522	1 940
June . .	922	31 448	579 204	3 137	105 798	3 830	1 994
July . .	944	31 487	575 924	4 166	127 778	2 431	3 602
August .	943	30 701	567 613	3 420	125 476	3 533	2 187
September	953	30 485	573 258	3 617	128 625	2 912	1 729
October .	972	30 647	588 399	2 921	119 270	2 475	2 071
November	979	30 847	592 305	2 755	115 055	2 067	1 090
December	979	30 870	596 615	2 204	102 503	2 141	745
1864 — January .	960	30 073	600 597	1 865	91 748	2 530	874
February .	952	29 683	619 030	1 603	88 618	2 109	1 603
March . .	961	30 077	657 607	1 562	89 679	2 749	1 413
April . .	937	29 408	649 508	1 456	84 936	1 938	2 116
May . .	929	28 682	636 550	2 951	121 023	1 259	2 047
June . .	963	29 284	656 192	4 018	152 108	1 334	2 035
July . .	960	28 950	647 810	4 154	167 160	1 052	2 218
August .	919	26 946	605 325	3 875	168 047	1 194	3 271
September	907	25 366	587 621	3 143	148 918	1 168	2 076
October .	914	24 607	601 822	2 685	146 613	1 423	3 317
November	889	23 672	607 158	2 026	138 791	1 154	2 801
December	829	22 463	571 820	1 808	124 704	1 296	2 294

TABLE VI.—(*Continued.*)

Month	Died during the Month — Of Wounds		Of Disease		Total		Missing in Action	
	Officers	Men	Officers	Men	Officers	Men	Offic'rs	Men
1861—June . .	–	2	–	–	–	2	–	–
July . .	–	17	–	4	–	21	6	98
August .	1	5	1	33	2	38	–	9
September	2	16	2	114	4	130	–	73
October .	1	46	9	162	10	208	17	364
November	2	15	8	296	10	311	3	11
December	2	31	4	507	6	538	–	22
1862—January .	1	28	2	496	3	524	–	7
February .	12	215	14	397	26	612	2	34
March .	22	246	31	1 001	53	1 247	2	- 54
April . .	61	987	33	1 020	94	2 007	37	638
May . .	50	610	36	1 096	86	1 706	23	749
June . .	49	995	38	1 047	87	2 042	68	2 078
July . .	12	241	33	1 261	45	1 502	10	284
August .	131	1 770	77	2 079	208	3 849	110	2 161
September	152	2 705	44	1 654	196	4 359	35	574
October .	105	1 985	57	2 724	162	4 709	30	12
November	26	603	68	3 212	94	3 815	18	- 844
December	205	2 661	74	4 156	279	6 817	83	813
1863—January .	105	1 773	57	4 483	162	6 256	32	148
February .	23	643	66	4 653	89	5 296	13	- 1 138
March .	26	394	77	4 281	103	4 675	54	- 201
April . .	29	422	71	3 366	100	3 788	34	- 3
May . .	263	3 236	41	2 309	304	5 545	134	2 962
June . .	111	1 389	40	2 144	151	3 533	111	2 496
July . .	319	3 412	62	2 764	381	6 176	186	4 617
August .	54	999	91	3 341	145	4 340	42	- 1 263
September	155	1 782	68	2 813	223	4 595	195	2 822
October .	77	922	67	2 329	144	3 251	79	- 2 187
November	130	1 550	37	2 070	167	3 620	49	- 1 165
December	45	633	42	2 277	87	2 910	9	- 769
1864—January .	12	322	34	1 969	46	2 291	37	175
February .	24	375	36	1 730	60	2 105	32	355
March .	11	213	46	2 217	57	2 430	24	- 25
April . .	40	505	54	2 485	94	2 990	180	3 849
May . .	418	6 469	47	1 656	465	8 125	238	6 568
June . .	425	6 810	59	2 183	484	8 993	173	4 204
July . .	276	4 242	50	2 734	326	6 976	202	2 373
August .	185	2 988	58	3 191	243	6 179	254	3 445
September	170	2 349	40	2 819	210	5 168	75	- 102
October .	162	2 021	51	2 784	213	4 805	97	1 604
November	70	935	30	2 266	100	3 201	49	- 1 321
December	85	1 131	25	2 327	110	3 458	41	- 886

TABLE VII.

Average Regimental Strength, and Monthly Rates of Sickness, Mortality, etc., in the United States Volunteers.

Month	Av. Regim'l Strength		Sick at close of Month		Discharged for Disability	Deserted
	Officers	Men	Officers	Men		
1861 — June . .	39	797	191	464	119	119
July . .	37	814	622	711	144	300
August .	34	815	499	747	153	106
September	34	828	685	858	67	45
October .	35	834	610	836	84	50
November	35	842	656	1 066	44	29
December	35	882	710	1 132	74	38
1862 — January .	34	826	895	1 427	49	11
February .	35	833	666	1 094	69	33
March .	36	846	732	1 250	71	21
April . .	36	836	893	1 463	77	35
May . .	35	808	1 085	1 764	101	37
June . .	34	762	1 307	1 990	94	78
July . .	35	755	1 317	2 070	139	75
August .	34	746	1 244	2 013	114	96
September	34	768	1 286	2 113	88	83
October .	34	763	1 112	1 988	129	135
November	35	758	1 000	1 968	124	62
December	35	740	1 079	2 053	129	86
1863 — January .	34	716	1 168	2 143	154	99
February .	34	697	966	1 967	178	90
March .	35	676	822	1 757	226	49
April . .	35	658	894	1 518	175	36
May . .	34	641	873	1 675	88	31
June . .	34	628	997	1 826	66	34
July . .	33	610	1 323	2 219	42	62
August .	33	602	1 114	2 211	62	38
September	32	602	1 186	2 244	51	30
October .	32	605	953	2 027	42	35
November	32	605	893	1 943	35	18
December	32	609	714	1 718	36	12
1864 — January .	31	626	620	1 528	42	15
February .	31	650	540	1 432	34	26
March .	31	684	519	1 364	42	21
April . .	31	693	495	1 308	30	33
May . .	31	686	1 029	1 901	20	32
June . .	30	681	1 372	2 318	20	31
July . .	30	675	1 435	2 580	16	34
August .	29	659	1 438	2 776	20	54
September	28	648	1 237	2 534	20	35
October .	27	658	1 091	2 436	24	55
November	27	683	856	2 286	19	46
December	27	690	805	2 181	23	40

TABLE VII. — (*Continued.*)

Month	Died during the Month — Of Wounds		Of Disease		Total		Miss'g in Action	
	Officers	Men	Officers	Men	Officers	Men	Officers	Men
1861 — June	–	6	–	–	–	6	–	–
July	–	19	–	4	–	23	149	109
August	11	2	11	15	22	17	–	4
September	8	3	8	20	17	23	–	13
October	3	6	30	22	33	29	56	50
November	6	2	22	34	28	36	8	1
December	6	3	11	57	17	60	–	2
1862 — January	3	4	6	65	9	68	–	1
February	25	19	29	35	53	54	4	3
March	22	10	31	43	53	53	2	-2
April	57	40	31	41	87	81	34	26
May	52	28	37	50	90	78	24	34
June	51	46	39	48	90	95	70	96
July	12	12	34	60	47	72	10	14
August	74	46	43	54	117	99	62	56
September	68	54	20	33	87	87	16	11
October	39	33	21	46	60	79	11	0
November	8	9	22	47	30	56	6	-12
December	62	38	22	59	85	97	25	12
1863 — January	30	24	16	62	47	86	9	2
February	6	9	19	65	25	74	4	-16
March	7	6	21	61	29	67	15	-3
April	8	6	20	51	28	57	10	0
May	79	52	12	37	91	89	40	47
June	35	24	13	37	48	61	35	43
July	101	59	20	48	121	107	59	80
August	18	18	30	59	47	76	14	-22
September	51	32	22	49	73	80	64	49
October	25	16	22	40	47	55	26	-37
November	42	26	12	35	54	61	16	-20
December	15	11	14	38	28	49	3	-13
1864 — January	4	5	11	33	15	38	12	3
February	8	6	12	28	20	34	11	6
March	4	3	15	34	19	37	8	0
April	14	8	18	38	32	46	61	59
May	146	102	16	26	162	128	83	103
June	145	104	20	33	165	137	59	64
July	95	65	17	42	113	108	70	37
August	69	49	21	53	90	102	94	57
September	67	40	16	48	83	88	30	-2
October	66	34	21	46	86	80	39	27
November	29	15	13	37	42	53	21	-22
December	38	20	11	41	49	60	18	-15

The sickness rates for enlisted men are seen to have increased in a nearly uninterrupted progression, until the middle of 1862, after which the average rate was not far from 19 per cent., being less in the winter and spring than during the summer and autumn. If we arrange them by months, — taking the average of the values for the three years 1862–64, but omitting the results for 1861 on account of their incompleteness, — we find the influence of the seasons strongly manifested, both for officers and men.

The average rates of sickness and of mortality from disease, thus classified by months, are shown in the next table, in which, as in that just given, these rates are represented by the proportionate number of men in each 10 000.

TABLE VIII.

Average Monthly Rates of Sickness, and of Mortality from Disease.

Month	Deaths by Disease		Sick at close of Month.	
	Officers	Men	Officers	Men
January . . .	11	53	894	1 699
February . . .	20	43	724	1 498
March	22	46	691	1 457
April	23	43	761	1 430
May	22	38	996	1 780
June	24	39	1 225	2 045
July	24	50	1 358	2 290
August . . .	31	55	1 265	2 333
September . .	19	43	1 236	2 297
October . . .	21	44	1 052	2 150
November . .	16	40	916	2 066
December . . .	16	46	866	1 984

The rate, as well as the number, of discharges for disability seems to have reached a maximum in the early part of the year 1863, after which it rapidly declined; and, during the year 1864, the average number thus discharged monthly was less than 26 in each 10 000, or scarcely more than one fourth of one per centum.

The number of desertions followed apparently a somewhat similar course to that of discharges for disability, being a maximum at nearly the same epoch, while during the year 1864 the monthly average was but 35 in each 10 000 men, or slightly above one third of one per centum. It should be stated that these numbers have been obtained by subtracting the "number of men returned from desertion" from the reported number of desertions; and that a very large number of the reported desertions at one period were probably "constructive," consisting of drafted men who failed to respond to the summons; a very large proportion of the remainder were "bounty-jumpers."

It may be remarked that the sums of the values for the Eastern and the Western armies do not always accord with the values for the total army, in the same month. This is due in part to the fact that the regiments in rendezvous near home were not included with either the Eastern or the Western army, and in part to the different method adopted for enumerating the regiments, as already explained on page 584.

The rates here deduced for the volunteer army, from the records of those organizations only whose monthly reports were on file in September 1865, may be extended to the whole body of troops, excepting only the colored men, with a near approximation to accuracy. For this purpose we make use of the table for the Strength of the army, given on pages 7, 8, and by applying the ratios just obtained to the number of white troops there given, we form our Table IX., which thus affords an independent and probably a close estimate of the actual experience of our soldiers in these respects, excepting perhaps for the first few months of the war, for which the statistics are not adequate to a trustworthy generalization.

TABLE IX.

Statistics of the White Troops as inferred from the Regimental Reports on file.

Month	Strength at close of Month		Sick at close of Month		Discharged for Disability	Deserted
	Officers	Men	Officers	Men		
1861 — June	8 780	178 220	168	8 276	2 124	2 124
July	9 920	221 080	617	15 719	3 183	6 639
August	9 961	238 039	498	17 779	3 635	2 521
September	14 114	338 886	967	29 081	2 260	1 513
October	17 686	423 314	1 080	35 402	3 552	2 100
November	19 963	483 037	1 310	51 478	2 116	1 383
December	22 151	553 849	1 573	62 679	4 126	2 114
1862 — January	23 046	553 954	2 062	79 049	2 720	598
February	25 078	588 922	1 671	64 428	4 052	1 970
March	26 207	610 793	1 919	76 373	4 346	1 303
April	26 498	612 502	2 367	89 609	4 747	2 163
May	26 437	604 563	2 868	106 663	6 100	2 240
June	25 465	568 535	3 328	113 167	5 338	4 453
July	27 130	590 470	3 574	122 340	8 219	4 410
August	30 146	657 854	3 750	132 426	7 526	6 315
September	35 472	793 528	4 562	167 672	6 999	6 555
October	38 501	851 499	4 281	169 278	10 959	11 495
November	40 255	879 745	4 025	173 134	10 926	5 490
December	40 952	874 048	4 415	179 442	11 284	7 517
1863 — January	40 979	858 021	4 786	183 874	13 205	8 529
February	41 800	841 200	4 039	165 464	14 948	7 537
March	41 915	817 085	3 447	143 560	18 482	3 987
April	42 177	797 823	3 772	121 110	13 978	2 840
May	40 457	757 543	3 533	126 888	6 688	2 348
June	39 912	735 088	3 981	134 227	4 859	2 529
July	39 138	715 862	5 178	158 850	3 021	4 474
August	38 228	706 772	4 259	156 267	4 396	2 721
September	38 425	722 575	4 557	162 146	3 671	2 182
October	39 011	748 989	3 718	151 820	3 153	2 636
November	39 651	761 349	3 541	147 930	2 657	1 400
December	40 342	779 658	2 880	133 945	2 799	975
1864 — January	39 912	797 088	2 475	121 795	3 357	1 164
February	39 259	818 741	2 120	117 244	2 789	2 121
March	39 276	858 724	2 040	117 130	3 589	1 846
April	39 504	872 496	1 956	114 122	2 600	2 844
May	40 271	893 729	4 144	169 898	1 770	2 878
June	39 175	877 825	5 375	203 480	1 782	2 721
July	37 986	850 014	5 451	219 304	1 377	2 907
August	36 183	812 817	5 203	225 638	1 601	4 389
September	34 427	797 573	4 265	202 105	1 587	2 815
October	32 564	796 436	3 553	194 012	1 880	4 388
November	31 371	804 629	2 685	183 938	1 529	3 709
December	32 015	814 985	2 577	177 748	1 850	3 268

TABLE IX. — (*Continued.*)

Month	Died during the Month — Of Wounds		Of Disease		Total		Missing in Action	
	Offic'rs	Men	Offic'rs	Men	Offic'rs	Men	Offic'rs	Men
1861 — June . . .	–	112	–	–	–	112	–	–
July . . .	–	419	–	99	–	518	148	2 419
August . .	11	54	11	357	22	411	–	97
September .	12	95	12	676	24	771	–	433
October . .	6	268	52	945	58	1 213	99	2 124
November .	11	84	45	1 664	56	1 748	17	62
December .	12	193	25	3 152	37	3 345	–	137
1862 — January .	7	202	14	3 577	21	3 779	–	50
February .	62	1 107	72	2 047	134	3 154	10	175
March . .	57	641	81	2 610	138	3 251	5	- 141
April . .	150	2 438	81	2 518	231	4 956	91	1 574
May . . .	138	1 681	99	3 017	237	4 698	63	2 062
June . . .	129	2 621	100	2 758	229	5 379	179	5 475
July . . .	34	685	94	3 574	128	4 259	28	804
August . .	222	3 006	131	3 533	353	6 539	187	3 671
September .	240	4 269	70	2 611	310	6 880	55	905
October . .	150	2 835	82	3 891	232	6 726	43	17
November .	34	782	88	4 161	122	4 943	23	- 1 091
December .	255	3 313	92	5 174	347	8 487	104	1 014
1863 — January .	124	2 094	67	5 285	191	7 379	38	174
February .	27	759	78	5 493	105	6 252	15	- 1 346
March . .	30	462	90	5 025	120	5 487	63	- 236
April . .	35	509	86	4 061	121	4 570	41	- 4
May . . .	318	3 916	50	2 795	368	6 711	162	3 591
June . . .	141	1 764	51	2 720	192	4 484	141	3 168
July . . .	396	4 237	77	3 436	473	7 673	231	5 741
August . .	67	1 244	113	4 163	180	5 407	52	- 1 576
September .	195	2 291	86	3 548	281	5 839	246	3 555
October . .	98	1 176	85	2 966	183	4 142	101	- 2 786
November .	167	1 995	48	2 657	215	4 652	63	- 1 500
December .	58	826	55	2 978	113	3 804	12	- 1 006
1864 — January .	16	428	45	2 614	61	3 042	49	232
February .	32	496	48	2 284	80	2 780	42	469
March . .	14	278	60	2 894	74	3 172	31	- 33
April . .	54	679	73	3 342	127	4 021	242	5 174
May . . .	587	9 080	66	2 324	653	11 404	334	9 223
June . . .	568	9 112	79	2 923	647	12 035	231	5 627
July . . .	362	5 559	66	3 587	428	9 146	265	3 111
August . .	249	4 015	78	4 283	327	8 298	341	4 624
September .	231	3 190	54	3 828	285	7 018	102	- 139
October . .	214	2 676	67	3 687	281	6 363	128	2 126
November .	92	1 239	40	3 001	132	4 240	65	- 1 754
December .	121	1 614	35	3 317	156	4 931	59	- 1 263

From this table we find, for the forty-three months which it comprises, the following aggregates, which probably differ but little from the truth.

	Officers	Men	Both
Killed in action, etc. .	5 726	84 444	90 170
Died of disease . . .	2 746	129 575	132 321
Total deaths	8 472	214 019	222 491
Missing in action . . .	4 106	54 959	59 065

We have already seen[1] in Table II. of Chapter I., that the total number of deaths among the soldiers there considered — being less than those here estimated upon, by the number from the Pacific slope and that from the rebel States — was about 216 000, up to the close of the year 1864, and about 239 000 for the whole duration of the war. The materials of that table were derived from those employed in our present estimate ; and if, preserving the same ratio between the troops comprised in the two tables, we adopt the estimate there given for the deaths in 1865 before the end of the war, we shall find the probable number of these to be about 23 500, making the total number of deaths among the white soldiery during the war to be 246 000. The totally independent estimates[2] of the Provost Marshal General, cited in the same place give 250 384, — affording a most satisfactory accordance.

These must not be regarded as correct estimates of the number of deaths among our soldiers in consequence of the war, since they only comprise those which occurred in the military service, and exclude the large number who lost their lives after discharge for disability or the expiration of their term of service, yet in consequence of wounds received or disease contracted in the field.

The inordinate mortality and singular susceptibility to fatal disease exhibited by the colored troops is omitted from the topics here discussed, since our materials are inadequate for the proper investigation of the subject. It may not be amiss to express the hope that some of the able medical officers of the War Department may soon make this a subject of special discussion from official data.

The aggregates of the numbers in our Table IX. do not accord well with the numbers given by the Provost Marshal General on page 79 of his Report. Since our results are only estimates, and based upon the data on file in the offices of the U. S. and State Adjutant Generals, a close agreement ought not to be expected. Probably the accordance between the two sources of information

[1] Page 10. [2] *Report*, pp. 73–83.

is as good as could reasonably have been awaited excepting for the "Missing in Action." The most plausible explanation of the discrepancy in the figures for this class is, that out of the large numbers entered on the regimental reports as gained or lost, "for causes not named," a considerable part may have been traced by the Provost Marshal General's Bureau to the category of Missing in Action. This may possibly have been done through the agency of the Paymaster's Department, since it appears from the Provost Marshal General's Report that recourse was had to the pay-rolls in preparing the tables of casualties.[1]

Our tables give the number of desertions also considerably different from those of the Provost Marshal General.

4. *Effect of Long Marches.*

The schedule of questions prepared by Mr. Olmsted was placed in the hands of three inspectors soon after the battles of Gettysburg, which took place on the 2d and 3d of July, 1863, and was designed to elicit the general effect of the hurried, and frequently severe, marches to which our men were subjected immediately before that memorable struggle. A large part of the troops there engaged had hastened from Virginia, to repel the invasion of Pennsylvania by the insurgent army. By forced marches from Fredericksburg to Gettysburg our army succeeded in maintaining its positions in the interior of the curve whose circumference the enemy was compelled to describe ; but this was only possible by dint of severe exertions, and inordinate marches, — from which the soldiers had no time to rest before engaging in the battles, which they brought to so triumphant an issue. The inspectors proceeded immediately to an investigation of the condition and experience of the several regiments, and reports were obtained as follows : —

From Dr. Isaac Fairchild .	25	regiments	of	the	6th	Army	Corps
" Mr. Wm. F. Swalm .	26	"	"	"	1st	"	"
" " " " " .	28	"	"	"	2d	"	"
" Mr. Gordon Winslow	31	"	"	"	3d	"	"
" " " " .	34	"	"	"	5th	"	"
In all	144	regiments.					

[1] Page 72.

The blank form of return used is as follows: —

1. Name of regiment.
2. Name and title of officer commanding.
3. Date of inquiry.
4. Name of Inspector.
5. Was the regiment actively engaged in the battles of July 1863, at Gettysburg? If so, on what days? How long engaged?
6. What long marches since the 10th of June up to the time of the engagement — specifying dates and distances?
7. What long marches since the engagement?
8. What supplies of food and drink taken on march?
9. Numbers excused from duty at divers periods, before, during, and since engagement, according to adjutants' records?
10. What amount of straggling in consequence of forced marches? (Numerical statements desired when practicable.)
11. Opinion of colonel or adjutant as to the effect of long marches on the health of the men.
12. Opinion of surgeon concerning the influence of long marches —
    On the number of stragglers?
    Amount of sickness?
    Character of sickness? — distinguishing such sickness from the sickness commonly prevailing.

The replies to these questions are tabulated in detail and in summary, as are likewise the special tri-monthly returns of the regimental adjutants; but in this place, only a concise abstract of the results is needful. An excellent preliminary report to the Commission on this subject was made in 1863 by Mr. O'Connell, then temporarily in charge of the statistical investigations, from the returns obtained from forty regiments.

The distances marched by the 144 regiments under consideration in less than three weeks ending with July 2, were almost without exception in long marches of from 20 to 30 miles a day, although halts for a day or two intervened in many instances. The extent of these marches may be exhibited by a table showing the number of regiments in each army corps, which traversed the several distances.

No. Miles	1st Corps	2d Corps	3d Corps	5th Corps	6th Corps	Total
Over 350	–	–	2	–	–	2
200–230	–	–	5	13	19	37
180–190	17	16	8	–	–	41
168-175	4	–	–	2	–	6
140-150	–	4	–	1	–	5
125–135	–	4	9	4	–	17
105-115	–	4	–	9	3	16
75-100	–	–	3	3	1	7
Under 60	5	–	4	2	2	13
	26	28	31	34	25	144

The 71st N. Y. Volunteers marched 365 miles before, and 210 miles after, the battle; the 3d Michigan 350 miles before, and 200 afterward.

The distances traversed in July by the same regiments after the battles of Gettysburg were as follows, being in moderate daily marches, except for a short time, while in pursuit of the enemy.

No. Miles	1st Corps	2d Corps	3d Corps	5th Corps	6th Corps	Total
Over 300	–	–	–	5	–	5
250–270	–	–	2	1	–	3
230-235	–	–	3	1	–	4
200-220	–	–	8	2	–	10
175-180	–	1	1	–	–	2
145-165	22	24	1	3	–	50
130-145	4	3	1	5	21	34
100-125	–	–	1	2	4	7
90-100	–	–	1	6	–	7
Under 75	–	–	7	–	–	7
Not stated	–	–	6	9	–	15
	26	28	31	34	25	144

During the march before the battle, the rations issued to the men consisted of "hard tack," with salt pork, and coffee in most cases; fresh beef was occasionally given to two fifths of the regiments, as shown in the following table.

	1st Corps	2d Corps	3d Corps	5th Corps	6th Corps	Total
Coffee, pork, fresh beef occasionally	6	10	12	20	9	57
Coffee, pork, salt beef	–	3	–	–	–	3
Coffee and pork	10	6	15	9	11	51
The same in insufficient quantity	–	1	1	3	4	9
Coffee but no meat	–	1	1	2	–	4
Not even coffee	–	7	–	–	–	7
Not fully stated	10	–	2	–	1	13
	26	28	31	34	25	144

Assorting these next by their general health according to the opinion of the commanding officers, we find their condition to have been —

	1st Corps	2d Corps	3d Corps	5th Corps	6th Corps	Total
Better than when in camp	3	4	1	2	6	16
As good as when in camp	10	8	16	23	8	65
Debilitated by the march	5	14	3	3	2	27
Exhausted at first, afterwards better	8	1	1	–	–	10
Imperfectly stated	–	1	10	6	9	26
	26	28	31	34	25	144

According to the opinion of the surgeon, the health of the men was —

	1st Corps	2d Corps	3d Corps	5th Corps	6th Corps	Total
Better than when in camp	–	–	3	1	–	4
As good as when in camp	17	9	9	6	5	46
Exhausted by fatigue	1	10	6	6	5	28
Exhausted at first, afterwards better	–	2	–	–	–	2
Tendency to disease developed (excl. sunstroke) .	8	6	11	14	12	51
Imperfectly stated	–	1	2	7	3	13
	26	28	31	34	25	144

The character of the diseases from which the men suffered is particularly mentioned by the surgeons, in many instances, as follows: —

	1st Corps	2d Corps	3d Corps	5th Corps	6th Corps	Total
Sunstroke	3	10	9	1	2	25
Tendency to malarial or typhoid fever	–	1	1	1	–	3
" " diarrhœa and fever	1	1	4	1	2	9
" " diarrhœa alone	17	7	6	13	6	49

Of the two regiments which made the very severe marches already mentioned, the 71st New York is reported, both by the colonel and the surgeon, to have been in as good health as when in camp, but the 3d Michigan suffered from sunstroke, from malarial fever, and from diarrhœa. The latter had rations of hard tack, coffee, and salt pork; the former had in addition to these fresh beef from time to time.

In order to discover to what extent the endurance of the men was affected by the character of the rations furnished them, we will first tabulate the same reports in such a way as to exhibit an assortment according to the statement of the commanding officers as to the sanitary condition of the regiments, receiving each class of rations. In the column "rations" are named all articles of diet furnished, with the exception of hard tack, which was the staple for all. The men had no opportunities for getting food from the country through which they marched. The other columns refer to the grades of health as given in our previous table of statements by commanding officers: —

a denoting condition better than when in camp,
b denoting condition quite as good as when in camp,
c denoting that they suffered from exhaustion,
d denoting that condition was good after a preliminary exhaustion,
n denoting that our information is inadequate.

Rations	*a*	*b*	*c*	*d*	*n*	Total
Coffee, pork, fresh beef occasionally .	6	33	6	2	10	57
Coffee, pork, salt beef	–	1	2	–	–	3
Coffee and pork	4	20	8	6	13	51
The same, in insufficient quantity .	2	2	2	–	3	9
Coffee but no meat	1	1	2	–	–	4
Not even coffee	–	1	6	–	–	7
Not fully stated	3	7	1	2	–	13
	16	65	27	10	26	144

Considering next the statements of the surgeons, and assorting these similarly, we have the next table, which differs only from the preceding one in its arrangement in that it contains an additional column, *e*, to indicate the number of regiments in which a decided tendency was manifested toward the development of disease.

Rations	*a*	*b*	*c*	*d*	*e*	*n*	Total
Coffee, pork, fresh beef occasionally .	2	21	8	2	18	6	57
Coffee, pork, salt beef	–	3	–	–	–	–	3
Coffee and pork	2	12	13	–	19	5	51
The same, in insufficient quantity .	–	2	2	–	5	–	9
Coffee but no meat	–	–	1	–	2	1	4
Not even coffee	–	–	2	–	4	1	7
Not fully stated	–	8	2	–	3	–	13
	4	46	28	2	51	13	144

As to the character of the diseases manifested we have information regarding 86 regiments; but our tabular view which follows includes merely those 51 regiments which manifested a decided tendency to disease in consequence of the march, together with 24 additional ones reported to have suffered from sunstroke, although their health in other respects was as good as when in camp.

Rations	No. Regt's	Sun-stroke	Malarial or Typhoid Fever	Diarrhœa and Fever	Diarrhœa alone
Coffee, pork, fresh beef occasionally .	57	3	1	2	15
Coffee, pork, salt beef	3	1	–	–	–
Coffee and pork	51	10	2	5	12
The same, in insufficient quantity .	9	1	–	–	5
Coffee but no meat	4		–	1	1
Not even coffee	7	5	–	1	3
Not fully stated	13	4	–	–	3
	144	24	3	9	39

Three New York regiments of the second Army Corps were so much exhausted by their march of 186 miles as to be unfitted for duty on arrival. One of these had received rations of coffee, corned beef, and pork; one, of coffee and pork; and the third neither coffee nor meat. Apart from the temporary exhaustion the physical health of the first two was good; the last suffered severely from sunstroke.

The data thus presented seem to warrant some hygienic inferences.

Of the 57 regiments whose rations comprised fresh meat, 39 in the opinion of their colonels, and 23 in that of their surgeons, enjoyed as good health as when in camp, or even better. There were but three which suffered seriously from sunstroke, and of the 18 regiments which seemed to incur disease by the march, all but three suffered only from simple diarrhœa. Yet these severe marches were under a midsummer sun, in a warmer latitude than that to which the men belonged.

The three regiments to which two kinds of salted meat were furnished, did not suffer in general health, although two of them were for a time extremely exhausted.

Of the 51 regiments which received no meat excepting salt pork in full rations, 24 in the opinion of their colonel, and 14 in that of their surgeon, did not suffer in health from the march otherwise than by sunstroke, but 10 of them suffered severely from this affliction. The same is true of 4 according to the colonel, and 2 according to the surgeon, of those regiments which were placed upon short rations of the same kind. Special tendency to disease was manifested in 19 of these regiments, seven of them suffering from malarial or typhoid fever.

Of the 20 regiments whose supply of meat was either wanting or insufficient, there are but 7 whose health is reported as not impaired by the march, although some of these marched but a comparatively short distance.

The 16 regiments reported by their colonels as having actually gained in health by the march, had marched upon an average 170 miles, and 6 of them more than 200 miles, previous to the battle: 6 had received fresh meat. The 4 regiments so reported by their surgeon, had marched on the average 180, and 2 of them above 214 miles. Two of these had received fresh meat.

There were 25 others concerning which the colonels and surgeons coincided in the opinion that their physical condition was as good during and after the march as when in camp. Of these 16 (one of which marched 365 miles in 21 days) had received fresh meat as well as salt pork, and we have no information as to the diet of 4 others. Five of them had salt pork but no fresh meat.

The regiments which appear to have suffered especially from foot-soreness are 25 in number. The statistics of these indicate no connection between the suffering on this account, and the diet;

nor do those regiments appear to have been most troubled in this way, whose marches had been the longest.

In a large number of cases where the only prevalent disease was diarrhœa, this was ascribed by the surgeons to the immoderate use of cold water.

All accounts agree in representing the spirits of the army on the march as excellent. They bore their hardships cheerfully and hopefully, and the officers very generally attributed the good health of the men in a great degree to their state of mind, and confident anticipation of the decisive victory.

TABLES FOR CONVERTING INCHES INTO CENTIMETERS, AND THE REVERSE.

Inches into Centimeters.

1 inch = 0.02539979 m.

Inches	Centimeters	Inches	Centimeters	Inches	Centimeters
1	2.54	10	25.40	110	279.40
2	5.08	20	50.80	120	304.80
3	7.62	30	76.20	130	330.20
4	10.16	40	101.60	140	355.60
5	12.70	50	127.00	150	381.00
6	15.24	60	152.40	160	406.40
7	17.80	70	177.80	170	431.80
8	20.32	80	203.20	180	457.20
9	22.86	90	228.60	190	482.60
10	25.40	100	254.00	200	508.00

Centimeters into Inches.

1 meter = 39.3704 in.

Centim.	Inches	Centim.	Inches	Centim.	Inches
1	0.394	10	3.937	110	43.307
2	0.787	20	7.874	120	47.244
3	1.181	30	11.811	130	51.182
4	1.575	40	15.748	140	55.119
5	1.968	50	19.685	150	59.056
6	2.362	60	23.622	160	62.993
7	2.756	70	27.559	170	66.930
8	3.150	80	31.496	180	70.867
9	3.543	90	35.433	190	74.804
10	3.937	100	39.370	200	78.741

TABLES FOR CONVERTING POUNDS INTO KILOGRAMS, AND THE REVERSE.

Pounds into Kilograms.

1 lb. = 453.59264 g.

Pounds	Kilograms	Pounds	Kilograms	Pounds	Kilograms
1	0.45	10	4.54	100	45.36
2	0.91	20	9.07	200	90.72
3	1.36	30	13.61	300	136.08
4	1.81	40	18.14	400	181.44
5	2.27	50	22.67	500	226.75
6	2.72	60	27.22	600	272.16
7	3.18	70	31.75	700	317.51
8	3.63	80	36.29	800	362.87
9	4.08	90	40.82	900	408.23
10	4.54	100	45.36	1 000	453.59

Kilograms into Pounds.

1 kilogr. = 2.2046213 lbs.

Kilograms	Pounds	Kilograms	Pounds	Kilograms	Pounds
1	2.20	10	22.05	71	156.53
2	4.41	20	44.09	72	158.73
3	6.61	30	66.14	73	160.94
4	8.82	40	88.18	74	163.14
5	11.02	50	110.23	75	165.35
6	13.23	60	132.28	76	167.55
7	15.43	70	154.32	77	169.76
8	17.64	80	176.37	78	171.60
9	19.84	90	198.42	79	174.16
10	22.05	100	220.46	80	176.37

SYNOPSIS.

CHAPTER I.

MILITARY POPULATION AND ENLISTMENTS IN THE LOYAL STATES, AS DEDUCED FROM OFFICIAL REPORTS.

CHAPTER II.

NATIVITY OF UNITED STATES VOLUNTEERS.

CHAPTER III.

AGES OF THE ORIGINAL VOLUNTEERS.

CHAPTER IV.

AGES OF RECRUITS.

Order of other nativities by time of growth.
Similar inferences deduced from tabulation by States of enlistment.
This investigation is based upon an assumption.
Objection to this assumption, and answer to the objection.
Note illustrating the correctness of this answer.
More satisfactory answer afforded by manuscript tables.
The relative number of tall men slowly increases with the age.
This increase shows no superior vitality in this class.
Upon facts now presented, our knowledge of Law of Growth for the average man depends.
Inferences from the average of men may not apply to the average man.
Lehmann's memoir on application to individuals, of laws deduced from averages.
These laws may fail to indicate striking and unfailing phenomena.
Illustration from shoot in growth at entrance upon manhood.
The curve for any individual has two branches, meeting in a cusp.
This cusp is obliterated in the mean of many individuals.
The curve for such a mean shows no token of any shoot.
The epoch in question may be physiologically considered as a new birth.
May not a sudden accession of growth take place at other epochs?
Is there such an accession at the second dentition?
The curve of stature suggests some such phenomenon at about 24.
Growth in stature perhaps not fully terminated during life.
Influences which would conceal its effect.
The increase in length of the larger bones may cease at an earlier date.
Evidence of increase in stature after ossification of the epiphyses.
These hypotheses explain the diminution in height at 24.

5. FULL STATURE. 118

The full stature of man has been hitherto undetermined for any nationality.
Various statements by different authorities.
Wide range and uncertainty of these statements.
Even here the ages proper for deducing full stature are uncertain.
Suggestion of Dr. Villermé, that comfort and ease increase full stature, and hasten its attainment.
This idea not entirely confirmed by present results.
An element of correctness in it is indicated by our results for sailors.
Limits of age adopted in deducing full statures.
TABLE IX. — *Mean Statures for different Periods of Age, by States.* 122
TABLE X. — *Mean Statures for different Periods of Age, by Nativities.* 123
The decrease in stature after 45 years, exerts small influence here.
Its effect, supposing a given decrease in all soldiers over 45.
Principle adopted in computing the full statures.
TABLE XI. — *Full Statures, for Soldiers of* 18 *different States and* 14 *different Nativities.* 125
The full stature for any nativity seems to vary in different States.
This inference confirmed by the 684 manuscript tables of height and age.
TABLE XII. — *Statures of Natives of New England States, by Ages and Regions where enlisted.* 126
TABLE XIII. — *Statures of Natives of New York, by Ages and Regions where enlisted.* 127
Stature dependent both upon ancestry and influences during growth.
Residence in Western States during growth tends to increase stature.
Similar influences exist probably in many Southern States.
Those States which produce highest stature for natives, tend most to increase stature of immigrants.
No geographical law indicated in the order of relative full statures.
Possible explanation of the phenomenon by character of the soil.
Effect of residence in America upon stature of Europeans.
TABLE XIV. — *Full Statures of Irish and Germans enlisting in Eight different States, compared with each other, and with Natives of these States enlisting at Home.* 128

Similar phenomenon for natives of adjacent States, here aggregated.
TABLE XV. — *Comparison of Statures of Natives of Ohio and Indiana, enlisting in Indiana.* 129
Attempts to compare statures of men enlisted in cities and in country.
Other desirable researches, now found impossible.
Results of measures of students at Cambridge, England, and at Edinburgh.
Measurement of students at Harvard and Yale Colleges.
TABLE XVI. — *Heights of Harvard and Yale Students.* 130
Resultant mean statures for each year of age.
The same by periods of age.
Extreme statures found among these students.
Summary of inferences regarding full stature.
It does not chiefly depend upon the temperature of a region.
Nor is the nationality a controlling influence.
Nor does it depend upon the degree of comfort, as principal agency.
Nor upon the elevation of the district.
Yet all these influences doubtless contribute to the general result.

6. STATURE OF SAILORS. 132

Mean heights of men on New York naval musters, less than those of soldiers.
The difference averages an inch and a quarter for each age.
Table of excess in stature of New York soldiers over sailors, at each age.
Delay of development and real defect of full stature in sailors.
Collection of statures, and ages of sailors elsewhere enlisted.
Assistance of officers of the Navy Department.
Statistics of sailors collected, and their classification.
Epochs of full stature for different classes of sailors.
Explanation of these phenomena.
Note on ages of full stature for sailors of different nativities.
Table of these ages for 18 nativities, in three classes of sailors.
TABLE XVII. — *Heights of Sailors, by Ages and Nativities.* 135
TABLE XVIII. — *Heights of "Landsmen," by Periods of Age and Nativities.* 141
TABLE XIX. — *Heights of "Seamen," by Periods of Age and Nativities.* 142
TABLE XX. — *Heights of Sailors, by Periods of Age and Nativities.* 143
Inferior stature of sailors explained by enlistment of short men.
This explanation inadequate to account for all the facts observed.
The difference in height of soldiers and sailors, found after excluding from the data all statures above 66 inches.

9. STATURE OF OTHER RACES OF MEN. 144

Height of Laplanders and Patagonians, according to Tenon.
Esquimaux, according to Pauw.
Natives of Pacific Coasts, according to Rollin, of La Pérouse's expedition.
Chayma and Caribe Indians, according to Humboldt.
Patagonians, according to various authorities. D'Orbigny's observations.
Puelches, according to D'Orbigny.
Various races of South American Indians, according to D'Orbigny.
New Zealanders, according to Thomson.
Bushmen, according to Freycinet.
Obongoes, according to Du Chaillu.
Data in War Department might give stature and law of growth for negroes.
Descriptive musters are probably there for 180 000 colored men.
Access to these refused to the Commission by Mr. Stanton.
Data accessible only for 40 000 soldiers, and 4 000 sailors.
This number inadequate, on account of the large numbers of mixed race
Several varieties of negro in the Southern States.
These are intermixed with each other, and with Indian races.

TABLE XXXV. — *Number of Soldiers below* 61 *Inches, by Ages and States.* 170

TABLE XXXVI. — *Proportional Number of the same, in each* 10 000 *of same Age and State.* 172

TABLE XXXVII. — *Number of Soldiers below* 61 *Inches, by Ages and Nativities.* 174

TABLE XXXVIII. — *Proportional Number of the same in each* 10 000 *of same Age and Nativity.* 176

Influence, upon mean statures, of excluding all men below a given height.

Most statistics of height are derived from military records.

Some lower, but no upper, limit of height has there been prescribed.

Other conditions to be considered, in instituting comparisons.

Only men of the same age, or full stature, should be compared for determining differences of class.

SUPPLEMENTARY NOTES. 179

Memoir of Boudin, upon stature and weight of various peoples.

This memoir obtained too late for use in the preceding pages.

Notes to § 3, *Heights by Nativities.*

Mean stature of French conscripts from 1818 to 1828.

Mean age of the same, and inferior limit of stature.

Mean stature of French conscripts from 1831 to 1862.

Mean age of the same, and inferior limit of stature.

Natives of France in United States Army, taller than those of same age in France.

This inference not affected by our aggregation of French with Belgians.

This excess for Frenchmen aged 20, is nearly 3 centimeters.

The inference here accords with that deduced from other sources.

Relative statures of English, Irish, and French, from official documents.

Wide variance of these results from those here deduced.

Collation of our own statistics with the official British tables.

Explanation of Table XXXIX.

TABLE XXXIX. — *Comparative Distribution of Irish Soldiers, by Stature.* 181

Totally different distribution of statures in the American and British armies.

This is made manifest by the next table. Explanation.

TABLE XL. — *Comparative Distribution of Irish Soldiers, by Age.* 182

Inferences from this table.

Difference in distribution by statures, explained by the distribution by ages.

Number of Irish recruits to American army, above 25 years old, greater than that below 21 years to British army.

This fact accounts for the diversity in distribution by stature.

Alleged enormous difference in stature between English and French armies.

No account was taken of a difference of 4½ inches in lower limit of height.

Nor was regard had to the great difference in the mean age.

Yet the largest group is between 64 and 65 inches for each nation.

The case affords a good example of the misuse of statistical results.

Remark of Bischoff as to deductions from statistics of recruiting.

Notes to § 5. *Full Statures.* 183

Boudin's inferences regarding Villermé's theory are the same as ours.

His estimate of local influences upon stature is far below ours.

Notes to § 7. *Stature of other Races of Men.* 184

Mean stature of Esquimaux, according to Pauw.

Mean stature of Sepoy regiments in India.

The high limit of minimum stature here forbids ethnical inferences.

Notes to § 8. *Extremes of Stature.* 184

Discussion of geographical distribution of tall men in France.

Boudin finds ground for belief that the governing influences are hereditary rather than physiological.

Illustrations of this theory.

Ratio of recruits of minimum height in Brittany and in Normandy.

Different proportion of excessive statures in different districts.

The slopes of the Jura furnish the tallest men of France.
They also give the maximum number above the average height.
Similar inferences deducible from Belgian and Prussian military statistics.
These facts are analogous to those deducible from our own investigations.
But the effect of local influences is here seen to be as great as that of race or stock.

CHAPTER VI.

COMPLEXIONS, COLOR OF HAIR AND EYES.

Descriptive musters not made out in early part of the war.
These musters may increase our anthropological knowledge.
The descriptions tabulated by clerks who collected ages and statures.
No attempts made to render this collection complete.
Descriptive musters for about 669 000 men transcribed at different State Capitals.
Volunteers are distinguished from recruits in the tabulations.
The volunteers are of the later class; earlier ones not being described.
Recruits are of the earlier class; the later not being collected.
Above 425 000 volunteers here described, and about 243 000 recruits.
Results are presented in two forms; by States and by Nativities.

Deductions from these tables must be drawn with caution.
The descriptions were evidently entered very loosely in most cases.
Illustrations of this fact.
Proper caution will obviate danger of important error.
Marked and real differences between men from different States.
Differences in color of hair and color of eyes.

Variations between different nativities much more marked.
Comparison of natives of Scandinavia and Iberia.

CHAPTER VII.

PREVIOUS OCCUPATIONS. 208

Materials for this inquiry were obtained from descriptive musters.
Manner of classification.
Instructions for the collection of materials.
Occupations of two thirds of a million of our soldiers here assorted.
One half per cent. were officers who never served in the ranks.
Number of original commissioned officers from the "professional" class.
The enlisted rolls here tabulated do not fairly represent this class.
Explanation of the disproportion of the numbers here given.
True proportion of the professional class in the ranks.
It was probably about 94 for the whole army, and 102 for recruits.
For officers and men together it was probably about 3.2 per cent.
Large enlistments from seminaries of learning.
About three tenths of the enlisted men were under 21 years old.
The occupations of these were not definitely fixed.
Table I. — *Occupations of Volunteers, by States.* 210
Table II. — *Occupations of Recruits, by States.* 211
Table III. — *Occupations of U. S. Soldiers, by States.* 212
Table IV. — *Occupations of Volunteers, by Nativities.* 213
Table V. — *Occupations of Recruits, by Nativities.* 214
Table VI. — *Occupations of U. S. Soldiers, by Nativities.* 215
Table VII. — *Proportionate Numbers for different Occupations, by States.* 216
Table VIII. — *Proportionate Numbers for different Occupations, by Nativities.* 217

CHAPTER VIII.

MEAN DIMENSIONS OF BODY.

1. History of the Investigation. 218

Schedule of inquiries prepared by Messrs. Olmsted and Elliott.
Investigations had been commenced by Professor Henry.
Instruments constructed under Professor Bache's superintendence.
Two inspectors appointed, and duties assigned them.
Inquiry as to both physical and social characteristics of the men.
Copy of Form [E].
The author appointed Actuary to the Sanitary Commission in June 1864.
Extract from his first Report.
Number of men then examined and condition of the records.
Recommendations concerning prosecution of these inquiries.
Unity of method insisted on; more precise queries; and more activity.
Examination of colored men, and appointment of a chief examiner.
Twelve sets of instruments, and twelve examiners authorized.
Modification of the apparatus and schedule of qüestions.
Disadvantages from want of special training on part of the author.
Difficulty of obtaining apparatus promptly.
Measurements were made in inches instead of centimeters.
Regret that the metric system was not exclusively employed.
Copy of new schedule, "Form [EE]."
Dr. Buckley appointed chief examiner; — all examiners to practice with him.
Copy of "Instructions to Examiners."
The end of war soon ended opportunities for examinations.
Number of men measured and otherwise examined according to the new form.
Policy adopted in assignment of duties to the examiners.
Assistance and opportunities afforded by military officers.

Cordial and effective aid of naval authorities.
It was otherwise where permission from the Secretary of War was required.
Valuable opportunities, and important information were thus lost.
Mode of primary tabulation.
Classification of the results by nativities, like the statures.
Characteristic differences among men examined by Form [E].
Impossible to discover how far these were due to the examiners.
Errors of this sort doubtless exist to a considerable extent.
The personal differences have been determined for many dimensions.
Mean values, and assortment of individual discordances therefrom.
Objects and results of this assortment.
The computations would be more instructive were the ages considered.
Best mode of research was precluded by pecuniary considerations.
The materials are available for use of future inquirers.
Question to be investigated.
Reference of all the measurements to the stature as unit of length.
Proportions as well as dimensions thus determined for nearly 24 000 men.
Usefulness and success of this part of the work.
Its great extent and laborious character.
Much more might have been effectively done, had time and means allowed.
Results of the measurements by the Novara expedition hoped for.
Apparatus used has been distributed to institutions of learning.
Similar examinations of other races expected.

2. Measurements obtained. 232

Examinations of the earlier series (by Form [EE]).
Detailed statement of number of men measured.
Publication of some of the results, by Mr. Elliott.
Personal differences between examiners in mode of measurement.
Examples of influence of this source of error.
Vain attempts to determine difference between Messrs. Buckley and Fairchild.
Discordances between results of the earlier and of the later examinations.
They may often be explained by the phraseology of the questions.
Instruments used in the measurements.
Andrometer. Its graduation.
Great delay in construction of the apparatus.
The later series of measures chiefly made in first eight months of 1865.
Examiners appointed. Practice with Dr. Buckley.
Stations and transfers of the several examiners.
Measures of students at Cambridge and New Haven.
Measures of Southern-born men at New Orleans.
Measures of Iroquois Indians in Western New York.
Classified statement of materials collected in the later series.
Manner of measuring.
Number of cases, assorted according to amount of clothing.
Proportionate number of men of various nativities.
Dimensions wrongly measured. These measurements made available.
Tabulation of the returns kept up without intermission.
Mean results for the several examiners frequently collated.
Relative trustworthiness of the two series of measures.
Classification by nativities different for the two series.
Actual and linear dimensions only, are discussed in this chapter.
Inferences legitimately deducible from these materials.
The present work does not claim to be a thorough discussion.
It aims at furnishing materials in a form convenient for the investigator.

3. Averages, Types, etc. 240

The value of our results depends upon the correctness with which their means represent normal dimensions.

A numerical measure of the degree of approximation is important.
True significance of averages. Criterion for typical character.
Laws of error illustrated by distribution of shots at a target.
Laws deducible from experience whatever mark has been aimed at.
The point of aim is indicated by the average of results.
If the real and intended points coincide, correctness of aim is shown.
The difference between the two shows the personal error.
Influences of the accidental class which affect single cases.
Character of distribution of single shots around their mean.
Regular and known law of decrease of their number with the distance.
Nature and limits of application of this law. Measure of precision.
In the case cited, regularity, not correctness, of aim is measured.
Accordance with law of error affords a criterion for value of the mean.
Illustration extended to the mean of many individual means.
Here the same law is found to hold good.
The measure of precision then shows the influence of extraneous agencies.
Analogy with Laws of Nature when aiming at production of typical forms.
The manifestation of the law of error indicates typical character.
Typical forms exist throughout the organic creation.
They are susceptible of numerical determination.
Varieties in the same species correspond to constant errors of aim.
Individual dissimilarities correspond to accidental errors.
Here we seek the types of human form and physical capability.
This implies the types for many races, nationalities, classes, etc.
Our materials are chiefly limited to American soldiers, and certain ages.
Still they comprise a wide territory and varied ancestry.
The existence of a human type first demonstrated by Quetelet.
There are two sorts of mean results deducible from measurement.
The mean of many measures of one object represents a material thing.
That of measures of many similar objects represents only an ideal.
The idea of a type practically abolishes this wide distinction.
Quetelet's illustration by measurements of a statue.
The human type, and types of classes and races may thus be discovered.
Here we seek only the type of some physical manifestations.
That of external form is a standard of beauty and model for art.
Quetelet has shown that the mental and moral type may be investigated.
He is thus the founder of Social Science, in the true sense of this term.
Statistical investigation a safe method only when it demonstrably elicits some type or law.
The discredit, in which some hold it, is due to its misapplication.
It is the only mode of discovering or demonstrating many and various laws.
The average man. Computation of theoretical variations.
General formula for law of error. Probability of any given discordance.
Tables of numerical value of such probability.
Probable error, mean error, probable error of mean.
Necessary, though incorrect, assumption of adequate measurements.
Assortment of the several measures by magnitude. Determination of r, e, and r_0.
Cautions as to interpretation of results.
Degree of typical character is shown by accordance with law of error.
This accordance is susceptible of numerical expression.

Number examined in the later series; number of examiners.
Those in, and those not in, usual vigor, have been discussed separately.
Number of men in each of these classes.
Classification by nativities.
Details of incomplete and erroneous measurements.
Number of white soldiers included in the earlier series.

5. SAILORS. 286

Their mean height is less than that of the soldiers by 1.14 inches.
The mean stature of the marines is between that of soldiers and sailors.
Larger value for mean distance between finger-tip and patella.
Greater length of legs observed in sailors; and possible explanation.
Table of mean values of the dimension 4½, for soldiers and sailors.
These values are in large excess for sailors in each nativity.
Table of mean height to perinæum, for soldiers and sailors.
Table of mean distance from middle of sternum to finger-tip, for same.
The legs were actually as well as relatively longer in sailors.
The excess of length is in the thigh, and not below the knee.
Table of mean distance from knee to perinæum for soldiers and sailors.
Relative lengths of the thigh and the leg below the knee.
The neck is larger for sailors.
Length of arm and hand is both actually and relatively less.
Table of mean lengths of arm and hand for soldiers and sailors.
Table of mean length of upper arm for the same.
Distance from perinæum to pubes.
Actual and relative mean value of this dimension from 1013 sailors.
Mean distance between nipples, and ratio to circumference of chest.
This mean distance smaller than for soldiers, but the ratio is greater.
The foot-dimensions resemble those of soldiers, but thickness is greater.
TABLE III. — *Mean Dimensions of Sailors.* 291

6. STUDENTS. 294

Occasion of the measurements. Data collected.
Full stature corresponding to the mean height at the mean age.
Reason why these numbers are only roughly approximate, and too small.
Nativities of the students measured.
The students nearly an inch taller than soldiers of same nativity.
Other points of difference in the mean dimensions.
Table of mean distance between nipples, and its ratio to circumference.
Comparison between the students of the two universities.
TABLE IV. — *Mean Dimensions of Students of Harvard and Yale Colleges.* 296

7. COLORED SOLDIERS. 297

Endeavors to assort and classify the materials with more nicety.
Different races of negroes in the Southern States.
Admixture with each other, and with the white and various red races.
Final assortment in two classes, full blacks, and men of mixed race.
Natives of free and slave States separately considered.
Those not in ordinary health, and those examined naked, are distinguished.
Average height less than as deduced from more copious data in Chapter V.
The material on file at Washington would be very valuable.
All access to rolls in War Department was denied the Commission.
Distance from tip of finger to upper margin of patella.
This dimension the most striking in its contrast between the races.
Mean value, maximum, and minimum for full blacks and mulattoes.
The mean value is less for natives of the late slave States.
Table of comparison for natives of free and slave States.
Length of head and neck, and length of body.
Both of these are less for the colored men than for the whites.
For the full blacks they are less than for the mixed races.
Table of mean length of body.
Men examined in New Orleans after the close of the war.
Height to perinæum is greater than for white men.
The excess is both in length of thigh, and in the height to knee.
Table of mean heights to perinæum and to knee.
Distance from perinæum to pubes greater than for whites.

The mean age is usually below that of full stature.
Therefore the mean dimensions are smaller than belong to mean age.
The dimensions, when expressed in terms of the stature show less variation.
This assumes a proportional growth for all parts after age of 18.
Also that the same type of form belongs to men of the same class.
Our assumption may be tested by the law of probability.
If warrantable, we may determine the normal form apart from its magnitude.
If unwarrantable, this fact will be disclosed by the discordances.
Characteristic differences between human types thus manifested.
Exceptions to this statement.
The limits of normal variation form part of the typical character.
Small comparative variation in size of the head.
Height to the 7th cervical vertebra might have been a better unit.
The results of Chapter V. are directly applicable to those found here.
Reduction of measurements of 23 685 men to decimals of stature.
Necessary hypothesis. Its test possible and desirable.
The records of relative dimensions are carefully preserved.
Tables of assortment computed for each dimension.
Amount of labor involved. Satisfactory character of results.
A close approximation to typical proportions seems attained.
The present research does not aim at any exhaustive discussion.
Opportunity for obtaining important anthropological knowledge.
The classes and races are here considered in same order as in Chapter VIII.
Scale of relative dimensions published by Bougery and Jacob.
Their values in general corroborated by those here deduced.

2. WHITE SOLDIERS. 325

Head and Neck.
Extreme range of the mean values in the nineteen groups.
This range is less than one seventh of that in the actual dimensions.
Constancy of the mean value in all the larger groups.
Maximum and minimum mean values for the nativity-groups.
Probable variation for individuals and probable error of mean.
Discordances found in actual dimensions disappear in the relative.
Results deduced from the earlier series.
Length of Body. 325
Table of results for different nativities, from each series.
Predominance for certain nativities in Chapter VIII. is due to stature.
Distance from Finger tip to Patella. 326
Variable character of this dimension. Its limits.
Probable individual variation; error of mean.
Height to Perinæum. 327
Values for different nativity-groups.
Probable variation and error of mean. Extreme values.
Results from the earlier series of measures.
Perinæum to Pubes. 327
Value for sailors only, among white men.
Corresponding total height to pubes.
Height to Knee. 327
Average proportional value; range of variation with nativity.
Probable variation and error of mean.
Table of ratios between height to knee and length of thigh.
These ratios differ from those deduced from actual dimensions.
Breadth of Neck. 328
Mean value; variation for different nativities.
Probable variation and error of mean.
Results of the earlier series of measures.
Girth of Neck. 328

Order of classes and races examined, according to distance between eyes.
The same according to relative length of feet.
Red man preeminent in length of body and of arms; black man in that of legs.
Classification by mobility of thorax.
Superiority of the white race in this respect; inferiority of mulattoes.
Large diversity in the dimension 4½ among white men.
Only the soldiers represent the population of the land.
Difference between dimension 4½ and the height to neck less than that to knees.
The soldiers differ here from the other classes in the slope of shoulders.
The mean values of.
They may be safely adopted for scientific or artistic purposes.
Numerical determinations desirable in biological researches.
The statistical method also applicable to researches in inanimate nature.
Many individuals are needed for determining normal limits of variation.
Absurdity of determining characteristics of a type from a single specimen.
The fact of typicality must be established, as well as the type.
Simple numerical ratios exist in the human type only approximately.
Freedom of the creative energy; only limited when a purpose is to be attained.
Symmetry and harmony are perfect when requisite; otherwise dispensed with.
Incommensurability not inconsistent with nature's higher symmetry.
Supposed harmonic relations not confirmed by these investigations.
Carus regards the normal dimensions as measurable by the length of hand.
Table of his results with their equivalents in decimals of stature.
These are near approximations to the true values.
The smallness of his unit masks the small error of results.
A larger amount of material might have modified his views.
Schadow's theories in his *Polyklet*.
He considers the height of the head as two fifteenths of the stature.
We have not the height of head without the neck.
The head and neck together stand in no simple relation to the stature.
He considers the foot a better unit of measure than the head.
Vitruvius made its length one sixth of the stature.
Schadow's own measures did not confirm this hypothesis.
Our results show that it has no simple ratio to the height.
Zeising's theory of extreme and mean ratio.
Nature of this theory. Inferences therefrom.
Its analogy with deductions from phyllotaxis and similar laws in zoology.
Theoretical and inductive arguments for these views.
Zeising considers dimensions determined by muscular outlines.
Numerical proportions deducible from this theory.
Our dimensions have reference, so far as may be, to the bony frame.
Where comparable with Zeising's inferences, they do not confirm them.
Remark of Zeising as to the ideal character of his inferences.
Careful and thorough spirit exhibited in his investigations.
Yet our more copious data show an absence of simple numerical proportion.
Liharžik's theory of harmonic relations.
Results deduced regarding proportions of body.
Relations in detail between different portions of the body.
His inferences also apply to the law of growth.
Our results do not corroborate these deductions.
Liharžik's treatise on the square of 7 as the basis of human symmetry.
Brent's hypothesis of numerical ratios in proportions of the human body.
List of such ratios, supposed by him to exist.
Tested by our measurements, these also fail of confirmation.
Similar suppositions by Silbermann and others.
Beauty in organized form seems independent of simple numerical ratios.
Nor does observation render their existence probable.

CHAPTER X.

DIMENSIONS AND PROPORTIONS OF HEAD.

Wide variation of relative cranial dimensions in Table IX.
The relative circumference varies in the ratio of five to two.
The relative length over the top of head differs nearly as three and one.

4. Linear Measures of Heads of Other Races. 379

Description of the tables.
Table X. — *Mean Dimensions of the Heads of Blacks and Indians.* 380
Table XI. — *Mean Relative Dimensions of Heads of Blacks and Indians.* 380

5. General Inferences from the Linear Measures. 381

Table XII. — *Comparison of Mean Dimensions of Head.* 381
The values for white soldiers are derived from both series.
Horizontal circumference. Its significance.
Its mean value for different races varies very slightly.
Its maximum is for the full blacks; its minimum for the Indians.
The Indian breadth of face is especially large.
Width between angles of jaws, for students, affected by personal error.
This width is smallest for white men.
Width between the condyloid processes smallest for blacks.
These relations are simple when width at the hinge is considered.
Frontal semicircumference small for all the white groups.
Occipital semicircumference relatively large, especially for students.
Large lateral semicircumferences in mulattoes.
Inference from these facts.
Loss of cerebral space at forehead overbalanced by shape of head.
Table XIII. — *Comparison of Proportional Dimensions of Head.* 383
Explanation of the preceding table.
Ethnical distinctions appear manifest in each of the nine columns.
Comments upon these characteristic differences.
Position of mulattoes relatively to their component races.
They frequently differ more from the whites than the full blacks do.
The last six columns of Table XIII. contain ratios only.
Frontal circumference smaller than the occipital in white men.
With Indians, full blacks, and mulattoes, the reverse is the case.
Ratios of the transverse semicircumferences to their common diameter.
Ratios of the longitudinal to the transverse semicircumference.
Ratios of the horizontal to the transverse semicircumference.
Ratios of the two longitudinal peripheries in perpendicular planes.

6. Facial Angles. 384

Unsatisfactory character and discordance of the recorded measures.
The personal differences have however proved tolerably constant.
Instrument contrived for measuring facial angles.
Description of the manner of its use.
The measures in the earlier series are especially discordant.
Amount of the discrepancy, and consequent untrustworthiness.
The results of earlier series are only given solely for their historical interest.
Probable origin of the discordances.
Table XIV. — *Mean Facial Angles according to the Earlier Series.* 387
The later series contains two classes of results.
In the first and smaller, the superciliary ridge was used for measuring the angle.
In the second, the frontal eminence was used.
Investigation of personal differences for the second class.
Reference to the mean of seven examiners, for white soldiers and sailors.
Method of computation.
Second method employed as a control; accordance of the results.
Table of corrections thus obtained, for each examiner and each nativity.

CHAPTER XI.

WEIGHT AND STRENGTH.

CHAPTER XII.

PULMONARY CAPACITY.

TABLE VI. — *Pulmonary Capacity of Negroes in Usual Vigor, by Height.* 478
TABLE VII. — *Pulmonary Capacity of Indians in Usual Vigor, by Height.* 479
The number of Indians did not allow symmetrical distribution by stature.
This fact is also manifest in difference from whites, in capacity of lungs.
We may construct normal curves of lung-capacity graphically.
These show that it increases regularly with the height.
The rate for white men is about 6 cubic inches for each inch of stature.
The values in the next table have thus been deduced.
TABLE VIII. — *Empirical Determination of Pulmonary Capacity, by Stature.* 480
Close accordance between these empirical values and those observed.
Inferior limit of application of this law.

3. RELATION TO LENGTH OF BODY. 480

Differences in height are dependent upon the length of the legs.
Hence dimensions of thorax would seem a better basis of assortment.
Hutchinson's investigations led him to reject this idea.
He inferred that size of chest has no relation to pulmonary capacity.
Quotations from his memoir, bearing on this point.
Our more copious materials demanded a repetition of this inquiry.
The results are contained in the next following section.
Tabulation of our results according to the length of the body proper.
This length is the distance from perinæum to 7th cervical vertebra.
Its variation in individuals is more restricted than that of the height.
Inferences from this tabulation.
Pulmonary capacity is less related to length of body than to height.
A graphic representation of this relation shows not a straight but a curved line.
The accordance with individual determinations is not so good.
The maximum capacity belongs to a length of body of about 30 inches.
TABLE IX. — *Pulmonary Capacity of White Soldiers, by Length of Body.* 482
TABLE X. — *Pulmonary Capacity of White Men, by Length of Body* 483
TABLE XI. — *Pulmonary Capacity of Negroes, by Length of Body.* 484
TABLE XII. — *Pulmonary Capacity of Indians, by Length of Body.* 485
TABLE XIII. — *Empirical Determination of Pulmonary Capacity, by Length of Body* 486
Length of body seems related to lung-capacity, only as representing a mean stature.
Men of same stature do not show a capacity varying with length of body.
Men of the same length of body do not show a capacity varying with stature.
TABLE XIV. — *Pulmonary Capacity, by Length of Body, for White Soldiers 67 Inches high.* 487

4. RELATION TO CIRCUMFERENCE OF CHEST.

Mean circumference of chest for white men in usual vigor.
The same relation is not indicated for the physical dimensions as for stature.
This is shown by the facts developed in the last section.
The range of variation, for a given stature, often exceeds that of the stature itself.
This circumstance explains the apparent difficulty.
The ratio of girth of chest to height is subject to great fluctuations.
Hutchinson's inference and explanation.
Our results do not corroborate the general inference.
This will be seen from the next five tables.
The relation of lung-capacity to circumference of chest is clearly marked.
The curve which represents it for white soldiers differs little from a straight line.
TABLE XV. — *Pulmonary Capacity of White Soldiers, by Circumference of Chest.* 489
TABLE XVI. — *Pulmonary Capacity of White Men, by Circumference of Chest.* 490
TABLE XVII. — *Pulmonary Capacity of Negroes, by Circumference of Chest.* 491
TABLE XVIII. — *Pulmonary Capacity of Indians, by Circumference of Chest.* 492
TABLE XIX. — *Empirical Determination of Pulmonary Capacity, by Circumference of Chest.* 493

5. Relation to Play of Chest.

Difference between "play of chest" and actual change in size of thorax.
One is the difference between exterior girth at full inspiration and at full expiration.
The other expansion is both laterally and downwards.
Ordinary breathing is accomplished by a different process from that here used.
In unconscious respiration the expansion is chiefly downward.
And the lateral expansion is rather abdominal than thoracic.
Motion of the ribs in men is often nearly imperceptible.
Its average amount Hutchinson found not more than one thirtieth of an inch.
The deep inspiratory movement here considered is very different.
Increase of sectional thoracic area is not proportional to that of girth.
Our results therefore apply to an unusual mode of respiration.
Yet they must bear some relation to the amount ordinarily respired.
And this latter amount cannot well be directly measured.
Tables XX.–XXII. show the mean capacity found for six classes, by play of chest.
This tabulation was originally made by tenths of inches.
Table XX. — *Pulmonary Capacity of White Men, by Play of Chest.* 495
Table XXI. — *Pulmonary Capacity of Negroes, by Play of Chest.* 496
Table XXII. — *Pulmonary Capacity of Indians, by Play of Chest.* 497
Tabular view of the mean play of chest in the several classes.
These numbers are not proportional to the average pulmonary capacity.

6. Relation to Age. 497

The maximum capacity was found by Hutchinson to be at the age of 35.
Our tabulation shows a strongly marked maximum at 21 years.
The capacity is then nearly 200 cubic inches.
Possible effect of increased strength of muscles of thorax.
Table XXIII. — *Pulmonary Capacity of White Soldiers in Usual Vigor, by Age.* 498
Table XXIV. — *Empirical Table for Pulmonary Capacity of White Men, by Age.* 499

CHAPTER XIII.

RESPIRATION AND PULSE.

1. Preliminary. 500

Uncertainty of observations of the frequency of breathing and pulse.
Very slight excitement often modifies the phenomenon.
Special precautions were enjoined upon our examiners.
Difficulty of maintaining or enforcing the needful conditions.
Manner of observation prescribed.
These sources of error cannot be supposed entirely obviated.
Indications of personal differences are perceptible.
Possible explanations of such constant differences.
Our limits preclude detailed investigation of personal errors.
Improbability that the omission will affect our mean results.
The materials remain available for future investigators.
The frequency both of pulse and breathing varies with time of day.
It is also known that these are affected by the posture.
Our observations were chiefly made while the men were standing.
But there were many exceptions to this general usage.

2. Respiration, by Age. 501

The frequency of breathing greatest in childhood.
Our results show frequency greater for soldiers below, than above, 18 years.
It would seem to decrease until puberty, and then to remain constant.

Tables of distribution, by age and frequency of respiration.
This distribution suggests some misgivings as to our results.
More than 1-90 of the records indicate above 20 respirations a minute.
For men not in full vigor the proportion is greater still.
In the majority of cases the number is stated as 24 to the minute.
Suspicions created by this circumstance.
It would seem as though the counting had been made for only part of a minute.
Injunctions were strict that it should continue for a full minute.
And the general fidelity of the examiners is well established.
Wide differences between results of the earlier and of the later series.
Hence they are separately presented in all cases.
Mr. Fairchild's results are kept distinct from those of Dr. Buckley.
The former were made in the winter, and mostly confined to prisoners.
It is also clear that the counting was during half a minute only.
TABLE I. — *Distribution by Age and Number of Respirations. Soldiers in Usual Vigor. Earlier Series.* 504
TABLE II. — *Distribution by Age and Number of Respirations. Soldiers not in Usual Vigor. Earlier Series.* 506
TABLE III. — *Distribution by Age and Number of Respirations. White Soldiers in Usual Vigor. Later Series.* 510
TABLE IV. — *Distribution by Age and Number of Respirations. White Soldiers not in Usual Vigor. Later Series.* 512
TABLE V. — *Distribution by Age and Number of Respirations. Full Blacks in Usual Vigor.* 514
TABLE VI. — *Distribution by Age and Number of Respirations. Mulattoes in Usual Vigor* 516
TABLE VII. — *Distribution by Age and Number of Respirations. Indians.* 518
For students and sailors the results are omitted.
All the students were examined by Dr. Elsner.
Illustrations of systematic error in his countings.
His observations both of pulse and respiration are rejected throughout.
All his other determinations appear entitled to full confidence.
Of the sailors all but 324 were measured by Mr. Phinney.
The circumstances were unfavorable for these observations.
Consequently no attempt was made to carry them out.
The remainder were chiefly examined by Dr. Elsner.
The negroes not in usual vigor number in these tables but 294.
This comprises both the full blacks and the mulattoes.
The two were therefore aggregated in the tabulation.
For the men in full vigor we find a wide difference between these classes.
Our tables are given in detail in order to permit and invite criticism.
They exhibit the weak points of our determinations clearly.
Results as tested by the distribution of individual cases.
Character of distribution of individual cases among white soldiers.
This seems inconsistent with a normally constant typical number.
It is equally unexplained by any supposition of carelessness.
These results are given more compactly in the next three tables.
The mean frequency of respiration seems constant during early manhood.
The greater frequency for the black race is conspicuous.
The black troops were mostly examined in a warmer climate.
Indications that white men breathe more frequently in warm regions.
Regret that our limits prevent further inquiry at present.
Mr. Fairchild's examinations were chiefly confined to rebel prisoners.
This cannot explain the discordance between his results and Dr. Buckley's.
There must be some very large personal influence.
TABLE VIII. — *Mean Frequency of Respiration, by Age. White Soldiers. Earlier Series.* 520
TABLE IX. — *Mean Frequency of Respiration, by Age. White Men. Later Series.* 521
TABLE X. — *Mean Frequency of Respiration, by Age. Other Races than the White.* 522
Comparative constancy of the mean values for different ages.
Greater frequency in the respiration of the blacks.

The outer limit of distinct vision diminishes with advancing age.
Uncertainty as to whether the normal far-point changes.
Age of maximum distance of vision.
The inner limit increases with the age.
So that advancing years curtail the range at each limit.
The mean distance for men not in usual vigor is less than for others.
Uncertainty of ages of the colored men.
Apparent influence of health upon range of vision.
Object of the Tables X. to XIII. Inferences from them.
The students give a larger proportion of far-sighted and near-sighted than sailors.
The distribution for Indians is improved by increasing the size of groups.
Their normal distance is about 54 inches; their average distance about 52.
TABLE VIII. — *Distribution of Soldiers according to Distance of Vision.* 538
TABLE IX. — *Distribution of Sailors according to Distance of Vision.* 539
TABLE X. — *Distribution of Students, according to Distance of Vision.* 539
TABLE XI. — *Distribution of Full Blacks according to Distance of Vision.* 540
TABLE XII. — *Distribution of Mulattoes according to Distance of Vision.* 541
TABLE XIII. — *Distribution of Indians according to Distance of Vision.* 542
Proportional number whose outer limit falls within given distances.
TABLE XIV. — *Comparison of the Vision of different Classes of Men.* 542

3. COLOR-BLINDNESS. 543

Nature of this peculiarity.
Its frequency much greater than is generally supposed.
Estimates of the proportion of persons thus affected.
One fiftieth of the white men examined by us cannot well discriminate colors.
There is another class who do not readily observe contrasts of color.
These are not included in our statistics.
TABLE XV. — *Number of Color-blind found in each Class of Men.* 544
This defect of vision apparently not related to color of the eye.
Assortment of these color-blind by hue of the iris.
TABLE XVI. — *Color-blindness among White Men, by Nativities.* 545
Color-blind assorted by degree of education.
The imperfection not connected with social grade.
Character of the peculiarity observed in different cases.
Incompleteness of this classification, and inferences from it.
Cause of color-blindness. Dalton's supposition disproved.
It appears due to a limited range in the sensibility of the retina.
This view is analogous to that of Seebeck and Helmholtz.
What it does, and what it does not, imply.
Deductions from this theory.
It may be decisively tested by the spectroscope.
The proportion in the black and red races much smaller than in the white.
Only two instances were found among mulattoes.
Among mulatto natives of Slave States, no case was found.
More observations needed on this point.

CHAPTER XV.

MISCELLANEOUS CHARACTERISTICS.

1. PRELIMINARY. 549

Many questions in our schedule could not be here discussed.
Problems which might be investigated from our data.
A few of these have been partially examined.
These minor topics are here collected in a single chapter.
Although incongruous, this seems their only place.

From discussion of these the Sanitary Commission anticipated its chief usefulness.
Organization of system of Camp Inspections.
Object of these inspections.
Account of them, and of their results in the History of the Sanitary Commission.
About 1500 reports of these inspections are in our archives.
Each report contains answers to between 60 and 180 questions.
All these have been assorted, tabulated, and discussed.
Character of the information which they contain.
The Hospital Directory is described in the History of the Commission.
Tabulation of daily reports of military hospitals.
Prohibition in July 1864, of further information to the Commission.
This the first of a series of orders of similar character.
These discouragements led to abandonment of the investigations.
Similar researches were subsequently undertaken by the Surgeon-General.
Materials now in the archives of the Statistical Bureau.
The most extensive labor has been upon the monthly regimental returns.
Collection of data prosecuted for nearly three years.
In October 1865, 32 000 reports had been transcribed and tabulated.
These comprised all returns for volunteers except for last three months.
Access to the rolls here also suddenly forbidden by the Secretary.
Our work brought to a close before Mr. Stanton left office.
No means then existed for resuming these investigations.
Other vain efforts to procure data for rendering our statistics available.
For want of these data our vast collection of material lies unused.
The State Adjutant-generals enabled us to complete the work of collection.
Our statistics of the loss and gain, casualties, etc., of the volunteer army, to January 1865, are thus quite complete.
For the remaining three months of the war, three fourths of the returns are transcribed.
A detailed account of our materials is given in § 3.
Inquiry into the effect of forced marches.
For this the experience of regiments at Gettysburg is available.
Long and hurried marches were made just previous to this battle.
Special inquiries to determine the effect upon our men.
A few inferences from these are in the final section of this chapter.

2. Camp Inspections. 579

Tabulated and discussed results of these are with our archives.
They are too extensive for convenient or useful publication.
The diversity of circumstances renders a comparison of averages delusive.
We present but one table from these materials.
This shows the relative number of camps for each of nine grades of goodness.
It comprises twelve principal subjects of inquiry, in each of four periods.
The inspection reports chiefly contain verbal statements.
These have been translated into a numerical scale.
The values of the table indicate the proportionate number in each thousand.
Periods employed for this table, number of camps inspected in each period.
Table I.—*Results of Camp Inspections. Proportionate Numbers.* 580

3. Sickness, Mortality, Discharges, etc. 582

Many discordances detected in the records, and adjusted by means of State archives.
For the nine months ending February 1862, the data were discussed by Mr. Elliott.
In that discussion, the Eastern and Western troops were separately considered.
Each of these classes was then serving in its own region.
The same is true for the next following six months.
The returns for this period have been partially published.
During later periods of the war, soldiers from both regions served in each.
Our statistics therefore require a classification by armies.
A knowledge of the regiments composing each army thus becomes needful.

Our materials would then afford a valuable addition to the history of the war.

They would give, for every army monthly, the mortality, strength, sanitary condition, number of desertions, etc.

Without the data required, our vast materials are comparatively useless.

Final effort of the Commission at the beginning of June 1867.

Its failure, although supported by distinguished statesmen and officers.

Our materials are carefully preserved for future use.

Very slight official data will suffice to render them valuable.

The next two tables show the character of the information they contain.

A few of the aggregated summaries are presented in Tables II. and III.

The corresponding proportionate numbers are in Tables IV. and V.

Some of the most important general facts are in Tables VI. and VIII.

Manner of formation of these tables.

Probable degree of correctness of Tables VI. and VII.

Insufficiency of military statistics at the beginning of the war.

Obstacles to their collection.

Gradual improvement in their completeness.

In August 1862, nearly two thirds of the whole army reported.

During 1863, nearly seven eighths of the volunteers reported.

It seems warrantable to apply our inferences to the total of white troops.

TABLE II. — *Summary of Regimental Reports for Eastern Soldiers, to August* 1862. 586

TABLE III. — *Summary of Regimental Reports for Western Soldiers, to August* 1862. 588

TABLE IV. — *Monthly Condition of the Eastern Forces, to August* 1862. 590

TABLE V. — *Monthly Condition of the Western Forces, to August* 1862. 592

TABLE VI. — *Strength, Sickness, Mortality, Discharges, and Desertions, recorded for the total Armies.* 594

TABLE VII. — *Average Regimental Strength and Rates of Sickness and Mortality in the total Armies.* 596

The sickness rates increased continually until the middle of 1862.

After that time the average rate was a little less than one fifth.

Influence of the season of the year.

Classification of the sickness and mortality from disease according to months.

TABLE VIII. — *Average Monthly Rates of Sickness and of Mortality from Disease.* 598

The discharges for disability were most frequent early in 1863.

They rapidly decreased soon afterwards.

In 1864 they numbered about a quarter of one per cent.

The number of desertions followed a similar course.

The monthly average in 1864 was little more than a third of one per cent.

Extension to the whole army (except black troops), of inferences from Tables VI. and VII.

This is readily accomplished by means of materials in Chapter I.

Our Table IX. is thus formed, and affords an independent estimate.

TABLE IX. — *Statistics of White Troops, inferred from Regimental Reports.* 600

Estimated deaths in the service to the end of the year 1864.

Probable number during the remainder of the war.

Near accordance of our results with those of the Provost Marshal General.

These numbers give the deaths during the war, of men in actual service.

Those occurring after discharge from military service are not included.

The singular mortality of colored soldiers is not here discussed.

It is much to be desired that it should soon be investigated by medical men.

Comparison of the aggregates in Table IX. with the Provost Marshal General's statistics.

Probable explanation of the discordances.

4. EFFECT OF LONG MARCHES. 603

Questions prepared for regiments engaged in battle of Gettysburg.

Most of these regiments had made forced marches to reach the field.

Classification of 144 regiments examined.

Blank form of examination used.

Tabulation of the replies and of the special trimonthly returns.

Preliminary report by Mr. O'Connell, from returns of 40 regiments.

The marches of these 144 regiments were mostly above 20 miles a day.
Tabular view of distances marched immediately before the battle.
  Tabular view of distances afterward marched in same month.
Character of the rations issued during the rapid marches.
  Tabular view. Regiments of each corps assorted by character of rations.
General health of the regiments.
  Tabular assortment by general health.
    1. In opinion of commanding officers.
    2. In opinion of surgeons.
Character of diseases occurring on the march.
  Health of those two regiments whose marches were most severe.
Endurance of the troops as affected by the character of rations.
  Tabular assortment by condition of the troops and rations furnished.
    1. In opinion of commanding officers.
    2. In opinion of surgeons.
Character of diseases developed by the march.
  Tabular assortment by diseases, and by rations furnished.
  Rations of those three regiments which suffered most.
Inferences from the preceding statistics.
  Those regiments which had fresh meat suffered little or not at all.
  Those which had two kinds of salt meat suffered only from temporary exhaustion.
  Those which had salt pork only, but enough, suffered considerably.
    In about half of them the suffering was chiefly from sunstroke.
    More than one third of them exhibited special tendency to disease.
  Those which had not enough meat, suffered much even on short marches.
  Of those which had gained on the march, one half had received fresh meat.
  Of those others which had not suffered, two thirds had received fresh meat.
  The diarrhœa was mainly ascribed by the surgeons to excessive use of cold water.
Through these marches the moral condition of the army was excellent.

THE AMERICAN MILITARY EXPERIENCE

An Arno Press Collection

Brown, Richard C. **Social Attitudes of American Generals, 1898-1940.** 1979

Erney, Richard Alton. **The Public Life of Henry Dearborn.** 1979

Koistinen, Paul A.C. **The Hammer and the Sword.** 1979

Parrish, Noel Francis. **Behind the Sheltering Bomb.** 1979

Rutman, Darrett Bruce. **A Militant New World, 1607-1640.** 1979

Kohn, Richard H., editor. **Anglo-American Antimilitary Tracts, 1697-1830.** 1979

Kohn, Richard H., editor. **Military Laws of the United States, From the Civil War Through the War Powers Act of 1973.** 1979

Arnold, Isaac N. **The Life of Benedict Arnold.** 1880

Ayres, Leonard P. **The War with Germany.** 1919

Biderman, Albert D. **March to Calumny.** 1963

Chandler, Charles DeForest and Frank P. Lahm. **How our Army Grew Wings.** 1943

Collins, James Potter. **Autobiography of a Revolutionary Soldier.** 1859

Elliott, Charles Winslow. **Winfield Scott.** 1937

Gould, Benjamin Apthorp. **Investigations in the Military and Anthropological Statistics of American Soldiers.** 1869

Grinker, Roy R. and John P. Spiegel. **War Neuroses.** 1945

Hunt, Elvid. **History of Fort Leavenworth, 1827-1927.** 1926

Leahy, William D. **I Was There.** 1950

Lejeune, John A. **The Reminiscences of a Marine.** 1930

Logan, John A. **The Volunteer Soldier of America.** 1887

Long, John D. **The New American Navy.** 1903. Two vols. in one

Meyers, Augustus. **Ten Years in the Ranks U.S. Army.** 1914

Michie, Peter S. **The Life and Letters of Emory Upton.** 1885

Millis, Walter. **The Martial Spirit.** 1931

Mott, T[homas] Bentley. **Twenty Years as Military Attaché.** 1937

Palmer, John McAuley. **America in Arms.** 1941

Pyle, Ernie. **Here is Your War.** 1943

Riker, William H. **Soldiers of the States.** 1957

Roe, Frances M.A. **Army Letters From an Officer's Wife, 1871-1888.** 1909

Shippen, E[dward]. **Thirty Years at Sea.** 1879

Smith, Louis. **American Democracy and Military Power.** 1951

Steiner, Bernard C. **The Life and Correspondence of James McHenry.** 1907

Sylvester, Herbert Milton. **Indian Wars of New England.** 1910. Three vols.

[Totten, Joseph Gilbert]. **Report of General J.G. Totten, Chief Engineer, on the Subject of National Defences.** 1851

Truscott, L[ucian] K., Jr. **Command Missions.** 1954

U.S. Congress. **American State Papers.** 1834/1860/1861. Four vols.

U.S. Congress. **Military Situation in the Far East.** 1951. Five vols.

U.S. Congress. **Organizing for National Security.** 1961. Three vols. in two

[U.S. Bureau of Labor Statistics], U.S. Congress. **Wartime Technological Developments.** 1945. Two vols. in one

U.S. Congress. **Report of the Board on Fortifications or other Defenses Appointed by the President of the United States Under the Provisions of the Act of Congress, Approved March 3, 1885** *and* **Plates to Accompany the Report.** 1886. Two vols. in one

U.S. President's Air Policy Commission. **Survival in the Air Age.** 1948

U.S. Selective Service System. **Backgrounds of Selective Service.** 1947. Two vols. in four

White, Howard. **Executive Influence in Determining Military Policy in the United States.** 1925

Winthrop, William. **Military Law and Precedents.** 1920